CASES AND MATERIALS
ON LABOUR LAW

CASES AND MATERIALS ON LABOUR LAW

BY

K . W . WEDDERBURN

Cassel Professor of Commercial Law in the
University of London (London School of Economics),
of the Middle Temple, Barrister-at-Law

CAMBRIDGE
AT THE UNIVERSITY PRESS
1967

Published by the Syndics of the Cambridge University Press
Bentley House, 200 Euston Road, London, N.W. 1.
American Branch: 32 East 57th Street, New York, N.Y. 10022

© Cambridge University Press 1967

Printed in Great Britain
at the University Printing House, Cambridge
(Brooke Crutchley, University Printer)

CONTENTS

CHAPTER I. THE INDIVIDUAL EMPLOYMENT RELATIONSHIP

CHAPTER 2. TERMINATION OF EMPLOYMENT

PREFACE

Interest and research in Labour Law, or 'Industrial Law', have increased rapidly over the last decade in universities and elsewhere. The increase reflects, on the one hand, the growing importance of the subject in legal studies and in the neighbouring social sciences, and, on the other, the effect which social change itself has upon the very content of academic courses. The topics studied vary from place to place; but the core of a modern Labour Law course deals with the problems of employment and collective bargaining, with trade union law and industrial conflict, and with industrial injury and social security. The selection of materials which follows aims to provide the reader with sources relevant to that core of the subject.

The order is that in which I would choose to introduce the reader to the subject. First, the individual employment relationship is explored; second, the problem of loss of employment is examined, a chapter in which social security law is first introduced to a major degree; and third, the legal dimension of collective bargaining is taken up, especially in its relationship to that institution to which the lawyer is always driven back in England, the individual contract of employment. Fourth and fifth come the areas of industrial conflict and of trade union law; and sixthly, we return to the place of work for a brief look at compensation for injury suffered there.

The selection is, of course, a personal one. The book is lengthy; but originally it was even longer. Numerous extracts had to be excised, especially those concerned with background and sociological material. In some cases reference is now made to such material in footnotes. Similarly, I had to cut down the lengthy commentary with which I had once intended to introduce each chapter. A few discussions by way of note or excursus have survived; but often I have referred to what is written elsewhere so as to make way for primary source materials. I have also abbreviated most of the headnotes to cases.

The insistent demand to reduce the bulk of the volume served, at any rate, to re-emphasise both that a source book cannot be a text book, and that a student course on Labour Law cannot also be a full course on Industrial Relations. The law student must be taken through the legal complexities to see the social reality beneath them. But his primary raw material is in the legal sources; and this thought guided my hand in the unpalatable task of excission. What remains will, I hope, supply a firm structure on which the reader can build in discussion and in further reading. Fortunately, the subject inevitably demands that one goes outside statutes and decisions in the ordinary courts; and the reader will find decisions of Commissioners and the Minister on social security law; of the Industrial Court; of Industrial Tribunals; and of the Registrar of Friendly Societies. My hope is that these materials will be useful not only to lawyers but also to those interested in industrial relations and industrial sociology who seek to understand the increasing impact of law upon their subjects of study.

Two factors necessarily complicated the task of completing the basic selection of materials by December 1966. Whereas ten years ago the structure of Labour Law in Britain had remained relatively unchanged for decades, since 1960 everything has been on the move. Before this book appears, the Royal Commission under Lord Donovan may have reported; and certainly many of the impending appeals to the High Court on redundancy payments will have been heard. There is no telling what further developments will have occurred in the common law. Secondly, statute always presents a special problem for legal source books; and there is an increasing quantity of legislation on Labour Law. I have tried to tread a middle path by including those statutory materials which are essential to a comprehension of the main questions that arise.

Whatever new statutes, reports or decisions appear in the next few years, however, the student must still tackle the legal dimension of employment as it exists today. The significance of the new develop-ments cannot be understood or evaluated without a study of the present system. Nor will any new developments lightly shrug off our present structure of Labour Law, for its roots go deep into our society. My hope is that this book will help to explain the law as it is now.

I am grateful to many persons for help in compiling the book, first of course to those who gave permission for the reproduction of materials and whose names are enumerated in the list of acknowledge-ments which follows.

My very deep thanks are due above all to Richard Wilson for his assistance in the patient collection and preparation of materials. His work was continued at a later stage by Tony Grabiner; and the book owes much to both of them, not merely for their pertinacious industry but also for suggestions and criticisms which sprang from their deep understanding of Labour Law and of its social meaning. I am much indebted, too, to my secretary, Miss Gillian Hurley, for her help in typing; to the Librarians and library staffs of the Squire Law Library, Cambridge, the British Library of Political and Economic Science at the London School of Economics, and the Library of the Middle Temple; to Paul Davies, Jonathan Gilman, Martin Daly, Stephanie Daly, Michael Boyes, Roger Field, and Ralph Freeman for their timely assistance; and last, but not least, to my wife for her help and enduring patience. None of them, of course shares my responsibility for the faults which remain. Their own convention forbids that I thank my publishers, a fact which I mention only to show that I would otherwise have wished to do so.

The London School of Economics   K. W. WEDDERBURN
9 March 1967

ACKNOWLEDGMENTS

I am grateful to the following for allowing reproductions to be made: Messrs Butterworth & Co. Ltd for the *All England Law Reports* and *The Law Journal*; The Incorporated Council for Law Reporting for England and Wales for *The Law Reports*; Lloyd's List Law Reports for their reports; The Solicitors' Journal for one of their reports; Times Newspapers Ltd for their *Times Law Reports* and reports from *The Times*; W. Green & Son Ltd for a *Scots Law Times* report; The Irish Law Times and Solicitors' Journal for a report from *Irish Law Times Reports*; Browne and Nolan Ltd for *Irish Reports*; John Aiken & Son Ltd for *Northern Ireland Law Reports*; the Law Book Company Ltd for a report from *The Commonwealth Law Reports*; Her Majesty's Stationery Office for Statutes, extract from Reports of Commissioner's Decisions under National Insurance and National Insurance (Industrial Injuries) Acts, National Insurance Act 1946 Ministers' Decisions, Registrar's Decisions on Disputes under the Trade Union Act, 1913, Industrial Court Decisions and various other publications; Basil Blackwell & Mott Ltd for an extract from O. Kahn-Freund's chapter in *The System of Industrial Relations in Great Britain* edited by Flanders & Clegg; *The Guardian* for two reports from that newspaper; The International Labour Organisation for extracts from Conventions and a report; The Trades Union Congress for extracts from their Constitution and their 1965 report; The Transport and General Workers Union; The British Iron, Steel and Kindred Trades Association; The National Union of Printing, Bookbinding and Paper Workers (now Division A of the Society of Graphical and Allied Trades), and the Union of Shop, Distributive & Allied Workers all for extracts from their Rule Books; The Engineering Employers Federation and the Confederation of Shipbuilding and Engineering Unions for an extract from 'The York Agreement' 1922; the British Film Producers Association and the Association of Cinematograph, Television and Allied Technicians for extracts from their collective agreement; The British Footwear Manufacturers Federation and the National Union of Boot and Shoe Operatives for extracts from the collective agreement.

K.W.W

INDEX OF STATUTES

INDEX OF CASES

(Numbers in heavy type refer to the page on which the report appears)

INDEX OF INDUSTRIAL COURT AWARDS

INDEX OF DECISIONS OF NATIONAL INSURANCE COMMISSIONERS AND THE MINISTER

INDEX OF DECISIONS OF
INDUSTRIAL TRIBUNALS

INDEX OF DECISIONS OF REGISTRAR
OF FRIENDLY SOCIETIES AND
TRADE UNIONS

CHAPTER 1

THE INDIVIDUAL EMPLOYMENT RELATIONSHIP

Introductory Note

The realities of labour relations are to be found in the collective bargaining arrangements made by trade unions and employers, and in statutory provisions. Nonetheless, the lawyer, in his analysis of a problem, is compelled to inspect especially the *individual* employment relationship, the rights and duties of the particular worker and employer, on which, no doubt, statute and collective agreements have made their impact. The fundamental legal institution of Labour Law remains the contract of employment, increasingly perhaps taking on the flavour of 'status' rather than old-fashioned 'contract', but still the individual legal relation between that employee and that employer.

Chapters 1 and 2 offer materials which impinge on discussion of this relationship. First, Section A raises the question of definition. Who is a 'servant', 'employee', and the like for various legal purposes, at common law and under statute. This is a problem of increasing importance as the materials dealing with 'self-employed' workers show. Sections B and C remind the reader of fundamental contractual issues. First the personal character of the contract is illustrated (especially by reference to remedies). Next 'public policy' is touched upon, mainly in regard to restraint of trade, and Section C probes the formation of the contract. (Here materials have not been included fully on matters which the student will have touched upon elsewhere before studying Labour Law, e.g. capacity to contract).

In Section D are included cases relevant to the basic rights and dutie of the parties to the contract of employment. These are of the great importance when, in later chapters, we deal with problems of collect bargaining and industrial conflict, since the collective realities in t those areas tend often to be resolved, in litigation, in individual con terms in the last resort. In the same section is included statutory ma concerning the workmen's right to payment of his wages.

Chapter 2, Section A deals with termination of the contr frustration, breach and notice. Naturally, the cases concern

breach should be read in close conjunction with Section D of Chapter 1. Sections B and C deal with notice and damages for breach. Lastly, Section D of Chapter 2 adds selected topics concerned with social security: unemployment benefit and redundancy payments for the employee who has lost his job. The last heading is particularly apposite to the chapter, since the Redundancy Payments Act crosses the wires of employment and social security law by establishing a scheme whereby employers must make payments to redundant workers but can usually recover most of the sums paid from a national fund. (It has been possible too to include a selection of decisions by the new Industrial Tribunals, although only from their early cases.)

SECTION A

SERVANTS, WORKMEN AND EMPLOYEES

PERFORMING RIGHTS SOCIETY LTD *v.* MITCHELL AND BOOKER LTD

[1924] 1 K.B. 762

The defendants, management of the Palais de Danse, Hammersmith, engaged a jazz band, the Original Lyrical Five, to play for them at the Palais. The band infringed the plaintiffs' copyright in a tune called 'Mon Homme' by playing it. The question arose of whether the defendants were liable for this infringement on the ground that the band was their servant.

McCARDIE, J.: The case is to be decided on general principles. The decisions are numerous and not always easy to follow. The distinction between 'servant' and 'independent contractor' does not seem to rest merely on the magnitude of the task undertaken. Thus, whilst a labourer employed to cleanse drains at 5s. for the job was held to be a servant and not a contractor: see *Sadler* v. *Henlock*[1], a plumber called in by a landlord to mend a leaky cistern was held to be an independent contractor and not a servant: see *Blake* v. *Woolf*.[2] A licensed drover has been held to be an independent contractor and not a servant: see *Milligan* v. *Wedge*,[3] on the ground that he exercised an independent calling. So, too, in *Rapson* v. *Cubitt*[4] a gas-fitter was held to be an independent contractor. On the other hand, I conceive that a general

---

[1] (1855) 4 E. & B. 570. [2] [1898] 2 Q.B. 426.
[3] (1840) 12 Ad. & E. 737. [4] (1842) 9 M. & W. 710.

manager, at a high salary, of a partnership, or the managing director of a limited company at an even higher salary, are usually servants and not independent contractors, and in many cases a partnership or a limited company has been held liable for their negligence or breach of duty. The nature of the task undertaken, the freedom of action given, the magnitude of the contract amount, the manner in which it is to be paid, the powers of dismissal and the circumstances under which payment of the reward may be withheld, all these bear on the solution of the question...It seems, however, reasonably clear that the final test, if there be a final test, and certainly the test to be generally applied, lies in the nature and degree of detailed control over the person alleged to be a servant. This circumstance is, of course, one only of several to be considered, but it is usually of vital importance.

R. v. FOULKES

(1875) L.R. 2 C.C.R. 150; 13 Cox C.C. 63

The defendant acted as unpaid clerk to his father who was Clerk to the Local Board. Was he a servant for the purposes of embezzlement?

COCKBURN, C.J.: It is true that the relation of clerk or servant is generally founded on contract, but the relation may exist at will only. The evidence is that the prisoner did perform all those things which a clerk or servant might have done, and although he might have refused to go on doing them, yet so long as he continued to perform them he did them in the capacity of a clerk or servant to his father.

BRAMWELL, B., MELLOR, J., BRETT, J. and POLLOCK, B. concurred with COCKBURN, C.J.

HEDLEY v. THE PINKNEY AND SONS STEAMSHIP CO.

Court of Appeal   [1892] 1 Q.B. 58. Affirmed [1894] A.C. 222

During a storm, a seaman was swept through an opening in a ship's bulwarks and was drowned. An action was brought against the company which owned the ship. The doctrine of common employment was the law at this time. [The doctrine was of course abolished by the Law Reform (Personal Injuries) Act, 1948, post p. 683.]

In the course of his judgment LORD ESHER M.R. said: The question is whether, apart from the Merchant Shipping Act, the owners of the ship are liable for the negligence of the captain with regard to the safety of one of the crew. The basis of the liability in such a case is that the master is liable for the negligence of his servant; therefore, the first step the plaintiff must take to establish the owners' liability is to show that the captain is their servant. It is clear that the captain is the servant of the shipowners. He is appointed and paid by them; they can dismiss him, and he is subject to their orders. The seaman is a servant of the owners also. The captain, no doubt, is a superior servant, and the seaman is an inferior servant, bound to obey the orders of the captain; but they are both servants of the same master, employed in the same operation. They are, therefore, fellow-servants engaged in a common employment. The common law of England is that, where fellow-servants are engaged in a common employment, whether one is inferior to the other, whether one is bound to obey the other or not, the master is not liable for injury occasioned to the one through the negligence of the other.

WALKER v. CRYSTAL PALACE
FOOTBALL CLUB LTD

Court of Appeal   [1910] 1 K.B. 87

The defendant club engaged the plaintiff to play with the club for one year at £3. 10s. 0d. per week. In his contract he agreed to keep himself temperate, sober and fit, to attend regularly for training and to observe the training and general instructions of the club, to do all that the club might deem necessary to fit himself as an efficient football player and to conform to the rules and laws of the Football Association.

Was he a 'workman' within the Workmen's Compensation Act, 1906?

COZENS-HARDY, M.R.: It has been argued before us very forcibly by Mr Russell that there is a certain difference between an ordinary workman and a man who contracts to exhibit and employ his skill where the employer would have no right to dictate to him in the exercise of that skill; e.g. the club in this case would have no right to dictate to him how he should play football. I am unable to follow that. He is bound according to the express terms of his contract to obey all general directions of the club, and I think in any particular game in which he was engaged he would also be bound to obey the particular instructions of the captain or whoever it might be who was the delegate of the authority of the club for the purpose of giving those instructions.

FARWELL, L.J.:...The appellants...first of all say there is no contract of service with an employer because the football player is at liberty to exercise his own initiative in playing the game. That appears to me to be no answer. There are many employments in which the workman exercises initiative, but he may or may not be bound to obey the directions of his employer when given to him. If he has no duty to obey them, it may very well be that there is no service, but here not only is the agreement by the player that he will serve, but he also agrees to obey the training and general instructions of the club. I cannot doubt that he is bound to obey any directions which the captain, as the delegate of the club, may give him during the course of the game—that is to say, any direction that is within the terms of his employment as a football player. FLETCHER MOULTON, L.J. concurred.

In re ASHLEY AND SMITH

[1918] 2 Ch. 378

Alderman Huggins of Gravesend and Mr Hall were regular contributors to the *Sportsman*, the one for 20 years, the other for 40 years. A receiver was appointed to wind up the company. Could they claim preferential payments under s. 209 of the Companies (Consolidation) Act, 1908, (fore-runner of s. 319, Companies Act, 1948)?

SARGANT, J.: I must consider whether the main indications of service are present here or not; and having done so I have come to the conclusion that neither of these persons was a servant of the company. I particularly note four circumstances. In the first place, they were working entirely away from the company, and not in the office of the company at all. Secondly, they were not exclusively employed in the service of the company, but they might have taken up any amount of other work for other persons, and I think it is highly probable that they did so. Thirdly, they were not bound to render services generally, but only a particular class of service. Fourthly, and most important of all, they might perform the service in question practically as they pleased; they were not working under the control of the company or subject to the command of the master under whom they worked. I do not say that any one of those four circumstances which I have mentioned, except possibly the last, would be entirely conclusive; but I do think that, when all those four circumstances are taken together, it is impossible to say that either of those persons was a servant of the company...

CASSIDY *v.* THE MINISTRY OF HEALTH

Court of Appeal   [1951] 2 K.B. 343

At the end of a course of post-operational treatment on a patient's left hand, the hand was found to have been rendered useless. The patient brought an action against the hospital for negligent treatment.

The treatment was carried out under the care of a whole-time surgeon, Dr F., who had operated, a house surgeon, Dr R., and members of the nursing staff.

SOMERVELL, L.J.: With regard to the position of surgeons or doctors, Lord Greene, M.R., said in *Gold's* case[1] that the relationship of a consulting surgeon or physician precludes the drawing of an inference that the hospital authorities are responsible for their negligent acts. He treats the position of a house physician or surgeon as open. MacKinnon, L.J., said that the senior surgeon, Mr Lockwood, was certainly not a servant of the hospital, the others probably not. Goddard, L.J., said that he was not considering the position of doctors on the permanent staff: that must depend on whether there was a contract of service and the facts of any particular case.

The evidence as to Dr Fahrni's position is that he was an assistant medical officer: that he received a sum in lieu of residential emoluments which indicates that, if there had been accommodation, or perhaps if he had been a bachelor, he would have lived in; and that he was in whole-time employment. His engagement was subject to the standing orders of the council, but these are not before us. Dr Ronaldson was a house surgeon working under Dr Fahrni.

The first question is whether the principles as laid down in *Gold's* case cover them. In considering this, it is important to bear in mind that nurses are qualified professional persons. It is also important to remember, and MacKinnon, L.J., in *Gold's* case emphasized this, that the principle respondeat superior is not ousted by the fact that a 'servant' has to do work of a skilful or technical character, for which the servant has special qualifications. He instanced the certified captain who navigates a ship. On the facts as I have stated them, I would have said that both Dr Fahrni and Dr Ronaldson had contracts of service. They were employed, like the nurses as part of the permanent staff of the hospital. In *Gold's* case, Lord Greene, M.R., in considering what a patient is entitled to expect when he knocks at the door of the hospital, comes to the conclusion that he is entitled to expect nursing, and therefore the hospital is liable if a nurse is negligent. It seems to me the same must apply in the case of the permanent medical staff. A familiar example is an out-patients' ward. One may suppose a doctor and a sister dealing with the patients: it seems to me that the patient is as much entitled to expect medical treatment as nursing from those who are the servants of the hospital. I agree, that, if he is treated by someone who is a visiting

[1] [1942] 2 K.B. 293.

or consulting surgeon or physician, he will be being treated by someone who is not a servant of the hospital: he is in much the same position as a private patient who has arranged to be operated on by 'X'. SINGLETON and DENNING, L.JJ. delivered concurring judgments.

STEVENSON, JORDAN AND HARRISON LTD
v. MACDONALD AND EVANS

Court of Appeal   [1952] 1 T.L.R. 101

Mr Evans-Hemming was engaged by the plaintiff company as a management engineer and he later became a member of their executive committee. He wrote a book on business management. In an action by the company to restrain the publication of this book, the question of the legal nature of his relationship with the company arose.

DENNING, L.J.: As my Lord has said, it is almost impossible to give a precise definition of the distinction. It is often easy to recognize a contract of service when you see it, but difficult to say wherein the difference lies. A ship's master, a chauffeur, and a reporter on the staff of a newspaper are all employed under a contract of service; but a ship's pilot, a taxi-man, and a newspaper contributor are employed under a contract for services. One feature which seems to run through the instances is that, under a contract of service, a man is employed as part of the business, and his work is done as an integral part of the business; whereas, under a contract for services, his work, although done for the business, is not integrated into it but is only accessory to it.

It must be remembered, however, that a man who is employed under a contract of service may sometimes perform services outside the contract. A good illustration is *Byrne* v. *Statist Co.*,[1] where a man on the regular staff of a newspaper made a translation for the newspaper in his spare time. It was held that the translation was not made under a contract of service but under a contract for services. Other instances occur, as when a doctor on the staff of a hospital or a master on the staff of a school is employed under a contract of service to give lectures or lessons orally to students. If, for his own convenience, he puts the lectures into writing, then his written work is not done under the contract of service. It is most useful as an accessory to his contracted work, but it is not really part of it. The copyright is in him and not in his employers.

The present case affords a good example of a mixed contract which is partly a contract of service and partly a contract for services. In so far as Mr Evans-Hemming prepared and wrote manuals for the use of a

[1] 30 *The Times* L.R. 254; [1914] 1 K.B. 622.

particular client of the company, he was doing it as part of his work as a servant of the company under a contract of service; but in so far as he prepared and wrote lectures for delivery to universities and to learned and professional societies, he was doing so as an accessory to the contract of service and not as part of it. The giving of lectures was no doubt very helpful to the company, in that it might serve directly as an advertisement for the company, and on that account the company paid Mr Evans-Hemming the expenses he incurred. The lectures were, in a sense, part of the services rendered by Mr Evans-Hemming for the benefit of the company. But they were in no sense part of his service. It follows that the copyright in the lectures was in Mr Evans-Hemming.

SIR RAYMOND EVERSHED, M.R. and MORRIS, L.J. delivered concurring judgments.

MORREN v. SWINTON AND PENDLEBURY BOROUGH COUNCIL

Court of Appeal   [1965] 1 W.L.R. 576

The Court had to decide on a case stated by the Minister of Housing and Local Government whether the appellant was an employee of the respondent borough council for the purposes of the Local Government Superannuation Act, 1937. The council appointed the appellant, could dismiss him, paid his salary, mileage and subsistence allowances and his national insurance contributions. His work was not under their control or direction but under that of a consulting engineer (Kaufman) who had contracted with the council to execute sewage works. The consulting engineers also selected him, though they did not appoint him.*

LORD PARKER, C.J.: Sometimes it is said quite generally that the test is whether the master can order or require what is to be done, where the true contract is one for services, or whether the master can order or require not only what is to be done, but how it shall be done, in which case it is a contract of service.

That perhaps is an over-simplification, and in *Short* v. *Henderson*,[1] Lord Thankerton dealt with what he called the four indicia of a contract of service. These are, and he quoted the Lord Justice Clerk:[2] '(a) The master's power of selection of his servant; (b) the payment of wages or

---

[1] 1946 S.C. (H.L.) 24.   [2] *Ibid.* 33.

* Compare *Parker* v. *Orr* (1966) 1 I.T.R. 488: Congregational minister on staff of an 'Industrial Mission' subject to the 'directives' of Senior Chaplain not an employee within Redundancy Payments Act 1965, *post* p. 218.

other remuneration; (c) the master's right to control the method of doing the work, and (d) the master's right of suspension or dismissal.' Lord Thankerton went on:[1] 'The learned judge adds that a contract of service may still exist if some of these elements are absent altogether, or present only in an unusual form, and that the principal requirement of a contract of service is the right of the master in some reasonable sense to control the method of doing the work, and that this factor of superintendence and control has frequently been treated as critical and decisive of the legal quality of the relationship.'

The cases have over and over again stressed the importance of the factor of superintendence and control, but that it is not the determining test is quite clear. In *Cassidy* v. *The Minister of Health*[2] Somervell L.J.,[3] referred to this matter, and instanced, as did Lord Denning in the later case of *Stevenson, Jordan & Harrison* v. *McDonald & Evans*[4] that clearly superintendence and control cannot be the decisive test when one is dealing with a professional man, or a man of some particular skill and experience. Instances of that have been given in the form of the master of a ship, an engine driver, or a professional architect, or as in this case, a consulting engineer. In such cases there can be no question of the employer telling him how to do work, therefore the absence of control and direction in that sense can be of little, if any, use as a test.

In my judgment here all the other considerations point to a contract of service. It is true, as has been pointed out by Mr Threlfall, that in fact though the appellant was appointed by the respondents, the power of selection was delegated to the consulting engineers. That, as it seems to me, is nothing more than good practice since the appellant was going to have to work under and with those consulting engineers. Apart from that, he was appointed by the respondents, they had the right to dismiss him, he was paid such matters as subsistence allowance, National Insurance contributions and holidays, and in addition there was provision for one month's notice. Pausing there, it seems to me that looked at on those facts, the only possible inference is that he was engaged under a contract of service. How different is the contract with Kaufman, who is not paid a subsistence allowance, or National Insurance contributions and is not entitled to holidays. Further there is no provision for termination of his services or service by notice.... For my part I cannot see how the terms of the contract that he was to work under and accept the direction

---

[1] *Ibid.* 33.
[2] [1951] 2 K.B. 343; [1951] 1 T.L.R. 539; [1951] 1 All E.R. 514, C.A.
[3] [1951] 2 K.B. 343, 351.   [4] [1952] 1 T.L.R. 101, C.A.

and control of Kaufman, who had himself been appointed as the respondents' agent to supervise the works, could convert what otherwise was a contract of service into a contract for services. MARSHALL, J. and WIDGERY, J. agreed with LORD PARKER, C.J.

Re C. W. & A. L. HUGHES LTD

[1966] 2 All E.R. 702

H. Ltd engaged 'labour only' sub-contractors to carry out building work, the company supplying the materials. The company decided what work it wanted done, and the contract would be offered to a gang leader at a price. He would then recruit the members of the gang, and arrange the ultimate distribution of the money. The company paid the gang leader weekly sums on account, after inspection of the work. No deductions were made for tax on P.A.Y.E. nor did the company concern itself with the men's national insurance contributions. It made no contribution to the holiday scheme arranged in the building industry and to which it contributed for its own employees. The company went into liquidation. The issue arose whether sums advanced for the purpose of paying the gang leaders could fall within s. 319 (4) Companies Act, 1948 which deals with sums advanced where payment has been made 'to any clerk, servant, workman or labourer in the employment of the company'. It was held that the gang leaders and the members of the gangs were not in the employment of the company.

PLOWMAN, J.: . . . I conclude that the contracts with which I am concerned here were contracts between employer and sub-contractor— that is to say, gang leader—and not contracts between master and servant. The degree of control exercised by the company is not such in my opinion as to bring them into the latter category. This conclusion is, I think, supported by the decision of the Court of Appeal in the recent case of *Emerald Construction Co. Ltd* v. *Lowthian.**

MARLEY TILE CO. LTD AND J. CLARK†

Decision of the Minister under the National Insurance (Industrial Injuries) Act 1946
(Unreported); 2 August and 26 October 1965

Clark, a slater and tiler, was taken on by the Marley Tile Co. He was told he would receive details of the work to be done, and materials would be supplied to him. A price for the work would be agreed. He

---

* [1966] 1 All E.R. 1013; see *post* p. 492.
† Details kindly supplied by Amalgamated Slaters, Tilers and Roofing Operatives Society.

would be treated as a sub-contractor, dealing with his own tax and national insurance affairs. Although free to accept work from elsewhere he was to give priority to the work from the company. At first he worked with another tiler, who received the money and shared it out. Later he worked on his own. He used his own tools; he was not subject to constant supervision, but the company's representative visited the site occasionally. He came to take on a number of jobs at a time, and the company would sometimes ask him to switch from one to the other. From 1954 to 1964 he carried out only one job which was not for the company. He was injured in the course of one job for the company and claimed industrial injury benefit (see *post* p. 760). The issue arose whether he was an employee within the relevant Act. The Minister (with whom such a decision lay) decided that Clark was 'engaged by the Company under a separate contract on the day in question to carry out specific work for an agreed lump sum and that in the performance of that work he was not subject to detailed control by the Company as to the manner in which he carried it out' and that therefore he was not in insurable employment under the Act,* and not entitled to benefit.

W. CREIGHTON & CO. LTD AND AMALGAMATED SLATERS, TILERS & ROOFING OPERATIVES SOCIETY

Industrial Court: Case 3107   (25 July 1966)

This was a reference made to the Industrial Court by the Minister of Labour, following a claim by the union under the Terms and Conditions of Employment Act, 1959 section 8.† The union members carried out jobs of work on various building sites for W. Creighton &

---

* The class of insured person in which anyone should be placed is a question to be determined by the Minister (in practice an inspector appointed by him): see now s. 64 National Insurance Act 1965. Questions of law may be referred to or appealed to the High Court: s. 65. Similarly, the Minister decides whether an employee was in insurable employment for the purposes of the National Insurance (Industrial Injuries) Act 1965, s. 35, subject to a similar right of appeal. Both Acts repeat earlier versions in 1946. The Minister's Decisions used to be issued in a series of pamphlets; for examples see *post* p. 26 and p. 27. On the general question of 'self-employment' and the like, see G. Clark (1967) 30 M.L.R. 6. One of the problems of an increasingly statutory labour law is the fact that the statutory provisions tend to apply only to contracts of 'employment'. For various statutory definitions see *post* p. 30 *et seq.*

The Minister's power to determine the status of the worker has apparently been transferred to the question whether he is an 'employee' for Selective Employment tax: Finance Act 1966, s. 44; even though certain other questions have been given for determination to the new Industrial Tribunals: Selective Employment Payments Act 1966, s. 7. (On these tribunals see (1966) 29 M.L.R. pp. 65–7; and redundancy decisions, *post* p. 219 *et seq.*)

† See *post* p. 345.

Co. Ltd. The men were designated by the company as self-employed persons. The union claimed that the men were in fact employees and should be treated accordingly in relation to agreements carried out by the National Joint Council for the Building Industry; the Current Building (Safety, Health and Welfare) Regulations; the Contracts of Employment Act, 1963; the Redundancy Payments Act, 1965 etc. In effect, the question became: Could the employer, by declaring the men self-employed, successfully contract out of the whole field of employer's liability without providing favourable terms and conditions of employment as they existed in the rest of the industry?

Main submissions on behalf of the Society

4. It was submitted that the men concerned were employed by the Company on a simple piece-work basis in that they received a fixed payment in respect of each roof which they covered. They were, however, designated by the Company as self-employed persons and their conditions of employment were contrary to those established by the National Joint Council....

5. It was the Society's contention that the Company entered into a contract of service with their tilers and not a contract for services, and that the relationship between the Company and the workers concerned was therefore that of employers and employees. The Company were employers within the meaning of Section 8 of the Terms and Conditions of Employment Act, 1959 (hereinafter referred to as 'the Act') in that the workers approached them for employment, whereupon the Company directed them to a particular site and on completion of the work on that site they directed them to another. The Society accepted that roofing contractors, who normally undertook work over a much wider area than other employers in the Building Industry, found it impossible to exercise the usual continuous and direct control on the site: they could however determine by the end product whether or not a man was doing his fair share of work. The Company were able to control their workers effectively since they secured the initial contracts, directed the workers where to go, controlled the flow of materials to the site and satisfied themselves as to the quality of the work done....

National Working Rule 8—Sub-contracting for Labour only

18. The employment on a site by a main contractor of a sub-contractor for labour-only is subject to the following conditions:

(1) That the main contractor shall require the labour-only sub-con-

tractor to observe, and the sub-contractor shall observe, the Working Rule Agreement and the decisions of the National Joint Council.

(2) That in the event of a default by the labour-only sub-contractor, the main contractor shall accept responsibility for:

(a) Wages at the standard rate due (but not paid) to the sub-contractor's operatives in respect of time worked on the site during the pay week immediately prior to the default, plus any time worked in the pay week in which the default occurs; and

(b) Annual and public holidays credit stamps which should have but have not, been affixed to the cards of the sub-contractor's operatives during the period of their employment on the site.

(3) The main contractor shall satisfy himself that the operatives employed by the labour-only sub-contractor are covered by a current Employer's Liability Insurance Policy.

(4) The labour-only sub-contractor shall afford the same facilities for access of Trade Union Officers as are afforded by the main contractor.

Following a dispute which had arisen regarding the engagement of gangs of self-employed bricklayers, the National Joint Council Emergency Disputes Commission had issued their findings on the 28th August 1964 as follows:

(1) National Working Rule 8 provides the conditions governing labour-only sub-contracting.

(2) The rule refers to, and only to, bona fide labour-only sub-contracting and not to the engagement of gangs of self-employed men...

23. The Society submitted that the financial advantages enjoyed by the Company as a result of their present system of engaging labour included the following estimated items. The Company's annual commitments in respect of National Insurance, graduated pensions and holiday schemes would otherwise amount to about £6500, while the application of the Selective Employment Tax would cost them £4375 a year. They would also, as ordinary employers, incur additional expenses in respect of office administration, including the operation of P.A.Y.E. and probably of insurance premiums covering employers' liability. It was submitted that it was this financial saving which enabled the Company to induce their workers to be designated as self-employed by offering them gross remuneration which appeared to represent high earnings, whereas their terms and conditions of employment were in fact less favourable than those of ordinary employees in the Industry. The latter were not only better off financially in terms of net pay,

allowing for lawful deductions, but they also enjoyed guaranteed time, holiday and sickness payments and other benefits and legal protection while at work. . .

Main submissions on behalf of the Company

26. It was stated that the Company were roofing and tiling contractors and sub-contractors who in the main carried out work for large building contractors. The workers concerned in the claim undertook a specific job for an agreed price and when that job was completed they applied for another job in much the same way as the Company themselves undertook sub-contracts with main contractors.

27. It was the Company's submission that their relationship with their tilers was by way of contract for services and was not that of employer and employee in the generally accepted sense. There was no written contract between the Company and the workers concerned. . .

29. In support of their submission that the workers concerned were not 'employees' of the Company, the Company stated that the system was that the workers worked in pairs or, occasionally, in threes. The Company, on the basis described in paragraph 27 above, agreed with one of this group, who was a tiler, the remuneration to be paid for the job in hand: that tiler agreed with the other member (or members) of the group how the total remuneration was to be shared between them. It was only to that tiler that payments were made by the Company: he in turn paid the appropriate share to the other member (or members) of the group. . .

40. It was submitted that the self-employed status of the Company's tilers had been accepted without question by the Inland Revenue, the Ministry of Labour and the Ministry of Pensions and National Insurance: the men were treated as employers for taxation purposes and the Company understood that they received allowances for the use of their private cars in addition to certain other allowances appropriate to their trade. A few of the men employed accountants to keep proper records for income tax purposes. . .

43. If, however, the Company were to be required to observe the National Joint Council conditions, it would be necessary for them to ask all their tilers to become day workers, and not all of them would be likely to agree. Other labour would therefore need to be recruited in order that the Company could fulfil their obligations to their customers.

Award

44. Having given careful consideration to the evidence and submissions of the Parties the Court find and Award as follows:

(1) They find that, on the facts, the relationship between the Company and the workers concerned in the claim is by way of contract of service and not by way of contract for services; that the expression 'self-employed' is a misdescription of the true position of the said workers in relation to the Company; and that the Company are employers and the workers concerned are employees within the meaning of Section 8 of the Act.*

(2) There have been established in the Building Industry terms and conditions of employment, namely those laid down from time to time by the National Joint Council which conform with the requirements of Section 8 of the Act and are the recognised terms and conditions applicable to the workers concerned in the claim.

(3) The Company are not observing the recognised terms and conditions.

(4) The Court are not satisfied that the terms and conditions which the Company are observing are not less favourable than the recognised terms and conditions.

(5) The Court accordingly require the Company to observe the said recognised terms and conditions as respects all workers of the relevant description from time to time employed by them.

(6) This Award shall have effect from the beginning of the first full pay week following the 1 November 1966...

45. Although it is no part of their functions in this reference to do so, the Court think it right to suggest that the National Joint Council might consider whether, having regard to the special characteristics of roofing contract work, provision might be made in the National Working Rules whereby a roofing contractor might where it seemed appropriate employ his workers on a piece-work basis if the terms and conditions of such employment were not less favourable than those provided for by the National Working Rules as they now stand....

* Note: This decision by the Industrial Court was the first occasion on which a tribunal was prepared to pierce the veil of 'self-employment' and strike through to the realities of the relationship behind the parties' contract in order to hold one to be an 'employee'. Much will depend on whether the courts generally will adopt this approach. If they do not, many common law and statutory rules of law applicable to employees will be easily evaded.

MERSEY DOCKS AND HARBOUR BOARD
v. COGGINS & GRIFFITH (LIVERPOOL) LTD

House of Lords   [1947] A.C. 1

The board owned a number of cranes, and employed and paid a number of skilled men to work them. They hired out a crane and driver to the respondents and the contract provided that the driver should be the respondents' servant. The respondents had the immediate direction of his operations, for instance they could tell him to move a particular piece of cargo, but they had no power to direct how he should work and manipulate the crane and its controls. The driver crushed a man with his load. The House of Lords had to decide whether the Board or the respondents were liable: this involved deciding whether the respondents had become the driver's employer.

LORD SIMONDS: It is not disputed that at the time when the respondents entered into a contract with the appellants under which the latter were to supply the former with the service of a crane and craneman, Newall was the servant of the appellants. He was engaged and paid and liable to be dismissed by them. So also, when the contract had been performed, he was their servant. If then in the performance of that contract he committed a tortious act, injuring McFarlane by his negligence, they can only escape from liability, if they can show that pro hac vice the relation of master and servant had been temporarily constituted between the respondents and Newall and temporarily abrogated between themselves and him. This they can do only by proving, in the words of Lord Esher M.R. in *Donovan v. Laing, Wharton & Down Construction Syndicate, Ltd*[1] that 'entire and absolute control' over the workman had passed to the respondents. In the cited case the court held upon the facts that the burden of proof had been discharged and I do not question the decision. But it appears to me that the test can only be satisfied if the temporary employer (if to use the word 'employer' is not to beg the question) can direct not only what the workman is to do but also how he is to do it. In the case before your Lordships the negligence of the workman lay not in the performance of any act which the respondents could and did direct and for which, because they procured it, they would be responsible, but in the manner in which that act was performed, a matter in which they could give no direction and for which they can have no responsibility.

The doctrine of the vicarious responsibility of the 'superior',

1 [1893] 1 Q.B. 629, 632.

whatever its origin, is to-day justified by social necessity, but, if the question is where that responsibility should lie, the answer should surely point to that master in whose act some degree of fault, though remote, may be found. Here the fault, if any, lay with the appellants who though they were not present to dictate how directions given by another should be carried out, yet had vested in their servant a discretion in the manner of carrying out such directions.

LORD MACMILLAN, LORD PORTER, LORD UTHWATT and VISCOUNT SIMON delivered concurring speeches.

SPALDING v. TARMAC CIVIL ENGINEERING LTD

Court of Appeal   [1966] 1 W.L.R. 156

The plaintiff was injured when a crane, which had been hired out by the second defendants (the owners) to the first defendants (who employed the plaintiffs), collapsed.

The judge found that there were two causes of the accident: negligence of the driver in handling the crane and his failure to maintain the brakes of the crane. The judge apportioned responsibility for the accident as between these two causes as 60% and 40% respectively. The driver had been supplied by the owner under the contract.

The question arose as to which of the two defendants was liable to the plaintiff.

SALMON, L.J. referred to *Mersey Docks and Harbour Board* v. *Coggins & Griffith (Liverpool) Ltd* and continued: Viscount Simon L.C. there said:[1] '...the respondent company had the immediate direction and control of the operations to be executed by the crane driver with his crane, for example, to pick up and move a piece of cargo from shed to ship. The respondent company, however, had no power to direct how the crane driver should work the crane.'

His conclusion, therefore, was that, whatever the contract as between the board and the hirers may have said, the crane driver remained the servant of the board because the hirers had no power to direct the driver as to how he should operate the crane. There is a passage to the same effect in the speech of Lord Porter.[2]

But it was recognized in that case that this kind of contract may determine the liability of the employers inter se. Everything depends on the language used in the particular contract. The contract of course is only indirectly relevant in deciding whether the owners or the hirers of the

[1] [1947] A.C. 1, 10.   [2] Ibid. 17.

crane are responsible for the actions of the crane driver to the plaintiff who is injured by the operation of the crane. But as between the owners and the hirers the contract may determine liability. In the *Mersey Docks* case,[1] the House of Lords came to the conclusion that the contract then under consideration left the liability fairly and squarely on the shoulders of the owners and did not transfer any part of it to the hirers.

In the present case the contract is quite different. The parties state specifically in clause 8 that 'Such drivers or operators shall for all purposes in connection with their employment in the working of the plant be regarded as the servants or agents of the hirer...' If clause 8 had stopped there, it would be close to the contract in the *Mersey Docks* case, but it went on: '...who alone shall be responsible for all claims arising in connection with the operation of the plant by the said drivers or operators.'

It seems to me quite plain that this clause means that these two parties have agreed that any claim which arises in connection with the operation of the plant by the driver shall be the responsibility of the hirers.... Here you have the owners, who are hiring out a piece of equipment with one of their own skilled and experienced drivers who is for some time to act in many respects at any rate as the servant of the hirers; and what the parties are here doing in clause 8 is to agree as between themselves who it is who is to be responsible for any claim which arises out of the operation of the crane...The driver when he is maintaining the crane is in no sense a servant of the hirers...

I agree that this claim arose both out of the negligent operation of the crane and out of the negligent maintenance of the crane. The driver in operating the crane had left the boom in the air in a dangerous position: for that piece of negligence the hirers are liable. The driver had negligently failed to maintain the brake in the respects to which my Lords have referred: for that negligence the owners are responsible.

SELLERS and RUSSELL, L.JJ. concurred.

JOHN LEWIS BUILDING LTD
v. THE CONSTRUCTION INDUSTRY
TRAINING BOARD

(1966) 1 Industrial Tribunals Reports 231

The appellant company which is engaged in work within the Construction industry, is a subsidiary of another company ('the parent company'). The appellant company appealed against assessment to the levy imposed in the construction industry, contending that as all its workers were paid

[1] [1947] A.C. 1.

by the parent company it was not an employer and not therefore liable to assessment to the levy.

The decision of the Tribunal was as follows:...Article 3(2) of the Industrial Training Levy (Construction Board) Order 1965* provides that the construction industry levy shall apply to any person who on 23 June 1965 was an employer in the construction industry. The appellants contend that they were not. They concede that they were engaged in that industry, but they argue that they employed no one, and that their workers were employed in fact and in law, by the parent company.

The appellants contend that the contract of employment for each worker is with the parent company. They lay great stress on this, as they have a profit-sharing scheme for their employees, which is based upon all employees being employees of the parent company and not of subsidiary companies. For this reason, the appellants say that written particulars of the terms of employment, under Section 4 of the Contracts of Employment Act, 1963 specify the parent company, and not the appellants, as the employer of the employees working for the appellants.

The Respondents contend that, on all the facts, the appellants are the employers. The appellants' manager hires and fires. The appellants control not only the work the employees do, but the manner in which they do it. The appellants stamp the National Insurance Cards. The appellants deduct income tax. The appellants actually pay out the wages, from money drawn from the parent company. The appellants have their own yard and office. The appellants rendered a return to the Respondents in which they stated that they had 63 employees to whom they had paid remuneration in the year ended 5 April 1965...On all the facts, we find that the appellants were employers in the construction industry and liable to be assessed.

Appeal dismissed, assessment confirmed.

LEE v. LEE'S AIR FARMING LTD

Privy Council   [1961] A.C. 12

The appellant's husband was governing director of the defendant company. He was also the controlling shareholder since he held 2999 of the 3000 shares in the company which carried out the business of aerial top-dressing. The husband was also employed by the company, at 'a salary to be arranged by the governing director', as its chief pilot. While

---

* Made under the Industrial Training Act, 1964. As to what is an 'establishment' within that Act, see decisions noted in (1966) 110 Sol. Jo. 899.

piloting the plane he was killed. The Judicial Committee had to consider whether he was a 'workman' under a New Zealand statute, and whether he had entered into a contract of service with an employer. It was of the opinion that he had.

LORD MORRIS OF BORTH-Y-GEST: Their Lordships find it impossible to resist the conclusion that the active aerial operations were performed because the deceased was in some contractual relationship with the company. That relationship came about because the deceased as one legal person was willing to work for and to make a contract with the company which was another legal entity. A contractual relationship could only exist on the basis that there was consensus between two contracting parties. It was never suggested (nor in their Lordships' view could it reasonably have been suggested) that the company was a sham or a mere simulacrum. It is well established that the mere fact that someone is a director of a company is no impediment to his entering into a contract to serve the company...Control would remain with the company whoever might be the agent of the company to exercise it. The fact that so long as the deceased continued to be governing director, with amplitude of powers, it would be for him to act as the agent of the company to give the orders does not alter the fact that the company and the deceased were two separate and distinct legal persons. If the deceased had a contract of service with the company then the company had a right of control. The manner of its exercise would not affect or diminish the right to its exercise. But the existence of a right to control cannot be denied if once the reality of the legal existence of the company is recognized. Just as the company and the deceased were separate legal entities so as to permit of contractual relations being established between them, so also were they separate legal entities so as to enable the company to give an order to the deceased.

BOULTING v. ASSOCIATION OF CINEMATOGRAPH, TELEVISION AND ALLIED TECHNICIANS

[For the facts see Chapter 5 p. 567, *post*.]

Court of Appeal   [1963] 2 Q.B. 606

LORD DENNING, M.R. (in a dissenting judgment) said *obiter*: I would like to add this consideration. Suppose that there is a dispute between the company and the managing directors as to the amount of remuneration which the managing directors should receive. Is this a 'trade dispute' within s. 5 (3) of the Trade Disputes Act, 1906, with the result that the trade union could intervene on behalf of the managing directors with all the protection which the law affords? This depends on whether the managing directors are 'workmen', that is, 'persons employed' in industry. I cannot believe that a dispute between the company and its managing directors as to the amount of their remuneration is a 'trade dispute'. I am quite aware that a senior member of the staff (who is not a director) may properly be considered to be a 'person employed'. But I do not think that the chairman or directors or managing directors of a company can properly be considered 'persons employed' within the meaning of the Act. See *The Roundabout Ltd* v. *Beirne*,[1] where the directors did all the work of the company (which was running a public house), but were not held to be 'workmen'.

UPJOHN and DIPLOCK, L.JJ. did not deal with this point.

TRUSSED STEEL CONCRETE CO. LTD v. GREEN

[1946] Ch. 115

Directors of the plaintiff company, having resolved to remove the defendant managing director from office, sent him an appropriate sum in lieu of notice. This was a lawful dismissal provided they had the right to dismiss him. The defendant alleged that he was protected by a Ministry of Labour certificate made with regard to the company under the Essential Work (General Provision) (No. 2) Order 1942. The court had to decide whether the plaintiff was a workman under the Order. It found that he could be and was employed by the company, but that the terms of the order did not cover him because he was not employed 'at' or 'from' any address.

COHEN, J.: I am inclined to the view that I am not justified in construing the word 'workers' in sub-clause 4 (A) as so restricted as not to include persons in the position in which Mr Green was employed. But I do not think that that necessarily involves that every managing director would necessarily come within the description. I think you have to consider it in each case according to the facts of the case. When I find a man who is bound to devote his whole time to the affairs of the company, to do all in his power to develop and extend the business of the company, not to engage in any other business and who is engaged on the terms that his employment may be determined by the company by notice in writing, I find it impossible to say that he is not employed by the company.

[1] [1959] Ir.R. 423, 429.

I think the right way of stating the conclusion I have reached is that there is nothing to prevent me giving to the words 'persons employed in the undertaking' in clause 2 of the Essential Work (General Provisions) (No. 2) Order, 1942, a wide meaning, and that the Minister has power under reg. 58(A) to make an order affecting persons in the category of Mr Green. I cannot see any reason for limiting his power any more than the Court of Sessions did in the case to which I have referred of *Anderson* v. *James Sutherland (Peterhead), Ltd*[1]. In that case what the Court of Sessions had to decide was whether a managing director was within the meaning of an article 'a member of the company who is employed by the company in any capacity', and they came to the conclusion that he was such a person.

NATIONAL INSURANCE ACT, 1965

1. . . . (2) For the purposes of this Act, insured persons shall be divided into the following three classes, namely

(*a*) employed persons, that is to say, persons gainfully occupied in employment in Great Britain, being employment under a contract of service;

(*b*) self-employed persons, that is to say, persons gainfully occupied in employment in Great Britain who are not employed persons;

(*c*) non-employed persons, that is to say, persons who are neither employed nor self-employed persons.

GOULD *v.* MINISTER OF NATIONAL INSURANCE

[1951] 1 K.B. 731

The plaintiff, a music-hall artiste, entered a contract with Prince Littler, whereby he would appear with a female partner in a variety act described as a comedy duo. He agreed to abide by certain rules, and thereby agreed inter alia to produce a new or revert to an old song sketch or act if reasonably required of him; to obey certain rules as to the use of improper words or gestures; to obey the management's directions as to the taking of encores; to turn up for rehearsals at stated times; and gave the management power to prohibit any part of his performance which was unsuitable or unpleasing to the audience, himself agreeing not to depart from the script. The question arose as to whether he was 'an employed person' or a 'self-employed person' for

[1] 1941 S.C. 203. (Contrast *Robinson* v. *George Sorby Ltd* (1967) 2 I.T.R. 148.)

the purposes of the National Insurance Act, 1946 (the predecessor of the Act of 1965).*

ORMEROD, J.: It is clear that the real question is one of the degree of control exercised by the person employing the artiste, and this, as I see it, means not only the amount of control but the nature of that control and the direction in which it is exercised.

In *Short* v. *J. and W. Henderson Ltd*,[1] a case in the House of Lords under the Workmen's Compensation Acts, Lord Thankerton recapitulated with approval the four indicia of a contract of service derived by the Lord Justice Clerk in the Court of Session in *Park* v. *Wilsons and Clyde Coal Co. Ltd*[2] from the authorities referred to by him. These are: (*a*) the master's power of selection of his servant; (*b*) the payment of wages or other remuneration; (*c*) the master's right to control the doing of the work; and (*d*) the master's right of suspension or dismissal. He goes on to say 'that the principal requirement of a contract of service is the right of the master in some reasonable sense to control the method of doing the work, and that this factor of superintendence and control has frequently been treated as critical and decisive of the legal quality of the relationship'.

It is clear in this case that the management had the power to select the artiste, that the artiste was paid a remuneration which in the agreement is called a salary, and that in certain circumstances the management reserved the right to cancel the contract. There were, in addition, other conditions in the contract to which I have referred, by which the appellant agreed to be bound. In my view, however, they were simply conditions necessary to the proper working of the theatre. Indeed, they were conditions by which, in a suitably modified form, modified in a way which would not affect the issue, any concert artiste who was appearing at a concert for a single night might reasonably agree to be bound, and I cannot imagine that in such circumstances anyone would argue that the contract was a contract of service.

As I see this contract, there is nothing which imposes on the appellant any control over the method in which he performs his act. It is true that the management have the right to prohibit any part of the performance which they think may offend the audience, and that the right is reserved to require the appellant to produce a new song or sing an old one, and

---

[1] (1946) 39 B.W.C.C. 62.   [2] 1938 S.C. 121, 133.

* Self-employed persons may be entitled to sickness benefit, see R. (S) 2/61 *post* p. 97, but never to unemployment benefit, or injury benefit under the National Insurance (Industrial Injuries) Act, 1965.

so on; but the performing of the act depends entirely on the skill, the personality, and the artistry of the appellant, and this is a matter with which the contract gives the management no right to interfere. I am therefore of the opinion that the contract in question is a contract for services only, and not a contract of service, and that the Minister was right in treating the appellant as a self-employed person.

AMALGAMATED ENGINEERING UNION
v. MINISTER OF PENSIONS AND NATIONAL INSURANCE
[1963] 1 W.L.R. 441; [1963] 1 All E.R. 864

The Sick Steward of a local branch of the Amalgamated Engineering Union, Mr Walker, was injured in an accident while riding his motor bicycle in the course of carrying out his duties. He claimed injury benefit under the National Insurance (Industrial Injuries) Act, 1946* on the ground that his injury happened in the course of his employment as a sick steward. His stewardship was part-time: he was employed full-time by the British Transport Commission. It was a condition of membership of the Amalgamated Engineering Union that if a member was elected to some post he should accept it. He was paid 1s. per visit by the union.

The Minister's decision that he should receive benefit was opposed by the union on two grounds (amongst others): that this was only an incident of his contract of membership, not a contract of service; and that they did not anyway exercise sufficient control to make it a contract of service.

MEGAW, J.: Mr Cooke says, even looking at the matter from the point of view of rule 8 alone, there is no provision that the branch shall have any detailed control over the way in which the sick steward carries out his duties. Mr Cooke points out that nobody could give the applicant instructions as to the order in which he should make his visits; how long he should spend and the questions he should ask the sick member; how he should travel, whether by rail or bus or motor bicycle; what precautions he should take to safeguard his money or what matters he was to report on other than as provided in the rules; and how he found the sick.

Mr Cooke says that in all these circumstances this is not a contract of service. In my view, and I think this is supported by the authorities, the

---

* 'Insurable employment' is now defined in Schedule 1, National Insurance (Industrial Injuries) Act, 1965, of which para. 1 reads (as did the 1946 Act): 'Employment in Great Britain under any contract of service or apprenticeship, whether written or oral, and whether expressed or implied.'

question of control of the employee is an important element in deciding whether or not the contract is a contract of service but it is a test or criterion which is far from being an absolute one. The nature of the control which is required in order to bring the employment within the scope of a contract or service varies almost infinitely with the general nature of the duties involved. If, for example, one finds that the contract, whether a written contract or an oral contract, has laid down in considerable detail what the duties are which are to be performed, and that the employer, i.e. the union or the branch, has the right to dispense with the services of the employee if it is not satisfied with the manner in which he carries them out, the actual absence of any express provision as to the right of the employer to control the manner of carrying out the work may be of very much less importance than it would be in other cases. Here I think, having regard to the detail in which the sick steward's duties are defined in rule 8, clauses 4 and 5, it is a case where the control of the employer is sufficiently extensive to bring the case within the category of contract of service rather than contract for services. I think anyone reading these rules as a whole would more reasonably take the view that the relationship established here is the relationship of master and servant than of employer and independent contractor. In so far as it is a question of law—and I do feel some difficulty in seeing how it is really a question of law—I should hold that in this case the nature of the employment falls on the contract of service side of the line.

WILD v. JOHN BROWN & CO.

Court of Appeal   [1919] 1 K.B. 134

The plaintiff, a miner, was also the delegate of the Rotherham Branch of the Yorkshire Miners' Association and on occasions was appointed by the men to inspect the workings of the colliery and the condition of working places under the Coal Mines Acts of 1911 and 1912. On these occasions he was paid by the men. He was injured in the course of his employment and claimed to be compensated for loss of earnings from all his normal sources of income under various provisions of the Workmen's Compensation Acts. This raised the question of whether his part-time activities were performed under a contract of service.

SWINFEN EADY, M.R.: The question that arises is, what was his position as delegate of the Branch? Did it constitute a contract of service within the meaning of the Act, and was the relationship of employer and workman constituted between the applicant and either his branch or the Association? The applicant said that there was nothing in writing

specifying the duties of delegates except the rules of the Association which he produced, and that he was a delegate of the branch in pursuance of these rules...The evidence really comes to this, that in certain matters the delegate may well have to obey the instructions of the branch that sent him, or their mandate, as the applicant says, but that, with regard to other matters provided for by the rules, he would have to exercise his own judgment and discretion. Can it be said that a person elected in such circumstances to be a delegate is under a contract of service as a workman either to the branch or to the Association? It seems to me to be obviously impossible. It cannot therefore be maintained that there was in this connection any concurrent contract of service within the meaning of the Workmen's Compensation Act, 1906.
DUKE, L.J. and EVE, J. concurred.

M.64 JOBBING GARDENER

Decision of the Minister under the National Insurance Act, 1946

Mrs M. 'at her husband's request' advertised for a gardener. She interviewed and engaged Mr X. who answered the advertisement. He had been a gardener for some 15 years. It was arranged that he should do gardening for Mr and Mrs M. on Mondays and Wednesdays and that his wages should be 26s. a day. On Monday, 23 November 1953, he was taken round the garden by Mrs M. who told him what vegetables she wanted and the size of the household to be supplied.

From that day he worked in the garden from 8 a.m. to 4.30 p.m. on Mondays and Wednesdays...Mrs M. paid Mr X. out of money which her husband gave her for the purpose. He received £2. 12s. a week wages from her whether or not he worked two full days; he was also paid for the fortnight he was on holiday.

Decision. That...Mr X. was included in the class of employed persons for the purposes of the National Insurance Act, 1946; and was employed in insurable employment within the meaning of the National Insurance (Industrial Injuries) Act, 1946; that Mr M. was liable as employer for the payment of contributions under the said Acts in respect of the said Mr X. during the said period. (16 August 1956).

BRADDELL v. BAKER

(1911) 27 T.L.R. 182

Braddell employed William Taylor as a jobbing gardener for four days a week. Taylor was at liberty to work for someone else at other times; and to send along a substitute on any day when he could not attend at

Braddell's himself. An information was preferred against Braddell for employing a 'male servant' without a licence contrary to s. 19 (3) of the Revenue Act, 1869 (now repealed).

LORD ALVERSTONE, C.J.: They must recognize that in a large number of instances, especially in the case of persons who had a garden which was not large enough to occupy the whole time of a gardener it was a common practice for a nurseryman to do a gardener's work occasionally. The question, therefore, could not be solved by looking simply at the class of work that the man had to do.

If a taxable servant did work which made his master liable, the master would not escape the tax by reason of the servant doing some other work. But a master did not become liable in respect of a non-taxable servant simply because he did some work which would make a servant taxable. In each case it was a question of fact, and he was unable to say that the magistrates had gone wrong in taking the view that a nurseryman who was employed in this manner and with these privileges did not come within the expression 'male servant' in s. 19 (3) of the Revenue Act, 1869.

HAMILTON, J. and AVORY, J. concurred.

M.67 FOREIGN GIRLS PERFORMING PART-TIME DOMESTIC WORK

Decision of the Minister under the National Insurance Act, 1946

Mr J., and his wife who was employed full-time as a schoolmistress, had two young children. They wished to have a girl to live with them who would help with the domestic work and look after and be a companion to their younger child while Mrs J. was away from home.

During the period from March 1950 to June 1955, five Danish girls resided with them successively for periods varying from six months to nearly two years...The girls regularly performed part-time domestic work for Mr and Mrs J. and were paid weekly the sum agreed upon. Mrs J. told the girls they should normally be available for domestic work throughout the morning. She indicated to them from time to time what work they should do and on occasions how they should do it. Mr and Mrs J. sometimes helped the girls with their work. The girls had meals with the family, were introduced to their friends and treated as their social equals.

The girls improved their English by conversations with Mr and Mrs J. who from time to time would correct their mistakes...

Decision. That while performing domestic work for Mr and Mrs J. the girls were included in the class of employed persons for the purposes of the National Insurance Act, 1946; and were employed in insurable employment within the meaning of the National Insurance (Industrial Injuries) Act, 1946.   (27 February, 1957).

WHITTAKER v. MINISTER OF PENSIONS

[1966] 3 All E.R. 531

A claimant for industrial injury benefit was refused industrial benefit after suffering injury during the course of her trapeze act at a circus. She was engaged to give a specified number of performances and provide her own apparatus. She was also required to assist in moves, in seating the audience, and on occasion in full usherette duties. Rather less than half her working day was spent on her own act and preparation for it; but assisting in moving and seating the audience were customary for circus performers. She appealed against the Minister's decision that she was not 'employed in insurable employment'.

MOCATTA, J., reviewed the cases and, distinguishing *Gould's* case (*ante*, p. 22), concluded: It seems clear, therefore, from the more recent cases that persons possessed of a high degree of professional skill and expertise, such as surgeons and civil engineers, may nevertheless be employed as servants under contracts of service, notwithstanding that their employers can, in the nature of things, exercise extremely little, if any, control over the way in which such skill is used. The test of control is, therefore, not as determinative as used to be thought to be the case, though no doubt it is still of value in that the greater the degree of control exerciseable by the employer, the more likely it is that the contract is one of service.

The difficulty in this case is due to the hybrid character of the claimant's duties. Had she only been obliged to perform her trapeze act, even if she had also been under various constraints and controls in relation thereto, there would have been grounds for holding her contract to have been one for services. It is even clearer that, if she had been employed only to help in moving the circus from place to place and to act as an usherette during performances, her contract would have been one of service. Here she had both types of duty to perform.

I must apply here the test approved in *Cassidy's* case[1], namely, was

[1] [1951] 1 All E.R. 574; [1951] 2 K.B. 343.

her contract a contract of service within the meaning which an ordinary person would give to the words? In doing so I must have regard to the contract as a whole. Whilst it is no doubt true that the claimant would not have secured her contract had she not been a trapeze artiste, she equally, as it appears to me, would not have secured it had she not agreed to assist in moving the circus and to act as an usherette. It is noticeable that the special typed provisions in cl. 25 as to her undertaking full usherette duties went beyond the printed and general provision in cl. 14, applicable apparently to all artistes, regarding assisting in seating the audience at and before each performance as was required. The performance of her own highly skilled professional act and the preparations for it occupied, it would seem, rather less than half her working day. The first sentence of cl. 4 of the contract is ungrammatical but appears to mean that the claimant undertook to devote the whole of her working time during the period of the engagement to the company, a provision markedly alien to the usual position of independent contractors. Looking at the contract as a whole and the evidence as to how she was required to perform her duties under it, it seems to me that she had no real independence and had to carry out her contractual duties as an integral part of the business of the company during her engagement. In other words the feature of contracts of service to which DENNING, L.J., drew attention in his judgment in *Stevenson, Jordan and Harrison, Ltd* v. *MacDonald & Evans*[1], cited earlier, is clearly present here.

In my judgment, having regard to the test to be applied and all the circumstances of the case, the claimant was at the time of her accident employed under a contract of service and was therefore employed in insurable employment within the meaning of the National Insurance (Industrial Injuries) Act, 1946, at that time and I accordingly answer in her favour the question of law raised by the Case Stated.

I should add that after writing the above, my attention was drawn by Mr Patrick Atiyah, Fellow of New College, Oxford, to the decision of the High Court of Australia in *Zuijs* v. *Wirth Brothers Pty, Ltd.*[2] That case also concerned an accident to a trapeze artiste in a circus and the question whether he was or was not at the time employed under a contract of service. The similarities between the two cases are fairly close and I am glad to find that the conclusion at which I had arrived accords with the decision reached in that case and with a number of the interesting authorities therein cited.

[1] [1952] 1 T.L.R. 101.　　　　[2] (1955), 93 C.L.R. 561.

CONTRACTS OF EMPLOYMENT ACT, 1963

8. *Interpretation.*—(1) In this Act—'employee' means an individual who has entered into or works under a contract with an employer, whether the contract be for manual labour, clerical work or otherwise, be expressed or implied, oral or in writing, and whether it be a contract of service or of apprenticeship; and cognate expressions shall be construed accordingly.*

TRADE DISPUTES ACT, 1906

5. (3) In this Act and in the Conspiracy and Protection of Property Act, 1875, the expression 'trade dispute' means any dispute between employers and workmen, or between workmen and workmen, which is connected with the employment or non-employment, or the terms of the employment, or with the conditions of labour, of any person, and the expression 'workmen' means all persons employed in trade or industry, whether or not in the employment of the employer with whom a trade dispute arises...

INDUSTRIAL COURTS ACT, 1919

8. [The] expression 'workman' means any person who has entered into or works under a contract with an employer whether the contract be by way of manual labour, clerical work, or otherwise, be expressed or implied, oral or in writing, and whether it be a contract of service or of apprenticeship or a contract personally to execute any work or labour.

EMPLOYERS AND WORKMEN ACT, 1875

10. *Definitions:* 'Workman.'—In this Act the expression 'workman' does not include a domestic or menial servant, but save as aforesaid, means any person who, being a labourer, servant in husbandry, journeyman, artificer, handicraftsman, miner, or otherwise engaged in manual labour, whether under the age of twenty-one years or above that age, has entered into or works under a contract with an employer, whether the contract be made before or after the passing of this Act, be express or implied, oral or in writing, and be a contract of service or a contract personally to execute any work or labour.†

---

* Exactly the same definition is used in the Prices and Incomes Act, 1966, s. 34. On the Redundancy Payments Act, 1965, s. 25 see *post* p. 218 and on the contrast between the 1963 and 1965 Acts *post* p. 68.

† Note: this is the definition of relevance to the Truck Act, 1831: see *post* p. 119.

WAGES COUNCILS ACT, 1959

24. *Interpretation.*—In this Act the following expressions have the meanings hereby respectively assigned to them, that is to say: 'worker' means any person who has entered into or works under a contract with an employer, whether the contract be for manual labour, clerical work or otherwise, be expressed or implied, oral or in writing and whether it be a contract of service or of apprenticeship or a contract personally to execute any work or labour, except that it does not include any person who is employed casually and otherwise than for the purposes of the employer's business.

Section B

THE NATURE OF THE CONTRACT OF EMPLOYMENT

(i) personal character

NOKES *v.* DONCASTER AMALGAMATED COLLIERIES LTD

House of Lords   [1940] A.C. 1014

Two companies, one of which employed the appellant, amalgamated. The appellant shortly afterwards was prosecuted for absenting himself. The question arose whether he was under a contract of service with the new company. It was held that he was not, because he had not consented to a new contract.

In the course of his speech Lord Atkin said: I had fancied that ingrained in the personal status of a citizen under our laws was the right to choose for himself whom he would serve: and that this right of choice constituted the main difference between a servant and a serf...A winding-up order or resolution operated as a discharge of existing servants, resulting in the right to claim damages for wrongful dismissal. It is true that the transferee company would ordinarily offer to employ the former servants of the transferor company: and an unreasonable refusal to accept such offer would mitigate or perhaps get rid of any damages. But the servant was left with his inalienable right to choose whether he would serve a new master or not.

JOHNSON v. DREWSON'S DECOR LIMITED

(1966) 1 Industrial Tribunals Reports 267

In September 1960 the applicant commenced employment with James Drewitt & Son Ltd. He continued to work for this company but, on the 1 July 1963, he was told to go and work at another site. He was not told that his employers had changed, although the respondents claimed that they had taken over the services of the applicant on that date. He was dismissed and claimed a redundancy payment. (See *post* p. 215).

The Decision of the Tribunal was as follows: ... The applicant gave evidence to the effect that he was employed by James Drewitt & Son Ltd as a painter continuously up to the 1 July 1963, when he was called to the office and told to go to work on another site. He was not told of any change of employer either then or later, nor was any document ever given to him notifying him of any such change... We find that the applicant was not informed of any change of employer, still less was he given any opportunity to exercise his judgment as to whether he wished to take up employment with Drewson's Decor Ltd. He was originally employed by James Drewitt & Son Ltd as a painter and, up to the time of his dismissal, he was doing painting work for James Drewitt & Son Ltd, under Drewitt's foreman. It is clear there is a close association between James Drewitt & Son Ltd and Drewson's Decor Ltd, though the companies are not associated within the meaning of s. 48 of the Redundancy Payments Act 1965, and it may well be that from time to time Drewson's Decor Ltd took over the responsibility for members of staff of James Drewitt & Son Ltd. Whatever arrangement was made between the two companies, the contract between Mr Johnson and James Drewitt & Son Ltd was never terminated until such time as Drewson's Decor Ltd gave him notice, which he accepted as a valid notice of termination of contract. Mr Johnson... must at some indeterminate stage, have realized that Drewson's Ltd purported to be his employers, but he never terminated his employment with James Drewitt. Seeing that there was no change in the nature of the work he was doing nor as to the company for which it was being done, it cannot be said that he had left his employment with James Drewitt.

We do not accept that Mr Johnson was ever dismissed by James Drewitt & Son Ltd in 1963 nor had he accepted employment by Drewson's Decor, and we hold that the respondent has failed to discharge the burden of proof that there has been any break in his employment. We therefore hold that he is entitled to a redundancy payment for the whole period for which he claims.

FARROW v. WILSON

(1869) L.R. 4 C.P. 744*

Price Pugh employed the plaintiff to be his farmer-bailiff. Both sides had to give 6 months' notice; or 6 months' salary in lieu of notice could be given by Price Pugh. Price Pugh died. This was an action for wrongful dismissal against his personal representative who gave no notice or payment in lieu.

WILLES, J. (delivering the judgment of the court): In this case our judgment is for the defendants. Generally speaking, contracts bind the executor or administrator, though not named. Where, however, personal considerations are of the foundation of the contract, as in cases of principal and agent and master and servant, the death of either party puts an end to the relation; and, in respect of service after the death, the contract is dissolved, unless there be a stipulation express or implied to the contrary. It is obvious that, in this case, if the servant had died, his master could not have compelled his representatives to perform the service in his stead, or pay damages, and equally by the death of the master the servant is discharged of his service, not in breach of the contract, but by implied condition.

JOHNSON v. SHREWSBURY AND BIRMINGHAM RAILWAY CO.

(Court of Appeal in Chancery)   3 De G.M. & G. 914 (43 E.R. 358)

The defendants, a railway company, entered a seven year agreement with the plaintiffs whereby the latter were to run the railway. The contract was to end if the contractors failed to obey, within 48 hours, any instructions from the company. The company issued impossible instructions. An injunction to restrain them from determining the contract was sought.

KNIGHT BRUCE, L.J.: There is here an agreement, the effect of which is that the Plaintiffs are to be the confidential servants of the Defendants in most important particulars, in which, not only for the sake of the persons immediately concerned but for the sake of society at large, it is necessary that there should be the most entire harmony and spirit of co-operation between the contracting parties. How is this possible to prevail in the position in which (I assume for the purpose of the argument by the default of the Defendants) the Defendants have placed

* See too Termination of Employment *post*, p. 137.

themselves ? We are asked to compel one person to employ against his will another as his confidential servant, for duties with respect to the due performance of which the utmost confidence is required. Let him be one of the best and most competent persons that ever lived, still if the two do not agree, and good people do not always agree, enormous mischief may be done.

A man may have one of the best domestic servants, he may have a valet whose arrangement of clothes is faultless, a coachman whose driving is excellent, a cook whose performances are perfect, and yet he may not have confidence in him: and while on the one hand all that the servant requires or wishes (and that reasonably enough) is money, you are on the other hand to destroy the comfort of a man's existence for a period of years, by compelling him to have constantly about him in a confidential situation one to whom he objects. If that be so in private life, how important do these considerations become when connected with the performance of such duties—duties to society—as are incumbent upon the directors of a company like this. I think that by interfering in the present case there would be no equality.

TURNER, L.J., delivered a concurring judgment.

KEETCH & OTHERS v. LONDON PASSENGER TRANSPORT BOARD

Times, 20 September 1946

This was an application by the plaintiffs for an interim injunction and a declaration against the defendants, their employers, to prevent the employers from making it a condition of the plaintiffs' employment that they should become members of the Transport and General Workers' Union. The issue before the court being that even if the notice to terminate, given to those employees who refused to join the union, was notice in breach of contract would an injunction lie against the defendants ?

WYNN PARRY, J., said that: He proposed to assume in favour of the plaintiffs, without deciding the matter, that Mr Paull was correct in his submission that there was a term in each contract that the employee should not be discharged except on grounds of misconduct, age, ill-health, reduction of staff, or some similar ground. Even on that assumption, would it be right to intervene and grant an injunction restraining the defendants from making it a condition of the plaintiffs' employment that they should join the union ? There was a well established principle of that Court that it would not enforce specifically a contract for personal service.

It appeared from the observations of Lord Lindley in *Whitwood Chemical Company* v. *Hardman* (see *post*, p. 36) that for an injunction to be granted in the case of an agreement for personal service the onus was on the plaintiff to show that his case fell within some recognized exception to the general rule that the Court would not decree specific performance of a contract of personal service. It also appeared from Lord Lindley's observations that the Court must look at the matter broadly and would generally consider it much better not to interfere. Lord Lindley also described the remedy by injunction as an 'extraordinary' one. Finally, it was important to observe that his remarks were based on the assumption that the defendant had broken his contract or intended to do so.

Assuming for the purpose of the present judgment that the defendants intended to take a step which would amount to a breach of contract, the remarks of Lord Lindley provided him with a sure and safe guide, and he must be satisfied that the case did not fall within the general principle that the Court would not enforce a contract of personal service by injunction, but fell within such a recognized exception to that rule as was to be found in *Lumley* v. *Wagner* ((1852) 1 De M. & G. 604). That case was still law, and from it and other authorities it appeared that the Court would not interfere by injunction unless it was able to effect some substantial result by giving the party claiming it some substantial relief.

In his view that could not be achieved by an injunction in the present case. The policy of the board, as he understood it, was that they were simply saying that in the cases of employees who did not wish to join the union, they proposed to give them notice. That being so, and assuming that the following out of that policy would constitute a breach of the contract between the board and the plaintiffs, it was still manifest that the plaintiffs could not successfully claim the injunction for which they asked because that would amount to ordering specific performance of the contract in an indirect way. The remedy of the plaintiffs, if there were a breach of contract, was primarily in damages. Any injunction which that Court granted at the present time could at the most be only of a very limited nature as regarded the period during which it would be effective, and for that reason he did not regard the case as one which fell within the principle laid down in *Lumley* v. *Wagner*. Taking that view, he was thrown back on the guidance given by Lord Lindley in

Whitwood Chemical Co. v. *Hardman*, and accepting that guidance and applying it he had come to the conclusion that the case was not one in which he should interfere at that stage by granting an interlocutory injunction.

WHITWOOD CHEMICAL CO. *v.* HARDMAN

Court of Appeal   [1891] 2 Ch. 416

The manager of a manufacturing company agreed to give 'the whole of his time to the company's business' for 10 years. He became actively engaged in promoting a rival company: and was about to invest in it and become a director. His employers sought to restrain him.

LINDLEY, L.J.: The first point to observe is, that there is no negative covenant at all, in terms, contained in the agreement on which the plaintiffs are suing—that is to say, the parties have not expressly stipulated that the defendant shall not do any particular thing. The agreement is wholly an affirmative agreement, and the substantial part of it is that the defendant has agreed to give 'the whole of his time' to the plaintiff company...Now every agreement to do a particular thing in one sense involves a negative. It involves the negative of doing that which is inconsistent with the thing you are to do. If I agree with a man to be at a certain place at a certain time, I impliedly agree that I will not be anywhere else at the same time, and so on *ad infinitum*; but it does not at all follow that, because a person has agreed to do a particular thing, he is, therefore, to be restrained from doing everything else which is inconsistent with it. The Court has never gone that length, and I do not suppose that it ever will. We are dealing here with a contract of a particular class. It is a contract involving the performance of a personal service, and, as a rule, the Court does not decree specific performance of such contracts. That is a general rule. There has been engrafted upon that rule an exception, which is explained more or less definitely in *Lumley* v. *Wagner*[1]—that is to say, where a person has engaged not to serve any other master, or not to perform at any other place, the Court can lay hold of that, and restrain him from so doing; and there are observations, in which I concur, made by Lord Selborne in the *Wolverhampton and Walsall Railway Company* v. *London and North Western Railway Company*[2], to the effect that the principle does not depend upon whether you have an actual negative clause, if you can say that the parties were contracting in the sense that one

[1] 1 D.M. & G. 604.   [2] Law Rep. 16 Eq. 433.

should not do this, or the other—some specific thing upon which you can put your finger.

But there is this to be considered. What are we to say in this particular case? What injunction can be granted in this particular case which will not be, in substance and effect, a decree for specific performance of this agreement? It appears to me the difficulty of the plaintiffs is this, that they cannot suggest anything which, when examined, does not amount to this, that the man must either be idle, or specifically perform the agreement into which he has entered.

KAY, L.J., delivered a concurring judgment.

WARNER BROTHERS PICTURES INC. v. NELSON

[1937] 1 K.B. 209

Warner Brothers sought an injunction against Bette Davis to restrain her from acting for any other film company. By her contract she had agreed to render her services as a film artiste exclusively to Warner Brothers for a specified period.

BRANSON, J.: The conclusion to be drawn from the authorities is that, where a contract of personal service contains negative covenants the enforcement of which will not amount either to a decree of specific performance of the positive covenants of the contract or to the giving of a decree under which the defendant must either remain idle or perform those positive covenants, the Court will enforce those negative covenants; but this is subject to a further consideration. An injunction is a discretionary remedy, and the Court in granting it may limit it to what the Court considers reasonable in all the circumstances of the case...The case before me is, therefore, one in which it would be proper to grant an injunction unless to do so would in the circumstances be tantamount to ordering the defendant to perform her contract or remain idle or unless damages would be the more appropriate remedy ...The defendant is stated to be a person of intelligence, capacity and means, and no evidence was adduced to show that, if enjoined from doing the specified acts otherwise than for the plaintiffs, she will not be able to employ herself both usefully and remuneratively in other spheres of activity, though not as remuneratively as in her special line. She will not be driven, although she may be tempted, to perform the contract, and the fact that she may be so tempted is no objection to the grant of an injunction.

R. v. NATIONAL ARBITRATION TRIBUNAL, EX PARTE HORATIO CROWTHER & CO. LTD

[1948] 1 K.B. 424

The court had to consider whether the wartime Order 1305 gave the National Arbitration Tribunal power to order the reinstatement of a wrongly dismissed employee.

LORD GODDARD, C.J.: It seems to me it is a strong thing to say, looking at this regulation which alone gives force to the order, that a power is thereby impliedly given to the tribunal to grant a remedy which no court of law or equity has ever considered it had power to grant. If an employer breaks his contract of service with his employees, either by not giving notice to which the latter are entitled, or by discharging them summarily for a reason which cannot be justified, the workmen's remedy is for damages only. A court of equity has never granted an injunction compelling an employer to continue a workman in his employment or to oblige a workman to work for an employer. If a workman or any other employee who occupies a higher status than that usually implied by the term workman, breaks his contract with his employer, no injunction has ever been granted obliging that workman or employee to work for the employer. The most that has ever been done is that if the contract was one by which for a certain period a person has agreed to serve another exclusively, the workman or employee may be restrained from working for anybody else during the term for which he contractually engaged to serve his employer.

Nor is there any provision in the regulation which imposes a penalty on the employer if he refuses, after the award, to re-employ the man, nor on the workman, if, in spite of an award, he refuses to work for an employer.

CROOM-JOHNSON and HUMPHREYS, J.J., delivered concurring judgments.

TRANSPORT AND GENERAL WORKERS' UNION v. SILCOCK AND COLLING LTD

Industrial Court: Case 3081

This was a voluntary arbitration under the provisions of the Industrial Courts Act, 1919. The court was asked to determine whether a breach had occurred of an agreed procedure and whether a dismissed driver,

F. Murray, should be reinstated in his former employment. F. Murray was a car transporter driver at Halewood and shop steward of the Transport and General Workers' Union. He was convicted in a Magistrates' Court of dangerous driving. The same day a union official was asked if he could spare ten minutes in the depot manager's office. At this meeting Murray was summarily dismissed. The bewildered official asked if this action could be stayed until he could get in touch with the company's directors; but this was refused. The official discussed the matter with the shop stewards; considerable aggravation was felt; and a meeting of men resolved on a withdrawal of labour.

The disputes procedure provided that disputes would be discussed between appropriate management and union representatives; failing agreement, referred to the Chairman of the Employers' Association and Union officials; failing settlement, sent to a meeting of the Joint Committee; and, if agreement still was not reached, referred to the Ministry of Labour Conciliation Department. The agreement continued: ...(e) Failing settlement it is agreed that either party may ask for an arbitrator to be appointed by the Ministry of Labour Conciliation Department and this arbitrator's decision shall be binding on both parties. Disputes affecting all member firms of the association will be referred as a dispute with the Ford Collecting and Delivery Agents' Service Association. (f) No strike or lock-out will take place whilst the above procedure is being complied with, and both parties will ensure that it is not unnecessarily delayed or obstructed.

33. *Award.*—The findings and conclusions of the Court relating to the two items contained in the Terms of Reference are as follows:

Item 1...

(3) The key to the difference between the Parties lies mainly in the interview on the afternoon of the 17 August 1965, at which the depot manager dismissed Mr Murray...

(5) In the event, when the interview was over the district official did not get into telephone communication with the Chairman of the Association or indeed with any of the directors at Dagenham. Instead, he and the senior shop steward had a discussion with the other shop stewards and thereafter called a meeting of the Company's hourly-paid staff then on the site, following which those members of the staff and subsequently the remainder of the hourly-paid staff withdrew their labour. On the 19 August this strike was recognised as official by the General Executive Council of the Union.

(6) It is an express provision of the Procedure (see Clause 3 (*f*) of the Agreement quoted in paragraph 5 above) that 'No strike or lock-out will take place while the above procedure is complied with, and both parties will ensure that it is not unnecessarily delayed or obstructed'. In view particularly of this provision it is plain that, unless the submissions argued before the Court by the Union are correct, the strike mentioned in paragraph (5) above was started, and subsequently approved by the Union, in breach of the Procedure. The substance of the Union's argument is that the depot manager's refusal to suspend his dismissal of Mr Murray until the district official could take the matter up with the directors at Dagenham constituted itself a breach of and non-compliance with the Procedure; that it constituted an 'obstruction' of the Procedure within the meaning of the above-quoted Clause 3 (*f*) of the Procedure; that it nullified the operation or application of the Procedure in relation to the dispute in question; and that in consequence the strike did not constitute any breach of the Procedure. The Court are unable to accept this argument as correct....If at any stage of the Procedure it is agreed (or, in the case of the last stage, awarded) that the manager's decision was unjustified or should for any reason be reversed, the normal and right course is that if the driver has already been dismissed the agreement or award makes proper provision, if necessary, for his reinstatement. This is what commonly happens in industrial disputes. It may possibly, in the circumstances of any given case, be wise for a manager to suspend the dismissal pending the operation of the Procedure, but it is no breach or obstruction of the Procedure for him to adhere to his decision to dismiss the worker and to leave it to the Procedure to rectify that decision if it is wrong. The Court accordingly find that the Union are wrong in contending that by reason of the course taken by the depot manager the strike did not constitute a breach of the Procedure...

(9) The Court think it right to add, however, that there were certain mitigating factors in relation to the calling of the strike on the 17 August.

Item 2.

After considering carefully all the relevant evidence put before them, and the submissions of the Parties, the Court find, and so Award, that the Union's claim that Mr Murray should be reinstated in his former employment has not been established.*

* The availability of reinstatement as a remedy in voluntary arbitration contrasts with the common law approach. It is encountered occasionally in awards of the In-

VINE v. NATIONAL DOCK LABOUR BOARD

House of Lords [1957] A.C. 488

Vine was a registered dock worker under the scheme set up by the Dock Workers (Regulation of Employment) Act, 1946 and by an order made under that statute in 1947. He failed to attend for shift work with a company of stevedores. As a result he was brought before a disciplinary committee set up by the local board, and was given seven days notice. His appeal to a tribunal set up under the scheme failed. He challenged this decision on the ground that the local board had no power to delegate its disciplinary powers to the committee, and he claimed damages for wrongful dismissal and a declaration* that his dismissal was *ultra vires*.

VISCOUNT KILMUIR, L.C.: First, it follows from the fact that the plaintiff's dismissal was invalid that his name was never validly removed from the register and he continued in the employ of the National Board. This is an entirely different situation from the ordinary master and servant case; there, if the master wrongfully dismisses the servant, either summarily or by giving insufficient notice, the employment is effectively terminated, albeit in breach of contract. Here, the removal of the plaintiff's name from the register being, in law, a nullity, he continued to have the right to be treated as a registered dock worker with all the benefits which, by statute, that status conferred on him. It is therefore right that, with the background of this scheme, the court should declare his rights.

Secondly, it was said that the grant of a declaration would lead to further litigation; I cannot believe that the National Board would do other than comply with the declaration, and, in that case, I do not see why there should be further litigation. Thirdly, for the reasons given by Jenkins, L.J., I find it difficult to see that damages would be an adequate remedy.

LORD KEITH OF AVONHOLM: This is not a straightforward relationship of master and servant. Normally, and apart from the intervention of statute, there would never be a nullity in terminating an ordinary contract of master and servant. Dismissal might be in breach of contract and so unlawful but could only sound in damages.

dustrial Court, and very frequently in the decisions of *ad hoc* arbitrators, appointed by the Ministry of Labour under the Industrial Courts Act, 1919, to whom parties in industry often refer their disputes.

* Compare the remedy in *McClelland* v. *Northern Ireland General Health Services Board, post*, p. 161.

Here we are concerned with a statutory scheme of employment. One of its objects was to do away with the evils of casual employment at the docks. Another was to secure a regular supply of labour for the shipping and unshipping of merchandise. These objects are concisely stated in the scheme, echoing the words of the statute, to be 'to ensure greater regularity of employment for dock workers and to secure that an adequate number of dock workers is available for the efficient performance of dock work.' No employer can engage labour at the docks unless he is registered under the scheme and no dock worker can be employed at the docks unless he also is registered under the scheme. To be registered as a dock worker is, therefore, the first step in getting employment. Further, having been registered the worker comes on to the pay roll of the National Dock Labour Board, unless he is in the employ of a registered dock employer on a contract by the week or longer, whether there is work for him or not. He is in what the scheme calls the reserve pool and while in the reserve pool is in the employment of the National Dock Labour Board. While in the reserve pool a man has to be at call unless he is excused for illness or otherwise. When allocated for work at the docks he comes for the time being into the employment of the particular registered employer requiring his services, and when this employment is finished he falls back again into the reserve pool. The worker employed by a registered employer on a week's notice or longer does not properly come within the scheme apart from the fact that he must be registered. He is paid by his particular employer and is subject to his orders and control. But if he were dismissed by his employer it would seem that, as a registered dock worker, he would fall into the reserve pool and be in the employment of the National Board and subject to the directions of the local board. It is impossible, in my opinion, to equate the position of a registered dock worker in relation to the National Dock Labour Board with that of an employee under an ordinary contract of service.

LORDS MORTON OF HENRYTON, COHEN and SOMERVELL OF HARROW delivered concurring speeches.

BARBER v. MANCHESTER REGIONAL HOSPITAL BOARD

[1958] 1 W.L.R. 181

The plaintiff was a gynaecologist at a hospital which in 1948 came under the control of a regional hospital board. By a circular the board informed the hospital staff that new contracts on the basis of terms and conditions issued by the Minister of Health would be offered soon, but that meanwhile their duties would be continued 'subject to the terms and conditions of service above referred to'. The plaintiff refused to accept the permanent contract on the terms offered and was dismissed. The Minister refused to hear an appeal on the ground that he was not employed under a contract which incorporated the appeal procedure contained in the terms and conditions of service.

Inter alia, the plaintiff claimed a declaration that his employment with the board had never been validly determined.

BARRY, J.: However, Mr Scott Henderson's case is that the termination of the plaintiff's employment on 30 April 1952 was not only a breach of the plaintiff's contractual rights, but was in fact a nullity. In law, Mr Scott Henderson submits, the plaintiff's services were not terminated on 30 April 1952, and have never been terminated up to today. In consequence he relies on the third prayer, namely, for an order for payment of salary at the full rate of £2375 per annum from 1 May 1952, to the date of the writ. Mr Scott Henderson puts the case in a way which, at first sight, appears attractive. The terms and conditions, as he points out, provide in the clearest possible terms that the procedure laid down in clause 16 shall be completed before the board's decision to terminate a consultant's appointment is carried into effect. That procedure was never completed and, therefore, he argues, the board's decision to terminate the plaintiff's appointment can never have become effective; he is still in their service, and is still entitled to his agreed rate of remuneration.

Mr Scott Henderson relied on certain authorities and in particular on *Vine* v. *National Dock Labour Board*... Giving this matter the best consideration I can, I am unable to equate this case to the circumstances which were being considered by the Court of Appeal and the House of Lords in *Vine* v. *National Dock Labour Board*. There the plaintiff was working under a statutory scheme of employment, and clearly in those circumstances all the Lords of Appeal who dealt with the case in the House of Lords took the view that it could not be dealt with as though it were an ordinary master and servant claim in which the rights of the parties were regulated solely by contract. Here, despite the strong statutory flavour attaching to the plaintiff's contract, I have reached the conclusion that in essence it was an ordinary contract between master and servant and nothing more. In those circumstances I feel bound to apply the general rule stated by Lord Keith, and to reach the conclusion here that the plaintiff's only remedy against the board is the recovery of damages.

VIDYODAYA UNIVERSITY v. SILVA

Privy Council   [1964] 3 All E.R. 865

The appellant university was set up by statute and was empowered to institute professorships. Every appointment was to be by agreement in writing between the university and the professor on such terms as the executive council thought fit. The council was empowered by s. 18(e) of the statute to dismiss 'any officer or teacher on the grounds of incapacity or conduct which in the opinion of not less than two-thirds of the members of the council renders him unfit to be an officer or teacher of the university'.

The respondent, a professor, claimed that the council, in dismissing him, had to act judicially to terminate the appointment and should have told him of the accusations and given him an opportunity of being heard.

LORD MORRIS delivered the opinion: The law is well settled that if, where there is an ordinary contractual relationship of master and servant, the master terminates the contract the servant cannot obtain an order of certiorari. If the master rightfully ends the contract there can be no complaint: if the master wrongfully ends the contract then the servant can pursue a claim for damages...In a straightforward case where a master employs a servant the latter is not regarded as the holder of an office and, if the contract is terminated, there are ordinarily no questions affecting status or involving property rights. It becomes necessary, therefore, to consider whether in the present case there are any features which suggest a relationship other than that of master and servant. It was submitted on behalf of the respondent first that, if someone has the power to determine what the rights of an individual are to be, then a duty to act judicially arises simply from the nature of the power, and secondly, that where the power is a power to dismiss from an office (and it was contended that the respondent could be said to be the holder of an office) and to dismiss not at discretion but by reason of misconduct, then there is a duty to act judicially. In their lordships' opinion the first of these submissions is too wide and cannot be accepted. The second calls for an examination of the position which the respondent occupied, having regard to the facts concerning his appointment and having regard to the provisions of the Act of 1958. It was contended that the respondent had certain statutory rights and that certiorari could be granted in order to enforce them and in order to ensure obedience to the provisions of the Act...

It seems to their lordships that a 'teacher' who has an appointment with the university is in the ordinary legal sense a servant of the university unless it be that s. 18 (e) gives him some altered position. The circumstance that the university was established by statute and is regulated by the statutory enactments contained in the Act of 1958 does not involve that contracts of employment, which are made with teachers and which are subject to the provisions of s. 18 (e), are other than ordinary contracts of master and servant. Comparison may be made with the case of *Barber* v. *Manchester Regional Hospital Board**... It may be said that if those or some of those who are 'officers' of the university have a special position which takes them out of the category of employed servants, as to which matter their lordships express no opinion, and if as a result the council would in their case have to act judicially in exercising the power of dismissal under s. 18 (e) it would seem strange if it were different in the case of 'teachers' who are linked with 'officers' in s. 18 (e).... The present case depends, therefore, on ascertaining the status of the respondent. He invoked a procedure which is not available where a master summarily terminates a servant's employment, and for the reasons which have been expressed their lordships do not consider that the respondent was shown to be in any special position or to be other than a servant.

(ii) PUBLIC POLICY

HORWOOD v. MILLAR'S TIMBER AND TRADING CO. LTD

Court of Appeal [1917] 1 K.B. 305

A clerk, employed by the defendants, borrowed money from the plaintiff moneylender. In return he assigned to the plaintiff all his future salary; and undertook, *inter alia*, not to leave his employment nor to pledge any of his property without the plaintiff's permission. The plaintiff alleged that he had committed breaches of this covenant, and sued to recover salary due from his employer to the clerk.

LORD COZENS-HARDY, M.R.: It seems to me that if as a matter of construction I come to the conclusion that the contract is one which puts the covenantor in the position—I cannot think of a better word at the moment to express my view—of *adscriptus glebae*, as the villein

---

* *Ante*, p. 42. See too *Taylor* v. *National Union of Seamen* [1967] 1 All E.R. 767 (*post* p. 624) where a declaration was refused a union official *qua* employee, but was granted on other grounds.

used to be called in mediaeval times, on the ground of public policy the law will not recognize such a thing. No one has a right so to deal with a man's liberty of action as well as his property, and the law says it is contrary to public policy.

WARRINGTON and SCRUTTON, L.JJ., delivered concurring judgments.

ALLEN v. THORN ELECTRICAL INDUSTRIES

Edmonton County Court   *The Times*, 30 September 1966

The plaintiff, a chargehand supervisor, negotiated (as union representative) a rise with the employers on 12 July 1966—5 per cent backdated to April with a further 5 per cent in 1967. On 20 July the Government demanded a 'standstill' in wage increases not already paid. [Later the Prices and Incomes Act, 1966, was passed. In Part II, this would give the government power to impose a standstill of up to four months on wage settlements while they were considered by the National Board for Prices and Incomes. In Part IV, the government took powers for 12 months to forbid by order increases in wages, or payments higher than rates on 20 July; and employers were to be protected from breach of contract claims within the terms of s. 30*. Neither Part of the Act had been brought into operation by Order at the time of this action.]

The plaintiff's claim for arrears due under the negotiated increase succeeded before Judge Granville Smith. The defendants admitted that the increase had been negotiated and that it had become part of the contract of employment. [No question arose here therefore of the relationship between the individual employment contract and the collective bargain: see *post*, p. 289.]

MR. PAIN, Q.C., for the plaintiff, said: The defendants relied on the White Paper, *Prices and Incomes Standstill*; on the underlying economic situation thereby disclosed and on a letter from the Minister of Labour, Mr Gunter, to the Confederation of British Industry, dated 24 August 1966. They admitted that since 12 July Mr Allen had continued to work for them and that they had failed and refused to pay him the increase in salary.

MR PAIN said: 'The simple question is whether this £1 a week increase is payable or not, and whether by reason of either frustration

---

* See further on the Prices and Incomes Act, 1966, collective bargaining and employment contracts *post* p. 258; and its impact on industrial conflict law, *post* p. 520. Part IV of the Prices and Incomes Act was brought into operation on 6 October 1966: see *post* p. 262, and the first Order made against Thorn's under Part IV *post* p. 293.

or public policy the defendants are entitled to say: "We will not pay this money although we agree that we are otherwise contractually bound".'

MR R. I. THRELFALL, Q.C., for the defendants, said the agreement was made in free negotiations and the defendants would have honoured it without question but for supervening events.

Within eight days after concluding the agreement the Prime Minister made clear the view of the Government that Britain was in the grip of a serious economic crisis and called for a standstill on all forms of income up to the end of 1966. Subsequently the Government issued a memorandum which set out the position and called on all concerned to accept some deferments.

Part IV of the subsequent Act enabled orders to be made which, in effect, would make it unlawful to pay increases, but that part of the Act had not yet been brought into force.

He said: 'The position is, therefore, that there are no existing compulsory powers to interfere with the operation of agreements, but the defendants were faced with the strong expression of view on the Government's part that the country was in the grip of an economic crisis and to pay the increase which they had contracted would be contrary to the national interest. As a responsible and major concern, the company felt bound to respond, as far as it properly could, to the requirements of the Government's policy.'

There were two ways in which the impact of this might be said to release the parties to the agreement from their contractual obligations.

The first way was by the doctrine of frustration in the sense that the performance of the promise was different, through the supervening circumstances, from that which was contemplated when the agreement was made, and although the Court did not exercise an absolving power, nevertheless in the new circumstances the Court holds the agreement was not intended to apply.

If that were not sufficient grounds to hold that the agreement was frustrated then the defendants invited the Court to hold that the agreement had been frustrated because it had become unlawful as a result of circumstances and supervening events being contrary to public policy.

He submitted that the Government's White Paper was the foundation on which the Court could hold that the agreement, if made today, would be unlawful as being contrary to public policy.

He added: 'It is difficult to find authority where public policy has been expressly applied to considerations arising from inflation and an economic situation, but in this case I would submit that it is clear that the view of Parliament is that the application of an increase of this sort would be injurious to the overriding economic interests of the nation.'

MR PAIN replied: 'The conception of a contract being frustrated by new public policy emerging was something that was entirely contrary to authority and to these two branches of the law of contract. There was no difficulty here about the defendant carrying out this agreement —it was not onerous on them to do so.

So far as public policy was concerned, the suggestion appeared to be that no subject could lawfully do anything which had a tendency to be injurious to the public and apply this to all contracts. The statements on which the defendants relied were merely very broad statements made when the doctrine of public policy was being evolved. One could not take wide principles and seek to apply them generally in a modern context.

No evidence had been called as to what was public good. The White Paper on prices and incomes and a couple of letters had been put in. 'But', he went on, 'it cannot be right to say that one must look at a Government pronouncement and say that on economic matters the Government are the people best to judge and that we must accept their opinion of what the public interest demands.

If one were to follow that it would reduce judges to being mere pawns of Whitehall because they would be bound to accept any statement in a White Paper apparently whether or not it had the approval of the House of Commons. It would be subversive to our whole system of democratic Government.'

The Judge commented that what he was really being asked to do was to bring Part IV into operation. When Mr Pain agreed, adding that he would be doing it in such a way as to make Part IV unnecessary, the Judge added: 'Yes, I should be one step ahead of the Government.'

JUDGE GRANVILLE SMITH, giving judgment, said the defendants were in no way trying to get out of their obligations. 'It has not been suggested that is so, and I want to make it clear that is not the background. They are willing to pay', he said.

Dealing with the defence submissions on frustration, he said: 'Here, I think that argument fails, because in fact there is no frustration' There is no getting away from it. Both parties are anxious to perform a contract. The contract is perfectly capable of being performed. The only reason that it isn't is the Government.'

It had been argued, he said, that the agreement was discharged by frustration by reason of a change in circumstances undermining the whole basis thereof, and or because performance thereof became contrary to public policy.

'Acting purely from a legal point of view and acting in the belief that my only duty is to construe the law to the best of my ability I have come to the conclusion that to give effect to the defendants' plea would be to enter into matters which are not the province of a Judge at all.

Nothing I have heard gives me any ground for saying that the defendants can be absolved from performing this contract.'

PLOWMAN & SON LTD v. ASH

Court of Appeal   [1964] 1 W.L.R. 568; [1964] 2 All E.R. 10

The plaintiffs, agricultural and corn merchants, employed five sales representatives, one of whom was the defendant. By clause 8 of his contract of employment he agreed that for two years after leaving he would 'not canvass or solicit for himself or any other person or persons any farmer or market gardener who shall at any time during the employment of the employee hereunder have been a customer of the employers'. He was given a list of customers on whom to call but was never given a list of all the plaintiff's customers and he did not know ones not on his list. Having left the employment he worked for a competitor and began to solicit orders from the plaintiff's customers. The plaintiffs sought and obtained an interlocutory injunction.

HARMAN, L.J.: Here it is said that there are three reasons why this covenant ought not to be enforced. The first is that on its true construction the document applies to goods of all kinds and would prevent canvassing by the employee in articles of trade of any sort or kind. True it is that in the covenant not to canvass there is no mention of the kind of goods in which the employer is dealing. But, in my judgment, you must regard the contract (as you always must) as a whole, and this is a contract for a sales representative in South Lincolnshire serving a firm which, as appears from the very clause in question, clause 8, is a corn and agricultural merchant and animal feeding stuffs manufacturer. In my opinion, it is no wider than that: the articles in which he may not canvass are the very articles of which his employer employed him.

Secondly, it is said that this is not limited as to area, and that is quite true...But I do not see that that is any objection. It seems to me that the employer may well wish to preserve his connection even with a man who is 50 miles away or more. As for the suggestion of both of them moving to Australia, that seems to me to be a fantastication of which one need not take any account, anyhow on the trial of the motion.

Thirdly, it is said (and this is, in my opinion, the nub of the matter) that though customers are limited to those who were customers during the period of employment, it does not exclude people who have ceased to be customers and therefore form no part of the goodwill of the employer, nor does it confine itself to customers with whom in some way or other the employee has come into contact. It is on that ground, I think, that the judge refused the motion. I have felt great doubt on this point, but on the whole, if a man was a customer at the beginning of the employment I do not see why hope should be abandoned of his becoming a customer again at the end of it and why, therefore, people who have, for the time being at any rate, ceased to be customers, have fallen outside the proprietary interest.

As to knowledge, it is clear that the employee might be obliged under his contract to serve his employers anywhere in South Lincolnshire and the surrounding areas if he was asked to do so. Regarding the contract, as you must, at the date when it was entered into, I should have thought that anywhere within those areas was a potential ground for his activities and that, therefore, the employers might legitimately protect themselves against his solicitation anywhere in that area, that is to say, where they had customers, even though in fact he did confine his attention to the west or the south-west. Consequently, I do not think that that makes the covenant too wide.

DAVIES and RUSSELL, L.JJ., delivered concurring judgments.

M & S DRAPERS *v.* REYNOLDS

Court of Appeal   [1957] 1 W.L.R. 9; [1956] 3 All E.R. 814

The plaintiff's contract of employment as a collector salesman contained the following clause: 'For a period of 5 years following the determination of this agreement the servant shall not directly or indirectly either by himself or as the agent, servant or partner of another person or company sell or canvass or solicit orders and in either case by way of the business of a credit draper from any person whose name shall have been inscribed upon the books of the firm as a customer during the 3 years immediately preceding such determination upon whom the servant has called in the course of his duties for the firm.' He had brought customers with him when he entered the employment.

DENNING, L.J.: During the last 40 years the courts have shown a reluctance to enforce covenants of this sort. They realise that a servant has often very little choice in the matter. If he wants to get or to keep his employment, he has to sign the document which the employer puts before him; and he may do so without fully appreciating what it may involve. Moreover, if these covenants were given full force, they would tend to reduce his freedom to seek better conditions, even by asking for a rise in wages: because if he is not allowed to get work elsewhere, he is very much at the mercy of his employer.

While showing proper reluctance to enforce these covenants, the courts will, however, do so if they are shown to be reasonable as between the parties and as regards the public. In this case I think that the employers might reasonably protect their own trade connexion, that is, the connexion which was properly their own as distinct from the connexion which the traveller brought with him. But I do not see why the employers should be able to forbid him to call on the people whom he already knew before he worked for them—the people whom I will call 'his customers'. His knowledge of these people, and his influence with them, were due to his own efforts or at any rate they were nothing to do with these employers. His goodwill with those customers belonged to him, and cannot reasonably be taken from him by a covenant of this kind. Any other view would mean that, soon after employing him, they could dismiss him—at a fortnight's notice—and then prevent him for five years thereafter from calling on his own customers who had been his long before he entered the employment. When I find the clause so wide as to cover 'his customers' and is for so long as five years, I think it is an unreasonable restraint of trade. We were referred to the case of Gilford Motor Co. Ltd v. Horne,[1] but I think that case is quite distinguishable for the reasons given by Hodson, L.J. A managing director can look after himself. A traveller is not so well placed to do so. The law must protect him. I agree the appeal should be dismissed.

HODSON and MORRIS, L.JJ., delivered concurring judgments.

[1] [1933] 1 Ch. 935.

GLEDHOW AUTOPARTS LTD v. DELANEY*

Court of Appeal   [1965] 1 W.L.R. 1366; [1965] 3 All E.R. 288

The defendant was a traveller employed by the plaintiffs to obtain orders for them in those districts to which they sent him. He in fact operated in an area covering some fourteen or so counties. He was paid weekly and could be given a week's notice. By clause 6 of the contract he was bound for a period of three years from the termination of the contract not to seek orders 'in respect of any goods dealt in by the company (the sale of which the traveller is engaged to promote under this agreement) from any person firm or company situate or carrying on business within the districts in which the traveller has operated during the course of this agreement...'

SELLERS, L.J.: It is to be borne in mind that the law that has to be applied here is the law in respect of restraint in a contract of service between a master and a servant, which is to be distinguished and has been distinguished in the authorities from the restraints which may be imposed in a contract where there is a sale of a business. It is convenient to turn to *Attwood* v. *Lamont*[1], where this court reviewed the position which had been established by two leading decisions in the House of Lords, *Mason* v. *Provident Clothing and Supply Co. Ltd*[2] and *Herbert Morris, Ltd* v. *Saxelby*[3]. The judgment of Younger, L.J., was approved by Atkin, L.J. The effect of the decisions of the House of Lords was established to be: first, that it is for the covenantee to show that the restriction sought to be imposed on the covenantor goes no further than is reasonable for the protection of his business; secondly, that the restraint must be reasonable not only in the interests of the covenantee but in the interests of both the contracting parties; and thirdly, that an employer is not entitled by a covenant taken from his employee to protect himself after the employment has ceased against his former servant's competition, although a purchaser of goodwill is entitled to protect himself against such competition on the part of the vendor. Some other observations in that case were made about the severance of restrictive clauses such as this, but no such question arises in this case...

---

[1] [1920] All E.R. Rep. 55; [1920] 3 K.B. 571.
[2] [1911–13] All E.R. Rep. 400; [1913] A.C. 724.
[3] [1916–17] All E.R. Rep. 305; [1916] 1 A.C. 688.

* Compare *Commercial Plastics Ltd* v. *Vincent* [1965] 1 Q.B. 623 (C.A.); *Strange Ltd* v. *Mann* [1965] 1 All E.R. 1069; *Scorer* v. *Seymour-Johns* [1966] 3 All E.R. 347 (C.A.).

For the purpose of this case there is no need for consideration to be given to any trade secrets of an employer. This case must be judged on the other limb of that right, viz., to some protection for some proprietary right in the nature of trade connexion. It is on that basis that this case has been argued. In my view the protection here does go beyond what is necessary to protect the rights of the employer. That depends and is based on the nature of his trade. If this provision had been restricted to customers then, I think, there could be no doubt that it would have been enforceable and I would agree with the learned judge in that respect; but the learned judge continues, after holding that it would be appropriate to enforce that, that he would go further and that it would be applicable not only to established customers but to people on whom the defendant employee had called in the course of his employment with the plaintiff employers—potential customers, people with whom he had made some sort of initial contact which might be expected to develop afterwards. That perhaps is more questionable; but if that had been the case I would again have agreed with the learned judge. Then, however, he holds that an agreement such as this is enforceable notwithstanding that it would embrace all those people in the areas or districts in which the employee had been directed to operate on whom he had never called at all, who, therefore, had no relationship whatsoever with the employers and who, if they were canvassed by the employee, or anyone else, would only be canvassed in the ordinary way in competition with the employers. The facts seems to be that the area which was contemplated by the agreement— and that is what must be looked at initially—was a wide one, in terms an unlimited one. I am not prepared to make a fantastic interpretation of what might be involved; although the words of clause 2 are such that this employee could have been directed by the employers to take orders within the districts which the employers would from time to time direct, without any limitation, yet he was in fact known to be living in the Farnborough district and it may well be that some reasonable interpretation should be made of the limit of the provision...

I think that the duration of three years, while considerable, is not to be condemned. I certainly agree that the commodities were narrow. The area operated in itself would not matter, I think, if the restriction had been to customers or people who had been visited; but as soon as one goes beyond that it seems to me that the restriction is one which does go beyond what was necessary to protect the employers. I can see nothing which makes it anything other than a protection against competition; and so on that point, with respect, I would disagree with the learned judge and would allow this appeal.

DANCKWERTS, L.J.: The position is, of course, quite different from that where the owner of a business sells the goodwill of the business and engages not to compete with the purchaser; for in that case the purchaser needs the covenant to protect that which he has purchased. In the case of an employee it is against public interest that he should be deprived of the opportunity of earning his living: see per Lord Shaw of Dunfermline in *Herbert Morris, Ltd* v. *Saxelby*. The party seeking to enforce such a covenant has to show affirmatively that the covenant is reasonably required for the protection of his business, so that it is within the exceptions from the general rule that all covenants in restraint of trade are invalid.

DIPLOCK, L.J., delivered a concurring judgment.

BULL v. PITNEY-BOWES LTD

[1966] 3 All E.R. 384

The plaintiff had been the defendant's employee for 25 years, first as a clerk and eventually as sales manager. He, like all other eligible employees, had been required to enter the company's pension scheme. This was established by way of a trust fund. The scheme contained the following rule:

16. Notwithstanding the provisions of these rules, if in the opinion of the committee any retired member is engaged or employed in any activity or occupation which is in competition with or detrimental to the interests of [the defendants], and if he shall fail to comply with written notice from [the defendants] requiring him to discontinue such activity or occupation the committee shall be entitled to cancel all his rights and benefits under these rules.

On his retirement the plaintiff entered the employment of a competing company. He claimed a declaration that rule 16 was void and unenforceable, and that he was entitled under rule 7 to receive a pension, having satisfied all the other requirements of the scheme.

THESIGER, J.: The idea that a promise not to do certain work might be void and unenforceable because it was illegal as against public policy seems to have originated at the time of a shortage of labour after the black death had swept through England. The principle was applied in the Court of Appeal in a case relied on by the plaintiff before me in this case and conceded by counsel for the defendants in this case to constitute a difficulty in the way of the defendants argument. That case is *Wyatt* v. *Kreglinger and Fernau*[1]. That decision was very strongly criticized at the time it was reported in a long note in the 49 *Law Quarterly Review*, p. 465, a note, I imagine, for which Professor Goodhart was probably responsible. The note...concludes with these observations:

'And where do we find this injury to the public? It is based on the ground that, if it were not for the agreement the plaintiff "might continue to serve the community in the wool business", or in Scrutton, L.J.'s words[2] "the country is thereby being deprived without any legitimate justification of the services of a man of sixty years of age who is quite competent to enter into business, because he is given leave to enter into any kind of business other than the wool trade". This view is supported by the quotation of a dictum by James, V.-C., in *Leather Cloth Co.* v. *Lorsont*[3]...although the point at issue in that case was an entirely different one. But even assuming that in 1869 public policy took this strange shape, it is hardly a valid argument in 1933 when there are nearly two million unemployed'...In view of Lord Reid's approach to problems of policy in the last paragraph of his speech in *Rumping* v. *Director of Public Prosecutions*[4] one may perhaps note that we now, in 1966, have on the statute book the Restrictive Trade Practices Act, 1956, the Resale Prices Act 1964, and we may perhaps note that Parliament has discussed Commonwealth immigration from the point of view of the labour market, the alleged 'hoarding of labour' and the so-called 'brain-drain'. G. H. Treitel in his *Law of Contract* (2nd Edn.) p. 322, says of the *Wyatt* case: 'Reaction against this case has gone so far that it is sometimes said that public interest is not an independent ground of invalidity at all. But this view is too extreme. The principle of public interest may not operate very often, but is in the last resort a useful one. There might well be cases in which a restraint on a surgeon or on a skilled engineer would be reasonable in relation to the interest to be protected, but contrary to the interests of the public at large.'

To that comment I would add this consideration which, I think, is material to the present case. We hear nowadays of take-over bids. The bidder may be a corporation that may be far from interested in developing the exports of this country in competitive markets overseas.

---

[1] [1933] All E.R. Rep. 349; [1933] 1 K.B. 793.
[2] [1933] 1 K.B. at p. 807.   [3] (1869), L.R. 9 Eq. 345 at p. 354.
[4] [1962] 3 All E.R. 256 at p. 260; [1964] A.C. at p. 835.

Industrial and scientific techniques are now complicated. Machine tools and the use of computers and what is called industrial 'know-how' are important. It may be very much in the public interest that the services of experienced salesmen skilled in a particular technique should be available to promote sales from this country overseas in competition with other sellers from elsewhere...

The plaintiff's argument goes on: the provisions of rule 16 were imposed as a condition of the employment of all employees. It affected them all, and it might affect them at an early age. The plaintiff's argument is that the defendants cannot enforce a policy contrary to public policy by substituting an inducement by way of threat for a promise. The plaintiff relies very strongly on the words by Slesser, L.J., in particular in the case of *Wyatt* v. *Kreglinger and Fernau*[1], to which I have referred. The defendants point out that the *Wyatt* case[2] could be distinguished on the ground that Scrutton and Greer, L.JJ., imply a promise not to enter a particular trade whereas here, in the case before me, the defendants contend that there is no such promise and no automatic forfeiture, although they have to concede that the loss of the pension depends on the view of the committee. One may, perhaps, summarise the defendants' argument by saying that it is that to discourage is not the same as to restrain.

Now so far as the individual is concerned, I appreciate the distinction relied on by the defendants between (i) a covenant not to take up certain skilled work and (ii) the discontinuance of a pension if one does choose to take up that work. The latter does not involve the breach of any promise; but from the point of view of the public and of the reason behind the rule at common law there is little if any distinction in principle. The relevant factor is the inducement not to take up work in which one is skilled. One does not readily take up work unless it is worth one's while from the economic aspect. The attraction normally is that one requires, and is offered in return for the work, remuneration that will leave a larger sum in one's pocket than would otherwise be there. There is, therefore, in all probability a greater cost to the public as consumers if the remuneration offered has to include an element of compensation for the loss of pension.

Now the problem here arises from a principle of public policy and I emphasise the word 'public'. From the public point of view there is every justification for the plaintiff's argument in this case that the

[1] [1933] All E.R. Rep. at pp. 353, 354; [1933] 1 K.B. at pp. 808, 809.
[2] [1933] All E.R. Rep. 349; [1933] 1 K.B. 793.

employer cannot achieve by the inducement of a continued pension that which he could not achieve by obtaining a direct promise in return for particular wages or salary. It is, of course, an interesting and, indeed, vital feature of *Wyatt's* case that the actual decision in that case was adverse to the ex-employee's claim for a pension and in favour of the employer's right to stop the pension, although in that case the ex-employee was willing to abide by the condition and to refrain from doing the work of which he was capable and for which he had been trained. Unless *Wyatt's* case can be distinguished, the decision is not only binding on me but the criticisms that were levied at that decision at the time were based on conditions of employment and of the economy (within the jurisdiction of this court) which no longer prevail. These defendants cannot now and do not seek to rely on those criticisms.

Now *Wyatt's* case[1] seems to me to be a very strong authority indeed in favour of the plaintiff in this case. In *Wyatt's* case Macnaghten, J., avoided deciding what is now the relevant point by holding that there was no intention to enter into any contract. Scrutton, L.J., would have been ready to uphold Macnaghten, J.'s decision on that ground, but, as the other two members of the court were inclined to take a different view on that particular point, Scrutton, L.J., himself expressly decided the case on the point that is now relevant. He said[2]: 'Now this agreement, stated in the most favourable form for the plaintiff, namely a stipulation by the employer that he will pay the plaintiff so much a year if the plaintiff does not enter into the wool trade for the rest of his life in any part of the country or world, appears to me to be a contract in restraint of trade which is unenforceable just as much as a contract by the employee not to trade in the wool trade for the rest of his life in any part of the world, and that the country is thereby being deprived without any legitimate justification of the services of a man of sixty years of age who is quite competent to enter into business, because he is given leave to enter into any kind of business other than the wool trade...'

My first conclusion in this case is that the provisions of the pension fund were part of the terms and conditions of the plaintiff's employment and those provisions include rule 16. My next conclusion is that rule 16 would have been regarded by the Court of Appeal that decided *Wyatt's* case as equivalent from the public point of view to a covenant in restraint of trade. The state of affairs in 1933 in which that court

---

[1] [1933] All E.R. Rep. 349; [1933] 1 K.B. 793.
[2] [1933] 1 K.B. at p. 807; [1933] All E.R. Rep. at p. 352.

was then criticised for so holding as a matter of public policy that the covenant was unenforceable on the ground of illegality no longer prevails in this country. So far as that aspect of the decision is concerned, there is no inducement for me in 1966 to try to distinguish *Wyatt's* case. It would be a difficult, if not impossible, task in any case, and the inducement is rather the other way.

I therefore hold that the answer to the first question put to me, which is 'Is rule 16 of the pension fund a restraint of trade?', must be in the affirmative.

I next consider question 2, which reads: 'If rule 16 of the pension fund is a restraint of trade, is it a reasonable and enforceable restraint?' I hold that the answer to that question must be 'No'.

I therefore will make the declarations asked for, which are that rule 16 of the Frankopost pension fund is an unreasonable restraint of trade and is void and unenforceable, and that, subject to the provisions of rules 27, 30, 31 and 32, on reaching his normal retirement age the plaintiff will be entitled to receive a pension in accordance with sub-rules (*b*) and (*d*) of rule 7 of the pension fund.

KORES MANUFACTURING CO. LTD *v.* KOLOK MANUFACTURING CO. LTD

Court of Appeal   [1959] Ch. 108

Two companies manufacturing similar products agreed together not to employ any person who had been employed by the other company during the five years previous to that time. The contract was held to be unreasonable in the interests of the parties and therefore in restraint of trade.

JENKINS, L.J. [delivering the judgment of the court]: The mere fact that parties dealing on equal terms have entered into an agreement subjecting themselves to restraints of trade does not preclude the court from holding the agreement bad where the restraints are clearly unreasonable in the interests of the parties. In the present case, the restraint reciprocally imposed on the plaintiffs and the defendants by the agreement of 1934 was such as to preclude the plaintiffs from employing at any time any person who had, during the then past five years, been a servant of the defendants, and vice versa...

[We] are of opinion that (apart from the effect of the assumption that it was impliedly terminable by reasonable notice) the reciprocal restraints imposed by the agreement of 1934 were unreasonable in the interests of the parties to it, and that the agreement accordingly failed to satisfy the first of the two conditions which a contract in restraint of trade must satisfy in order to be held valid, and was, therefore, void and unenforceable.

We would add this. It is true that the agreement of 1934 was between two employers, and not between employer and employee. Nevertheless, it was wholly and solely directed to preventing the employees of either contracting party, on ceasing to be employed by them, from entering the employment of the other contracting party. Apart from the question of trade secrets and confidential information, we have described the matter requiring protection as being the adequacy and stability of the plaintiffs' and defendants' respective complements of employees. That, no doubt, is an interest which employers are entitled to protect by all legitimate means, as by paying good wages and making their employment attractive. We have further described the danger against which that interest required protection as being the unimpeded secession of employees of either of the parties to that of the other of them under the inducement of higher wages or better working conditions. But an employer has no legitimate interest in preventing an employee, after leaving his service, from entering the service of a competitor merely on the ground that the new employer is a competitor. The danger of the adequacy and stability of his complement of employees being impaired through employees leaving his service and entering that of a rival is not a danger against which he is entitled to protect himself by exacting from his employees covenants that they will not, after leaving his service, enter the service of any competing concern. If in the present case the plaintiffs had taken a covenant from each of their employees that he would not enter the service of the defendants at any time during the five years next following the termination of his service with the plaintiffs, and the defendants had taken from their employees covenants restraining them in similar terms from entering the employment of the plaintiffs, we should have thought that (save possibly in very exceptional cases involving trade secrets, confidential information and the like) all such covenants would on the face of them be bad as involving a restraint of trade which was unreasonable as between the parties. Here the plaintiffs and the defendants have, as it seems to us, sought to do indirectly that which they could not do directly by reciprocal undertakings between themselves not to employ each other's former employees, entered into over the heads of their respective employees, and without their knowledge. It seems to us to be open to question whether an agreement such as that, directed to preventing employees of the parties from doing that which they could not by individual covenants with their respective employers validly bind themselves not to do, should be accorded any greater validity than individual covenants by the employees themselves would possess. We prefer, however, to leave that question open, and to found our conclusions as to the invalidity of the agreement of 1934 on the reasons given earlier in this judgment...The view we have formed on the question of reasonableness between the parties makes it unnecessary for us to form any conclusion on the question of reasonableness in the public interest.

EASTHAM *v.* NEWCASTLE UNITED FOOTBALL CLUB LTD

[1964] Ch. 413; [1963] 3 W.L.R. 574

The plaintiff was a professional football player registered with a club of the Football League. This action in effect challenged the 'retain and transfer' system of the Football Association. The plaintiff had asked to be transferred to another club: his own club had refused and gave him notice of retention: and the plaintiff refused to re-sign with them. This meant that he was effectively prevented from playing for another club in almost all parts of the world; and the club did not have to pay him wages. He claimed this was in unreasonable restraint of trade.

WILBERFORCE, J., found that the retain and transfer system contained elements of restraint and were not justifiable. He then considered whether a declaration was available against the League and the Association and cited two cases *Mineral Water Bottle Exchange* v. *Booth* (1887) 36 Ch.D 465 C.A. and *Kores Manufacturing Co. Ltd* v. *Kolok Manufacturing Co. Ltd* (*ante*, p. 58) and continued:

So as a first step these two cases support the proposition that the court may examine contracts between employers only and declare them void on grounds on which such a contract would be declared void if it had been a contract between employer and employee.

But these were actions between employers only, and this is the next step: is it open to an employee to bring an action for a declaration that the contract between the employers is in restraint of trade? To my mind it would seem unjust if this were not so. The employees are just as much affected and, indeed, aimed at by the employers' agreement as the employers themselves. Their liberty of action in seeking employment is threatened just as much as the liberty of the employers to give them employment, and their liberty to seek employment is considered by the law to be an important public interest. Is the defence of that interest to be left exclusively in the hands of the employers themselves, who have set up the ring against the employees and who have (as here) shown every intention of maintaining it as long as they can; left to the chance that one day there may be a blackleg among the employers who will challenge it ? In my judgment to grant a remedy by way of declaration to the persons whose interests are vitally affected would be well within the spirit and intent of the rule as to declaratory judgments...

The effect of [earlier] cases may well be to prevent the plaintiff from bringing an action for damages for conspiracy against the members of the ring—in fact, he has not tried to bring such an action—but they do not seem to me to preclude him seeking a declaratory judgment, which may be granted whether or not the plaintiff has a legal cause of action against the defendants. The declaratory judgment is a comparatively modern remedy which is being found to have a usefulness which was probably not appreciated when those cases were decided.

If I am right so far, then the court has jurisdiction to grant a declaratory judgment, not only against the employer who is in contractual relationship with the employee, but also against the association of employers whose rules or regulations place an unjustifiable restraint on his liberty of employment. A case where the employee is himself contractually bound by the employers' rules (as the employee is here, by virtue of registration and the terms of his contract) is a fortiori to the case last mentioned.

Section C

FORMATION OF THE CONTRACT
OF EMPLOYMENT

CARUS *v.* EASTWOOD

Court of Appeal   (1875) 32 L.T. 855

The respondent weaver worked in a mill where he was paid by the piece. The works rules were posted up so that people passed them on their way to work. One of the rules required 14 days notice to terminate the employment. The respondent had left without notice and had been prosecuted under the master and servant statutes. It was not proved that he had read the rules or could have read them. It was held that it might be enough to sustain such a conviction to show that the rules had been posted up; or alternatively that there was a well known custom of the district concerning notice.

BLACKBURN, J.: ...Of course it would be very cogent evidence of a contract based upon these rules if a copy of them were proved to be posted in a prominent place, and it is not to be assumed, even if the servant could not read, that such rules would not be binding upon him. They might well be brought to his knowledge by other means ...A well known custom in the district might also be sufficient to establish a contract.*

MELLOR, J. and QUAIN, J. concurred.

NATIONAL COAL BOARD v. GALLEY

Court of Appeal   [1958] 1 W.L.R. 16

The terms of an employment contract must be reasonably unambiguous and certain to be legally enforceable: (see *post*, p. 184).

[Contrast *Loftus* v. *Roberts* (1902) 18 T.L.R. 532 (C.A.), a contract at 'a West End salary to be mutually arranged' insufficiently certain. But see too now *Sykes (Wessex) Ltd* v. *Fine Fare Ltd*, *The Times*, November 17, 1966; and *post* p. 288.]

WORKS RULES AND SIMILAR DOCUMENTS

In many employments certain terms are set out in a book of Works Rules or the like. Without reproducing those of any particular firm, the following may be taken as terms similar to those which are to be found in many areas of industrial employment:

ACCEPTANCE OF EMPLOYMENT AND TERMS OF ENGAGEMENT

FOR HOURLY-PAID OPERATIVE EMPLOYEES

1. I accept employment with XY COMPANY LIMITED in Grade......
at the wage of..............per hour, commencing on..............
....
2. I understand that such employment is subject to the terms of

* Note: The ordinary principles of contract law concerning 'tickets' and the like would obviously apply here. See too the discussion by DU PARCQ, L.J. (dissenting) in *Marshall* v. *English Electric Co. Ltd* [1945] 1 All E.R. 653.

Agreements made from time to time between the Company and the Trade Unions and to the Company's Rules and Regulations.

3. I acknowledge receipt of copies of:
   (a) Current Agreements made between the Company and the Trade Unions.
   (b) The Company's Rules and Regulations.
   (c) Safety Instructions to the New Employee.
   (d) A booklet explaining the Pension Fund.

4. I understand I must become a contributing member of XY Hourly-Paid Contributory Pension Fund at the earliest date on which, under the Rules of that Fund, I am eligible to become a member and I undertake to be bound by the provisions of the Trust Deed and Rules of that Fund. I apply to become a member and authorise XY Company Limited to deduct the appropriate contributions from my wages during any period while I am a contributing member, and to pay the contributions on my behalf to the Trustees of the Fund.*

Signature: A. N. Other   Date: 29 . 10 . 66

WORKS RULES

Overtime

Any employee if called upon to do so shall work all reasonable overtime by night or day and during weekends or holidays (but in the case of women and young persons only within the hours permitted by law). All possible notice will be given in advance.

Where a day worker is required to work overtime for more than two hours a meal break of half an hour without pay must be taken. In such circumstances when overtime is worked at short notice food will be provided at the company's expense...

Trade Unions

(a) The Company negotiates with the following Trade Unions:... Membership of a Union is a matter for the employee to decide for himself, though the Company in conducting negotiations would like to feel that it is dealing with associations truly representative of its employees.

Agreements between the Company and the above Unions (including those relating to negotiating machinery) are binding on all employees.

* Note: *Hewlett* v. *Allen post*, p. 126. *Quaere* the effect of the Shop Clubs Act, 1902.

(*b*) Employees must not take part in any unofficial strike or stoppage of work, but must accept the agreed negotiating machinery and procedure for the settlement of disputes.

Sickness

Employees who are absent through sickness or accident for more than two days must produce or send a medical certificate on the third day of absence...A similar certificate must be produced during each week of absence, and at the end of any period of absence exceeding three days, a doctor's certificate must be produced. If an employee is admitted to a hospital or similar institution, the production of a certificate of admission at the beginning and a certificate of discharge at the end of the period will be sufficient, but regular medical certificates will be required during any period of convalescence. If the above conditions are complied with, the Company will make up the wage, excluding bonus and overtime payments, of any employee absent through sickness, after taking into account the sums, if any, which the employee is entitled to claim under the National Insurance Act. Normally the Company will not pay, in respect of sickness, more than a total of 14 days' absence in any calendar year, and any payment beyond that period is at the Company's discretion.*

Search of Employees

In order to safeguard its property, the Company reserves the right to search employees while on the premises and to be satisfied as to the contents of any parcel or package taken away by an employee. Personal property brought to the Works not likely to be used in connection with the employee's duty must be left with the doorkeeper upon arrival and collected at the time of leaving. Personal property for use in connection with the employee's work cannot be brought on to the Company's premises unless a pass is obtained from the doorkeeper.

Disciplinary Action

It is within the power of the Works Manager or his Deputy, as a disciplinary measure alternative to dismissal, to suspend an employee without pay for a period up to a maximum of three days.

Smoking

Smoking is not permitted on any part of the Company's premises except where permission is granted.

* See *post*, p. 92.

Fidelity

It is a condition of employment that no employee shall disclose to anyone, during his employment or subsequently, any information of a confidential nature concerning the business of the Company, or any process, produce or appliance owned or operated by it, except to those members of the Company's Staff who are authorised to receive or deal with such matters. The Company may require, if it considers it necessary, that an employee shall become the subject of a Fidelity Bond Insurance.

Company's liability in the event of loss

The Company will not accept responsibility to any employee or any third party in respect of loss or damage to any employee's or third party's tools, clothing, cycle, car or personal property of any kind while on the Company's premises, whether in the Company's possession or not.

General

Employees must not carry out on Company premises any work for private purposes without management permission.

Employees must not behave in a disorderly manner on Company premises.

Employees must not bring intoxicants on to Company premises without management permission. No employee will be allowed to enter Company premises in an intoxicated condition. Any employee found to be under the influence of intoxicants while on Company premises will be deemed unfit for work and must leave the premises if requested.

Employees must not take part in any betting, gambling or gaming on Company premises unless it is lawful and permitted by the Management.

Unless they have management permission, employees must not hold meetings or take part in activities of clubs or other organisations on Company premises.

No poster or written matter may be exhibited or distributed on Company premises without management consent.

Employees' Signature

I hereby acknowledge receipt of a copy of the book containing Works Rules governing my employment.

I have read these Rules, I understand them and as a condition of my employment, I undertake to observe them.

Signed: A. N. Other. *Check Number:* 317824. *Date:* 24 July 1960.

CONTRACTS OF EMPLOYMENT ACT 1963

4. *Written particulars of terms of employment.* (1) Not later than thirteen weeks after the beginning of an employee's period of employment with an employer, the employer shall give to the employee a written statement identifying the parties, specifying the date when the employment began, and giving the following particulars of the terms of employment as at a specified date not more than one week before the statement is given, that is

(*a*) the scale or rate of remuneration, or the method of calculating remuneration,

(*b*) the intervals at which remuneration is paid (that is, whether weekly or monthly or by some other period),

(*c*) any terms and conditions relating to hours of work (including any terms and conditions relating to normal working hours),

(*d*) any terms and conditions relating to (i) holidays and holiday pay; (ii) incapacity for work due to sickness or injury, including any provisions for sick pay; (iii) pensions and pension schemes, and

(*e*) the length of notice which the employee is obliged to give and entitled to receive to determine his contract of employment:

Provided that paragraph (*d*) (iii) of this subsection shall not apply to the employees of any body or authority if the employees' pension rights depend on the terms of a pension scheme established under any provision contained in or having effect under an Act of Parliament and the body or authority are required by any such provision to give to new employees information concerning their pension rights, or concerning the determination of questions affecting their pension rights.

(2) If there are no particulars to be entered under any of the heads of paragraph (*d*), or under any of the other provisions of the last foregoing subsection, that fact shall be stated.

(3) If the contract is for a fixed term, the date when the contract expires shall be stated.

(4) If after the date to which the statement relates there is a change in the terms to be included, or referred to, in the statement, the employer shall, not more than one month after the change, inform the

employee of the nature of the change by a written statement and, if he does not leave a copy of the statement with the employee, shall preserve the statement and ensure that the employee has reasonable opportunities of reading it in the course of his employment, or that it is made reasonably accessible to him in some other way.

(5) A statement under subsection (1) or subsection (4) of this section may, for all or any of the particulars to be given by the statement, refer the employee to some document which the employee has reasonable opportunities of reading in the course of his employment, or which is made reasonably accessible to him in some other way.

(6) If the employer in referring in the statement to any such document indicates to the employee that future changes in the terms the particulars of which are given in the document will be entered up in the document (or recorded by some other means for the information of persons referring to the document) the employer need not under subsection (4) of this section inform the employee of any such change which is duly entered up or recorded not more than one month after the change is made.

REDUNDANCY PAYMENTS ACT 1965

38. (2) The following section shall be inserted in the Contracts of Employment Act 1963 after s. 4 of that Act:

4A. *References to tribunal as to particulars of employment.* (1) Where an employer is required by s. 4 of this Act to give to an employee a written statement under subsection (1) or subsection (4) of that section, and (*a*) the employer does not give such a statement to the employee within the time limited by that section, and (*b*) that time expires on or after the appointed day, the employee may require a reference to be made to a tribunal to determine what particulars ought to have been included or referred to in a statement given so as to comply with the requirements of that section.

(2) Where a statement purporting to be a statement under subsection (1) or subsection (4) of section 4 of this Act is given by an employer to an employee on or after the appointed day, and a question arises as to the particulars which ought to have been included or referred to in the statement so as to comply with the requirements of that section, either the employer or the employee may require that question to be referred to a tribunal...

(4) Where, on a reference under subsection (1) of this section, a tribunal determines particulars as being those which ought to have been included or referred to in a statement, the employer shall be deemed to have given to the employee a statement in which those particulars were included, or referred to, as specified in the decision of the tribunal.

(5) On determining a reference under subsection (2) of this section, a tribunal may either confirm the particulars as included or referred to in the statement given by the employer, or may amend those particulars, or may substitute other particulars for them, as the tribunal may determine to be appropriate; and the statement shall be deemed to have been given by the employer to the employee in accordance with the decision of the tribunal...

(7) Any matter required to be referred to a tribunal in pursuance of this section shall be referred to, and determined by, a tribunal in accordance with regulations made under Part III of the Redundancy Payments Act 1965.

(8) In this section 'tribunal' has the same meaning as in the Redundancy Payments Act 1965.*

---

* Note: In *Adams* v. *Macaire Mould Co. Ltd* (1966) 1 Industrial Tribunals Reports 411, the tribunal held that it had no jurisdiction to entertain a claim by an applicant who was no longer employed by the respondent in view of the words of s. 8 (1) Contracts of Employment Act, 1963 (*ante* p. 30). That section makes no provision for the ex-employee, though it is 'apt to include the situation which arises when a contract exists, but the employee has not begun to work under it' (p. 412). Contrast the wording of s. 25 Redundancy Payments Act, 1965 (*post*, p. 218). But it has also been held that an application by an ex-employee can be entertained under s. 4A (2): *Longden* v. *Ashton-under-Lyne* (1966) 1 I.T.R. 430. Later decisions have held that there is jurisdiction to hear an ex-employee's claim under s. 4A generally, which seems the better view. See *Mackay* v. *Henderson Ltd* (1967) 2 I.T.R. 98, where an analogy was drawn with actions brought by ex-employees under statutes to which s. 10, Employers and Workmen Act, 1875, (*ante* p. 30) applied.

EXAMPLES OF WRITTEN PARTICULARS

Conditions of Employment as at 6 July 1964

Employer: XY LTD. *Employee:* A. N. OTHER

Employment commenced: 12 June 1963. *Rate of pay:* 5s. per hour calculated on a 45 hour week (9 hours per day), plus overtime at standard rate for weekdays. After 45 hours work has been completed, time and a quarter for Saturday morning up to 1.0 p.m., time and a half for Saturday afternoon. (Sundays and Bank Holidays, etc., pay by special arrangement.) Pay is calculated from Thursday at 8.0 a.m. to Wednesday 5.30 p.m., wages being paid on Friday. (Two days kept in hand.) Normal hours of work are as follows:

8.0 a.m. to 10.0 a.m.	1.30 p.m. to 4.0 p.m.
10.15 a.m. to 1.0 p.m.	4.15 p.m. to 5.30 p.m.

Bonus. At the present time a bonus of a certain percentage is given to all employees according to production figures and paid on the basic weekly rate, excluding overtime. This bonus may not be paid in certain cases, where there has been absenteeism, lateness, etc. The Management reserve the right to adjust this scheme at their discretion.

Holidays and Holiday pay. According to law this firm is not obliged to pay any holiday pay, however, it is our normal practice at the present time to pay for 10 working days at 5/6th of a day per month for any employee having had 15 months service with the firm; less than 15 months service, 2/3rd of a day for every full month's service. Holiday year commences at the 1 May to the 30 April the following year. Although it is hoped to continue this scheme, the management reserve the right to alter or discontinue it at their discretion.

Sickness pay. The firm does not pay for loss of time through sickness, except by special arrangement. Employees are able to claim from the National Health Service if they are eligible (*sic*).

Pension scheme. A government pension scheme covers all employees Further particulars of this are available in the main office.

Notice of termination. Employers are required to give one week's notice after 26 weeks continuous weeks' employment, two weeks' notice after two years or more and four weeks' notice after 5 years or more, or other arrangements by mutual agreement. This notice of termination of employment is not required to be given when employment is terminated through misbehaviour.

Employees are required to give one week's notice only after 26 weeks or more continuous service.

CONTRACT OF EMPLOYMENT ACT 1963
Statement of Main Terms and Conditions of Employment

Name of Employer: XYZ LTD

Name of Employee: A. N. OTHER

Date of Statement: 19 July 1964	Date employment began: Over 5 years. (Note—if over five years sufficient to say so)
1. Pay	Your wage or salary will be paid at the rate agreed for Journeymen. A copy of the agreement setting out the rates applicable is available for reference at Works Manager's Office* The company undertake to ensure that future changes in the agreement will be entered up in the copy available or otherwise recorded for reference within one month of the change You are to be paid weekly
2. Holiday entitlement and pay	Your entitlement to holidays and to holiday pay are set out in the agreement already referred to. Your summer holidays will be as agreed with the Works Management and will be notified on the Works Notice Boards at least six months prior to the date of the holiday
3. Sickness and injury	Terms are as set out in the agreement referred to. Other payments may be made at the company's discretion
4. Pensions and pension schemes	The company's pension and Life Assurance scheme, details of which are available in the Works Managers Office, may be joined by an employee at his option on the 5 April following the date of commencing employment with the company. Failure to join at the first opportunity will mean that membership cannot be obtained at a subsequent date
5. Normal hours of work	Your normal hours of work will be as posted on the Works Main Notice Board. Changes will be notified as they occur. Tea breaks in the afternoon and morning are restricted to ten minutes
6. Termination and notice	You are entitled to receive one weeks' notice after six months continuous service; two weeks' notice after two years continuous service; and four weeks' after five years continuous service. You are required to give one weeks' notice during the first two years of employment; thereafter, you are required to give two weeks notice. By mutual agreement these periods of notice can be waived by the parties. Payment in lieu of notice can be given by the company

* Note: On the relationship between Collective Agreements and individual contracts of employment, see *post*, chapter 3, p. 289.

INLAND REVENUE COMMISSIONERS v. HAMBROOK

[1956] 2 Q.B. 641

The plaintiffs sued the defendant in an *actio per quod servitium amisit**, claiming as damages the sum which they had paid in sick pay to their tax officer who had been injured in a motor accident for which the defendant had been two-thirds responsible. The tax officer was an established civil servant.

The action was not successful. [On the civil servant's peculiar position see too *Riordan* v. *War Office post*, p. 160; *Rodwell* v. *Thomas post*, p. 294; *Dudfield* v. *Ministry of Works post*, p. 296.]

LORD GODDARD, C.J.: The question that falls for decision is whether the Crown are entitled to maintain the action commonly known as '*per quod servitium amisit*' in respect of the loss of the services of an established civil servant. There is no direct authority on this point in English law...This action has often been described as an anomaly, for instance, by Lord Sumner in *Admiralty Commissioners* v. *S.S. Amerika*,[1] where he said: 'It appears to be a survival from the time when service was a status'. Villein status gave the lord a proprietary interest in his villeins; by the time of Henry IV a master was regarded, in the old law, as having a like interest in his servant. At any rate, this class of action is referred to in the Year Book of the eleventh year of that king: f. 2, M. 22. In the same way a husband had a proprietary right in his wife which gave rise to actions of criminal conversation and for loss of consortium: see *Best* v. *Samuel Fox & Co. Ltd*[2]...So firmly established was the idea of a proprietary right in a servant that it is observable that the action was usually laid in trespass, showing that the infliction of an injury on a servant was regarded as a direct injury to the master...

Let me now consider the nature of the employment of an established civil servant. The terms 'servant' and 'service' are convenient expressions and in common use relating to civil employment under the Crown, but I have to consider the true legal relationship. In Bacon's Abridgment under the sub-title 'Prerogative' it is stated that 'the King hath an interest in all his subjects and is entitled to their services and

[1] [1917] A.C. 38, 60; 33 T.L.R. 135.
[2] [1952] A.C. 716; [1952] 2 T.L.R. 246; [1952] 2 All E.R. 394.
* By this action an employer can sue a defendant who tortiously injures his servant in defence of his proprietary interest in the servant. The Law Reform Committee proposed the abolition of the action in its Eleventh Report, Cmnd. 2017.

may employ them in such offices as the public good and the nature of our constitution require.' It was also said, in *Rex* v. *Burnell*,[1] that 'every man is a public officer who hath any duty concerning the public, and he is not less a public officer where his authority is confined to narrow limits, because it is the duty of his office and the nature of that duty which makes him a public officer and not the extent of his authority.' It is true that this was said in argument for the King in that case, but the quotation has found its way into works of authority such as the late Mr Stuart Robertson's work on the Civil Proceedings by and against the Crown and, in my opinion, is accurate. I think an established civil servant, whatever his grade, is more properly described as an officer in the civil employment of Her Majesty, and I can see no ground on which different rules of law in respect of his employment can be applied according to the grade or position he may occupy. They apply to a junior clerical officer as they do to a Permanent Secretary; as the Judicial Committee said in the *New South Wales* case,[2] the same rules of law in this respect apply in relation to the armed forces to a Field Marshal as to a private soldier. It is settled beyond controversy that the Sovereign can terminate at pleasure the employment of any person in the public service, except in special cases where it is otherwise provided by law. If authority be needed for what may now be considered as axiomatic, I need only refer to *Shenton* v. *Smith*[3] and *Dunn* v. *The Queen*,[4] but it is curious that there does not appear to be a definite and clear decision as to whether there is a contract of service between the Crown and its officers in the Civil Service. Mr Stuart Robertson, in the work to which I have already referred, after citing numerous cases and instances of petitions of right that have been presented, though not in all cases tried, says, at page 359: 'Even if there be a contract of service the Crown's absolute powers of dismissal must be deemed to be imported into it.' Lord Atkin said, in *Reilly* v. *The King*,[5] that 'a power to determine a contract at will is not inconsistent with the existence of a contract until so determined.'...It is, I think, fair to say that the trend of their Lordships' opinion seems to be that in the absence of some special term, such as engagement for a definitely expressed period, there is not a contractual relationship.

The Solicitor-General contended that in these cases there is a contract, though it is one which cannot be enforced against the Crown, so

---

[1] (1699) Carth. 478, 479.
[2] [1955] A.C. 457, 489.
[3] [1895] A.C. 229.
[4] [1896] 1 Q.B. 116; 12 T.L.R. 101.
[5] [1934] A.C. 176, 180; 50 T.L.R. 212.

that not only can no action lie for wrongful dismissal, but no action, or formerly no petition of right, could be brought for salary earned but not paid. This contention, if correct, would, I think, be enough, without more, to show the vast difference between the relationship of the Crown and its officers and the ordinary relation of master and servant· But, while it is clear that no action for wrongful dismissal can be brought by a discharged civil servant, I may be allowed to say that I adhere to the opinion I expressed in *Terrell* v. *Secretary of State for the Colonies*[1] that he could recover his salary for the time he has served. He would claim on a *quantum meruit*...If I may be bold enough to express a conclusion on a matter on which the Judicial Committee hesitated in *Reilly's* case,[2] it is that an established civil servant is appointed to an office and is a public officer, remunerated by moneys provided by Parliament, so that his employment depends not on a contract with the Crown but on appointment by the Crown, though there may be, as indicated in *Reilly's* case,[2] exceptional cases, as, for instance, an engagement for a definite period, where there is a contractual element in or collateral to his employment...Even if I am wrong in the opinion I have expressed above that the relationship is not contractual, a contract which gives no remedy to the employee against his employer for its breach is wholly different in kind from those which have hitherto supported the action.*

CHAPLIN v. LESLIE FREWIN
(PUBLISHERS) LTD

Court of Appeal   [1965] 3 All E.R. 764

The plaintiff, an infant aged 19,† together with his adult wife, entered into two contracts: one was with two ghostwriters who were to write his autobiography based on what he was to tell them about his life: the second was with the defendant publishers who were to have the exclusive right of producing, publishing and selling the book. The book—*I Couldn't Smoke the Grass on My Father's Lawn*—was written and the plaintiff saw the proofs. He and his wife discussed it and

---

[1] [1953] 2 Q.B. 482, 499; [1953] 2 All E.R. 490.

[2] [1934] A.C. 176.

* The judgment of GODDARD, L.C.J. was affirmed by the Court of Appeal on another ground, namely that the action *per quod servitum amisit* applied only to loss of the service of a domestic or 'menial' servant.

† Note: on the employment of young persons and children, statutory provisions are of greater importance than the common law rules concerning capacity. See, for example, Children and Young Persons Act, 1963, ss. 37 to 43; Young Persons (Employment) Act, 1938; Factories Act, 1961, Part VI.

certain proposed alterations at length with the publishers and then passed it for publication. Later the plaintiff repudiated the contract on the basis of his minority, stating it was untrue, libellous, and very unpleasant. He sought an interlocutory injunction against the publishers, but was unsuccessful.

DANCKWERTS, L.J.: I now turn to the first question—whether the contract is revocable or is binding on the infant. On this question we were referred to *Doyle* v. *White City Stadium, Ltd, and British Boxing Board of Control* (1929)[1] in which Doyle (an infant) had agreed to be bound by the rules regulating professional boxing because otherwise he could not pursue the career of a professional boxer. The contract and the rules were held binding on him. It is plain that it was a case treated as within or analogous to the exception to the general rule in respect of infants' contracts, and the contract was held binding on the infant because it enabled him to earn his living and so was for his benefit. I think that the principle of that case applies to the present case. The advantage of the contract to the plaintiff in the present case was that it would enable the plaintiff to make a start as an author and thus earn money to keep himself and his wife. The time to judge the question of whether the contract is beneficial must, I think, be the date when the contract is made (see 21 *Halsbury's Laws of England*, 3rd Edn., p. 145). It cannot be right to enable a contract made in good faith to be avoided because it turns out at a later date that the benefits are not as great as the parties anticipated.

It was contended by counsel for the plaintiff that this contract could not be beneficial to the plaintiff because (*a*) the book exposed him to the risk of actions for defamation, and (*b*) the book presented the plaintiff himself as being a bad character. As regards the first, the defendants allege that they can justify, and on this ground the learned judge declined, according to practice, to grant an injunction. As regards the second ground, the contract did confer substantial benefits. I find it difficult to sympathize with a person who, for the purpose of gain, has approved of a book which is calculated to denigrate his character and afterwards wishes to change his mind. How far the book will affect readers, I do not know, but it may be that the publicity which the book has now received will increase the sales of the book and thus increase the benefits to the plaintiff which were the object of the contract. The mud may cling, but the profits will be secured. Taste is a matter of opinion.

[1] [1934] All E.R. Rep. 252; [1935] 1 K.B. 110.

WINN, L.J., delivered a concurring judgment; LORD DENNING, M.R., dissented, saying that prima facie the contract was not for the infant's benefit.

SECTION D

CONTENTS OF THE EMPLOYMENT RELATIONSHIP

I. DUTIES OF CARE AND OBEDIENCE; EXPRESS, IMPLIED, AND CUSTOMARY TERMS*

LISTER v. ROMFORD ICE & COLD STORAGE CO. LTD

House of Lords   [1957] A.C. 555

The appellant, in the course of his employment by the respondents as a lorry driver, negligently knocked down his mate (his father). The latter successfully sued the respondents for their vicarious liability. The respondents brought another action—or rather, their insurance company did in their name—against the appellant for breach of an implied term that he would use reasonable care and skill in his driving. The appellant pleaded that it was an implied term that if the employer was insured or if as a reasonable man he ought to have been insured against this vicarious liability, then he could not claim contribution or indemnity from his employee. The House of Lords upheld the appellant's liability in damages.

VISCOUNT SIMONDS: It is, in my opinion, clear that it was an implied term of the contract that the appellant would perform his duties with proper care. The proposition of law stated by Willes, J. in *Harmer* v. *Cornelius*[1] has never been questioned: 'When a skilled labourer,' he said, 'artisan, or artist is employed, there is on his part an implied warranty that he is of skill reasonably competent to the task he undertakes,—*Spondes peritiam artis*. Thus, if an apothecary, a watch-maker, or an attorney be employed for reward, they each impliedly undertake to possess and exercise reasonable skill in their several arts....An express promise or express representation in the particular case is not necessary.' I see no ground for excluding from, and every ground for including in, this category a servant who is employed to drive a lorry which, driven without care, may become an engine of destruction

[1] (1858) 5 C.B.N.S. 236, 246.

* Compensation for breach of these duties is dealt with in Chapter 2 *post*, p. 169.

and involve his master in very grave liability. Nor can I see any valid reason for saying that a distinction is to be made between possessing skill and exercising it. No such distinction is made in the cited case: on the contrary, 'possess' and 'exercise' are there conjoined. Of what advantage to the employer is his servant's undertaking that he possesses skill unless he undertakes also to use it? I have spoken of using skill rather than using care, for 'skill' is the word used in the cited case, but this embraces care. For even in so-called unskilled operations an exercise of care is necessary to the proper performance of duty.

I have already said that it does not appear to me to make any difference to the determination of any substantive issue in this case, whether the respondents' cause of action lay in tort or breach of contract. But, in deference to Denning, L.J., I think it right to say that I concur in what I understand to be the unanimous opinion of your Lordships that the servant owes a contractual duty of care to his master, and that the breach of that duty founds an action for damages for breach of contract, and that this (apart from any defence) is such a case. It is trite law that a single act of negligence may give rise to a claim either in tort or for breach of a term express or implied in a contract. Of this the negligence of a servant in performance of his duty is a clear example.

I conclude, then, the first stage of the argument by saying that the appellent was under a contractual obligation of care in the performance of his duty, that he committed a breach of it, that the respondents thereby suffered damage and they are entitled to recover that damage from him, unless it is shown either that the damage is too remote or that there is some other intervening factor which precludes the recovery...Nor was it suggested that in the present case there were any features which distinguished the relation of the appellant and the respondents from that of any other driver and his employer. That is why at the outset of this opinion I said that this appeal raises a question of general importance. For the real question becomes, not what terms can be implied in a contract between two individuals who are assumed to be making a bargain in regard to a particular transaction or course of business; we have to take a wider view, for we are concerned with a general question, which, if not correctly described as a question of status, yet can only be answered by considering the relation in which the drivers of motor-vehicles and their employers generally stand to each other. Just as the duty of care, rightly regarded as a contractual obligation, is imposed on the servant, or the duty not to disclose confidential information (see *Robb* v. *Green*), or the duty not to betray secret processes (see *Amber Size and Chemical Co. Ltd* v. *Menzel*), just as the duty is imposed on the master not to require his servant to do any illegal act, just so the question must be asked and answered whether in the world in which we live today it is a necessary condition of the relation of master and man that the master should, to use a broad colloquialism, look after the whole matter of insurance. If I were to try to apply the familiar tests where the question is whether a term should be implied in a particular contract in order to give it what is called business efficacy, I should lose myself in the attempt to formulate it with the necessary precision. The necessarily vague evidence given by the parties and the fact that the action is brought without the assent of the employers shows at least ex post facto how they regarded the position. But this is not conclusive; for, as I have said, the solution of the problem does not rest on the implication of a term in a particular contract of service but upon more general considerations...But here we are in the realm of speculation. Is it certain that, if the imaginary driver had said to his employer: 'Of course you will indemnify me against any damage that I may do however gross my negligence may be,' the employer would have said: 'Yes, of course!'? For myself I cannot answer confidently that he would have said so or ought to have said so. It may well be that if such a discussion had taken place it might have ended in some agreement between them or in the driver not entering the service of that employer. That I do not know. But I do know that I am ever driven further from an assured certainty what is the term which the law imports into the contract of service between the employer and the driver of a motor-vehicle.

Another argument was at this stage adduced which appeared to me to have some weight. For just as it was urged that a term could not be implied unless it could be defined with precision, so its existence was denied if it would not be shown when it came to birth. Here, it was said, was a duty alleged to arise out of the relation of master and servant in this special sphere of employment which was imposed by the common law. When, then, did it first arise? Not, surely, when the first country squire exchanged his carriage and horses for a motor-car or the first haulage contractor bought a motor-lorry. Was it when the practice of insurance against third party risk became so common that it was to be expected of the reasonable man or was it only when the Act of 1930 made compulsory and therefore universal what had previously been reasonable and usual?

Then, again, the familiar argument was heard asking where the line is to be drawn. The driver of a motor-car is not the only man in charge of an engine which, if carelessly used, may endanger and injure third parties. The man in charge of a crane was given as an example. If he, by his negligence, injured a third party who then makes his employer vicariously liable, is he entitled to assume that his employer has covered himself by insurance and will indemnify him however gross and reprehensible his negligence? And does this depend on the extent to which insurance against third party risks prevails and is known to prevail in any particular form of employment?...The common law demands that the servant should exercise his proper skill and care in the performance of his duty: the graver the consequences of any dereliction, the more important it is that the sanction which the law imposes should be maintained. That sanction is that he should be liable in damages to his master: other sanctions there may be, dismissal perhaps and loss of character and difficulty of getting fresh employment, but an action for damages, whether for tort or for breach of contract, has, even if rarely used, for centuries been available to the master, and now to grant the servant immunity from such an action would tend to create a feeling of irresponsibility in a class of persons from whom, perhaps more than any other, constant vigilance is owed to the community...My Lords, I have come to the conclusion that the considerations which I have discussed do not permit me to imply a term such as is pleaded in any of the alternative forms adopted in the original and amended defence or advanced in argument at the bar, and that the appeal so far as it is founded on an implied term in the contract of service must fail.

LORD TUCKER: But, my Lords, apart from these objections which make it impossible for me to accept any of the pleaded implied terms, the case raises questions of importance going beyond the precise language used in this case by the pleader.

Some contractual terms may be implied by general rules of law. These general rules, some of which are now statutory, for example, Sale of Goods Act, Bills of Exchange Act, etc., derive in the main from the common law by which they have become attached in the course of time to certain classes of contractual relationships, for example, landlord and tenant, innkeeper and guest, contracts of guarantee and contracts of personal service. Contrasted with such cases as these there are those in which from their particular circumstances it is necessary to imply a term to give efficacy to the contract and make it a workable agreement in such manner as the parties would clearly have done if they had applied their minds to the contingency which has arisen. These are the 'officious bystander' type of case, to use Mackinnon, L.J.'s, well-known words. I do not think the present case really comes in that category, it seems to me to fall rather within the first class referred to above.

Without attempting an exhaustive enumeration of the duties imposed in this way upon a servant, I may mention: (1) the duty to give reasonable notice in the absence of custom or express agreement; (2) the duty to obey the lawful orders of the master; (3) the duty to be honest and diligent in the master's service; (4) the duty to take reasonable care of his master's property entrusted to him and generally in the performance of his duties; (5) to account to his master for any secret commission or remuneration received by him; (6) not to abuse his master's confidence in matters pertaining to his service: cf. *Robb* v. *Green*.[1]

It would, I think, require very compelling evidence of some general change in circumstances affecting master and servant to justify the court in introducing some quite novel term into their contract, for example, a term absolving the servant from certain of the consequences of a breach of his recognized duty to take care, or as to the provision of insurance covering the servant's liability to third parties or his master. I find it difficult to understand what, if any, are the limitations of this theory. Is it to be confined to the relationship of master and servant with reference to motor-cars, or is it to extend to all those employed in industry or transport who, in the very nature of things, are engaged on work in which negligence on their part may result in widespread and grievous damage amounting to thousands of pounds for which they may be liable to their employers and in respect of risks which it was customary for the employer to insure against long before the advent of the motor-car?

LORD MORTON concurred with VISCOUNT SIMONDS and LORD TUCKER. LORD RADCLIFFE and LORD SOMERVELL dissented, on the ground that the modern contract of employment contains an implied term that the employee shall derive the benefit of an insurance policy and not be open to suit of the insurance company who (as here) usually has the right to step into the shoes of the employer and sue in his name. [It may be noted that a 'gentleman's agreement' among insurance companies has, since 1957, in pratice meant that the views of the minority have so far triumphed, because the companies agreed not to bring such actions against workers.]

[1] [1895] 2 Q.B. 1, 315; 11 T.L.R. 330, 517

HARVEY v. O'DELL LTD

[1958] 2 Q.B. 78

McNair, J.: I do not read *Lister's* case as laying down a proposition of general application that whenever an employed person drives a motor-vehicle within the course of his employment he impliedly agrees *vis-à-vis* his employer to take reasonable care in such driving and to indemnify him for any failure.

Galway was engaged and employed by the first defendants as a storekeeper; as a concession to the first defendants he from time to time used his own motor-cycle on their business and was so using it at the time of the accident. I find it difficult to see on what grounds of justice and reason I should hold that by making his motor-cycle combination available for his employers' business on a particular occasion he should be held in law to have impliedly agreed to indemnify them if he committed a casual act of negligence.

Suppose in a time of labour disturbances in the docks, master stevedores, as sometimes happens, induce their office staff to man the cranes or to do stevedoring; if a third party is injured through the negligence of such staff, no doubt the master stevedores would be vicariously liable, as, indeed, they might be primarily liable, on the basis that they had employed unskilled persons. But it would surely be contrary to all reason and justice to hold that the willing office staff, by abandoning their ledgers and undertaking manual tasks, had impliedly agreed to indemnify their employers against liability arising from their negligence in performing work which they were not employed to do.

BROWNING v. CRUMLIN VALLEY COLLIERIES LTD

[1926] 1 K.B. 522

The defendant colliery had to close down their mines for a period while repairs were done to make the mine safe. The judge found that the mine had become unsafe through no fault of the defendants. The men claimed an implied term that the defendants should provide them with work so as to enable them to earn their wages.

Greer, J.: The consideration for work is wages, and the consideration for wages is work. Is it to be implied in the engagement that the wages are to be paid when through no fault of the employer the work cannot be done? The principle that ought to guide the Court when asked to say whether any term should be read by implication into a written contract was stated by Bowen, L.J., in *The Moorcock*,[1] and his words have ever since been accepted as the guiding principle. In any case in which it is necessary to ascertain whether any and what term should be implied in a written contract the correct application of this guiding principle has to be determined. Bowen, L.J., said: 'Now, an implied warranty, or, as it is called, a covenant in law, as distinguished from an express contract or express warranty, really is in all cases founded on the presumed intention of the parties, and upon reason. The implication which the law draws from what must obviously have been the intention of the parties, the law draws with the object of giving efficacy to the transaction and preventing such a failure of consideration as cannot have been within the contemplation of either side'...

It seems to me that there must in the circumstances of the present case be some implied term. The men did not work, they were not ready and willing to work in the state the mine was in, and the agreement is silent on the question whether they are in these circumstances entitled to be paid wages. Were the mineowners to bear 'all the chances of failure' due to the operation of natural forces without any fault on their part? Were the perils of the transaction in that event to be all on one side, or must the consequences be divided between the two parties, the employers losing the advantages of continuing to have their coal gotten and being compelled to undertake expensive repairs, and the men on their part losing their wages for such time as was reasonably required to put the mine into a safe condition? The latter, I think, must be presumed to have been the intention of both parties. I am satisfied that no employer would have consented to agree that the workmen should be free to withhold their work if the mine became dangerous through no fault on his part and yet should be entitled to be paid their wages. I think the employer would only have agreed to the workmen's right to withhold their labour under these circumstances, subject to the condition that they should not be entitled to their wages. Further, it seems to me clear from the way in which the present case was conducted, and from the evidence given by several witnesses, that this was the usual understanding of the effect of the men's contract of employment....

Great reliance was placed by Mr Matthews on the decision in *Devonald* v. *Rosser & Son*,[2] but in that case the defendant's failure to provide work for the plaintiff so as to enable him to earn his piecework

---

[1] (1889) 14 P.D. 64, 68.   [2] [1906] 2 K.B. 728, 740, 742.

pay was due to the employer deciding that owing to bad trade it would pay him better to close down. It was not due to a cause over which he had no control, it was neither illegal nor impossible for him to continue to find work for the plaintiff, and the Court expressly left open the question whether the plaintiff could have succeeded if the stoppage had been due to such a cause, indicating, I think, that they inclined to the opinion that he could not: see per Lord Alverstone, C.J., and per Sir Gorell Barnes, President, where the learned President uses these words: 'I can quite understand that, having regard to a certain set of circumstances, such as breakage of machinery, it may be reasonable to hold that it was the intention of the parties that those risks should be shared, that risks of that character which are known to both parties, and which prevent both from doing what was contemplated, should excuse from the obligation to maintain the continuance of the work.' I think these observations apply *a fortiori* to contracts between mineowners and their workpeople.

TURNER v. SAWDON & CO.

Court of Appeal   [1901] 2 K.B. 653

The defendants agreed to employ the plaintiff as their salesman for four years at a fixed salary. After a period they stopped giving him work to do but continued to pay him his salary. The plaintiff said this was a breach of contract.

A. L. SMITH, M.R.: The real question which the plaintiff thought to raise, and which was raised, was whether beyond the question of remuneration there was a further obligation on the masters that, during the period over which the contract was to extend, they should find continuous, or at least some, employment for the plaintiff. In my opinion such an action is unique—that is an action in which it is shown that the master is willing to pay the wages of his servant, but is sued for damages because the servant is not given employment. In *Turner* v. *Goldsmith*[1] the wages were to be paid in the form of commission, and that impliedly created a contract to find employment for the servant. This contract is different, being to employ for wages which are to be paid at a certain rate per year. I do not think this can be read otherwise than as a contract by the master to retain the servant, and during the time covered by the retainer to pay him wages under such a contract. It is within the province of the master to say that he will go on paying

[1] [1891] 1 Q.B. 544.

the wages, but that he is under no obligation to provide work. The obligation suggested is said to arise out of the undertaking to engage and employ the plaintiff as their representative salesman. It is said that if the salesman is not given employment which allows him to go on the market his hand is not kept in practice, and he will not be so efficient a salesman at the end of the term. To read in an obligation of that sort would be to convert the retainer at fixed wages into a contract to keep the servant in the service of his employer in such a manner as to enable the former to become *au fait* at his work. In my opinion, no such obligation arose under this contract, and it is a mistake to stretch the words of the contract so as to include in what is a mere retainer an obligation to employ the plaintiff continuously for the term of his service.

VAUGHAN WILLIAMS, L.J. and STIRLING, L.J., delivered concurring judgments.

DEVONALD *v.* ROSSER & SONS

Court of Appeal [1906] 2 K.B. 728

The plaintiff was employed on a piecework basis as a rollerman at the defendant's tinplate factory, under a contract which entitled him to one month's notice. Because the trade was slack, the defendant shut down the works and a fortnight later gave the plaintiff a month's notice. The plaintiff alleged an implied agreement by the defendants to provide him with work during those six weeks. The defendants tried to establish a custom that they were entitled to shut down when they wished.* The plaintiff succeeded. (It is noteworthy that the sum he was allowed to recover was calculated by reference to the worker's recent average earnings over six weeks.)

LORD ALVERSTONE, C.J.: The only facts that are material to be considered are that the plaintiff was in the defendants' regular employment, that he was paid by piecework, and that he was employed upon the terms of a rule which provides that 'No person regularly employed shall quit or be discharged from these works without giving or receiving twenty-eight days' notice in writing, such notice to be given on the first Monday of any calendar month.'...No distinction in principle can be drawn between wages by time and wages by piece. Piecework is only a method of ascertaining the amount of the wages which is to be paid to the workman. What, then, is the obligation of the employers under

* On custom note especially *Sagar* v. *Ridehalgh* (*post*, p. 132).

such a contract as the present? On the one hand we must consider the matter from the point of view of the employers who I agree will under ordinary circumstances desire to carry on their works at a profit, though not necessarily at a profit in every week, for it is matter of common knowledge that masters have frequently to run their mills for weeks and months together at a loss in order to keep their business together and in hopes of better times. On the other hand, we have to consider the position of the workman. The workman has to live; and the effect of the defendants' contention is that if the master at any time found that his works were being carried on at a loss, he might at once close down his works and cease to employ his men, who, even if they gave notice to quit the employment, would be bound to the master for a period of at least twenty-eight days during which time they would be unable to earn any wages at all. I agree with Jelf, J., that that is an unreasonable contention from the workman's point of view. In my opinion the necessary implication to be drawn from this contract is at least that the master will find a reasonable amount of work up to the expiration of a notice given in accordance with the contract. I am not prepared to say that that obligation is an absolute one to find work at all events, for the evidence showed that it was subject to certain contingencies, such as breakdown of machinery and want of water and materials. But I am clearly of opinion that it would be no excuse to the master, for nonperformance of his implied obligation to provide the workman with work, that he could no longer make his plates at a profit either for orders or for stock...

With regard to the question of the alleged custom, I may say that I have always understood that a custom cannot be read into a written contract unless, to use the language of Lord Denman, C.J., in *Reg.* v. *Stoke-upon-Trent*,[1] it is 'so universal that no workman could be supposed to have entered into' the 'service without looking to it as part of the contract.' But here the closing of the works is a matter that depends entirely upon the will of the employer, upon the particular circumstances of the case, and upon the view that the employer takes of the prospect of trade, and as to whether it is worth his while to make plates for stock or not. Under those circumstances there can be no element of certainty about the alleged custom at all, and the defence of custom must fail.

SIR GORELL BARNES, P. and FARWELL, L.J., delivered concurring judgments.

---

[1] (1845) 5 Q.B. 685.

BAUMAN v. HULTON PRESS LTD

[1952] 2 All E.R. 1121

The plaintiff was employed by the defendant company, owner of *Picture Post*, as a colour photographer. Under his contract he was to be paid at a fixed retaining fee per week and in addition payment at definite rates for work done. In return he gave them first option on all his ideas, agreed to be available at all reasonable times and not to accept commission from any other British weekly periodical.

STREATFEILD, J.: It is true that the plaintiff, as a highly skilled technician, could not be told by the defendants how to do his work. That is why they employed an expert to do it for them, but he was bound, so long as it was reasonable, to hold himself in readiness to go wherever they chose to send him on different commissions. To that extent, it seems to me, he was clearly subordinate to their commands and was bound to them by the terms of the contract. Just as in different circumstances Phillimore, J., in choosing between the fine distinctions in *Rhodes* v. *Forwood*[1] and *Turner* v. *Goldsmith*,[2] thought that *Northey* v. *Trevillion*[3] was more like *Rhodes* v. *Forwood*, in considering the facts of this case I must make my choice on the other side of the line. I think that this case is like *Turner* v. *Goldsmith*. Accordingly, in my judgment, this was a contract of service in which the servant was to be paid partly by way of salary and partly by way of remuneration at the rates provided for the work which he was to carry out. In those circumstances it seems to me that, to give business efficacy to the agreement, there is no difficulty in implying the term that throughout the duration of the contract, whatever it was, the defendants were bound to give the plaintiff a reasonable amount of work to enable him to earn that which the parties must be taken to have contemplated. I so hold, and imply such a term.

MEEK v. PORT OF LONDON AUTHORITY

[1918] 1 Ch. 415—[Affirmed [1918] 2 Ch. 96 (C.A.) on other grounds]

The Port of London Act, 1908, transferred the undertakings of the London and India Docks Company to the Port Authority: by s. 60 servants transferred were to hold office on like terms and conditions as they had previously. It had been the practice of the London and India Docks Co. to pay their servants' income tax for them. The

---

[1] (1876) 1 App. Cas. 256. [2] [1891] 1 Q.B. 544.
[3] (1902) 7 Com. Cas. 201.

plaintiffs, who were transferred under the 1908 Act, did not become liable to income tax until later. They claimed the benefit of this practice.*

ASTBURY, J.: Now it is quite true that, subject to the temporary exception in the case of the Millwall Dock Company, the defendants' predecessors for some years past, and apparently prior to the employment of the plaintiffs, had been in the habit of paying the income tax on the wages of their servants. But none of the plaintiffs when they entered the employment of those predecessors had ever heard of that practice, and none of them took up their employment with reference thereto. In these circumstances it is difficult to see how it can be held to be an implied term and condition of their service.

In *Reg.* v. *Inhabitants of Stoke-upon-Trent*[1] Lord Denman said: 'If the evidence had been admitted, it might have shown a custom so universal that no workman could be supposed to have entered into this service without looking to it as part of the contract.' That was cited in *Devonald* v. *Rosser & Sons*[2] as correctly stating the law with regard to contracts of service where 'custom' or 'usage' was raised.

The plaintiffs submitted, and I think accurately, that, assuming this practice to be a general usage within the meaning of the authorities, 'such usages are tacitly annexed to all contracts relating to the business with reference to which they are made unless the terms of such contracts expressly or impliedly exclude them.' Now there is no evidence as to how long this practice had existed at the date of the plaintiffs' original employment, but it is clear that the practice was either not sufficiently notorious to have reached their knowledge or that they entered into the employment without any reference thereto.

Prima facie a practice by an employer to pay a tax such as income tax on his servants' salaries ought to be regarded as in the nature of a bounty. It would require a very strong case indeed to turn a practice apparently of bounty into a usage of obligation. This was not a practice relating to the carrying on of a particular trade or business, but it was a method adopted, universally it may be, over a certain period of time by the employer for the purpose of assisting and benefiting his servants.

In the circumstances I do not think the plaintiffs, even if the practice had existed for a long time and was universal, have brought themselves within the authorities which provide that the implication of a term in a contract of this character, and *a fortiori* a contract affecting the amount

[1] 5 Q.B. 303, 307.   [2] [1906] 2 K.B. 728, 733, 741.

* Compare *Sagar* v. *Ridehalgh post*, p. 132, where Lawrence, L.J. takes a rather different view as to the importance of the worker's knowledge of an implied term.

of wages, can only be made, and ought only to be made, where the parties seeking the advantage of that implication can be deemed to have entered into the contract of employment on the faith and in consideration of the existence of that usage. There is no ground here for saying that the plaintiffs occupied this position at all, and for these reasons I am not able on the evidence before me to come to the conclusion that this was an obligatory practice or usage binding upon the London and India Docks Company at the date of transfer.

THOMAS *v.* VIVIAN

(1873) 37 J.P. 228

Thomas contracted to serve Vivian for a year, but if Vivian should cease to carry on the works from being unable to obtain ore, or for any other cause, then Vivian was to be at liberty to terminate the contract. Thomas absented himself, and was summoned before justices. Held, the contract was not bad for want of mutuality; and that the burden of proof was on Thomas to show that his absence was justifiable. This was a case stated by the magistrates (justices of the peace) acting for the borough of Swansea, in the County of Glamorgan, under Master & Servant Act, 1867. They had convicted Thomas and ordered him to fulfil his contract.

[Such criminal liability for breaches of employment contract, commonly invoked in the late nineteenth century, was abolished by s. 17, Conspiracy and Protection of Property Act, 1875.]

COCKBURN, C.J.: The master obliges himself to find work for the appellant unless from some unforeseen accident. That is surely mutuality enough, and that provision seems to have been inserted expressly to obviate such an objection as this.

BOWEN (Counsel): The second point is that there was no proof of the servant absenting himself. The burden of proof lay on the respondent. It is for the master to inquire into the cause of absence, and make out that it was without sufficient cause.

BLACKBURN, J.: Surely not. It is for the workman to explain why he was absent.*

MELLOR, J., and LUSH, J., concurred.

* Note: This, together with the fact that no right of unilateral 'suspension' of employment exists in English law (see *post*, p. 143), is the basis of the reason why many strikes are bound to be in breach of the contracts of employment of the workers involved. Even notice of a strike may be no more than notice of impending breach by absence. For a further Note on that see chapter 4, p. 525.

BOWES & PARTNERS *v.* PRESS

Court of Appeal   [1894] 1 Q.B. 202

Some miners gave fourteen days' notice to the colliery-owner that they would not go down into the mine with non-unionists. At the time when they were due to go down, a non-unionist got into the lift. They refused to go down with him. The cage took ten seconds to return. They offered to go down in it but were not allowed to. They remained at the pit's mouth for the whole shift. They were sued for damages.*

LINDLEY, L.J.: I pause here to ask, What right had the men to send that notice? What right had they to impose that as a condition of their service? It is not in accordance with their contract, neither was it any part of their contract, that they should be at liberty to say what they do say here, that 'all non-unionists must descend and ascend by themselves.' On the contrary, it is in the very teeth of the contract which embodies the regulations to which I have referred. The men had no right to take that course and to assert the power of dictating to the masters how the men should ascend or descend. However, there is the notice; and accordingly, after the expiration of those fourteen days, some of the miners came to the pit, and, there being a non-unionist who got into the cage to go down the pit, they would not go down. Was that in accordance with the contract or not? It was clearly a breach of contract—so clear a breach that even their own counsel could not hope to argue the contrary...Now, having regard to the fact that this was a preconcerted course of action, it appears to me that the real solution of the problem presented to us in this—that the men did 'absent themselves'; not that I attach much importance to that particular expression, but they did refuse to go to their place of work for three days in accordance with the rules and terms of their contract. I think, having regard to the preconcerted notice and the absence of all right on their part to impose those terms, that the true effect of what they did was this—to say, 'We will not go to our work according to our contract'; and if so, then it appears to me that the view taken of the damages was quite right....

The real difficulty is whether, by reason of the men's breach of

---

* On refusal to obey reasonable lawful orders see, too, *Stratford v. Lindley* (H.L.) *post*, p. 478; *Beale* v. *G.W.R. post*, p. 90; *Laws* v. *London Chronicle Ltd, post*, p. 147. *Stratford* v. *Lindley* shows that it makes no difference that the employee is following his union's instructions even where these are known to the employer before he gives the order.

covenant, the masters are entitled to merely nominal damages or to substantial damages. For the reasons I have given, I think they are entitled to substantial damages. It appears to me that the men deliberately put themselves in the wrong, and that they continuously and persistently refused to work except upon terms which they had no right to dictate.

A. L. SMITH, L.J., and DAVEY, L.J., delivered concurring judgments.

NATIONAL COAL BOARD *v.* HUGHES

Pontypridd County Court   (1959) 109 L.Jo. 526

The plaintiffs' claim before His Honour JUDGE ROWE HARDING at Pontypridd County Court was for damages for breach of contract against seven of their employees in consolidated actions. The defendants were members of a team of eight miners employed at the plaintiffs' Nantgarw Colliery and the first defendant was the team captain. Shortly after the defendants had arrived at the coal face on the day shift of 4 June 1958, the first defendant had refused to obey the instructions of the overman and deputy to work the whole of the coal face of no. 7 district that morning and he had thereupon been ordered out of the mine. The other defendants had thereafter refused to do any more work and had likewise been ordered out.

The defence of each defendant was that the orders given them were unlawful and that they involved work in a dangerous place and in unreasonably dangerous conditions; that the plaintiffs' officials were unjustified in ordering them out of the mine; that the plaintiffs had failed to observe certain terms of an agreement between themselves and the National Union of Mineworkers (as agents for the defendants) dated 1 March 1956, and further, that the plaintiffs had failed to invoke certain conciliation machinery set up by a similar agreement dated 1 January 1947. They all counterclaimed for wages lost.

JUDGE HARDING (having found that the overman had instructed the first defendant as captain how the seam was to be worked, and that the latter had replied that he was going to work it his way, and that the other defendants had refused to work as instructed) said that the question remained whether they were justified in refusing. As regards the other defendants, it was said that, whatever their reasons, they were entitled to refuse because their team captain had instructed them otherwise, and they—and the first defendant—relied upon para. 5 of the agreement of 1 March 1956, which in wide and general terms made the team captain responsible for general supervision in coal-getting operations. But that agreement must be construed so as to have a legal effect and not so as to conflict with any statutory duty imposed on the plaintiffs, and regulation 9 (1) of the Coal and Other Mines (Managers and Officials) Regulations, 1956, provided that charge and supervision should be vested in deputies appointed by the manager. The onus of proving the order unreasonable being on the defendants, they must prove that there was no way of carrying out the order without exposure to unreasonable danger. Here the order envisaged a method of working the face in a particular way, but the defendants had refused to work in part of the area at all. It seemed to him [His Honour] that in that situation the defendants could not successfully plead an unlawful order unless they showed that there was no method of working the face with reasonable safety. He was satisfied that the conveyor worked normally in the afternoon shift for four unskilled men and that it followed that it could have worked equally successfully for the skilled defendants, and he was not satisfied its condition constituted a danger. As regards the failure to adopt the conciliation procedure, it was for the defendants to initiate it and they had not done so. There would be judgment against each defendant for £37 16s. 4d. and the counterclaims would be dismissed.

BEALE v. GREAT WESTERN RAILWAY CO.
(1901) 17 T.L.R. 450

The present action was a test case brought by an employee of the company claiming to recover five days' 'suspension money' and a week's wages in lieu of notice for wrongful dismissal. The conditions of the plaintiff's employment as a platelayer included a clause giving the company power to dismiss or suspend in any case of 'intoxication, disobedience of orders, negligence, or misconduct', without paying wages. Gangs of platelayers usually worked from 6.0 a.m. to 6.0 p.m., and occasionally at night when required. They travelled to work in their own time, and from work in the company's time, usually a quarter of an hour each way. The plaintiff's gang was ordered to report at 11.0 p.m. and make a journey of one hour to a place of work that night. They refused, and were suspended and later dismissed.

Counsel for the plaintiff contended that the Judge was wrong in holding that the plaintiff was not entitled to a week's notice or a week's wages in lieu of notice, because though it was true that the plaintiff had refused to obey the order given to him, the order was not one which he was bound to obey, being unreasonable in that it required him to travel for an hour without extra payment.

The Divisional Court upheld the decision of the County Court judge in favour of the defendant company.

LORD ALVERSTONE, C.J., said that they were not concerned with the question whether the railway company were entitled to make their servants go to work in their own time. That was obviously a matter on which a reasonable employer and his servants ought to be able to come to some agreement. All the Court had to consider was whether there was evidence on which the learned Judge could find that the order given to the plaintiff was a reasonable order. There was, in fact, no evidence to show that the order was not a proper or reasonable one. That order having been disobeyed by the plaintiff, the company were justified in dismissing him.*

GREGORY v. FORD

[1951] 1 All E.R. 121

The plaintiff was injured by a lorry driven by the third defendant, who was employed by the first and second defendants. The latter owned the lorry.

BYRNE, J.: The third defendant further contends that it was an implied term of his employment that the first and second defendants should at all times keep the lorry insured against third-party risks. It seems to me that, when a person is employed to drive a lorry, there must be an implied term in the contract of service that the servant shall not be required to do an unlawful act. If that be so, it appears to me to follow that it is an implied term of the contract that the employer will comply with the provisions of the statute. There is no evidence before me that the third defendant knew that the policy of insurance did not cover the errand on which he was engaged at the time of the accident. . . .

In my view, there was an implied term in the contract of service that the employer would comply with the statute, from which it would follow that the servant would be indemnified by insurers for any damage caused by his negligence. I have, therefore, come to the conclusion that on this ground the third defendant is entitled to succeed.

* Note: The problem as to the territorial area within which the employer can properly require the employee to work arises now particularly under the Redundancy Payments Act, 1965: see the decisions of Industrial Tribunals, *post*, p. 219 and p. 239 .

2. SICKNESS

(a) Many employees will today have express terms of employment covering payments during periods of sickness when they cannot work. For an example see *ante* p. 64 and p. 70.

(b) Nonetheless, in 1964 Government surveys suggested that not more than half the working population was covered by any kind of sickness scheme, and many of those who were covered received only small sums for a limited period of the sickness (see summary in *The Worker and the Law*, Penguin, p. 66; McGibbon & Kee, p. 65). In consequence the problem of the 'implied term' is likely to remain important in many of contracts employment when the worker is ill. (For a collective agreement on sick pay see *post* Chapter 3, p. 251.)

(c) The reader should remember that if the illness lasts, or seems likely to last, for such a long period that it strikes at the foundation of the contract, under the ordinary doctrines of the law of contract, the employment contract will terminate by reason of 'frustration': see *ante* p. 33, *post* p. 137–8. Otherwise, sickness does not break continuity of employment: Contracts of Employment Act, 1963, *post* p. 168; *Tarbuck* v. *Wilson Ltd* (1967) 2 I.T.R. 157. (But pregnancy may break it since that is not 'sickness or injury' within the Act: *Whiteley* v. *Garfield Spinning Ltd* (1967) 2 I.T.R. 128.)

(d) Under the national insurance scheme, sickness benefit will be payable to those incapable of work, normally without limit in duration; but for those who have paid less than 156 contributions, the time limit (subject to requalification) is 312 days: National Insurance Act, 1965, s. 21(2). Under the National Insurance Act, 1966, sickness benefit, like unemployment and industrial injury benefit, now has a graduated 'earnings-related' supplement in addition to flat rate benefit, payable for six months from the thirteenth day of incapacity. On the Act see J. Reid (1966) 29 M.L.R.537.

ORMAN v. SAVILLE SPORTSWEAR LTD
[1960] 1 W.L.R. 1055

The production manager in a skirt factory fell ill and was away for over two months. Nothing was said in his contract of employment as to payment of salary in periods of illness.*

* See now s. 4, Contracts of Employment Act, 1963, *ante*, p. 66. But *quaere* the evidential quality of written particulars under that section in case of a dispute about such employment terms?

PILCHER, J.: Having considered all these cases and the careful argument addressed to me by counsel, it seems to me that they establish the following proposition. Where the written terms of the contract of service are silent as to what is to happen in regard to the employee's rights to be paid whilst he is absent from work due to sickness, the employer remains liable to continue paying so long as the contract is not determined by proper notice, except where a condition to the contrary can properly be inferred from all the facts and the evidence in the case. If the employer—and, of course, it will always be the employer—seeks to establish an implied condition that no wages are payable, it is for him to make it out, and the court, in construing the written contract, will not accept any implied term which will not pass the test laid down by Scrutton, L.J., in *Reigate* v. *Union Manufacturing (Ramsbottom) Co. Ltd*, to which I have referred earlier in this judgment.*

In my view, it is clear, from the evidence in this case that if the matter had been mooted when the contract of service was made between the plaintiff and the defendants' managing director, the situation envisaged by Scrutton, L.J., in the *Reigate* case, namely, that the plaintiff and the managing director would at once have disagreed, would have obtained. I am accordingly of the opinion that in this contract no implied term in regard to payment during the period of illness can properly be introduced at all. It follows, therefore, that on the authorities the defendants remain liable to pay the plaintiff from the time when he ceased work until the contract of service was determined.

PETRIE *v.* MACFISHERIES LTD†

Court of Appeal   [1940] 1 K.B. 258

In 1926 the defendants posted up a notice in their fish-smoking department stating that workmen who were away through illness would be paid half their weekly wages for a period of up to three weeks in any one

---

* See [1918] 1 K.B. 592 at p. 605: 'The first thing is to see what the parties have expressed in the contract; and then an implied term is not to be added because the Court thinks it would have been reasonable to have inserted it in the contract. A term can only be implied if it is necessary in the business sense to give efficacy to the contract; that is, if it is such a term that it can confidently be said that if at the time the contract was being negotiated some one had said to the parties, "What will happen in such a case," they would both have replied, "Of course, so and so will happen; we did not trouble to say that; it is too clear." Unless the Court comes to some such conclusion as that, it ought not to imply a term which the parties themselves have not expressed.'

† See too *O'Grady* v. *Saper* [1940] 2 K.B. 469: commissionaire sued for wages not paid in three periods of illness when he was off work. His contract of employment was silent on the point. Held: the evidence pointed to the terms, 'not expressed but no doubt implied, upon which this man was employed were that he should not be paid wages whilst he was sick' (MacKINNON, L.J.).

year, and that this would be done as an act of grace and not as of right. In 1930 they took on the plaintiff as a smoker-packer. He knew of this sickness arrangement, though it was not shown that he had ever seen the notice. He claimed his full weekly wages for the period in which he had been ill, less the money he had been paid as an act of grace.

DU PARCQ, L.J.: The first thing to remember is that one must find out what the contract is. It is plain that Lord Cozens-Hardy did not mean that every contract of service, whatever terms were contained in it, must result in a liability to pay a workman during the time that he is ill. The terms in the contract may be express, or they may be implied. You may have a custom. It appears in one of the cases that there is a custom that agricultural labourers are not paid during the time they are off work through illness. It would be idle in such a case to assert that Lord Cozens-Hardy said that under a contract of service the servant must always be paid wages during his absence through illness. Apart from express terms, or terms imported through some well known custom, the terms may obviously be implied in other ways. I do not dwell on that, because in this case, when the whole of the facts are looked at, it seems to me plain—and I think that if the judge had not attached undue importance, as I think he must have done, to the isolated passage from *Marrison* v. *Bell*[1] to which I have referred, he could have come to no other conclusion—that there was here, at the material time in 1938, a contract, one of the terms of which was that during absence through illness the workman was to have no right to any remuneration whatever. It is, in my view, impossible to draw any other conclusion from the facts.... If you assume that the plaintiff is a reasonable man—and if I do not assume that I am quite unable to put any construction at all on the conduct of the parties—he knew, as he admits that he knew, long before 1938, that if he was away ill he would not be paid a penny as of right. It is not suggested that he thought, when he was paid ex gratia, that he was still entitled to wages over and above the ex gratia payment. He knew that it was the intention of the firm to pay him nothing whatever as of right if he was ill, and he knew that it was on that footing that the defendants understood that they contracted with him. If one finds that, knowing that, he makes no objection and makes no claim for wages, but goes back to work, and accepts, as he later did, an increase in his wages, it appears to be quite impossible for him to say that he did not agree to work for the defendants on the footing that that was a term of the contract.

SLESSER, L.J., and ATKINSON, J., delivered concurring judgments.

[1] [1939] 2 K.B. 187.

NATIONAL INSURANCE ACT, 1965
SICKNESS BENEFIT

R(S) 2/63

Claimant understood that on being appointed to the staff he would no longer have his wages reduced during sickness. At the end of a spell of sickness he discovered that a reduction had been made in his wages and he promptly claimed sickness benefit for the whole of the spell.

DECISION OF THE TRIBUNAL...

4. The claimant had previously claimed sickness benefit, his last claim being in 1959. At that time he knew that National Insurance benefit would be deducted from his wages paid during sickness, and he claimed benefit in time accordingly. In 1961 he was appointed to the staff, and one of the inducements offered to him, as a result of which he agreed to accept slightly reduced wages, was that he would be entitled to wages during sickness. Nothing was said about any deduction for National Insurance benefits, and, in view of what his position had been before, it was in our opinion reasonable that he should understand what was said as meaning that wages would in future be paid in full during sickness. He believed down to a date at least as late as 5 March 1962 that he was not entitled to claim sickness benefit whilst drawing full wages; he thought that it would be 'false pretences'. This is a common mistake....

7. The conditions of entitlement to sickness benefit are laid down by s. 11 of the National Insurance Act, 1946,* and the regulations made under it. Under that section sickness benefit and unemployment benefit are closely linked for certain purposes. Regulations prevent a person from receiving sickness benefit whilst working (subject to certain exceptions) (see regulation 6(1)(g) of the National Insurance (Unemployment and Sickness Benefit) Regulations, 1948 [S.I. 1948, no. 1277] as amended). A person cannot receive unemployment benefit if he is working (subject to certain exceptions) (see regulation 6(1)(h) of the same regulations), nor even if he is receiving wages (regulation 6(1)(d)). A person can receive sickness benefit and full wages at the same time, but this is not because the Act or any regulation says that he can, but because they give him an entitlement to the benefit in certain circumstances and they do not say that he cannot....

---

* The relevant sections are now ss. 19, 20, 48 and 49(3) National Insurance Act, 1965.

8. Regulations made under s. 28(2) of the Act prescribe the periods within which sickness benefit (of the kind in question in this case) must be claimed.... If the claimant proves good cause for the delay during *the whole* period, he can escape disqualification altogether. If he proves good cause for the delay during *the latter part* of the period, he can escape disqualification for that part. If however he proves good cause for only the *earlier part* of the delay, he cannot escape disqualification....

10. The result of the regulations is that, even though a person has paid the necessary contributions, and even though the conditions for the receipt of sickness benefit are satisfied, nevertheless he may be disqualified for receiving benefit to which he is entitled, unless he claims within the prescribed time, subject to extension where good cause is shown for the delay....

11. 'Good cause' in these regulations has the same meaning as 'reasonable cause' in the corresponding regulations made for the purposes of claims for industrial injury benefits (Decision C.S.I. 10/50 (reported))....In Decision C.S. 371/49 (reported) the Commissioner said '''Good cause'' means, in my opinion, some fact which, having regard to all the circumstances (including the claimant's state of health and the information which he had received and that which he might have obtained) would probably have caused a reasonable person of his age and experience to act (or fail to act) as the claimant did.' This description of good cause has been quoted in countless cases. It has stood the test of time. In our judgment it is correct....

13. Ignorance of one's rights is not of itself good cause for delay in claiming. It is in general the duty of the claimant to find out what they are, and how and when they should be asserted. But an examination of numerous Commissioner's decisions shows that over the years there has been a gradual but appreciable relaxation of the strictness with which problems of good and reasonable cause have been approached. The Commissioner has long recognized a wide variety of circumstances, in which it would not be expected that a reasonable person would make inquiries or think that there was anything to inquire about: see e.g. Decisions R(S) 18/52, where a schoolmaster in perfect health was prevented from working because he had been in contact with infectious disease and did not know that in those circumstances he was entitled to receive sickness benefit; R(P) 5/58, where a widow who had emigrated to America in 1946 did not learn of her right to a retirement pension until 15 months after she attained pensionable age in 1955; R(S) 10/59,

where a woman who contributed as a non-employed person knew that, as such, she was not entitled to sickness benefit but did not know she had certain residual rights derived from former employment which entitled her to sickness benefit; see also Decisions R(S) 11/59 and R(I) 25/61. In all these cases a claimant has been held to have had good cause for delay in claiming because the right to benefit was unlikely and not such as to provoke inquiry into its existence....

16. Having fully considered the matter and taken into consideration the fact that the rules hitherto applied are of long standing, we feel justified in holding that cases of the present type may be regarded as special cases. We do not doubt that the earlier decisions were justified when they were given, but we think that experience over later years justifies modification of them....

17. In the present case the claimant was under two misapprehensions. He had been led by the events when he was promoted to the staff to believe that he would be paid his wages in full. The payment in full on the 23 February may well have confirmed that belief; it certainly would not have corrected it. That was a mistake of fact. He also believed that he was not entitled to claim sickness benefit whilst receiving his wages in full. That was mistake of law.

18. In our judgment, in the absence of special circumstances, there should be held to be good cause for delay in claiming sickness benefit:

(*a*) during any period throughout which the claimant did not claim because he had reasonable grounds for believing and believed that he was being or would be paid his salary or wages in full during sickness and he believed that it was not permissible for him to claim sickness benefit whilst being so paid; and

(*b*) during such further brief period thereafter as was reasonably necessary to enable him to claim promptly.

R(S) 2/61

A farmer who normally ran his small dairy farm of about 50 acres with the aid of one man had suffered injury to his left shoulder, as a result of which he was unable to carry out a number of duties such as using the milking machines, the tractor and wheelbarrow and doing heavy lifting. He had to employ an extra man at week-ends to do work which, before his injury, he had done himself. He was able to let in the cows, feed the poultry, drive a car, keep the accounts and do such little supervising work as was necessary.

Held that, applying the test in R(S) 11/51, the claimant was not incapable of work.

DECISION OF THE COMMISSIONER...

6. The local tribunal by a majority, the chairman dissenting, allowed the claimant's appeal. It seems clear, however, that they must have overlooked the meaning of 'incapable of work'....

7. The test to be applied is to be found in Decision R(S) 11/51. In that decision a tribunal of three Commissioners stated that a person is incapable of work within the meaning of that section 'if, having regard to his age, education, experience, state of health and other personal factors, there is no work or type of work which he can reasonably be expected to do'. They then explained that by 'work' in that connection they meant remunerative work, including work as a self-employed person in some gainful occupation.

8. It is true that there are some cases in which the work of a self-employed person which a claimant claiming sickness benefit is able to do is of so trivial a character that it can be disregarded as negligible. Instances of work which has been held to be negligible are a claimant who helped his wife occasionally to cut, or pack, a few flowers (see Decision C.S. 5/54 (not reported)) or a woman who ran a guest house, capable of taking no more than six or seven visitors at the most, and who did no more than order the meals and interview visitors (see Decision C.S. 9/53 (not reported)) or a farmer who even had to be helped by his wife in doing such paper work as was necessary on a farm, where very little paper work was involved, and who ordered seeds from an agent who called and attended marts a few times a year to buy or sell stock. See Decision C.S. 17/55 (not reported). It is impossible to say on the facts of this case that the work which the claimant is able to do, despite his disability, is so trivial as to be negligible.

9. In the circumstances, I must hold that the claimant was not incapable of work on the 27 March 1959....

12. In certain cases, a pension or gratuity is payable in respect of an injury caused by accident arising out of and in the course of a person's employment. Such benefit, however, is payable under the National Insurance (Industrial Injuries) Acts, which do not apply to self-employed persons.[*]

[*] See *post.* p. 760, chapter 6.

3. FIDELITY, INVENTIONS, AND DUTIES OF DISCLOSURE

ROBB v. GREEN

Court of Appeal   [1895] 2 Q.B. 315

The defendant, an employee of the plaintiff who was a tradesman, left his service and set up a similar business on his own. Before he left, he copied out lists of the plaintiff's customers, and tried to get them to transfer their custom to himself.

LORD ESHER, M.R.: I think the judge was perfectly justified in holding that such conduct was a breach of the trust reposed in the defendant as the servant of the plaintiff in his business. The question arises whether such conduct is a breach of contract. That depends upon the question whether in a contract of service the Court can imply a stipulation that the servant will act with good faith towards his master. In this case it it said that the contract of service was in writing; but there is nothing in the express terms of the contract that contradicts such an implication. I think that in a contract of service the Court must imply such a stipulation as I have mentioned, because it is a thing which must necessarily have been in view of both parties when they entered into the contract. It is impossible to suppose that a master would have put a servant into a confidential position of this kind, unless he thought that the servant would be bound to use good faith towards him; or that the servant would not know, when he entered into that position, that the master would rely on his observance of good faith in the confidential relation between them. Where the Court sees that there is a matter of this kind which both parties must necessarily have had in their minds when entering into a contract, that is precisely the case in which it ought to imply a stipulation. We have the authority of Bowen, L.J., in the case of *Lamb* v. *Evans*[1] that there is such an implication in a contract of service.

KAY, L.J., and A. L. SMITH, L.J., concurred.

WESSEX DAIRIES LTD v. SMITH

Court of Appeal   [1935] 2 K.B. 80

MAUGHAM, L.J.: The question to be determined essentially depends upon the term to be implied in the ordinary case of a contract of employment in the absence of express agreement. In the present case an

---

[1] [1893] 1 Ch. 218, 229.

express agreement has been mentioned which states the duty of fidelity, but I should like to decide the case on a wider ground.... For myself I prefer the more general implication stated thus by A. L. Smith, L.J.:[1] 'I think that it is a necessary implication which must be engrafted on such a contract that the servant undertakes to serve his master with good faith and fidelity. That is what was said in the case of *Lamb* v. *Evans*,[2] and I entirely agree with it.' The Lord Justice then asked himself whether the defendant in *Robb* v. *Green*[3] acted with good faith and fidelity. The same question has to be answered in the present case. In dealing with it certain considerations should not be left out of sight. First, after the employment terminates, the servant may, in the absence of special stipulation, canvass the customers of the late employer, and further he may send a circular to every customer. On the other hand, it has been held that while the servant is in the employment of the master he is not justified in making a list of the master's customers, and he can be restrained, as he was in *Robb* v. *Green*, from making such a list, or if he has made one, he will be ordered to give it up. But it is to be noted that in *Robb* v. *Green* the defendant was not restrained from sending out circulars to customers whose names he could remember. Another thing to be borne in mind is that although the servant is not entitled to make use of information which he has obtained in confidence in his master's service he is entitled to make use of the knowledge and skill which he acquired while in that service, including knowledge and skill directly obtained from the master in teaching him his business. It follows, in my opinion, that the servant may, while in the employment of the master, be as agreeable, attentive and skilful as it is in his power to be to others with the ultimate view of obtaining the benefit of the customers' friendly feelings when he calls upon them if and when he sets up business for himself. That is, of course, where there is no valid restrictive clause preventing him doing so.

In this case the question is whether the defendant acted with fidelity when, on the Saturday afternoon in question and perhaps on the previous days of the week, in going his round he informed the customers that he would cease on Saturday to be in the employment of the plaintiffs, that he was going to set up business for himself, and would be in a position to supply them with milk. He was plainly soliciting their custom as from Saturday evening. In my opinion that was a deliberate as it was a successful canvassing at a time when the defendant was under

---

[1] [1895] 2 Q.B. 320.   [2] [1893] 1 Ch. 218.
[3] [1895] 2 Q.B. 1, 315, 320.

an obligation to serve the plaintiffs with fidelity. I am of opinion therefore that he committed a breach of his implied contract....

GREER, L.J., and TALBOT, J., concurred.

WORSLEY & CO. LTD v. COOPER

[1939] 1 All E.R. 290

The defendants had both been directors of the plaintiff company, a paper company. One of them had travelled for the company for several years and had prepared a sample book and price list of the papers sold by the company, listing the names of the various types of paper and so on. The defendants were bought out of the plaintiff company. They then set up business selling paper on their own account, sending a circular to the plaintiff's customers which could give the impression that the defendant company was a successor to the plaintiffs. Later they sent out a price list, identical to the plaintiffs' except for some of the names of the types of paper being different, even including a key whereby a customer could relate the defendant's new name to that used by the plaintiff company.

The plaintiff company sued, alleging *inter alia* that the defendants had disclosed confidential information or had made an improper use of such confidential information in breach of duty or an implied contract. The claim failed under this head; though it succeeded under another (namely, the tort of passing off).

MORTON, J.: The position as regards the divulging or improper use of confidential information is this. I think that it is the fact, as I have already said, that paper merchants would not wish the source from which each one of their whole range of papers came to be disclosed to their customers, who are generally printers, or to their competitors. However, they might, in any individual instance, tell a good customer, if he wanted to know, where a particular paper came from. The first circular sent out by Mr Cooper, junior, contains this remark: 'My intention is to market the same products as before...'. That is to say, he is saying, as I read it: 'The same products as I have previously marketed I shall continue to market.' Only a man with an intimate knowledge of the plaintiff company's business could be quite certain that every paper which he himself, having left the plaintiff company's employment, was going to sell was exactly the same as a particular paper sold by the plaintiff company. That knowledge was acquired by Mr Cooper.... However, I have arrived at the conclusion, with some hesitation, that, apart from the fact that the price list and key were a breach of copyright, Mr Cooper, junior, did not commit an actionable wrong under this heading.... There was nothing surreptitious in the way in which Mr Robert Cooper acquired intimate knowledge of the source of origin of each of the plaintiffs' papers. He has not sought to disclose that source of knowledge, but the information which he acquired during his service with the plaintiffs he has used in advancing his own business and in damaging the plaintiffs' business. As I say, I cannot feel any particular approval of the particular methods he adopted, but I think that what he did under this heading of the case amounts to no more than to say of each paper sold by the plaintiffs: 'If you order the paper which I sell under the name of so-and-so, you will be getting paper which the plaintiffs sell under the name of such-and-such.' That statement was true. It was the use of his knowledge, skill and experience gained in the plaintiffs' service, and I do not think that it can be said that the origin of the paper was anything in the nature of a secret process. I have come to the conclusion, though with some hesitation, that, on the case as pleaded in paras. 13, 14 and 15 of the statement of claim, the plaintiffs have not made out any ground of relief against the defendants.

HIVAC LTD v. PARK ROYAL SCIENTIFIC INSTRUMENTS LTD

Court of Appeal   [1946] Ch. 169

The plaintiff company discovered that some of their skilled employees were working for a rival company in their spare time making midget valves for deaf aids, which was also their work for the plaintiff. There was no evidence that confidential information had been divulged. The plaintiff company sought an interlocutory injunction against the rival company. [It is to be noted that because of the Essential Work Order the plaintiff could not dismiss the employees concerned without considerable difficulty. The plaintiff company had manufactured the valves for many years; the rival company was a newcomer in the business and, to the employees' knowledge, would seriously damage the plaintiff by its competition, if it succeeded, in a field where competition had been non-existent.]

LORD GREENE, M.R.: It has been said on many occasions that an employee owes a duty of fidelity to his employer. As a general proposition that is indisputable. The practical difficulty in any given case is to find exactly how far that rather vague duty of fidelity extends.... The law would, I think, be jealous of attempting to impose on a manual worker restrictions, the real effect of which would be to prevent him utilizing his spare time. He is paid for five and a half days in the week. The rest of the week is his own, and to impose upon a man, in relation to the rest of the week, some kind of obligation which really would unreasonably tie his hands and prevent him adding to his weekly money during that time would, I think, be very undesirable. On the other hand, if one has employees of a different character, one may very well find that the obligation is of a different nature.... One example was discussed in argument, that of a solicitor's clerk who on Sundays it was assumed went and worked for another firm in the same town. He might find himself embarrassed because the very client for whom he had done work while working for the other firm on the Sunday might be a client against whom clients of his main employer were conducting litigation, or something of that kind....

First of all, what was done here was done in the spare time of the employees. That leads to this: we have to consider what implication, if any, needs to be read into the contract of service with regard to the employee's use of his spare time. Does that implication in any way restrict him, or, rather (which is the practical question here) did that implication make it a breach of duty on his part to do what he did, with the consequential result that the defendants, in persuading the employees to do what they did, procured a breach of contract? I think the judgment of Maugham, L.J., in *Wessex Dairies, Ltd* v. *Smith*, which is quite deliberately placed by him on a broad ground, does lead to this. Although the case before him was concerned with an employee who had done certain things in his employers' time, I cannot find that in his reasoning that was regarded as an essential part of the offence. I cannot read the judgment as meaning that if the roundsman had on a Saturday afternoon, when his work was over, gone round to all these customers and canvassed them, he would have been doing something he was entitled to do. It would be a curious result if, quite apart from making use of the list of customers or his special knowledge or anything of that kind, he could set himself during his spare time deliberately to injure the goodwill of his master's business by trying to get his customers to leave him. Then again the question here is not a question of getting the customers to leave the business but a question of building up a rival in business to the prejudice of the goodwill of the employer's business.

I am not ashamed to confess that in the course of the argument my mind has fluctuated considerably on this question. As I see it, the court stands in a sense between Scylla and Charybdis, because it would be most unfortunate if anything we said, or any other court said, should place an undue restriction on the right of the workman, particularly a manual workman, to make use of his leisure for his profit. On the other hand, it would be deplorable if it were laid down that a workman could, consistently with his duty to his employer, knowingly, deliberately and secretly set himself to do in his spare time something which would inflict great harm on his employer's business. I have endeavoured to raise the questions in the way that they appeal to me and, on the best consideration I can give to the matter, I think that the plaintiffs are *prima facie* right in this case.

MORTON, L.J., delivered a concurring judgment; BUCKNILL, L.J., concurred.

BENTS BREWERY CO. LTD *v.* HOGAN

[1945] 2 All E.R. 570

In order to be able to prepare a programme of wages and conditions of service for some of their members who were managers of on-licensed premises, a union sent out to these managers a questionnaire which included questions as to the expenses of the houses, their takings, trade and total wages bill. Brewery companies, who owned these houses, sought a declaration that their employees were not entitled to give this information.

LYNSKEY, J.: In my view, it is quite clear that an employee is under an obligation to his employers not to disclose confidential information obtained by him in the course of and as a result of his employment. Different judges, in various cases, have given different grounds for the existence of this obligation. Sometimes it has been said that the obligation was the result of an implied term in the contract of service; sometimes that it was an obligation arising out of the employee's position or status as such, and sometimes that the obligation arises because of the trust or confidence which an employee owes of necessity to his employer.

Whatever the true ground may be, in my view the obligation exists upon an employee not to disclose such confidential information. In my opinion, such obligation arises from an implied term in the contract of service, but for the purpose of this case it does not matter so long as it is clear that the obligation, apart from any express term, exists, and I think it does.... In considering what questions asked seek confidential information it seems to me that the terms and conditions of the individual manager's employment are contained in the contract of service made by such manager. Such information is not acquired as a result of the opportunities afforded by his service or acquired in the course of such service. In my view, therefore, the terms and conditions of the particular manager's service cannot be treated as confidential information which the manager is under an obligation not to disclose....

I have come to the conclusion that the questions the answers to which would disclose confidential information are those contained in questions 7 and 9, that is weekly sales and total wages bill. The information sought in the remaining 16 questions is information which an applicant for the position of manager would seek to know before making his contract of service. I do, however, feel that information as to the weekly sales and the total wages bill for the licensed house of which he is manager is information which the manager could only acquire as a result of and in the course of his service. It is also information of a confidential character which the brewery company employer would not desire to be disclosed. Having come to the conclusion that there was an obligation on the manager-employees not to disclose confidential information acquired by them as a result of and in the course of their service, and that the questionnaire contained in the document requested information of a confidential character in so far as it related to weekly sales and total wages bill of each particular house, it follows, in my view, that if any manager should disclose such information to the defendant the manager would be committing either a breach of his contract with his employer or a breach of the duty he owed to his employer.

CRANLEIGH PRECISION ENGINEERING LTD *v.* BRYANT

[1965] 1 W.L.R. 1293

Bryant was an engineer and inventor, and managing director of the plaintiff company for some years. The plaintiffs marketed a swimming pool, one of his inventions. He also formed another company under the control of his family. Letters patent for Bryant's pool were never obtained; but, in his capacity as managing director, he learned of another patent (Bischoff's patent) having been granted for a pool which was similar but which lacked certain essential features of his pool.

These features could be understood only by someone with the technical knowledge of Bryant. Bryant left the plaintiff company's employment, taking files, assets, and correspondence. He shortly afterwards acquired the Bischoff patent, of which he had never informed the plaintiff company.

The plaintiffs successfully claimed an injunction to prevent Bryant from using any confidential information obtained while managing director; and from making use of the Bischoff patent.

[It is to be noted that the defendant was here a managing director. Company directors are under stringent 'fiduciary duties' towards their companies. Nevertheless, in this judgment, as in others recently, the matter is discussed on the basis of employment law. For a further discussion of directors' duties, see *post* p. 567.]

ROSKILL, J.: The essence of the defendants' case was that neither of these particular features of the plaintiffs' pool was susceptible of being the subject of confidence because of their very simplicity. It was said that anybody could buy a plastic strip and use it for clamping, and any competent engineer or sheet metal worker could without difficulty construct the interfit. It was said that the plastic strip manufacturer might have his secrets of manufacture of the plastic strip, but those secrets were not the secrets of the swimming pool manufacturer, and once the latter had received from the plastics manufacturer a plastic strip suitable for clamping the liner to the top of the vertical plates, there could, in the nature of things, be no secrecy attaching to the user of the clamping strip as such. . . . In my judgment the plaintiffs are correct in their contentions on this issue. I think the knowledge that this particular clamping strip was the right type of clamping strip to use for this particular purpose, coupled with the knowledge of how to define to a plastics manufacturer what was required for this particular purpose and that a plastics manufacturer could readily supply this particular form of strip, is and was a trade secret of the plaintiffs. . . . Did Bryant therefore receive this knowledge in circumstances of confidence? There are many authorities which have been cited to me where this question has arisen for determination; some on one side of the line, some on the other side. . . . The essential fact is that Bryant was the managing director of the plaintiff company. He alone of the directors appreciated the technical importance of the clamping strip and of the interfit. He had devised them both. There was no one else in the plaintiffs who could have informed him of these matters. It is no answer to say that Bryant himself was responsible for the development in question.

Bryant, in my judgment, acquired this information, which, as I have held, was confidential information, as the plaintiffs' managing director, and he acquired it in confidence. He has sought to take advantage of it since he left the plaintiffs to his own advantage and to that of the defendant company. In my judgment, that, on the authorities, involves a breach of his duty of confidence to the plaintiffs, and he should be restrained from committing such breach and the defendant company should also be restrained from taking advantage of that breach.... In the present case, Bryant, as possessor of what I have held to be the plaintiffs' confidential information, is seeking to free himself from his obligations of confidence, not because of what the plaintiffs have published, for they have published nothing, but because of what Bischoff published—a publication of which Bryant only became aware because of his contractual and confidential relationship with the plaintiffs.

I have dealt with this question at length for the matter was argued at length before me. Applying the law as I conceive it to be, I have no doubt that Bryant acted in grave dereliction of his duty to the plaintiffs in concealing from the plaintiffs' board the information which he received from the plaintiffs' patent agents, and in taking no steps whatsoever to protect the plaintiffs against the possible consequences of the existence and publication of the Bischoff patent. I also have no doubt that Bryant acted in breach of confidence in making use, as he did as soon as he left the plaintiffs, of the information regarding the Bischoff patent which he had acquired in confidence and about its various effects on the plaintiffs' position, for his own advantage and for that of the defendant company. Any other conclusion would involve putting a premium on dishonesty by managing directors.

In reaching this conclusion I have not lost sight of the fact that P1, unlike the draft service agreement which Bryant refused to sign, contained no express obligation not to divulge confidential information, but this makes no difference, for, were it necessary, I would not hesitate to imply into the contract of employment between Bryant and the plaintiffs the relevant obligation. It is both reasonable and necessary so to do.

The plaintiffs relied on the decision of the Court of Appeal in *Swain* v. *West (Butchers) Ltd*,[1] in support of their argument that Bryant was under a duty to report to the plaintiffs' board that of which the plaintiffs' patent agents had informed him. I need only say that my conclusion on

---

[1] [1936] 3 All E.R. 261.

that part of the case is, I think, consistent with that decision. I reject the argument that it was a mere error of judgment on Bryant's part not to report this. It is difficult to think that as Bryant was able to buy the Bischoff specification in October–November 1963, for a relatively trivial sum, the plaintiffs could not have done so at least as cheaply, had Bryant given them the opportunity of so doing.

TRIPLEX SAFETY GLASS CO. *v.* SCORAH
[1938] 1 Ch. 211

While he was employed by the plaintiffs as an assistant chemist, the defendant at the plaintiff's request discovered a method of producing acrylic acid. Later he left and set up on his own as a glass-manufacturer, and applied for and was granted a patent for the discovery. The plaintiffs then tried to patent it and discovered the patent had already been granted. They claimed *inter alia* a declaration that they were entitled to the letters patent granted to the defendant.

FARWELL, J.: In a case of this sort it is a term of all such employment, apart altogether from any express covenant, that any invention or discovery made in the course of the employment of the employee in doing that which he was engaged and instructed to do during the time of his employment, and during working hours, and using the materials of his employers, is the property of the employers and not of the employee, and that, having made a discovery or invention in course of such work, the employee becomes a trustee for the employer of that invention or discovery, and he is therefore as a trustee bound to give the benefit of any such discovery or invention to his employer, and in my judgment that applies in this case notwithstanding the express contract is not enforceable.

PATENTS ACT, 1949

56.—(1) Where a dispute arises between an employer and a person who is or was at the material time his employee as to the rights of the parties in respect of an invention made by the employee either alone or jointly with other employees or in respect of any patent granted or to be granted in respect thereof, the comptroller may, upon application made to him in the prescribed manner by either of the parties, and after giving to each of them an opportunity to be heard, determine the matter in dispute, and may make such orders for giving effect to his decision as he considers expedient:

Provided that if it appears to the comptroller upon any application under this section that the matter in dispute involves questions which would more properly be determined by the court, he may decline to deal therewith.

(2) In proceedings before the court between an employer and a person who is or was at the material time his employee, or upon an application made to the comptroller under subsection (1) of this section, the court or comptroller may, unless satisfied that one or other of the parties is entitled, to the exclusion of the other, to the benefit of an invention made by the employee, by order provide for the apportionment between them of the benefit of the invention, and of any patent granted or to be granted in respect thereof, in such manner as the court or comptroller considers just.

STERLING ENGINEERING CO. LTD
v. PATCHETT

House of Lords   [1955] A.C. 534

During the war, the respondent who was an employee of the appellants, invented the 'paragun' in the course of his employment; and after the war he invented numerous domestic electrical appliances for them. A dispute arose about the patents.

VISCOUNT SIMONDS: The patents in question stand in the joint names of the company (or the company which it controls) and the respondent, i.c. in the names of employer and employee. It is elementary that, where the employee in the course of his employment (i.e. in his employer's time and with his materials) makes an invention which it falls within his duty to make (as was the case here) he holds his interest in the invention and in any resulting patent as trustee for the employer unless he can show that he has a beneficial interest which the law recognizes. Here the respondent first asserted the 'understanding and agreement' to which I have so often referred. It was for reasonable remuneration and nothing else. It failed: there was no 'agreement' and 'understanding' meant nothing...

It is true enough that the rule that inventions made by an employee belong to the employer is sometimes spoken of as an implied term of the contract of service. In a sense, no doubt, it is an implied term in that it is not written out in the contract of service, but it is a term which, given the conditions which are here present, namely, inventions made by the employee in the course of his employment which it was part of his duty to make, the law imports into the contract. It appears to me that it is only an implied term in the same sense that it is an implied term, though not written at large, in the contract of service of any workman that what he produces by the strength of his arm or the skill of his hand or the exercise of his inventive faculty shall become the property of the employer. If the employment is of a designer that which he designs is thus the property of the employer which he alone can dispose of. If it is patentable it is for the employer to say whether it shall be patented, and he can require the employee to do what is necessary to that end. And if it is patented in their joint names, the employee holds his interest as trustee for the employer: see *Adamson* v. *Kenworthy*.[1] If this is, as I think it clearly is, the law, it can only be excluded by an express agreement that it shall be varied and some other legal relationship created.... I am therefore of opinion that the counterclaim should succeed, subject only to what may be said about s. 56 (2) of the Patents Act, 1949.

But that jurisdiction only arises if the court is not satisfied that one or other of the parties is entitled to the exclusion of the other to the benefit of an invention. The word 'entitled' refers to legal right. The court must therefore determine the legal rights just as it must determine them in any other case, and if the issue is, as it is here, whether one party is entitled to the exclusion of the other, it must decide that question 'Aye' or 'No' and, having decided it in the affirmative, it is not for the court to say that it is not satisfied. So here, having examined every plea which has been adduced to support the contention that the respondent has some beneficial interest in the patents and rejected them all, the court must declare itself satisfied that the company is entitled, to the exclusion of the respondent, and decline the jurisdiction conferred by the subsection.

It was urged that this construction of the subsection reduces its operation to negligible proportions.... If, in the result, its scope is less wide than may have been expected, that is not the affair of the courts.

LORD PORTER, LORD REID, LORD TUCKER and LORD SOMERVELL OF HARROW concurred.

BRITISH SYPHON CO. LTD v. HOMEWOOD

[1956] 1 W.L.R. 1190

The defendant, while chief technician to the plaintiff company, invented a low-pressure system of dispensing soda water, without being asked to do this. He patented it, left the company and started work with a rival company.

---

[1] (1931) 49 R.P.C. 57.

ROXBURGH, J.: It is common ground that the defendant had not been expressly asked to design any new method of dispensing soda water by a low-pressure system or any other system, and that he had not been asked to give any advice in relation to any such problem. This is the circumstance which, as far as I can see, differentiates this case from all that have gone before....He was employed to give the plaintiffs technical advice in relation to the design or development of anything connected with any part of the plaintiffs' business. No particular problem had been put before him, but if, and as often as, any problem of that kind was put before him, it was his duty to be ready to tender his advice and to assist in any matter of design or development. He was paid to stand by in that respect. He had other functions, but those are not material to the present case.

Would it be consistent with good faith, as between master and servant, that he should in that position be entitled to make some invention in relation to a matter concerning a part of the plaintiffs' business and either keep it from his employer, if and when asked about the problem, or even sell it to a rival and say: 'Well, yes, I know the answer to your problem, but I have already sold it to your rival'? In my judgment, that cannot be consistent with a relationship of good faith between a master and a technical adviser. It seems to me that he has a duty not to put himself in a position in which he may have personal reasons for not giving his employer the best advice which it is his duty to give if and when asked to give it.

He has a duty to be free from any personal reason for not giving his employer the best possible advice. *A fortiori*, it seems to me that he is not entitled to put himself into the position of being able to say: 'You retained me to advise you, and I will tell you what I advise you. Do it this way, but you will have to buy the method from your rival, because I have just sold it to him, having invented it yesterday.' That seems to me to be reasoning which, in the absence of authority, makes it right and proper for me to decide that this invention (which, in my judgment, plainly relates to and concerns the business of the plaintiffs, namely, the distribution of soda water to the public in containers of a satisfactory character), if made during a time during which the chief technician is standing by under the terms of his employment, must be held to be in equity the property of the employer. Accordingly, my decision is for the plaintiffs.

READING v. ATTORNEY-GENERAL

House of Lords   [1951] A.C. 507

The appellant, a sergeant in the Royal Army Medical Corps, while wearing uniform accompanied a number of civilian lorries carrying illicit brandy and whisky in and about Cairo. His presence meant that the police did not inspect the lorries. He earned £20,000 this way. Having been court-martialled and sent to prison for two years he claimed the return of the money.

LORD PORTER: I am content for the purposes of this case to accept the view that it forms no part of the law of England and that a right to restitution so described would be too widely stated.

But, indeed, this doctrine is not of the essence of Denning, J.'s judgment. His reasoning is to be found in the passage which succeeds that quoted. He says: 'In my judgment, it is a principle of law that if a servant, in violation of his duty of honesty and good faith, takes advantage of his service to make a profit for himself, in this sense, that the assets of which he has control, or the facilities which he enjoys, or the position which he occupies, are the real cause of his obtaining the money, as distinct from being the mere opportunity for getting it, that is to say, if they play the predominant part in his obtaining the money, then he is accountable for it to the master. It matters not that the master has not lost any profit, nor suffered any damage. Nor does it matter that the master could not have done the act himself. It is a case where the servant has unjustly enriched himself by virtue of his service without his master's sanction. It is money which the servant ought not to be allowed to keep, and the law says it shall be taken from him and given to his master, because he got it solely by reason of the position which he occupied as a servant of his master'. And again: 'The uniform of the Crown: and the position of the man as a servant of the Crown were the sole reasons why he was able to get this money, and that is sufficient to make him liable to hand it over to the Crown.' The learned judge, however, also says: 'This man Reading was not acting in the course of his employment: and there was no fiduciary relationship in respect of these long journeys nor, indeed, in respect of his uniform'. If this means, as I think it does, that the appellant was neither a trustee nor in possession of some profit-earning chattel, and that it was contrary to his duty to escort unwarranted traffic or possibly any traffic through the streets of Cairo, it is true, but, in my view, irrelevant. He nevertheless was using his position as a sergeant in His Majesty's Army and the uniform to which his rank entitled him to obtain the money which he received. In my opinion any official position, whether marked by a uniform or not, which enables the holder to earn money by its use gives his master a right to receive the money so earned even though it was earned by a criminal act. 'You have earned', the master can say, 'money by the use of your position as my servant. It is not for you, who have gained this advantage, to set up your own wrong as a defence to my claim'.

ASQUITH, L.J., in the Court of Appeal, points out[1] that there is a well-established class of cases in which a master can recover whether or not he has suffered any detriment in fact, e.g. those in which a servant or agent has realized a secret profit, commission or bribe in the course of his employment, and that the sum recoverable is the amount of such profit. It is perhaps sufficient to refer in this connexion to *Boston Deep Sea Fishing & Ice Co.* v. *Ansell.*[2]

LORD NORMAND: Though the relation of a member of His Majesty's forces to the Crown is not accurately described as that of a servant under a contract of service or as that of an agent under a contract of agency, the Court of Appeal has held that he owes to the Crown a duty as fully fiduciary as the duty of a servant to his master or of an agent to his principal, and in consequence that all profits and advantages gained by the use or abuse of his military status are to be for the benefit of the Crown. I respectfully think that these are unassailable propositions, and further that the appellant cannot be allowed to propone as a defence to the Crown's claim his own criminal conduct either in accepting a bribe in breach of military discipline or in participating in an offence against the municipal law of Egypt.

VISCOUNT JOWITT, L.C., LORD OAKSEY and LORD RADCLIFFE concurred.

BELL *v.* LEVER BROS.

House of Lords   [1932] A.C. 161

The appellant B. was employed by the respondent company as chairman of the board of directors for a term of years. The parties entered an agreement whereby the respondent company was to pay B. £30,000 as compensation for terminating his contract of service. Later the company discovered that B. had committed breaches of his contract of service for which they could have dismissed him without paying any compensation. They claimed repayment of the money but were unsuccessful. In the course of his speech LORD ATKIN said: Nor can I find anything in

---

[1] [1949] 2 K.B. 232, 236.   [2] 39 Ch.D. 339, 367-8 [see *post,* p. 156].

the relation of master and servant, when established, that places agreements between them within the protected category. It is said that there is a contractual duty of the servant to disclose his past faults. I agree that the duty of the servant to protect his master's property may involve the duty to report a fellow servant whom he knows to be wrongfully dealing with that property. The servant owes a duty not to steal, but, having stolen, is there superadded a duty to confess that he has stolen? I am satisfied that to imply such a duty would be a departure from the well established usage of mankind and would be to create obligations entirely outside the normal contemplation of the parties concerned. If a man agrees to raise his butler's wages, must the butler disclose that two years ago he received a secret commission from the wine merchant; and if the master discovers it, can he, without dismissal or after the servant has left, avoid the agreement for the increase in salary and recover back the extra wages paid? If he gives his cook a month's wages in lieu of notice can he, on discovering that the cook has been pilfering the tea and sugar, claim the return of the month's wages? I think not. He takes the risk; if he wishes to protect himself he can question his servant, and will then be protected by the truth or otherwise of the answers.

LORD THANKERTON and LORD BLANESBURGH agreed with LORD ATKIN; LORD WARRINGTON OF CLYFFE (with whose speech VISCOUNT HAILSHAM agreed) left this point open.

SWAIN v. WEST (BUTCHERS) LTD

Court of Appeal   [1936] 3 All E.R. 261

The appellant was employed under a 5-year contract to be general manager of the respondent company. It was a special term of his contract that 'during the continuance of the agreement the general manager shall devote all his time to the business of the company and do all in his power to promote, extend and develop the interests of the company'. He was ordered by the managing director to sell non-Empire beef and mutton as Empire produce, which was unlawful. The chairman of the board promised that if he gave conclusive proof of the managing director's actions he would not be dismissed. The plaintiff gave proof and was then dismissed for his own part.

GREENE, L.J.: It was submitted to us that there was some general principle of law applicable to contracts of service in general and to this contract in particular that a servant is under no duty to disclose the improper conduct of his fellow servant. I am unable to accept such a proposition. Whether there is such a duty or not must depend upon the circumstances of each particular case. Under clause 7 of the agreement between the appellant and respondent in this case the appellant is given the general control of the company subject to the overriding power of the managing director. He is made responsible for the business as a whole, subject to the lawful orders of the managing director, and he is obliged to 'promote, develop and extend the interests of the company'. The plaintiff received instructions from the managing director to do acts which were a dishonest contravention of an order in council. These acts were done on the instructions of the managing director and from the plaintiff's own evidence it was clear that the plaintiff said: 'the managing director told me to do this'. The plaintiff was responsible for the management of the business and was responsible for seeing that the business was conducted honestly and efficiently by all who came under his control. If the dishonesty of a fellow-servant came within his notice he should tell the board. The true position in my view is this: what are the obligations undertaken in this particular contract? The managing director gave the plaintiff unlawful orders. The plaintiff's duty was to report to his employer that the managing director had endeavoured to persuade him to do something which was dishonest and which would, if carried out, be a breach of his duties in controlling the business of the company. If this was his duty it is not altered by the circumstance that he carried out the suggestion made to him. The fact that he carried out the suggestion made it none the less his obligation to inform his directors of the orders which had unlawfully been given to him. He was invited thereafter to give the board details of the complicity of the managing director in these proceedings. He gave a statement of his knowledge of the facts. Can it be said that what he was invited to do was not already his duty to do? His duty to give information to the board arose at the moment when the original improper orders were given to him, and this duty is not lessened by the fact that he obeyed those orders himself.

GREER, L.J. delivered a concurring judgment; MACKINNON, J. agreed.

CORK v. KIRBY MACLEAN LTD

Court of Appeal   [1952] 2 All E.R. 402

A workman employed by the defendants did not disclose to them that he was subject to epileptic fits. He fell to the ground from a platform and was killed. The cause was partly that he had an epileptic fit and partly that the defendants had not complied with building regulations.

The decision was that the plaintiff was guilty of contributory negligence. The judgment may be read as suggesting that such a workman owes a common law duty to his employer to disclose personal factors which increase the dangers involved in employing him.*

SINGLETON, L.J.: In *Blyth* v. *Birmingham Waterworks Co.* ALDERSON, B., said (11 Exch. 784): 'Negligence is the omission to do something which a reasonable man, guided upon those considerations which ordinarily regulate the conduct of human affairs, would do, or doing something which a prudent and reasonable man would not do'. I take that definition of negligence as, again, it seems to me to cover this case in every sense. A man who knew himself to be in the condition in which Mr Cork knew that he was ought to have told his employers. However anxious he was to get work, he owed a duty to his employers and to his fellow workmen as well as to himself, and failure to inform the employers followed by instructions from them to work at some height above ground involved risk to other workmen as well as risk to himself. I am satisfied that that is 'fault' within the definition in s. 4 of the Act of 1945, and within the natural and ordinary meaning of the word in s. 1....When the plaintiff seeks to recover damages from the defendants, the defendants may properly say that Mr Cork was guilty of contributory negligence.

DENNING, L.J. and ROMER, L.J. delivered concurring judgments.

4. PAYMENT OF WAGES†

MORIARTY v. REGENT'S GARAGE CO.
[1921] 1 K.B. 423

As part of an express contract, the director of a company was to be paid £150 per annum for as long as he was a director; and he was to be a director for as long as he held debentures. In the middle of one year his debentures were paid back, and he claimed proportionate remuneration out of the £150 for the work he had so far performed in that year. The issue arose whether he fell within the Apportionment Act, 1870: s. 2: 'From and after the passing of this Act all rents, annuities, dividends, and other periodical payments in the nature of income...shall, like interest on money lent, be considered as accruing from day to day, and

---

* The older cases suggest that the employee is under no duty to disclose personal 'defects': see *Fletcher* v. *Krell* (1872) 42 L.J.Q.B. 55; *Hands* v. *Simpson Fawcett Ltd* (1928) 44 T.L.R. 295. Today, however, the courts might place such a duty upon a worker where failure to disclose created danger for fellow-workers or the employer.

† On Wages Councils see *post* p. 366.

shall be apportionable in respect of time accordingly'.... s. 5: 'In the construction of this Act...the word "annuities" includes salaries and pensions.'

McCARDIE, J.: Was the present plaintiff in receipt of a 'salary'? A director is not, I agree, a servant of the company in the ordinary sense, but he may be a servant under the terms of his agreement as director, so that he may be indicted for embezzlement as a 'clerk or servant', as was decided in *Reg.* v. *Stuart.*[1]

Here the agreement says by clause 4 that the fees of the plaintiff for acting as director shall be £150 per annum, that is, in my view, a fixed yearly remuneration for a substantial office to be held for a substantial period of time. In my opinion the plaintiff was in receipt of a 'salary'; his reward could not be called 'wages'; it was not contingent on profits; it did not depend upon a vote of the shareholders; and it was a permanent contractual right to a fixed yearly amount. Therefore the plaintiff comes within the Apportionment Act, 1870, unless there are decisions which compel us to take a contrary view....

I do not fail to see the wide stretch of the results which follow from the decision we are now giving, and one of the questions that must arise in the future is whether or not the Apportionment Act will destroy the operation of the rule under which a servant who is dismissed for misconduct loses the whole of the money accruing to him, although he is entitled to get the money that has actually accrued. The rule has been clear since *Ridgway* v. *Hungerford Market Co.*[2] and *Lilley* v. *Elwin*[3]...

On the other hand I am not altogether satisfied as to the justice of denying the benefit of the Apportionment Act to a man who may have been guilty of misconduct. Suppose a salary is payable half yearly to a man, and suppose he has fulfilled his duties with absolute propriety up to the last week; that he then commits an act which justifies his master in dismissing him. Upon the law as it stands the man gets nothing for his five and a half month's work. Is it right that he should be deprived of remuneration for five and a half months' work because during the last fortnight he has done something for which he has been dismissed? I express no opinion upon that point. Ere long it must arise for decision.

LUSH, J. delivered a concurring judgment.

[1] [1894] 1 Q.B. 310.   [2] (1835) 3 A. & E. 171.
[3] (1848) 11 Q.B. 742.

GRIEVE v. IMPERIAL TOBACCO LTD

Bristol County Court   *The Guardian*, April 30, 1963

The plaintiff claimed £21 allegedly due under his contractual conditions of employment. For 50 years the company had made a gift to employees who had fulfilled certain conditions, calculated on a percentage of earnings. In 1961, following a strike in which the claimant took part, the company gave a 12½ per cent bonus to many employees, but only 9 per cent to those who had struck. The company claimed that the payments were and always had been gifts, which it could withhold at discretion. The first gift had been paid in 1911 and regular resolutions of the board of directors had been passed stating the conditions and changing them from time to time. In 1927, those who took part in the General strike did not receive the bonus.

JUDGE PATON: The payments of the gifts were announced on the factory and office notice boards stating that a payment of a gift would be made and showing the amount and qualifying conditions. In two cases in 1948 and in 1956 the notices gave the warning not to count on the gift. The 1960 strike was the eleventh since 1911 in which the company had withheld from strikers payment of gift or reduced it. At no time had the gift been the subject of negotiation with the unions.* The company had refused to negotiate and the secretary of the Tobacco Workers Union had admitted this in evidence and said that he had accepted the position.

What then was the real nature of the payments? First they were invariably described by the company as a gift, and there was no evidence that it was described as anything else by any other person...The only factor which lent any plausibility to the contention that there was some kind of contractual obligation was that the payment was made each year for 50 years. But mere repetition of gratuitous payments cannot convert that which was gratuitous into a contractual obligation. The defendants were extremely careful to preserve the gratuitous nature of the payments and to make clear to potential recipients that in the matter of payment they had an unfettered discretion.

FACTORIES ACT, 1961

S. 135: (1) In every textile factory the occupier shall for the purpose of enabling each person employed who is paid by the piece to compute the total amount of wages payable to him in respect of his work, cause

* Note: contrast the decision in *Edwards* v. *Skyways Ltd*, *post* p. 286.

particulars of the rate of wages applicable to the work to be done, and also particulars of the work to which that rate is to be applied, to be published as follows:

...(*b*) in the case of weavers in the cotton trade, the particulars of the rate of wages applicable to the work to be done by each weaver shall be furnished to him in writing at the time when the work is given out to him and the basis and conditions by which the prices are regulated and fixed shall also be exhibited in each room on a placard not containing any other matter and posted in a position where it is easily legible;...

(*f*) the particulars either as to rate of wages or as to work shall not be expressed by means of symbols...

(3) If any person employed in a factory having received any such particulars whether they are furnished directly to him or to a fellow workman, discloses the particulars for the purpose of divulging a trade secret, he shall be guilty of an offence...

(5) The Minister, on being satisfied by the report of an inspector that the provisions of this section are applicable to any class of factories other than textile factories, may if he thinks fit, by regulations apply the provisions of this section to any such class subject to such modifications as may in his opinion be necessary...

S. 136 Save as otherwise expressly provided under this Act, the occupier of a factory shall not, in respect of anything to be done or provided by him in pursuance of this Act, make any deduction from the sum contracted to be paid by him to any person employed or receive or allow any person in his employment to receive any payment from any such person.

TRUCK ACT, 1831

An Act to prohibit the Payment, in certain Trades, of Wages in Goods, or otherwise than in the current Coin of the Realm.

I. WHEREAS it is necessary to prohibit the Payment, in certain Trades, of Wages in Goods, or otherwise than in the current Coin of the Realm; be it therefore enacted by the King's most Excellent Majesty, by and with the Advice and Consent of the Lords Spiritual and Temporal, and Commons, in this present Parliament assembled, and by the Authority of the same, That in all Contracts hereafter to be made for the hiring of any Artificer* in any of the Trades herein-after enumerated,

* Note: After the Amendment Act of 1887, s. 2, the term 'Artificer' was extended to include all 'workmen' within the definition of the Employers and Workmen Act 1875, s. 10, *ante*, p. 30.

or for the Performance by any Artificer of any Labour in any of the said Trades, the Wages of such Artificer shall be made payable in the current Coin of this Realm only, and not otherwise; and that if in any such Contract the Whole or any Part of such Wages shall be made payable in any Manner other than in the current Coin aforesaid, such Contract shall be and is hereby declared illegal, null, and void.

II. And be it further enacted, That if in any Contract hereafter to be made between any Artificer in any of the Trades herein-after enumerated, and his Employer, any Provision shall be made directly or indirectly respecting the Place where, or the Manner in which, or the Person or Persons with whom, the Whole or any Part of the Wages due or to become due to any such Artificer shall be laid out or expended, such Contract shall be and is hereby declared illegal, null, and void.

III. And be it further enacted. That the entire amount of the Wages earned by or payable to any Artificer. . .in respect of any Labour done by him shall be actually paid in the Current Coin of this Realm and not otherwise; and Payment made to any such Artificer by his Employer of or in respect of any such Wages by the delivering to him of Goods or otherwise than in the current Coin as aforesaid except as hereinafter mentioned shall be and is hereby declared illegal null and void.

CAMERON v. ROYAL LONDON OPTHALMIC HOSPITAL

[1941] 1 K.B. 350

The plaintiff was employed as a stoker and mechanic at a hospital; he lived in the hospital. The question arose whether he was a domestic or menial servant for the purposes of the Truck Acts (see Employers and Workmen Act, 1875, s. 10, *ante*, p. 30).

DU PARCQ, L.J.: In *In re Junior Carlton Club*[1], also a case under the Unemployment Insurance Act, 1920, the learned judge, after a reference to a text-book and after saying, as I do, that he was not attempting to formulate a definition of what is a domestic servant 'even for the purposes of this Act', went on to say: 'But if I had, in my own words, to describe what are the characteristics of such a servant I should express it, and do express it for present purposes, in the way that I sought to express it in the course of the argument in this case—namely, that domestic servants are servants, whose main or general function it is to be about their employers' persons, or establishments, residential or

[1] [1922] 1 K.B. 166, 170.

quasi-residential, for the purpose of ministering to their employers' needs or wants, or to the needs or wants of those who are members of such establishments, or of those resorting to such establishments, including guests.... There is no doubt, of course, that the plaintiff was a servant. Was he a domestic servant?' Roche J.'s words may, in my opinion, be applied to this case. The phrase 'domestic servant' calls up a definite idea to the mind of everybody. To the mind of a man with a small house and of modest means it probably calls up a picture of a maid servant. Others will be more likely to think of a butler, a footman, a chauffeur, gardeners and so forth. What quality have all these people in common? They all come within the description given by Roche J. in *In re Junior Carlton Club* quoted above. Consideration of the Truck Acts justifies the statement that what Parliament had in mind in framing the definition of 'workman' in s. 10 of the Employers and Workmen Act, 1875, was that in modern civilized society the Truck Acts would work hardship, or at any rate the greatest inconvenience, unless they excluded those working in a home for the purposes of the upkeep and maintenance of the home. That is a truism. If it were not permissible to pay the general servants of a household partly in food and by the provision of sleeping accommodation the position of the householders would be almost impossible. The reason for that is not merely that the servant is treated as part of the family—to use the expression in the wider sense—but because he assists in the maintenance of the home and does work in and about it which, if it were not done by servants would have to be done either by the employer himself or, at the greatest inconvenience, by someone from outside....

Applying these observations to the facts of this particular case, the first question is whether or not this hospital can be brought within the description of a domestic establishment or domus. Such a description would no doubt apply to a boarding-school. It could, in my opinion, be applied also to a residential college in a university, and I have no doubt that it applies to a hospital. Indeed some hospitals are now commonly referred to as homes. A 'nursing home' is the expression used to describe a hospital run as a paying concern. There is also the expression 'mental home'. The term 'domestic' may be applied to establishments of that kind. Those who live there regularly, as members of the staff, and temporarily as patients, may be regarded as a family in a wide sense, and certainly the establishment is of a domestic character as a whole....

The evidence of the chief maintenance engineer of the defendant hospital shows that the work done by the plaintiff at first was that of a stoker, and that as he acquired more experience he was promoted and better paid, gathered a good deal of knowledge, and was eventually styled a mechanic. As a mechanic he did certain things requiring skill, such as boiler-cleaning and repairing the conveyor which carries coal and which was introduced in place of the old hand-firing system. He also executed minor operations on pumps and turbines, he burnt rubbish and did odd jobs in the way of minor repairs, attending to the lamps and lighting, and helping to keep the department clean.

In a home, whether it be a private house or a large hospital, the heating arrangements are of a different character from what was considered sufficient in 1831 when the first Truck Act was passed, or even when the Employers and Workmen Act, 1875, was passed. In most large country houses central heating has been adopted, so that there are boilers which need attendants. That is a normal state of affairs in a large establishment. In a small establishment a small boiler may be left to the care of the gardener, or even of one of the female staff. That cannot be the case in a large establishment; and it is equally impossible, or at any rate inconvenient, in such an establishment to have to rely on calling in assistance from outside to attend to the boilers. There is no doubt that the plaintiff very often did things which a domestic servant ordinarily might not have been able to do....

I have come to the conclusion that the plaintiff was a domestic servant in the employ of the defendants. Most people might very well, if they had been asked, not have spoken of him as a domestic servant, using the expression colloquially; nevertheless, in my opinion, he was one according to the true meaning of that phrase, which is not limited to those who do only what is called house-work in the narrower interpretation.

DU PARCQ, L.J. was sitting as an additional judge in the King's Bench Division.

BOUND v. LAWRENCE*

Court of Appeal   [1892] 1 Q.B. 226

LORD ESHER, M.R.: The question in this case is whether, on the facts stated by the magistrates, the appellant can be said to be engaged in

---

* Contrast *Morgan* v. *London General Omnibus Co.* (1884) 13 Q.B.D. 832, C.A. (omnibus conductor engaged daily not employed on 'manual labour') with *Smith* v. *Associated Omnibus Co.* [1907] 1 K.B. 916 (driver of omnibus who started it with a handle and did any necessary repairs was held to be engaged in manual labour). For recent discussion of the problem in the context of the Factories Act, 1961, see *Stone Lighting and Radio Ltd* v. *Haygarth*, *post*, p. 709.

manual labour within the meaning of this Act of Parliament. It seems to me that the decision in *Morgan* v. *London General Omnibus Co.*[1] assists us to this extent, that it shows that we must not look at what the appellant may do incidentally in the course of his employment, but must see what is his real and substantial work. Now, I take it that if we examine this case it appears that the appellant was employed as a grocer's assistant in a shop, and his business was to take orders from the customers and to carry them out. In doing this he may have to show goods, and if the customers take away the goods he has to make up the parcels. In doing this he has to use his hands, and the question is whether that makes him a manual labourer. There can be no manual labour without user of the hands; but it does not at all follow that every user of the hands is manual labour, so as to make the person who does it a manual labourer. Now, the principal part of the appellant's employment is selling to the customers across the counter. That is his substantial employment, and if he has to do other things which involve physical exertion we must see whether that is not incidental to his real employment. In this case I cannot doubt that that is so. The findings of fact seem to me to negative the idea that the work described was any part of his real and substantial employment. If the mere user of the hands in matters incidental to a man's employment is to constitute him a manual labourer, it would extend the Act to every shop-assistant in every shop, great or small, which cannot have been the intention of the legislature.

FRY, L.J. and LOPES, L.J. concurred.

KENYON v. DARWEN COTTON MANUFACTURING CO.

Court of Appeal   [1936] 2 K.B. 193

Workers agreed with the defendant company to finance it by subscribing for shares in it and paying for them in most cases by frequent and small instalments. At first the employee received each week his net wages, and an envelope containing the amount of the instalment which he immediately handed back. After a while this practice was dropped and employees received their net wages plus a receipt for the share deduction. The plaintiff claimed back these instalments as infringing the Truck Act, 1831.

SCOTT, L.J.: 'Wages' and 'contract' being so defined, s. 1 makes it expressly illegal for the employer to give to the workman for his labour

---
[1] 13 Q.B.D. 832.

any consideration whatsoever except current coin of the Realm. In addition it forbids any promise—whether in the hiring agreement itself, or in some separate agreement entered into by way of consideration for, or as a condition of the making of the hiring agreement—by the employer to give to the workman money's worth instead of current coin. If the employer for instance is a company and persuades a workman to enter into or remain in its service on the terms of his accepting a portion of his wages in the form of certificates for shares in the company or in signed receipts for payment of instalments of the cost of such certificates, the wages are in part 'payable in a manner other than payment in current coin', and the transaction falls within the express prohibition. And by whatever device or understanding and however indirectly this result is brought about, the inhibition of the statute attaches. If the agreement took the form of an independent and voluntary application by the workman for shares, and an arrangement for weekly payments of the application money with nothing else said, but there was an understanding that the workman would out of his wages make the weekly payment, I think the wages would be payable in shares and not in current coin and therefore in defiance of s. 1, just as much as if the hiring agreement itself said that the employer would pay the workman so much in current coin and the balance in signed receipts for instalments of application money. The former would be merely an 'indirect device' for bringing about the same result as the latter arrangement would achieve 'directly'. The provisions of s. 25 that a mere 'understanding', and a fortiori a mere 'endeavour to impose an obligation' is to be deemed a 'contract' are in my view conclusive that this extremely wide view of the scope of s. 1 is right. If it is, then the whole network of 'agreements, understandings, devices, contrivances, collusions whatsoever on the subject of wages, whether written or oral, whether direct or indirect, to which the employer and workman are parties or are assenting, or by which they are mutually bound to each other, or whereby either of them shall have endeavoured to impose an obligation on the other of them' is made illegal by the last line of the section.

S. 2 proceeds on the basis of this same wide conception of the contractual relationship. It assumes a case in which there is no contravention of s. 1, and is aimed only at arrangements as to the way in which wages in current coin of the Realm are to be 'laid out or expended'. It expressly prohibits the insertion of any such arrangements in the 'contract', and as a sanction for enforcement the whole 'contract' (defined as above) is, in the event of breach of the prohibition, made illegal and void: the collateral arrangements and understandings are swept away as unequivocally as the hiring agreement itself.

If ss. 1 and 2 have the above effect, s. 3 would seem at first sight superfluous; and for that reason might afford ground for argument that ss. 1 and 2 cannot have the meaning I attribute to them. There are, however, two answers to that argument. In the first place the statute was intended to be a charter of liberty to workmen which they could easily understand; and in 1831 the education of the working classes was not what it is to-day. It was for this reason important for Parliament to make very plain—even to the point of repetition—the workman's right to receive his whole remuneration in current coin of the realm. In the second place the phrase 'actually paid' both bears out the same intention, and, as it seems to me, imports something further. The money must be paid over so completely and finally that it then and there becomes the workman's very own, being received into his possession subject to no sort or kind of understanding however tacit that he is either to return any part of it or use it in a particular manner or lay it out for a particular purpose. The phrase precludes the idea of any payment which is not final and absolute, it calls for a payment which shall leave the payee wholly free and untrammelled in his enjoyment of it, and by implication forbids the exaction of any condition or promise or obligation from him as recipient as to what he will do with his money after receipt.

S. 4 manifests the same intention to make the workman's rights absolutely clear; but it is in addition an indispensable provision. The whole of the contractual arrangements between the parties being void, the workman is left with no contract upon which to found a cause of action for wages. It is therefore necessary to give him a statutory right of action, and this is the main purpose of s. 4. But for the extremely wide definition of the word 'contract', contained in s. 25, it might have been arguable that the 'contract' avoided by ss. 1 and 2 was only so much of the contract of hiring as offended against the provisions of those sections. But that definition precludes any such limiting construction, and makes it clear, as I have said above, that the whole set of arrangements between employer and workman which contain or are directly or indirectly concerned with the agreement of hiring are brought within the statutory net and avoided lock, stock and barrel, if any one provision offends against the statute....

S. 4 does not expressly state what is to be the measure of the statutory right to wages, nor what the conditions of service are to be; but I think the proper construction of the section is to treat it as repeating those terms of the agreement of hiring which do not offend directly or indirectly against the statute: there is no other measure of amount or time of payment or of the necessary terms of the mutual obligations under the hiring relationship....

There can be no question that as from 3 November 1932, when the practice of putting the amount of the weekly share subscription into a separate envelope was discontinued, the procedure followed was an offence against the statute, and that the whole set of arrangements was avoided by the express provisions of the statute. I do not think that the device of putting part of the wages into one envelope, and another part equal to the amount of the weekly subscription which the employee had undertaken to make in part payment of his shares into a second envelope, makes any difference in law. It was, I think, a mere 'understanding, device, contrivance, collusion or arrangement' within the meaning of s. 25 and was therefore forbidden by the express prohibitions of ss. 1 to 4 of the Act of 1831.

SLESSER, L.J. and EVE, J. concurred.

HEWLETT v. ALLEN*

House of Lords   [1894] A.C. 383

Under her contract the plaintiff had to conform to the works rules, and one works-rule stated that 'All employees will have to become members of the sick and accident club'. Each week her subscription was deducted from her wages and she was handed the rest with a ticket showing the deductions. She claimed back the amount she had paid weekly in subscriptions, under s. 4 of the 1831 Truck Act.

LORD HERSCHELL, L.C.: My Lords, I do not think it can be doubted that the object of this enactment was to strike at the practice which had grown up of employers making their payment in part by the supply of goods in the sale of which they were interested, which it was thought would place the person employed at an unfair disadvantage, and which it was thought was calculated to result in the person employed obtaining something less than the agreed remuneration for services. The contrast in those sections is between payment in current coin of the realm and payment in some other fashion; and I can myself entertain no doubt that

---

* Note that but for this decision it would be difficult legally to operate the increasing practice of the 'check-off', whereby an employer deducts trade union subscriptions at source.

a payment made by an employer at the instance of a person employed to discharge some obligation of the person employed, or to place the money in the hands of some person in whose hands the person employed desires it to be placed, is in the sense and meaning of those sections a payment to the person employed as much as if the current coin of the realm had been placed in his or her hands.

It is said that money paid in that way would not be a payment of the debt—that it could not have been pleaded as payment—that the defence must have been one of set-off. My Lords, whether that be so or not, in accordance with the system of pleading which previously prevailed, I do not think it at all necessary to inquire. The distinction between payment and set-off was often a very fine one in old days. But, however, that may be as a matter of pleading, I cannot myself doubt, looking at the purpose and object as well as the words of this statute, that a payment made in that fashion would be a payment in the current coin of the realm and not otherwise within the meaning of the Truck Act. The case obviously would not be in the slightest degree within the mischief against which that statute was directed.

LORD WATSON, LORD MORRIS and LORD SHAND delivered concurring judgments.

PENMAN v. THE FIFE COAL CO. LTD

House of Lords   [1936] A.C. 45

The plaintiff agreed in writing that his employers should deduct from his wages each week the rent which his father owed the employers. He claimed this sum back.

LORD MACMILLAN: Here there was no payment at all, whether in current coin or otherwise, by the respondents to any one. The respondents simply retained part of what they were bound to pay, and applied what they retained in discharge of the liability of the appellant's father. No doubt it may be said in popular parlance that they paid themselves. But I cannot think that this was payment in current coin to the workman within the meaning of the statute. I adopt the words of Bowen, L.J. in *Hewlett's* case,[1] where he said: 'The employer cannot, for the purpose of compliance with the statute, be both payer and payee. To hold otherwise would be to make the statute idle.' Nothing that was said in this House detracted from the soundness of this view, which was subsequently referred to with approval by Lord Davey in *Williams* v. *North's Navigation*

[1] [1892] 2 Q.B. 662, 666.

Collieries (1889) *Ltd*[1]. In *Hewlett's* case[2] the payment which was upheld was payment by the employers to a third party. The employers themselves derived no personal benefit. In the present case the retention was for the employer's own benefit, and it is a cardinal object of the Truck Act to prevent the employer from making deductions from his workmen's wages in his own interest.... There is, in my opinion, all the difference in the world between the case where the workman directs his employers to pay part of his wages to a third party and the case where the workman assents to his employers retaining part of his wages for their own behoof, whether in discharge of a debt due to them by the workman himself or in discharge of a debt due to them by some third party.

LORD WRIGHT: *Hewlett* v. *Allen* is based on the fact that the sums in question were paid on the worker's mandate to a third party in order to discharge a debt of the worker due to that third party. The worker's request to pay the third party on her behalf made, so it was held, the third party the worker's agent or hand to receive the current coin. In the present case the respondents retained the sums now in suit in order to pay a debt due, not to a third party, but to themselves, and not due from the appellant, but due from another party—namely, his father; and, furthermore the father's debt was for rent in respect of premises belonging to the respondents of which the father was tenant. If express provision was required in s. 23 of the Act to validate a deduction for the rent of premises demised or let to the workman, it would seem impossible to justify a deduction of the rent of premises not demised or let to the appellant, but to another person. The fact that the appellant lived with his father in the premises is, I think, immaterial. That *Hewlett's* case went to the limit of what is permissible in the way of liberal construction of the Act is in my opinion clear from a consideration of *Williams* v. *North's Navigation Collieries* (1889) *Ltd*; it is not true to say that *Williams'* case was distinguished from *Hewlett's* case on the ground that in the former case the workman did not assent, whereas in the latter he did assent, to the deduction. Lord Davey, in *Williams'* case,[1] thus sums up the statutory position: 'By s. 23 and s. 24, certain deductions are permitted to be made, or, to use the language of the marginal note, "particular exceptions to the generality of the law", are made under strictly defined conditions, and no other deductions or particular exceptions are in my opinion authorized.' Subsequent statutes have

[1] [1906] A.C. 136, 142.
[2] [1894] A.C. 383.

enlarged the list of permissible deductions but have not affected the principle.*

LORD THANKERTON, LORD ALNESS and LORD TOMLIN concurred.

TRUCK ACT, 1896

1. (1) An employer shall not make any contract with any workman for any deduction from the sum contracted to be paid by the employer to the workman, or for any payment to the employer by the workman, for or in respect of any fine, unless

(a) the terms of the contract are contained in a notice kept constantly affixed at such place or places open to the workmen and in such a position that it may be easily seen, read, and copied by any person whom it affects; or the contract is in writing, signed by the workman; and

(b) the contract specifies the acts or omissions in respect of which the fine may be imposed, and the amount of the fine or the particulars from which that amount may be ascertained; and

(c) the fine imposed under the contract is in respect of some act or omission which causes or is likely to cause damage or loss to the employer, or interruption or hindrance to his business; and

(d) the amount of the fine is fair and reasonable having regard to all the circumstances of the case.

(2) An employer shall not make any such deduction or receive any such payment, unless

(a) the deduction or payment is made in pursuance of, or in accordance with, such a contract as aforesaid; and

(b) particulars in writing showing the acts or omissions in respect of which the fine is imposed and the amount thereof are supplied to the workman on each occasion when a deduction or payment is made.

(3) This section shall apply to the case of a shop assistant in like manner as it applies to the case of a workman.†

---

* See now, for example, Wages Councils Act 1959, s. 14; Income Tax Act 1952, and Regulations, 1962, S.I. 1003; Maintenance Orders Act, 1958, s. 6; National Insurance Act, 1965, s. 12 (2); Dockworkers Pensions Act, 1960 and Payment of Wages Act, 1960 (authorising cheques for payment if the worker so requests).

† Sections 2 and 3 make parallel provision for deductions in respect of damaged goods and of materials.

PRITCHARD v. JAMES CLAY LTD

[1926] K.B. 238

A moulder of iron pipes was employed on piece work. He was to be paid 5¾d. for each 6 ft pipe he made free from defects. If it was defective he was to be paid an agreed price according to the defect. An information was laid against the respondents for making deductions contrary to the Truck Act, 1896. The requirements for affixing a written contract, made by s. 2 of the Act, had not been complied with; but the justices refused to convict on the ground that the lower payments were merely payments for faulty pipes. Their decision was reversed.

LORD HEWART, C.J. stated the facts, read s. 2 of the Truck Act, 1896, and continued: What was the contract with the appellant? Was it a contract to produce incomplete and defective pipes, or was it a contract to produce complete pipes of a certain length and free from defects? To my mind it is clear that the contract was that the appellant should produce a complete pipe 6 ft long and free from defects, for which he was to be paid 5¾d. That was the standard or normal pipe, and that was the basis of the contract of employment. There follows in the statement of facts a series of variations of the sum of 5¾d. These depend upon whether the pipe was of the right length, whether it was straight or bent or was short or too rough, or whether the holes in it had been properly cored; in other words, the variations depended upon the performance of the appellant in producing his work. One can scarcely imagine a more exact repetition of what is struck at by s. 2 of the Truck Act, 1896—a deduction 'for or in respect of bad or negligent work or injury to the materials or other property of the employer'. In my opinion this was, in the words of Mr Joy, an ingenious attempt to get round the Act which does not succeed.

SANKEY, J. and TALBOT, J. concurred.

BIRD v. BRITISH CELANESE LTD

Court of Appeal   [1945] K.B. 336

The plaintiff was employed as a spinner under an oral contract which had incorporated various internal works rules. One of these provided that in the event of various transgressions, including refusal to obey an order, the employer was entitled 'temporarily to suspend the workman from his employment'. The plaintiff refused to do certain cleaning work before the end of a shift. He was 'suspended' for the day. The same thing happened on the next day. He brought an action claiming the sum due as wages for those two days, alleging that they were deducted illegally under the Truck Act, 1896.

SCOTT, L.J.: [Of the requirements of the 1896 Act, s. 1] one at least—an exhibited notice or signed contract containing the suspense clause—was not fulfilled; therefore, if the judge's interpretation were right, his result of illegality would follow; for the 'suspension' term was clearly as the judge said, a 'contract' within the definition in the Truck Act, 1831, s. 25, with which the 1896 Act is to be read as one: but I think that he misconstrued the enacting words at the commencement of the section. There are only two types of contractual stipulation within the provisional prohibition—(i) deductions from wages; and (ii) payments made by the workman unconnected with his wages. Both are, I think, qualified by the last seven words 'for or in respect of a fine.' Those words are an essential limitation on both prohibitions, because without that limitation all deductions from wages, and also all payments by the workman out of his own pocket would be brought within the ban—for example, subscription to a pension or welfare or sports fund. It is quite clear that the 'suspense' clause in the particular contract of employment before the court is not within the second category of prohibited stipulations; no payment by the workman was called for by it. Is it within the first? Clearly not because you cannot deduct something from nothing. The suspense clause may act in two ways. It may be a merciful substitute for the procedure of dismissal, and a possible re-engagement. Under the suspense clause the right to wages ceases and the wages are not earned; no deduction can be made from wages which are not payable. In the present case, as the workman was adjudged guilty of serious misconduct, the operation of the clause was merely merciful; it enabled the workman, when the suspension ended, to claim as of right to continue in his old job. The clause operates in accordance with its terms; the whole contract is suspended, in the sense that the operation of the mutual obligations of both parties is suspended; the workman ceases to be under any present duty to work, and the employer ceases to be under any consequential duty to pay. That is the natural meaning of the word 'suspend' when applied to a contract of employment, and I think it is also its legal meaning. If so, this suspense clause is not obnoxious to the veto of s. 1 of the Act. It was suggested in argument that the words 'for or in respect of a fine' should be read as applying only to the second limb of the prohibition, and not to deductions from wages. I do not think that is the right construction; it applies to both limbs. My interpretation is strongly supported by a comparison of ss. 2 and 3 with their parallel provisions and language. Those two sections forbid two specific types of deduction from wages; they would both have been superfluous if s. 1 had contained a general prohibition of all types of deductions from wages. Under all three sections the deduction is from wages which have been earned under the contract and for which the employer is under a present duty to make payment. In this sense the deductions from wages under s. 1 are generically similar to those under ss. 2 and 3; for in all three cases the deductions are from wages earned and payable in accordance with the terms of the contract: on the other hand, where there is a suspension in accordance with the terms of the contract, there are no wages so to become payable.

For these reasons I think the Truck Act veto is inapplicable; and the appeal must be allowed with costs here and below.

LAWRENCE, L.J.: Apart from the Truck Act, there is nothing in law or in fact which prevents two contracting parties contracting on the terms that either during holidays or illness, or any other period, the obligations of the contract shall be suspended. By the terms of such a contract the contracting party, if he be an employer, never contracts to pay wages during the period referred to, any more than the other party, if he be a workman contracts to work during that period...It follows in my opinion that such a contract is not a contract for any deduction from the sum contracted to be paid since no sum was ever contracted to be paid during a period of suspension.

MORTON, L.J. concurred.

SAGAR v. RIDEHALGH & SON LTD

Court of Appeal   [1931] 1 Ch. 310

The plaintiff, a weaver, was employed by the defendant under an oral contract of service. His wages were determined by reference to a collective agreement between the employers' and workers' unions. Evidence showed a custom observed by most mills in Lancashire for deductions to be made for work which was not done with reasonable care and skill. The plaintiff claimed this practice was rendered illegal by the Truck Act, 1831, s. 3. (The Act of 1896 does not apply to persons engaged in weaving by reason of an Order (no. 299) made in 1897 under s. 9 of that Act). The Court of Appeal followed Hart v. Riversdale Mill Co. [1928] 1 K.B. 176, in deciding that the arrangements were not illegal deductions but part of the calculation of wages. The judgment of LAWRENCE, L.J. is of general interest.

LAWRENCE, L.J.: In the case of *Williams* v. *North's Navigation Collieries* (1889), *Ltd*,[1] the House of Lords decided that s. 3 of the Truck Act, 1831, does not allow an employer when paying wages rightly earned by or payable to a workman to deduct a sum due from the workman to the employer in respect of an antecedent breach of his contract to work. In the case of *Hart* v. *Riversdale Mill Co.*[2] the Court of Appeal decided that when a deduction made by the employer was not a deduction from wages rightly earned or payable, but a loss which accrued to the workman in the ascertainment of what sum for wages had been earned by or was payable to him, the deduction did not contravene the provisions of s. 3 of the Truck Act, 1831. The question we have to decide is whether the facts of the present case bring it within the decision in *Williams'* case or within the decision in *Hart's* case.

Three alternative views of the terms of the plaintiff's contract of service have been suggested in the course of the arguments before us— namely: (1) that the employers agreed to pay the workman a specified lump sum for every piece of cloth whether well or ill woven, leaving the employers to their remedy for damages in case the workman should have committed a breach of his implied obligation to exercise reasonable skill and care; or (2) that the employers agreed to pay the workman a specified lump sum for every piece of cloth woven if of good merchantable quality, leaving the workman, in case of bad workmanship, entitled to a *quantum meruit* only; or (3) that the employers agreed to pay the workman a specified lump sum for every piece of cloth woven subject to a deduction (not exceeding the actual or estimated loss sustained by the employer) if the workman did not exercise reasonable skill and care. . . . As regards the first of these alternatives, it is not disputed, and indeed it is pleaded by the plaintiff, that the Uniform List of Prices agreed between the Amalgamated Weavers' Association and the Cotton Spinners' and Manufacturers' Association were incorporated in the plaintiff's contract for service. . . . I find myself unable to agree with the finding of Farwell J. that under the plaintiff's contract of service the standard prices fixed by the Uniform List of Prices had been earned and were payable to him, whether the work had been well or ill done, and that the only remedy open to the employers if the plaintiff failed to exercise reasonable care and skill was to dismiss him or to sue him for damages for breach of contract.

That leaves the question whether the second or third alternative view of the plaintiff's contract for service is the true one. If the matter had

---

[1] [1906] A.C. 136.   [2] [1928] 1 K.B. 176.

rested simply on the fact that the prices in the Uniform List of Prices were for good work only the logical result would have been that the true terms of the contract were those mentioned in the second alternative, and that the plaintiff, in the circumstances of the present case, would only have been entitled to a *quantum meruit*, in which case no question under s. 3 of the Truck Act, 1831, would have arisen. . . .

The employers based their contention on two alternative grounds: either that the established practice of making reasonable deductions for bad work in the defendants' mill was incorporated into the plaintiff's contract of service by reason of his having agreed to be employed upon the same terms as the other weavers in that mill, or else that the general usage of making reasonable deductions for bad work prevailing in the cotton weaving trade of Lancashire was so well known and understood that every weaver engaging in that trade must be taken to have entered upon his employment on the footing of that usage.

As regards the first of these grounds, it is clearly established by the evidence of Mr George Ridehalgh that the practice of making reasonable deductions for bad work has continuously prevailed at the defendants' mill for upwards of thirty years, and that during the whole of that time all weavers employed by the defendants have been treated alike in that respect. The practice was therefore firmly established at the defendants' mill when the plaintiff entered upon his employment there. Further, I think that it is clear that the plaintiff accepted employment in the defendants' mill on the same terms as the other weavers employed at that mill. I draw this inference not only from the statement of claim (as explained by the particulars) and from the plaintiff's own evidence, but also from the fact that this action is avowedly brought to test the legality of the practice prevailing at the defendants' mill, and not to determine whether this particular plaintiff was employed upon some special terms which would make that practice inapplicable to his contract of service. Although I entirely agree with the learned judge in finding it difficult to believe that the plaintiff did not know of the existence of the practice at the mill, I think that it is immaterial whether he knew of it or not, as I am satisfied that he accepted his employment on the same terms as to deductions for bad work as the other weavers at the mill. In the result, I have come to the conclusion that the practice of making reasonable deductions for bad work prevailing at the defendants' mill was incorporated in the plaintiff's contract of service.

Further, I am of opinion that the second ground is also established by the evidence—namely, that the practice in the defendants' mill is in accordance with the general usage of making reasonable deductions for bad work prevailing in the weaving trade of Lancashire, which usage, in the absence of any stipulation to the contrary, would be incorporated into every contract of service as a weaver in a Lancashire cotton mill without special mention.... The main contention of the plaintiff on this part of the case was that both the practice in the defendants' mill and the general usage in the weaving trade in Lancashire sought to be incorporated into the plaintiff's contract of service were illegal, as contravening the provisions of the Truck Act, 1831. In my judgment, this contention is completely answered by the fact that the practice of making reasonable deductions for bad work from wages has been recognized as legal...by the Court of Appeal in *Hart's* case[1]...

It is significant, on the question of the existence and notoriety of the general usage in the weaving trade in Lancashire, Cheshire, Derbyshire and the West Riding of Yorkshire, to note that in the year 1897 the workmen employed in that trade, being apprehensive that a compliance with the provisions of ss. 1 and 2 of the Truck Act, 1896, might lead to the more rigid enforcement of the usage of making deductions for bad work, persuaded the Secretary of State that the provisions of the Act were unnecessary for their protection, and procured him to make an order under s. 9 granting an exemption from those provisions in respect of the persons engaged in all branches of that trade, thus leaving the usage to continue as theretofore without any of the restrictions imposed by the Act.

Apart from the question of illegality under the Truck Act, 1831, Farwell, J. has held that the usage is not a good usage, because it is neither universal nor reasonable nor certain, and accordingly does not comply with the tests laid down in *Devonald* v. *Rosser & Sons*[2]....In the first place, it is to be noticed that in *Hart's* case[1] the justices found that 'deductions for bad work are, and have been for many years, the usage and custom in the cotton weaving trade of Lancashire, and have always been, and are, an incident of a weaver's contract of service, and have always been, and are, taken into account in calculating the correct wages.' The Court of Appeal decided that this usage was not illegal under the Truck Acts and gave effect to it....In the next place, I am of opinion that the usage is not, as held by the learned judge, unreasonable. The deductions are not arbitrary deductions at the will and pleasure of the employers; they are limited to cases where there has been bad work, and they are limited to an amount which does not exceed the actual or

[1] [1928] 1 K.B. 176, 178. [2] [1906] 2 K.B. 728.

estimated damage or loss occasioned to the employer by the act or omission of the workman.... In the next place, a trade usage allowing an employer to make deductions for bad work at his discretion not exceeding a certain defined limit does not, in my opinion, render the usage uncertain. It would be altogether unreasonable if the usage were to make certain definite deductions in every case. There are degrees of negligence, and it is reasonable that employers should not exact the full amount of the loss occasioned to them in every case. From a business point of view there is no uncertainty about such a usage. A Lancashire weaver knows, and has for very many years past known, precisely what his position was as regards deductions for bad work on accepting employment in a Lancashire mill. There would be no uncertainty in his mind on this point as to the effect of his engagement.

LORD HANWORTH, M.R. and ROMER, L.J. delivered concurring judgments.

CHAPTER 2

TERMINATION OF EMPLOYMENT

SECTION A

TERMINATION WITHOUT NOTICE— FRUSTRATION; SUMMARY REPUDIATION

POUSSARD v. SPIERS

[1876] 1 Q.B.D. 410

The plaintiff was engaged to sing the chief part in Lecocq's opera, *Les Pres Saint Gervais*. She fell ill, and a substitute, Miss L. was found who would, however, only perform if she was engaged for a month; which was agreed. After Miss L. had performed four performances the plaintiff returned and offered to take over.*

BLACKBURN, J.: This inability having been occasioned by sickness was not any breach of contract by the plaintiff, and no action can lie against him for the failure thus occasioned. But the damage to the defendants and the consequent failure of consideration is just as great as it if had been occasioned by the plaintiff's fault, instead of by his wife's misfortune. The analogy is complete between this case and that of a charterparty in the ordinary terms, where the ship is to proceed in ballast (the act of God, &c., excepted) to a port and there load a cargo. If the delay is occasioned by excepted perils, the shipowner is excused. But if it is so great as to go to the root of the matter, it frees the charterer from his obligation to furnish a cargo: see per Bramwell, B., delivering the judgment of the majority of the Court of Exchequer Chamber in *Jackson* v. *Union Marine Insurance Co.*[1]

And we think that the question, whether the failure of a skilled and capable artiste to perform in a new piece through serious illness is so important as to go to the root of the consideration, must to some extent depend on the evidence; and is a mixed question of law and fact....If a temporary substitute capable of performing the part adequately could have been obtained upon such a precarious engagement on any reasonable

[1] Law Rep. 10 C.P. at p. 141.

* On frustration and the personal nature of employment contracts, see *ante*, p. 33.

terms, that would have been a right course to pursue; but if no substitute capable of performing the part adequately could be obtained, except on the terms that she should be permanently engaged at higher pay than the plaintiff's wife, in our opinion it follows, as a matter of law, that the failure on the plaintiff's part went to the root of the matter and discharged the defendants.

CONDOR *v.* BARRON KNIGHTS LTD
[1966] 1 W.L.R. 87

The plaintiff, aged 16, was employed by the defendant company to be the drummer in a group called 'The Barron Knights'. Under his contract he agreed to perform for them for five years wherever he was directed and to devote all his time to serving them, the contract being terminable by six months written notice on either side except in the case where the plaintiff committed any breach of his obligation or misconducted himself, the defendants then being able to dismiss him summarily. The group was engaged on one-night stands, performing seven nights weekly, sometimes twice a night, travelling between engagements, sleeping when they could and rehearsing as much as possible. The plaintiff collapsed, and his doctor said he should not be employed for more than three or four nights a week: there was a possibility he might develop schizophrenic symptoms if he came under strain again. The defendant company decided it was not practicable to employ a substitute drummer for the remaining nights in a week and dismissed him summarily. The summary dismissal was held to be justified.

THOMPSON, J.: The engagement of the plaintiff, both by the express words of the agreement and by the clear basis on which he and the defendants knew that the group was working, was an availability by the plaintiff to perform on seven nights a week if there were engagements on seven nights a week and more than once on such of them as they were offered and were able to accept double engagements. Therefore, in my judgment, it was quite a reasonable and proper conclusion for the group to take that it was not from their point of view a business proposition to employ the plaintiff on the only basis on which the doctor had said he might reasonably and safely be employed.

That brings one accordingly to the question whether at that date the plaintiff was capable of and available to work as the contract contemplated, that is to say, not merely to play drums, but to play drums on seven nights a week, if need be travelling from one one-night stand to another. The plaintiff thought he was and the plaintiff said that at a later date in the year he did, but I am satisfied that at the time when the defendants had to consider the situation, not merely was it a reasonable view for them to take that he was not then fit, but that he was not in fact fit, that is to say, fit to work, as the contract contemplated, seven days a week. In my judgment for this purpose fitness involves not merely being able to do the work, though with the virtual certainty that at the end of a week or a very short period such as a month there will be a breakdown of a worse kind, but it does involve the ability to do it without the likelihood of such damage to health and so as, within the contract, to continue with the continuity which the contract contemplated. I am satisfied that at the date when Tony Avern saw him, which was 1 February, and said what I accept Tony Avern said, because I do not accept what the plaintiff told me he had said (namely, that the plaintiff had become too expensive), in my judgment on 1 February 1963, the situation was that the plaintiff was not fit to perform his part of the contract and at that date there was no reasonable likelihood that he would in the near future become so able.

Accordingly in my judgment, by reason of the impact upon his health and well-being of his life, far too strenuous and exhausting for a boy of 16, talented though he was and ambitious though he was, the impact was such in my judgment that that had in a business sense made it impossible for him to continue to perform or for the defendants have him perform the terms of the contract as a member of their group. It follows that in my judgment there was no wrongful dismissal in this case and the defence so far as that is concerned prevails.*

Re FOSTER CLARK INDENTURE TRUSTS
[1966] 1 All E.R. 43

In 1925 Foster Clark Ltd established a contributory pension fund for its employees under a trust fund and rules, rule 16 of which stated *inter alia* that members were entitled to benefit if their services were 'dispensed with by the company before retiring age'. In 1963 on 7 February a receiver was appointed by a debenture-holder and the receiver sold F. Ltd's business to a wholly-owned subsidiary of F. Ltd named Alimentary Paste Ltd. On 8 February the receiver sent a letter to F.

* Note that the case may be seen either as one of breach or as of frustration: compare *Storey* v. *Fulham Steel Works* (1907) 24 T.L.R. 89, C.A.

Ltd's employees which said 'All employees...will be retained by me on the terms of one week's notice on either side'. From then on A.P. Ltd gave the employees their particulars under the Contracts of Employment Act, 1963, paid their salaries and wages, paid their insurance contributions and deducted their tax. It was the receiver's intention that 'the contracts of employment...should be transferred to the subsidiary in the same way as the company's trading contracts.'

PLOWMAN, J.: The question is what was the effect of what happened on 8 February, or on 7 February. Did the employees of the company cease to be employees of the company and so become entitled to benefit under the rules of the trust deed?...In other words, as I said, did the employment of those persons terminate at the time when the receiver was appointed or at the time of the sale agreement, or did that employment notwithstanding those matters remain employment with the company? So far as the question whether the appointment of the receiver itself operated to determine the employment is concerned, I do not propose to decide that as a question of law because it is unnecessary for me to do so.

At first sight there appears to be no very good reason in principle why an appointment out of court of a receiver who is the agent of the company should determine contracts of employment, and the two passages which I have cited from Palmer and from Kerr suggest that such an appointment does not have that effect. As I have said, however, it becomes unnecessary for me to decide that matter because it seems to me that the sale by the receiver of the company's business as a going concern on 8 February 1963, to another company, albeit a subsidiary of Foster Clark, Ltd, must have had the effect of determining the employment of all employees who were employed in the business. After 8 February 1963, Foster Clark, Ltd had no business in which to employ the employees. That, I think, is supported by the decision of the Court of Appeal in the case of *Brace* v. *Calder*.[1] In that case the defendants, a partnership consisting of four members, agreed to employ the plaintiff as manager of a branch of their business for a certain period. The plaintiff entered into their service under the agreement, but, before the period had expired, two of the partners retired, and the business was transferred to and carried on by the other two. The continuing partners were willing to employ the plaintiff on the same terms as before for the remainder of the period, but he declined to serve them. It was held in an action for wrongful dismissal, by Lopes and Rigby, L.JJ., Lord Esher, M.R., dis-

[1] [1895–99] All E.R. Rep. 1196; [1895] 2 Q.B. 253.

senting, that the dissolution of the partnership operated as a wrongful dismissal of the plaintiff, but that he was only entitled to nominal damages.... Similarly, it seems to me here that the transfer of the business from one company to another operated as a dismissal of the employees who were employed in that business. That conclusion, I think, is sufficient to dispose of the first question raised by the originating summons and for that purpose I do not think it is necessary to go on and consider exactly what the position of the employees was after 8 February. It is fairly clear that their employer was the subsidiary company. However that may be, the point I am concerned with is that on 8 February 1963, their employment by Foster Clark, Ltd was terminated. That answers the first question; the answer is, in effect, 'yes'.

Re RUBEL BRONZE & METAL CO. LTD AND VOS
[1918] 1 K.B. 315

Vos was employed by the defendants as general manager for three years at a fixed salary plus commission. After a year they suspended him pending an investigation of his efficiency: they refused to let him work. He claimed he was entitled to treat the contract as repudiated.

MCCARDIE, J.: Hence it is desirable to briefly consider the meaning of the words 'wrongfully dismiss'. The phrase has often been used, but never defined. Does it indicate a peculiar contractual feature of the relationship between master and servant, or does it denote a mere application to such relationship of the well-known principles of law as to the repudiation of contracts? The relation of master and servant differs in important respects from other contracts. The power of dismissal sprang into existence at a late stage of the development of the common law (see the useful note in Macdonell on Master and Servant, 2nd ed., pp. 191–2). It was practically unknown in the eighteenth century. It first took clear form in the year 1817, when Lord Ellenborough tried the case of *Spain* v. *Arnott*. There the servant refused to obey his master's orders, and Lord Ellenborough held that the master was justified in terminating the employment. In my view the ratio of that decision was that the servant had, in substance, refused to fulfil his essential obligations under the contract, whereby the master was entitled to treat the contract as ended. Thenceforward the law as to dismissal developed rapidly, though the principles are but rarely revealed and the jurist may seek in vain for the ordered rules of growth.

Today it is well settled that a master may dismiss his servant for many reasons, such as misconduct, substantial negligence, dishonesty, and the like. Such matters may, I think, be said to constitute such a breach of duty by the servant as to preclude the further satisfactory continuance of the relationship and to justify the master in electing to treat the contract as repudiated by the servant. But the point is one of doubt, as the light of formulated ratio illuminates but few of the decisions. Perhaps the modern view has been that continued good conduct by the servant is a condition, either express or implied, of the contract of service the breach of which entitles the master to end the employment: see the doubt of Lush, J., in *Hanley* v. *Pease*.[1] Such view is certainly consistent with the effect of the decisions in *Ridgway* v. *Hungerford Market Co.*,[2] and *Baillie* v. *Kell*.[3] It is clear, however, that if a dismissal be without just cause the master is deemed to have wrongfully repudiated his contractual obligations to the servant: see *General Billposting Co.* v. *Atkinson*.[4] 'Wrongful dismissal' is, I think, a mere illustration of the general legal rule that an action will lie for unjustifiable repudiation of a contract. The doctrine of repudiation equally applies when the master wrongfully refuses, before the period of employment has arrived, to take the servant into his service: see *Hochster* v. *De la Tour*.[5]

CLOUSTON & CO. LTD *v.* CORRY

Privy Council   [1906] A.C. 122

The plaintiff was employed as manager of the defendant's grain and produce department under a five-year contract. He was dismissed after fourteen months and claimed damages. On the present appeal the Judicial Committee of the Privy Council was of the opinion that the verdict of the jury was so unsatisfactory that it should be set aside and a new trial ordered.

LORD JAMES: In an action brought to recover damages for alleged wrongful dismissal from service, a defence, which in former days would have been embodied in a plea of justification, is set up. Allegations of misconduct, drunkenness, the use of foul language in public, resulting in conviction, are made, supported by strong evidence virtually admitted by the plaintiff to be true...Now the sufficiency of the justification depended upon the extent of misconduct. There is no

¹ [1915] 1 K.B. 698, 705.   ² (1835) 3 Ad. & E. 171.
³ (1838) 4 Bing. N.C. 638.   ⁴ [1909] A.C. 118, 122.
⁵ (1853) 2 E. & B. 678.

fixed rule of law defining the degree of misconduct which will justify dismissal. Of course there may be misconduct in a servant which will not justify the determination of the contract of service by one of the parties to it against the will of the other. On the other hand, misconduct inconsistent with the fulfilment of the express or implied conditions of service will justify dismissal. Certainly when the alleged misconduct consists of drunkenness there must be considerable difficulty in determining the extent or conditions of intoxication which will establish a justification for dismissal. The intoxication may be habitual and gross, and directly interfere with the business of the employer or with the ability of the servant to render due service. But it may be an isolated act committed under circumstances of festivity and in no way connected with or affecting the employer's business. In such a case the question whether the misconduct proved establishes the right to dismiss the servant must depend upon facts—and is a question of fact.

HANLEY *v.* PEASE & PARTNERS LTD

[1915] I K.B. 698

The plaintiff stayed away from work one day without consent of his employers. They did not discharge him but instead suspended him from working for one day so that he lost the wages for that day. The plaintiff brought an action for damages for wrongful dismissal.*

LUSH, J.: Whether the right of a master to dismiss a servant for misconduct or breach of duty or anything else of the kind is treated as a right arising out of the ordinary right of a contracting party to put an end to the contract when there has been a repudiation by the other party, or whether it is treated as a right which the master has on the ground that obedience to lawful orders must be treated as a condition of the contract, is wholly immaterial. I do not think it is necessary to say which is the proper way to regard it, because in either view the right of the master is merely an option. The contract has become a voidable contract. The master can determine it if he pleases. Assuming that there has been a breach on the part of the servant entitling the master to dismiss him, he may if he pleases terminate the contract, but he is not bound to do it, and if he chooses not to exercise that right but to treat the contract as a continuing contract not withstanding the misconduct or breach of duty of the servant, then the contract is for all

* See examples of express terms giving power to suspend, *ante,* p. 64.

purposes a continuing contract subject to the master's right in that case to claim damages against the servant for his breach of contract. But in the present case after declining to dismiss the workman—after electing to treat the contract as a continuous one—the employers took upon themselves to suspend him for one day; in other words to deprive the workman of his wages for one day, thereby assessing their own damages for the servant's misconduct at the sum which would be represented by one day's wages. They have no possible right to do that. Having elected to treat the contract as continuing it was continuing. They might have had a right to claim damages against the servant, but they could not justify their act in suspending the workman for the one day and refusing to let him work and earn wages.

ROWLATT and ATKIN, J.J., delivered concurring judgments.

MARSHALL v. ENGLISH ELECTRIC CO. LTD

Court of Appeal   (1945) 61 T.L.R. 379; [1945] 1 All E.R. 653

This case arose during war-time under the Essential Work (General Provisions) (No. 2) Order 1942. The plaintiff, whose contract could be terminated by either side at an hour's notice, had been suspended for three days without pay for disciplinary reasons.

LORD GODDARD: As is well known, the Essential Work Order drastically restricts the right of either master or workman to determine a contract of service to which the order applies, and no doubt this has in some cases proved an obstacle in the way of maintaining discipline in places where work of national importance is in progress. It may well be that it was for that reason that the original order was amended by introducing the paragraph which we have to consider. Its wording is involved, but the effect is that an employer may suspend a workman without pay for a period not exceeding three days as a disciplinary measure if the conditions of his service permit, and subject to an appeal. We are here dealing with a man whose contract of service was liable to be determined by an hour's notice given by either side, as indeed are those of the great majority of manual workers in factories and kindred establishments throughout the country. Sagar v. Ridehalgh and Son, Ltd [ante, p. 132] shows that an established practice at a particular factory may be incorporated into a workman's contract of service, and, indeed, whether he knew of it or not—as it must be presumed that he accepted employment on the same terms as applied to other workers in that factory. The findings of the Judge show that there was this practice at the defendant's factory. The employers had always asserted a right to suspend; the workmen had acquiesced in it and, moreover, in one instance, had insisted on this penalty being imposed on an inspector who had struck a youth. It seems, therefore, that in the days before the Essential Work Order men, including the plaintiff, who could have left at an hour's notice if they did not like this practice have continued in their employment with knowledge of it and have insisted on its enforcement when they thought it right to do so. In my opinion it follows that the practice ought to be regarded as incorporated in the contract of service.

But it is said that, when analysed, this practice is not suspension but dismissal in the case of a man subject to an hour's notice. As to this, the defendants say that the contract is continuous; it does not renew from hour to hour but exists until notice is given and may last, and very likely in many cases does, for 20 years or more. So they contend that, if they merely suspend and do not give a man notice, they do not dismiss him but merely tell him that he is not to work for a specified time and that they are not going to pay him during that time. What, then, is left of the contract of service during that time? Everything, say the defendants, except the obligation to work on the one side and to pay on the other. But in the case of an hourly servant are there any rights or obligations left except, possibly, the obligation to pay for one hour? It was suggested that there might be pension rights, but there was no evidence that the plaintiff had any right to a pension, nor would one expect that a pension was secured as of right to a man subject to dismissal at one hour's notice. In my opinion, what is called suspension is in truth dismissal, with an intimation that, at the end of so many days, or it may be hours, the man will be re-employed if he chooses to apply for re-instatement.

This indeed seems to be the effect of the evidence, as the witnesses called for the defendants appear to agree that a suspended man can go off and seek employment elsewhere if he chooses to do so; he is under no obligation to return if he does not wish to submit to suspension. The fact is that, were the order not in existence, the question could not in practice arise.

MACKINNON, L.J. delivered a concurring judgment; DU PARCQ, L.J. dissented on the grounds that the practice of suspension had not been incorporated into the plaintiff's contract of service.

TURNER *v.* MASON

(1845) 14 M. & W. 112; 153 E.R. 411

The plaintiff while in the defendant's employ as a maid heard that her mother was dying and wanted to see her. She asked permission to be away from her job until the next day, but this was refused. Nevertheless the plaintiff went to see her mother and was summarily dismissed. This was an action for wrongful dismissal.

In argument the following passage occurs: [Parke, B. The obligation of a domestic servant is to obey all lawful commands. This plea sets out that which *prima facie* is a lawful command, which you must answer by the replication. Now here the replication alleges the extreme illness of the plaintiff's mother, but does not say the plaintiff gave the defendant notice of that fact; it only says that was the ground on which she applied for his permission, but not that she communicated it. Alderson, B. If the mother be very poor, is the daughter to absent herself from her service to work for her, to prevent her starving? Pollock, C.B. Or, if she has a right to go to the death-bed of her mother or father, why not of any other near friend?] The replication alleges expressly that the defendant had no need of her services. [Parke, B. The master is to be the judge of the circumstances under which the servant's services are required, subject to this, that he is to give only lawful commands.]

The Court gave judgment for the defendant.

ALDERSON, B.: The plea is a good answer to the action, because it shows the discharge of the plaintiff to have been for wilful disobedience of the defendant's order to stay in his house all night. Then is the replication a good answer to the plea? It is informal, because it does not show that the mother was likely to die that night, or that it was necessary to go that night to see her, or to stay all night. But if this were otherwise, these circumstances would amount only to a mere moral duty, and do not show any legal right. We are to decide according to the legal obligations of parties. Where is a decision founded upon mere moral obligation to stop? What degree of sickness, what nearness of relationship, is to be sufficient? It is the safest way, therefore, to adhere to the legal obligations arising out of the contract between the parties. There may, undoubtedly, be cases justifying a wilful disobedience of such an order; as where the servant apprehends danger to her life, or violence to her person, from the master; or where, from an infectious disorder raging in the house, she must go out for the preservation of her life. But the general rule is obedience, and wilful disobedience is a sufficient ground of dismissal.

ROLFE, B.: In truth, the cases suggested by my brother Alderson are cases in which there is not legally any disobedience, because they are cases not of lawful orders. It is an unlawful order to direct a servant to continue where she is in danger of violence to her person, or of infectious disease.

POLLOCK, C.B., and PARKE, B., delivered concurring judgments.

LAWS v. LONDON CHRONICLE LTD

Court of Appeal   [1959] 1 W.L.R. 698

The plaintiff was employed by the defendant company. Her direct superior, Delderfield, quarrelled with the managing director at a meeting. When Delderfield rose to walk out in the middle of the meeting, she got up to follow him. The managing director told her to stay but she nevertheless went out, out of loyalty to Delderfield. She was dismissed summarily.

LORD EVERSHED, M.R., stated the facts and continued: It is the corner-stone of Mr Stable's case that there was in truth nothing that a self-respecting employer could do but to dismiss summarily: for here was an order given—'Stay where you are'—and disobeyed.... I will not read the judgments of Parke, C.B., and Barons Alderson and Rolfe; but it would in my judgment be going too far to say that any of those judges [in *Turner* v. *Mason, ante,* p. 146] laid it down as a proposition of law that every act of disobedience of a lawful order must entitle the employer to dismiss. I think that cannot be extracted from the judgments; and I am satisfied that it is too narrow a proposition as one of law.... To my mind, the proper conclusion to be drawn from the passages I have cited and the cases to which we have been referred is that, since a contract of service is but an example of contracts in general, so that the general law of contract will be applicable, it follows that the question must be—if summary dismissal is claimed to be justifiable—whether the conduct complained of is such as to show the servant to have disregarded the essential conditions of the contract of service. It is, no doubt, therefore, generally true that wilful disobedience of an order will justify summary dismissal, since wilful disobedience of a lawful and reasonable order shows a disregard—a complete disregard—of a condition essential to the contract of service, namely the condition that the servant must obey the proper orders of the master, and that unless he does so the relationship is, so to speak, struck at fundamentally.

In the present case, the judge, in the course of his judgment, said: 'It is clear and sound law that to justify dismissal for one act of disobedience or misconduct it has to be of a grave and serious nature'; and later he concluded, in the plaintiff's favour, that what she had done, or not done, on 20 June was not sufficiently grave to justify dismissal.

With all respect to the judge, I think that his proposition is not justified in the form in which he stated it. I think it is not right to say that one act of disobedience, to justify dismissal, must be of a grave and serious character. I do, however, think (following the passages which I have already cited) that one act of disobedience or misconduct can justify dismissal only if it is of a nature which goes to show (in effect) that the servant is repudiating the contract, or one of its essential conditions; and for that reason, therefore, I think that you find in the passages I have read that the disobedience must at least have the quality that it is 'wilful': it does (in other words) connote a deliberate flouting of the essential contractual conditions...the judge...said: 'She had served loyally up to then. There was this row between her immediate superior, Delderfield, and Brittain. The only thing Brittain said to her was "You stay where you are." She did not do so but walked out of the room. Till then she had been a good girl. This was the one and only act of disobedience. She was put in a difficult position.' As I have said, I take it (and no ground for a contrary view has been put to us) that the judge did accept her as a witness of truth. The situation was plainly one which was as embarrassing as it was unpleasant for her; and in the circumstances, with her immediate superior walking out and asking her to follow, I am satisfied that it cannot be said that her conduct did amount to such a lawful disobedience of an order, such a deliberate disregard of the conditions of service, as justified the employer in saying 'I accept your repudiation: I treat the contract as ended: I summarily dismiss you.'*

* But note the decision of the Court of Appeal in *Sinclair* v. *Neighbour* [1966] 3 All E. R. 988. The plaintiff, employed by the defendant bookmaker as manager, had taken £5 from the till for his expenses, and £15 for gambling, having, he later alleged, left his wallet at home. He put an IOU in the till for £15; and replaced the money next day after his bet had been successful. He knew that his employer would not have approved of his taking the money for gambling. He was peremptorily dismissed. The County Court judge found his actions to be reprehensible, but not dishonest and not, therefore, sufficiently serious to merit summary dismissal The Court of Appeal reversed that decision. Sellers L. J. said that this conduct was 'on the face of it incompatible and inconsistent

LORD JENKINS and WILLMER, L.J., agreed with the judgment of LORD EVERSHED, M.R.

SAVAGE v. BRITISH INDIA STEAMSHIP NAVIGATION CO.

(1930) 46 T.L.R. 294

The chief officer and the captain of a mail steamer were both summarily dismissed after an incident on one voyage when a valve was opened and Persian rugs in the hold were damaged by water.

MR JUSTICE WRIGHT reviewed the evidence and said that the onus was on the defendants to prove that the dismissal was not wrongful. If the dismissal was justifiable in law it was immaterial that it might be a decision of great severity. There was no written contract of employment, and the only documents relating to employment were various circulars dealing with the age at which officers must retire, their rights to pension, and their right to leave on full pay after certain periods of service. The circulars made it clear that pensions were only to be paid at the discretion of the company.

The first question to be decided was whether the contract was one under which the officer was to serve until the age for retirement, the contract not being determinable by either party on reasonable notice meanwhile; or whether it was a contract of employment which was determinable by either party at any time on reasonable notice. He held that it was the latter...

Could the defendants justify the dismissal? Dealing with the case of Captain Power first, his Lordship discussed the evidence and said that the captain had committed a grave breach of good seamanship. Would that single lapse after many years of service justify the dismissal? An employer was entitled to dismiss a servant for a single act of misconduct or serious negligence. In determining the seriousness of an act of negligence regard must be had, not to the consequences of the act, but to its nature. With great reluctance he held that the negligence here was incompatible with the captain's duty and with his position in charge of the vessel. It was not a mere error of judgment,

with his duty' so as to justify instant dismissal. As a new manager it was 'incumbent on him to keep the till inviolate'. Davies L.J. agreed because of the 'breach of the confidential relationship'. Sachs L.J. would have described all such illicit taking of money, even if temporary, as 'dishonest' where the employee knew the employer would disapprove.

Note, too, that where an employer waives a breach going to the root of the contract by continuing the employee in his service after he has full knowledge of it, he cannot thereafter rely upon it as a ground for summary dismissal: *Beattie* v. *Parmenter* (1889) 5 T.L.R. 396 (C.A.).

but was gross negligence. The company, therefore, was entitled to refuse to continue to employ the captain, and his dismissal was justified. ...As to the chief officer, Savage, it was impossible to attribute to him the same degree of misconduct.

His Lordship dealt with the evidence and said that in his opinion the company had failed to show sufficient ground for summary dismissal. Savage was, therefore, entitled to damages based on the fact, which he had found, that either party was able to terminate the contract on reasonable notice. He held that in this case reasonable notice would be 12 months, and Savage would, therefore, have judgment for 12 months' salary, with costs.

JUPITER GENERAL INSURANCE CO. *v.* SHROFF

Privy Council   [1937] 3 All E.R. 67

The manager of the life insurance department of the appellant insurance company recommended the issue of an endowment policy on a third party, knowing that a few days earlier the managing governor had refused to re-insure the life. Did this justify summary dismissal? The Privy Council was of the opinion that it did.

LORD MAUGHAM: On the one hand, it can be in exceptional circumstances only that an employer is acting properly in summarily dismissing an employee on his committing a single act of negligence; on the other, their Lordships would be very loath to assent to the view that a single outbreak of bad temper, accompanied, it may be, with regrettable language, is a sufficient ground for dismissal. Sir John Beaumont, C.J., was stating a proposition of mere good sense when he observed that in such cases one must apply the standards of men, and not those of angels, and remember that men are apt to show temper when reprimanded....It must be remembered that the test to be applied must vary with the nature of the business and the position held by the employee, and that decisions in other cases are of little value. We have here to deal with the business of life insurance. A mistake in accepting a risk may lead to a very considerable loss, and repetition of such mistakes may lead to disaster....If an officer of a life insurance company, whatever his motive may be, withholds from his superiors information which will in all probability lead them to refuse a risk, and *a fortiori* if it is one of exceptional character and magnitude, it would seem to be very difficult for his superiors to be confident that he will, in the future, properly carry out the important duties entrusted to him. In other words, if a person in charge of the life assurance department, subject to the supervision of superior officers, shows by his conduct or his negligence that he can no longer command their confidence, and if, when an explanation is called for, he refuses apology or amendment, it seems to their Lordships that his immediate dismissal is justifiable.

LEAROYD v. BROOK

[1891] 1 Q.B. 431

P. was apprenticed with the defendant by his guardians, the plaintiffs. When he discovered that P. was an habitual thief, the defendant refused to continue the apprenticeship. He was sued for breach of the apprenticeship deed.*

A. L. SMITH, J.: The question now arises, Is a master under articles of apprenticeship bound to keep, teach, and maintain at his own risk an habitual thief for the term stipulated for by the articles?...It has unquestionably been held that, in an ordinary apprenticeship deed, the covenants by the master are independent covenants, the performance of which does not depend upon the performance by the apprentice on his part of the obligations imposed upon him by the deed....It appears, however, to me that this does not decide what I have to determine in the present case. Where an apprentice by his own wilful act prevents a master from teaching him, the master can set this up as a defence when sued upon his covenant to keep, teach, and maintain the apprentice, irrespective of the question whether the apprentice has performed his obligations under the deed or not. This is settled by the case of *Raymond* v. *Minton*.[1] The *ratio decidendi* of that case is not that the master is absolved because the apprentice has not performed the obligations imposed upon him by the articles, but because the apprentice by his own acts has put it out of the power of the master to carry out what he had contracted to do. Apply this reasoning to the present case. The master has contracted to teach the apprentice how to carry on a pawnbroker's trade honestly. That must be the contract by the master. The apprentice, by becoming an habitual thief, has rendered that impossible. Then why does not the principle laid down in *Raymond* v. *Minton* apply? Moreover, the remedy suggested in some of the cases as being the sole one which the master had upon

[1] Law Rep. 1 Ex. 244.

* On the special legal principles governing apprenticeship contracts see chapter IV of Mansfield Cooper and Wood *Outlines of Industrial Law* (5th ed. 1966).

default of the apprentice and loss consequent thereon, namely, to sue for the loss, can hardly exist in a case where the apprentice becomes an habitual thief; he cannot sue at once for his loss, but must first prosecute his apprentice, get him convicted and sentenced if he can, then take him back for the residue of the term, and sue for the loss he has sustained—an inapt procedure, beyond all question.

GENERAL BILLPOSTING CO. LTD v. ATKINSON

House of Lords   [1909] A.C. 118

Where a manager, employed under a contract which included a restriction on his right to trade when the contract ended, was wrongfully dismissed he recovered damages for this and started trading contrary to the restriction. The former employers tried to enforce this restriction.

LORD COLLINS: But I think this case may be, and in fact has been, decided on broader lines than those laid down in the notes to *Pordage* v. *Cole*[1] as to mutual and independent covenants. I think the true test applicable to the facts of this case is that which was laid down by Lord Coleridge, C.J., in *Freeth* v. *Burr*[2], and approved in *Mersey Steel Company* v. *Naylor*[3] in the House of Lords, 'That the true question is whether the acts and conduct of the party evince an intention no longer to be bound by the contract.' I think the Court of Appeal had ample ground for drawing this inference from the conduct of the appellants here in dismissing the respondent in deliberate disregard of the terms of the contract, and that the latter was thereupon justified in rescinding the contract and treating himself as absolved from the further performance of it on his part.

LORD ROBERTSON delivered a concurring speech; THE EARL OF HALSBURY agreed with the speech of LORD COLLINS.

HOWARD v. PICKFORD TOOL CO. LTD

Court of Appeal   [1951] 1 K.B. 417

The plaintiff, managing director of the defendant company, employed under a six year contract, sought a declaration that the defendant's conduct amounted to a repudiation of his contract of employment. He continued to carry out his duties.

---

[1] 1 Wms. Saund, 319.   [2] (1874) L. R. 9 C. P. at p. 213.
[3] (1884) 9 App. Cas. 434.

EVERSHED, M.R.: It is quite plain (and I refer, if it be necessary to quote authority, to the speech of Lord Simon, L.C., in *Heyman* v. *Darwins Ltd*[1]) that if the conduct of one party to a contract amounts to a repudiation, and the other party does not accept it as such but goes on performing his part of the contract and affirms the contract, the alleged act of repudiation is wholly nugatory and ineffective in law.

ASQUITH, L.J.: ...An unaccepted repudiation is a thing writ in water and of no value to anybody: it confers no legal rights of any sort or kind. Therefore a declaration that the defendants had repudiated their contract with the plaintiff would be entirely valueless to the plaintiff if it appeared at the same time, as it must appear in this case, that it was not accepted....The plaintiff's having stayed on and continued to perform the contract for something like two months and being still in the act of performing it, seems to me to be a sufficient reason for saying that the remedy asked for is an academic one such as cannot properly be sought....

SINGLETON, L.J., delivered a concurring judgment.*

RIDGE *v.* BALDWIN

House of Lords [1964] A.C 40.

A chief constable claimed that the Watch Committee was not entitled to dismiss him without observing the rules of 'natural justice', such as giving him an opportunity to answer charges of misconduct.

LORD REID, in the course of his speech, said: So I shall deal first with cases of dismissal. These appear to fall into three classes: dismissal of a servant by his master, dismissal from an office held during pleasure, and dismissal from an office where there must be something against a man to warrant his dismissal.

The law regarding master and servant is not in doubt. There cannot be specific performance of a contract of service, and the master can terminate the contract with his servant at any time and for any reason or for none. But if he does so in a manner not warranted by the contract he must pay damages for breach of contract. So the question in a pure case of master and servant does not at all depend on whether the master

---

[1] [1942] A.C. 356, 361.

* But see on the use of the declaration as a remedy *McClelland* v. *N. Ireland General Health Services Board* [1957] 2 All. E.R. 129 (*post*, p. 161); *Vidyodaya University* v. *Silva* [1964] 3 All E.R. 865, (*ante*, p. 44). The declaration is appropriate only where some statutory *status* relationship has supervened, as in *Vine* v. *N.D.L.B.* [1957] A.C. 488, *ante*, p. 41. See *Taylor* v. *National Union of Seamen* [1967] 1 All E.R. 767. But compare Zamir, *The Declaratory Judgement* pp. 129–48.

has heard the servant in his own defence: it depends on whether the facts emerging at the trial prove breach of contract. But this kind of case can resemble dismissal from an office where the body employing the man is under some statutory or other restriction as to the kind of contract which it can make with its servants, or the grounds on which it can dismiss them. The present case does not fall within this class because a chief constable is not the servant of the watch committee or indeed of anyone else.

Then there are many cases where a man holds an office at pleasure. Apart from judges and others whose tenure of office is governed by statute, all servants and officers of the Crown hold office at pleasure, and this has been held even to apply to a colonial judge (*Terrell* v. *Secretary of State for the Colonies*[1])....So I come to the third class, which includes the present case. There I find an unbroken line of authority to the effect that an officer cannot lawfully be dismissed without first telling him what is alleged against him and hearing his defence or explanation.

RIDGWAY *v.* HUNGERFORD MARKET CO.

3 Ad & E. 171 (111 E.R. 378)

A clerk employed by the defendants had to enter in the minute book a resolution to call a meeting to elect his successor. In his own handwriting he added a protest against this and was dismissed. The dismissal was held to be justified.

LORD DENMAN, C.J.: Now it is not necessary that a master, having a good ground of dismissal, should either state it to the servant, or act upon it. It is enough if it exist, and if there be improper conduct in fact. Suppose a servant had heard that his master intended to dismiss him without notice, and were to insult him in consequence: it is clear that the insult would justify the master in dismissing the servant; and yet, if he intended to dismiss him independently of the insult, the motive for the dismissal would be different from such ground of justification. It is unnecessary to discuss how it would be, if the master, at the time of the dismissal, had no knowledge of the fact which was to justify it; yet I think the justification would be good, even if the fact, existing at the time, were not known to the master.

COLERIDGE, J.: As to the existence of a sufficient cause, the jury have found it; and they were right in so doing. The act of entering the

[1] [1953] 2 Q.B. 482; [1953] 3 W.L.R. 331; [1953] 2 All E.R. 490.

protest on the minute book was inconsistent with his service; a servant of this kind, if allowed to do such acts, would be useless. But then it is said that it should have been put to the jury, whether this cause was the operating motive for the dismissal. I own that I was impressed for a considerable time with the weight of this argument. But I think that when a master, sued for wages, defends himself upon the ground that he had dismissed the servant, and that there was in fact something which justified the dismissal, that presents an intelligible issue to a jury: whereas, if the inquiry were to be, whether this justifying cause operated in the master's mind, a jury, in the great majority of cases, could not pronounce a satisfactory verdict. I think it is enough to show a justification existing in point of fact.

LITTLEDALE and PATTESON, J.J., delivered concurring judgments.

DIGGLE v. OGSTON MOTOR CO.

(1915) 84 L.J.K.B. 2165

The plaintiff was employed as works superintendent of the defendant company for one year 'subject of course to your carrying out your duties to the satisfaction of the directors...'

In an action for wrongful dismissal the jury found that the directors were 'really and genuinely dissatisfied' with the plaintiff's work but that they had no good reasons for such dissatisfaction.

LAWRENCE, J.: In this contract the engagement was to be for a year 'subject, of course, to your carrying out your duties to the satisfaction of the directors and to economical costs of production.' The action was brought because the plaintiff was dismissed within the year. I think it was a conditional engagement for a year, and that it lies upon the plaintiff to prove that the directors were in fact satisfied with his services, or dishonestly professed to be dissatisfied, or at least were capriciously dissatisfied. I do not agree that the contract must have the word 'reasonably' introduced into it. The only question of reasonableness in the matter is this: if it can be said that a reasonable man could not honestly have come to the conclusion, then a ground is made out for saying that the defendants came to the conclusion dishonestly. But if you admit that a reasonable man could have come to the conclusion, then the only question is, Did they in fact do so? and the decision is for them and not for the jury.

RIDLEY, J., delivered a concurring judgment.

BOSTON DEEP SEA FISHING & ICE CO.
v. ANSELL

Court of Appeal   (1888) 39 Ch.D. 339

The plaintiff was employed as managing director of the defendant company who dismissed him on grounds which they were later unable to substantiate. However, subsequent to the dismissal they discovered various acts, in particular taking commission from certain shipbuilders in connexion with a contract between the shipbuilders and the company without disclosing it, which they claimed were justification for the dismissal.

COTTON, L.J.: Now we come to the counter-claim, and there is an appeal against the allowance of the counter-claim. What we have to consider first is this, had the company—although they knew it not at the time when they dismissed the defendant in October—a good ground of dismissal? In my opinion, they had. I have stated that he was engaged not only by the Plaintiff Mr Garfit, but that he agreed with the company to be their general manager, and had authority given to him with reference to the contract to be entered into with the Earle's Shipbuilding Company. Then when he was engaged in that contract, in respect of the matters of that very contract, he in one instance got a percentage of 1 per cent from the Shipbuilding Company, and, in the other case, he insisted on getting—that is the evidence—and did get, a lump sum of £50. It is suggested that we should be laying down new rules of morality and equity if we were to so hold. In my opinion if people have got an idea that such transactions can be properly entered into by an agent, the sooner they are disabused of that idea the better. If a servant, or a managing director, or any person who is authorized to act, and is acting, for another in the matter of any contract, receives, as regards the contract, any sum, whether by way of percentage or otherwise, from the person with whom he is dealing on behalf of his principal, he is committing a breach of duty. It is not an honest act, and, in my opinion, it is a sufficient act to show that he cannot be trusted to perform the duties which he has undertaken as servant or agent. He puts himself in such a position that he has a temptation not faithfully to perform his duty to his employer. He has a temptation, especially where he is getting a percentage on expenditure, not to cut down the expenditure, but to let it be increased, so that his percentage may be larger. I do not, however, rely on that, but what I say is this, that where an agent entering into a contract on behalf of his principal, and without the knowledge or assent of that principal, receives money from the person with whom he is dealing, he is doing a wrongful act, he is misconducting himself as regards his agency, and, in my opinion, that gives to his employer, whether a company or an individual, and whether the agent be a servant, or a managing director, power and authority to dismiss him from his employment as a person who by that act is shown to be incompetent of faithfully discharging his duty to his principal. It was said by Mr Justice Kekewich that this was an isolated transaction, and, therefore, in his opinion, it did not give legal authority or power to the company to dismiss him. But I cannot accede to that view. As far as we know it may have been an isolated transaction, but if we find at the very beginning of the employment that this agent, whose duty it was not to receive anything from the persons with whom he was dealing, did in fact do so, and in fact kept the receipt secret for months after the money was received, I am not satisfied that he did not do other things equally inconsistent with his duty to his principals; and in my opinion the discovery of that fact—even if it was an isolated transaction, showing that he would put himself in a position not faithfully to discharge his duty, that he would put himself in a position to regard the interest of someone else rather than that of his employer—did justify his employers in discharging him from the office which he held. It was urged before us that it was a long time ago, and it was said, suppose this happened eight years ago; supposing the act had been done eight years ago, would that in law have justified the employer in discharging him? In law, I say yes. It is very true that if an employer was a reasonable man, and found that a servant who had served him faithfully for eight years, had, in the early time of his employment, done an act which was wrongful and which justified his dismissal, probably he might have said: 'This is a man who has been in my employ for years, and he has always behaved himself honestly in the discharge of his duties, except in regard to this one transaction which took place such a long time ago, and, therefore I do not insist on my legal right.' But, although a man would ordinarily act in that way, yet, in my opinion, that has no effect on the question whether the act is not of such a character as to justify the employer in dismissing him when he finds it out. Of course if he knows of the act and still continues to employ him, it might have been held by Judges of fact or by a jury that he had condoned it and prevented himself from insisting on the legal right. But assuming that the act of misconduct was unknown, it cannot be said that the mere fact that it happened eighteen months before, prevents the company from insisting upon their legal right to discharge a person who has so misconducted himself.

BOWEN and FRY, L.JJ. delivered concurring judgments.

ARBITRARY DISMISSALS IN THE FUTURE?

INTERNATIONAL LABOUR ORGANISATION:
RECOMMENDATION NO. 119

('Termination of Employment at the Initiative of the Employer')

Extracts from White Paper (Cmnd. 2548, December 1964) explaining the attitude of the United Kingdom Government.

Some of the provisions of the Recommendation on Termination of Employment (No. 119) apply to all kinds of termination of employment at the initiative of the employer, while others are particularly concerned with redundancy. The underlying principle of the instrument is that 'termination of employment should not take place unless there is a valid reason... connected with the capacity or conduct of the worker or based on the operational requirements of the undertaking, establishment or service.'* The Recommendation lists certain things that, among others, are not to be regarded as valid reasons, e.g., union membership or participation in union activities outside working hours, or with the consent of the employer, within working hours; seeking office as or acting as a worker's representative; the filing in good faith of a complaint against an employer alleging violation of laws or regulations; or race, colour, sex, marital status, religion, political opinion, national extraction or social origin.

Other provisions of the Recommendation concern appeals against termination; period of notice or compensation in lieu; protection of dismissed workers and criteria determining the selection of workers to be affected by redundancy and the re-engagement of workers....

The Recommendation provides that effect may be given to its provisions through national laws or regulations, collective agreements, works rules, arbitration awards, or court decisions or in such other manner consistent with national practice as may be appropriate under national conditions. This flexibility in methods of application is welcome to the United Kingdom, where some of the matters included in the Recommendation are dealt with by voluntary means, whilst others are

* Note: This would apply whether or not notice were given to terminate the employment.

the subject of legislation. For example, the principle that workers should not be dismissed without a valid reason has very general acceptance in practice but has not been made the subject of legislation, whereas minimum periods of notice of termination of employment have been laid down by the Contracts of Employment Act, 1963.

The Government consider that the application of the principles embodied in the Recommendation can play a useful part in promoting a sense of security at work and that this is in the interests both of work-people and of the efficiency of the economy. Certain reservations are, however, necessary in the light of practice in this country, and they are mentioned in the following paragraphs...

The Recommendation... envisages that an appeal by a worker against dismissal should normally be dealt with by appropriate machinery at the level of the undertaking, establishment or service, or established by collective agreement, or, in the absence of such machinery, by a neutral body. It is not the general practice in the United Kingdom for appeals against dismissal to be dealt with through collective machinery or through a neutral body. However, in the docks and—provided that the union supports the employee concerned—in coalmining, and also in a very few individual undertakings, appeals against dismissal may be heard through special joint machinery set up for the purpose. More generally, dismissals are often the subject of trade union representations and of negotiations between employers and trade unions, and in many industries disagreements over dismissals may be dealt with through the established joint procedures for the resolution of disputes.

The Government accept these recommendations. They propose to discuss with representatives of employers and trade unions the provision of procedures to give effective safeguards against arbitrary dismissal.

Paragraph 18 of the Recommendation provides that the instrument shall apply to all branches of economic activity and all categories of workers, except that the following may be excluded from its scope:

(a) workers engaged for a specified period of time or a specified task in cases in which, owing to the nature of the work to be effected, the employment relationship cannot be of indefinite duration;

(b) workers serving a period of probation determined in advance and of reasonable duration;

(c) workers engaged on a casual basis for a short period; and

(d) public servants engaged in the administration of the State, to the extent that constitutional provisions preclude the application of the Recommendation to them...

As regards (d), established civil servants in the United Kingdom have very great security of employment and the interests of temporary civil servants in the event of redundancy are safeguarded by the terms of agreements with the Staff Side of the National Whitley Council, and in the case of industrial civil servants with the appropriate trade unions. However for constitutional reasons it is important that the ultimate right of the Crown to dismiss at its pleasure should not be impaired and it is, therefore, proposed to exclude category (d) from the scope of the Recommendation.

A further exclusion will be made in the case of merchant seamen and fishermen, since the terms of their employment are not appropriate to the application of the Recommendation.

Subject to these reservations the Government accept the Recommendation.

SECTION B

NOTICE TO TERMINATE*

RIORDAN v. WAR OFFICE
[1959] 3 All E.R. 552 (affd. on other grounds C.A. [1960] 3 All E.R. 774n.)

An unestablished civil servant sued for wrongful dismissal. The Crown's right to dismiss at pleasure was upheld in this judgment. The plaintiff had handed in a notice of termination himself which he attempted to withdraw 55 minutes later.

DIPLOCK, J.: ... I think that the regulations relating to the termination of employment must be regarded if not as terms of a contract of employment at least as analogous to the terms of such a contract, and that the giving of a notice terminating the employment, whether by employer or employee, is the exercise of the right under the contract of employment to bring the contract to an end either immediately or in

---

* Note: It has become the practice of many employers to give 'warning notices' of impending dismissal, especially where groups of workers are about to become redundant. In *Morton Sundour Fabrics Ltd* v. *Shaw, The Times*, 26 November 1966, a worker who was given notice that the works would be closing in the near future argued that this was notice to terminate his employment for the purposes of Redundancy Payments Act, 1965, the termination occurring at the end of the period of notice to which he was entitled under the Contracts of Employment Act, 1963. The Divisional Court rejected the contention. The notice was not a notice to terminate at all. Such a notice, Parker, L.C.J. said, must specify the date of termination or at least contain facts from which such a date could be inferred. The reader should therefore carefully distinguish a 'warning notice' from a formal notice to terminate. The point is of particular importance under the Redundancy Payments Act, 1965, *post*, p. 215. See too strikes, *post* p. 525.

the future. It is a unilateral act requiring no acceptance by the other party and, like a notice to quit a tenancy, once given it cannot in my view by withdrawn save by mutual consent.

In re AFRICAN ASSOCIATION LTD & ALLEN
[1910] 1 K.B. 396

A clerk was employed in Africa under a contract which contained the following term: 'Provided always, however, that the employers may at any time hereafter, at their absolute discretion, terminate this engagement at any earlier date than that specified if they may desire to do so.'

LORD ALVERSTONE, C.J.: The employers may in their discretion terminate the engagement at any time, but in my opinion the proper construction to place upon the language of clause 2, particularly when one bears in mind that the agreement relates to service abroad, is that it means that that discretionary power to terminate the engagement at any time can only be exercised after reasonable notice of their intention has been given by the employers.

BRAY, J. delivered a concurring judgment; BUCKNILL, J. agreed with the judgment of LORD ALVERSTONE, C.J.

McCLELLAND v. N.I. GENERAL HEALTH SERVICES BOARD

House of Lords   [1957] 1 W.L.R. 594; [1957] 2 All E.R. 129

The plaintiff was employed as a senior clerk by the defendant board. The terms and conditions of her service laid down various grounds on which she could be dismissed, e.g. 'gross misconduct' or failure to take an oath of allegiance. She could terminate the employment with one month's notice. They tried to terminate her employment on grounds of redundancy with six months' notice. There was no express provision for dismissal on this ground. It was held that the employers could not terminate the employment by notice. It should be noted that the employee obtained the remedy of a declaration.

LORD OAKSEY: Counsel for the respondent in your Lordship's House based their arguments upon the fact that in the case of a general hiring for an indefinite time a master is entitled to give his servant a reasonable notice and contended that the contract in question was a contract of master and servant for a general hiring. It is, no doubt, true that a general hiring without more is terminable on reasonable notice, but, in

6   W C A

my opinion, the contract in question was not a simple contract of general hiring for an indefinite time. It began by an offer of a permanent and pensionable post. That offer did not, of course, conclude a contract but it cannot be ignored in the construction of the contract which was then concluded. That contract incorporated provisions under which the appellant, after a period of probation, was entitled to an annual pension on a contributory basis on completing ten years' service in circumstances of ill health or on attaining the age of sixty, a short service gratuity for five years and other pension rights and allowances for sickness. Moreover, the contract was expressly subject to the September conditions.

The clauses I have set out all contain express powers of termination and, in my opinion, there is no ground for suggesting that it is necessary to imply a further power to terminate the contract in order to give the contract the efficacy which the parties must have intended it to have. With the greatest respect to the Court of Appeal in Northern Ireland and those of your Lordships who take a different view, I think, on the contrary, that to offer an officer a permanent and pensionable post on such terms and then to claim the right to give him notice which will deprive him of all the pension and other rights offered by the express terms of the contract, not only is not a right which the parties must have intended the master to have, but is one which no reasonable person could have contemplated he would claim.

For these reasons I move your Lordships that this appeal be allowed.

LORDS GODDARD and EVERSHED delivered concurring speeches; LORDS TUCKER and KEITH OF AVONHOLM dissented on the grounds that the terms and conditions of service could not be taken as exhaustive on the subject of dismissal, to the exclusion of a right to give notice.

ADAMS v. UNION CINEMAS

Court of Appeal   [1939] 3 All E.R. 136

Adams was employed by the defendants to control 120 cinemas.

DU PARCQ, L.J.: I have felt a little more doubt about the question of the 6 months' notice, but, on reflexion, it seems to me to be clear that there again the judge's decision, not only can be supported, but ought to be supported. The position one has is that this man was employed in most responsible duties, a position which was worth £2000 per annum, in control of all these theatres. It was a most important thing, from his point of view, that he should not be dismissed without reasonable notice, and most important, equally, from the point of view of his employers, that they should not be suddenly left without a controller. In those circumstances, one has an indefinite agreement, which may come to an end by a proper agreement being put forward, but which otherwise, if the defendants do not choose even to tender an agreement, will only come to an end by notice. I do not think, having regard to the importance of it, that one can possibly say that 6 months' notice is too much. I think that it is reasonable. Viewing the case as I do, I think that it is the notice which I myself should have thought the proper one in the circumstances.

ATKINSON, J.: The second point is that, if the plaintiff had not got an agreement for two years, at any rate he had an engagement for one year certain, to date from 28 June. It is said that that is a presumption of law which we are bound to apply. If it be so, it would be wholly contrary to the facts in this case, but I do not myself think that that presumption of law arises, and, if it does, it seems to me that the circumstances displace it....In *Fisher* v. *Dick & Co., Ltd*[1] Branson, J.,...added, at p. 469: 'If I may respectfully say so, they appear to me to state the common sense of the matter. When you are dealing with agreements which are not agreements between agricultural labourers and their employers, there is not the same kind of reason for treating the agreement as a yearly hiring, but rather the contrary'....I think that that all applies here. The agreement contemplated was not one for a year certain at all. It was, as du Parcq, L.J., has put it, an agreement to go on, for a period which might well be less than 12 months, until it was displaced either by a written agreement for a longer period or by a reasonable notice given by one side or the other.

Like du Parcq, L.J., I was rather worried about the length of 6 months' notice. It seems to me that it might be thought that that was rather long notice for an engagement of rather a temporary character. When one remembers, however, the importance of the position and the size of the salary, and the fact that the plaintiff had continued in that position for over 4 months, I am not prepared to differ from the view formed by the judge, who had the evidence before him.

MACKINNON, L.J. delivered a concurring judgment.

[1] [1938] 4 All E.R. 467.

MULHOLLAND v. BEXWELL ESTATES CO.
(1950) 66 2 T.L.R. 764

The plaintiff was employed on trial as general manager of three estate agency companies. He was paid weekly. After six months he was given one week's notice. He was awarded damages on the basis of being entitled to three months' notice, that being the 'reasonable' period in the circumstances.

PARKER, J.: Though it may be surprising it is old law that an employment, an engagement, for an indefinite period is what is called a general hiring for a year unless something is shown to the contrary. In other words, there is a presumption of yearly hiring. Mr Caplan argues that there is really nothing here to rebut that presumption, and that the only possible point which could be taken in rebuttal is the fact that the salary, or the wage, is payable by the week. He referred however, to *Levy* v. *Electrical Wonder Company* ((1893) 9 *The Times* L.R. 495), a case of wrongful dismissal, in which Lord Coleridge, C.J., in summing up to the jury, pointed out to them that the words 'at a salary of £5 per week, payable weekly' did not make it a weekly hiring but only indicated the mode of payment. He then went on, it is to be observed, to refer to other terms of the contract which were far more consistent, if not only so, with a yearly hiring than with a weekly hiring.

The whole of the facts of a case such as this must be considered. Not only, as it seems to me, is the salary payable weekly—though, as I say, that is not in any way conclusive to rebut the presumption: it may only indicate the time and method of payment. It must be remembered that the plaintiff was being taken on (and I do not think that he really denies it; but at any rate I accept the managing director's evidence on this point) on trial. It seems to me that that is far more consistent with a hiring for a period, indefinite, it is true, but not a hiring for a year certain; for if this be treated as a general hiring then it would be quite impossible for the defendants, whatever the plaintiff did, to terminate his employment before 22 January 1951. It seems to me, having regard to the way in which this contract was made, to the parties concerned, and to the method of payments, that I am entitled to treat the presumption of a yearly hiring as rebutted.*

If I am right on that, I come lastly to the question what was reasonable notice. I have very little assistance on this point. I am entitled to bear in mind the decisions—very often the findings of juries and sometimes

* See too *De Stempel* v. *Dunkels* [1938] 1 All E.R. 238 (C.A.).

very old—in regard to what is a reasonable notice in other employments. I think I can also take into consideration that the managing director himself clearly thought a week's notice was reasonable, and that the plaintiff (true, when rather pressed by me) said that he felt that three months would be the sort of notice which he could give if he desired to leave. It seems to me that I must take into consideration the responsibilities involved in the job and the nature of the employment in order to determine what is a reasonable notice. It is to be observed that, although the plaintiff's position is stated to be that of general manager of three companies, when one analyses the position one finds that that gives a very glorified idea of what his duties were. Above all, it is quite clear that whatever he was called he was to work under and to the order of the managing director. After all, it was the latter's business; he had worked up these three companies, and whatever individual he employed was clearly to be under him and to take orders from him.

WILSON v. UCCELLI

(1929) 45 T.L.R. 395

The plaintiff was employed by the defendant as a private tutor to his son. He was summarily dismissed having lost his charge on the Underground Railway.

HUMPHREYS, J.: It was quite impossible to say that the engagement of the plaintiff, who was an educated man—a public school man—was a monthly one. Having regard to his position, to the fact that the service was to be performed abroad, and that both parties contemplated that it would last for several years, he (his Lordship) thought that three month's notice was reasonable, and he, therefore, awarded the plaintiff three months' salary at £25 a month and £3 a week for a corresponding period for board and lodging, or £114 in all.

There were certain subsidiary matters. The plaintiff contended that it was an implied term of his agreement that he should have a month's holiday, and that as he did not have the holiday he was entitled to a month's salary in lieu thereof. He (his Lordship) was not aware of any law which entitled a tutor to any particular holiday or to salary for the period during which he ought to have had a holiday. The plaintiff had suffered from asthma, and went to Mont Dore to undergo the cure. The defendant agreed that his son should accompany him and paid the whole of the expenses. It seemed, therefore, to be somewhat impudent for the plaintiff to suggest that he was entitled to a month's salary in lieu of a holiday which he said he ought to have had.

DAVSON *v.* FRANCE

Westminster County Court   (1959) 109 L.Jo. 526

The plaintiff claimed £14 being certain wages in lieu of notice. He had been engaged to play the trumpet at the defendant's club after an audition at which both the defendant and the bandleader were present. After a few days the plaintiff was given fourteen days' notice, but at the end of the first seven days he was told to stop work in two days' time. The plaintiff claimed that the customary notice for musicians was one of fourteen days.

JUDGE WRIGHT said that he was not sure that it was necessary to decide what was customary as regards notice, because on the facts of the case fourteen days' notice had been given but the plaintiff had not been allowed to work it out. However, on the evidence, he was quite satisfied that there was such a custom of fourteen days' notice where musicians were engaged otherwise than for a single day or a fixed-term engagement, in the absence of any agreement to the contrary. There would be judgment for the amount claimed.

CONTRACTS OF EMPLOYMENT ACT, 1963

1. *The rights of employer and employee to a minimum period of notice.*
(1) The notice required to be given by an employer to terminate the contract of employment of a person who has been continuously employed for twenty-six weeks or more—

(*a*) shall not be less than one week's notice if his period of continuous employment is less than two years, and

(*b*) shall be not less than two week's notice if his period of continuous employment is two years or more but less than five years, and

(*c*) shall be not less than four weeks' notice if his period of continuous employment is five years or more.

(2) The notice required to be given by an employee who has been continuously employed for twenty-six weeks or more to terminate his contract of employment shall be not less than one week.

(3) Any provision for shorter notice in any contract of employment with a person who has been continuously employed for twenty-six weeks or more shall have effect subject to the foregoing subsections, but this section shall not be taken to prevent either party from waiving his right to notice on any occasion, or from accepting a payment in lieu of notice.

(4) Any contract of employment of a person who has been continuously employed for twenty-six weeks or more which is a contract for a

term certain for four weeks or less shall have effect as if it were for an indefinite period and, accordingly, subsections (1) and (2) of this section shall apply to the contract.

(5) Schedule 1 to this Act shall apply for the purposes of this and the next following section for ascertaining the length of an employee's period of employment and whether that period of employment has been continuous.

(6) It is hereby declared that this section does not affect any right of either party to treat the contract as terminable without notice by reason of such conduct by the other party as would have enabled him so to treat it before the passing of this Act....

2. *The rights of employee in period of notice.* (1) If an employer gives notice to terminate the contract of employment of a person who has been continuously employed for twenty-six weeks or more, the provisions of Schedule 2 to this Act shall have effect as respects the liability of the employer for the period of notice required by s. 1 (1) of this Act.

(2) If an employee who has been continuously employed for twenty-six weeks or more gives notices to terminate his contract of employment, the provisions of Schedule 2 to this Act shall have effect as respects the liability of the employer for the period of notice required by s. 1 (2) of this Act.

(3) This section shall not apply in relation to a notice given by the employer or the employee if the notice to be given by the employer to terminate the contract must be at least one week more than the notice required by s. 1 (1) of this Act.

(4) So far as a contract purports to exclude or limit the obligations imposed on an employer by this section it shall be void.

3. *Measure of damages in proceedings against employers.* If an employer fails to give the notice required by s. 1 of this Act the rights conferred by the last foregoing section (with Schedule 2 to this Act) shall be taken into account in assessing his liability for breach of the contract....

SCHEDULE 1

COMPUTATION OF PERIOD OF EMPLOYMENT

Preliminary

1. (1) The employee's period of employment shall be computed in weeks in accordance with this Schedule, and the periods of two and five years mentioned in s. 1 of this Act shall be taken as 104 and 260 weeks respectively.

(2) Save as otherwise expressly provided, the provisions of this Schedule apply to periods before it comes into force as they apply to later periods.

(3) For the purpose of computing an employee's period of employment (but not for any other purpose), the provisions of this Schedule apply to periods during which the employee is engaged in work wholly or mainly outside Great Britain, and periods during which the employee is excluded by or under s. 6 of this Act, as they apply to other periods.

General provisions as to continuity of period of employment

2. Except so far as otherwise provided by the following provisions of this Schedule, any week which does not count under paragraphs 3 to 6 of this Schedule breaks the continuity of the period of employment.

Normal working weeks

3. Any week in which the employee is employed for twenty-one hours or more shall count in computing a period of employment.

Employment governed by contract

4. Any week during the whole or part of which the employee's relations with the employer are governed by a contract of employment which normally involves employment for twenty-one hours or more weekly shall count in computing a period of employment.

Periods in which there is no contract of employment

5. (1) If in any week the employee is, for the whole or part of the week—

(a) incapable of work in consequence of sickness or injury, or

(b) absent from work on account of a temporary cessation of work, or

(c) absent from work in circumstances such that, by arrangement or custom, he is regarded as continuing in the employment of his employer for all or any purposes,

that week shall, notwithstanding that it does not fall under paragraph 3 or paragraph 4 of this Schedule, count as a period of employment.

(2) Not more than twenty-six weeks shall count under paragraph (a) of the foregoing sub-paragraph between any two periods falling under paragraphs 3 and 4 of this Schedule.

(3) Paragraph (*b*) of sub-paragraph (1) of this paragraph shall not apply to a temporary cessation of work on account of a strike in which the employee takes part....*

Change of Employer

10. ...(2) If a trade or business or an undertaking...is transferred from one person to another, the period of employment of an employee in the trade or business or undertaking at the time of the transfer shall count as a period of employment with the transferee, and the transfer shall not break the continuity of the period of employment.

[Sub-paragraphs (3), (4), and (5) make parallel provisions for continuity in the cases, respectively, of modification or transfers of employment under an Act of Parliament; employment by personal representatives on death of an employer; and changes of partners, personal representatives or trustees who are employers.]

SECTION C

COMPENSATION FOR WRONGFUL TERMINATION OR OTHER BREACH†

ADDIS v. GRAMOPHONE COMPANY LTD

House of Lords [1909] A.C. 488

The plaintiff was given six months notice and subsequently was wrongfully dismissed. The question arose as to the proper heads of damage.

LORD LOREBURN, L.C.: To my mind it signifies nothing in the present case whether the claim is to be treated as for wrongful dismissal or not. In any case there was a breach of contract in not allowing the plaintiff to discharge his duties as manager, and the damages are exactly the same in either view. They are, in my opinion, the salary to which the plaintiff was entitled for the six months between October 1905, and April 1906, together with the commission which the jury think he would

---

* On the effect of strikes, see now s. 37 Redundancy Payments Act, 1965, *post*, p. 421. On 5 (1) (*b*) see *Wilson* v. *Courtaulds Ltd* (1966) 1 I.T.R. 442: four months' 'lay off' counted as employment period for continuity; a 'temporary cessation'; *Houston* v. *Murdoch Mackenzie* (1967) 2 I.T.R. 125: cessation must be regarded as 'temporary' by both employee and employer. On (5) 1 (*c*), see *Smith* v. *G. K. Purdy Trawlers Ltd* (1966) 1 I.T.R. 508: chief engineer sailed under separate contract for each voyage, but employment held to be continuous because of shore work done between voyages. Alternatively, the tribunal would have applied 5 (1) (*c*) to the shore periods. Held to be dismissed by reason of redundancy when his coal burning ship was replaced by diesel vessels, see *post*, p. 215.

† As to the remedies of injunction and declaration see *ante*, p. 41 and p. 153.

have earned had he been allowed to manage the business himself. I cannot agree that the manner of dismissal affects these damages. Such considerations have never been allowed to influence damages in this kind of case....If there be a dismissal without notice the employer must pay an indemnity; but that indemnity cannot include compensation either for the injured feelings of the servant, or for the loss he may sustain from the fact that his having been dismissed of itself makes it more difficult for him to obtain fresh employment. The cases relating to a refusal by a banker to honour cheques when he has funds in hand have, in my opinion, no bearing. That class of case has always been regarded as exceptional. And the rule as to damages in wrongful dismissal, or in breach of contract to allow a man to continue in a stipulated service, has always been, I believe, what I have stated. It is too inveterate to be now altered, even if it were desirable to alter it.

Accordingly I think that so much of the verdict of £600 as relates to that head of damages cannot be allowed to stand. As there is an additional dispute how much of it does relate to that head of damages, the best course will be to disallow the £600 altogether, and to state in the order that plaintiff is entitled to be credited, in the account which is to be taken, with salary from October 1905, to April 1906.

As to the £340 I think there was evidence on which the jury were entitled to find that the plaintiff could have earned more commission if he had been allowed to remain as manager.

In the result I respectfully advise your Lordships to order judgment for the plaintiff for £340, with a declaration that he is entitled to be credited, in the account now under investigation, with salary from October 1905, to April 1906, and with all commission on business actually done during that period which he would have been entitled to receive if he had been acting as manager.

LORDS JAMES OF HEREFORD, ATKINSON, GORELL and SHAW OF DUN-FERMLINE delivered concurring speeches; LORD COLLINS dissented and said that exemplary damages could be awarded.

YETTON v. EASTWOODS FROY LTD

[1966] 3 All E.R. 353

The plaintiff had worked all his life for Eastwoods Ltd of which he had become managing director in 1960. Eastwoods Ltd was taken over by another company, which sold part of the business to a third company. This part the defendant company acquired, and combined with a similar business. The plaintiff had been told by the third company that he would be required until retiring age. In 1964 his contract was replaced by a five-year contract with the defendant company as joint managing director with another person. But early in 1965, the company told him that it had been decided to appoint a director of the third company as managing director of the company; and he and his co-managing director were offered posts as *assistant* managing directors at their existing salaries. He objected; made a request for an extension of his five-year contract, which was refused; and eventually dismissed. The offer of assistant managing director was repeated, but he again refused it. His salary under his contract was £7500 per annum. He successfully sued for damages for wrongful dismissal.

BLAIN, J.: The basic principle of damages is *restitutio in integrum*: the plaintiff should have what he has lost through the defendants' fault but, of course, if a plaintiff in fact, in the case of a contract of service, earns something elsewhere through being at liberty so to do, then he has lost that much less as the consequence of the default. Moreover if he can minimize his loss by a reasonable course of conduct, he should do so, though the onus is on the defaulting defendant to show that it could be, or could have been, done and is not being, and has not been, done. Thus, the opportunity to reduce damages by finding reasonable (I repeat reasonable) alternative employment, should be taken and, indeed, sought, whether such employment is by the same defaulting employer or by someone else; in either case the test being whether it is reasonable to refuse it or not in the circumstances of each case. So that no one of the decided cases is necessarily binding in the circumstances of other cases, though great help is to be found in applying the principles by having a look at them....

In *Brace* v. *Calder*[1] the plaintiff had been an employee of a partnership comprising four partners under a service agreement. The partnership was dissolved during the term of the agreement at the instance of the partners, and a majority of the Court of Appeal held that such dissolution operated as a wrongful dismissal of the plaintiff. He could have mitigated his damage by taking employment under the new partnership, which happened to be two of the four original partners, and he declined to do so, and he lost his case on an award of nominal damages. The report does not indicate why he declined, but as he was awarded nominal damages only, I must assume that the refusal was regarded as unreasonable in the circumstances of that case.

[1] [1895–99] All E.R. Rep. 1196; [1895] 2 Q.B. 253.

Then I was referred to *Payzu, Ltd* v. *Saunders*[1] which was a case of breach of contract for delivery of goods under a contract of sale.... However there are passages which I find of some assistance to read. In the course of Bankes, L.J.'s, judgment,[2] he quoted the words of Lord Haldane, L.C., in *British Westinghouse Electric and Manufacturing Co., Ltd* v. *Underground Electric Rys. Co. of London, Ltd*[3] where Lord Haldane said: 'The fundamental basis is thus compensation for pecuniary loss naturally flowing from the breach; but this first principle is qualified by a second, which imposes on a plaintiff the duty of taking all reasonable steps to mitigate the loss consequent on the breach, and debars him from claiming any part of the damage which is due to his neglect to take such steps.'

Bankes, L.J., then quoted James, L.J., in *Dunkirk Colliery Co.* v. *Lever*[4] and then himself put the matter (if I may say with respect) most succinctly in this way:[5] 'It is plain that the question what is reasonable for a person to do in mitigation of his damages cannot be a question of law, but must be one of fact in the circumstances of each particular case. There may be cases where as matter of fact it would be unreasonable to expect a plaintiff, in view of the treatment he has received from the defendant, to consider any offer made. If he had been rendering personal services and had been dismissed after being accused in presence of others of being a thief, and if after that his employer had offered to take him back into his service, most persons would think he was justified in refusing the offer, and that it would be unreasonable to ask him in this way to mitigate the damages in an action of wrongful dismissal. But that is not to state a principle of law, but a conclusion of fact to be arrived at on a consideration of all the circumstances of the case. Counsel for the plaintiffs complained that the defendant had treated his clients so badly that it would be unreasonable to expect them to listen to any proposition that she might make. I do not agree. In my opinion each party to the contract was ready to accuse the other of conduct unworthy of a high commercial reputation, and there was nothing to justify the appellants in refusing to consider the defendant's offer. I think the learned judge came to a right conclusion on the facts, and that the appeal must be dismissed.'

The last words of a short concurring judgment of Scrutton, L.J.,

---

[1] [1918–19] All E.R. Rep. 219; [1919] 2 K.B. 581.
[2] [1918–19] All E.R. Rep. at p. 220; [1919] 2 K.B. at p. 588.
[3] [1911–13] All E.R. Rep. 63 at p. 69; [1912] A.C. 673 at p. 689.
[4] (1878), 9 Ch.D. 20 at p. 25.
[5] [1918–19] All E.R. Rep. at p. 221; [1919] 2 K.B. at p. 588.

read:[1] 'In certain cases of personal service it may be unreasonable to expect a plaintiff to consider an offer from the other party who has grossly injured him; but in commercial contracts it is generally reasonable to accept an offer from the party in default. However, it is always a question of fact. About the law there is no difficulty.'

Addis v. *Gramophone Co., Ltd,*[2] a well known House of Lords authority, is authority for the proposition that a dismissed servant cannot claim for damages for injured feelings or (to quote Lord Atkinson's own opinion in that case[3]) 'in respect of the harsh and humiliating way in which he was dismissed', but counsel for the plaintiff is not advancing any such head of damages in this case, and I do not regard *Addis* as ruling out the circumstances of dismissal as relevant in so far as they affect a dismissed servant's state of mind when he has to decide whether he should accept alternative employment with the same employer. Indeed, the dicta of Scrutton, L.J., and of Bankes, L.J., in the *Payzu* case[4]—that is why I have just read them—could hardly have been uttered in forgetfulness of such a case as *Addis*.

The last case in point of time to which I have been referred is *Shindler* v. *Northern Raincoat Co., Ltd.*[5]...Now those cases as cited afford guidance only, but very clear guidance. As I see the matter, it is a plain question of fact for the court in any particular case, whether any particular refusal to accept alternative employment which would reduce a plaintiff's loss is a reasonable or an unreasonable refusal, and factually, even if not as a strict matter of law, personal factors clearly are more likely to be of weight or are likely to be of greater weight in cases of personal services than in what I call (for want of a better word) soulless cases of sale of goods contracts where money may often be the only important factor. Certainly personal factors do not have to be ignored in the making up of a dismissed servant's mind when he comes to make a decision reasonable or unreasonable.

Now to the position of the plaintiff in this case and to the first of those two contentions. As I have said, the first question is whether he acted unreasonably in refusing the offer in the defendants' solicitors' letter of 26 March 1965.

[His Lordship reviewed the facts relating to the offer, including the fact that it involved an 'important reduction in status', and continued:]

[1] [1918–19] All E.R. Rep. at p. 221; [1919] 2 K.B. at p. 589.
[2] [1908–10] All E.R. Rep. 1; [1909] A.C. 488.
[3] [1908–10] All E.R. Rep. at p. 4; [1909] A.C. at p. 493.
[4] [1918–19] All E.R. Rep. 219; [1919] 2 K.B. 581.
[5] [1960] 2 All E.R. 239; *post*, p. 175.

I unhesitatingly find that it was perfectly reasonable for the plaintiff to refuse that offer.

That, of course, does not absolve him, if he is to obtain his full damages, from the need to act reasonably to mitigate those damages elsewhere or thereafter. What did he do? The evidence about this was reliable, though not voluminous. He made some fifty-seven applications for employment in answer to advertisements within a twelve month period from April 1965 to April 1966. He made also a number of applications (I think eight altogether) or himself inserted press advertisements, those being listed separately because they were not in answer to advertisements. Also, he wrote to some twenty-four people with whom he was in personal contact, that being a little later, in fact appreciably later, from December last onwards. In terms of remuneration he first started as an applicant in the £8000 to £10,000 a year class, telling the court that he would probably have accepted £7500 if it had been put forward to him. It was not unreasonable, in my view, in view of his past history, to start at a high level. He said he was not expecting endowment or top hat benefits as well as salary because of his age. In about September 1965, he came down to £5000 and a little later to £4000, and he told me that he never went below that. Finally, he deliberately refrained from following up a possible job—that is all we know about it—at £2500 a year early in October 1965. As I have said, I take the view that he was right to try for something like the previous salary in the early stages. Indeed, supposing he had taken an appointment at something very much less, I might have had to try an argument why he had not set his sights higher. His achievements justify this, in my view, even though they were confined to work in one group. That is a circumstance which might be thought by some potential employers to limit his potential versatility, it might be thought by others to be a tribute to his reliability, his integrity, and in view of the high position on the ladder which he had reached, to his sheer ability and value to those who knew his work. I tend to think myself—this is hindsight, and in any case it was his mind (so long as it was a genuine and reasonably exercised mind) that matters—that he might have started to drop his sights a little sooner, but I see no reason to assume that he would have obtained any employment, which he has in fact failed to obtain thus far.*

* Note: *Jackson* v. *Hayes Candy Ltd* [1938] 4 All E.R. 587, where refusal of an offer of re-engagement at a lower salary was held to be reasonable for purposes of the rules on mitigation of damage. Compare the common law rules on mitigation with the statutory pressure to take 'suitable' employment under s. 22 National Insurance Act, 1965: *post*, p. 210.

Doing the best that I can in a necessarily arbitrary way, I will assume that it would be fair to guess that after the conclusion of this litigation and the passage of a month or so, I will say by the end of the summer, he will be able to find employment at an average rate of not less than £3000 per year, on average over the remaining relevant period. That period I put as from the end of August 1966, to the end of the period of employment under the contract that was broken, that is to say, the end of March 1968. I think that means nineteen months at an average of £250 per month. If that is right, it would reduce the full claim by some £4750. I shall be told if there should be any tax adjustment to that; but before I formally deal with the consequences of that, I think it right to say this. I have no doubt that in commercial and City circles the views of elderly lawyers on non-legal matters may not carry great weight, but having seen the plaintiff in the witness box and having read in correspondence and in minutes how he conducted himself in the trying circumstances of the disputes and knowing what I do of the history of his career, I do not myself doubt that his commercial value is in truth much higher than that figure of £3000 a year which I have mentioned. I have thought it right to go on that figure as a matter of legal assessment of damages allowing for the risks of not finding suitable work at suitable times in suitable circumstances. It does not mean that that is my assessment of his value, which I do not doubt is very much higher, and I say that in case the contrary should be assumed in any circumstances to which it may be relevant hereafter.

Unless there are other factors, such as taxation matters,[1] that would result in judgment for £25,250.

SHINDLER v. NORTHERN RAINCOAT CO. LTD

[1960] 1 W.L.R. 1038

The plaintiff was managing director of the defendant company under a ten-year contract. Loyds Co. who owned the share capital offered him alternative employment to which he seemed agreeable and sold the capital to M. Co. who did not want to continue his employment. Nothing came of this offer of fresh employment. Later he was removed from office, and Loyds Co. again made offers of fresh employment which he refused.

DIPLOCK, J.: It does, however, seem to me that all five of their

---

[1] The parties had agreed an appropriate reduction in respect of income tax (see on this question *post*, p. 190).

Lordships in the *Southern Foundries* case[1] were agreed upon one principle of law which is vital to the defendants' contention in this case. That principle of law is that laid down in the case of *Stirling* v. *Maitland*,[2] where Cockburn, L.J., said: 'if a party enters into an arrangement which can only take effect by the continuance of a certain existing set of circumstances, there is an implied engagement on his part that he shall do nothing of his own motion to put an end to that state of circumstances under which alone the arrangement can be operative.' Applying that respectable principle to this case, there is an implied engagement on the part of the company that it will do nothing of its own motion to put an end to the state of circumstances which enables the plaintiff to continue as managing director: that is to say, an undertaking that it will not revoke his appointment as a director and will not resolve that his tenure of office be determined....

The position was that, on the correspondence, the defendants had, by the letter dated 2 September 1958, told the plaintiff that his service with them would terminate not later than 30 November 1958. That was a wrongful repudiation of contract which the plaintiff had an opportunity either to accept by rescinding the contract and thus entitle himself to sue for damages, or to continue to treat the contract as subsisting and to continue to serve as managing director. He elected to do the latter and there was accordingly no breach of the contract on which he could sue until his office as director was terminated on 21 November, and between 2 September and 21 November the defendants had a *locus poenitentiae* in which they could have changed their minds and decided to go on employing him. It seems to me that on a matter of law it cannot be said that there is any duty on the part of the plaintiff to mitigate his damages before there had been any breach, which he has accepted as a breach.

The objection in fact seems to be this. In his solicitor's letter dated 27 September 1958, the plaintiff expressed willingness to accept, or, as it was put, was 'not unwilling to accept', the alternative post offered by Loyds Retailers Ltd, provided his functions were clearly defined and the letter continued: 'the acceptance is on the strict understanding that in so doing he does not in any way prejudice his claims arising out of the breach of his contract...' The letter in reply, dated 1 October, stated that the proviso 'is of course not acceptable to our clients...' Therefore, the only offer which was before him at that moment was an offer

---

[1] [1940] A.C. 701.
[2] (1865) 5 B. & S. 840. [L.J. in report; but correctly C.J.]

of employment on the terms that he should not act on such legal righ. as he had for damages for breach of contract against the defendants. It seems to me that it was not reasonable to ask him, or to require him, to accept such an offer. That matter is self evident.

The second contention of the defendants is that whatever may be said about the earlier offers, namely, those made in February and March 1959, after he had been dismissed, there were further offers which ought to have been accepted by the plaintiff if he were acting reasonably. The plaintiff invites me to say that these offers were not sincerely made. They were merely offers designed to reduce the possible damages in this litigation. Since that charge has been made, I think it right to say that I am satisfied that these offers were genuine offers and that Loyds considered that the plaintiff was a man with a flair who could be useful to them in their business and they were prepared, despite what had gone before, to make use of his services. But the fact that I have found that the offers were genuine offers, of course, does not conclude the matter, because I have to consider whether it was reasonable for the plaintiff to refuse them. I may have indicated that I have no great moral admiration for the attitude which the plaintiff has taken in this case, but I have still got to consider, using common sense, whether it was reasonable in all the circumstances to expect the plaintiff to accept the offer of employment from Loyds made in February and March 1959. The plaintiff said that he thought that the offers were not genuine, and I have no doubt that he did so think.

It seems to me that in all the circumstances, having regard to the row which had taken place between the plaintiff and Mr Symons of Loyds at their last significant meeting, to the fact that there had already been litigation about the calling of the meeting on the question of the dismissal of the plaintiff, to the fact that the litigation in this action had already reached the stage at which the pleadings were being delivered thick and fast, and to the fact that the letter offering the employment was not sent, as it might well have been at that stage, through the solicitors; and having regard especially to the fact that the employment was one of personal services where the plaintiff would have to act under the direction of Mr Amelan, the managing director of Loyds, and Mr Symons. I think as a matter of common sense it would not be right to say that the plaintiff was unreasonable, at that time in those circumstances, in refusing the offer.

LINDSAY *v.* QUEEN'S HOTEL CO.

[1919] 1 K.B. 212

A domestic servant gave one month's notice; and six days before she was due to leave was wrongfully dismissed. The customary damages were one month's wages; but the employer contended her damages should be limited to her wages until the date on which she would have left. This contention of the employer was upheld; but in addition the plaintiff was awarded the value of six days' board and lodging.

BRAY, J.: The county court judge held that the plaintiff was entitled to a month's wages in addition to the wages due to her. There is a custom that the damages ordinarily recoverable by a servant who has been wrongfully dismissed are a month's wages, and the reason is that a master has the right by custom to dismiss a servant at any time on payment of a month's wages, in addition to whatever is due for wages. But in this case by reason of the notice which the plaintiff herself had given, the contract of service would in any event have terminated six days after the date when the plaintiff was dismissed. I do not think that there is any law or custom by which the ordinary rule of a month's wages as damages applies to a case of this sort. I think the damages must be ascertained according to the principles applicable to any other case of wrongful dismissal, that is to say, the damages are the actual pecuniary loss which has been sustained. Then, what was the plaintiff's loss ? She has lost the value of six days' board and lodging, in addition to wages up to 4 March.

AVORY, J., delivered a concurring judgment.

MANUBENS *v.* LEON

[1919] 1 K.B. 208

The plaintiff was employed by the defendant as a hairdresser's assistant at a weekly wage and commission on the takings. It was also an implied term of the contract that he should be at liberty to receive tips from customers. The plaintiff was wrongfully dismissed without notice.

LUSH, J.: The plaintiff was entitled, upon the defendant's breach of the contract, to recover for the loss he had sustained by reason of the breach, the loss being measured by, or represented by, the damages flowing from the breach within the contemplation of the parties to the contract. It was clearly within the contemplation of the parties to the contract that the plaintiff would receive these tips. The deputy county court judge found that it was an implied term of the contract that the plaintiff should be allowed to receive tips. The defendant, therefore, knew and contemplated, when the contract was entered into, that if it should be broken by the plaintiff being summarily dismissed, the plaintiff would sustain a loss in respect of tips which he would otherwise have received. I do not say that the defendant undertook to allow the plaintiff to cut the hair of customers, but the contract was that the defendant would not prevent the plaintiff from receiving the remuneration which he would have received in the ordinary course if he fulfilled the duty for which he was engaged.*

BAILHACHE, J., concurred in the opinion of LUSH, J.

LAVARACK *v.* WOODS OF COLCHESTER LTD

Court of Appeal   [1966] 3 All E.R. 683

The plaintiff entered into a service agreement for five years with the defendants in 1962 at £4000 per annum, plus such bonus as the directors determined from time to time. He also agreed not to engage in other concerns (except as holder of quoted shares). In 1964 he was wrongfully dismissed. He immediately accepted employment with Martindale Co. at the low salary of £1500 per annum, and bought half the shares in that company, hoping to improve the value of his holding by his work. He also invested £14,000 in Ventilation Co., a company competing with the defendants and formed by a colleague who had also left them in 1964. In 1965 the defendants discontinued their bonus scheme, replacing it by fixed higher salaries. Had he stayed, the plaintiff's salary would have been £5000. Two questions arose in assessing damages: (i) Was the plaintiff entitled to £2000, two years' increase of salary in lieu of the discretionary bonus payments? (ii) Should the plaintiff give credit for prospective profits on his holding in

---

* Contrast *McGrath* v. *de Soissons* (1962) 112 L.Jo. 60 (County Court), where an architect employed at £2000 a year who had lawfully been given one month's notice, claimed for the value of luncheon vouchers. When at work he was entitled to such vouchers to the value of 15s. per week. The vouchers were not given to employees who were on holiday or who were away ill. Judge Leslie held that it was an implied term in the contract of employment that the vouchers were to be given only to employees who were actually at work. His employers were not obliged to find work for the plaintiff during the period of his notice. The plaintiff was not therefore entitled to their value in addition to the month's salary paid to him in lieu of notice.

See now *White* v. *Bloomfield Ltd, The Guardian,* 8 December 1966: manager appointed to 65 or until he elected to retire had got 'rather set in his ways'. The defendants dismissed him for misconduct. Roskill J. rejected the allegation of misconduct and awarded £2379 damages for wrongful dismissal, much of that sum representing loss of a pension at £6 a week. (Compare, on misconduct and efficiency, the decisions *post,* p. 239.)

Ventilation or in the likely improvement in value of Martindale shares ? (He did not dispute that credit must be given for his drawings of salary from Martindale.)

DIPLOCK, L.J.: The learned master took the view that if the defendants had retained the plaintiff in their employment—and, presumably, despite their manifest desire to dismiss him, also retained a favourable opinion of his merits—his salary would have been raised by £1000 per annum. The learned master accordingly treated his salary as being £5000 per annum for two years after 31 March 1965, instead of the contractual sum of £4000 per annum. I think that he was wrong to do this. I accept as correct the principle stated by Scrutton, L.J., in *Abrahams* v. *Herbert Reiach, Ltd*,[1] that in an action for breach of contract...a defendant is not liable for not doing that which he is not bound to do, has been generally accepted as correct and in my experience at the Bar and on the Bench has been repeatedly applied in subsequent cases. The law is concerned with legal obligations only and the law of contract only with legal obligations created by mutual agreement between contractors—not with the expectations, however reasonable, of one contractor that the other will do something that he has assumed no legal obligation to do. So if the contract is broken or wrongfully repudiated, the first task of the assessor of damages is to estimate as best he can what the plaintiff would have gained in money or money's worth if the defendant had fulfilled his legal obligations and had done no more. Where there is an anticipatory breach by wrongful repudiation, this can at best be an estimate, whatever the date of the hearing. It involves assuming that what has not occurred and never will occur has occurred or will occur, i.e., that the defendant has since the breach performed his legal obligations under the contract, and, if the estimate is made before the contract would otherwise have come to an end, that he will continue to perform his legal obligations thereunder until the due date of its termination. But the assumption to be made is that the defendant has performed or will perform his legal obligations under his contract with the plaintiff and nothing more. What these legal obligations are and what is their value to the plaintiff may depend on the occurrence of events extraneous to the contract itself and where this is so, the probability of their occurrence is relevant to the estimate.

The cases cited by Lord Denning, M.R., only one of which was referred to in the argument at the hearing, do not in my respectful

[1] [1922] 1 K.B. at p. 482.

view involve any departure from this principle. In *Richardson* v. *Mellish*,[1] the contract sued on obliged the defendants in the events that happened to appoint the plaintiff as master of a vessel for two voyages so far as such appointment lay within their power. Their power to do so was dependent on the approval of the East India Company and, of course, on the continued existence of the vessel and of the plaintiff himself. It was argued that, because the plaintiff's right to employment was dependent on these contingencies extraneous to the contract, he could not recover damages for the loss of the second voyage which had not yet started when the action came on for trial. It is not surprising that this argument failed. *Inchbald* v. *Western Neilgherry Coffee, Tea & Cinchona Plantation Co., Ltd*,[2] was a case of anticipatory breach in which the defendants by their own act put it out of their power to perform their contractual obligations. So was *Brace* v. *Calder*.[3] In *Turner* v. *Goldsmith*,[4] it was held that on the true construction of the contract the defendants undertook to provide the plaintiff with the opportunity of earning commission for five years and that the event which happened, viz., a fire at their factory, did not absolve them from this obligation. In *Manubens* v. *Leon*,[5] it was held to be an implied term of the contract that the plaintiff should be given the opportunity of earning tips from customers. This was an example of a contract under which one party accepted a legal obligation to give the other party an opportunity of obtaining a benefit from a third party. *Chaplin* v. *Hicks*,[6] which was cited in argument, is the well-known instance of a contract under which the defendant assumed a legal obligation to give the plaintiff a chance of winning a prize in a competition. The only question argued was whether the damages for loss of a chance were too speculative to be capable of estimation. Under the contract the final selection of the prize winners was left to the defendant himself but it was accepted by his counsel that he was under an implied obligation to make a *bona fide* selection based on the merits of the candidates.

The events extraneous to the contract, on the occurrence of which the legal obligations of a defendant to a plaintiff thereunder are dependent, may include events which are within the control of the defendant: for instance, his continuing to carry on business, even though

---

[1] [1823–24] All E.R. Rep. 258; (1824), 2 Bing. 229.
[2] [1861–73] All E.R. Rep. 436; (1864), 17 C.B.N.S. 733.
[3] [1895–99] All E.R. Rep. 1196; [1895] 2 Q.B. 253.
[4] [1891–94] All E.R. Rep. 384; [1891] 1 Q.B. 544.
[5] [1918–19] All E.R. Rep. 792; [1919] 1 K.B. 208.
[6] [1911–13] All E.R. Rep. 224; [1911] 2 K.B. 786.

he has not assumed by his contract a direct legal obligation to the plaintiff to do so. Where this is so, one must not assume that he will cut off his nose to spite his face and so control these events as to reduce his legal obligations to the plaintiff by incurring greater loss in other respects. That would not be the mode of performing the contract which is 'the least burdensome to the defendant'.

The decision of Phillimore, J., in *Bold* v. *Brough Nicholson & Hall, Ltd*,[1] is an example of this and does not involve any departure from the principle that the injured party is entitled to be compensated only for the loss of those benefits which he would have been legally entitled to claim if his contract had been performed. There the plaintiff was employed on terms whereby he was legally entitled to claim pension contributions from his employers so long as a pension scheme for their employees was continued. The employers had a right to discontinue the scheme as a whole, but no discretion to withhold contributions in respect of the plaintiff so long as the scheme continued. Their relevant undertaking was in effect: 'If as a matter of general business policy we continue the scheme, in that event we will pay contributions for you.' They had not in fact discontinued the scheme by the time when the plaintiff's action for damages for wrongful dismissal was brought: there was, therefore, no question that if his contract of employment had been performed up to that date, he would have been legally entitled to claim his pension contributions under the scheme. As respects the balance of the unexpired period of his service agreement, Phillimore, J., was faced with the familiar task of estimating what his legal entitlement to pension contributions would be likely to be if his contract had been performed during that period, and that depended on the likelihood that the event would occur on which his entitlement to pension contributions under his contract would have ceased. The employers' discretion to continue or discontinue the pensions scheme was not a discretion as to the manner of performing their contract of service with the plaintiff but a discretion as to the way in which they would conduct their business as a whole. On this the amount which they would be under a legal liability to pay to the plaintiff under his contract of service depended—in the same way as the amount which they would be under a legal liability to pay to employees remunerated in whole or in part by commission would depend on the exercise of their discretion as to expansion or contraction of their trade in a particular article or as to its price. The plaintiff was accordingly entitled to be

[1] [1963] 3 All E.R. 849.

recompensed for the likelihood that his employers would have continued to conduct their business as a whole in such a way as to produce the event which would have entitled him to claim pension contributions under his service agreement if it had been performed.

This case is to be contrasted with *Beach* v. *Read Corrugated Cases, Ltd*,[1] where under the contract of employment the employers had an option to discontinue retirement contributions to the plaintiff whether or not the general scheme continued. The likelihood of their continuing the general scheme was thus irrelevant to their legal obligation to the plaintiff. They could perform their contract in the manner least burdensome to themselves by discontinuing his retirement contributions.

In the present case if the defendants had continued their bonus scheme, it may well be that on the true construction of this contract of employment the plaintiff would have been entitled to be recompensed for the loss of the bonus to which he would have been likely to be legally entitled under his service agreement until its expiry. But it is unnecessary to decide this. They were under no contractual obligation to him to continue the scheme and in fact it was discontinued. His legal entitlement under the contract on which he sues would thus have been limited after 31 March 1965, to his salary of £4000 per annum. And there, in my view, is the end of the matter. I know of no principle on which he can claim as damages for breach of one service agreement compensation for remuneration which might have become due under some imaginary future agreement which the plaintiffs did not make with him but might have done if they wished. If this were right, in every action for damages for wrongful dismissal, the plaintiff would be entitled to recover not only the remuneration that he would have received during the currency of his service agreement but also some additional sum for loss of the chance of its being renewed on its expiry.

RUSSELL, L.J. concurred, and on question (ii) said, with the agreement of DIPLOCK, L.J.: I turn to the question of the Ventilation company and the plaintiff's investment therein. I can see no justification for considering this investment as of any relevance to the damage occasioned by the wrongful dismissal. It was an investment of money and nothing more. Its profitability or otherwise cannot be attributed to his release from his obligation to devote his time to the service of the defendants; because such minimal time as he devoted to the affairs of the Ventilation company cannot seriously be regarded as having been made available

[1] [1956] 2 All E.R. 652.

to him by his dismissal. It is of course true that during his employment he was barred from such investment in a company carrying on this particular type of business, which is in France in competition with the defendants. But that does not suffice to entitle the defendants to set off any improvement in the value of the plaintiff's shareholding against his loss of salary and bonus. It is simply a question of turning his private money or credit to account, and not his time and work. It is no different from an investment which he could have made during his continued service.

Finally, there is the question whether any and what deduction should be made from the damage suffered on account not only of his salary earned and expected in the period from Martindale, but also on account of the undoubted fact that the expenditure of the time released to him by the wrongful dismissal has enabled him by his work and management during that time to enhance the value of the half interest in Martindale that he bought for £1500 shortly after his dismissal. I agree that account should be taken of this, though of necessity a fairly high degree of estimation is involved. The master held that in all the circumstances it was reasonable that the plaintiff should go into Martindale on the terms on which he did, rather than hawk his services around. One of the reasons for saying that it was reasonable is that avowedly the plaintiff was hoping to gain in part by improving by his own efforts the value of his holding as well as, in other part, by a relatively low salary. To the extent that this hope has been fulfilled in the relevant 2⅔ years, it seems right to set it against his loss of salary from the defendants.

LORD DENNING, M.R. concurred as to (ii), but dissented as to question (i).

NATIONAL COAL BOARD v. GALLEY

Court of Appeal   [1958] 1 W.L.R. 16

The defendant was a deputy employed by the Board under a written contract. By clause 4 the defendant declared that he 'will serve the board as regularly as the state of trade and interruptions from accident or repairs to its mines and works or the non-arrival of wagons or general holidays will from time to time permit and that my wages shall be regulated by such national agreement and the county wages agreement for the time being in force and that this contract of service shall be subject to those agreements and to any other agreements relating to or in connexion with or subsidiary to the wages agreement and to statutory provisions for the time being in force affecting the same.' In 1952, his trade union (N.A.C.O.D.S.) negotiated a variation of the system then current which included working voluntary shifts on Saturdays at over-time rates, a practice which had started as an emergency measure in 1947. The new agreement, which was subsequently recorded in writing, provided for deputies to have an upstanding weekly wage to include overtime. Clause 12 included the following words... 'deputies shall work such days...as may reasonably be required by the management.' Contrary to expectation overtime working on Saturdays did not soon become unnecessary. By 1957 when the miners had received sub-stantial wage-increases compared to the deputies and the latter were still working long hours without overtime, the deputies were very dis-satisfied. As a result they put a ban on working the Saturday shifts. This meant that no productive work was possible in the mines on Saturdays. After two months the plaintiffs brought in substitute deputies at £3. 18s. 2d.* each and the Saturday voluntary shift was continued. Over the period of the ban the plaintiff's loss of production was well over £3000. The plaintiff brought an action for damages for breach of contract.

PEARCE, L. J. (delivering the judgment of the court): The judge thought that, since one of the objects of Nacods was to negotiate the wages and conditions of all members and the defendant was a member of the local trade union which was itself a member of Nacods, the defen-dant was individually bound by the Nacods agreement. But in any event, by the defendant's personal contract his wages were to be regulated by national agreements for the time being in force and the contract was to be subject to those agreements; and therefore, since the Nacods agree-ment was a national agreement, the defendant was bound by it. 'He has', continued the judge, 'in fact accepted it and worked under it. He has taken the advantages of it and accepted the responsibilities of it for a period of some four years before this particular trouble arose. On the point that the agreement itself was not properly made, I think the com-plete answer would be that it is expressly admitted in the defence that the Coal Board, the plaintiffs, and the union did enter into an agreement which in fact contains the vital matters which are in dispute here.'

Mr Gardiner contends that the judge was wrong in holding that the defendant was personally bound by the Nacods agreement. If that point fell to be decided it might well be a matter of some difficulty. But, as the judge said, it is clear that the defendant's personal contract of service is

* The figure is 10d. at p. 21 of W.L.R., but 2d. at p. 29.

regulated by the Nacods agreement, and the defendant by working on the terms of the Nacods agreement has entered into an agreement which contains the term now in dispute.

The defendant next contends that, even though the Nacods agreement was applicable to the defendant's employment, yet it had no contractual force, because it was too vague. It is an industrial agreement, he argues, covering a wide area, with no intention that it shall have a specific or enforceable effect. Collieries differ, and what is reasonable in one will be unreasonable in another. The court has no yardstick to measure what are reasonable requirements. For instance, the stringency of those requirements depends on the number of deputies employed. It is a case within the principle of *May and Butcher* v. *The King*[1] rather than *Foley* v. *Classique Coaches Ltd.*[2]

But it seems to us, on a consideration of the Nacods agreement, that it was meant to have a binding effect. Realising the difficulties inherent in the situation, it provided for discussions, if it appeared to be working out unfairly for the deputies. To define with exactitude what are the duties of a servant is no easy task. The court will supply an implied condition as to reasonableness in many contracts where duties are not fully defined, as in *Hillas & Co. Ltd.* v. *Arcos Ltd*[3] and *Foley* v. *Classique Coaches Ltd.*[4]

Mr Gardiner also relies on the provision in clause 15 for discussion in the event of complaints. He contends that this is typical of an industrial agreement not intended to be enforceable in the courts. We do not, however, see how in principle such a provision differs from that in *Foley* v. *Classique Coaches Ltd*[5] which provided for the price to be agreed between the parties. It may be that discussion is a condition precedent to action, but once discussion is repudiated or fails the matter falls to be determined by the courts. Moreover, the defendant is in this further difficulty. He is asserting that the agreement as a whole exists, while seeking to deny the enforceability of clause 12. If clause 12 is too vague to be enforceable the whole agreement is not legally binding on either side: see *Bishop & Baxter Ltd* v. *Anglo-Eastern Trading Co. Ltd.*[6]

In this contract the parties have expressly provided that reasonableness shall be the test. The fact that it is difficult to decide in a given case, should not deter the court from deciding what is a reasonable requirement by a master in the light of the surrounding circumstances. In our

[1] [1934] 2 K.B. 17n.   [2] [1934] 2 K.B. 1.
[3] (1932) 147 L.T. 503.   [4] [1934] 2 K.B. 1.   [5] Ibid.
[6] [1944] K.B. 12; 60 T.L.R. 37; [1943] 2 All E.R. 598.

view, therefore, the judge was right in deciding that the term as to working was legally binding.

We come now to the central point in this appeal, namely, whether the defendant became in breach of his contract of employment when he refused to obey his employer's request to work the Saturday voluntary shift on 16 June 1956.... Ultimately the question must be whether the defendant himself was being required to work reasonable hours. If, of course, he was being required to work longer hours than other deputies, that, in the absence of some exceptional circumstances, would be evidence that the requirement made on him was unreasonable. There is, however, no suggestion of that in this case.

[His Lordship reviewed the evidence and said that the court had come to the conclusion that there was no evidence to justify the contentions that the defendant was being required to work in breach of the 1952 agreement. He continued:] Two points arise on damages.

The first is the question of whether in assessing damage the court can take into account matters that occurred after the issue of the writ.... It is not contended that apart from the provisions of R.S.C., Ord. 36, r. 58, there would be power to take account of the breaches of contract on Saturdays subsequent to the writ.

The terms of the rule are: 'Where damages are to be assessed in respect of any continuing cause of action they shall be assessed down to the time of the assessment'....

Here the obligation broken by the defendant was the obligation to work the Saturday voluntary shift every other Saturday. The defendant having failed to perform this obligation on Saturday, 16 June 1956, the writ in the action was issued on 21 June. Can it be said that the defendant's failure thereafter to work the Saturday voluntary shift on each of the alternate Saturdays on which it was his turn to do so was a continuation of the cause of action constituted by his failure to work the Saturday voluntary shift on 16 June? We cannot see that it was.... The fact that the defendant prior to 16 June manifested an intention not to work the Saturday voluntary shift any more, coupled with his actual failure to do so on 16 June, might have entitled the plaintiffs to treat the contract as repudiated and to claim damages on that footing, but they did not do so. They chose to allow the contract to remain in force, and while it stood their cause of action in respect of his failure to work the Saturday voluntary shift on any given Saturday when it was his turn to do so arose if and when he failed to work the shift on that day and not otherwise. A continuing cause of action is not in our view constituted by repeated breaches of recurring obligations nor by intermittent breaches of a continuing obligation....

The last point which arises concerns the measure of damages. The judge found that the plaintiffs had proved a loss of profit of £535 due to the impossibility of working the Saturday voluntary shift on 16 June 1956. He then went on to hold that the defendant and others—namely, all the deputies and shotfirers concerned with the loss—should be treated as being responsible for that loss and that the defendant was liable to the plaintiffs for his share. Having regard to the view he took on the first point in connexion with damages, it became unnecessary for him to fix the number of those responsible.

For the defendant it is contended that the judge was wrong in assessing the damage in this way. In contract, as opposed to tort, it is argued, a defendant is only liable for the damage caused by his own breach, not that caused by others even if they have all acted in concert. The mere failure of the defendant to work on June 16 would not have prevented the working of the shift, and accordingly he is only liable for a proportion of his wages or for the cost of a substitute.

In our judgment, it is going too far to say that in no circumstances can A be liable for a share of the loss caused by A and B acting in concert. Indeed, were this not so it would in many cases be impossible to compensate a plaintiff for his real loss. This was recognized in *Ebbw Vale Steel, Iron and Coal Co.* v. *Tew*.[1] In that case the court was concerned with the measure of damages where a face-worker broke his contract. Having stated that the correct measure was the value of the output lost less the expenses which would have been incurred in obtaining it, Roche, L.J. said:[2] 'In the case of a hewer such as Tew, the application of these principles is not difficult. It may be more difficult with another class of workman not so directly concerned in getting coal from the seam. But with another class of workman, a tribunal must do its best either to assess the contribution of the workman in question to output and arrive at a figure representing his notional output during the period of default, or if it cannot do that, it must decide upon the evidence what would have been the value to the employer of the services he did not give'....

Here the defendant is charged with breach of his contract of service in that he failed to work the Saturday voluntary shift on 16 June 1956, when it was his turn to do so. It is said that he took this course in concert with his fellow deputies. But he is not charged with the tort of inducing his fellow deputies to break their contracts or of the tort of conspiracy

[1] [1935] 1 L.J.N.C.C.R. 284.   [2] Ibid., 288.

which might be constituted by the defendant and his fellow deputies mutually inducing each other to break their contracts in this respect. Therefore the matter must be dealt with as being simply a matter of breach of contract, albeit the defendant knew when he committed the breach that his fellow deputies intended to do the same.

What, then, is the measure of damages in this particular case? If the defendant alone and on his own initiative had failed to work the Saturday voluntary shift on 16 June, the measure of damages would, we apprehend, have been the net value to the plaintiffs of the work which he would have performed if he had worked that shift as he ought to have done. *Prima facie*, the measure of damages cannot be different because when he broke his contract in this respect he knew that his fellow deputies intended to commit similar breaches, except in so far as it would then be apparent that any damage likely to flow from the breach could not be avoided or lessened by their presence.

Suppose that no question of supervision entered into the matter and that five face-workers were obliged by the terms of their contracts of service to work a special shift. Suppose further that if they did work it they would produce between them coal of the net value to their employers of £500, each contributing equally to the total. Suppose further that one of these face-workers failed, in breach of his contract, to work the special shift. The damages resulting from the breach would, we should have thought, be £100, whether or not the other four face-workers intended, to his knowledge, to absent themselves as well. There would be no question of charging him with the whole loss of £500.

The present case only differs from that hypothetical one in that deputies exercise supervisory functions, so that the absence of any one of them may entail a far greater loss of output than the absence of one more face-worker. The question still is: what loss of output did the absence of the particular deputy charged with breach of his contract entail? The question in each case must be: what would his services have contributed to the net value of the output of the shift if the deputy concerned had duly worked it? This is in each case a question of fact.

In the present case, though the defendant was undoubtedly acting in concert with others, it is not shown that his breach contributed to the loss. He would not, as we understand it, have worked at a coal face, but would have been doing safety work. How, then, can it be said that loss of output is any measure of his liability? In these circumstances we do not think it can be said that any damage has been proved against him. beyond the cost of a substitute, say £3. 18s. 2d.

BRITISH TRANSPORT COMMISSION v. GOURLEY

House of Lords   [1956] A.C. 185

The respondent having suffered personal injuries was successful in an action for negligence against the appellant. One head of damages under which he claimed was 'loss of earnings'. The trial judge assessed damages under this head to be £37,720; and also held that if he had earned this sum the respondent would have had £6695 left after paying income tax. The appellants claimed that they need only pay the latter sum.

LORD GODDARD: A plaintiff may seek to increase or a defendant to diminish damages by items which are held to be too remote. The mere fact that the item arises as between the plaintiff and a third party would not seem to be the test. In a wrongful dismissal or personal injuries action the fact that a plaintiff has obtained remunerative employment with a third party is normally relevant, though it would fall within the words *res inter alios acta*. The question is whether taxation is or is not too remote to be taken into account. A plaintiff claims loss of earnings because he has been prevented from fulfilling a contract of service or earning wages or, if a professional man, earning fees from clients or, if a trader, from dealing with customers....The simplest case to take, no doubt, is that of a person assessed under Schedule E. A certain salary is attached to the office, but that which he will receive is, at the present rate of taxation, the salary less a very substantial percentage, which is deducted for tax before payment. If, therefore, he is disabled by an accident from earning his salary, I cannot see on what principle of justice the defendants should be called upon to pay him more than he would have received if he had remained able to carry out his duties....The principles set out above would be applicable in wrongful dismissal actions in which the court has to calculate damages for loss of earnings which would have been subject to tax had they been earned.*

LORDS RADCLIFFE and SOMERVELL OF HARROW concurred in the speech of LORD GODDARD; LORD TUCKER and EARL JOWITT delivered concurring speeches; LORD KEITH OF AVONHOLM dissented.

* Note: After *Gourley's* case, therefore, the defendant has to pay only the smaller amount where (1) the sums for the loss of which the damages awarded constitute compensation would have been liable to tax; *and* (2) the damages awarded to the plaintiff would not themselves be subject to tax: see *Mayne and McGregor* on 'Damages', p. 251.

PARSONS v. B.N.M. LABORATORIES LTD

Court of Appeal [1964] 1 Q.B. 95

In assessing the damages in an action for wrongful dismissal, the court had to decide whether it should take account of what the plaintiff would have paid in income tax out of that sum if he had earned it; and also of the amount he received in unemployment benefit during the period he was out of work.

The Finance Act, 1960, rendered damages for wrongful dismissal of £5000 or more taxable in the hands of the recipient. But the Court held that statute could have no application to damages of less than that amount; and the majority of the Court applied the principle in *Gourley's* case (*ante*, p. 190) that tax at the standard rate should be taken into account and deducted from the sum payable as damages. The Court of Appeal also deducted the sum paid as unemployment benefit.*

SELLERS, L.J.: ...There is no doubt that the plaintiff had to act reasonably to mitigate the loss which his unemployment created. He had family responsibilities and he very properly received unemployment benefits to which he was entitled and these amounted to £59 2s. 6d. Master Jacob took the view that this sum should not be deducted, holding, I think, that it was to be likened to an insurance policy held by the plaintiff and that it was a benefit to which the plaintiff whilst unemployed would be entitled whether wrongfully dismissed or not. The benefit which the plaintiff obtained was just that provision made by employer, employee and the State to bridge over or attenuate the hardships of a period of unemployment by providing a weekly payment when earnings are not forthcoming. With the employer as a contributing party I do not regard the payments as comparable to benefits received under a purely personal insurance policy or by way of pension or benefit arising out of a man's employment. In the one case the employee has paid a premium and in the other he has a contract of employment and his services given under it form the reward (equivalent to a premium) which entitles him to the benefit. I can see no reason why a defaulting party should obtain the benefit of a payment for which he had not paid any part of the premium or given the services which command the benefit...but I think that where, as here, the employer has made a contribution to the unemployment insurance he should get the benefit of it, if he finds it necessary to put one of his employees

---

* Contrast the arrangements made under the Law Reform (Personal Injuries) Act, 1948, s. 2, *post*, p. 684.

into unemployment, even in circumstances where he is liable to compensate him in damages.

PEARSON, L.J.; It is possible that in some other case there might be special hardship or other exceptional features which would require taxation to be taken into account in one of the ways suggested for the purpose of doing justice in the particular case. For instance, if in some future case a large sum of damages for wrongful dismissal is awarded, the effect of ss. 37 and 38 of the Finance Act, 1960, will be that the first £5000 of the damages will be free of tax and the excess over £5000 will be subject to tax, and that discrepancy will raise an awkward problem as to the effect, if any, of such taxation on the assessment of the damages.... I am inclined to think the right evaluation of *Gourley's* case[1] is to say that it was dealing with a very special case of tax discrepancy, or tax anomaly, and was not intended and should not be construed as generally requiring or authorizing the incidence of taxation to be taken into account in the assessment of damages. The tax discrepancy or tax anomaly is that, whereas the lost earnings or profits would have been taxable, the damages which are provided in replacement of them—as counsel vividly said, to fill the hole made by the wrongful act—are free of tax. The facts of *Gourley's* case show that, if the notional taxation on the lost profits or earnings had not been taken into account in assessing the damages, the plaintiff would have received an enormous fortuitous windfall in addition to compensation.... The evident intention of ss. 37 and 38 is to bring within the scope of income tax and surtax large sums paid to employees on the termination of their employments, because such sums have hitherto been tax-free. It was necessary to cover payment of large damages for wrongful dismissal, because the machinery of a wrongful dismissal followed by a claim for damages could easily be used for the purpose of arranging and effecting such a payment. It was not, however, intended to impose tax on damages for wrongful dismissal in an ordinary case, where the damages are small or medium-sized. Such damages remain tax-free....

There remains the question whether there should be a further deduction of £59. 2s. 6d. in respect of the unemployment benefit received by the plaintiff in the period of about three months of unemployment following his leaving the defendants' employment in consequence of the wrongful dismissal. The question can be put in this form: Are the sums of unemployment benefit received by the plaintiff to be brought into account in reduction of the damages for

[1] [1956] A.C. 185.

wrongful dismissal, or are they too remote to be brought into account for this purpose?...The principal passages dealing with remoteness in *Gourley's* case[1] are in the speech of Lord Reid. He said[2]: 'The general principle on which damages are assessed is not in doubt. A successful plaintiff is entitled to have awarded to him such a sum as will, so far as possible, make good to him the financial loss which he has suffered and will probably suffer as a result of the wrong done to him for which the defendant is responsible.' He went on to say later[3]: 'But the general principle is subject to one qualification. A loss which the plaintiff has suffered, or will suffer, or a compensatory gain which has come or will come to him following on the accident, may be of a kind which the law regards as too remote to be taken into account.'

In the end one comes back to the question: Is the plaintiff's receipt of unemployment benefit a matter too remote to be taken into consideration in ascertaining his net loss resulting from the wrongful dismissal? The common-sense answer is that of course it is not too remote. It is not 'completely collateral'. The dismissal caused the plaintiff to become unemployed, and therefore entitled, as a matter of general right under the system of state insurance and not by virtue of any private insurance policy of his own, to receive unemployment benefit. The effect of the dismissal was not to deprive him of all income but to reduce his income by substituting unemployment benefit for his salary. It would be unrealistic to disregard the unemployment benefit, because to do so would confer on the plaintiff, to the extent of £59. 2s. 6d., a fortuitous windfall in addition to compensation. Sir Andrew Clark also put his argument in this way: the plaintiff has a duty to mitigate the damage, resulting from the wrongful dismissal, by seeking other employment and drawing unemployment benefit in the meantime. I think that is correct, although the word 'duty' is used in a special sense, meaning only that the plaintiff cannot charge the defendant with any part of the loss which the plaintiff could have avoided by taking reasonable steps.

SELLERS, L.J., dissented from the decision regarding deduction of income tax. HARMAN, L.J., delivered a judgment concurring with PEARSON, L.J., on both points.

[1] [1956] A.C. 185.   [2] Ibid. 212.
[3] Ibid.

CLAYTON AND WALLER LTD *v.* OLIVER

House of Lords [1930] A.C. 209

The appellants agreed to engage the respondent to play one of three leading parts in a musical play ('Hit the Deck') for six weeks, but failed to cast him in one of the three parts. The respondent claimed damages for loss of enhancement of his reputation and for loss of publicity.

LORD BUCKMASTER: It is true that as a general rule the measure of damage for breach of contract is unaffected by the motives or manner of its breach. What are known as vindictive or exemplary damages in tort find no place in contract nor accordingly can injury to feelings or vanity be regarded. The action of breach of promise of marriage is an exception to the general rule, for, strictly assessed, the loss to a woman as a husband of a man who declines with insult to marry her might be assumed to be nil, but that is not the way such damages are determined.

In the present case the old and well established rule applies without qualification, the damages are those that may reasonably be supposed to have been in the contemplation of the parties at the time when the contract was made, as the probable result of its breach, and if any special circumstances were unknown to one of the parties, the damages associated with and flowing from such breach cannot be included. Here both parties knew that as flowing from the contract the plaintiff would be billed and advertised as appearing at the Hippodrome, and in the theatrical profession this is a valuable right.

In assessing the damages, therefore, it was competent for the jury to consider that the plaintiff was entitled to compensation because he did not appear at the Hippodrome, as by his contract he was entitled to do, and in assessing those damages they may consider the loss he suffered (1) because the Hippodrome is an important place of public entertainment and (2) that in the ordinary course he would have been 'billed' and otherwise advertised as appearing at the Hippodrome. The learned judge put the matter as a loss of reputation, which I do not think is the exact expression, but he explained that as the equivalent of loss of publicity and that summarizes what I have stated as my view of the true situation.

LORDS BLANESBURGH and TOMLIN concurred in the speech of LORD BUCKMASTER; VISCOUNT DUNEDIN and LORD WARRINGTON delivered concurring speeches.

ALDER v. MOORE

Court of Appeal   [1961] 2 Q.B. 57

The defendant, a football player, was paid £500 under an insurance scheme when his right eye was injured in a match. One condition of his receiving this money was that he agreed not to play professional football again and would 'be subject to a penalty of the amount stated above', i.e. £500, if he did. He began to play football again and resisted a claim for the return of the £500 on the ground that it was a penalty.

SELLERS, L.J.: The requirement of repayment in this case does not appear to me to be unreasonable or unjust and, like the judge, I can see no reason why the court should not enforce it. Far from being extravagant or unconscionable it is the precise sum which the defendant had received from the underwriters and which he would not have received at all if the future could have been foreseen only four months ahead. If the sum claimed is to be regarded as damages it is, in effect, an agreed and fair pre-estimate of the loss which the underwriters have suffered. However, that way of putting it does not seem to me to be quite appropriate. Neither do I think the obligation is in any way in the nature of a threat held over the defendant *in terrorem*. The underwriters had no concern or desire to preclude the defendant from playing football for reward. They wished if he did so to be reimbursed that which they had paid on a basis proved to be false by events and no more.... The defendant's argument here has the advantage that the underwriters have chosen to call the payment they wish to recover a 'penalty'. Why they did so I cannot understand, but whilst they run a risk of being taken at their word the law looks at the substance of the matter and not at the words used, whether 'penalty' or 'liquidated damages'. I would regard it, as the judge did, as a repayment of a sum in circumstances which are entirely equitable. It is in no way an imposition of a fine or penal payment, and if it has to be made to fall under one head or the other, it is to be regarded as a payment by way of damages for breach of an undertaking which is not unfair or unconscionable and therefore not a penalty.

SLADE, J., delivered a concurring judgment; DEVLIN, L.J., dissented.

SECTION D

SOCIAL SECURITY LAW AND LOSS OF EMPLOYMENT

(i) UNEMPLOYMENT BENEFIT*

(a) Whether Entitled to Benefit

R(U) 11/64

A casual dock worker attended at the docks one Sunday night, expecting to start work at midnight. The work did not become available, and, as was the practice in the circumstances, he was paid the sum of £1 as 'disappointment money'. Such a payment was provided for in an Industrial Agreement, which the claimant contended did not apply to casual workers. He claimed that the sum paid to him was an *ex gratia* payment which did not prevent him from being unemployed; further, that if he was engaged at all the engagement came to an end before midnight, so that he was unemployed on the Monday.

The decision of the Commissioner was as follows:

4. The rights and duties of registered dock workers in these docks are regulated by a scheme which as amended is set out in the Dock Workers (Regulation of Employment) (Amendment) Order, 1961 [S.I. 1961 No. 2107]. The scheme is to be found in the schedule to that Order, to which the claimant has helpfully referred me. The claimant contends that he is not a registered dock worker and on the evidence I must accept that as being correct. The scheme is concerned mainly with registered dock workers but it is clear that others can in certain circumstances be employed in the docks (see paragraph 10 of it).

5. There was in force also an Agreement dated the 30 January 1956 between the Grimsby Trawler Owners Association and the Transport and General Workers Union. On the face of it this Agreement applies to all lumpers irrespective of whether they are registered dock workers (see Clause 1) and the Agreement provides that where labour has been engaged for midnight landing and the vessel fails to arrive in dock by 12.30 a.m. each man shall be entitled to payment of 20s. disappointment money unless transferred to another vessel...(see paragraph 10(3) of the schedule). The claimant however contends that this Agreement does not apply to a casual worker like him, and that the payment made to him

---

* *Note:* Unemployment benefit normally lasts for only 312 days: see National Insurance Act, 1966, s. 3 (2), amending s. 21, National Insurance Act, 1965. The unemployed worker must thereafter requalify. On 'wage related' benefits under National Insurance Act, 1966, see J. Reid (1966) 29 M.L.R. 537.

on this occasion was an *ex gratia* payment which does not prevent him from being unemployed....

7. To qualify for unemployment benefit the first thing that the claimant must prove is that the Monday was a day of unemployment within the meaning of s. 11 of the National Insurance Act, 1946* (see regulation 6(1)(a) of the National Insurance (Unemployment and Sickness Benefit) Regulations, 1948 [S.I. 1948 No. 1277]).

8. Having fully considered everything that has been said, I am satisfied that the true inference from the facts is as follows. The payment of 20s. (less the stamp money) was made in pursuance of what amounted to a guarantee of part wages for the period which the claimant would work on Monday if the ship docked in time. I do not think that it matters whether it was paid before or after midnight. What does matter is in respect of what period it was paid, which in my judgment was from midnight onwards. If the written Agreement applied to the claimant then the payment was made under the Agreement in accordance with the claimant's agreed rights. If on the other hand the written Agreement did not apply to the claimant nevertheless in my judgment this was not an *ex gratia* payment. It is not suggested that it was made only on one isolated occasion. It was the payment always made in such circumstances. I think that, if the employers had on this occasion said that they chose not to pay the claimant anything, he would not only have been extremely angry but would have felt that he was not being given something to which he was legally entitled. Put in a somewhat different way, if this Agreement did not apply to the casual workers, in my judgment it was a term of the arrangements between the employers and the claimant, to be implied from the course of conduct of the employers and persons in the position of the claimant, that he should be paid 20s. disappointment money in the same way as the registered workers.†

9. In the circumstances in my judgment the claimant cannot be regarded as having been unemployed on the Monday. Although I see the force of the argument of the claimant's association, I think that any other conclusion would be inconsistent both with the whole theory relating to guaranteed weekly wages and with decisions relating to individual days such as Decision R(U) 5/58. Where employers have agreed to pay and do pay a certain wage for a week, whether the employee works or not, no day in that week can be regarded as a day of unemployment. In Decision R(U) 5/58 the claimant's agreement

* See now ss. 19 and 20, National Insurance Act, 1965.
† Compare the problems discussed, *post*, p. 289.

provided that he was entitled to double wages plus a fixed sum if he worked on Whit-Monday, and to the fixed sum only if he did not work on that day. A day or two beforehand he was notified that he would not be required to work on Whit-Monday. He was paid the fixed sum. It was held that he could not be regarded as unemployed on that Monday. That case seems to me indistinguishable from the present one.

R(U) 1/55
Availability—absent on holiday

A rigger, a casual dock worker, who normally made himself available for employment by taking his place twice daily at a stand, went away for a holiday. He left his address with the employment exchange and contended that he was available for employment at short notice, being only two hours rail journey away. Employment at the time was slack and he alleged that no vacancy arose during his absence.

Held that claimant was not available for employment—the question was not whether employment was available for him but whether he was available for employment; employers of dock labour expect to find labour at the stand, and it was not shown that the claimant could reasonably expect an opportunity of employment to be brought to his notice whilst he was away.

(b) Disqualifications

NATIONAL INSURANCE ACT, 1965*

22:...(2) A person shall be disqualified for receiving unemployment benefit for such period not exceeding six weeks as may be determined in accordance with Part IV of this Act if

(*a*) he has lost his employment in an employed contributor's employment through his misconduct, or has voluntarily left such employment without just cause;

(*b*) after a situation in any suitable employment has been notified to him by an employment exchange or other recognized agency, or by or on behalf of an employer, as vacant or about to become vacant, he has without good cause refused or failed to apply for that situation or refused to accept that situation when offered to him;

(*c*) he has neglected to avail himself of a reasonable opportunity of suitable employment;

(*d*) he has without good cause refused or failed to carry out any written recommendations given to him by an officer of an employment exchange with a view to assisting him to find suitable employment,

---

* For the disqualification under s. 22 (1) in trade disputes see *post*, p. 407.

being recommendations which were reasonable having regard to his circumstances and to the means of obtaining that employment usually adopted in the district in which he resides; or

(e) he has without good cause refused or failed to avail himself of a reasonable opportunity of receiving training approved by the Minister of Labour in his case for the purpose of becoming or keeping fit for entry into or return to regular employment.

(3) Regulations may provide for disqualifying a person for receiving sickness benefit for such period not exceeding six weeks as may be determined in accordance with Part IV of this Act if

(a) he has become incapable of work through his own misconduct; or

(b) he fails without good cause to attend for or to submit himself to such medical or other examination or treatment as may be required in accordance with the regulations, or to observe any prescribed rules of behaviour....

...(5) For the purposes of this section, employment shall not be deemed to be employment suitable in the case of any person if it is either

(a) employment in a situation vacant in consequence of a stoppage of work due to a trade dispute; or

(b) employment in his usual occupation in the district where he was last ordinarily employed at a rate of remuneration lower, or on conditions less favourable, than those which he might reasonably have expected to obtain having regard to those which he habitually obtained in his usual occupation in that district, or would have obtained had he continued to be so employed; or

(c) employment in his usual occupation in any other district at a rate of remuneration lower, or on conditions less favourable, than those generally observed in that district by agreement between associations of employers and of employees, or, failing any such agreement, than those generally recognised in that district by good employers;

but, after the lapse of such an interval from the date on which he becomes unemployed as in the circumstances of the case is reasonable, employment shall not be deemed to be unsuitable by reason only that it is employment of a kind other than employment in his usual occupation if it is employment at a rate of remuneration not lower, and on conditions not less favourable, than those generally observed by agreement between associations of employers and of employees or, failing any such agreement, than those generally recognised by good employers.

(6) In this section

(*a*) the expression 'place of employment' in relation to any person, means the factory, workshop, farm or other premises or place at which he was employed, so, however, that, where separate branches of work which are commonly carried on as separate businesses in separate premises or at separate places are in any case carried on in separate departments on the same premises or at the same place, each of those departments shall for the purposes of this paragraph be deemed to be a separate factory or workshop or farm or separate premises or a separate place, as the case may be....

(*c*) Disqualification for 'Misconduct'

R(U) 34/52

A claimant was dismissed because although the quality of his work was satisfactory, his output was not up to the standard required.

1. My decision is that the claimant is not disqualified for receiving unemployment benefit...through his industrial misconduct, under s. 13(2)(*a*) of the National Insurance Act, 1946.[*]

3. The evidence shows that the claimant was dismissed by his employers, after 12 weeks of employment as a thread tapper, because his output of work was not up to standard. A bonus was paid on output, and the claimant wished to earn it, but he could not. He had been spoken to by a chargehand about a fortnight before he was dismissed and had been asked to increase his output, but he failed to do so. He was doing about 6000 to 6500 threads a day; his employers wanted 7000 to 8000. Some employees were turning out 13,000 a day. The quality of his work was satisfactory, but the quantity was deficient. The claimant was incapable of turning out more. There is nothing at all to suggest that he was deliberately restricting his output. It is not that he would not, but that he could not, improve his output. He seems to be by nature a slow worker.

4. A physical handicap of this kind does not constitute industrial misconduct.

[*] See now s. 22 National Insurance Act, 1965, *ante*, p. 198.

R(U) 41/53

A mobile crane driver, a shop steward, was summarily discharged for refusing to operate his crane on a jetty which his trade union regarded as being involved in a trade dispute. He disregarded the negotiating procedure which was available for the adjustment of disputes to avoid stoppage of work.

1. My decision is that the claimant is disqualified....The claimant told the local tribunal that men in his section had been paid 5d. an hour extra for this hazardous operation, but that the payment had been stopped on the day of his dismissal. A meeting of men in the section took place during the dinner break on that day, the 17 June 1953, at which it was agreed that the jetty 'be put in dispute'. The claimant was himself the steward of the section. After dinner he was ordered by an engineer to reverse his crane on to the jetty, but he told the engineer that owing to the fact that the jetty was 'in dispute' he could not carry out the instructions. He was thereupon summarily discharged. The claimant contends that as a loyal trade union member he was bound to carry out the decision of the sectional meeting, which was a meeting of members of the union, and to carry out the rules of the union.

4. The claimant, however, is mistaken in thinking that he was carrying out the rules of his union. He was in fact acting directly contrary to an agreement to which his trade union had been a party. An elaborate agreement, dated the 9 March 1953 had been drawn up....

5. The claimant, who was himself a steward, completely ignored this scheme for settling disputes. One of the principal objects of the scheme is the avoidance of stoppages, but instead of taking his grievance to the convenor of shop stewards at a convenient time, the claimant stopped working on the jetty. It is clear that he stopped not because the work was hazardous but because the extra 5d. an hour had been put an end to. The claimant contends that he was loyally carrying out the decision of the sectional meeting which had put the jetty 'in dispute', but as I understand the matter that meeting had no right or power to rule that work must be stopped on the jetty. By purporting to place the jetty 'in dispute' the meeting was ignoring the agreed procedure and was doing something it had no right to do.

6. Where a person like a shop steward, who is in a position of authority and responsibility, disregards the method of procedure which his trade union has agreed to, and purports of his own accord to refuse to carry out a reasonable order, he is, in my judgment, undoubtedly guilty of industrial misconduct.

A 19-year-old apprentice draughtsman was held to have lost this employment through misconduct. The local tribunal were informed of his trouble with the police but recorded the evidence inadequately. The claimant argued that he was dismissed for misconduct 'outside working hours'.

The decision of the Commissioner was as follows:

1. My decision is that the claimant is disqualified for receiving unemployment benefit from the 2 June 1958 to the 12 July 1958 (both dates included) on the ground that he lost his employment through his misconduct, in terms of s. 13(2)(a) of the National Insurance Act, 1946....

8. The insurance officer now concerned with the case submits that 'although the claimant's detention in police custody may have precipitated his discharge it was not the sole reason for it' and that 'the claimant lost his employment partly through his failure to attend night classes.' Having regard to the time table of events given by the claimant (see the preceding paragraph) I think it is very plain that it was the claimant's trouble with the police which precipitated his discharge.... I am now informed that the claimant (along with another youth) was charged on two counts of breaking into premises and stealing therefrom: and that he was put on probation for two years. This involves a finding of guilt by a competent Court, which I must accept.

11. In any event the claimant does not dispute that he committed these acts. His argument is that they constituted what he himself calls 'misconduct outside working hours', and that misconduct outside working hours is not relevant for purposes of s. 13(2)(a) of the Act.

12. This is a misapprehension. It may be that this misapprehension has been fostered, to some extent, by the popular use of the term 'industrial misconduct' as a paraphrase of the statutory provision. The Statute speaks of 'misconduct' without any such qualifying adjective. No doubt misconduct in order to be relevant to s. 13(2)(a) of the Act must be misconduct of a kind which has a bearing on the suitability of the person concerned for the employment in question. But it is a fallacy to suppose that conduct which takes place outside working hours and away from the place of work is necessarily irrelevant for purposes of s. 13(2)(a). This was pointed out in Decision R(U) 10/53, and again (more recently) in two unreported decisions, C.U. 18/55 and C.W.U. 1/56. In Decision C.U. 18/55 the Commissioner said '...Even

though the misconduct committed may not be directly connected with the particular duties required of that person and even though it is committed outside working hours (see Decision R(U) 10/53), nevertheless the offence may directly or indirectly affect the suitability for continued employment and, in those circumstances, such a person would incur disqualification for benefit under s. 13 of the Act.' In Decision C.W.U. 1/56 the Commission (after pointing out that the word 'industrial' does not appear in s. 13(2)(a) of the Act) said 'The section does not define misconduct or enact that it must have some connection with a person's employment. The general intention of subsection (a) of s. 13 appears to be to impose a limited period of disqualification for receiving unemployment benefit in order to deter employed persons from conducting themselves in a manner likely to make them unnecessarily a charge upon the National Insurance Fund. Whether a person's conduct amounts to misconduct for the purposes of s. 13(2) (a) of the Act is a question to be determined by the statutory authorities.'

13. On a consideration of the whole circumstances of the case I am satisfied that the claimant's behaviour which brought him into police custody was misconduct which affected his suitability for continued employment as an apprentice draughtsman.

R(U) 14/57

An airframe fitter was discharged when a customer complained about the claimant's drunkenness which had occurred outside working hours whilst lodging in the customer's premises. The employers agreed that there were other contributory reasons for his dismissal.

The decision of the Commissioner was as follows:

...2. The claimant is a married man aged 33 years. He was employed by an aviation company as an airframe fitter, and was dismissed from that employment on the 16 November 1956. Asked whether the discharge was due to unsatisfactory conduct of any kind, the employers wrote—'Yes. As an undesirable employee. While on Company's work on Continent his conduct [was] not conducive to good relations between customer and company (drunkenness).' They subsequently amplified this by saying that although the offence did not take place within working hours, 'the worker was lodging in Canadian Govt. property and was in receipt of subsistence from this firm. His conduct was not conducive to good relations between us and the R.C.A.F.' Invited to comment upon this, the claimant stated as follows: 'I was A.E.U.

Convener of Shop Stewards at —— Ltd, and played an active part in improving wages and conditions of Trade Union members employed there. I was sent to Germany to work on Royal Canadian Air Force aircraft in mid-July and returned in mid-September. On November 16 at 4.45, approximately two months after my return I was informed that I was sacked as undesirable. In negotiations, the Shop Stewards demanded my reinstatement. The Management referred to an incident in Germany which took place *in my own time* and went on to say that I was responsible for unofficial strikes, as justifying them in sacking me....' Asked to comment upon this the employers explained that action was not taken upon the claimant's conduct in Germany until two months after his return, 'because the official report on [the claimant's] activities in Germany was not received from the Royal Canadian Air Force until that time': and in answer to the question—'Had his connexion with unofficial strikes anything to do with his dismissal?'— they replied on L.T. 53 (Rev.)—'Not completely but his conduct in this connection had to be taken into cognisance when considering his behaviour under (4) below:

(4) His dismissal followed upon certain incidents relating to his conduct when employed by this Company on a Government Contract on the Continent to which the Government concerned objected and which incidents, coupled with certain other incidents in the home establishment satisfied us beyond doubt that [the claimant] was an undesirable employee.'...

5. In order to justify disqualification, two matters must be proved. It must be proved that the claimant was guilty of misconduct of the kind contemplated by s. 13 of the Act, and also that it was through his misconduct that he lost his employment. Plainly, for purposes of s. 13 of the Act, the misconduct must bear some relation to the workman's ability to contribute to the requirements of the employers' business. But that does not mean that misconduct exhibited outside working hours is necessarily irrelevant: see Decision R(U) 10/53. What a man does in his own time is not necessarily his personal concern alone. It may be that, as the tribunal say, if the claimant had been working in Scotland, his conduct similar to that in Germany would not have amounted to misconduct involving disallowance of benefit. But that would be so, as I see it, on the assumption that working in Scotland did not involve lodging in the quarters of the employers' customer. It seems to me that when a job requires that a workman lodge in the quarters of his employers' customer, wrongous conduct on the part of

the workman, of such a character as reasonably to cause the customer to complain to the employers, may well constitute misconduct for purposes of s. 13....

7. I think it is admittedly the case that the employers had additional reasons for wanting to get rid of the claimant. But in terms of the Statute, what the statutory authorities have to inquire is whether the claimant 'lost his employment through his misconduct.' This formula does not, in my view, require the authorities to be satisfied that the misconduct in question was the *sole* reason for dismissal....

8. I hold that the claimant lost his employment through his misconduct, and that in terms of s. 13(2)(a) of the Act he is disqualified for receiving unemployment benefit for a period of six weeks.

R(U) 2/60

Part of claimant's duty on night shift was to attend to frost fires. It was alleged that on one night he allowed them to go out. The claimant admitted that one fire had gone out during the night but said he had rekindled it immediately. The only evidence of the alleged neglect was given by the manager of the works, but he came on duty at 8.30 a.m. and the claimant had finished at 6 a.m. No evidence, either written or oral, was obtained from the man who took over duty from the claimant.

Held that misconduct had not been proved. The onus of proving misconduct is on those who allege it, and it must be clearly proved. When the claimant denies the allegations it is desirable that the most direct evidence should be adduced.

(d) Leaving 'Voluntarily' without 'Just Cause'

R(U) 9/59

A claimant was discharged after one year's employment because he refused to join the firm's superannuation scheme. His reason was that he could not afford the weekly contribution. It was not shown that at the time of his engagement he knew he would be expected to join the scheme.

The decision of the Commissioner was as follows:

...8. I will assume that acceptance into the superannuation scheme would not (on the long view) be disadvantageous to the claimant; but this does not seem to me very relevant. In fairness to the claimant it must be borne in mind that the immediate effect, so far as he was concerned, was a deduction from his weekly pay-packet, of 7s. 5d., which (in his view) he could not afford.* If he was discharged for refusing to suffer a deduction from his net weekly earnings which he genuinely

* Consider the impact on such a situation of the Shop Clubs Act, 1902.

thought he could not afford, and which he had not previously been told that he would have to suffer, I do not see how he can be said to have left his employment voluntarily.

9. In the case to which Decision R(U)-4/51 relates the Commissioner had to consider the position of an employee who refused to pay his membership subscription to a trade association of which the employers required their employees to be members. There the Commissioner took the view that a claimant who for a genuine reason refused to pay and so 'invited discharge' could not be regarded as having left voluntarily. This view was in conformity with the view expressed, in similar circumstances, by the Umpire under the now repealed Unemployment Insurance Acts: and I respectfully agree with it. In the present case one starts from the position that the claimant was in fact discharged, and that there is no evidence that he wished to leave. It is for the insurance officer to show that, in the circumstances, he left his employment voluntarily. In my judgment, this has not been established. I hold that the claimant is not shown to have rendered himself liable to disqualification under s. 13(2)(a) of the Act. The disqualification imposed is therefore set aside.

R(U) 20/64

A police sergeant retired after 25 years' service, although it was open to him to remain in his employment for several years longer. At the time of retirement he was living in his own house, which he had arranged to buy about a year previously, and found difficulty in travelling to and from his place of employment because he had recently been transferred. Before retiring he had consulted several prospective employers, and he began other employment about two weeks later.

Held by a Tribunal of Commissioners that the claimant voluntarily left his employment without just cause.

The decision of the Tribunal was as follows:

...7. Section 13(2)(a) of the National Insurance Act, 1946, provides that a person shall be disqualified for receiving unemployment benefit for a period not exceeding six weeks if he has voluntarily left his employment without just cause. A similar provision has been part of the law continuously since s. 87 of the National Insurance Act, 1911, was enacted. Both the previous statutes and the present Act have always been interpreted as meaning that those who assert that the claimant left voluntarily must prove it, and that, when they have done so, it is then for the claimant to prove that he did not leave without just cause. This is the strictly accurate way of putting the matter; a slight change of emphasis may be involved in the phrase, frequently used in practice, that the claimant must prove that he had just cause for leaving. Each of these matters must be proved on balance of probabilities.

8. The basic purpose of unemployment benefit is to provide against the misfortune of unemployment happening against a person's will. Section 13(2) however clearly recognizes that it may be payable in certain cases where the claimant leaves voluntarily, if he does not do so without just cause. It is not sufficient for him to prove that he acted reasonably, in the sense of acting reasonably in his own interests. The interests of the National Insurance Fund and other contributors have to be taken into account as well. 'The notion of "just cause" involves a compromise between the rights of the individual and the interests of the rest of the community. So long as he does not break his contract with his employer, the individual is free to leave his employment when he likes. But if he wishes to claim unemployment benefit he must not leave his employment without due regard to the interests of the rest of the community...' (Decision C.U. 164/50 (not reported)). This has been expressed in different ways in many decisions; see Decisions R(U) 14/55, paragraph 5 and R(U) 23/59, paragraph 12. The difficulty however lies in making a comparison between such very different elements.

9. In deciding the question of just cause it is essential to remember throughout that the question is the one arising on the very words of the statute, and it is not permissible to substitute any other test. Further, 'It is not practicable to lay down any hard and fast rule to guide the Statutory Authorities as to the precise circumstances in which just cause or no just cause for leaving is shown. Each case must depend upon its own particular circumstances' (Decision R(U) 14/52, paragraph 5). Nor should the various elements in the case be considered in water-tight compartments. It is necessary to look at the whole circumstances at the relevant time in order to determine whether in a fair sense it can be said that he did not leave without just cause. It may however be helpful to draw attention to certain types of case which occur frequently, in order to give guidance as to the way in which the Commissioner has regarded these problems.

10. In Decision R(U) 14/52 already referred to the Commissioner approached the matter by considering the necessity of being assured of suitable alternative employment unless there were circumstances justifying the claimant in leaving without it. We think that it may be helpful to approach the matter from the opposite direction, considering

first some circumstances in which a person may be held to have just cause for leaving his employment although he has no alternative employment to go to, and discussing then the effect of alternative employment or a prospect of it where there are no such circumstances or they are not sufficient to constitute just cause.

11. It is clearly established that some feature of the claimant's existing employment may justify him in leaving it immediately without any regard to the question of other employment. This is illustrated by many decisions including C.U. 248/49 (reported), R(U) 15/53, R(U) 38/53, R(U) 18/57, C.U. 46/59 and C.U. 1/64, the two last not reported. But the circumstances must be pressing. If, for example, the claimant has a grievance in connection with his employment, it may be reasonable to expect him to take such steps as are open to him through the proper channels to get it remedied rather than to leave immediately without doing so.

12. It is equally well established that circumstances in the claimant's personal or domestic life may become so pressing as to justify him in leaving without regard to the question of other employment. Illustrations of this are to be found in decisions such as R(U) 14/52 itself, R(U) 19/52 and R(U) 31/59. The need to take a quick decision about housing accommodation sometimes creates an urgency justifying the claimant in leaving; see, for example, Decision C.U. 49/57 (not reported). Many cases of this type depend on some circumstance affecting the health of the claimant or some person living with him.

13. In both the classes of case referred to in the last two paragraphs there must be some urgency in the matter. Otherwise it often has to be held that the claimant could have taken some step other than leaving his employment when he did so. This is merely a particular application of the more general statement that the claimant ought to take such steps as are reasonably open to him to avoid voluntarily becoming unemployed and dependent on the National Insurance Fund.

14. Where the claimant either gives no reason at all for leaving or gives reasons which do not amount to just cause for doing so, the question frequently arises how the situation is affected by his having made arrangements for other employment or having prospects of other employment either immediately following his old employment or shortly afterwards. This commonly arises in cases where either the claimant moves house to some other district, which necessitates his moving his employment, or he leaves his employment simply because he wants a change of employment.

15. In our judgment the fact that a man moves house to a different district does not automatically or in itself provide him with just cause for leaving his employment in his old district when he does so. If a sentence in Decision C.U. 21/59 (not reported) had meant this in our judgment it would have been erroneous. But the fact that a man has moved or is moving house is an element to be taken into account with all the other circumstances in considering whether he has just cause. And the reasons for his moving may make it an important element. Further, there may be developments and difficulties in connection with his move which may make it an extremely important element, for example, if a situation unexpectedly develops whereby it becomes impracticable for him to avoid a short period of unemployment. Manifestly, a mere desire to change one's employment does not of itself constitute just cause.

16. In such cases it has been said that, generally speaking, a man should be assured of having suitable alternative employment to go to before he leaves that which he already has, or at least he ought to have very good reason for supposing that his chances of securing alternative employment in the immediate future are such that he will not be relying on unemployment benefit (Decision R(U) 14/52). In other decisions the matter has been put somewhat differently by saying, for example, that in general a person should not leave settled employment before he is reasonably assured of another situation at no distant date (Decision C.S.U. 13/56 (not reported)) or that he should take all reasonable steps to secure alternative employment before leaving that which he has (Decision C.U. 20/59 (not reported))....

19. There is no doubt in this case that the claimant voluntarily left his employment. It is therefore for him to show that he did not do so without just cause. There is no suggestion that there was any unsatisfactory feature about his employment in the police force which would help him to prove just cause. We are not satisfied that the true inference from the facts is that the purchase of his house caused him to retire. From the evidence it seems to us much more probable that he had decided to retire after 25 years, hoping perhaps to obtain civilian work with the police force after his retirement, and that he bought or took steps to buy the house at H. to live in when he retired after 25 years. We should need strong evidence to show that he bought it in order to retire many years later. We cannot accept his suggestion that the purchase of the house of itself provides just cause for leaving his employment. The question then is whether the prospects of employment

which he had, combined with the other circumstances, could justify a finding of just cause for leaving. In our judgment they do not do so. In fact there was a gap of a fortnight between the end of the one employment and the beginning of the other, and there is no evidence justifying the inference that the claimant ever thought that that gap would be either shorter or longer. Although the case is somewhat near the line, we do not feel justified in holding that the claimant has established that there were no steps which he could reasonably have been expected to take to avoid a gap between the two employments. All the events occurred in a comparatively small area, and this is not one of those cases where a claimant's new home is so far from his old one that it was impracticable to make arrangements at a distance. And we do not see how those efforts which he had made to obtain employment which he knew to have been unsuccessful—such as his attempt to obtain civilian employment with the police—can help him to prove just cause.

20. In our judgment however there are circumstances in this case, including his efforts to obtain employment, which justify a modest reduction in the period of disqualification. As the claimant was unemployed for only a fortnight this presumably will not help him, but we make the reduction as this decision may be a precedent in future cases.*

(e) Refusal of 'Suitable' Employment

R(U) 1/52

A tool maker lost employment on 10 May 1951 by reason of a stoppage of work due to a trade dispute. On 22 August 1951 he refused an offer of suitable employment as a tool maker with another firm on the ground that the offer was an interference in the dispute and he was not prepared to accept employment other than with his old firm until the dispute was settled. He contended that there were vacancies with his old firm and that the Employment Exchange would not submit him; but the firm stated they had no vacancies and were not prepared to reinstate him. The dispute was eventually settled on 24 October 1951 and he was

---

* See too on this provision of (now) s. 22, National Insurance Act, 1965: R(U) 18/52: claimant left employment with a non-union firm because of an objection by his union as to demarcation of his duties. He knew the firm did not recognize the union.
Held: just cause not proved. 'What the employers chose to do in their own establishment was a matter for them to decide'.
R(U) 38/53: electrician who was not a member of a union, left his employment voluntarily rather than yield to pressures to join the union.
Held: he had just cause for leaving. His action was 'reasonable in the circumstances as he wished to exercise his undisputed right to decide whether he would become a member of a trade union'.

reinstated on 29 October 1951. The stoppage of work due to the trade dispute ended on 30 June 1951.

Held that the claimant had refused an offer of suitable employment without good cause and was disqualified for benefit for six weeks; also that from 22 August 1951 to 29 October 1951 he was not entitled to benefit as he was not available. On 22 August 1951 a settlement of the dispute was not in sight and he should have accepted the employment offered which was suitable within the meaning of the Act.

R(U) 34/58

An unmarried labourer aged 22, living in Shetland, had been unemployed for 7 months and had no prospects of local employment. He refused employment as an unskilled worker at a place about 750 miles distant from his home.

1. My decision is that the claimant is disqualified for receiving unemployment benefit for six weeks immediately following the end of the benefit week in which this decision is given.

2. The claimant is an unmarried man aged 22 years, who lives in Shetland. He was registered for employment as a labourer. On the 25 February 1958 he was notified of a vacant situation as an unskilled worker at a brickworks in Bletchley in Buckinghamshire, the offered rate of wages being 3s. 7¼d. an hour. At that date the claimant had been unemployed for over seven months. He refused to apply for the situation. His stated reason for refusal was recorded as follows—'Would consider job if wages were higher. I was getting 4s. on last job per hr.' If the claimant had accepted the job he could have lodged in the employers' hostel for 45s. a week....

6. The first reason given is that the rate of wages offered was lower than the claimant had been receiving locally. The rate offered was the rate generally observed in the district, and when examined in detail it is found not to be lower than the claimant had been receiving: for the rate was in fact 3s. 7¼d. an hour for day work, with time and a quarter for night work, day shift and night shift being taken week about.

7. The second reason given is that no subsistence allowance was offered. Looking to the rate of wages offered and to the fact that hostel accommodation was available at 45s. a week, I do not regard this as a tenable objection.

8. The third reason given is that no offer of travelling expenses was made. I agree that in the present case travelling expenses would come to a substantial sum (the claimant says 'probably £10 including food').

This objection was apparently not mentioned to the employment exchange when the situation was refused. If inquiry had been made on this matter the claimant would have learned that there are arrangements whereby an advance of fare may be made against an undertaking to repay by instalments, and in fact in certain circumstances repayment of such advances may be partially remitted.

9. It is of course true that the situation offered was a very long distance from the claimant's home. But as has already been stated he is an unmarried man of 22; and he has at no time indicated any personal or domestic reasons which require him to stay at home. He had been unemployed for over seven months, and there were no prospects of local employment. The claimant should have taken the job offered, rather than continue to stay at home drawing unemployment benefit. In the circumstances I entirely agree with the dissenting opinion of the chairman of the local tribunal who considered that the claimant had failed to show good cause for refusing a situation which could not be regarded as unsuitable.

R(U) 15/62

Refusal of suitable employment—claimant having no usual occupation

After a period of sickness following employment as a builder's labourer the claimant registered for employment as a light labourer. He obtained very little work, and nearly five years later was offered employment as a trainee machine operator with Remploy Ltd at a rate of wages lower than that paid by other employers. He declined the offer on the ground that, as a family man, he could not manage on the wages offered.

The decision of the Commissioner was as follows:

1. My decision is that the claimant would have been disqualified for receiving unemployment benefit for the period 15 November 1961 to 26 December 1961 (both dates included) because without good cause he did not accept a suitable situation which was offered to him....

3. The claimant is a married man, aged 43, and has three young children. Up to 3 February 1956 he was employed as a builder's labourer, but thereafter he became ill with cardiac debility on 30 April 1956. He again registered for work on 12 February 1957 as a light labourer, having been found fit for suitable employment: since then he has not worked except for 10 weeks from 20 January 1958 to 28 March 1958 when he was employed at the Industrial Rehabilitation Unit. At the relevant time he as receiving £7. 19s. 0d. per week from the National Assistance Board.

4. On 10 November 1961 the claimant was submitted to and accepted for employment as a trainee at Remploy Ltd, which exists for the purpose of training and providing sheltered employment for disabled persons. The claimant was interviewed but refused the employment on the grounds:

'That I was willing to take the job offered me, but when told the weekly rate of pay, I found it to be impossible to accept. That sort of job with pay so small is alright for single persons, but for a married man with family it would be starvation. It would mean that I should take home pay packet of £6 10s. 0d. and out of that would be rent of £1 14s. 5d. We could not manage on such pay.'

He has since written to the Commissioner saying (*inter alia*):

'If I am working my wife cannot do with less than £9 10s. 0d. per week housekeeping money, so it was impossible to have such low rate job which would only suit single person. Give me job where I can live and not starve and I will do it'....

8. Accepting, as I think I must, the report of the manager of Remploy Ltd, the figures accepted by the local tribunal should be somewhat higher, but I need not dwell on this point because it was clearly laid down in Decision R(U) 10/61:

'In our opinion therefore the question whether a claimant would have been worse off financially by accepting a situation is not in itself relevant to the question whether he is disqualified under s. 13(2)...'.

In that case the claimant alleged that by accepting the employment he would lose £1 per week and the tribunal held that even if accepted 'that fact would not in itself show that the situation was not "suitable" or that the claimant had "good cause" for refusing to accept it within the meaning of s. 13(2)(*b*).' Following this principle it seems to me that the claimant's only objection to the employment offered does not in itself show that the situation was not suitable or that he had good cause for refusing to accept it.

9. It is necessary to consider s. 13(5)...In the present case it is not disputed that the standard rate of pay at Remploy Ltd, is less than the rate paid by other employers but this is because Remploy provide sheltered employment for disabled persons who cannot reasonably expect to be remunerated on the same scale as the able-bodied.

11. No difficulty arises in this case as to the lapse of time, which was long. The difficulty arises over the words 'employment in his usual occupation'. If the claimant's usual occupation is regarded as that of a

builder's labourer, it is difficult to give an acceptable meaning to the proviso to s. 13(5) because it is extremely unlikely that as a disabled person he will be offered employment at a rate of remuneration not lower, and on conditions not less favourable, than those of able-bodied men. The insurance officer now concerned submits:

'Since [the claimant] registered for work on 12 February 1957 after having been declared fit for suitable employment he has not worked and in my submission he has no "usual occupation" within the meaning of s. 13(5) of the Act. If this submission is accepted, the employment offered must be considered in the light of the general tests of suitability and the provisions of s. 13(5) of the Act are not relevant.'

12. Upon consideration I accept this submission because I think it is necessary in order to give meaning to s. 13(5): it is clearly futile to offer work to a man for which he is not registered and which he is not capable of doing. I therefore find that the situation offered to the claimant cannot be deemed unsuitable on the ground that it was employment of a kind other than employment in his usual occupation and at a lower rate of pay than is generally recognized by good employers.

13. If s. 13(5) does not apply, the question whether employment is suitable is a question of fact to be decided in the light of all the circumstances, which would include the physical and mental capabilities of the claimant, the nature and accessibility of the work and the earnings, and also the length of time the claimant has been away from work. In the present case I have considered all the available factors, including some which were not before the local tribunal, and have come to the conclusion that the employment offered was suitable for the claimant and that he had no good cause for refusing it. Having regard to the evidence set out in paragraph 5 hereof, which the claimant has not attempted to challenge, I am unable to find that the wages offered to the claimant were so low as to render the employment not suitable.

R(U) 9/64

Refusal of employment—conditions of employment which a claimant might reasonably have expected to obtain

A joiner refused employment with a building firm because he would not be allowed to take tea breaks without loss of pay. Most building firms in the area paid for tea breaks but a few of the smaller firms did not. The claimant had lost no pay because of tea breaks in his last employment.

He contended that the employment was not suitable because the conditions were less favourable than those which he might reasonably have expected to obtain; alternatively, that he had good cause for refusing it because acceptance of such employment was contrary to the policy of his trade union, of which he was a branch secretary.

Held: the employment offered was *prima facie* suitable. There was no national or local agreement on tea breaks; it was a matter of arrangement at each site or job. The claimant could not expect to be paid for them always when employed by any employer in the district. Further, following his union's policy of insisting upon pay for tea breaks could not be a 'just cause' for leaving employment under s. 13(2) of the Act; and this policy did not provide him with good cause for refusing suitable employment. He was therefore disqualified.

(ii) REDUNDANCY PAYMENTS

REDUNDANCY PAYMENTS ACT, 1965

1. *General provisions as to right to redundancy payment.* (1) Where on or after the appointed day* an employee who has been continuously employed for the requisite period

(*a*) is dismissed by his employer by reason of redundancy, or

(*b*) is laid off or kept on short-time to the extent specified in sub-s. (1) of s. 6 of this Act and complies with the requirements of that section,

then, subject to the following provisions of this Part of this Act, the employer shall be liable to pay him a sum (in this Act referred to as a 'redundancy payment') calculated in accordance with Schedule 1 to this Act.

(2) For the purposes of this Act an employee who is dismissed shall be taken to be dismissed by reason of redundancy if the dismissal is attributable wholly or mainly to

(*a*) the fact that his employer has ceased, or intends to cease, to carry on the business for the purposes of which the employee was employed by him, or has ceased, or intends to cease, to carry on that business in the place where the employee was so employed, or

(*b*) the fact that the requirements of that business for employees to carry out work of a particular kind, or for employees to carry out work of a particular kind in the place where he was so employed, have ceased or diminished or are expected to cease or diminish....

2. *General exclusions from right to redundancy payment.* (1) An

* 6 December 1965.

employee shall not be entitled to a redundancy payment if immediately before the relevant date the employee

(a) if a man, has attained the age of sixty-five, or

(b) if a woman, has attained the age of sixty.

(2) Except as provided by s. 10 of this Act, an employee shall not be entitled to a redundancy payment by reason of dismissal where his employer, being entitled to terminate his contract of employment without notice by reason of the employee's conduct, terminates it either

(a) without notice, or

(b) by giving shorter notice than that which, in the absence of such conduct, the employer would be required to give to terminate the contract, or

(c) by giving notice (not being such shorter notice as is mentioned in paragraph (b) of this subsection) which includes, or is accompanied by, a statement in writing that the employer would, by reason of the employee's conduct, be entitled to terminate the contract without notice.

(3) An employee shall not be entitled to a redundancy payment by reason of dismissal if before the relevant date the employer has offered to renew his contract of employment, or to re-engage him under a new contract, so that

(a) the provisions of the contract as renewed, or of the new contract, as the case may be, as to the capacity and place in which he would be employed, and as to the other terms and conditions of his employment, would not differ from the corresponding provisions of the contract as in force immediately before his dismissal, and

(b) the renewal or re-engagement would take effect on or before the relevant date,

and the employee has unreasonably refused that offer.

(4) An employee shall not be entitled to a redundancy payment by reason of dismissal if before the relevant date the employer has made to him an offer in writing to renew his contract of employment, or to re-engage him under a new contract, so that in accordance with the particulars specified in the offer the provisions of the contract as renewed, or of the new contract, as the case may be, as to the capacity and place in which he would be employed, and as to the other terms and conditions of his employment, would differ (wholly or in part) from the corresponding provisions of the contract as in force immediately before his dismissal, but

(*a*) the offer constitutes an offer of suitable employment in relation to the employee, and

(*b*) the renewal or re-engagement would take effect on or before the relevant date or not later than four weeks after that date,

and the employee has unreasonably refused that offer....

3. *Dismissal by employer.* (1) For the purposes of this Part of this Act an employee shall, subject to the following provisions of this Part of this Act, be taken to be dismissed by his employer if, but only if,

(*a*) the contract under which he is employed by the employer is terminated by the employer, whether it is so terminated by notice or without notice, or

(*b*) where under that contract he is employed for a fixed term, that term expires without being renewed under the same contract, or

(*c*) the employee terminates that contract without notice in circumstances (not falling within s. 10(4) of this Act) such that he is entitled so to terminate it by reason of the employer's conduct.

(2) An employee shall not be taken for the purposes of this Part of this Act to be dismissed by his employer if his contract of employment is renewed, or he is re-engaged by the same employer under a new contract of employment, and

(*a*) in a case where the provisions of the contract as renewed, or of the new contract, as the case may be, as to the capacity and place in which he is employed, and as to the other terms and conditions of his employment, do not differ from the corresponding provisions of the previous contract, the renewal or re-engagement takes effect immediately on the ending of his employment under the previous contract, or,

(*b*) in any other case, the renewal or re-engagement is in pursuance of an offer in writing made by his employer before the ending of his employment under the previous contract, and takes effect either immediately on the ending of that employment or after an interval of not more than four weeks thereafter....

9. *Reference of questions to tribunal.* (1) Any question arising under this Part of this Act as to the right of an employee to a redundancy payment, or as to the amount of a redundancy payment, shall, in accordance with regulations made under Part III of this Act, be referred to and determined by a tribunal.

(2) For the purposes of any such reference

(*a*) a person's employment during any period shall, unless the contrary is proved, be presumed to have been continuous;

(b) an employee who has been dismissed by his employer shall, unless the contrary is proved, be presumed to have been so dismissed by reason of redundancy....*

11. *Exemption orders.* (1) If at any time there is in force an agreement between one or more employers or organisations of employers and one or more trade unions representing employees, whereby employees to whom the agreement applies have a right in certain circumstances to payments on the termination of their contracts of employment, and, on the application of all the parties to the agreement, the Minister, having regard to the provisions of the agreement, is satisfied that s. 1 of this Act should not apply to those employees, he may make an order under this section in respect of that agreement.

(2) The Minister shall not make an order under this section in respect of an agreement unless the agreement indicates (in whatsoever terms) the willingness of the parties to it to submit to a tribunal such questions as are mentioned in paragraph (b) of the next following subsection.

(3) Where an order under this section is in force in respect of an agreement

(a) s. 1 of this Act shall not have effect in relation to any employee who immediately before the relevant date is an employee to whom the agreement applies, and

(b) s. 9 of this Act shall have effect in relation to any question arising under the agreement as to the right of an employee to a payment on the termination of his employment, or as to the amount of such a payment, as if the payment were a redundancy payment and the question arose under this Part of this Act....

25. *Interpretation of Part I, and supplementary provisions.* (1) In this Part of this Act 'business' includes a trade or profession and includes any activity carried on by a body of persons, whether corporate or unincorporate, and 'employee' means an individual who has entered into or works under (or, in the case of a contract which has been terminated, worked under) a contract with an employer, whether the contract is for manual labour, clerical work or otherwise, is express or implied, oral or in writing, and whether it is a contract of service or of apprenticeship, and 'employer' and any reference to employment shall be construed accordingly.†

---

* But note that the burden of proof of the dismissal itself remains on the employee: *Connop* v. *Unit Metal Construction Ltd* (1966) 1 I.T.R. 486.

† For other sections see *post*, p. 420; and for an analysis of the Act as a whole, see Wedderburn (1966) 29 M.L.R. 55. Note that among the classes of employees expressly excluded by s. 16 are: dock workers; spouses of employers; and civil servants (for

DECISIONS OF INDUSTRIAL TRIBUNALS

[*Note:* The tribunals consist of a chairman who is a barrister or solicitor of seven years' standing, and two 'wing men', one from each of an employers' and employees' panel: Industrial Tribunals Regulations, 1965, S.I. 1101. Their procedure is governed now by S.I. 359 and S.I. 361 of 1967. Appeals lie to the High Court under the Tribunals and Inquiries Act, 1958, on points of law by virtue of S.I. 1403 of 1965. At the time of writing a large number of such appeals are pending: see *post* p. 239.]

(*a*) '*Dismissals*' *by reason of* '*redundancy*' *within* s. 1.

HODGKINSON *v.* BRAINTREE & BOCKING U.D.C.†

(1966) Industrial Tribunals Reports 258

The applicant was a dust cart driver. In December 1965 he fell ill and when he returned on the 13 January 1966 the respondents told him that

whom equivalent arrangements are made). Note too that the Act (except for s. 13) *does* apply to 'domestic servants' unless they are close relatives: s. 19. On the meaning of 'domestic servant' see *ante*, p. 120. The Act, in effect, combines features of employment law and social security law, by obliging the employer to make the payments to redundant workers but allowing him to claim a rebate of (usually) about two-thirds of what he paid from a national Fund, financed by employers' contributions.

† Contrast *Irvine* v. *National Fishcuring Co. Ltd* (1966) 1 I.T.R. 151: applicant who had been employed for many years by respondents was provided with a woman assistant who had become redundant in the Kipper Section of the firm. He was also given notice of termination of employment. The respondents claimed that he had been dismissed for incompetence.

Held: they had failed to discharge the onus of proof. The applicant was dismissed by reason of redundancy. (Note: the woman had taken over at a lower rate of pay.)

See too: *Ross* v. *Alexander Campbell Co. Ltd* (1966) 1 I.T.R. 189: employee dismissed by reason of illness and advancing age which makes him unable to carry out all his duties, is not dismissed by reason of redundancy.

Sweeney v. *Engelhard Industries Ltd* (1966) 1 I.T.R. 317: employee who heard that employing company were about to move to another area sought other employment because he knew that he could not obtain accommodation in that area. He left for a new job before the employing company actually moved. *Held:* he had not been 'dismissed' at all within the meaning of s. 3 of the Act. No redundancy payment was payable.

Dixon v. *Evernden* (1966) 1 I.T.R. 248: employee informed while on holiday that she was no longer needed as the business had 'managed quite well with reduced staff for some time'. The Tribunal was in some doubt on the reason for the dismissal; but as the employer had failed to prove otherwise, it held that this was a dismissal attributable to redundancy.

Petrie v. *Yarrow & Co.* (1966) 1 I.T.R. 382: worker employed as electrician became a 'marker-off', then moved back to electrician, which meant he lost the marker-off allowance. *Held:* his employment had not been terminated by the employer. He was employed as an electrician. Indeed, a 'yard conference' agreement made it clear that when marking-off work was reduced workers automatically reverted to normal rates for electricians.

See too *post* p. 224 note; and now *North Riding Garages Ltd.* v. *Butterwick* [1967] 1 All. E.R. 644 (D.C.), Appendix *post* p. 239.

his job had been filled by another man and that he would be required to do a different driving job. He refused, left the respondents' employ, and claimed a redundancy payment.

The Decision of the Tribunal was as follows:...It has been argued for the applicant that he became redundant because while he was away sick, but still in the Council's employment as a driver, a fresh dust cart driver had been taken on. This meant that there were three effective drivers plus Mr Hodgkinson, who was sick, which made a total of four drivers, and when he was dismissed the number was reduced to three. He then became redundant. This reduction is, it is contended, clear evidence that Mr Hodgkinson was dismissed for redundancy, because there was not any work for a fourth driver. It is urged that we should look at the number before and after his dismissal as a decisive factor in answering the question of whether he was dismissed because of redundancy.

We do not agree. The Act applies a different test. It provides that an employee shall be taken to be dismissed by reason of redundancy if the dismissal is attributable wholly or mainly to the fact that the employers need to carry out work of a particular kind has ceased or diminished or is expected to cease or diminish. We have heard that the dustbins of Braintree and Bocking proliferate rather than diminish owing to increase in the local population, at the rate of some 350 houses a year. We are satisfied that the work had not ceased or diminished. We are satisfied that the reason Mr Hodgkinson was dismissed was that, having been replaced by someone else, he was not prepared to do another job for the council. We are satisfied that the reason he had been replaced was that the dustbins had to be emptied while he was sick. We are satisfied that he was not dismissed for redundancy.

ESSEN v. VANDEN PLAS (ENGLAND) 1923 LTD
(1966) 1 Industrial Tribunals Reports 186

The applicant was employed by the respondents from September 1963 until 28 January 1966 when he was dismissed having been given notice. He was told the reason for his dismissal was bad timekeeping.

The Decision of the Tribunal was as follows:...Weighing all those circumstances, we find as a fact that this dismissal was attributable wholly or mainly to misconduct, i.e. bad timekeeping and not wholly or mainly to the shortage of work....

Section 2 of the Act sets out a number of general exclusions from the right to a redundancy payment. For example, if a man is over 65 or a woman is over 60 they cannot get a redundancy payment. The section also provides that if, after notice has been given for redundancy, the employer offers suitable alternative employment and the employee unreasonably refuses to take it, then he is not entitled to a redundancy payment. The other general exclusion is the one raised by Mr Cowlard. The section provides that where an employer is entitled to dismiss an employee summarily (that is without notice) the employee shall not be entitled to a redundancy payment even though the employer has in fact allowed the employee to serve out his notice. In such a case the employer is required to give the employee a statement in writing that the employer would, by reason of the employee's conduct, be entitled to terminate the contract without notice. The applicant argues that as he was given no such written statement, he is entitled to a redundancy payment.

We find s. 2(2) of the Act very difficult to understand. It provides that an employee dismissed for conduct justifying summary dismissal shall have no entitlement to a redundancy payment. It is not clear why it is necessary for the subsection to make this specific provision, as an employee is only entitled to a redundancy payment if his dismissal is attributable wholly or mainly to redundancy. He is dismissed for redundancy if the sole or main reason for his dismissal is that his employer's need for employees to do work of a particular kind has ceased or diminished. If his dismissal is wholly or mainly due to some other cause, e.g. incompetence or ill-health or that the employer wanted to replace him by someone else, he is not entitled to a redundancy payment. It is therefore otiose to provide in s. 2(2) that an employee dismissed for incompetence so serious as to justify summary dismissal is not entitled to a redundancy payment.

The subsection goes on to provide that where an employer dismisses an employee for conduct justifying summary dismissal, but allows him to work out a normal notice, the employer shall set out, in writing, the fact that he is entitled to dismiss the employee without notice. We also find it difficult to understand why this provision was inserted in the Act, and what its effect is. If an employee commits some minor misconduct and is given notice, the employer need not give him a written statement. If the employee is guilty of misconduct so bad as to justify summary dismissal but is given notice, he must be given a written statement. We cannot see why the latter employee should receive this special treatment.

Another question left unanswered by s. 2(2) is what effect a failure to give such a written statement shall have on a claim for a redundancy payment. No sanction is provided for such a failure. We do not think that such a failure can make the employee entitled to a redundancy payment, as he would still fail to qualify under s. 1(1)(a), because his dismissal would be for misconduct and not redundancy. The reason for dismissal would not become redundancy because the employer had failed to give the statement in writing required by s. 2(2)(c). The dismissal must either be attributable wholly or mainly to redundancy as defined, or it must be attributable wholly or mainly to some other cause. In the former case an employee is entitled to a redundancy payment. In the latter case he is not.

MEGER v. GREENS FOOD FARE LIMITED

(1966) 1 Industrial Tribunals Reports 244

The Tribunal held that a redundant employee who, during the period of notice, left her employment with the agreement of her employers but without giving the written notice required under s. 4(1)(b), lost the right to a redundancy payment...

The general rule is that an employee is not entitled to a redundancy payment unless he is dismissed by his employer. 'Dismissed' means that the employee's contract of employment is terminated by the employer. In circumstances such as arise in the present case, the contract of employment was terminated not by the employer but by the employee because she wanted to leave early in order to take up other employment. Parliament has made provision in the Act to deal with cases such as those in order that an energetic employee who has been given notice and finds alternative employment during the period of that notice shall not be penalised. That provision is contained in s. 4 of the Act. The provisions of that section, relevant to the present case, are that where an employee is given notice by his employer, but wants to leave before the notice expires, the employee may himself give notice in writing to his employer to terminate the contract of employment. If the employer does not object then the termination of employment shall be deemed to be a dismissal by the employer and the employee can qualify for a redundancy payment.*

* When the employer does object, he can give to the employee a notice in writing stating that unless the employee withdraws his notice to leave, the liability to pay will be contested. In such a case, the tribunal, if it thinks it just and equitable that some payment should be made, having regard to the employee's reasons for wishing to leave and the employer's reasons for wanting him to serve out the longer notice, may award

Our difficulty in this case is that it is quite clear on the facts that no notice in writing was given by Mrs Meger. She telephoned to Mr Horlick, told him she had got this new job which was starting before her notice expired and asked if she could be released to take it up immediately. The respondents allowed her to do so.

We are divided on this. Two of us feel that the specific provisions of the Redundancy Payments Act (which says that s. 4 shall only apply where the employee gives notice in writing to her employer) are binding upon us. The other member of the Tribunal feels that because oral notice, given over the telephone, was accepted by the employer, then the employee should be entitled to the benefit of this provision and to a redundancy payment.

All of us feel sympathy for Mrs Meger but, as I have said, the majority of us feel that we are bound by the specific provisions of the section. In those circumstances, the application fails and is dismissed.

Application dismissed.

(b) *Transfer of Job or Place of Job and 'Dismissal'; and Offers of Re-engagement under s. 2*

VINCENT *v.* WILLIAM CAMPBELL & SONS (BISCUITS) LIMITED

(1966) 1 Industrial Tribunals Reports 319

The applicant was employed by the respondents, who are biscuit manufacturers, as a charge hand in the packing department. She refused to go and work in the creaming and chocolate department, although the work she would have been required to do there would not have been substantially different from the work she was doing. She was dismissed and claimed a redundancy payment.

Held: the applicant was dismissed because she had refused to obey an order and not because she had become redundant. She was, therefore, not entitled to a redundancy payment.

the whole of the redundancy payment or such part of it as it thinks fit: s. 4(3)(4). See, for example, *Duncan* v. *Fairfield Rowan Ltd* (1966) 1 I.T.R. 153, where the respondents showed no particular reason for wanting to keep the worker, but the worker wanted to leave in order to take up another job. He was awarded his payment. But the employee must take care to observe s. 4 strictly. See, for example, *Armit* v. *McLauchlan* (1966) 1 I.T.R. 280, where the employee failed because he gave his notice verbally instead of, as s. 4(1) requires, in writing. He also gave his notice too early. He was entitled to four week's notice; but was given some three months. He gave his own notice to quit in the second month. Section 4 only operates when the employee gives his notice during the currency of the 'obligatory' period of notice from his employer, i.e. the minimum period to which he is entitled: s. 4(5). See *Phillips* v. *Morganite Carbon Ltd* (1967) 2 I.T.R. 53.

NOQUET v. ESSEX PUBLISHING CO. LTD
(1966) 1 Industrial Tribunals Reports 160

On 1 December, 1965 the applicant was informed by her employers the respondents, that the office at which she worked in Walthamstow was being closed and that, in future, she would be required to work at their other premises, about two miles away. She refused to do so and her employment with the respondents ceased on 31 December 1965. She claimed a redundancy payment.

The Decision of the Tribunal was as follows:. . . Can it be said, in the circumstances of this case, that the respondents' conduct in asking the applicant to work in an office less than two miles away was conduct such as to justify an employee in terminating the contract without notice? We think not. We find that the employee terminated the contract of employment herself, and that she was not dismissed by her employer. We are supported in that view by a statement made by the applicant in her Originating Application, in which she set out her case where she first applied to this tribunal and in which she said 'I did not wish to go to the Leytonstone Office, so I left the company's employ'.

We think this was not a dismissal but a transfer of employment. The employee left because the terms of the transfer were not to her liking and because of her personal circumstances.*

* See too: *Bounds* v. *Smith Co. Ltd* (1966) 1 I.T.R. 53: applicant employed at Dungeness Nuclear Power Station; after 1961, he was paid at the rates for 'travelling' men by arrangement with his union. He was required to move to another site, but refused.
Held: his dismissal stemmed from this improper refusal, not from redundancy.
Stannard v. *Dexion Ltd* (1966) 1 I.T.R. 274: employing company decide to close a department, and in consequence require applicant to move to another department. The applicant refused and was dismissed.
Held: he had been engaged not, as he claimed, as a woodworker, but as a general production worker. He had voluntarily terminated his own employment because he did not like the work he was to do in the new department.
Richards v. *Thomas Ward Ltd* (1966) 1 I.T.R. 246: applicant employed as a plate-layer's labourer at respondent's Scunthorpe works, told he will be moved elsewhere. (It would have been to Barnsley.) He refused to move, left the employment and claimed a redundancy payment. Evidence was given that it was a custom in the industry to transfer gangs of men in this way. Also, he was paid a 'subsistence allowance', shown as such on the wage sheet; and the foreman had explained that this meant he must be prepared to transfer elsewhere if required to do so.
Held: the employee was required under his contract of employment to 'transfer to whatever place he was directed to'. No dismissal had occurred; he had discharged himself.
See too now, *Morton Sundour Fabrics Ltd* v. *Shaw, The Times*, 26 November 1966 (Div. Ct.): A worker who gives notice and leaves after an informal warning notice that the works will soon be closing down is not 'dismissed' within the meaning of s. 3 of the Act. He left voluntarily. The Court rejected counsel's view that the payments were a 'poor man's golden handshake'. But use by employers of informal 'warnings' instead of long notice to terminate probably could, as counsel claimed, drive a 'coach and horses'

COLLIER v. E. POLLARD (DISPLAY) LTD

(1966) 1 Industrial Tribunals Reports 399

The burden of proving that an offer of employment under s. 2(4) of the Redundancy Payments Act, 1965, was not an offer of suitable employment or that the offer was not unreasonably refused, lies upon the employee to whom the offer was made, and not upon the employer.

The Decision of the Tribunal was as follows:...The general rule of law is that he who affirms must prove, that is, that the onus of setting up a *prima facie* case rests upon the plaintiff, appellant, or applicant. There are two statutory exceptions to that rule in relation to the Redundancy Payments Act, which are dealt with at s. 9(2) but with which we are not concerned here. We are accordingly satisfied that the onus in relation to s. 2(4) of the Act lies upon the applicant to satisfy the Tribunal that the offer made to him in accordance with the subsection was not an offer of suitable employment in relation to himself, and that he did not refuse that offer unreasonably.

In our view he has tendered no evidence which would enable us to make either finding. He has told us that he lives in Edgware and has for many years been employed at Highbury by the respondents as a wood machinist engaged in the manufacture of display and cabinet work. It is not disputed that the applicant's employment was terminated on grounds of redundancy within the meaning of s. 1(2) and 3(1) of the Act. At the beginning of this year a group of companies, including the respondent's, was in course of reorganisation, and that in February 1966 it was known that the applicant's work would shortly come to an end at Highbury, and that he would be asked to go to a workshop at Walthamstow. Though, as we understand, the work which he would have been required to do there would have been the same as that on which he was engaged at Highbury, he refused before a formal offer was made to him, because of the extra time and travelling involved. This was not an offer made in writing within the provisions of s. 2(4), and we are not further concerned with it.

Some time later he received a written offer of alternative employment at a different address—St John Street, Clerkenwell—addressed to him personally and in conformity with the requirements of s. 2(4).

through the Act. Unsettled workers would leave for other jobs and lose their right to redundancy payments. The case also illustrates how easy it is for tribunal decisions to reach the High Court on a 'point of law'. Such appeals are likely to become as frequent, and as unpopular, as in the cases on 'workmen's compensation' before the national insurance schemes of 1946.

He has told us today that he had two reasons for declining the written offer:

(1) He believes that the Clerkenwell workshops are to be closed down in the early part of next year, and the woodworking department moved to Walthamstow, and he has already explained why he felt obliged to refuse the offer of work there, though we may say that we did not find his reasons cogent or compelling.

The question of the suitability of a move to Walthamstow is not before us now, but we should comment here that there is no evidence of this anticipated move from St John's Street; the applicant can speak only of his belief and understands that the Clerkenwell premises have 'already been sold'; an assertion which the respondents, however, deny. The respondents submit that the Tribunal should not in any case take into account the possibility of a future move to Walthamstow, since we are concerned only under the terms of s. 2(4), with particulars specified in the offer of work at Clerkenwell. We do not find it necessary to consider this question further.

(2) The new work offered to him at Clerkenwell was unsuitable. He agrees that he would still have been working on machines as a wood machinist. But he says that the work at St John's Street would have been quite different, and would have involved different skills. The Clerkenwell work was 'shop fitting' work, requiring the use of heavier and more dangerous machines. The applicant said that he did not feel that he could properly undertake such work instructing others as a chargehand on machines with which he was himself unfamiliar.

We are of opinion that a skilled machinist, as the applicant is, should be competent to adapt his skills to different types of machine; at any rate, after some period of training or adjustment. This was also the employer's view, since they offered to employ him as a chargehand, and at an increased rate of pay. We cannot believe that they would have made such an offer had they thought that the applicant was so incapable of undertaking the work offered. We note, moreover, that the applicant does not know exactly what machines he would have been called upon to operate, and that he made no effort to inquire, but refused the offer without more ado, and without even mentioning his doubts as to his capacity to his employer.

We find accordingly that, though the applicant was dismissed on grounds of redundancy within the meaning of s. 1(2) and 3(1)(a) of the Act, he has set up no *prima facie* case that the offer of employment made to him on 24 March in compliance with s. 2(4), was an offer of employment which was not suitable in relation to himself, or that it was not unreasonably refused.

Application dismissed.

COOPER *v.* FIAT (ENGLAND) LTD

(1966) 1 Industrial Tribunals Reports 310

The applicant had been employed by the respondents for a number of years as a 'body work inspector'. He only spent about one third of his time performing his duties of a body work inspector, and for the rest of the time he had been employed as a Driver and on body finishing work. On 5 January 1966 he was told that he was to work as a body finisher, and was later informed that he would be paid the same rate of pay and enjoy the same benefits as previously. The applicant refused the offer and was dismissed. He claimed a redundancy payment.

Held: the work which the applicant had been offered, i.e., as a body finisher, was substantially similar to his previous work and was, therefore, suitable. He had acted unreasonably in refusing the offer.

The Decision of the Tribunal was as follows:...The applicant was not able to make it clear to us why he considered work as a body finisher—*prima facie* similar to his old work—to be unsuitable alternative employment. He sought to persuade us that for an inspector to 'return to the bench', even though the other circumstances of his employment were precisely the same, was in some sense a 'retrograde step'. The Tribunal has heard no evidence to satisfy it that such a change would be retrograde, nor does it see why this should be so. There seems to be some element of prestige connected with this question; the applicant thought that he would have more opportunity of meeting persons of higher status as an inspector than he would have as a body finisher; but again the Tribunal is not impressed by that submission. It has never been suggested that the applicant's chances of promotion as an inspector would have been greater than as a body finisher. Mr Cowlard (the applicant's representative) submitted that employment involving the use of tools could not be considered suitable alternative employment for a man who had been performing inspection tasks which did not require them; but, even if we found substance in that submission, which we do not, the fact remains that the applicant in any event had recently been employed as a body inspector for only about a third of his time.*

* *Note:* The offer of alternative employment must be unambiguous and not vague: *McNeil* v. *Vickers Ltd* (1966) 1 I.T.R. 180. Further, acceptance of it must be clearly proved: *Crosby* v. *Steel Nut & Joseph Hampton Ltd* (1966) 1 I.T.R. 270 (redundant man who worked for one and a half days at alternative work which required training, not shown to have 'accepted' it).

RAMAGE v. HARPER–MACKAY LTD

(1966) 1 Industrial Tribunals Reports 503

The applicant was employed as sales representative. The respondents instituted a policy of reducing the number of their sales representatives. He was required to increase his sales but failed to do so. He was relieved of his position and told that, in future he would work in the warehouse and as a relief representative. By this move he would have lost the right to qualify for certain bonus payments and the car with which he had been provided. The applicant refused to accept the move and resigned, the respondents' paying him four weeks pay. No other person was employed in his place. He claimed a redundancy payment.

Held: by relieving him of his duties, the respondents had repudiated their obligations to him and he was entitled to terminate his contract without notice, the case falling within s. 3(1) (c) of the Redundancy Payments Act, 1965. The termination of his employment was attributable to the respondents' policy of reducing the number of their sales representatives and consequently was due to redundancy. The work offered was not suitable as it involved a loss of position and would affect his prospects as a sales representative. His claim therefore succeeded.

The Tribunal said:...We were of the view that the offer of employment made was not suitable and that the applicant was not unreasonable in refusing it. The alternative employment involved a loss of bonuses of about £1 10s. 0d. weekly. It involved the loss of the use of a car for a large part of the year. It involved a loss of position which would affect his prospects as a sales representative. Such employment is considered to require higher qualities of responsibility and initiative than a warehouseman's employment. To accept the alternative employment would have undermined the applicant's relationship with his customers if he required to meet them as a relief salesman. The applicant also objected to being reduced to the position of making up orders for his fellow representatives.*

SHEPPARD v. NATIONAL COAL BOARD

(1966) 1 Industrial Tribunals Reports 177

The applicant's employment with the respondents was terminated by notice expiring on the 1 January 1966. On the 3 December 1965, the respondents offered, in writing, the applicant alternative employment which he rejected. The alternative employment offered was of a similar nature to his present employment but required the applicant to travel further to and from work and his opportunity for overtime was diminished.

* On the 'status' element in this argument, compare *Yetton* v. *Eastwoods Froy Ltd*, *ante*, p. 170; and see now *Skillen* v. *Eastwoods Froy Ltd* (1967) 2 I.T.R. 112.

Certain benefits would not be available in the new employment. The applicant claimed a redundancy payment.

Held: that the offer made by the respondent was of suitable employment. The availability of overtime was not a factor to be considered in deciding whether the employment was suitable or its rejection reasonable However, the loss of the other benefits (cheap coal, travelling and insurance assistance) were matters to be considered and, in the circumstances, the applicant had not been unreasonable in rejecting the offer. He was entitled to a redundancy payment.

LEE *v.* ASHTON BROTHERS AND COMPANY LIMITED

(1966) 1 Industrial Tribunals Reports 344

In considering whether an offer of alternative employment is an offer of suitable employment, the fact that the employee will be required to work on a 'double shift' system is a factor to be taken into account.

In the view of the Tribunal, it is not possible (even if desirable) to lay down any hard and fast general rule on the point, and we consider that no general principle emerges. We decline to hold either that double shift working—to which alone this decision relates—is always necessarily unsuitable; or that it can never constitute a valid objection. We consider that it is always a most relevant factor to be taken into consideration, but that it is not by itself decisive. The answer must depend upon the special circumstances of each individual case.

In the case of Mrs Lee we conclude that in spite of the need for acceptance of double shift working the offer of employment was suitable, and that in all the circumstances of the case she unreasonably refused it. The following three main factors lead us to this conclusion.

(*a*) Mrs Lee has previously worked the double shift system....
(*b*) At Mrs Lee's age acceptance of the offer would in any event have involved only a comparatively short period of double shift working before she reached the age of retirement.*...(*c*) We find no special personal or family difficulties occasioned or increased by working double shifts. Mrs Lee has a husband, and a son aged 20, resident at home. Her husband is a bus driver and her son a salesman working irregular hours. Neither would be seriously affected....Mrs Lee was unquestionably entitled, at her age, to elect to retire from work. But for the

---

* She was 58 years old. Note that men at 65, and women at 60, lose their rights to redundancy payments. In the twelve months before that, a worker loses one twelfth of his payment for every month he is over 64 (or, women, 59) at the date of eventual dismissal: Schedule 1, paragraph 4 of the Act.

purposes of s. 2 of the Redundancy Payments Act, 1965, we hold that the offer constituted an offer of suitable employment in relation to the employee, and that she unreasonably refused it.

RAWE v. THE POWER GAS CORPORATION LIMITED

(1966) 1 Industrial Tribunals Reports 154

The applicant worked for the respondents at various sites in South East England from December 1961 to 24 December 1965. During December 1965 he was offered work by the respondents on Tees-side which he refused and he ceased to work for them. He claimed a redundancy payment, but the respondents claimed that he was a 'travelling man' and had refused to work within the terms of his contract by refusing to go to Tees-side and that this was the reason for his dismissal, and not because he was redundant.

Held: that on the evidence it was clear that the applicant was not a 'travelling man'. He had become redundant and had been offered alternative employment by the respondents. This offer was not one of suitable employment for the applicant as it required him to leave his family and risk domestic troubles, and previously he had only been required by the respondents to work in South East England, and therefore his refusal was not unreasonable. He was entitled to a redundancy payment.

The decision of the Tribunal was as follows:...'...It seems to us that the expression "in relation to the employee" means that we have to apply a subjective test to see whether in the particular circumstances of the employee the offer was reasonable and refusal unreasonable. The reason for the refusal was domestic. The applicant is married, has a rented house in South-East England, a family of two boys aged 16 and 17, the younger still at school. His wife objected to his going away so far....He wished to accept this employment on Tees-side but had to decide whether to risk breaking up his marriage by domestic upset or whether to forego the job. In this difficult position he made the choice he thought was right, to give up the employment. On all the facts of the case, we are satisfied that it was not an unreasonable refusal of the offer and in relation to him this was not an offer of suitable employment.'*

---

* The tribunals certainly take account of domestic factors in interpreting 'unreasonable' and 'suitable'. See *Silver* v. *J. E. L. Group* (1966) 1 I.T.R. 238 (production manager at Hounslow factory refused to move with firm to Dorset; he had very recently bought a larger house undertaking large commitments, and did not wish to live far from his sick father; the Dorset employment was not 'suitable' even though the firm offered a car for week-end travel back to Hounslow), and *Cahuac* v. *Allen Amery Ltd* (1966) 1 I.T.R. 313 (offer of employment to women working at premises in Hackney E.2 in premises to which firm was moving in E.C.1, a forty minutes journey from their homes,

(c) Continuity of Employment, Change of Ownership and Associated Companies

KINCEY *v.* PARDEY & JOHNSON LIMITED

(1966) 1 Industrial Tribunals Reports 182

The applicant was employed in a sub-post office from 1959 to 15 January 1966. Her working hours were arranged on a two week system, in the first she worked on Mondays, Wednesdays and Fridays from 9 a.m. to 5.30 p.m. and in the second she worked on Tuesdays and Saturdays from 9 a.m. to 5.30 p.m. and on Thursday from 9 a.m. to 1 p.m. The employment ceased on the closing of the office and she claimed a redundancy payment.

Held: that in order to be entitled to a redundancy payment it was necessary to be satisfied that the applicant had been 'continuously employed' for the requisite period. The provisions of Schedule 1 to the Contracts of Employment Act, 1963 [*ante*, p. 167] apply to determine this question and the effect of those provisions is that the applicant's continuity of employment would be broken by any week in which she worked less than 21 hours. On the facts she worked 22½ hours in one week and 19 in the next, and therefore she was not continuously employed for the requisite period.

ROWLATT (LIQUIDATOR OF ISLAND MUTUAL SUPPLIES LIMITED) *v.* BUDDEN AND HARRIS

(1966) 1 Industrial Tribunals Reports 269

The provisions of s. 13 of the Redundancy Payments Act 1965 will not operate where employees are engaged by a new employer who purchases only the fixtures and fittings of the former employer, because this purchase

judged to be unsuitable. In one case account was taken of the applicant's caring for her widowed mother at home.)

But the decisions concerning children's interests vary widely. Compare with *Rawe's* case *Rose* v. *Shelley and Partners Ltd* (1966) 1 I.T.R. 169: wife of husband employed at Tottenham insistent that she will not move to alternative job offered in Huntingdon. She even found a job herself to support herself and family, a daughter of 17 at work, and a son of 11 at school. The tribunal found the offer 'suitable'; but the offer was invalidated by being made the day after the termination of the employment instead of, as s. 2(4) demands, before that date. In *Bainbridge* v. *Westinghouse Brake and Signal Co. Ltd* (1966) 1 I.T.R. 55, employee at Newcastle was offered work at Glasgow for a few months, and thereafter at Leeds. The tribunal apparently considered the offer 'suitable' to the employee; but by a majority went on to accept his refusal as reasonable in the light of domestic circumstances. These included the difficulties of finding a house in the new areas; and the fact that his children were at 'a crucial stage' of their education, one about to sit the '11 plus', the other the GCE examination. Similarly, in *White and Others* v. *John Boulding Ltd* (1966) 1 I.T.R. 446, the wife's refusal to move which would 'break up the marriage' was accepted as ground for a reasonable refusal.

See now *Freer* v. *Kayser Bondor, post* p. 239.

does not constitute a change in the ownership of the 'business' carried on by the former employer.

The Decision of the Tribunal was as follows:...The first question we have to determine is whether Mr Budden and Mrs Harris were re-engaged by the same employer, having regard to s. 13(1) and (2) of the Act. The effect, in brief, of both sections is that where a change occurs in the ownership of a business and the employee's contract is terminated in consequence, if by agreement with the employee the new owner renews the contract or re-engages him s. 3(2) of the Act, shall have effect as if the renewal of re-engagement had been by the previous owner.

Section 3(2) provides that in certain circumstances an employee shall not be taken to be dismissed if his contract is renewed or he is re-engaged by the same owner. Section 13(1) refers to where a change occurs (whether by virtue of a sale or other disposition or by operation of law) in the ownership of a business or part of a business, etc. Here if s. 13 applies there has to be a sale of the business or part of the business.*

It is clear that the Provident Clothing & Supply Co. have stepped into the shoes of the Island Mutual Supplies Company carrying on the same kind of business, acquiring their clientele and purchasing their fixtures and fittings, but they have paid nothing for good-will and the Island Mutual Supplies Company retain their own debts and liabilities. The business, the activities carried on by the Island Mutual Supplies Company far from being sold to anybody are in process of ceasing to exist (we refer to the definition of 'business' in s. 25(1) of the Act). All that has been sold are the fixtures and fittings necessary to the carrying on of the business.

Both respondents have not in consequence been re-engaged by the same business except that Mr Budden has assisted, and is assisting, the liquidator to collect debts owing to the Island Mutual Supplies Company. It is accepted by both sides that he does this as an independent contractor and not under any contract of service. He, therefore, falls

---

* See too *Curtis* v. *Collett & Sons Ltd* (1966) 1 I.T.R. 402: company ceases to manufacture certain items and arranges for another firm to do it; employees transferred to that firm; s. 13 does not apply and employees can claim payments. Contrast *Anderson* v. *David Winter Ltd* (1966) 1 I.T.R. 326 (purchase of premises by new company: no break in continuity of employment). Section 13 brings into play paragraph 10 of Schedule 1, Contracts of Employment Act, 1963, *ante*, p. 169. See now *Dallow Industrial Properties Ltd.* v. *Else*, [1967] 2 All E.R. 30 (D.C.): Continuity of employment is broken under para. 10(2) and s. 13 if the employee transfers his employment when the old employer has sold not the business or a separate part thereof, but only property or assets to the new employer.

outside the definition of employee in s. 25(1) of the Act. In the result we held that both respondents are entitled to redundancy payments and we awarded £63 to Mrs Harris and £144 to Mr Budden.

COLLORICK v. W. JAMES & COMPANY LIMITED

(1966) 1 Industrial Tribunals Reports 322

Early in 1966 the applicant was dismissed by the respondents. On leaving their employ he was engaged, on less favourable terms, by the CM Co. Ltd which, in relation to the respondents, is an 'associated company' within the terms of s. 48 of the Redundancy Payments Act, 1965. He claimed a redundancy payment.

Held: as the respondents and the CM Co. Ltd were associated companies, the applicant's employment by the CM Co. Ltd must be construed as re-employment by the same employer, as provided by s. 48 of the Act.* Consequently, the provisions of s. 3(2)(b) applied and the applicant was not entitled to a redundancy payment.

The Decision of the Tribunal was as follows:...The position then is that the respondent, as the wholly owned subsidiary of a company which is an associate subsidiary company to the Crittall Manufacturing Co. Ltd, is also an associated company to the Crittall Manufacturing Co. Ltd within the meaning of s. 48 of the Redundancy Payments Act....The right of Mr Collorick to a payment under the Redundancy Payments Act 1965 depends on the interpretation of s. 3 of the Act. Under s. 48(1), where the employer is a company, any reference in Part I of this Act to re-engagement by the employer shall be construed as a reference to re-engagement by that company or by any associated company.

There are obviously, I have set them out, substantial differences between the new contract in this case and the old contract. It is quite clear that paragraph (a) of subsection (2) deals with the case where the new conditions of employment are exactly the same as the old conditions of employment and, in addition to that, the new employment carries on and takes effect immediately on the ending of his old employment so that (b), when it opens with the words 'In any other case', must be dealing with someone else.

It seems that the provisions of s. 3(2) correspond to those of s. 2(3) and (4). In each case there is first the case dealt with where the contract is exactly the same and, secondly, the case dealt with where the contract

* Section 48 causes a holding company and subsidiaries within the meaning of s. 154, Companies Act, 1948, to be treated as one group unit for the purposes of re-engagements.

differs from that which had earlier been in force. If an employee refuses the second type of contract which is offered, the contract which differs from the old one, the Tribunal has to consider whether that is suitable employment to have been offered in relation to the employee and it has to consider whether the refusal of it was reasonable or not. But under sub-paragraph 2(*b*) of s. 3, if the employee has himself accepted the employment there is no provision made for the Tribunal to consider in any way whether the offer or the terms of the new contract are an offer of suitable employment in relation to what he had been doing. The scheme of the Act seems to be that payment is not made if there has been an offer of somewhat different employment in two circumstances. It is not made if the offer is regarded by the Tribunal as suitable and the refusal of it is regarded as unreasonable, and it is not made if the employee himself has decided to accept it. If he does accept re-engagement he has some benefit in that his earlier service with his previous employer counts as service with the associated company which re-engages him. That is not of much value, because with firms in good business there is not anticipation that there will be dismissal by reason of redundancy. But the Act is designed to make provision for those who have lost their positions as a result of redundancy, and if they have seen fit themselves to take the alternative employment the Act does concern itself with the nature of that. They can if they please, when an offer is made which does not seem to them to be apt to the work which they had earlier been doing, refuse that offer and take the chance that their refusal will be held to have been reasonable, but if they themselves accept the offer they must, it seems, be regarded as having been re-engaged in terms of s. 3(2)(*b*).

(*d*) Calculation and Payment of Redundancy Payments

HARPER *v.* TAYLOR WOODROW CONSTRUCTION LTD

(1966) 1 Industrial Tribunals Reports 259

For the purposes of calculating a redundancy payment, an employee's normal working hours will not include regular periods of overtime which he is expected to work, but which are not obligatory under the terms of the contract of employment.

The decision of the Tribunal was as follows:... The applicant, in common with all the similar employees of the respondent's firm, received on his engagement a document setting out the terms of employment which by reference fixed his working hours at 40 hours per week, and these working hours did not include overtime. That being the case, the provisions of § 1(2) of Schedule 2 of the Contracts of Employment Act, 1963, would not apply, and it would appear that the matter is governed by § 1(1) of Schedule 2 of the Contracts of Employment Act. In this case the applicant's normal working hours would be 40 as fixed under his contract.

The only matter which causes difficulty in this case is that the applicant and his fellow employees habitually did overtime work every week day and habitually also worked at the weekend, with the result that the hours they habitually worked were over 48. It was established that it is convenient both for the employers and the employees generally that the work should be accelerated in this way, and it was so done as a result of agreement between the employers and employees' representatives.

In these circumstances Mr Jones, the Office Manager of the employers, agreed that the men were not expected to work the 40 hour week but the longer week, though he added that an employee who refused to work over 40 hours in the week would not be regarded as in breach of contract. As, however, the employees are to a large extent dependent on one another, it is clear that such a refusal to work would be unpopular both with the employers and his fellow employees.... It may well be that in some cases the contract may be incapable of fulfilment without the working of longer hours than those fixed, as in the case of a milkman who is physically incapable of completing his stipulated work in the fixed working hours.... The fact that the parties have agreed to work longer hours is a matter of convenience and does not affect either position. We therefore hold that the applicant is entitled to a redundancy payment on the basis of a 40 hour week, namely, £41. 6s. 8d.*

---

* Compare *Pioli* v. *B.T.R. Industries Ltd* (1966) 1 I.T.R. 255, where the tribunal accepted evidence that the employee had been told overtime was compulsory, even though his written conditions of employment did not refer to this. His normal hours were therefore computed by reference to overtime. See now *post* p. 239.

See too, *O'Connor* v. *Montrose Canned Food Ltd* (1966) 1 I.T.R. 171, where the employee was offered temporary employment on the same conditions except that there would be no overtime. The tribunal held he was justified in refusing this offer of alternative employment and that his payment must be computed by reference to his 54-hour week, not the 40-hour week worked by most workers at the plant. No statement of his employment contract was produced; but the tribunal accepted that, as a maintenance fitter, he was *required* to work the 54-hour week to keep the machinery running.

WELSH v. JOHN THOMPSON WATER TUBE BOILERS LTD

(1966) 1 Industrial Tribunals Reports 272

The applicant, a piece-worker, was dismissed as redundant. He claimed that his redundancy payment should be based on 'normal working hours' of 48⅛ weekly, which included overtime. The respondents contended that he was employed on a 40-hour week and that any overtime worked should be excluded when considering his 'normal working hours'

The decision of the Tribunal was as follows:...It is conceded that the applicant is a piece-worker and that his redundancy payment should be calculated by reference to the formula specified in paragraph 2(3) of Schedule 2 to the Contracts of Employment Act, 1963. That formula takes into account normal working hours and average hourly rate.* It is on these two factors that there is a divergence between the parties. In order to calculate normal working hours the general rule is that only those hours which are paid at a basic rate should count, and that hours which are paid at an overtime rate should be ignored. An exception to this general rule is that where an employee's contract requires him to work for more than the number of hours paid at basic rates then the higher number fixed by the contract is to be taken, even though some of the hours in that higher number are paid at overtime rates....The statement of terms of employment given to the applicant pursuant to s. 4 of the Contracts of Employment Act, 1963...provides as follows: *Normal Working Hours*: Your normal working hours and the terms and conditions relating to such hours are in accordance with the notices on the site notice boards. In addition, overtime hours will be required as circumstances require and notice will be given when possible.

The respondents point out that under the Steam Generating Plant Erection Agreement the working week was laid down as 41 hours, which was reduced, in March 1965, to 40 hours. The applicant points out that if he only did 40 hours per week he would be classed as a bad time-keeper, that he did not work less than 48⅛ hours in a week unless on holiday, on weekend leave, or sick or off from accident. He pointed out that in his work he could not work precise hours because, as a chargehand erector, he could never leave until the job was safe.... Under the terms of his contract, and on the evidence given, we find

---

* Note the amendment of paragraph 2(4) of that Schedule in s. 39, Redundancy Payments Act, 1965.

as a fact that overtime hours were at the discretion of the management and had to be done by employees as required by the respondents. The words 'overtime hours will be required as circumstances require and notice will be given when possible' are mandatory. They give the management power to impose compulsory overtime. They do not provide for negotiated or voluntary overtime. We find that the applicant's normal working hours were 48⅛ per week.

(e) Lay-Off and Short-Time
POWELL v. SHERIDAN
(1966) 1 Industrial Tribunals Reports 331

P., an employee, was told that he was to be put on 'short-time'. He objected and, forthwith, left his employment. He claimed a redundancy payment from S., his employer.

Held: no redundancy payment was payable as the conditions laid down in s. 6 of the Redundancy Payments Act, 1965 had not been satisfied. The minimum qualifying period was four weeks' continuous short-time, [or any six weeks in a period of thirteen]*.

TAYLOR v. DUNBAR (BUILDERS) LTD
(1966) 1 Industrial Tribunals Reports 249

Lay-off—recall—notice of intention to claim redundancy payment—counter notice—likelihood of period of normal employment—ss. 5, 6(1)(a), 6(3), 6(4), 6(5) and 7(5)(c), Redundancy Payments Act, 1965.

The applicant was suspended from work by the respondents from the 5 January 1966. On the 31 January 1966 he commenced work with another employer. On the 2 February 1966 the respondents ordered the applicant, by telegram, to return to work. The following day a written claim for a redundancy payment was made on his behalf and, on the 4 February 1966, the respondents gave notice that they disputed the claim. The applicant had not returned to work for the respondents.

Held: the conditions required by s. 6(1)(a) of the Redundancy Payments Act, 1965 ('laid off...for four or more consecutive weeks') had been satisfied, but the respondents had served a counter notice in terms of s. 6(5), and it was reasonably to be expected that the applicant would have entered upon a period of normal employment as specified in s. 6(4) of the Act. It followed that the applicant was not entitled to a redundancy payment.

* These cases call to the attention of the reader ss. 5, 6 and 7 of the Act. Lack of space prevented their inclusion in full. Briefly they may entitle to a redundancy payment a worker who is either completely laid off, or on 'short time' (earning less than half normal pay), or partly laid off or partly on short time for four weeks, or for a broken period of six weeks in thirteen weeks. For a summary of the Act's provisions on these 'lost' weeks, see (1966) 29 M.L.R. p. 64.

The decision of the Tribunal was as follows:...that the applicant was either laid off or put on short-time working during the week ending Friday, 7 January 1966 (according as whether the holiday credits are treated as remuneration under his contract of employment or not); and that he had been laid off for the next three weeks ending Friday, 28 January 1966. We accordingly found that the provisions of s. 6(1)(a) had been satisfied.

Secondly, we found that the employer had served a counter notice in terms of s. 6(5) of the Act on 4 February 1966. The respondents contended that, on 3 February 1966, it was reasonably to be expected that the applicant would, not later than four weeks after that date, enter on a period of normal employment for not less than 13 weeks in terms of s. 6(4) of the Act. They led evidence, which we accepted, of new contracts involving a substantial amount of joiner work which they entered into in January 1966, and of joiner work on the Kingshouse Hotel which recommenced in January 1966. Despite the fact that the immediate reason for the recall of the applicant was probably the verbal claim for a redundancy payment, we were satisfied that, when the telegram was sent, the respondents had work which would have enabled them to employ the applicant on normal full-time employment for at least 13 weeks. We thought it likely that, had the applicant not been recalled on 2 February 1966, he would probably have been recalled during February even if no claim for a redundancy payment had been made. None of the suspended joiners returned to the respondents' employment—there being a local shortage of joiners—so that the respondents' offer was never tested. We accordingly find that the applicant is not entitled to a redundancy payment by reason of the provisions of s. 6(4) of the Act.

It was also contended that the applicant was not entitled to a redundancy payment because he had not given a week's notice of termination of his employment to the respondents in terms of s. 6(3) of the Act. We considered that the present case fell under s. 7(5)(c) of the Act and that the applicant's failure to give a week's notice of termination of employment prior to the decision of the Tribunal is of no significance.

APPENDIX ON REDUNDANCY DECISIONS

At the time of correcting final proofs, five appeals to the Divisional Court have been reported. Two are *Morton Sundour Fabrics Ltd* v. *Shaw, ante* p. 160 and p. 224 [now reported in (1967) 2 I.T.R. 84], and *Dallow Industrial Properties Ltd* v. *Else, ante* p. 232.

In *North Riding Garages Ltd* v. *Butterwick* [1967] 1 All E.R. 644, an employee, who had satisfied employers as a workshop manager for 30 years was dismissed ten months after a take-over of the firm. The new company introduced new methods and alleged that he was 'inefficient'. The tribunal awarded a payment because it thought that the requirement for a manager of the old type had ceased. *Held:* the decision was wrong in law. An employee who remained in the same kind of work could be expected to adapt to new methods, new duties and higher standards of efficiency. This employee had been dismissed not because of any diminution in the volume of the work, but because he failed to reach new standards of efficiency. 'We think that the tribunal has fallen into error by applying the wrong test, in that they have not looked at the overall requirements of the business but at the allocation of duties between individuals.': at p. 648 *per* Widgery J. [Note. This strict interpretation of s. 1 (2) (*b*) of the Act, *ante*, p. 215 limits considerably the ambit of 'redundancy' caused by the cessation or diminution of requirements of a business for work of a particular kind.]

In *McCulloch Ltd* v. *Moore, The Times,* 1 March 1967, an employee of contractors was told they had 'no further work in the Sussex area'. They offered him work in Reading, East Midlands, Luton or Scotland. He refused the offers. The employers (apparently not arguing s. 2) contended he was not dismissed, because of an agreement allowing employers to transfer workers. *Held:* The employers 'had nowhere involved the agreement' in his employment contract (see p. 282 *post*). The notice was therefore a dismissal by reason of redundancy. The 'place' of employment in s. 1 (2) means a defined area in which the employee is employed to work.

In *Turiff Construction Ltd* v. *Bryant, The Times,* 2 March 1967, a worker was employed on terms of agreement for civil engineering industry stating working hours to be 40 a week. The tribunal had calculated his redundancy payment on a basis of 51 hours a week, because, as recorded on site notices and in minutes of meetings between shop stewards and management, weekend overtime had been arranged averaging eleven hours a week (see *ante* p. 234). *Held:* although this local arrangement was referred to as the 'agreed site hours' and 'agreed working week', it was on a basis of co-operation not contract. Men who failed to work the 51 hours, as often happened, were not in breach of contract. The redundancy calculation should be based on a 40 hour week. (Consider the problems raised *post* p. 293 and p. 306.)

Further decisions of tribunals:

(*a*) *Howarth* v. *Delta Bureau* (1966) 1 I.T.R. 568: employee dismissed because 'she knew too much' and for personal reasons flowing from her relationship with director; not dismissed by reason of redundancy.

(*b*) *Freer* v. *Kayser Bondor* (1967) 2 I.T.R. 4: offer of alternative work on night shift not suitable because of wife's poor health. Further offer of less skilled work held to be suitable; but employee held to have refused it not unreasonably. The tribunal considered many factors on 'reasonableness' including whether the worker could use his skill elsewhere and even the *reason* for the redundancy. A refusal, it said, might be *more* reasonable if the employer created redundancy by rationalisation or automation or reorganisation for economy or efficiency than if caused by trading conditions: *sed quaere*.

(*d*) *Lyford* v. *Turquand* (1966) 1 I.T.R. 554: a 'week's pay' means only the money payable and does not include emoluments in kind. (The tribunal discusses various judicial pronouncements on the meaning of 'wages'.)

(*e*) *Sneddon* v. *Ivorycrete Ltd* (1966) I.T.R. 538: employers wishing to lay off worker dismiss him when union advise that their agreements make no provision for suspension. Worker offered work three weeks later but refuses to return. *Held:* he was dismissed, not 'laid off'; therefore he was entitled to redundancy payment. 'Lay off is a common feature of employment in certain industries but seems to be almost unknown to the common law'. The right to lay off may arise by usage of the trade; or from an express or implied term of the contract of employment; or by agreed modification of that contract. [Note. consider materials *ante* p. 64, p. 80 and pp. 143–5.]

CHAPTER 3

COLLECTIVE BARGAINING AND THE LAW

SECTION A

COLLECTIVE BARGAINING STRUCTURES

INDUSTRIAL RELATIONS HANDBOOK

(Ministry of Labour, 1961), pp. 18–19

The term 'collective bargaining' is applied to those arrangements under which wages and conditions of employment are settled by a bargain, in the form of an agreement made between employers or associations of employers and workers' organisations. In unorganised trades, the normal practice was and sometimes still is for the individual workman, when applying for a job, to accept or refuse the terms offered by the employer, without communication with his fellow workmen and without any other consideration than his own position. In other words, he made with his employer an entirely individual bargain. The position is different when the employer is party to an agreement which settles the principles and conditions upon which for the time being all workmen of a particular class or grade will be engaged. When the agreement is made by a number of different employers or, as is often the case, by an employers' association acting on behalf of the whole or the greater part of the firms in a given industry within a wide area, all the workers employed by the employers concerned are secured equality of treatment, while each employer is protected against unfair competition by reason of lower wages costs in so far as his competitors are parties to the agreement. For many years collective agreements have played a most important part in the regulation of working conditions in this country. They cover a great variety of matters including not only rates of wages, but also hours of work, overtime conditions, special allowances, piece-work arrangements, holidays, allocation of work, employment of apprentices, redundancy, guaranteed week arrangements, and working conditions generally. The terms and conditions laid down in agreements are applied not only to members of trade unions but also to non-unionists. Trade agreements are also largely observed by employers who are not party to them.

This system of collective bargaining could not function smoothly without agreements between the parties regarding the procedure for dealing with questions as they arise, and much work has been done towards evolving machinery for the avoidance of strikes and lock-outs in connection with trade disputes.

The whole of the collective system rests upon the principle of mutual consent, and the value of the agreements and the machinery for settling disputes has depended upon the loyal acceptance by the constituent members on both sides of the decisions reached. This acceptance is voluntary. Loyal acceptance has in fact been the rule in all the trades concerned. Although the question has been raised from time to time of the adequacy of these methods, the view has always been taken that it was not desirable to adopt some alternative based upon principles other than that of mutual consent or to introduce any system of penalties for non-observance of agreements.[1]

From time to time, however, certain steps have been taken by Parliament in the interests of the community to encourage joint voluntary machinery and to assist, where necessary, in the settlement of disputes. The main legislative measures are the Conciliation Act, 1896, and the Industrial Courts Act, 1919, and statutory provision has also been made, in times of national emergency, for a form of compulsory arbitration. The Conciliation Act (see chapter VII) was introduced upon the recommendation of a Royal Commission set up in 1891 'to inquire into the relations between employers and workmen and to report whether legislation could be directed to remedy any faults discussed'. From this Act the Ministry of Labour's conciliation service derives. The Industrial Courts Act (see chapter VII) gave effect to the recommendations of the Fourth Report dated January 1918 of the Whitley Committee and brought into existence a standing body for the voluntary arbitration of industrial disputes in cases in which the parties, having failed to come to any agreement through their ordinary procedure, jointly consent to refer the differences to arbitration.

---

[1] Under the general law of contract, although the terms of a collective agreement do not automatically become part of the individual contracts of employment made between employers and their employees, an employer and an employee will be bound by such terms if it can be shown that they were, either expressly or by implication, incorporated in an individual contract of employment made between them. An award made by the Industrial Court under s. 8 of the Terms and Conditions of Employment Act, 1959 [See post p. 345], has effect as an implied term of the contract of employment.

The Industrial Courts Act also established the Ministry of Labour's power to set up courts of inquiry to inquire into the causes and circumstances of industrial disputes.

TRANSPORT ACT, 1962

72. *General provisions as to terms and conditions of employment of staff.* (1) It shall be the duty of each Board, except as far as they are satisfied that adequate machinery exists for achieving the purpose of this subsection, to seek consultation with any organisation appearing to the Board to be appropriate, with a view to the conclusion between the Board and that organisation of such agreements as appear to the parties to be desirable with respect to the establishment and maintenance of machinery for—

(a) the settlement by negotiation of terms and conditions of employment of persons employed by the Board, with provision for reference to arbitration in default of such settlement in such cases as may be determined by or under the agreements, and

(b) the promotion and encouragement of measures affecting the safety, health and welfare of persons employed by the Board and the discussion of other matters of mutual interest to the Board and such persons, including efficiency in the operation of the Board's services.

(2) Where the Board conclude such an agreement as is mentioned in the foregoing subsection or any variation is made in such an agreement, the Board shall forthwith transmit particulars of the agreement or the variation to the Minister and the Minister of Labour.

(3) Nothing in this section shall be construed as prohibiting a Board from taking part together with other employers in the establishment and maintenance of machinery for the settlement of terms and conditions of employment, and the promotion and encouragement of measures affecting the health, safety and welfare of their workers, and the discussion of other matters of mutual interest to them and their workers.*

Re WALKER

Court of Appeal   [1944] 1 All E.R. 614

Birmingham Corporation decided, following discussions with staff representatives and inquiries into the practices of other employers, to pay their employees a fixed weekly rate of war bonus. This was dis-

---

* *Quaere:* What legal or political methods of enforcement might be used to enforce such duties?

allowed by the district auditor; the payments were held not to be 'unreasonable' within the principles governing the exercise of local authorities' powers established in *Roberts* v. *Hopwood* [1925] A.C. 578.

DU PARCQ, L.J.; The following further observations with regard to *Roberts* v. *Hopwood* may, I think, properly be made. First, that decision re-affirmed the well-established proposition that the statutory discretion as to the reasonable nature of the wages is to be exercised by the local authority and no one else, that it is a 'very wide' discretion, and that 'the court ought to show great reluctance before they attempt to determine how, in their opinion, the discretion ought to be exercised' (see *per* Lord Buckmaster, L.C., at p. 588, and *per* Lord Carson, at p. 616). Secondly, what is a reasonable wage must depend on the circumstances presently existing in the labour market...

Thirdly, it may, I think, be deduced from the speeches of the learned Lords that a local authority not only may, but ought to, have regard to the practice of private employers. The practice of such employers is one of the relevant circumstances which exist in the labour market, and it may generally be assumed that private employers are guided by commercial rather than philanthropic motives, since, to quote Lord Sumner (at p. 609) they 'must make both ends meet and have not the ratepayers' purse to draw on'.

I would add, as a corollary to these propositions, that the local authority must be judged according to prevailing practices and conditions. The practice of collective bargaining between associations of employers and workers has greatly developed in the present century. It is nowadays often impossible to regard the employment of each individual worker as the result of a separate bargain struck between master and servant. It is commonly convenient and satisfactory to settle wages by means of negotiations and discussion between the representatives of employers and employed. In the case of local authorities it appears that it is customary to establish joint committees for this very purpose. The evidence shows that the salaries now in question were paid as a result of the recommendation of such a joint committee, who thought it expedient, instead of granting the general increase in salaries which the cost of living would have justified, to grant a smaller increase to men without children, and to add what are called 'children's allowances' to the salaries of married men with children. In so doing the Birmingham corporation, far from setting themselves up as model employers, arc following the example of many of the joint stock banks and insurance companies. If local authorities were to be debarred from following a course which has commended itself to such profit-making employers, it is possible that they might be seriously hampered in their efforts to obtain the best services available, and that the efficiency of local government would suffer accordingly...Here the corporation has approved a collective bargain by which, in lieu of a flat rate of increase, the workers accept a graduated increase with discrimination in favour of men with families. We are not concerned to inquire whether this was a wise arrangement, or might have been improved upon. The question is whether the salaries of which complaint is made so manifestly exceed any sums which could have been arrived at on economic principles that the district auditor, or the court, can override the decision of the local authority.

GODDARD, L.J. delivered a concurring judgment; SCOTT, L.J. agreed with the judgments of GODDARD and DU PARCQ, L.JJ.

THE CONCILIATION ACT, 1896

2. *Powers of [Board of Trade]* as to trade disputes.* (1) Where a difference exists or is apprehended between an employer, or any class of employers, and workmen, or between different classes of workmen, the [Board of Trade] may, if they think fit, exercise all or any of the following powers namely,

(*a*) inquire into the causes and circumstances of the difference;

(*b*) take such steps as to the [Board] may seem expedient for the purpose of enabling the parties to the difference to meet together, by themselves or their representatives, under the presidency of a chairman mutually agreed upon or nominated by the [Board of Trade] or by some other person or body, with a view to the amicable settlement of the difference;

(*c*) on the application of employers or workmen interested, and after taking into consideration the existence and adequacy of means available for conciliation in the district or trade and the circumstances of the case, appoint a person or persons to act as conciliator or as a board of conciliation;

(*d*) on the application of both parties to the difference, appoint an arbitrator.

---

* Since 1916, these powers have been vested in the Minister of Labour. On their use and the operation of this Act and the Industrial Courts Act, 1919, see: Industrial Relations Handbook (1961) chapter VII; and the Evidence of Ministry of Labour to Royal Commission on Trade Unions and Employers Associations (1965 H.M.S.O.), Fourth Memorandum, pp. 101–13.

(2) If any person is so appointed to act as conciliator, he shall inquire into the causes and circumstances of the difference by communication with the parties, and otherwise shall endeavour to bring about a settlement of the difference, and shall report his proceeding to the [Board of Trade].

(3) If a settlement of the difference is effected either by conciliation or by arbitration, a memorandum of the terms thereof shall be drawn up and signed by the parties or their representatives, and a copy thereof shall be delivered to and kept by the [Board of Trade].

4. *Power for [Board of Trade]*to aid establishing conciliation boards.* If it appears to the Board of Trade that in any district or trade adequate means do not exist for having disputes submitted to a conciliation board for the district or trade, they may appoint any person or persons to inquire into the conditions of the district or trade, and to confer with the employers and employed, and, if the Board of Trade think fit, with any local authority or body, as to the expediency of establishing a conciliation board for the district or trade...

INDUSTRIAL COURTS ACT, 1919

1. *Constitution of Industrial Court.* (1) For the purpose of the settlement of trade disputes in manner provided by this Act, there shall be a standing Industrial Court, consisting of persons to be appointed by the Minister of Labour (in this Act referred to as 'the Minister') of whom some shall be independent persons, some shall be persons representing employers, and some shall be persons representing workmen, and in addition one or more women...

2. *Reference of disputes to Industrial Court or to arbitration.*† (1) Any trade as defined by this Act, whether existing or apprehended, may be reported to the Minister by or on behalf of either of the parties to the dispute, and the Minister shall thereupon take the matter into his consideration and take such steps as seem to him expedient for promoting a settlement thereof.

(2) Where a trade dispute exists or is apprehended, the Minister may, subject as herein-after provided, if he thinks fit and if both parties consent, either

(a) refer the matter for settlement to the Industrial Court; or

---

* See note on p. 244.
† For the exceptional cases where the Industrial Court has power to make legally enforceable awards by statute, see *post*, p. 344, and p. 345.

(*b*) refer the matter for settlement to the arbitration of one or more person appointed by him; or

(*c*) refer the matter for settlement to a board of arbitration consisting of one or more persons nominated by or on behalf of the employers concerned and an equal number of persons nominated by or on behalf of the workmen concerned, and an independent chairman nominated by the Minister, and, for the purpose of facilitating the nomination of persons to act as members of a board of arbitration, the Minister of Labour shall constitute panels of persons appearing to him suitable so to act, and women shall be included in the panels.

(3) The Minister may refer to the Industrial Court for advice any matter relating to or arising out of a trade dispute, or trade disputes in general or trade disputes of any class, or any other matter which in his opinion ought to be so referred.

(4) If there are existing in any trade or industry any arrangements for settlement by conciliation or arbitration of disputes in such trade or industry, or any branch thereof, made in pursuance of an agreement between organisations of employers and organisations of workmen representative respectively of substantial proportions of the employers and workmen engaged in that trade or industry, the Minister shall not, unless with the consent of both parties to the dispute, and unless and until there has been a failure to obtain a settlement by means of those arrangements, refer the matter for settlement or advice in accordance with the foregoing provisions of this section...

4. *Inquiry into trade disputes.* (1) Where any trade dispute exists or is apprehended, the Minister may, whether or not the dispute is reported to him under Part I of this Act, inquire into the causes and circumstances of the dispute, and, if he thinks fit, refer any matters appearing to him to be connected with or relevant to the dispute to a court of inquiry appointed by him for the purpose of such reference, and the court shall, either in public or in private, at their discretion, inquire into the matters referred to them and report thereon to the Minister...

(4) The Minister may make rules regulating the procedure of any court of inquiry, including rules as to summoning of witnesses, quorum, and the appointment of committees and enabling the court to call for such documents as the court may determine to be relevant to the subject-matter of the inquiry.

(5) A court of inquiry may, if and to such extent as may be authorised by rules made under this section, by order require any person who

appears to the court to have any knowledge of the subject-matter of the inquiry to furnish, in writing or otherwise, such particulars in relation thereto as the court may require, and, where necessary, to attend before the court and give evidence on oath, and the court may administer or authorise any person to administer an oath for that purpose...

7. *Remuneration and expenses.* Any expenses incurred by the Minister in carrying this Act into operation, including the expenses of the Industrial Court and of any court of inquiry, shall be paid out of moneys provided by Parliament.*

8. *Definition of 'trade dispute'.* For the purposes of this Act: The expression 'trade dispute' means any dispute or difference between employers and workmen, or between workmen and workmen connected with the employment or non-employment, or the terms of the employment or with the conditions of labour of any person: [See on 'workman' *ante*, p. 30].

COURT OF INQUIRY (SCAMP)

Report by Mr A. J. SCAMP of a Court of Inquiry into the causes and circumstances of the dispute between employers in membership of the Longbridge Group of Delivery Agents and their employees (1966).

Whereas by the Industrial Courts Act, 1919, the Minister of Labour (hereafter referred to as 'the Minister') is empowered to refer any matters appearing to him to be connected with or relevant to a trade dispute, whether existing or apprehended, to a Court of Inquiry and to make rules regulating the procedure of any such Court;

And whereas a trade dispute exists between employers in membership of the Longbridge Group of Delivery Agents and their employees;

Now, therefore, the Minister by virtue of the powers vested in him by the Act and of all other powers enabling him in that behalf, appoints a Court of Inquiry consisting of A. J. Scamp, Esquire, J.P.;

And the Minister directs that the terms of reference to the Court shall be as follows:

'To inquire into the causes and circumstances of the dispute and to report.'

And the Minister further directs that the following Rules regulating the procedure of the Court shall have effect, that is to say:

* *Quaere* whether this covers the Court's acting as arbitrator under the 'Fair Wages Resolution' procedures? See *post*, p. 333.

(1) (i) Any person may, by notice in writing signed by Mr Scamp, be requested to attend as a witness and give evidence before the Court, or to attend and produce any documents relevant to the subject matter of the Inquiry, or to furnish, in writing or otherwise as the Court may direct, such particulars in relation to the subject matter of the Inquiry as the Court may require;

(ii) The Court may require any witness to give evidence on oath, and Mr Scamp, or any person duly authorised by him, may administer an oath for that purpose;

(2) The Court may at any time, if it thinks expedient so to do, call in the aid of one or more assessors specially qualified, for the purpose of assisting the Court in its Inquiry...

[Reference made 17 December 1965]

REPORT...

3. I carried out this inquiry and prepared my report with the help of two assessors:

Mr H. Briggs, Employee Relations Adviser to Unilever Ltd and Mr G. H. Doughty, General Secretary of the Draughtsmen's and Allied Technicians' Association...

74. There was little trade union organisation in the car delivery business in Birmingham before 1958. In the main, the employers were originally men of little capital and no management experience. The L.G.D.A. did not emerge in its present form until 1961 and still lacks professional expertise in industrial relations. This has impaired their ability to deal with unofficial action and may at times have helped to bring about such action...

77. In my view, the five-point claim presented by the Union was set too high and, if conceded, would have made it uneconomical to use transporter vehicles for ferrying cars from the factory to dealers' compounds, and I am forced to believe that the claim was intended to achieve that object.

78. Unfortunately, there was no serious attempt to bridge the gap between the Union's claim and the initial counter-offer of the employers and there was resort in the Union's name to unconstitutional action in pursuance of the claim. Both sides were remiss in not pressing the use of the agreed disputes procedure between 18 November and 10 December 1965, and in not resolving differences in the interpretation of the procedure...

82. The state of industrial relations in the car delivery business in Birmingham is far from satisfactory. A radical change of attitude on both sides is particularly needful in Autocar and Transporters Ltd.

83. The machinery for consultation and discussion on matters of common interest is no longer adequate for the scale of operations now achieved in the car delivery industry. Recognizing that a breakdown in industrial relations in this industry can have such widespread effects, there should be provision whereby all the interested parties could come together and this would include not only the delivery agents and the trade union, but also the motor manufacturers, British Rail, and British Road Services...

86. With regard to the current dispute between the L.G.D.A. and the Union, the two sides should meet together again as early as possible. The meeting would best be regarded at the outset as a resumption of the discussions which were broken off on 18 November 1965, and should be the occasion of a sincere attempt to narrow their differences and, if possible, to reach a settlement. If a settlement is still not reached, the parties should, without delay, have recourse to the next stage in the disputes procedure as set out in their Agreement dated 7 December 1964—namely to seek the aid of a conciliation officer of the Ministry of Labour. Failing a settlement by that means, one party or the other has the right to ask for the appointment of an arbitrator whose findings, must, as laid down in the present Agreement, be binding on both parties...

89. A National Joint Industrial Council for the car delivery industry should be set up under an independent chairman. On the employers' side, representatives should be drawn from each operational area in the country. On the trade union side, there should be representation from each region concerned, preferably by officers who can have regard for the interests of the Union's memberships in both motor manufacture and car delivery...

91. The employers' side of the industry should consider the need to employ, whether at national level or regional level, persons with professional training in industrial relations...

I have the honour to be, Sir,
Your obedient Servant,
(Sgd) A. J. SCAMP
31 January 1966

INTERPRETATION OF AGREEMENT OF
28 OCTOBER 1965

Between the British Railways Board, the Associated Society of Locomotive Engineers and Firemen and the National Union of Railwaymen

The agreement made under Mr Scamp's guidance between the parties in 1965 included the following paragraph D(4):

'Footplate staff surplus to requirements at a depot as a result of the introduction of the arrangements set out in this Agreement, will be allowed to remain at their depot until absorbed into permanent posts by the normal processes of the Promotion Arrangements, or transferring, should they wish, to another depot in accordance with the Redundancy Arrangements.'

A question arose whether this paragraph covered all members of A.S.L.E.F. or whether, as the British Railways Board contended, the arrangements were to cover only certain groups of footplate staff. The Agreement had contained paragraph E in which it was stated:

'Negotiations will be resumed immediately for a national incentive bonus scheme for freight train crews, and the inclusion of shunting drivers in marshalling yard, shed and works incentive bonus schemes'.

The parties referred the matter to Mr A. J. Scamp agreeing to abide by his interpretation. In the course of his award Mr Scamp said:

'6. I have not attempted to make a legal interpretation of the agreement. It was not conceived, drafted or to be implemented by lawyers. It attempted to record the understanding of each of the parties as to what was contemplated. I have therefore directed my attention to what I conceive to be the spirit and intention of the agreement.

7. Section E which looked forward to resumed negotiations on incentive bonus schemes neither specifically includes nor excludes any undertaking as to possible redundancy arrangements. In fact, the wording of the agreement as a whole does not substantiate either the contention of the British Railways Board or the Unions.

8. The Unions have told me that if they had thought that there was any possibility that the arrangements for redundancy in the agreement were not to be applied to staff covered by negotiations on incentive schemes, they would not have been parties to it. I accept this contention.

9. For their part, the British Railways Board have told me that they regarded the negotiations which were to follow as being on a distinct and separate issue and that in signing the agreement their representa-

tives in no way contemplated that similar redundancy arrangements would necessarily be provided...I believe that the British Railways Board contemplated considering the whole question of redundancy in the negotiations which were to follow. But these negotiations were explicitly foreshadowed in the agreement. In the view of the Unions, they were an integral part of the 'package deal' which would not be finally established until the negotiations had been successfully concluded.

10. As I have indicated, it is very likely that the agreement would not have been possible if the British Railways Board had made clear their understanding to the Unions. This is not to say that the Board representatives were in any way remiss for not having done so. I can accept that they believed, and did not question, that their understanding was also that of the Unions.

11. This was clearly, however, not the case. The agreement was reached and has been implemented only because the Unions thought they had the assurance they sought. This is the present position. In the Unions' view one of the essential foundations of the agreement is now in question. Unless it is maintained, there will be widespread discontent among their members. Mutual trust is essential also for the negotiations on other matters to produce greater efficiency to the benefit of the British Railways Board and their employees.

12. *For all these reasons, I have concluded in interpreting the Agreement that the arrangements in Section D(4) must be held to apply to the staff to be covered in the negotiations referred to in Section E of the agreement.*

13. I hope that negotiations on incentive bonus schemes can be resumed quickly. If it is the wish of the parties, I am willing to give such assistance as I can in the process of such negotiations. It will be appreciated that this interpretation of the agreement will have financial implications which the British Railways Board will need to take into account in the formulation of the incentive schemes.'

A. J. SCAMP

12 *January* 1967

INDUSTRIAL COURT: CASE 3017

Employers' Side of the Joint Committee for Retail Multiple Grocery and Provisions Trade in England and Wales, and the Trade Union Side of the same Joint Committee (Voluntary Arbitration).

The two sides of the Joint Committee for the Retail Multiple Grocery Trade were in dispute following a proposal of the Employers' side to vary a term of a collective agreement concerning payment during sickness. The present term provided for payment to certain workers of the minimum rate of pay applicable to them when at work, less the amount of National Insurance benefit payable to a person with no dependants.

The proposal was for the deduction to be equivalent to the National Insurance benefit actually paid.

Terms of Reference

'To determine the difference between the Employers' Side and the Trade Union Side of the Joint Committee for the Retail Multiple Grocery and Provisions Trade in England and Wales arising from a proposal of the Employers' Side to vary the terms of Clause 9 of the Agreement between the Parties relating to payment during sickness absence'...

1. The matter was referred to the Industrial Court for settlement in accordance with the provisions of the Industrial Courts Act, 1919...

Main submissions on behalf of the Employers' Side

4. Tables were placed before the Court showing the amounts of national insurance benefit payable in respect of sickness or industrial injury...It was submitted that it was wrong and not conducive to good order in the trade that the sick pay arrangements should produce a much higher income for people when they were absent from work. It was not disputed that these arrangements had been in force since 1952, but the excesses were then considerably smaller...

5. While the Employers' Side did not believe that those working in the multiple grocery trade had any lower standards of honesty or self-respect than any other class of the community, they believed that as a safeguard for themselves and for those employees who would not take advantage of the opportunity of staying away from work unnecessarily, the sick pay arrangements now needed to be put on a rational and healthy footing.

6. The principle adopted in their proposals was that the employee entitled to benefit under the National Insurance Acts should be put in as good a position as he would be under the Agreement if he were at work...

Main submissions on behalf of the Trade Union Side

14. It was stated that payment of wages during absence through sickness had, since long before the last war, been a common feature of the distributive trades, the practice being to pay full wages for a specified period without any deduction...

17. It was stated that the Employers' Side's proposal would have its impact mainly on those classes of worker most entitled to consideration when unable to work through sickness. A very high percentage of the workers were women, including an increasing proportion of married women, the majority of whom would not contribute to national insurance...

20. The present Clause 9 in the Agreement had been modelled on the principle voluntarily agreed by all the retail trades Joint Industrial Councils in operation at the time the National Insurance Act was introduced. Although certain of the J.I.C.s had ceased to function with the introduction of the Wages Councils Orders for the retail trades in 1949–50 the sickness absence pay conditions had been incorporated in the collective agreements which had been introduced in various sections of the retail trades from 1951 onwards...

21. With regard to the contention of the Employers' Side that it was wrong for a worker to be better off when absent sick it was argued that, in addition to the considerations already mentioned, the liability of the employer to make payments under the Agreement had been progressively mitigated by every increase in national insurance benefit which had taken place and that there was no justification for the multiple grocery trade to seek a worsening of the present widely accepted arrangement. The period of sickness entitlement under the Agreement did not go beyond six weeks, and then not until the worker had had five years continuous service with the employer...

Award

24. Having given careful consideration to the evidence and submissions of the Parties, the Court find that the claim by the Employers' Side has not been established and Award accordingly.

COURT OF INQUIRY REPORT: PEARSON 1964

Report of a Court of Inquiry into the causes and circumstances of a dispute between the parties represented on the National Joint Industrial Council for the Electricity Supply Industry under the chairmanship of Lord Justice Pearson (Cmnd 2361; 1964.)

[The Court of Inquiry was appointed following the decision of trade unions in the industry to impose an overtime ban and work to rule. This was a climax to years of negotiation with the Electricity Boards. In 1961, discussions began about improved 'status' for ordinary employees. In January 1962, a 'Three Year Agreement' was made about pay and productivity. Union claims in 1962 led to further disagreement and a 'package deal' was concluded of which paragraph (f) stated that no revision of wage rates should take place during the Three Year Agreement 'subject to the outcome' of the status discussions. The unions accepted this reluctantly in 1963 in the face of unofficial action already being taken by dissatisfied members. Their request for a Court of Inquiry in 1963 was not accepted by the Ministry of Labour. In December 1963 the unions submitted four sets of claims on wages and hours (for a 40 hour week especially). The Board claimed that these were a breach of the Three Year Agreement. The unions denied this; refused to go on with the 'status' discussions on which they alleged the Boards had been dilatory; and in March 1964, walked out of the National Joint Industrial Council meeting, thereby making it impossible for the Boards to go to arbitration under the N.J.I.C. constitution.]

The following passages are taken from (a) Union submissions, (b) the Boards' submissions, and (c) the Report's conclusions, as they appear in Cmnd. 2361:

(a) 72. Mr Tudor said that the almost completely negative attitude of the Board's Members at this stage [in 1964] was causing matters to approach a point of crisis. Feelings among workers in the industry were becoming intense and, as the Board's Members had been warned on 10 February, the Trade Unions' Members were under increasing pressure to terminate the three-year agreement in view of movements in wages and hours in other industries...

73. ...Mr Tudor pointed out that the formal procedure contained in the arbitration provisions was not carried out, and that the Trade Unions had shared the general reluctance of Trade Unions to go to arbitration owing to the actions of the Government and the influence

of its policies on arbitration since July 1961 when the 'pay pause was introduced...'

79. Mr Cannon went on to explain why his union had voted unilaterally for the ban on overtime early in 1963. He contended that, as it had been accepted that an overtime ban was not illegal, his Union, in exercising such a ban, were merely employing a legitimate method of exerting pressure on an employer in the course of an industrial dispute. He appreciated that an overtime ban in the electricity supply industry was a serious matter, but he could not accept that for this reason his Union, or indeed any other, could agree to forego its right to exert legitimate pressure to bring about parity between the industry and other industries.

(b) 111. ...[Mr Roberts for the Boards]:...The Government had no standing in connection with wage settlements in the electricity supply industry and, in the opinion of the Electricity Council, the Minister of Power could not give directions concerning a particular wage claim and its treatment.

112. Mr Roberts then spoke on the matter of arbitration. Under paragraph 20 of the First Schedule to the Constitutional Agreement, he said, if agreement on a matter could not be reached, either side might refer it to arbitration. In recent years Trade Unions had shown a reluctance to go to arbitration for reasons related to allegations of Government influence on arbitrators and possible interference with their awards. During the series of negotiations which ended in deadlock in March, the Boards' Members had expressed their readiness to refer the difference to arbitration but, notwithstanding a public statement by the Chairman of the Electricity Council that he would resign if there were any attempt to interfere with an arbitration award, the Unions' Members had continued to prevent reference of the difference to arbitration...116...The Boards' Members had a responsibility for judging between the respective interests of employee, consumer and the community. This was a heavy responsibility which they could not escape; they were entitled—indeed obliged—to take account of Government pronouncements on wages policy and to balance them fairly against other factors in the wage negotiations in just the same way as any other employers in the country should; they were naturally influenced by these pronouncements but not unduly so. He again emphasised that the Electricity Council and Boards had not and were not under any political pressure in the matter of wage negotiations; they had received no direction from the Government in this matter...

(c) Conclusions and Recommendations...

Breach of the three-year agreement

139. The effect of paragraph (f) was to make the schedule wage rates, with their annual increases, 'sacrosanct' for the period of three years, except in so far as they might be altered by the outcome of the status discussions. Other elements in the employees' remuneration, e.g. the additional weekly payments for employees with two years' service, were distinct from the schedule wage rates and so were not 'sacrosanct'.

140. The word 'sacrosanct' is convenient but needs to be explained in two respects. First, the three-year agreement was not intended to be legally binding, but the parties by entering into it assumed a moral obligation as is usual in industrial relations. Secondly, when the parties had made this agreement for a period of three years, either party would have liberty to approach the other party within that period and ask for consent to a revision or modification of the agreement, but the other party would be entitled to refuse consent. The party making the request would be bound to accept the refusal of consent, and would be contravening the agreement by persisting in the request and making it into a claim, and especially by supporting it with industrial action. In that sense the schedule wage rates were 'sacrosanct' and a claim for alteration of them was ruled out by the three-year agreement, except in so far as they might be altered by the outcome of the status discussions...

143. ...[The] Trade Unions' Members acted in contravention of the three-year agreement, which they had entered into and impliedly promised to keep. Indeed by stopping the status discussions and making and pressing their priority claims which conflicted with the agreement, they were setting aside the agreement.

Breach of the agreement for arbitration

144. At the meeting of the 19 March 1964, the N.J.I.C. was unable to determine the matter of the Trade Union Members' 'priority' claims, and the Trade Union Members, for the purpose of preventing the exercise by the Boards' Members of their right to refer the matter to arbitration, withdrew from the meeting so that no vote could be taken and no request for arbitration could be made. That was a subterfuge, and it was a breach of the implied term of the arbitration provision [of the N.J.I.C. Constitutional Agreement]...*

* These passages are interesting pointers to the use which might be made of 'implied' obligations if collective agreements had legal effect, in particular of an implied 'peace' obligation.

146. We express no view on the difficult and important general question whether or not there are reasonable grounds for the Trade Unions' reluctance to go to arbitration... We wish to state that arbitration is a most valuable instrument for preserving industrial peace; and we regret that for whatever causes faith in it has diminished...

The Way Ahead:...

157. The reasons why they have not so far made the progress that both sides had hoped they would were: (a) Apart from the broad objectives, there was not proper recognition of what the proposals involved until the negotiations had almost broken down. There was, therefore, insufficient appreciation on both sides of the far reaching nature of the changes. (b) It was unrealistic for the Boards to think that changes of this magnitude could be agreed and introduced in one fell swoop and at a fairly early date. (c) The Boards in the early stages, by seeking to establish that the changes had to be made with no addition to the existing wage bill, did not create an encouraging atmosphere for the discussions. This was to some extent rectified at a late hour by the 'cushioning' proposals, but by this time the Trade Unions had despaired of making progress and had decided to submit their 'priority' claims.

158. It seems obvious now, largely as a result of this Inquiry, that the status scheme involves decision on a number of thorny problems, and that even with goodwill on both sides it is unlikely to be agreed in full for an appreciable period. The present basis of discussion adopted by the Boards, in which the improvements in working methods or in the conditions and payments to the employees are not introduced until everything in the concept is agreed, is most unlikely to provide an avenue for early settlement of some of the outstanding points of difference (e.g. craftsmen's rates). It must be repeated that the scheme is a very worthy conception and one which both parties have accepted in principle as being in the overall best interests of the Boards, the employees and the consumers. Accordingly, there should be renewed efforts on the part of both sides to make progress towards its practical implementation and they should treat the problem with a sense of urgency and real purpose.

NATIONAL BOARD FOR PRICES AND INCOMES. REPORT NO. 9 (Interim). WAGES IN THE BAKERY INDUSTRY

...THE PURPOSE OF THIS REPORT

5. The fact that the references were made to us after strike action by both the production and the distribution workers raises the question of the relationship of this Board to the normal procedures for conciliation and arbitration. We do not regard ourselves as a substitute for the normal process of collective bargaining. This would not be a practical proposition, and most wage and salary claims will still have to be settled by negotiation. It follows from this that the Board does not replace conciliation and arbitration, which are parts of the process of collective bargaining. We interpret the role of the Board rather as being to influence over a period of time the way in which the general collective bargaining process works, and in the words of our Commission 'to have regard to the considerations set out in Command Paper Number 2639 on Prices and Incomes Policy and to such further considerations as one or more of Our Ministers may from time to time determine'...

PRICES AND INCOMES ACT, 1966

PART I

[Section 1 establishes the National Board for Prices and Incomes on a statutory basis, with power to compel witnesses etc., and within the normal limits of the High Court's rules of evidence, compel production of 'such estimates, returns, or other information as may be specified' Schedule 1, paragraph 14.]

2. (1) The Secretary of State, or the Secretary of State and any other Minister acting jointly, may refer to the Board any question relating to wages, salaries or other forms of incomes, or to prices, charges or other sums payable under transactions of any description relating to any form of property or rights or to services of any description or to returns on capital invested in any form of property, including company dividends; and without prejudice to the generality of the foregoing provisions of this subsection the Secretary of State, or the Secretary of State and any other Minister acting jointly, may refer to the Board any question

(a) relating to a proposal to increase any prices for the sale of goods or any charges for the performance of services, including charges for the application of any process to goods, or

(*b*) relating to any pay claims or other claims relating to terms and conditions of employment, or any awards and settlements relating to terms and conditions of employment...

5. ...(3) Subject to subsection (4) below (*a*) any report of the Board under s. 2 above must be published...within three months from the date on which the reference...is published in the Gazette...

(4) The Minister or Ministers concerned may...extend...the period of three months...by such further period as is specified in the direction.

PART II*

13. (1) The Secretary of State may by order apply this section to any pay claims relating to terms and conditions of employment made on behalf of employees.

(2) Notice of a claim to which this section applies shall be only given to the appropriate Minister within a period of seven days beginning with the day on which the claim is presented to the employers or employers' organisation concerned.

(3) The notice may be given

(*a*) by the trade union or other person by whom the claim is presented, or by any trade union or trade union organisation acting on behalf of that person, or

(*b*) by the person or any of the persons to whom the claim is presented, or by any employers' organisation representing the interests of employers to whom the claim is presented.

(4) The responsibility for ensuring that notice of the claim is given in accordance with subsection (2) above shall lie both on the person by whom the claim is presented (or the trade union or trade union organisation substituted for that person under the following provisions of this section) and on the employers or employers' organisation to whom the claim is presented, and if there is a failure to comply with subsection (2) above all of those persons shall be liable on summary conviction to a fine not exceeding fifty pounds.

(5) If a trade union or trade union organisation by notice to the Secretary of State accepts responsibility for persons specified in the

* To be brought into effect by Order. This had not yet been done at the time of writing. But the Government intends to do so before August 1967, and to amend ss. 14 and 19 to provide for 'standstill' powers of seven months instead of four.

notice subsection (4) above shall apply while the notice has effect as if the trade union or trade union organisation giving the notice were substituted in subsection (4) above for the persons specified in the notice...

14. (1) The Secretary of State may by order apply this section to awards and settlements relating to terms or conditions of employment.

(2) Within seven days of the making of an award or settlement to which this section applies the employers affected by the award or settlement shall duly give notice, with particulars of the award or settlement, to the appropriate Minister; and an employer failing to comply with this subsection shall be liable on summary conviction to a fine not exceeding fifty pounds.

(3) The notice to be given as required by subsection (2) above may be so given by a trade union or other person representing the employees affected by the award or settlement, or by a trade union organisation acting on behalf of those employees, and, if so given within the period specified in that subsection, shall absolve the employers affected by the award or settlement from the responsibility imposed by that subsection; and notices to be given by any employers under subsection (2) above may be so given on their behalf by any one of them, or by any employers' organisation representing their interests..

(5) An award or settlement to which this section applies shall not be implemented unless the notice required by this section has been duly given to the appropriate Minister.

(6) When the notice required by this section has been duly given to the appropriate Minister

(a) the award or settlement shall not be implemented until after the expiration of a period of thirty days beginning with the date on which the notice is so given, except that if at any earlier time the said Minister publishes in the Gazette a notice stating that it has been decided not to refer the award or settlement to the Board, this paragraph shall apply only until that earlier time;

(b) if under s. 2(1) or 2(3) of this Act the award or settlement is referred to the Board by a reference published in the Gazette within the said period of thirty days, the award or settlement shall not without the written consent of the Minister or Ministers who referred it be implemented until the date of publication of the Board's report on the reference...

34. ... 'awards and settlements', in relation to terms or conditions of employment, includes any agreement, whether or not enforceable

in law and whether or not concluded under recognised arrangements for the settlement by negotiations of terms and conditions of employment, to which any employer or any organisation representing employers is a party*...

16. (1) It shall be an offence for an employer to implement an award or settlement in respect of employment at a time when the implementation of the award or settlement is forbidden under the foregoing provisions of this Part of this Act.

(2) Subsection (1) above shall not make it unlawful for an employer at a time when the implementation of an award or settlement is not forbidden by the foregoing provisions of this Part of this Act, to pay any sum in respect of remuneration for employment at an earlier time.

(3) A person guilty of an offence under subsection (1) of this section shall be liable

(a) on summary conviction to a fine not exceeding one hundred pounds, and

(b) on conviction on indictment to a fine which, if the offender is not a body corporate, shall not exceed five hundred pounds.

(4) If any trade union or other person takes, or threatens to take, any action, and in particular any action by way of taking part, or persuading others to take part, in a strike, with a view to compel, induce or influence any employer to implement an award or settlement in respect of employment at a time when the implementation of that award or settlement is forbidden under the foregoing provisions of this Act, he shall be liable

(a) on summary conviction to a fine not exceeding one hundred pounds, and

(b) on conviction on indictment to a fine which, if the offender is not a body corporate, shall not exceed five hundred pounds.

(5) This section shall not give rise to any criminal or tortious liability for conspiracy or any other liability in tort†...

19. (1) If the report of the Board on a question referred to the Board under s. 2 (1)...is not published in accordance with s. 5 (1) of this Act by a date within three months from the publication of the

---

* This definition does not seem to include the contract of employment itself. A rise in pay granted unilaterally by an employer would not, therefore, be caught.

† *Note:* This subsection (5) was an attempt to prevent the spread of liability beyond the offence in subsection (4) by way of, for example, judicial views on 'conspiracy to commit an unlawful act': see *post*, chapter 4, 'Industrial Conflict', especially Section D, p. 520. *Quaere:* will subsection (5) succeed in this attempt in view of the words 'This section...'?

reference, the following provisions of this Act: s. 7(3)(*b*); s. 8; s. 14(6) (*b*); s. 15, shall apply as if the report had been so published on the last day of that period...

PART IV

[Brought into effect by Order on 6 October 1966, S. I. 1262. By reason of s. 25, it will expire on 11 August 1967.]

25. (1) At any time in the period of twelve months beginning with the date of the passing of this Act Her Majesty may by Order in Council bring the provisions of this Part of this Act into force for the remainder of the said period of twelve months.*...

28. (1) The Secretary of State may by order apply this section to remuneration under contracts of employment for any kind of work to be performed wholly or substantially within the United Kingdom or on British ships or aircraft.

(2) An employer shall not pay remuneration to which this section applies at a rate which exceeds the rate of remuneration paid by him for the same kind of work before the date of the coming into force of the order applying this section to that description of remuneration by any amount unless the appropriate Minister has given his consent in writing to the increase of the remuneration by that amount, or by a greater amount.

(3) If an employer contravenes this section he shall be liable

(*a*) on summary conviction to a fine not exceeding one hundred pounds, and

(*b*) on conviction on indictment to a fine which, if the offender is not a body corporate, shall not exceed five hundred pounds.

(4) Subsections (4), (5) and (6) of s. 16 of this Act shall apply in relation to the payment of remuneration by an employer which would be in contravention of this or the next following section as they apply in relation to the implementation by an employer of an award or settlement which would be in contravention of the said s. 16...

(6) Section 17 of this Act shall apply as if references to Part II of this Act included references to this Part of this Act.

29. (1) The Secretary of State may give notice published in the Gazette that he is considering the making of an order under this section.

---

* These sections have been included despite the temporal limitation of s. 25 because they will form the basis of certain litigation during 1967; and because they are bound to be referred to in the discussion of what is to follow the period of 'severe restraint' called for by the Government in increases of incomes until August 1967.

(2) A notice under subsection (1) above shall give particulars of the order proposed to be made, and shall specify a period, which shall not be less than fourteen days from the first publication of the notice, within which any employer, or any employers organisation, trade union organisation or other person representing employers or employees may make representations in writing to the Secretary of State.

(3) The Secretary of State may, if he thinks fit, after the expiration of the period specified in the notice for the making of representations, and after considering any representations duly made, by order apply this section to remuneration under contracts of employment for any kind of work.

(4) An employer shall not pay remuneration to which this section applies for work for any period while the order is in force at a rate which exceeds the rate of remuneration paid* by him for the same kind of work before 20 July 1966 by any amount unless

(a) the appropriate Minister has given his consent in writing to an excess of that amount or of a greater amount, or

(b) the order authorises an excess of that amount, or of a greater amount.

(5) If an employer contravenes this section he shall be liable

(a) on summary conviction to a fine not exceeding one hundred pounds, and

(b) on conviction on indictment to a fine which, if the offender is not a body corporate, shall not exceed five hundred pounds...

30. (1) This section applies to any contract of employment made before the date of the coming into force of this Part of this Act under which any person who has worked for the employer since before that date is to receive remuneration for the same kind of work for any period after that date which is at a higher rate than that at which he was being remunerated for work of that kind immediately before that date.

(2) If after having given not less than one week's notice in writing, the employer pays or tenders to the employee remuneration for work for any period after the said date and while this Part of this Act is in force at a rate which is not less than that at which he was paid for the same kind of work immediately before that date, the employer shall not be liable in respect of a breach of a contract to which this section

---

* *Quaere:* whether this means 'actually paid' or 'the rate legally payable'. The former appears to be the intention of the legislature, but the point has been much disputed in trade union circles where it is pointed out that an Order might then protect an employer paying less than he legally should have been paying on 20 July 1966.

applies for failure to pay remuneration at the rate provided by the contract.

(3) Subsection (2) above shall not take away the employee's right to rescind the contract...

INTERNATIONAL LABOUR ORGANISATION CONVENTIONS RATIFIED BY THE U.K.

FREEDOM OF ASSOCIATION AND PROTECTION OF THE RIGHT TO ORGANISE CONVENTION, 1948, no. 87

Article 2. Workers and employers, without distinction whatsoever shall have the right to establish and, subject only to the rules of the organisation concerned, to join organisation of their own choosing without previous authorisation...

Article 8 (1) In exercising the rights provided for in this Convention workers and employers and their respective organisations, like other persons or organised collectivities, shall respect the law of the land. (2) The law of the land shall not be such as to impair, nor shall it be so applied as to impair, the guarantees provided for in this Convention...

Article 11. Each Member of the I.L.O. for which this Convention is in force undertakes to take all necessary and appropriate measures to ensure that workers and employers may exercise freely the right to organise.

RIGHT TO ORGANISE AND COLLECTIVE BARGAINING CONVENTION, 1949, NO. 98

Article 1. (1) Workers shall enjoy adequate protection against acts of anti-union discrimination in respects of their employment. (2) Such protection shall apply more particularly in respect of acts calculated to (a) make the employment of a worker subject to a condition that he shall not join a union or shall relinquish trade union membership; (b) cause the dismissal of or otherwise prejudice a worker by reason of union membership or because of participation in union activities outside working hours, or with the consent of the employer, within working hours...

Article 2. (1) Workers' and Employers' Organisations shall enjoy adequate protection against any acts of interference by each other or each other's agents or members in their establishment, functioning or administration. (2) In particular, acts which are designed to promote the establishment or workers' organisations under the domination of employers or employers' organisations, or to support workers' organisations by financial or other means, with the object of placing such organisations under the control of employers or employers' organisations, shall be deemed to constitute acts of interference within the meaning of the Article.

Article 3. Machinery appropriate to national conditions shall be established, where necessary, for the purpose of ensuring respect for the right to organise as defined in the preceding articles.

Article 4. Measures appropriate to national conditions shall be taken where necessary to encourage and promote the full development and utilisation of machinery for voluntary negotiation between employers or employers' organisations and workers' organisations, with a view to the regulation of terms and conditions of employment by means of collective agreements.

I.L.O. GOVERNING BODY COMMITTEE ON FREEDOM OF ASSOCIATION

Case 341

(PAN HELLENIC FEDERATION OF TEXTILE WORKERS AGAINST GOVERNMENT OF GREECE)

The Federation complained of a number of breaches of Conventions 87 and 98. Among them was the Greek Law, 3239 of 1955, which in s. 20(2) provided:

'...In the event of any collective agreement...being contrary to the general economic or social policy of the Government, or to any such policy in particular matters, the Ministers of Co-ordination and of Labour may...amend or withold approval of all or part of such agreement...'

The following are extracts from Reports of the Committee dealing with this aspect of that complaint:

75th Report, 1964, paragraph 78

'[The Committee has] had occasion to point out that the need for prior approval of a collective agreement by official authorities was contrary to the whole system of voluntary negotiation envisaged in the Right to Organise and Collective Bargaining Convention, 1949, (No. 98), and to emphasise the importance that it attaches to the principle that public authorities should refrain from all interference which would restrict the right of trade unions to seek through collective bargaining or other lawful means to improve the living and working conditions of those whom they represent, or impede the lawful exercise of this right.'

85th Report, 1966, paragraph 184 et seq.

184. In its reply the Government states that the draft Bill for the Labour Code, the text of which has already been submitted to the I.L.O., provides for a new system of collective bargaining and arbitration, and amends several provisions of Act No. 3239.

185. If reference is made to the text of the draft Bill, it would appear that under s. 327, paragraph 2, the Minister of Labour is empowered, in certain circumstances which are not specified, to refuse to allow a collective agreement to be filed.

186. The Committee considers that if such a refusal may be based on grounds only of errors of pure form the provision in question is not in conflict with the principle of voluntary negotiation laid down by the Right to Organise and Collective Bargaining Convention, 1949 (No. 98), ratified by Greece. The Committee feels, on the other hand, that if this provision implies that the filing of a collective agreement may be refused on grounds such as those set forth in s. 20 of Act No. 3239, as quoted in paragraph 181 above, it amounts to a requirement that prior approval be obtained before a collective agreement can come into force, which infringes the principle of voluntary negotiation laid down by the aforementioned Convention. In this connection the Committee feels compelled, as on a number of occasions in the past, to emphasise the importance that should be attached to the principle that the public authorities should refrain from any interference which would restrict the right of trade unions to seek, through collective bargaining or other lawful means, to improve the living and working conditions of those whom they represent, or impede the lawful exercise of this right.

187. Having said this, the Committee considers none the less that its objections to the requirement that prior approval of collective agreements be obtained from the Government do not signify that ways could not be found of persuading the parties to collective bargaining to have regard voluntarily in their negotiations to considerations relating to the economic or social policy of the Government and the safeguarding of the general interest. But to achieve this it is necessary first of all that the objectives to be recognised as being in the general

interest should have been widely discussed by all parties on a national scale through a consultative body such as the National Social Policy Advisory Board, in accordance with the principle laid down by the Consultation (Industrial and National Levels) Recommendation, 1960 (No. 113). It might also be possible to envisage a procedure where by attention of the parties could be drawn, in certain cases, to the considerations of general interest which might call for further examination of the terms of agreement on their part. However, in this connection, persuasion is always to be preferred to constraint. Thus, instead of making the validity of collective agreements subject to governmental approval, it might be provided that every collective agreement filed with the Ministry of Labour would normally come into force a reasonable length of time after being filed; if the public authority considered that the terms of the proposed agreement were manifestly in conflict with the economic policy objectives recognised as being desirable in the general interest, the case could be submitted for advice and recommendation to an appropriate consultative body, it being understood, however, that the final decision in the matter rested with the parties to the agreement.

188. Since the Government is in the process of revising its legislation on the subject, the Committee hopes that the foregoing observations and suggestions will be taken into account, and therefore recommends the Governing Body to draw the Government's attention thereto.

SECTION B

IS THE COLLECTIVE AGREEMENT AN ENFORCEABLE CONTRACT BETWEEN THE COLLECTIVE PARTIES?

O. KAHN-FREUND in *The System of Industrial Relations in Great Britain* (edd. A. Flanders and H. Clegg; Blackwell, 1954) pp. 56–8.*

In the first place, then, a collective agreement is intended to give rise to mutual obligations imposed, let it be understood, upon the associations, not upon their members. One might be tempted to conclude that, for this reason, the agreement was a contract in the legal sense, i.e. that these obligations could be enforced by actions for

---

* See too the view expressed by Lord Pearson in the Electricity Supply Report: *ante*, p. 256.

damages or for an injunction in a court of law. In the writer's opinion this conclusion would be erroneous. This opinion cannot be supported by clear judicial authority. Such occasional judicial 'asides' (*obiter dicta*) as exist are contradictory, and there is to the writer's knowledge no express decision on the point. This is important. In the long history of British collective bargaining it does not ever seem to have happened that either a trade union or an employer or an employers' association attempted to prevent the violation of a collective agreement by an action for an injunction or to seek compensation by an action for damages. The reason can certainly not be found in the absence of such violations...

The true reason for the complete absence of any attempts legally to enforce the mutual obligations created by collective agreements can, in the writer's opinion, only be found in the intention of the parties themselves. An agreement is a contract in the legal sense only if the parties look upon it as something capable of yielding legal rights and obligations. Agreements expressly or implicitly intended to exist in the 'social' sphere only are not enforced as contracts by the courts. This appears to be the case of collective agreements. They are intended to yield 'rights' and 'duties', but not in the legal sense; they are intended, as it is sometimes put, to be 'binding in honour' only, or (which amounts to very much the same thing) to be enforceable through social sanctions but not through legal sanctions. This may seem to some a very theoretical observation. It is, however, a matter of at least potential practical importance that a strike or lockout, whether legal or illegal in other respects, cannot be complained of in a court by reason of its being a breach of a collective agreement. The court cannot, on that ground, suppress it through an injunction, or make either side liable to compensate the other. If, say, an employers' association refuses to induce its members to pay the 'union rate' or even instigates them not to do so, the union cannot make it liable in a court and must seek its remedies outside the law.

ARDLEY and MOREY v. LONDON ELECTRICITY BOARD

The Times, 16 June 1956

Under the terms of a co-partnership scheme, which was incorporated into each individual contract of employment, the directors had power to exclude any employee from the benefits of the scheme who in their opinion, *inter alia*, failed to take an interest in the welfare of the company. During negotiations arising out of an unofficial strike the directors issued a statement saying they would not exercise this power, and in return the trade union side agreed to the directors' proposals. The plaintiffs sued to recover their share in the benefits of this scheme.

PEARSON, J.: The defendants relied on clause 4 of the co-partnership scheme; the plaintiffs went on strike without giving any notice. They relied also on their alleged exercise of the right under rule 2 of the rules, which provided: 'The directors reserve the right to decline to allow any employee to share in the co-partnership scheme who in their opinion does not take an interest in the welfare of the company and its co-partnership, or who is wasteful of the company's property, or is careless or, negligent in the performance of his duty.'

A meeting took place on 22 January 1952, when an agreement was made for settlement of the strike. A 'declaration' after it stated: 'In the expectation that the agreement will operate smoothly and in the spirit in which it has been negotiated, the board will not exercise its rights to make reductions under the co-partnership scheme.'...

Clause 4 of the co-partnership agreement provided that an employee should not be entitled to the co-partnership bonus should he 'break his agreement for service with the company by going on strike without giving due notice to the company or otherwise unlawfully.' That created a problem, because the employee's breach of contract by going on strike without due notice did not of itself terminate the contract of employment.

In his Lordship's judgment, as the clause, on a strict construction, gave rise to difficulty, it had to be interpreted benevolently in accordance with the maxim *ut res magis valeat quam pereat*. He (his Lordship) felt no doubt that the intention was that the unlawful striking employee should lose his bonus for the period from the beginning of the bonus year to the moment when he broke his agreement for service with the company by unlawfully going on strike. That interpretation, though inaccurate, was quite intelligible.

When an employee unlawfully went on strike there was a termination of the performance of the contract of service on both sides, because the employee ceased to render services and the employer presumably ceased to pay wages. Also, the employee lost his right to continuance of the contract of employment, giving the employer a right to dismiss him. This was a difficult question, but in his (his Lordship's) judgment on the true construction of the clause an employee who unlawfully went on strike lost his bonus for the period from the beginning of the bonus year to the date of the unlawful strike....

After the failure to agree at the meetings of the District Industrial Joint Council and the National Joint Industrial Council the matter might have gone to arbitration, but instead Mr. Foulkes communicated with the Conciliation Officer of the Ministry of Labour. He (his Lordship) saw no reason why he should not have taken that action. There was no ground for suggesting that he had done so for a wrong reason. It was at that stage of the proceedings that it was alleged that a legally binding promise was made.

It was at the meeting of 22 January 1952, that the material declaration was made and certain terms were agreed. As a result of Sir Robert Gould's efforts the trade union side said that they would agree to the board's proposals providing that there was an undertaking given in regard to co-partnership and sick pay. Mr. Randall immediately agreed that an undertaking should be given on sick pay and after the trade union side returned Sir Robert Gould said: 'To put on record the board say they will take no action on sick pay and make the following declaration in regard to co-partnership: "In the expectation that the agreement will operate smoothly and in the spirit in which it has been negotiated, the board will not exercise its rights to make reductions under the co-partnership scheme." ' The Press notice agreed provided for (1) resumption of work; (2) supply to the trade unions of data relating to redundancy; (3) an undertaking by the trade unions to consider the data; and (4) arrangements for the selection of men found to be redundant.

One had to consider whether that so-called 'declaration' was or was not intended to have contractual force. If it was, there could be no difficulty in making it operative, probably as a collateral warranty to the main agreement. What were the facts so far as they appeared from the document? The factor which had impressed him (his Lordship) was the wording of the statement itself. It was called a declaration. That was not normally a contractual word. If one was seeking to describe some statement that involved contractual obligation one would not normally use that word. Next there was the word 'expectation', not normally a contractual word. Next, 'the agreement will operate smoothly'—that was not fully suitable for contractual provisions; on the other hand it was suitable for what the defendants suggested was called a 'gentleman's agreement'. It was very difficult to construe the 'declaration' as carrying contractual force.

What was said on 'no victimisation' was not intended to be a legally binding contract. It was hardly bilateral at all, but it was not to be expected that there would be any victimisation and if there was some contractual arrangement about victimisation it would not apply to the co-partnership bonus which was subsequently mentioned. For those reasons he held, on the material if it stood alone, that the Press declaration did not contain a legally binding promise.

Sir Hartley Shawcross had raised the question, if the parties used apparently contractual words, but both intended that there should be no contractual obligation, was the Court to impose upon them a contract which neither of them intended to enter into? That question did impress his Lordship, and he did not see how an affirmative answer could reasonably be given to it. There was evidence by both parties that they did not intend the declaration to create legal relations, and, for that reason, as well as the others, he (his Lordship) held that the declaration did not create legal relations and was not contractually binding.

AYLING *v.* LONDON AND INDIA DOCKS COMMITTEE

(1893) 9 T.L.R. 409

In 1889 there was a general strike in the docks which were managed by the defendant committee, and most of the casual labourers refused to continue work, going away without giving notice. The plaintiff, employed on a week's notice, went too. Representatives of the strikers met with representatives of the defendants for negotiations and eventually an agreement was reached under the auspices of Cardinal Manning, Sir James Whitehead and Mr Buxton. Clauses 5, 6 and 7 of the agreement ran as follows:

(5) The existing strike to be terminated, and all the men connected with the dock, wharf, or river work to return to work forthwith.

(6) The strikers and their leaders undertake that all labourers who have been at work during the strike shall be unmolested.

(7) In employing fresh men after the strike is ended the directors will make no difference between those who have and those who have not taken part in it, and will not show resentment to any of the men who have participated in the strike.

The men returned to work, but the defendants refused to take the plaintiff back. The plaintiff brought this action unsuccessfully claiming *inter alia*, damages for failure to reinstate him. The defendants successfully counterclaimed for damages for breach of contract.

Mr Justice Day, in giving judgment, said that it was admitted that the plaintiff had left his work to join the strike without any notice. It was said that the agreement was an answer to the employer's claim for that breach of contract. But he could not find in the agreement anything to show that claims by or against individuals were to be settled by it. It was only for the settlement of the strike. It appeared that certain persons had met to terminate the strike, which related to general objects and matters, and these were what were to be settled by the agreement. They were terms of arrangement for the settlement of the strike, not for the adjustment of claims by or against individuals. The persons who refused to abide by it would be in a false position, for a small number of men could not carry out a strike. In that sense only the persons who signed the agreement represented the men. No one contemplated incurring any legal liability; nor could the agreement affect any claim by or against individuals, or be an accord and satisfaction of any individual claims. The signatories of the agreement were not acting as agents for individuals, but for the general benefit of the men.

Bruce, J., concurred in the judgment of Day, J.

EAST LONDON BAKERS' UNION *v.* GOLDSTEIN

Court of Appeal   *The Times*, 9 June 1904

[In this action, the Court of Appeal (Henn Collins M.R., Stirling and Matthew L.JJ.) seemed to be prepared to look upon a local collective agreement as a contractual bargain, though their Lordships refused the discretionary remedy sought by the plaintiffs. But the date of the case must be noted; and the agreement was, as was then common, restricted to a locality.]

The East London Bakers' Union were the proprietors of a copyright label which was duly entered at Stationers'-hall on 25 September 1903. The copyright label consisted of a drawing of two bakers in a bakehouse, two loaves, and a peel and trough, and two cottage loaves, with a motto, 'Unity is strength, Union Bread for Union Men, East London Bakers' Union.' The plaintiff union, which consisted of 250 working bakers, brought this action, alleging that the defendant had used the copyright label in connection with his business of baker without the sanction of the union, and after receiving an intimation from

COLLECTIVE BARGAIN A CONTRACT ?

them that he was not authorized to use it. It appeared that on 17 May 1904, the defendant, who was a master baker, entered into and signed the following agreement with the plaintiff union:— 'I, the undersigned, agree to accept the following terms of work as expressed in this agreement:— (1) A trade union label to be used on each loaf of bread (masters now using their own label can continue or cease from doing as they please). (2) Twelve hours shall be recognized as a term of work every day, but on Thursday two hours extra. (3) No overtime shall be worked on ordinary days except the day before a holiday. (4) All overtime to be paid as per time and a half. (5) No man to be employed at baking at a wage less than 26s. as a *minimum*. (6) No master shall personally work as a baker, and one class of men shall not do the work of another class, higher or lower. (7) One full day rest in seven. (8) Only union men of the East London Bakers' Union shall be employed, and a delegate of the union shall at any time be permitted to enter the bakehouse for trade union business. I further agree that in case I receive an intimation from the secretary of the above organization that I have broken one or any of the terms of this agreement, or if I am in dispute with the above organization on any point, I have no right to use the trade union label on the bread baked by me. I further agree to pay to the above organization the sum of 5s. per year for the use of the label. I also recognize that the trade union label is the property of the organization mentioned above, and can only be used by me with their consent. If the union's label is to be taken away from me, the reason for so doing must first be submitted to arbitration. The arbitration is to deal only with the terms of this agreement.' The plaintiffs alleged that the defendant also orally agreed not to enter into unfair competition with master bakers who were producing their bread under trade union conditions. They alleged that the defendant was selling bread at less than cost price, so as to ruin the trade of the master bakers, who were paying trade union wages, and that the result of permitting the defendant to use their label would be that the defendant would have a label by which he could impose on the public and ruin the trade of the masters who paid fair wages, and compel bakers to work at inadequate wages and under insanitary conditions. They further alleged that the affixing of the label to a loaf was a representation to the general public that the loaf was made by members of the East London Bakers' Union, and with the sanction of the East London Bakers' Union; and that loaves baked by the defendant and exhibited and sold by him with the label attached were not baked by members of the East London Bakers'

Union; and that there were not any members of the East London Bakers' Union in the defendant's employment. The plaintiffs, on commencing the action, applied for an injunction restraining the defendant from using the label until the trial of the action. The defendant denied the alleged oral agreement, and said that he was selling his bread at the same price as the majority of bakers in the East-end of London, and that he was and always had been, willing to pay the rate of wages and abide by the conditions set out in the above written agreement. Mr Justice Bucknill granted the plaintiff's application for an interim injunction, but on the application of the defendant Mr Justice Grantham made an order dissolving the injunction. The plaintiffs appealed.

The Court dismissed the appeal.

The Master of the Rolls said that in this case the plaintiff trade union claimed an injunction against the defendant restraining him from putting a certain label on bread baked and sold by him. The plaintiffs' rights in the matter depended on the particular agreement entered into between them and the defendant. His Lordship referred to the agreement as above set out. The plaintiffs said that there was also another agreement, made orally, quite outside the written agreement. They alleged that by this oral agreement the defendant undertook not to compete unfairly with other masters. No such undertaking was to be found in the written agreement, and in his opinion there was no foundation for the allegation of an oral agreement. As the matter now stood the injunction which the plaintiffs asked for would entirely destroy the defendant's trade. In his opinion the Court would not be justified in allowing an injunction to go having that effect and based on an allegation not made out. The defendant having undertaken by his counsel to keep an account of all bread sold by him, to which the label was attached, the appeal would be dismissed.

The LORDS JUSTICES concurred.

SMITHIES v. NATIONAL ASSOCIATION OF OPERATIVE PLASTERERS

Court of Appeal   [1909] 1 K.B. 310

Where a trade union financed men on strike in breach of contract with knowledge of the contract, and believed bona fide that the employers were going to evade a settlement of the dispute by means of an agreed arbitration procedure, the court held that this did not constitute justification for the union procuring the breach by the workmen of their contracts.* Some of the *dicta* appeared impliedly to treat the procedure agreement as the equivalent of a contractual agreement.

KENNEDY, L.J.: The agreement of 1904 between the masters' association and the operatives' association and the agreements between the plaintiff and Forrester and Ecclesby were independent contracts. The breach by B. of his contract with A. cannot, I think, properly be held to justify or excuse A. in procuring C. to break an independent contract with B.

BUCKLEY, L.J.: But, lastly, it is said that the act was justified. No doubt there are circumstances in which A. is entitled to induce B. to break a contract entered into by B. with C. Thus, for instance, if the contract between B. and C. is one which B. could not make consistently with his preceding contractual obligations towards A., A. may not only induce him to break it, but may invoke the assistance of a Court of Justice to make him break it. If B. having agreed to sell a property to A. subsequently agrees to sell it to C., A. of course may restrain B. by injunction from carrying out B.'s contract with C., and the consequence may ensue that B. will be liable to C. in damages for breaking it. *Read* v. *Friendly Society of Operative Stonemasons*[1] was relied on upon this part of the case. That was an action by C. against B. in my supposed parties, and C. recovered damages. Where the action is by A. against B. wholly different considerations arise. That is the present case. I have no doubt that it might be a justification (to take the facts of the present case) if the union had done no more than induce Forrester to break a contract which Smithies, having regard to the provisions of the National agreement, never ought to have made with Forrester. But this is not the contention which is raised. The contention of the defendants here is: 'We were entitled to induce Forrester to break his contract with you because you had broken your contract, as contained in the National agreement, with us.' This is setting up that, where there are two independent contracts, the breach of the one by the one party entitles a breach of the other by the other party. This contention, in my opinion, cannot be maintained.

---

[1] [1902] 2 K.B. 732.

* Before the Trade Disputes Act, 1906, *post*, p. 385.

READ v. FRIENDLY SOCIETY OF OPERATIVE STONEMASONS

Court of Appeal   [1902] 2 K.B. 732

Where a man was apprenticed to an employer as a stonemason, and a union protested against this on the ground that it was in breach of a written agreement between the union and the employer, there was a threat to strike, and the apprentice was dismissed. The apprentice sued the employer and union officers and was successful.

[*Note.* The case ante-dated the Trade Disputes Act, 1906. The *dicta* cited are directed solely to the point of the collective bargain being discussed as a contract.]

COLLINS, M.R.: In these circumstances they conspired to enforce, by threats of a formidable character which they had the means of carrying into effect, a breach by his employers and instructors of the contract which the latter had with him; and the only justification they can suggest for this conduct is that Messrs. Wigg & Wright had come under an obligation to them, not perhaps legally enforceable, if not illegal, not to make such a contract as they had made with the plaintiff.

STIRLING, L.J.: [It] was contended on behalf of the defendants that there was a sufficient justification for their interference, because Messrs Wigg & Wright had, previously to the contract with the plaintiff, entered into a contract with them, the defendants, which is said to be inconsistent with the contract between Messrs Wigg & Wright and the plaintiff. Some difficulty appears to have arisen in the Divisional Court as to what the terms of this contract were; but at the hearing before us counsel on both sides agreed and invited us to decide the case on the footing that the terms of this contract are contained in a printed document put in evidence which purports to be 'working rules agreed to and signed by the employers and the operative stonemasons of Ipswich and district,' and to have been signed by (amongst others) Wigg & Wright, as employers, and the president and other officers of the defendant society. It was contended in argument that this agreement was illegal as being in restraint of trade. As at present advised, I am not satisfied that this is so; but in the view which I take it is unnecessary to decide the point, and I shall assume for the purpose of the present judgment that the agreement between Wigg & Wright and the defendants was in all respects valid and binding. The particular clause relied on is rule 6: 'That boys entering the trade shall not work more than three months without being legally bound apprentice, and in no case to be more than sixteen years of age, except masons' sons and step-sons.' This I refer to as the first part of the rule. It proceeds: 'Employers to have one apprentice to every four masons on an average.' This I refer to as the second part of the rule. It is contended, on behalf of the defendants, that the first part of the rule prohibits employers from taking apprentices over sixteen years of age; and if this were the true construction of the rule, and it were applicable to persons in the position of the plaintiff, there would be, to say the least, a serious question whether the justification set up by the defendants was not made out. But whatever the true construction of this part of the rule may be, it does not, in my opinion, apply to the plaintiff. He was a mason's son.

SPRING v. NATIONAL AMALGAMATED STEVEDORES' AND DOCKERS' SOCIETY

[1956] 1 W.L.R. 585; [1956] 2 All E.R. 221

[The Court was concerned with the expulsion of a member from his trade union, which it declared invalid: *post*, p. 619. The expulsion had been effected in order to honour the decision of the T.U.C. Disputes Committee, which decides disputes over membership between affiliated unions (*post*, p. 672) according to principles laid down at the Bridlington Congress in 1939. The 'Bridlington Agreement', while not being an ordinary collective agreement determining hours, wages, etc., can be thought of as a parallel type of agreement made between trade unions.]

SIR LEONARD STONE, V.C. referred to certain clauses of the rules and standing orders of the T.U.C. and to clause 13, saying: Now those clauses become of importance in this case. Clause (b) is as follows: 'If after such investigation the general council decides that the activities of the organisation concerned are detrimental to the interests of the Trade Union Movement or contrary to the declared principles of Congress, the general council shall direct the organisation to discontinue such activities forthwith and undertake not to engage therein in the future.

(c) Should the organisation disobey such direction, or fail to give such undertaking, the general council is hereby empowered in its discretion to order that the organisation be forthwith suspended from membership of the Congress until the next annual congress.

(d) The general council shall submit a report upon the matter to the next annual congress.'

Mr Victor Feather, the assistant secretary of the Trades Union

Congress and the officer whose duty is the settlement of inter-union and industrial differences before they reach the stage of open dispute, said in his evidence that the principles laid down at Bridlington were not points of law. He described them as being a morally binding code of conduct made between persons of similar views. I understand from his evidence that that is the view of the Trades Union Congress, and it is one which I think it would be difficult to challenge as being otherwise than an accurate definition of the Bridlington principles.

McLUSKEY v. COLE

Court of Appeal   [1922] 1 Ch. 7

An unregistered trade union brought this action against another trade union, also unregistered, of which it was a constituent member. It claimed a declaration that an expulsory resolution was invalid and an injunction to restrain the Federation from acting on the resolution. [Section 4(4) of the Trade Union Act, 1871, prevents the 'direct' enforcement of an agreement made between one trade union and another: see *post*, p. 539. Because of the peculiarities of the legal definition of a 'trade union' (see *post*, p. 537) many employers' associations are probably trade unions.*]

LORD STERNDALE, M.R.: It is necessary now to turn to the Trade Union Act of 1871. [His Lordship referred to the material sections and continued:] The question here is whether this is an action brought directly to enforce an agreement which comes within sub-s. 4 of s. 4: 'Any agreement made between one trade union and another.' That it is brought directly to enforce an agreement of some sort is in my opinion quite clear. I cannot see a much more direct way of enforcing an agreement than by an injunction to prevent a person from breaking it, and if an injunction to prevent a person from breaking an agreement is claimed, in my opinion that is an action brought directly to enforce that agreement.

Now was this an agreement between one trade union and another, if there was any agreement at all? It is admitted by counsel for the appellants that if this be an action by the plaintiff society as a society (and that is the basis on which I am dealing with it at the moment) the claim must arise out of a contract, and out of a contract by the plaintiff society with the defendant society. That, if it exist, must be an agree-

---

* See M. A. Hickling, 'Trade Unions in Disguise' (1964) 27 M.L.R. 625. As to registered and unregistered unions see *post*, chapter 5, p. 541 and p. 546.

ment between one trade union and another within the meaning of this sub-section. The agreement, if it exist, is an agreement that the plaintiff society should be a member of the defendant Federation upon the terms of the rules.

WARRINGTON and YOUNGER L.JJ. delivered concurring judgments.

PITMAN v. TYPOGRAPHICAL ASSOCIATION

The Times, 22 September 1949

The plaintiff sued on behalf of himself and all other members of the British Federation of Master Printers, following notice on the part of the defendant Association, a large trade union of craftsmen, that they intended to terminate an agreement made in 1919 in a fortnight's time. The plaintiff sought an interlocutory injunction claiming, *inter alia,* that the agreement was perpetual, and seeking to stop a strike being called.

Mr SCOTT CAIRNS, in opening the motion, said that it asked for interlocutory injunctions against the Typographical Association, which was a large and influential trade union of craftsmen in the printing industry. The plaintiffs were two out of three of the main organizations of employers in the same industry, and were represented by Mr Pitman and Mr Grime, that form of procedure being necessary as neither of the organizations which they represented was an incorporated body or a registered trade union. The British Federation of Master Printers was a national orgnization representing the general body of printers all over the country, and the Newspaper Society was the representative body of newspaper proprietors in the provinces and in the suburbs of London. For the last 30 years the terms of employment in the printing industry had been governed by a number of agreements entered into between the British Federation and the Newspaper Society on the one hand and the various unions of workers on the other, which were linked together in a federation called the Printing and Kindred Trades Federation. A basic wage agreement between the plaintiffs and the Typographical Association was entered into on 24 May 1919. That agreement contained no provisions for its being terminated in any circumstances, and he (counsel) would submit that the effect of the absence of any provision for its termination was that the agreement was one which was not terminable, in fact, that it was a perpetual agreement. In the alternative he would submit that the agreement could only be terminated by a reasonable notice, and that, having regard to the circumstances in which it was entered into and to the long period for which it had been in existence, a reasonable notice would be something considerably more than a fortnight. What had happened was that on 12 September the defendants gave notice to both of the masters' organizations purporting to determine the agreement on 26 September. ...Mr GARDINER said he would confine himself to the question of the length of notice to be given to put an end to the agreement. Apart from that, however, he would wish to submit that the agreement sought to be terminated was not really a contract at all, and was not intended to have legally binding force. The plaintiffs' federation, as a legal entity, did not exist, and so could not contract, and, certainly, no contract was made with the individual plaintiffs. If there was an enforceable agreement, he submitted that 14 days would be a reasonable notice to determine it.

MR JUSTICE DEVLIN said the first matter he had to consider was whether the plaintiffs had made out a *prima facie* case that there was a real likelihood of their succeeding in their contentions when the action came on for trial. He did not think that on its merits the plaintiffs' case was sufficiently strong to afford a basis for an interlocutory injunction at that stage of the proceedings. It was undesirable that he should say more regarding the contentions put forward, which would have to be finally decided when the case came on for trial. The motion would be dismissed.

BELLSHILL AND MOSSEND CO-OPERATIVE SOCIETY *v.* DALZIEL CO-OPERATIVE SOCIETY LTD

House of Lords   [1960] A.C. 832

The plaintiff and defendant societies, both members of a co-operative union, were in dispute as to their trading rights in a certain area of Lanark. Under the rules of their union such a dispute had to go to arbitration and the decision was to be final and binding: and also, under the rules, a member might withdraw from the union by sending in a written notice. The arbitral award went against the respondents who refused to comply but instead withdrew from the union. The appellants unsuccessfully claimed the respondents were still bound by the award.

LORD REID: My Lords, by becoming a member of the Co-operative Union the respondents agreed to be bound by the rules of that body....

But rule 15 provides that a society may withdraw from the union and the respondents withdrew from the union in 1957. Thereafter they were free to carry on their business in any area and this is admitted by the appellants with one exception. Rule 10 provides: '...Any disagreement that may arise as to overlapping or any other matter which cannot be settled in consultation between the parties shall, in failure of conciliation, be submitted to persons appointed by the Co-operative Union Ltd. as arbitrators and their decision shall be final and binding on all parties.' The appellants maintain that if a disagreement as to overlapping has been submitted to arbitrators in terms of this rule and the arbitrators decide that a society shall not trade in a particular area, as happened in this case, then that society remains bound by that award even after it has withdrawn from the union.

I cannot so interpret rule 10....the respondents only agreement, was its agreement as a member of the union to be bound by the rules of the union, and it could only be by virtue of the rules that the respondents could still be bound by the award made against them while they were members. The rules ceased to bind the respondents when they withdrew, and it would, in my opinion, at least require some very clear provision in the rules to render an award made under the rules effective after the rules themselves had ceased to be binding. I can find no such provision.

I am confirmed in my opinion by considering what would be the alternative. Is the award to be binding for ever ?*

VISCOUNT SIMONDS and LORDS KEITH OF AVONHOLM and DENNING delivered concurring speeches; LORD RADCLIFFE agreed with the opinion of VISCOUNT SIMONDS.

* Compare the problem where a union wishes to withdraw from a 'no strikes' agreement, if the collective bargain were given contractual effect. *Quaere* the effect of such a withdrawal on the individual employment contracts of workers concerned: see *post*, p. 283.

SECTION C

THE 'NORMATIVE' EFFECTS OF COLLECTIVE AGREEMENTS; THE RELATIONSHIP WITH INDIVIDUAL EMPLOYMENT CONTRACTS

INTRODUCTION

The problems concerning the incorporation of the collective agreement into the employment contract are likely to become more, rather than less complicated. At the time at which these materials are being compiled, various actions are pending brought by employees against employers who have failed to pay what are alleged to be wages contractually owing by reason of the Government's 'standstill' on rises, announced on 20 July 1966. (See on this *Allen* v. *Thorn Electrical Ltd*, *ante*, p. 46.) Some of the pending cases are likely to raise these problems.

The reader faced with this question should consider, in particular, the following problems in the light of the cases and materials that follow, and the discussion in 'The Worker and the Law', chapter 4:

(*a*) Can the employee be regarded as a principal, the union officers having bargained as his agent? This may be particularly relevant at local level. Also much can depend on the words used: see, e.g., Materials, *post*, p. 329.

(*b*) Have the collective terms, in whole or in part, been expressly incorporated into the employment contract? What are the documents to which one turns to answer this question? There may be correspondence or Works Rules. There may be only an oral hiring.

(*c*) What is the evidential value of the written statement of employment particulars issued under s. 4, Contracts of Employment Act, 1963? (See *ante*, p. 68.) In particular, if the statement states a certain wage, does that prevent the employee arguing that he is contractually entitled to a rise collectively negotiated?

(*d*) This leads to the question how far the collective terms, if not expressly incorporated, may be regarded as implied or 'customary' terms of an employment. (Cases in both chapter 1 and 2 may here be relevant: see note *post*, p. 290.)

(*e*) How far is the *form* of the collective machinery important? Note the stress placed in *Dudfield's* case, *post*, p. 296, on the fact that the Joint Council had functions which were 'purely consultative...not executive'.

(*f*) If, by either express or implied incorporation, the collective terms are to be included into the employment contract, the further question may arise as to whether any particular term in the collective agreement is 'appropriate' for incorporation. Is it intended to be, for example, merely a code adopted between the collective parties? Or is it a clause that can be given no certain meaning at individual rather than collective level? (In this connection, the reader should have in mind 'no strikes' and procedure clauses. See, for example, O. Kahn-Freund in 'Labour Relations and the Law' (1965), p. 27: 'In a recent case [*Rookes* v. *Barnard*, *post* p. 284 and p. 503] it was admitted that the 'no strike' obligation had become a term of the individual contracts of employment, but this must be quite exceptional.'

(i) *Does the Union bargain as Agent?**

HOLLAND *v.* LONDON SOCIETY OF COMPOSITORS
(1924) 40 T.L.R. 440

A provincial trade union made an agreement with a London trade union whereby a member of the provincial union who came to London should be entitled to membership of the London union. The plaintiff, a provincial member, came to London but was unable to accept a job because the London union refused him membership. He sued for a declaration that he was entitled to membership and for an injunction and damages.

[In argument, Lush, J. said that he must say that it would seem to him a most chaotic state of affairs if an individual could do what his union was expressly prohibited from doing (i.e. by s. 4(4) of the Trade Union Act, 1871, see *post* p. 539.)].

Lush, J., giving judgment, said that the case raised an issue of considerable importance, not only to members of this trade union, but to all trade unionists. No doubt it might prove an interesting question whether a member leaving London to seek work elsewhere, or, conversely, coming to London from another area, was entitled to lodge his

---

* *Note:* If the agency analysis is adopted, it is not easy to incorporate the collective agreement into the employment contracts of non-unionists. But collective agreements are frequently couched in terms which appear to make them applicable to the employment of all workers, whether in the union or not. See, for example, *Ross* v. *Alexander Campbell & Co. Ltd*, *ante*, p. 219; see too note *post* p. 290.

card in the new district, but his Lordship was not called upon to decide that question, as he was clearly of opinion that the present action was not maintainable, and that the plaintiff was a stranger and no party to the contract. He (the learned Judge) could not accept the contention that the contract was made for any individual, or for his behoof and benefit, but it was made by the trade unions concerned for their own purposes. Were he to decide to the contrary he would be laying down an entirely new principle of law, and Mr Morris had already pointed out some of the curious consequences that would ensue. He found as a fact that the agreement was not made between the member and the trade union, but between two trade unions, and as the plaintiff was neither directly nor indirectly a party, he must give judgment for the defendants, with costs.

ROOKES v. BARNARD

House of Lords   [1964] A.C. 1129
Court of Appeal   [1963] 1 Q.B. 623; [1962] 2 All E.R. 579
                                [1961] 2 All E.R. 825 (Sachs, J.)

[This case is dealt with fully *post*, p. 503. The points raised in these *dicta* were not the subject of comment in the House of Lords. The following passages are taken from the All England Reports.]

SACHS, J. (in the High Court): On 1 April 1949, there had come into force an agreement, referred to as the 1949 agreement, between the employers' and employees' sides of the draughtsmen, planners and tracers panel of the National Joint Council for Civil Air Transport. That panel is called the joint panel and consisted on the one hand of representatives of a number of trade unions, including A.E.S.D., and on the other side representatives of employers, including the corporation. The representatives of A.E.S.D. on that panel were authorised by their executive to bind the trade union as a whole and the members individually. The terms of the 1949 agreement thus became part of the terms of each individual contract of employment between the corporation and members of A.E.S.D.*...

The 1949 Agreement included the following provisions: 'Clause 4. Disputes. The employers on the one hand and the employees on the other hand undertake that no lock-out or strike shall take place. In the event of dispute occurring whether arising in connexion with this agreement or otherwise the matter shall be dealt with as provided for

---

* This comment is doubly *obiter* because the defendants had *conceded* that the 'no strike' clause bound each employee.

in the constitution of the National Joint Council for Civil Air Transport...'

In addition to the 1949 agreement there existed as between the trade unions on the joint panel and the corporation an understanding which apparently was not legally binding, and which has never been reduced to writing despite the desire of the trade unions that this be done. It was referred to as the '100% membership agreement'.

DONOVAN, L.J. (in the Court of Appeal): On 1 April 1949, an agreement had been entered into between employers and employees in the civil air transport industry, with the expressed object of maintaining good industrial relationships. A memorandum of this agreement is exhibited. Exactly who the parties to it were is not clear: but they are described in the memorandum as being on the one hand 'The Employer's Side of the Draughtsmen, Planners and Tracers Panel' and on the other hand 'The Employees' Side' of the same panel. The corporation is not expressly named as a party, nor is A.E.S.D. But Sachs, J., found that the panel in question is a panel of the National Joint Council for Civil Air Transport, and included representatives of the corporation on the employers' side, and representatives of A.E.S.D. on the employees' side. The representatives of A.E.S.D. were, so the judge finds, authorised to bind that trade union as a whole, and its members individually, so that the terms of the 1949 agreement, which deal among other things with hours of work, pay, holidays, and discipline (and here I quote the learned judge), 'thus became part of the terms of each individual contract of employment between the corporation and members of A.E.S.D.' Whether Barnard and Fistal, the first and third defendants, were members of A.E.S.D. and employed by the corporation at the date of this agreement is not disclosed in the judgment; and if there were an issue whether the agreement was part of the terms of their individual contracts of employment more proof would be needed.* But the fact was admitted. The second defendant, Silverthorne, however, was not an employee of the corporation at any material time, and his case, therefore, calls for separate consideration. But on the admission made, clause 4 of the agreement of 1949 was part of Barnard and Fistal's contracts of employment...

* This point is illustrative of the difficulties caused by the adoption of the 'agency' view. For further problems of this kind see Wedderburn, *The Worker and the Law* (1965) p. 112, (1966) p. 108.

DEANE v. CRAIK

The Times, 16 March 1962

[This case is dealt with *post*, p. 459. It was undoubtedly a judgment where, contrary to the usual view, union officials were treated as agents of members. But the number of members was small; the matters in dispute were personal to them; and the issues were localised to one employer.*]

EDWARDS v. SKYWAYS LTD

[1964] 1 W.L.R. 349

A meeting between representatives of a pilots' association and representatives of the defendant company who employed members of the association, took place to discuss threatened redundancies. It was agreed that redundant pilots who chose to claim back their contributions to the pension fund rather than take up a paid-up pension later on 'would be given an *ex gratia* payment equivalent to the company's contribution to the pension fund'. Later the company attempted to rescind this decision.

A pilot who was declared redundant and who had exercised his option to take up the *ex gratia* payment, successfully sued to recover it. It is to be noted that the union was conceded to be its member's agent; but the court treated the contract as one made when the *employee* accepted the company's standing offer.

[This concept of the 'standing offer' made by the employer in negotiation with the union, and accepted by each employee, can answer a number of juridical conundra.]

MEGAW, J.: A meeting took place between representatives of the association and representatives of the company on 8 February 1962. It was not in dispute that the representatives of the association were the duly authorised agents of the plaintiff, and that the representatives of the company had full authority from that company in respect of all that was done and agreed at that meeting affecting the plaintiff.... The issue in this action is whether, as a result of what was agreed at

* As far as the 'agency' problem is concerned three further points should be borne in mind: (i) The Terms and Conditions of Employment Act, 1959, s. 8(1)(b) appears to indicate that the legislature sees the collective parties not as agents but as principals (see *post*, p. 345): but (ii) The courts might more easily see an *employers'* trade association as the agent of the companies who are its members: consider *Thompson & Son Ltd.* v *Chamberlain* [1962] 2 Lloyds L.R. 399; and (iii) If trade union officials are seen as agents of members in negotiations, questions are bound to arise as to the extent of their authority to bind members.

the meeting, the plaintiff acquired a legal right, when he decided not to accept any of the offered alternatives but to leave the company's service and withdraw his own pension contributions, to be paid by the company a sum equal to the contributions which it had paid to the pension fund on his behalf. The plaintiff says that there was a legally binding contractual right. The company says that, while there may have been a moral right, or an obligation binding in honour, there was not a legally enforceable right....

Was there a legal obligation on the part of the company? The company admits, as I understand it, that at the meeting a promise was made on its behalf with its authority, although the actual word 'promise' was not used. In the defence it was pleaded that no consideration moved from the plaintiff. That plea was expressly abandoned at the hearing. It was conceded that there was consideration. The company admits that it was its intention to carry out its promise when it was made, and that the plaintiff's representatives, and the plaintiff himself, believed, and acted in the belief, that the promise would be fulfilled. Everyone, at the end of the meeting, believed that there was an agreement which would be carried out. But the company says that the promise and the agreement have no legal effect, because there was no intention to enter into legal relations in respect of the promised payment.

It is clear from such cases as *Rose and Frank Co.* v. *J. R. Crompton & Bros. Ltd.*[1] and *Balfour* v. *Balfour*[2] that there are cases in which English law recognises that an agreement, in other respects duly made, does not give rise to legal rights, because the parties have not intended that their legal relations should be affected. Where the subject-matter of the agreement is some domestic or social relationship or transaction, as in *Balfour* v. *Balfour*, the law will often deny legal consequences to the agreement, because of the very nature of the subject-matter. Where the subject-matter of the agreement is not domestic or social, but is related to business affairs, the parties may, by using clear words, show that their intention is to make the transaction binding in honour only, and not in law; and the courts will give effect to the expressed intention....

In the present case, the subject-matter of the agreement is business relations, not social or domestic matters. There was a meeting of minds —an intention to agree. There was, admittedly, consideration for the company's promise. I accept the propositions of counsel for the plaintiff

---

[1] [1923] 2 K.B. 261. [2] [1919] 2 K.B. 571; 35 T.L.R. 609, C.A.

that in a case of this nature the onus is on the party who asserts that no legal effect was intended, and the onus is a heavy one...I do, however, think that there are grave difficulties in trying to apply a test of the actual intention or understanding or knowledge of the parties: especially where the alleged agreement is arrived at between a limited liability company and a trade association; and especially where it is arrived at at a meeting attended by five or six representatives on each side. Whose knowledge, understanding or intention is relevant? But if it be the 'objective' test of the reasonable man, what background knowledge is to be imputed to the reasonable man, when the background knowledge of the ten or twelve persons who took part in arriving at the decision no doubt varied greatly between one and another?

However that may be, the company says, first, as I understand it, that the mere use of the phrase *ex gratia* by itself, as a part of the promise to pay, shows that the parties contemplated that the promise, when accepted, should have no binding force in law....As to the first proposition, the words *ex gratia*, in my judgment, do not carry a necessary, or even a probable, implication that the agreement is to be without legal effect....I see nothing in the mere use of the words *ex gratia*, unless in the circumstances some very special meaning has to be given to them, to warrant the conclusion that this promise, duly made and accepted, for valid consideration, was not intended by the parties to be enforceable in law....

Lastly, the company say that, even if the agreement were otherwise in all respects a binding agreement, it is not enforceable because its terms are too vague. This is founded on the submission that the precise words used by Davies at the meeting were 'approximating to'; that these precise words are a part of the agreement; that they leave a discretion to the company; that therefore there is no enforceable agreement, and they can refuse to pay anything. I have already indicated my conclusion on the evidence as to what was indeed agreed at the end of the meeting. If this be right, there is nothing in this point. Even if it were wrong, I do not think that English law provides that in such circumstances the plaintiff would be entitled to nothing. At most 'approximating to', if that were the contractual term, would on the evidence connote a rounding off of a few pounds downwards to a round figure.

(ii) *Incorporation of the Collective Bargain in the Individual Employment Contract—Express and Implied Incorporation*

NATIONAL COAL BOARD v. GALLEY

[1958] 1 W.L.R. 16

[*Note:* (*a*) In this case there was clear *express* incorporation, see *ante*, p. 184.

(*b*) In other cases, the point has been conceded that the relevant collective terms are part of the individual contract: see e.g. *Allen* v. *Thorn Electrical Ltd.* (*ante*, p. 46); *Rookes* v. *Barnard* (*ante*, p. 284 and *post*, p. 503); *Tomlinson* v. *L.M.S.* [1944] 1 All E.R. 537 (C.A.).

(*c*) Since 1963, the written statement given by the employer may refer to the collective agreement: Contracts of Employment Act, 1963, s. 4: see *ante*, p. 66 and p. 68. But it is to be remembered that this statement is not necessarily conclusive evidence of the terms of the employment contract: see 'The Worker and the Law', (1965) p. 44; (1966) p. 45.]

YOUNG v. CANADIAN NORTHERN RY CO.

Privy Council   [1931] A.C. 83

The plaintiff, a machinist in the employ of the Railway company, was dismissed in contravention of a clause in a Wage Agreement which, he claimed, secured him a right that junior men would be dismissed first.

LORD RUSSELL OF KILLOWEN: Before their Lordships' Board the appellant's counsel sought to establish the existence of the necessary contractual obligation from the following facts which, as he claimed, the evidence proved: That the railway company (whose shops were open shops) treated all its employees alike, whether members of Division No. 4 or not; that when the appellant was hired he was promised 'the going rate' and was placed as regards salary under 'schedule', which meant the Wage Agreement No. 4; that he was placed on the seniority list referred to in rule 31; that when he was dismissed the railway company gave him the number of days' notice required by rule 27; that when he complained to various officials of the railway company he was referred to the committee, as provided by rule 35. From these facts their Lordships were invited to hold that the necessary contractual obligation had been established.

There can be no doubt upon the evidence that in fact, the provisions of Wage Agreement No. 4 were applied by the railway company to all its employees in its locomotive and car department....

Their Lordships, however, are unable to treat these matters as establishing contractual liability by the railway company to the appellant. The fact that the railway company applied the agreement to the appellant, is equally consistent with the view that it did so, not because it was bound contractually to apply it to him, but because as a matter of policy it deemed it expedient to apply it to all....

But the matter does not quite rest there. When Wage Agreement No. 4 is examined, it does not appear to their Lordships to be a document adapted for conversion into or incorporation with a service agreement, so as to entitle master and servant to enforce *inter se* the terms thereof. It consists of some 188 'rules', which the railway companies contract with Division No. 4 to observe. It appears to their Lordships to be intended merely to operate as an agreement between a body of employers and a labour organization by which the employers undertake that as regards their workmen, certain rules beneficial to the workmen shall be observed. By itself it constitutes no contract between any individual employee and the company which employs him. If an employer refused to observe the rules, the effective sequel would be, not an action by any employee, not even an action by Division No. 4 against the employer for specific performance or damages, but the calling of a strike until the grievance was remedied.

MACLEA *v.* ESSEX LINE *

(1933) 45 Lloyd's List Rep. 254

The plaintiff claimed that he was entitled to 14 days' wages in lieu of leave for each complete year of his service. There was no mention of

---

* *Note:* Where there are existing collective terms that are applied to other workers, it is plainly easier to import them into the particular employee's contract of employment, especially where he is a new worker joining a plant: see *Sagar* v. *Ridehalgh, ante,* p. 132, and *Marshall* v. *English Electric Co., ante,* p. 144. Where the conditions are changing, at common law it may be of importance to determine whether the worker knew of the new terms: see *Meek* v. *Port of London Authority, ante,* p. 85. In practice, that problem would now usually be solved by use of the machinery of automatic incorporation of new collective terms provided by the Contracts of Employment Act, 1963, s. 4(6).

Furthermore, if the implied term is alleged to be 'customary', the usual requirements for incorporation of a 'custom' in a contract must be met, in particular that it is both clear and reasonable. In *Hooker* v. *Lange Bell & Co.* (1937) 4 L.J.N.C.C.R. 199, the Mayor's Court of the City of London was faced with a claim that extra payments would be made for unloading timber in the docks with greater speed than normal. It was alleged that the extra money would customarily be payable to and shared out by the union men, to the exclusion of non-unionists. The court held that the plaintiff, a such a right to leave in his written contract; but it was provided for in the rules of the National Maritime Board. Those rules were not referred to in his contract. He claimed that they were impliedly incorporated therein.

ACTON, J.: When the articles are signed and when, at the conclusion of the voyage, a settlement is signed by a member of the crew—in this case it is the second mate who receives his pay and who is discharged—*pro tanto* I think it is reasonably clear that all he is then signing is a settlement in full of everything that arises in respect of and by reason of that particular voyage and that thereafter he could not—it may well be—be heard to say that he had some other claim to bring forward which was a claim to which he was entitled by reason of any services rendered, or it may be any incidents occurring, during that particular voyage; so with all the other settlements which were signed by this officer was each separate voyage so concluded. But it seems to me that there is nothing in that which is in any way inconsistent with there being an agreement between the officer and the shipowner by whom he is engaged that, if he serves for a certain period of time, or it may be for a certain number of voyages, he shall be entitled to a certain amount of leave or to some payment in lieu of leave under such conditions and terms as may be agreed upon between the parties. It is clear that there is nothing under s. 114 of the Merchant Shipping Act of 1894 which would make any such agreement illegal; and indeed we know that such an agreement is an agreement which is contemplated by and often applied to relations of this kind between the crew and the shipowner by the rules and regulations of the National Maritime Board. Now, all this, of course, up to this point, has nothing whatever to do with the rules and regulations of the National Maritime Board; it is something which might have been arranged orally between the parties without any legal objection being possible to it. But in the present case the plaintiff says that the terms upon which he was engaged were in fact the terms and conditions of the National Maritime Board, and those terms and conditions as they might be revised from time to time, with all the variations that thereupon would be found in those rules as those alterations or revisions took place from time to time....

What was the evidence there? The evidence was that all that happened between the superintendent of this line and the plaintiff was that

non-union man, had been hired on the same terms as union men, and that a custom whereby non-unionists were excluded from such payments would be 'unreasonable' and would not in any case have been regarded as an implied term of the employment contracts.

he was told simply to join a certain ship belonging to the defendants on the next day. There was no sort of chartering or bargaining or any indication of what the terms were to be; and the plaintiff said that he assumed, and had no hesitation whatever in assuming, that in those circumstances he was being engaged at the rates of pay laid down by the rules and regulations of the National Maritime Board, and in all respects upon the terms and conditions of the National Maritime Board Year Book as it was revised from time to time. His case was that this is a perfectly familiar form of engagement which indeed had been applied to him on many occasions before—it had always been followed, that being regarded as an implied term of the contract—and that accordingly on this occasion he assumed, and always has assumed ever since, that those were the terms and conditions upon which he was employed. In support of his case the two witnesses to whose evidence objections were taken were called to give evidence, which they did quite shortly, supporting the plaintiff's contention that in the shipping industry when people are engaged in this way simply by being told to join a ship without anything more, it is always assumed on both sides that that engagement is upon the terms and conditions of the National Maritime Board and upon those conditions as they may from time to time be altered by the revision of the rules, which appears to take place with some frequency in the management of this National Maritime Board.

The evidence...seems to me, however, to be very definitely evidence upon which, along with the other evidence there was in the case, the learned Judge was entitled to come to the conclusion at which he did arrive, that as a matter of fact the agreement between these parties was that the plaintiff should be engaged upon the terms and conditions of the National Maritime Board, and that those terms and conditions were to be binding as between the parties however they might be varied from time to time upon a revision of those rules by the National Maritime Board itself.

GODDARD, J. delivered a concurring judgment.

THE TEMPORARY RESTRICTIONS ON PAY INCREASES (20 July 1966 Levels) ORDER 1966

S.I. NO. 1365 OF 1966, MADE UNDER THE PRICES AND INCOMES ACT, 1966, S. 29 (*ante*, p. 262)

[The Order required the employers, Thorn Electrical Industries Ltd (who were parties to the litigation noted *ante*, p. 46), not to pay remuneration at a rate which exceeded that paid for the same kind of work before 20 July 1966, in respect of the remuneration described in the Schedule:]

SCHEDULE

Description of Remuneration for Work

Remuneration for work performed under any contract of employment the terms of which include, expressly or by implication, all or any of the terms of the verbal agreement entered into on 12 July 1966 by or on behalf of Thorn Electrical Industries Ltd, the Association of Supervisory Staffs, Executives and Technicians, and the National Association of Clerical and Supervisory Staffs, which provides for periodic increases in the salaries of members of either of the contracting unions in the employment of Thorn Electrical Industries Ltd as from 4 April 1966 to 6 October 1968.

[*Quaere:* Is there implicit in this Order any view about the character of collective bargaining, e.g. any 'agency' concepts? Further, what would be the position of employees who were not members of the union?]

CLIFT v. WEST RIDING COUNTY COUNCIL

The Times, 10 April 1964

The plaintiff was an ambulance driver employed by the defendant council. The nationally agreed 'scheduled' rates for stand-by duty had been modified by a local collective agreement in 1955 between his union and his employers.* He claimed damages, alleging that he should have been paid the scheduled rates.

* *Note:* The transcript of this slenderly reported case discloses a most complex relationship between national and local bargaining structures. Where there are national, district and plant arrangements, all over-lapping, which terms become part of the employment contracts? Since 1963, the language used in the 'written particulars' of the employment contracts can be of great importance on this issue. See *ante* p. 239.

WIDGERY, J. said that Mr Clift's contract of service provided that in addition to his normal working week of 44 hours, he was required to stand-by for service during the night. For each night that he undertook stand-by duties at the depot he was paid 10s., and additional payment when he was actually carrying out his duty.

Agreed mathematical calculation showed that the difference between what he was actually paid, under a local agreement made between his union and his employers in 1955, and what he claimed he should have been paid at scheduled rates of pay plus overtime, amounted to £155 4s. 9d. if the local agreement was terminated, as he claimed, in November 1956, or £116 13s. 8d. if the local agreement was terminated, as he claimed in the alternative, in March.

Had the West Riding County Council continued the existing stand-by rotas and put them on scheduled rates of pay plus overtime, it would have involved an additional expenditure of something in the order of £30,000.

His Lordship concluded that, throughout the period concerned, until November 1957, Mr Clift's rates of pay for stand-by duties were covered by the local agreement made in 1955, that he—and other West Riding County Council ambulance drivers in a position similar to his—had, in fact been remunerated in accordance with that agreement, and that his claim failed and had to be dismissed.

RODWELL v. THOMAS

[1944] 1 K.B. 596

A civil servant, accused of stealing and selling an Air Ministry radio set, was dismissed from the service of the Tithe Redemption Commission. The National Whitley Council had established a disciplinary procedure for serious disciplinary charges other than ones which might give rise to criminal proceedings, and this had been sent round to all departments by a Treasury Circular. The plaintiff complained that since the charge against him could lead to criminal proceedings, the wrong procedure had been used against him; and that this was a term of his contract.

TUCKER, J.: The result of this Treasury Circular containing the recommendations or agreed finding of a joint committee of the National Whitley Council for the Civil Service appears to be that a specific form of procedure is laid down in cases where a serious disciplinary charge, other than one which may give rise to criminal proceedings, is brought against an established civil servant, e.g. where the penalty may be dismissal, but there is no recommendation laid down as to what is to be the appropriate procedure for dealing with charges which may give rise to criminal proceedings.... The plaintiff's case, therefore, fails at the outset because even on the assumption that the provisions of this report are to be regarded as contractual, I am unable to see that there has been any breach of them by the defendants.

Having regard, however, to the argument addressed to me by Mr Platts Mills, I think that it is only right to consider whether the contents of the report can be considered to form part of the contract between the plaintiff and the defendants. By the word 'contract', I mean a 'legally binding contract' which would give the plaintiff a right of access to a court of law to enforce compliance with its provisions. I have not been shown any written contract which established the terms of the plaintiff's employment, but it is said that because members of the trade union which represents him have been parties to this report of the joint committee he has the right to come to a court of law and say: 'Every one of the findings of this committee must be considered as part of the terms of my contract of employment for breach of which I am entitled to seek redress.' It is well-known that it has been found convenient to settle questions relating to conditions of employment through the medium of a representative body such as the joint committee, but I am at a loss to understand how every matter which is disposed of by give and take in that way can be said to be incorporated into a civil servant's contract of employment, so that, on a deviation from any term or condition, there is a breach of contract affording him a cause of action. In my opinion, Mr Platts Mills has failed to get within measurable distance of establishing that the recommendations of the joint committee enclosed with the Treasury Circular No. 12/35 form part of the plaintiff's contract of employment with the Tithe Redemption Commission....

There is a further difficulty in the plaintiff's way. The authorities show, not only that *prima facie* an established civil servant can be dismissed at pleasure, but that the court will disregard any term of his contract expressly providing for employment for a specified time or that his employment can only be terminated in specified ways. The court regards such a provision in a contract as a clog on the right of the Crown to dismiss at pleasure at any time. This action, being one which, in substance, seeks to establish that the plaintiff has been wrongfully dismissed because the procedure adopted at the inquiry was wrong and, therefore, ineffective legally to terminate his employment, in my opinion, does amount to an attempt to interfere with the right of the Crown to dismiss an established civil servant at any time for any reason, stated or unstated.

DUDFIELD *v.* MINISTRY OF WORKS

The Times, 24 January 1964

The plaintiff was an industrial civil servant, a lift attendant employed by the defendant Ministry. A committee of the Joint Council for Government Industrial Employees recommended that the class of workers to which the plaintiff belonged should be given a rise of 2*s.* per week. This was ratified by the Joint Council; but its operation was postponed because of the Chancellor of the Exchequer's 'pay pause'. The plaintiff claimed that he had a right to this money under his contract of employment.

GORMAN, J. said that Mr Dudfield became, in 1937, a lift attendant with the Ministry of Works. He was, at all times, a member of the Transport and General Workers' Union. In 1950 the industrial staff at the Ministry became established, and from January 1955, Mr Dudfield was an established chargehand lift man. He retired from his service on 22 November 1963.

On 26 November 1953 he was issued with the Ministry of Works' *Industrial Handbook,* and he signed for it in the terms that he had received an up-to-date copy of it and he understood that the rules in it applied to him. In rule 23 there was a reference to the joint council, which was in existence before 1948, and of which the constitutional powers and procedure were of great importance in this case. It was composed of 24 members appointed, as to the official side, by the Ministers of the Departments concerned, including the Treasury and Ministry of Labour, and as to the employees' side by the trade unions.

On 24 September 1959, at a meeting of the joint council, at which, among others, were present representatives of the Treasury and Mr Dudfield's trade union, the joint council ratified an agreement between the official side and the trade union side as the basis for determining the 'Miscellaneous "M"' rate. This provided that the male 'M' rate operative in London should be 177*s.*, that the next review of those rates should be in April 1960, and at six-monthly intervals after that, and that the agreement should remain in force for at least five years and be subject to review at any time thereafter at the request of either side. By the summer of 1961 the 'Miscellaneous "M" ' rate was 187s.

On 10 August 1961, a letter was sent from the Treasury to Mr Heritage, the Transport and General Workers' Union's representative on the joint council, and this stated that it was written 'to put on record what the Chancellor of the Exchequer told the representatives of the Industrial Civil Service this afternoon about the Government plans for applying to the Civil Service their general policy of securing the pause in wage and salary increases which in the Government's view is essential in all employments in present economic circumstances...The Government must ensure that during the period of the pause there are no other increases of pay in the Industrial Civil Service.' The document was a long one; its effect had been described as a 'pay pause'.

A further review of the 'Miscellaneous "M" ' rate was due in October 1961. A meeting of the committee of the joint council was held on 9 November 1961. According to the defence it was agreed at this meeting that, by application of the basis for determining that rate, an increase of 2s. a week resulted, effective from 1 October 1961. It was that increase which was the subject of Mr Dudfield's claim.

On 3 January 1962 a meeting of the joint council was held, and the minutes stated, under the heading 'Ratification of the "M" Rates', that the council ratified the rate of 189s., but the chairman pointed out that the ratification of the rates did not imply any departure from the decision conveyed in the Treasury letter of 29 September 1961, postponing any increase in the rate until circumstances permitted with no retrospection. On behalf of the trade union side the vice-chairman reiterated their objection to this limitation; he said that, in accordance with the council's agreement, the above rates should operate as from 1 October 1961.

Mr Dudfield's case was that he had a binding legal contract with the defendants by virtue of which he was entitled to this payment of 2s. a week, and that what had been called the pay pause could have no legal effect in depriving him of this sum.

His claim was put forward in very simple terms. The defence was much more complicated, and alleged that there was no contract of service between him and the defendants. It was denied that the Crown or the Ministry of Works on behalf of the Crown assumed an contractual obligation towards him as alleged or at all. That was not merely to say that there was no contract between him and the defendants as alleged in his statement of claim, but it went further and said that there was no contract of employment at all between him and the defendants. This was, of course, a very much wider allegation, and involved the right of Mr Dudfield to bring an action at law for his wages.

The case really gave rise to two considerations: first, if Mr Dudfield had been employed by some industrial company, could he have succeeded in his claim? Secondly, did it make any difference that the defendants were a government department?

On the issues raised in the case, the main matters for consideration were: first, on the facts of this case, and on the assumption that there was a contract between Mr Dudfield and the defendants, and disregarding any special relationship between him and the defendants, as a government department, was there any contract between him and the defendants for the payment of the increase of 2s. a week as from 1 October 1961, as claimed? Secondly, on the same assumptions, was there a legal right in him to this extra payment of 2s. a week, and was there any obligation upon the defendants to pay this increase? These two matters were really treating the defendants as though they were an ordinary industrial undertaking....

It was agreed on behalf of Mr Dudfield that his claim depended on contract. Lord Gardiner had said that he had to show that there was Treasury assent to the 2s. claimed, and he contended that the increase was, in fact, agreed by the Treasury through its representatives on the joint council.

The defendants submitted that, because of s. 3(1) of the Ministry of Works Act, 1942, and rule 21 of the 'Industrial Handbook'—which provided that rates of wages were authorized by Headquarters (Establishment Division), by whom any negotiations with the appropriate trade union were conducted—payment of the 2s. increase required the double sanction of a Treasury minute and the authority of the Director of Estabishment.

It was clear to his Lordship that, in respect of the increase claimed there was, in fact, no statutory authority for that payment, nor was there any authority of the Establishment Division as provided by rule 21. The contention made on behalf of the defendants was right.

In his Lordship's view rule 21 had to be read together with rule 23, which provided that employees were paid the appropriate rates as agreed on the joint council in negotiation with the trade unions concerned, and he did not think that they were intended to be contractual terms between Mr Dudfield and the defendants. Rule 23 set out the position of the joint council as a negotiating body.

Mr Dudfield never became in law entitled to the 2s. a week increase claimed.

The functions of the joint council were purely consultative. They were not executive. His Lordship was not saying, for a moment, that, within the ambit of its constitution, the joint council did not perform very important functions, but it did not create legally enforceable rights either for or against the Crown, or for or against a person employed in the miscellaneous trades.

It was submitted to his Lordship on behalf of Mr Dudfield that long-continued practice might form a contract, and in this case the Court should hold that there was, by reason of the practice, in fact a contract; and that the Court should imply a term as to payment claimed. It was his Lordship's view on the facts of this case, and on the assumpion that there was a contract between Mr Dudfield and the defendants, and disregarding any special relationship between him and them as a government department, that there was no contract between him and them for the payment of 2s. a week as from 1 October 1961. There was no legal right in him to the sum claimed, nor any legal obligation on them to pay it.

If there were a contract between Mr Dudfield and the defendants, he was entitled only to such sum as was authorized by the Treasury. In his Lordship's view, no claim on a *quantum meruit* could arise in this case.

On the view which his Lordship had formed of the facts, Mr Dudfield was not entitled to succeed; and, therefore, there did not arise for his Lordship's consideration the wider question as to the right of an industrial civil servant to sue the defendants, as a government department, for his wages. Any such decision on his Lordship's part would be *obiter*. He had, however, considered the submissions, and the authorities submitted to him on this aspect of the case, and had formed a view upon it.

He had considered those submissions, and upon due consideration, and in the exercise of his discretion, his Lordship decided not to state his view on this wider aspect of the case.*

The claim was dismissed with costs.

* On the status of a civil servant see *ante*, p. 71, and p. 294.

FAITHFUL *v.* THE ADMIRALTY

The Times, 24 January 1964

The plaintiff, a storehouse assistant employed by the Admiralty, sued for arrears of wages, arguing that an award of the Industrial Court entitled him to more money than he had been paid.

GORMAN, J. said that he was satisfied that no contract existed between Mr Faithful and the Admiralty to pay any award determined by the Shipbuilding Trades' Joint Council or, in the event of the trade union side and the official side of the joint council being unable to agree and referring the dispute to the Industrial Court, as the Court might award.

If a contract of employment existed between Mr Faithful and the Admiralty he was entitled only to such sums as were directed to be paid in Admiralty Fleet Orders.

HULLAND *v.* SANDERS AND SON

Court of Appeal   [1945] K.B. 78

Under the Conditions of Employment and National Arbitration Order, 1940,* all employers were to observe terms and conditions which were in force in their district having been settled by collective negotiations in which a substantial proportion of employers and workers in the area were represented. The question of whether an employer was observing these terms could be reported by a trade union to the Minister, who would then refer it to the National Arbitration Tribunal. It was then to become an implied term of each worker's contract that he was to be paid in accordance with the award of the National Arbitration Tribunal giving him a right to sue if he was not.

The plaintiff was paid below the local wage-level. He claimed he could recover a sum to make up the balance of what he should have been paid in the past provided he could prove this failure by his employer.

The judgement of the court was read by DU PARCQ, L.J.: ...The plaintiff's claim in this case was founded on the proposition that, if he could satisfy the court that his employer had failed to comply with article 5, paragraph 1, of the order in question, he would be entitled under the order to judgment for an amount representing the wages which his employer ought to have, and had not, paid to him. It was one of the

* Although this wartime Order was repealed in 1951, the reader should note this case as revealing the reluctance of the Court to disturb the express individual employment contract except where statute compels it.

defendants' contentions that, on the true construction of the order, no action would lie under it for wages at the suit of a workman except where, by its express provisions, a term is to be implied in the contract of service that a certain rate of wages is to be paid.... The plaintiff relies on the general proposition stated by Parke B. in *Shepherd* v. *Hills*[1]: 'There is no doubt that wherever an Act of Parliament creates a duty or obligation to pay money, an action will lie for its recovery, unless the Act contains some provision to the contrary.' This proposition is unquestionably correct, if its final words are understood as expressing the reservation that an action will not be held to lie for the recovery of such a sum when the enactment, read as a whole, manifests a contrary intention. It is thus necessary to look closely at the language of the order and to consider the words on which the plaintiff relies in association with their context....

The plaintiff founds his claim on the words of article 5, paragraph 1, in part III of the order: 'all employers... shall observe the recognized terms and conditions.' In our opinion, the argument put forward on his behalf, which the learned judge accepted, gave too little attention to the remaining provisions of article 5, in particular, paragraphs 3 and 4 of that article. The article must be read in the light of the words which we have quoted from regulation 58AA, paragraph 1 (*c*), to which part III of the order is referable. The terms and conditions of employment are to be 'determined in accordance with the order.' Part I of the order which is referable to regulation 58AA, paragraph 1 (*a*), has enacted (by article 2, paragraph 5) that it shall be an implied term of a contract of employment to which an agreement, decision or award, made under article 1, relates, that the rate of wages to be paid shall be in accordance with the agreement, decision or award. Now by part III, article 5, paragraph 3, provision is made for the determination of any question that may arise 'as to the nature, scope or effect of the recognized terms and conditions in any trade or industry in any district or as to whether an employer is observing the recognized terms and conditions or is observing terms and conditions which are not less favourable than the recognized terms and conditions.' This question (under the same paragraph) may be reported to the minister by an organization of employers or a trade union, and be by him referred to the National Arbitration Tribunal. Here, again, as in the case of an agreement, decision or award under part I, a term is to be implied in contracts of employment governed by the award of the tribunal (article 5, paragraph 4). The

---

[1] 11 Exch. 55, 67.

implication of such a term will necessarily give the workman a right under his contract to the wages fixed by the tribunal.

In spite of the persuasive argument addressed to us on behalf of the plaintiff, we are satisfied that to accept it would be to ignore, or to render in large part nugatory, the carefully framed provisions of these paragraphs of article 5. When the order is viewed as a whole, it is, we think, manifest that the provisions by which terms are to be implied in contracts of employment are essential to its scheme. Their principal, if not their only, object must be to give the workman a contractual right, and so a right to sue. If he had such a right, apart from these provisions, there would hardly be any need for them, and there would certainly be no need for the careful provision which, in fact, we find as to the date from which the implied term is to be incorporated in the contract. It must in all cases be so incorporated at least from the date of the award. So much is mandatory, but power is given to the tribunal to make it operative from an earlier date....

If the workman's right to sue arises in this way independently of any implied term which an award may bring into existence, it would seem that, in the event of a reference to the National Arbitration Tribunal under article 5, paragraph 3, neither a direction given under article 5, paragraph 4, nor the fact that the tribunal designedly abstained from giving any direction under that paragraph, would prevent the workman from successfully suing under article 5, paragraph 1, for arrears of wages in respect of a period anterior to any date fixed by the tribunal, or to the date of the award if the tribunal fixed no date. On this view (for which counsel for the plaintiff did not hesitate to contend) any individual workman might await a reference to the National Arbitration Tribunal, and then, if the award were given against the employer, lawfully demand payment from the employer of arrears of pay according to the quantum of wages fixed by the award, without regard to the date from which the implied term began to be operative, and subject only (as to time) to the statutes of limitation. The elaborate provisions introduced for the protection of the employer would thus be rendered nugatory.* Although he might have acted in good faith, honestly believing that the terms and conditions which he observed were no less favourable than those in force, or, it may be, believing that, on the true construction of the order, no terms and conditions could properly be held to be 'in force' in his district, he might be exposed to a multitude of actions in which the

---

* Compare the procedures under Terms and Conditions of Employment Act, 1959, s. 8, *post*, p. 345.

court would be bound to order him to pay sums greatly exceeding any amount which, in the considered judgment of the National Arbitration Tribunal, he ought justly to be called on to pay.... The order is contemplating, at least primarily, not separate agreements made between individuals, but terms arrived at after negotiations between associations of employers and of workmen. We apprehend that the National Arbitration Tribunal may properly regard such collective bargains (if we may so term them) as a whole when they compare their terms and conditions with the terms and conditions which a particular employer is observing.

R. *v.* INDUSTRIAL DISPUTES TRIBUNAL *ex parte*
PORTLAND URBAN DISTRICT COUNCIL

Court of Appeal   [1955] 1 W.L.R. 949; [1955] 3 All E.R. 18

A dispute arose in connexion with the Industrial Disputes Order 1951* as to whether a scheme of conditions of service approved by a Whitley Council applied to a workman. The employer—Portland U.D.C.—argued that the question should be settled in accordance with paragraph 25(2) of the scheme which provided machinery for settling whether an employee was within the scheme.

DENNING, L.J.: The third point which was strongly pressed on us by Mr Threlfall was that the difference ought to have been referred by the trade union in the first place to the Whitley council for the miscellaneous class. It ought not, he said, to have been referred straight away to the Minister. This point finds its origin in paragraph 25(2) in the red book (the scheme for the miscellaneous class), which says that 'a question as to whether or not an employee is an officer to whom the scheme applies, as distinct from a question arising out of the application of the scheme, shall be dealt with under the procedure for the settlement of differences as set out in the constitution for the provincial council.'

Perhaps the strongest way of putting this point for the local authority is this: The only thing that can be reported as an 'issue' to the Minister is whether an employer should observe the recognized terms and conditions. One of those terms is paragraph 25(2) in the red book. So long as the local authority are prepared to let the matter be decided in the way laid down in paragraph 25(2) in the red book, it cannot be said that they are not observing the recognized terms and conditions.

* Order 1376, revoked by S.I. 1796 in 1958.

The short answer to this point is that the local authority here repudiate the red book altogether. They say that it does not apply to Mr Carter. They cannot be heard to say that he is bound by it when they say they are not bound by it themselves.

Furthermore, paragraph 25(2) is not, properly speaking, one of the 'terms and conditions of employment' at all.* It is only machinery for settling a difference. The existence of such machinery is no bar to a report to the Minister. It is often of the greatest public importance that an issue should be reported to the Minister at once before resort is had to the trade machinery for settlement. It may be the only way in which a strike can be averted. It is then a matter for the Minister to decide what steps to take to settle the difference. It is for him to say whether there is suitable machinery for settlement of the difference and whether it should go first to the Whitley Council or be sent straight to the Industrial Disputes Tribunal. It would be very unfortunate if a difference could not be reported to the Minister until all trade machinery for settlement had been exhausted. The Order does not so require, and I do not think the courts should require it either. I think the trade union were entitled to report this matter to the Minister without first going to the Whitley Council.

ROMER, L.J.: I do not regard paragraph 25(2) as forming a part of the 'recognized terms and conditions' within the purview of that phrase as used in article 2 of the Order of 1951. The scheme admittedly formulates a complete code of terms and conditions but that is not to say that a term or condition of employment emerges from every paragraph of the scheme. No such term or condition emerges from paragraph 25(2), which does no more than provide administrative machinery for the purpose of settling questions whether or not an employee is in fact an officer to whom the scheme applies. From this it follows that the purported adoption by the urban district council of paragraph 25(2) does not enable them to say that they are conforming to even one of the recognized terms and conditions of employment and they cannot therefore displace the application of article 2 of the Order on that ground.

BIRKETT, L.J. delivered a concurring judgment.

* Compare Terms and Conditions of Employment Act, 1959, s. 8, as interpreted in *National Society of Metal Mechanics* against *Newtown Polishing Ltd* (No. 2), *post*, p. 359.

BARBER v. MANCHESTER REGIONAL HOSPITAL BOARD

[1958] 1 W.L.R. 181. [For facts see chapter 1, p. 42.]

BARRY, J.: Thirdly, (Counsel) submitted that even if the letter and the words 'subject to the terms and conditions of service above referred to' can be said to incorporate some of the terms and conditions, they cannot be said to incorporate all of them. In a sense, of course, as Mr Scott Henderson conceded, this argument is obviously correct. The terms and conditions are a code and obviously there cannot be incorporated into the contract with a part-time officer the terms and re-muneration applicable to whole-time officers. Similarly, certain other paragraphs in the terms and conditions are more applicable to the board itself, and really contain directions to the board rather than directions which may be incorporated in any contract between either a whole-time or a part-time officer and the board.

However, in my judgment, clause 16 is a clause which can quite clearly be incorporated in a contract made with either a whole-time or a part-time consultant, and if a whole-time or a part-time consultant is employed by the board subject to these terms and conditions, clause 16 is one of the terms and conditions incorporated into his contract. That clause gives him a measure of security of tenure in his employment, and prevents its termination, if he considers such termination to be unfair, until the procedure laid down in clause 16 has been carried out. I can see no foundation for saying that the words 'subject to the terms and conditions of service' can on any reasonable interpretation be said to exclude clause 16. If any terms and conditions are to be incorporated in the contract, why should clause 16 be excluded? I have been unable to find any satisfactory answer to that question. It is a clause clearly appropriate to inclusion in the contract of a consultant, just as appro-priate as the clauses relating to his terms of remuneration, leave and other matters of a similar kind.... I see no reason to suppose that in the negotiations which took place between the Ministry and the representa-tives of the medical profession it was ever doubted that this clause would have contractual force. I am quite satisfied it has contractual force.

CAMDEN EXHIBITION & DISPLAY LTD *v.* LYNOTT

Court of Appeal   [1965] 3 W.L.R. 763; [1966] 1 Q.B. 555

A dispute arose between the plaintiffs who were the employers and the defendants who were two shop stewards employed by them, about the working of overtime. The National Joint Council for their industry laid down working rules for the industry, one of which (6(a)) ran as follows:

'Overtime required to ensure the due and proper performance of contracts shall not be subject to restriction, but may be worked by mutual agreement and direct arrangement between the employer and the operatives concerned.'

A number of the men were dissatisfied with a wage increase of 6d. an hour. L. told the general manager about this and said none of the men would work overtime after a certain date, a decision which was implemented.

The plaintiffs sought an interim injunction to restrain the shop stewards from inducing the men to break their contracts by banning overtime.

LORD DENNING, M.R.: First of all, we must look at the working rules. In an ordinary contract of employment a man is bound to work his proper hours during his working week. But he is not bound to do overtime. Overtime is a matter for agreement between him and his employers. Do these working rules alter the position? It seems to me that, since the Contracts of Employment Act, 1963, these working rules are incorporated into the terms of employment of all men in the industry. A notice was issued under that Act saying to every man: 'Your rate of wages, hours of work, holidays and holiday pay are in accordance with the provisions of the constitution and working rule agreement issued by and under the authority of the national joint council.' In view of that notice these working rules are not only a collective agreement between the union and the employers. They are incorporated into the contract of employment of each man, in so far as they are applicable to his situation.

What is the true interpretation of this working rule 6(a)? I think it is clear that the unions agreed that when overtime was necessary to ensure the proper performance of contracts, the unions would not impose a restriction on overtime, and would not authorise their stewards, or anyone on their behalf, to impose a restriction on overtime. Overtime was to be arranged by mutual agreement and direct arrangement between the employers and the men.

Suppose that no authority is given by the unions for a ban on overtime, but some of the men seek together to restrict overtime, without any official sanction. Does this rule prevent it? Can the men put a collective unofficial embargo on overtime? This is a difficult point. On the whole I think this working rule means that the man will not, officially or unofficially, impose a collective embargo on overtime when it is required to ensure the due and proper performance of contracts. It follows that, if the defendants did induce the men to put a collective embargo on overtime, they were inducing them to break the working rules and hence their contracts of employment. But even so, the question is whether their conduct can be restrained by injunction....

[His Lordship read the Trade Disputes Act, 1906, ss. 3 and 5 (*post*, p. 385) and continued]: On the very face of the demands made by the men, the dispute here does seem to be connected with the terms of the employment of the men.... Sir Peter Rawlinson said that this was not a genuine dispute about the terms of employment. The demand for extra wages was really a specious cover for other ends which the men sought. He said that it was done solely for disruptive purposes. In the recent case of *Stratford (J.T.) & Son Ltd* v. *Lindley*,[1] the House of Lords held that, on the evidence before them, there was not a trade dispute. There was a quarrel between two unions as to which of them should have recognition from the employers. So here I quite agree that if it were proved that this demand for wages was a mere cover for disruptive or subversive elements, then it would not be 'in contemplation or furtherance of a trade dispute.' There is no evidence of this. All the evidence before us points to it being a dispute concerned with the terms and conditions of employment of the men and therefore a trade dispute.

But it is said that even though there was a trade dispute, s. 3 of the Act of 1906 does not prevent the grant of an injunction. It only prevents damages being given for torts already committed. It is said that s. 3 is in a like situation to s. 4. On s. 4 we were referred to the *obiter* dictum of Upjohn, L.J., with the concurrence of Diplock, L.J., in *Boulting* v. *Association of Cinematograph, Television & Allied Technicians*,[2] where he said[3] that s. 4 did not exclude the grant of an injunction. But that goes contrary to the view of Scrutton and Atkin, L.JJ., long ago in *Ware & de Freville Ltd* v. *Motor Trade Association*.[4] They thought that it did exclude an injunction. I prefer to follow Scrutton and Atkin, L.JJ. In any case the reasoning of Upjohn, L.J., has no application to

[1] [1965] A.C. 269; [1964] 3 W.L.R. 541; [1964] 3 All E.R. 102, H.L.(E.).
[2] [1963] 2 Q.B. 606, 643, 644, 649; [1963] 1 All E.R. 716, C.A.
[3] [1963] 2 Q.B. 606, 643, 644.
[4] [1921] 3 K.B. 40, 75, 92; 37 T.L.R. 213, C.A. [see *post*, p. 529].

s. 3. In *Stratford (J. T.) & Son Ltd* v. *Lindley*[1] it was accepted by all the members of this court and also by Lord Pearce in the House of Lords that s. 3 not only applies when a person has actually induced some other person to break a contract of employment, but also when he has threatened to induce it. It would indeed be absurd to suppose otherwise. If it is not actionable to induce such a breach, I cannot see that it is actionable to threaten to induce it. It seems to me, therefore, that the actions of the defendants are not actionable by reason of s. 3 of the Trade Disputes Act, 1906, and an injunction cannot be granted in the face of that section.

I might say a word on a further point which Sir Peter Rawlinson raised. He sought to say that this was a case where the men might be charged with inducing their employers to break their contracts with their own customers, relying on the principles stated in *Thomson (D. C.) & Co. Ltd* v. *Deakin*.[2] All I need say on this point is that that cause of action does not come within this writ at all.

DAVIES, L.J.: Like my Lord, I am quite satisfied that working rule no. 6 was a term of the employment of these men. But also, like my Lord, I find the meaning of the first part of that rule somewhat obscure. But it is not, I think, necessary for the purposes of this case to pass any final opinion upon it. It may very well mean, as my Lord has suggested, that it is a term not merely between the two sides of the National Joint Council but a term of the employment of all the men, it being incorporated in their contracts, that there shall be no collective maximum, or, to use the word that Russell, L.J., used in the course of the argument, no collective imposition of a ceiling on the amount of overtime. That of course would necessarily involve that there should be no collective refusal to do overtime, though the precise amount of the overtime is, as the rule expressly states, to be decided between the employers and the individual operatives.

But even if there has been a breach or a procurement or inducement to commit a breach of that rule by these two defendants, it is, I think, despite Sir Peter Rawlinson's attractive argument, plainly on the facts here a trade dispute....

[On the Trade Disputes Act, 1906, s. 4:] For myself I would respectfully agree with those observations of Scrutton, L.J., and I would reserve my view with regard to the precise meaning of s. 4....It seems to me, whatever may be the position under s. 4, that s. 3, when saying

---

[1] [1965] A.C. 269; [1964] 2 All E.R. 209, C.A.
[2] [1952] Ch. 646; [1952] 2 All E.R. 361 [*post*, p. 472].

that no action shall be brought for the act done, necessarily involves that no injunction can be granted to prevent the doing of or a threat to do the act. Otherwise the results would indeed be absurd.

RUSSELL, L.J.: First of all, my present view of the construction of working rule 6(a) is that it merely states that on the National Joint Council no ceiling is imposed by the working rules upon hours of over-time, the extent of overtime working being left to agreement between employers and operatives. As I see it, in my mind's eye, the parties of the joint council round the table said: 'Are we in these rules going to fix a ceiling on the hours of overtime worked by any man?' Answer: 'No'. Hence the first part of rule 6(a). They then proceeded to say, by way of addition: 'It is to be left to agreement between operative and em-ployer.' If that be so, it certainly cannot import into the contract of any particular operative an agreement not to limit or refuse to work over-time save for a reason special to himself. Therefore, in my view no breach of contract has been induced or procured.

But in any event the evidence shows that any steps that may have been taken by the defendants would only have been actionable on the ground that they induced other employees of the plaintiffs to break their contracts of employment, and also that such steps have been taken in furtherance of a genuine trade dispute. I cannot accept, any more than did the general manager of the plaintiffs, that the purpose was other than to improve wages and conditions....

Next, I agree with the views expressed by Lord Denning, M.R., and Salmon, L.J., in the *Stratford* case,[1] that s. 3 of the Trade Disputes Act, 1906, also prevents injunctions against future relevant acts. This was in fact decided by Sargant, L., in *Fowler* v. *Kibble*,[2] the contrary not having been argued at all. There would be something odd about a situation in which a man might be imprisoned for contempt of court when, on his way to Brixton Prison, he could truthfully say: 'What I did was made by s. 3 of the Act not actionable.' I wish to reserve my final opinion on the difference of judicial view on the construction of s. 4, a section which is differently framed....

I would only add in connection with *Thomson* (*D. C.*) & *Co. Ltd* v. *Deakin*,[3] which was mentioned by my Lord, that in the present case it is a breach of contract by the plaintiff which is alleged, whereas the injury to the plaintiff in the other cases arises from the breaches by others of their contracts with the plaintiff, which may be a very different thing.

---

[1] [1965] A.C. 269, 304.　　　　[2] [1922] 1 Ch. 487; 38 T.L.R. 271.
[3] [1952] Ch. 646 [on this see *post*, p. 472].

BARON *v.* SUNDERLAND CORPORATION

Court of Appeal   [1966] 2 W.L.R. 363

The plaintiff and his employer, the defendant corporation, were in dispute as to whether the plaintiff was entitled, under the scales set out in the Burnham report, to an additional sum for teaching deaf children. The plaintiff sued for this sum. The Burnham report set up a joint committee, which was incorporated into a statutory scheme for remuneration, and provided that questions about the interpretation of the report should be taken to the committee by a local education authority or 'by any association of teachers acting through the teachers' panel' or by the chairman of the Burnham Committee. The corporation argued in the present case as a preliminary point that this provision was an *arbitration clause* incorporated into the plaintiff's contract thereby entitling them to a stay of the proceedings. The court held this was not an arbitration clause having that effect.

DAVIES, L.J.: The first statutory instrument is the Remuneration of Teachers (Primary and Secondary Schools) Order, 1961 (S.I. 1961 No. 2361), which refers to the Burnham report, and provides as follows:

'Article 3. In respect of any period after December 31, 1961, the remuneration paid to full-time teachers in primary and secondary schools maintained by local education authorities shall be in accordance with the scales contained in the above-mentioned report....'

That statutory instrument was revoked in 1963 by the Remuneration of Teachers (Primary and Secondary Schools) Order, 1963 (S.I. 1963 No. 1234), the relevant article of which in force thereafter is article 3(1):

'With effect from April 1, 1963, the remuneration payable to full-time teachers in primary and secondary schools maintained by local education authorities shall, subject to the provisions of this Order, be determined in accordance with the scales and other provisions contained in the report as amended by the Schedule to this Order, and local education authorities shall pay to such teachers remuneration so determined.'

There is no express reference in the Order of 1963 to the committee which was set up. But it does obviously in its terms include all the provisions of the Burnham report....

[His Lordship turned to the report, s. V:] That is the constitution of the committee—10 representatives of the local education authorities, 10 representatives of the teachers, and the *ex officio* honorary secretaries. Now these are the important words:

'...and any question relating to the interpretation of the provisions of this report brought forward by a local education authority acting through the authorities' panel or by any association of teachers acting through the teachers' panel or by consent of the Chairman of the Burnham Committee shall be considered and determined by the joint committee.'...

It seems to me that this is about as unlike an arbitration clause as anything one could imagine. It is necessary in an arbitration clause that each party shall agree to refer disputes to arbitration; and it is an essential ingredient of an arbitration clause that either party may, in the event of a dispute arising, refer it, in the provided manner, to arbitration. In other words, the clause must give bilateral rights of reference. The present clause, as I see it, does nothing of the kind. It provides that the local education authority, acting through the authorities' panel, may 'bring forward' (to use the words in the report) the question, or the association of teachers, acting through the teachers' panel, may do so, or, alternatively, by consent of the chairman, someone else may do so. In the present case we do not know whether the teacher is a member of the union or whether the teachers' panel would be prepared to bring forward his contention. We do not know whether the chairman would consent to the matter being brought forward....

It may be asked: What then does this clause mean? It is not necessary to decide that for the purposes of this case. But I think that there is a great deal to be said for the submission made in opening by Mr McKinnon that really this is not primarily designed to deal with individual claims at all, although I suppose that they might be brought with the consent of the Chairman of the Burnham Committee. What it is really meant to deal with is a question brought up by the teachers' side on the one side or the local authorities' body on the other in order to obtain a decision on a broad question of interpretation which may affect a large number of teachers up and down the country. This, I think, is no such case. This is a simple common law claim by an employed person for salary which he claims to be due to him under his contract of service. And I can see nothing, either in the ground on which the judge proceeded, or on the alternative ground proposed by Mr Percy this afternoon, which would justify the court in interfering with the normal process of this action.

SALMON, L. J.: The judge approached this case as if s. V of the Burnham report were an arbitration clause which is written into the contract of service between the teacher and the local authority by the relevant statutory instrument. For my part, in spite of the valiant attempts of Mr Percy to persuade us to the contrary, I think that this is the wrong approach and I agree entirely with the reasons given by Davies, L.J., for concluding that the judge's view is not tenable. Whilst the jurisdiction of the courts cannot be ousted by agreement between the parties, Parliament may do anything; and, as his second point, Mr Percy argued that s. V was mandatory and in effect took away the common law right of a teacher to come to the courts for redress when his contract of service had in his view been broken by his employers. No doubt Parliament could take away that common law right; but it would need plain, express and unambiguous language for any court so to construe any statutory enactment.

For my part, I think that s. V does not come within measurable distance of taking away the ordinary common law right. I do not think that this section has any reference to litigation at all. The purpose of this section, as I see it, is an excellent one. It was designed to prevent disputes arising between teachers' associations and local authorities in relation to the interpretation of the Burnham report. If any such disputes arose between those bodies, this section provided machinery for settling those disputes. A dispute between those two bodies is something quite different from an individual teacher seeking to enforce what he conceives to be his common law rights against his employers. This section does not make any reference at all to the case of a teacher suing his employers.

RUSSELL, L.J., delivered a concurring judgment.

SECTION D

MATERIALS FROM COLLECTIVE BARGAINING DOCUMENTS

[The extracts that follow come from various types of collective agreements, not all of them currently extant. Their object is the provision of material for readers to discuss legal questions which have not yet been fully explored in decided cases, against the background of real industrial examples; and also to try, in an inadequate space, to introduce concrete industrial illustrations. The legal questions which may be of interest in connexion with the extracts include: Who are the parties to the agreement and are they legally identifiable? In what capacity do they bargain, or do they say they bargain? Are there special indications that the parties in an agreement *have* undertaken to be bound by legally enforceable obligations? Which of the terms of the agreements are 'appropriate' for incorporation into individual employment contracts? Do some clauses contain language ('recommend', etc.) not appropriate for contractual enforcement at any level? What legal meaning is to be given to 'procedure' clauses?]

JOINT INDUSTRIAL COUNCIL for the FOOD MANU-FACTURERS' INDUSTRIAL GROUP—Constitution and Working Agreement

2. COUNCIL

(a) Membership

The Council shall consist of thirty-six members having adequate knowledge of the industries concerned, appointed as follows:

Eighteen members (hereinafter called 'the employers' side') appointed by the Food Manufacturers' Industrial Group.

Eighteen members (hereinafter called 'the workpeople's side') appointed by the following Trade Unions: Transport and General Workers' Union; National Union of General and Municipal Workers; Union of Shop, Distributive and Allied Workers....

3. SETTLEMENT OF DIFFERENCES

(a) If, after full deliberation, the Council fails to reach a decision on any general question relating to wages, hours and conditions of employment, it may either endeavour to determine arbitration procedure, or refer the matter to the Ministry of Labour with a request that an Independent Arbitrator be appointed. An arbitration award shall be binding on both parties.

(b) Any questions relating to the observance or interpretation of an agreement made by the Council, or any other differences affecting workers within the scope of the Agreement arising between an employer and a trade union or trade unions represented on the Council shall, in the first place, be discussed by the parties concerned, and every effort shall be made to settle the difference locally. Any such settlement shall not contravene any agreement or arrangements made or recommended by the Council.

Failing such a settlement, the question or difference shall be referred to a Disputes Committee of the Council, who shall then endeavour to settle the matter by discussion, if necessary, with the parties concerned. If this procedure does not result in a settlement, the Council may refer the matter for settlement in accordance with paragraph (*a*) of this section.

(*c*) The Council undertakes to prevent strikes, lock-outs or unauthorised stoppages of work.

For their part employers, who are members of the Food Manufacturers' Industrial Group, either severally or jointly, will not order a lock-out, and the unions or any one union represented on the Joint Industrial Council, will not instruct their members to cease work, either nationally or locally, and will not encourage their members to take, or support their members, in taking individual action until the procedure laid down in paragraphs (*a*) and (*b*) of this section has been followed.

4. WORKS COUNCILS OR COMMITTEES

In order to facilitate the maximum understanding between the firms belonging to the Joint Industrial Council and the Trade Unions affiliated thereto it is recommended that where Works Councils or Committees are appointed, such bodies shall be restricted to the consideration of matters outside those determined by the agreements of the Joint Industrial Council.

NATIONAL JOINT COUNCIL: CEMENT MANUFACTURING INDUSTRY

14. CONCILIATION PROCEDURE

(*a*) *Local Disputes*

(i) A worker desiring to raise any question on a matter directly concerning him shall, in the first instance, discuss the same with his foreman, accompanied by his shop steward if he so desires.

(ii) Failing settlement, the question shall be taken up through the foreman with the works manager or other officer of the Company nominated by the Management.

(iii) Failing settlement under clause (*a*(ii)) the question shall be reported to the full-time district officer of the worker's Trades Union, either by the worker or by his shop steward for negotiation with the Management or for reference to the Union's Head Office.

(iv) Failing settlement under clause (a(iii)), the question shall be referred to the Fact-Finding Committee of this National Council and that Committee shall have executive authority to arbitrate upon and settle the dispute after hearing both sides of the case from the representatives of the interested parties. The decision of the Committee shall be binding upon all the parties concerned and, pending such decision, there shall not be any stoppage or disturbance of normal working.

(b) National Disputes

If after full deliberation this National Council fails to reach agreement on any question relating to wages, hours of work or conditions of employment, it shall refer the matter to an independent Arbitrator to be appointed by the Minister of Labour. Any settlement by such arbitration shall be binding upon all the parties concerned and, pending such settlement, there shall not be any stoppage or disturbance of normal working.

JOINT INDUSTRIAL COUNCIL FOR ELECTRICAL CABLE MAKING INDUSTRY (amended 1962)

THE PROCEDURE FOR DEALING WITH DISPUTES AND FOR ARBITRATION

1. A dispute shall be deemed to have arisen where a question has been raised by either side and there has been a failure to agree either locally or nationally.

2. Should a local dispute arise which has not been resolved through the procedure laid down in Clause 3 of the Memorandum of Agreement recognising Shop Stewards, such dispute shall be referred immediately by either party or the parties jointly to the appropriate District Council....

4. Failing settlement by a District Council the matter shall be referred to the Joint Industrial Council which may invoke the assistance of the Negotiating Committee in seeking a settlement. Alternatively, the Chairman, Vice-Chairman and the Joint Secretaries of the Joint Industrial Council shall have authority to call a special meeting of the Council or to refer the matter direct to the Negotiating Committee.

5. Notwithstanding any of the above provisions, either party may refer a matter direct to the Joint Industrial Council, but it is expressly agreed that only in exceptional circumstances or in matters not within

the executive powers of the District Councils shall the machinery provided by such Councils be circumvented.

6. In the event of the Joint Industrial Council being unable to resolve a dispute, or of a difference arising between the two sides of the Council, both sides, with the assistance of the Negotiating Committee, shall use their best endeavours to reach a speedy settlement. If the Council is unable to reach a settlement, both sides shall give the most serious consideration to a reference to arbitration and the Council, the Employers or the Trades Unions may refer the matter to the Minister of Labour.

7. Should it be agreed to refer the matter to arbitration, the decision of the arbitrating body shall be final and binding on all parties concerned....

9. The Employers and the Trades Unions, individually and collectively, undertake that they will exert every effort to maintain maximum production and in particular to ensure that no stoppage of work or any unauthorised action shall take place as a result of any dispute in which the employers and employees are directly or indirectly concerned before the full procedure as agreed herein has been exhausted. Should any stoppage of work or unauthorised action take place the same will be declared to be unconstitutional action and it is expressly agreed that work must be resumed before the commencement of proceedings as herein provided to effect a settlement.

DRUG AND FINE CHEMICAL JOINT CONFERENCE AGREEMENT (Wage Rates and Working Conditions)

...HOLIDAYS:...

7. The additional Joint Conference holidays shall be substituted for extra holidays where given by individual companies. It is not the intention that any employee shall lose any additional days of holiday given by the individual firm but an additional holiday shall not be given except in cases where the number of additional days of holiday for the particular year are less than in this Agreement.

8. Member firms are not entitled to give nor trade unions to apply locally for additions to holidays....

REDUNDANCY (agreed 1959)

It is recommended that in dealing with cases of redundancy employers should have regard to the following practices:

1. When redundancy is foreseen the earliest possible consultation with the local trade union officials concerned.

2. The planning of recruitment well ahead to take account of changes in labour requirements.

3. A stop to the recruitment of employees when a prospect of any redundancy arises.

4. An order of discharge beginning with the employees with least service, other things being equal.

5. Consultation with the local trade union officials on the management's lists of redundant employees.

6. Not less than four weeks prior warning to employees who are likely to become redundant, which will include the customary one week's notice of termination of employment.

7. Co-operation between firms locally in the placing of redundant employees.

8. Advance consultation with the local office of the Ministry of Labour.

9. The question of any payment in respect of redundancy to be a matter for consultation between the firm and the local trade union officials.

10. These recommendations would not apply to redundancy arising from industrial disputes.

RECOMMENDATION UPON THE PROVISION OF FREE PROTECTIVE CLOTHING

It is recommended that the employers should supply on loan:

1. Two suits of overalls to all process workers employed in wet, dusty and other processes liable to damage clothing at the commencement of employment, the overalls to be renewed when necessary....

4. Gloves, goggles and respirators as required where the employee is exposed to hazardous dusts, liquids, vapours or gases.

5. Waterproof covering for employees regularly on outside work in wet weather.

AGREEMENT between THE ENGINEERING AND
ALLIED EMPLOYERS' NATIONAL FEDERATION and
THE CLERICAL AND ADMINISTRATIVE WORKERS'
UNION (1920; revised 1946)

(1) EMPLOYMENT OF CLERICAL WORKPEOPLE

That every employer may belong to the Federation and every clerical worker may belong to a Union or not as either of them may think fit.

That every employer may employ any clerical worker and every clerical worker may take employment with any employer whether the clerical worker or the employer belong or not to a Union or to the Federation respectively.

That the Union recommend all their members not to object to work with non-Union clerical workpeople and that the Federation recommend all federated firms not to object to employ Union clerical workers on the ground that they are members of the Union.

That no clerical worker shall be required as a condition of employment to make a declaration as to whether he belongs to a Union or not....

CONCILIATION BOARD for CIVIL ENGINEERING
CONSTRUCTION: Working Rule Agreement...

XIVB. EXPOSED WORK

Operatives employed on 'Exposed Work' at heights on structures shall receive in respect of conditions additional allowances on the following scale:

Above 125 ft. and up to 175 ft.	1*d*. per hour
„ 175 ft. „ „ 200 ft.	2*d*. „ „
„ 200 ft.	3*d*. „ „

Heights are to be calculated from ground level.

'Exposed Work' shall mean work on a structure, above the heights specified, while there is no temporary or permanent protection from the weather....This Rule does not apply to drivers of tower cranes, drivers of power-driven derricks on high stages or linesmen-erectors and their mates.

XV. TEA BREAKS

Only where systematic overtime of not less than two hours each day is worked on a job shall a tea break (to be taken in the afternoon) be permitted. When permitted, a tea break shall not exceed 10 minutes.

'THE YORK AGREEMENT, 1922' (as amended)

[National Agreements between Engineering Employers' Federation and various Unions in the Confederation of Shipbuilding and Engineering Unions]*

PROCEDURE—MANUAL WORKERS

Agreement between the Federation and the Trade Unions

I. GENERAL PRINCIPLES

(*a*) The Employers have the right to manage their establishments and the Trade Unions have the right to exercise their functions.

(*b*) In the process of evolution, provision for changes in shop conditions is necessary, but it is not the intention to create any specially favoured class of workpeople.

(*c*) The Employers and the Trade Unions, without departing in any way from the principles embodied in Clause (*a*) above, emphasise the value of consultation, not only in the successful operation of the Procedure set out in Section II but in the initial avoidance of disputes.

II. PROCEDURE FOR DEALING WITH QUESTIONS ARISING

(1) *General*

(*a*) The procedure of the Provisions for Avoiding Disputes so far as appropriate, applies to:

(i) General alterations in wages;

(ii) Alterations in working conditions which are the subject of agreements officially entered into;

(iii) Alterations in the general working week;

but such alterations shall not be given effect to until the appropriate procedure between the Federation and the Trade Union or Unions concerned has been exhausted.

* See on the operation of these agreements A. Marsh, *Industrial Relations in Engineering* (1966).

(b) When the Management contemplates alterations in recognised working conditions which do not involve a change in material, means or method, and would result in work currently done by one class of workpeople in future being done by another class of workpeople in the establishment, the Management shall give the workpeople directly concerned or their representatives in the shop intimation of their intention, and afford an opportunity for discussion with a deputation of the workpeople concerned and/or their representatives in the shop. In the event of no settlement being reached, the Procedure outlined in s.(2)—Provisions for Avoiding Disputes—shall be operated. The alterations concerned shall not be implemented until settlement has been reached or until the Procedure has been exhausted....

(c) Where any class of workpeople is displaced by reason of any act of the Management, consideration shall be given to the case of workpeople so displaced with a view, if practicable, of affording them in the establishment work suitable to their qualifications.

(d) Questions arising which do not result in one class of workpeople being replaced by another in the establishment and on which discussion is desired, shall be dealt with in accordance with the Provisions for Avoiding Disputes and work shall proceed meantime under the conditions following the act of the Management....

(f) Where any local agreement conflicts with the terms of this Agreement, the provisions of this Agreement shall apply.

(g) Nothing in the foregoing shall affect the usual practice in connexion with the termination of employment of individual workpeople....

(2) Provisions for Avoiding Disputes

(a) When a question arises, an endeavour shall be made by the Management and the workman directly concerned to settle the same in the works or at the place where the question has arisen. Failing settlement deputations of workmen who may be accompanied by their Organiser (in which event a representative of the Employers' Association shall also be present) shall be received by the Employers by appointment without unreasonable delay for the mutual discussion of any question in the settlement of which both parties are directly concerned. In the event of no settlement being arrived at, it shall be competent for either party to bring the question before a Local Conference to be held between the Local Association and the local representatives of the Society.

(b) In the event of either party desiring to raise any question a

Local Conference for this purpose may be arranged by application to the Secretary of the Local Association or to the local representative of the Society.

(c) Local Conferences shall be held within seven working days, unless otherwise mutually agreed upon, from the receipt of the application by the Secretary of the Local Association or the local representative of the Society.

(d) Failing settlement at a Local Conference of any question brought before it, it shall be competent for either party to refer the matter to a Central Conference which, if thought desirable, may make a joint recommendation to the constituent bodies.

(e) Central Conference shall be held on the second Friday of each month at which questions referred to Central Conference prior to fourteen days of that date shall be taken.

(f) Until the procedure provided above has been carried through, there shall be no stoppage of work either of a partial or a general character.

(3) Shop Stewards and Works Committee Agreement*

With a view to amplifying the provisions for avoiding disputes by a recognition of Shop Stewards and the institution of Works Committees it is agreed as follows:

(a) Appointment of Shop Stewards

(1) Workers, members of the Trade Unions employed in a federated establishment may have representatives appointed from the members of the Unions employed in the establishment to act on their behalf in accordance with the terms of this Agreement.

(2) The representatives shall be known as Shop Stewards.

(3) The appointment of such Shop Stewards shall be determined by the Trade Unions concerned and each Trade Union party to this Agreement may have such Shop Stewards.

(4) The names of the Shop Stewards and the shop or portion of a shop in which they are employed and the Trade Union to which they belong shall be intimated officially by the Trade Union concerned to the Management on election.

* See: 'The Role of Shop Stewards in Industrial Relations', by W. E. J. McCarthy (1966; Research Paper No. 1 for the Royal Commission on Trade Unions and Employers Associations). Paragraphs 105–7 of this study are of particular interest to the student of Labour Law. See too *post*, p. 364, Industrial Court Case 3059, *National Union of Vehicle Builders* against *Fairview Caravans Ltd.*

(b) Appointment of Works Committees

(5) A Works Committee may be set up in each establishment consisting of not more than seven representatives of the Management and not more than seven Shop Stewards, who should be representative of the various classes of workpeople employed in the establishment.

The Shop Stewards for this purpose shall be nominated and elected by ballot of the workpeople, members of the Trade Unions parties to this Agreement, employed in the establishment.

The Shop Stewards elected to the Works Committee shall, subject to re-election, hold office for not more than twelve months....

(c) Functions and Procedure

(7) The functions of Shop Stewards and Works Committee, so far as they are concerned with the avoidance of disputes, shall be exercised in accordance with the following procedure:

(a) A worker or workers desiring to raise any question in which they are directly concerned shall, in the first instance, discuss the same with their foreman.

(b) Failing settlement, the question shall be taken up with the Shop Manager and/or Head Shop Foreman by the appropriate Shop Steward and one of the workers directly concerned.

(c) If no settlement is arrived at the question may, at the request of either party, be further considered at a meeting of the Works Committee. At this meeting the O.D.D. may be present, in which event a representative of the Employers' Association shall also be present.

(d) Any question arising which affects more than one branch of trade or more than one department of the Works may be referred to the Works Committee.

(e) The question may thereafter be referred for further consideration in terms of the 'Provision for Avoiding Disputes'.

(f) No stoppage of work shall take place until the question has been fully dealt with in accordance with this Agreement and with the 'Provisions for Avoiding Disputes'.

(d) General

(8) Shop Stewards shall be subject to the control of the Trade Unions and shall act in accordance with the Rules and Regulations of the Trade Unions and agreements with Employers so far as these affect the relation between employers and workpeople.

(9) In connection with this Agreement, Shop Stewards shall be afforded facilities to deal with questions raised in the shop or portion of a shop in which they are employed. Shop Stewards elected to the Works Committee shall be afforded similar facilities in connection with their duties, and in the course of dealing with these questions they may, with the previous consent of the Management (such consent not to be unreasonably withheld), visit any shop or portion of a shop in the establishment. In all other respects, Shop Stewards shall conform to the same working conditions as their fellow workers....

(12) For the purpose of this Agreement the expression 'establishment' shall mean the whole establishment or sections thereof according to whether the Management is unified or sub-divided....

STAFF

The following broad line of demarcation has been agreed between the Federation and the Amalgamated Engineering Union

[If a man is employed on staff conditions but is subject to the authority of the foreman and is not responsible for engagement or dismissal of other workers, and works with the tools or uses instruments in the normal course of his work, he should be regarded for the purpose of representation by a Trade Union as a workman. If, however, he is in the position of having authority over other workers and does not in normal circumstances work with tools, although he may use measuring instruments in the case of appeal or final test or in the course of exercising his duties over his subordinates, he should not be regarded as in the category covered by the machinery of negotiations between the parties.

It is recognized that even with this broad definition there may here and there be border-line cases which will require to be considered between the parties.

Dated 2 October 1941]...

PARTICULAR AGREEMENTS ON RATES, HOURS, etc.

WORKERS RECALLED TO WORK

(a) A workman required to return to work and not so notified until after he has ceased work and gone home for the day shall be guaranteed payment equivalent to three hours at the appropriate overtime rate for the period from the time he restarts until the time he finishes work....

COUPLING-UP

Overtime worked by dayshift men in coupling-up day and night-shifts shall be paid at the rate of time-and-third for the first two hours and time-and-half thereafter. Overtime worked by nightshift men in coupling-up night and day shifts shall be paid at the rate of time-and-half. Such overtime shall not be included in the 30 hours limitation in any four weeks. The Federation undertakes to recommend to federated firms that the hours required for coupling-up dayshift and nightshift, or *vice versa*, shall, as far as practicable, be equally divided between the two shifts....

1957 WAGES SETTLEMENT

The National Wages Agreement of 23 May 1957, provided that every adult male manual worker received an increase for 44 hours of 11s. for skilled workers, 10s. for intermediate grades, and 9s. for unskilled workers.

An Annex to the Agreement read as follows:

ANNEX TO AGREEMENT OF 23 MAY 1957

In consideration of the Agreement of 23 May 1957, relating to adult male manual workers it is mutually agreed:

1. (a) The increases set out in the Agreement referred to above are in full settlement of all existing national and district claims, whether by the Confederation or by individual Unions, for increased wages and differentials for adult male manual workers (subject to (b) below) and no further applications for such increases in wages or differentials shall be submitted for at least one year from the date of this Agreement...

(e) The Executives of all the Manual Workers' Unions affiliated to the Confederation of Shipbuilding and Engineering Unions will use their full influence to bring to an end without delay all practices which are contrary to the well-being of the Industry, including, for example: (1) Unconstitutional stoppages of work; (2) Embargoes on overtime; (3) All restrictions on output or earnings. This provision will not, by itself, be used to reduce piecework prices.

(f) The Executives of all the Manual Workers' Unions affiliated to the Confederation of Shipbuilding and Engineering Unions agree to use their full influence to facilitate the introduction of new machines and techniques and their efficient and safe operation for effective production....

GUARANTEE OF EMPLOYMENT FOR HOURLY RATED MANUAL WORKERS

Agreement between the Federation and the Confederation of Shipbuilding and Engineering Unions, 1957

Note: This Agreement replaces the 'Guaranteed Week' Clauses (*a*) and (*b*) in the Agreement of 3 April 1946, as amended 10 March 1956, and the proviso thereto.

All hourly rated manual workers who have been continuously employed by a federated firm for not less than four weeks shall be guaranteed employment for four days in each normal pay week. In the event of work not being available for the whole or part of the four days, employees covered by the guarantee will be assured earnings equivalent to their consolidated time rate for 34 hours.

This guarantee is subject to the following conditions:

(*a*) That the employees are capable of, available for, and willing to perform satisfactorily, during the period of the guarantee, the work associated with their usual occupation, or reasonable alternative work where their usual work is not available.

(*b*) In the case of a holiday recognised by agreement, custom or practice, the period of guarantee shall be reduced proportionately.

(*c*) In the event of a dislocation of production as a result of strike action, the operation of the period of guarantee shall be automatically suspended in respect of workpeople affected in the establishment where the strike is taking place.

(*d*) In computing the assured earnings referred to above, premium payments due for overtime worked on week days, and premium payments for work done on Sundays and holidays, shall be ignored....

AGREED NOTES

...6. The suspension of the guarantee in the event of a strike applies to all workpeople on strike or laid off by the strike in the establishment where the strike occurs. The guarantee is not suspended in regard to workpeople in an establishment other than the establishment where the strike takes place even though they may be indirectly affected through dislocation arising from the strike.

EXTRACTS FROM AN AGREEMENT BETWEEN A COMPANY AND A TRADE UNION*

CONSOLIDATED WAGES SCHEME

At all Depots (except those where all the staff concerned have determined by ballot held in 1961 that they wished to opt out of the arrangement permanently) the following provisions of this Scheme will apply to all operatives on the permanent staff, excluding canteen attendants, office cleaners and ancillary employees....

STRENGTH OF ESTABLISHMENT

It is a condition of the Consolidated Wages Scheme that each Depot will carry a nominated establishment of manual staff based on the consistently reasonable levels of performance which the Company's experience in operating techniques leads it to expect. Allowance is made for the local peculiarities of each Depot, Depot strengths being determined at Divisional level as reasonable for normal tonnage throughput. The scheme requires that there should be flexibility in the use of the labour force, by other than normal duties being undertaken according to need, in the interests of the Depot operations as a whole....

GUARANTEED WORKING WEEK

Subject always to the employees' compliance with the Company's Rules and Regulations:

The normal working week for staff paid on a weekly basis shall be of 42 hours, at present distributed over five days. The length of the working day and the spread of those days over the working week shall be as considered necessary by the local management to meet local operational daily requirements or contingencies arising, but $8\frac{1}{2}$ hours will be the maximum normal hours of any one day. The guaranteed working week shall not apply that week to employees not reporting for duty (unless certified unfit) on the first working day following a customary holiday.

No payment will be made by the Company in respect of loss of hours or assumed hours of overtime arising out of a stoppage or partial stoppage caused by circumstances outside the Company's control, outside the ordinary course of business, or occasioned by an industrial dispute either inside or outside of Depots.

* How far are these clauses 'appropriate' for incorporation into employment contracts?

If the dispute has not arisen within a Depot, employees may be requested to transfer temporarily to other Depots unaffected; such additional time and travelling expenses as are necessary will be paid for by the Company.

TRUST DEED OF 1898

[On which is based the National Conference Agreement between British Footwear Employers' Federation and National Union of Boot and Shoe Operatives (now 1962)]

On 8 March 1898, a Trust Deed was entered into between representatives of the Federation and the National Union whereby the Guarantee Fund of £2000 was vested in Trustees, upon the trusts declared in the following clauses extracted from the Deed:

1. The said sums of £1000 and £1000 making together the sum of £2000 shall be held by the Trustees upon the Trusts hereinafter declared concerning the same, that is to say: Upon Trust (a) to invest the same in any securities allowed by law for the investment of trust money with power to vary or transpose the investments as they shall think fit and in trust to accumulate the income thereof in the like investments and (b) to stand possessed of the same sums and investments and accumulations thereof upon the following trusts (that is to say):

2. If any dispute or question shall at any time arise between the Federation and the Union as to the breach or non-fulfilment of any of the provisions contained in the settlement or in any decision agreement or award of any such Local Board as aforesaid or of any Arbitrators or Umpire of any such Local Board...in every such case every such dispute or question shall be referred for determination to the Right Honourable Lord James of Hereford or other the person for the time being appointed to as as Umpire for the purposes of the Settlement and of these presents.

3. If the said Umpire shall determine that any of the provisions of the Settlement or of any such decision agreement or award as aforesaid has been broken or not fulfilled...the Umpire shall have the power to determine that all or any part of the sum deposited with the Trustees by the Federation or by the Union (as the case may be) shall be forfeited to the other of them in whose favour the Award shall be made and by his award to determine the amount to be so forfeited and such amount may include a sum for costs of the Reference and Award which shall be in the discretion of the said Umpire....

NATIONAL CONFERENCE AGREEMENT (BOOT AND SHOE)

9. *Boy Labour.* In the Clicking, Press, Lasting, Finishing, Heel Building, Preparing, Fitting-up, Stock or Shoe Room Departments, the proportion borne by the aggregate number of boys to the aggregate number of men employed throughout those departments shall not exceed one boy to every four (or fractional part of four) men, but in no one of those departments shall the proportion exceed one boy to every three men or fractional part of three.

For the purpose of this Clause the expression 'Boys' means male employees under 19 years of age, and the expression 'Men' means male employees of and over 19 years of age....

27. *Strikes and Lock-outs.* (*a*) No strike or lock-out shall be entered into on the part of any body of workmen, members of the National Union, or any manufacturers represented on any local Board of Arbitration.

(*b*) Where disputes or grievances exist they shall be investigated immediately by representatives of the Local Manufacturers' Association and of the local branch of the Union concerned, with a view to adjustment, and in the event of failure to adjust them, they shall be dealt with in accordance with the Rules of the Local Board of Arbitration of the district for dealing with disputes between employers and their employees.

(*c*) Where any strike or lock-out takes place and is continued beyond the period of three days allowed by the Agreement of 31 March 1910, the right of the Federation or Union, as the case may be, to claim upon the monetary guarantee under that agreement and the Trust Deed, may be exercised by application to a National Umpire appointed in accordande with Clause 9 of the Trust Deed and on the recommendation of the Minister of Labour for a forfeiture either (*a*) by way of fine or penalty, or (*b*) by way of damages or compensation for loss sustained, and in any case where the latter alternative is adopted the amount of such loss shall be assessed by a Committee of three representatives of the Federation and three representatives of the Union, and, if they disagree, by the National Umpire....*

---

* On procedure clauses generally, see the Research Papers for the Royal Commission by A. Marsh, 'Disputes Procedures in British Industry' (H.M.S.O.).

BRITISH FILM PRODUCERS ASSOCIATION and ASSOCIATION of CINEMATOGRAPH, TELEVISION AND ALLIED TECHNICIANS

THIS AGREEMENT is made the twenty-fourth day of February, One thousand nine hundred and fifty-eight, between the BRITISH FILM PRODUCERS ASSOCIATION... (hereinafter called 'the Association') representing the FILM PRODUCERS AND STUDIO OWNERS, members of the Association (hereinafter called 'the Associates') of the one part and the ASSOCIATION OF CINEMATOGRAPH, TELEVISION AND ALLIED TECHNICIANS...being a Trade Union properly registered, constituted and recognised and affiliated to the Trades Union Congress...(hereinafter referred to as 'the Union') representing the members thereof (hereinafter called 'the members') of the other part, and replaces an Agreement made on the 5 August 1947 and includes all amendments thereto up to the date hereof. Furthermore, the provisions of this Agreement shall be read, understood and operated as a Ratifying Agreement between each of the Associates and the Union, and each shall sign two copies of this Agreement, one copy thereof to be retained by the Associates and one by the Union....

Clause 2. Notice to Terminate the Agreement

This Agreement shall continue in full force and effect until determined by three months' notice in writing given by either of the parties.

Clause 3. Undertakings of the Association and the Associates

The Association and the Associates undertake and agree: (1) To recognise the Union for the purpose of representing and negotiating minimum salaries and conditions of employment of the members within the grades tabulated in the schedule to this Agreement and any additional grades which may be included by agreement of both parties during the currency of this Agreement.

(2) That the terms and conditions of this Agreement shall be applicable to all the members in the grades tabulated in the schedule to this Agreement.

(3) That during the period of this Agreement, so long as the Union and the members accept and comply with all the conditions of employment herein set out and faithfully and diligently promote the interests

of the Associates, they shall pay the members whilst employed by them in the grades concerned not less than the minimum salaries and allowances set out in this Agreement....

Clause 4. *Undertakings of the Union and the Members*

The Union and the members undertake and agree: (1) That provided and so long as the Associates by whom the members are for the time being employed shall observe the conditions and provisions of this Agreement, the Union and the members shall accept, comply with and observe all the conditions of employment herein set out, and the members shall faithfully and diligently promote the interests of such Associates, and shall carry out and perform to the best of their ability any reasonable requests or instructions which they may receive from time to time from the Associates, and shall guard and protect the interests of the Association and the Associates.

(2) That the members so instructed by the Associate shall work or be available for work, in accordance with the provisions of this Agreement.

(3) That the Associates shall provide each of the members with a copy of this agreement and each of the members shall sign a receipt for same, and further acknowledging that the terms of the Agreement are accepted and shall be observed by the members as a condition of their employment, or their continued employment with the Associates....

SECTION E

FAIR WAGES RESOLUTION, 1946*

'That, in the opinion of this House, the Fair Wages Clauses in Government Contracts should be so amended as to provide as follows:

1.—(a) The contractor shall pay rates of wages and observe hours and conditions of labour not less favourable than those established for the trade or industry in the district where the work is carried out by machinery of negotiation or arbitration to which the parties are organisations of employers and trade unions representative respectively of substantial proportions of the employers and workers engaged in the trade or industry in the district.

(b) In the absence of any rates of wages, hours or conditions of labour

---

* For the historical background, see O. Kahn-Freund (1948) 11 M.L.R. 269 and 429. Compare with clause 1(a) of the Resolution, s. 8 Terms and Conditions of Employment Act, 1959, and decisions thereunder: see *post*, p. 345.

so established the contractor shall pay rates of wages and observe hours and conditions of labour which are not less favourable than the general level of wages, hours and conditions observed by other employers whose general circumstances in the trade or industry in which the contractor is engaged are similar.

2. The contractor shall in respect of all persons employed by him (whether in execution of the contract or otherwise) in every factory, workshop or place occupied or used by him for the execution of the contract comply with the general conditions required by this Resolution. Before a contractor is placed upon a department's list of firms to be invited to tender, the department shall obtain from him an assurance that to the best of his knowledge and belief he has complied with the general conditions required by this Resolution for at least the previous three months.

3. In the event of any question arising as to whether the requirements of this Resolution are being observed, the question shall, if not otherwise disposed of, be referred by the Minister of Labour and National Service to an independent tribunal for decision.

4. The contractor shall recognise the freedom of his workpeople to be members of trade unions.

5. The contractor shall at all times during the continuance of a contract display, for the information of his workpeople, in every factory, workshop or place occupied or used by him for the execution of the contract a copy of this Resolution.

6. The contractor shall be responsible for the observance of this Resolution by sub-contractors employed in the execution of the contract, and shall if required notify the department of the names and addresses of all such sub-contractors.'

SIMPSON *v.* KODAK LTD

[1948] 2 K.B. 184

The plaintiff, a film worker, was employed at £6 7s. 6d. per week by the defendant company. The National Arbitration Tribunal made an award between the plaintiff's trade union and an employers' association as to the wages of film workers of the plaintiff's grade as the plaintiff claimed. The defendant did not belong to the employers' association. The award was £8 18s. od. per week. While the plaintiff was employed by them, the defendants received government contracts which contained the Fair Wages clause.

The plaintiff claimed arrears of wages.

SELLERS, J.: There have been, as I have said, slight amendments to the order, which have made some modification, and also the numbering of the paragraphs has been altered, but there is no alteration in the order which in any way affects or alters the decision which was arrived at by the Court of Appeal in *Hulland's* case.[1] Therefore, it seems to me concluded against the plaintiff that there is any implied term of his contract, or any statutory right to sue, for what he alleges to be the insufficiency of the wages which he has received. He has not established any contractual or other right to recover anything more than that which he has accepted.

The next ground on which he bases his claim is under the Cinematograph Films Act, 1938.* He relies on s. 34, subsection 1. The question which arises for consideration in this case, is whether that section entitles the plaintiff to sue, and to recover, if he establishes the facts which are necessary to show that what he was receiving was less favourable than that which he ought to have received, if the fair wages clause had been applied. The section itself seems to me clearly to defeat his claim in this action on very much the same grounds as are shown in *Hulland* v. *Sanders & Son*, because provision is made in this Act, as provision was made under the Arbitration Rules, for dealing with any disputes; it is provided by subsection 1 of s. 34: 'If any dispute arises as to what wages ought to be paid, or what conditions ought to be observed, in accordance with this section, it shall, if not otherwise disposed of, be referred by the Board of Trade to the industrial court for settlement.'

It was argued that 'if not otherwise disposed of' would not oust the jurisdiction of this court, but when one turns to s. 34, subsection 3, it makes it clear, I think, that there is no right of action other than that which arises on the original contract between the parties, until some implication has been established that some different rate of wage prevails. So that there again on like grounds to those which prevailed in *Hulland* v. *Sanders & Son*, the plaintiff has not taken those steps which entitle him to sue for those differences which he alleges would be established if the case was investigated on its facts.

That does not end his claim, because he advances it on a third ground. The third ground is this, that it is said and admitted that the defendant company was at some time during the plaintiff's employment (which

---

[1] [1945] K.B. 78 [*ante*, p. 300].

* For similar statutory enforcement of 'Fair Wages' see *post*, p. 343; and now Films Act, 1960.

started in 1937), under contract with various government departments, which contained the fair wages clause. The matter has not been gone into in great detail, but it is conceded that there were such contracts, and a sample of one of them has been put in before me. It is a Ministry of Aircraft Production document. I do not know that I have, on the conditions which have been supplied to me, got the date of the particular contract from which they have been extracted, but there is no doubt that certainly during the later years of the plaintiff's employment, a great deal of work was done by the defendant company for this particular department of the government. The fair wages clause in the sample conditions of the Ministry of Aircraft Production document which has been put before me, is clause 11. There is evidence that at some time, not clearly specified, the fair wages clause was exhibited at the defendant company's premises, as no doubt it would be, having regard to that obligation. There is no evidence that the plaintiff ever saw it.

Even if he had seen it, it does not seem to me that that clause, which exists in a contract between the employers and the government, impose any right upon the plaintiff to sue upon it so as to recover wages different from those which he was getting. It might be that if he knew of it, and certain things were done and said with regard to it, that that might give rise to some implications as to the rates of wages to which he was entitled, but there is quite insufficient evidence before me to show that there was any implied term other than that on which he had been paid as to his remuneration for the work he was doing. If he knew about this fair wages clause, and week by week accepted the wages which he did, it seems to me very strong evidence that he was accepting them as a compliance with the standard which was imposed on the defendant company by their contract with the government. It is very far from showing that he was in any position to enforce any different rate by any implied contract to the contrary.

R. *v.* INDUSTRIAL COURT *ex parte* ASSET
[1965] 1 Q.B. 377

A company which manufactured anti-glare spectacles entered a contract with the Ministry of Health for the supply of spectacles. The contract bound the Company to observe the Fair Wages Resolution. ASSET complained to the Ministry of Labour that the company was in breach of this term, and the Minister of Labour referred the matter to the Industrial Court. The company challenged the jurisdiction of the

Industrial Court; the union moved for an order of *mandamus* directing the Industrial Court to hear and determine the reference.

LORD PARKER, C.J.: In my judgment, the real question here turns on the true construction of clause 3 of condition 17 of the Standard Conditions of Government Contracts for Stores Purchases, 1962, which is incorporated into the contract. Condition 17, which is headed 'Fair Wages, etc.' begins by saying: 'The contractor shall, in the execution of the contract, observe and fulfil the obligations upon contractors specified in the Fair Wages Resolution passed by the House of Commons on 14 October 1946, namely,' and thereafter follow clauses 1, 2, 4, 5, and 6, all putting specific obligations upon the contractor, obligations of the contractor towards the government department entering into the contract, in this case the Ministry of Health. Clause 3, which might perhaps more aptly have come at the end and been clause 6, provides that: 'In the event of any question arising as to whether the requirements of this resolution are being observed, the question shall if not otherwise disposed of, be referred by the Minister of Labour and National Service to an independent tribunal for decision.'

It seems to me that on a fair reading of that clause it is not a simple arbitration clause providing for reference by one of the parties to the contract to an independent tribunal, or indeed to a tribunal appointed by the Minister of Labour. It does not take that form; the clause is making it a term of the contract that if the Minister of Labour is satisfied that a question has arisen as to whether the contractor is observing the contract in relation to the Fair Wages Resolution, he, the Minister of Labour, shall have the right, and I venture to think the duty, to refer the matter as there set out. Looked at in that way, it matters not whether the suggestion that there has been non-observance is made by the other contracting party or by a third party; it is not a question of the third party having any rights, but of the Minister of Labour being satisfied that there is a question whether the contractor is observing his obligations, and for the purpose of satisfying himself as to that, the Minister of Labour can consider, and indeed should consider, representations by third parties, in this case, representations by the applicants.

Indeed, I venture to think that approached in that way there is nothing inapt in the wording of the reference itself, because the reference itself is: whether, in the execution of contracts placed by the Ministry of Health, the Fair Wages Resolution, that is, the obligations of the contractor, are being observed by the company, that is the question raised.... The second objection, if I understand it rightly, is this, that even if the Minister of Labour had power to refer the question to an independent tribunal, the tribunal to which it was referred, namely, the industrial court, had itself no power to decide the matter. Reference in this connection is made to the fact that this is a statutory court set up under the Industrial Courts Act, 1919. Its jurisdiction, the purpose for which it was set up, was for the settlement of trade disputes, and it is quite clear that the dispute or question arising in the present case is not a trade dispute....

It is accordingly quite clear that the reference in this case did not purport to be and was not intended to be a statutory reference as provided by the Act itself. What the Minister of Labour has done is to ask the court if they will undertake the reference as an arbitral tribunal and they, the court, have agreed to do so and have only failed to deal with the matter as a result of the objections taken to their jurisdiction.... I cannot see for my part why such a reference cannot be made to a body constituted for some different purpose, provided that that body is willing to undertake it. It is just as if somebody, maybe a High Court judge, was appointed by consent of the parties. It is no part of his jurisdiction to decide such a matter, but if he were to undertake to do so, there would be no question of his having jurisdiction to do so.

The third objection is to the effect that this tribunal was not an independent tribunal. I find it very difficult to follow that...[I]t seems to me that such a tribunal is clearly an independent tribunal for the purpose of considering whether, as between the Ministry of Health and the contractor, the contractor is fulfilling his obligation.

Finally, I come to what in some ways can be looked upon as a technical point, but it is one which has given me very considerable difficulty. It is quite clear, as I have said, that the reference to the industrial court was not a reference to the industrial court in its statutory capacity, to exercise its statutory jurisdiction. It was a reference to the industrial court as an arbitral tribunal. Condition 23 of the contract, which is the general arbitration clause, provides that: 'All disputes, differences or questions between the parties to the contract with respect to any matter or thing arising out of or relating to the contract, other than a matter or thing as to which the decision of the authority is under the contract to be final and conclusive and except to the extent to which special provision for arbitration is made elsewhere in the contract, shall be referred to the arbitration of two persons,' etc....It seems to me quite clear that here the Minister was appointing the independent tribunal as an arbitral tribunal. The question that has concerned me here is whether the

Minister, having the power to appoint an arbitral tribunal or an arbitrator or arbitrators, can properly do so without naming them. The point, although not clearly taken in the correspondence, has been taken by Mr Lewis before us, and I have said it has worried me. It can be said that really what the Minister of Labour is doing here is to delegate his powers of appointing arbitrators or an arbitral tribunal to the president of the court, because the president of the court under s. 1(3) of the Act has power to do so. That section provides: 'For the purpose of dealing with any matter which may be referred to it, the court shall be constituted of such of the members of the court as the president may direct.' As I understand it, he has power under that not merely to select individuals, but to select the number of individuals who shall sit.

It is true that that is for the purpose of dealing with what I may call statutory references, but what is said here is that he will go through the procedure which he would go through in the case of statutory references in the case of any outside reference, such as this, which the court has undertaken.

I have had great doubts on the matter, but it seems to me that this practice, because there is no doubt that is the first time any question of this sort has been raised, is justifiable in this way, that when clause 3 of the Fair Wages Resolution says that the matter shall be referred by the Minister of Labour to an independent tribunal for decision, it is really an implied term or contractual term between the parties that, if the Ministry of Labour refers the matter to an existing tribunal which *ex hypothesi* is not a tribunal specially set up with statutory powers for the purpose, the arbitration tribunal will be constituted in a way that the tribunal in question would be constituted if it was undertaking one of its statutory functions.

If one looks upon it as a matter of implied contract, it seems to me that this can well be justified. It is really no different from the many cases that occur in the City of London of contracts providing for arbitration in regard to wheat, or some other produce, with an appeal to an appeal committee of the trade association with their rules, and in such a case although the appeal committee may consist of 25 or more persons, one of the rules will be to allow a certain number to be chosen, maybe five, under the rules, and those five, though not named and though selected by somebody else, are a perfectly good arbitral appeal tribunal.

So here it seems to me, that, although there is no reference to 'subject to the rules of', there is an implied term that the parties agree to the actual numbers being chosen according to the normal practice of the industrial court, and indeed may it be also, although it is unnecessary to decide it, that the reference shall be conducted according to the procedural rules of the court. Accordingly I have come to the conclusion in the present case that the industrial court, who have undertaken the reference and only stayed their hand because of these objections, have full jurisdiction to continue and decide the question.

That, however, is not an end of the matter so far as these proceedings are concerned, since the question arises whether an order of *mandamus* or any other prerogative order can go to the court when exercising its present function. As I have already said, it is not acting as a court in accordance with the Act which set it up; it is only acting as an arbitral tribunal. In these circumstances it seems to me clear that on general principles *mandamus* cannot go to a private arbitrator. The remedy of the parties in such a case, if there is thought to be an excess of jurisdiction, is I think to proceed in an appropriate case for an injunction, or to get a declaration of the court that he has no jurisdiction, or to await the award and have it set aside, or indeed still further, when sued upon the award to set up lack of jurisdiction as a defence.

It has been urged on us that really this arbitral tribunal is not a private arbitral tribunal but that in effect it is undertaking a public duty or a quasi-public duty and as such is amenable to an order of *mandamus*. I am quite unable to come to that conclusion. It is abundantly clear that they had no duty to undertake the reference. If they refused to undertake the reference they could not be compelled to do so. I do not think that the position is in any way different once they have undertaken the reference. They are clearly doing something which they are not under any public duty to do and, in those circumstances, I see no jurisdiction in this court to issue an order of *mandamus* to the industrial court.

WINN and WIDGERY, JJ., agreed with the judgment of LORD PARKER, C.J.*

* The appropriate remedy to prevent a private arbitrator from hearing a case in regard to which he has no jurisdiction is a declaration. But the High Court will be slow to exercise its discretion to grant a declaration against the Industrial Court in regard to the Fair Wages Resolution. Where there is any kind of 'question' within clause 3 of the Resolution, the court will consider that the Industrial Court has jurisdiction to determine all questions arising under the dispute: see *B.B.C.* v. *A.C.T.T.*, *The Times*, 30 November 1966. B.B.C. argued that the Fair Wages Resolution, incorporated in its Agreement of 1952 with the Postmaster General, did not apply to its own staff conditions (*a*) because, on its proper construction, the clause did not there refer to contracts of employment with the B.B.C.; and (*b*) because the B.B.C. was 'unique' and not in any trade or industry, or not one which could be compared with any other undertaking. Megaw, J., held that neither point went to the *jurisdiction* of the Industrial Court, since the reference to that court could include any problem of construction of the Resolution in the 1952 Agreement which the Industrial Court could decide.

NATIONAL ASSOCIATION OF TOOLMAKERS
against THE PRESSED STEEL COMPANY
LIMITED, COWLEY, OXFORD

Industrial Court   Case 3009

1. A question having arisen on a complaint by the National Association of Toolmakers, Room 11, Shaftsbury Buildings, 61 Station Street,
Birmingham 5, as to whether, in the execution of a contract placed by
the War Office, the requirements of the Fair Wages Resolution adopted
by the House of Commons on the 14 October 1946 are being observed
by the Pressed Steel Company Limited, Cowley, Oxford, and the
matter, which concerns the observance of Clause 4 of the Resolution
relating to the freedom of workpeople to be members of Trade Unions,
not having been otherwise disposed of, it was referred by the Minister
of Labour to the Industrial Court for decision....

Main submissions on behalf of the Association

4. It was stated that the Association was a recognised Trade Union
which conformed to all the requirements laid down for such organisations: it was founded in 1956 and was registered as a trade union on the
26 May 1960. The Association's national membership, as returned at
June 1963, had been 647: the figure at the present time stood at
around 1200.

5. By the 29 July 1963, out of approximately 670 toolmakers employed at the Employers' Cowley Works, some 91 had resigned from the
Amalgamated Engineering Union (A.E.U.) and joined the Association.
On that date the Employers sent a printed statement entitled 'Trade
Union Membership—Toolmakers' to all toolmakers in their employ in
which, in the Association's view, they referred unjustly to the Association as 'a breakaway Union' and sought to dissuade the toolmakers
from joining it....

8. It was stated that at all material times the Employers were
executing a contract placed by the War Office and that the Fair Wages
Resolution applied to that contract. In the Association's view the
Employers had failed to observe the requirements of clause 4 of that
Resolution (see paragraph 3 above) by refusing to employ toolmakers
who were members of the Association unless they resigned and rejoined
the A.E.U.: in the requirement that the contractor should recognise
'the freedom of his workpeople to be members of Trade Unions',

Trade Unions meant trade unions of the workpeople's own choice and not trade unions specified by the contractor....

11. There was no good reason, in the Association's view, why they should not have been recognised by the Employers as a representative trade union for the toolmakers. Out of approximately 623 trade unions in the country only 177 were affiliated to the Trades Union Congress, and 37 were affiliated to, or parties to the agreements of, the Confederation of Shipbuilding and Engineering Unions: thus over 400 trade unions were in a situation similar to the Association's, yet they were not classed as 'unrecognised'.

Main submissions on behalf of the Employers

12. It was stated that, so far as clause 1 (*a*) of the Fair Wages Resolution was concerned (see paragraph 3 above) the organisations of employers and trade unions representative respectively of substantial proportions of the employers and workers engaged in the Engineering Industry were the Engineering Employers' Federation and its constituent Associations and the trade unions affiliated to the Confederation of Shipbuilding and Engineering Unions.

13. The Employers had been members of the Engineering Employers' Federation since 1934 and the Federation had always dealt with officially recognised trade unions, that is to say unions which were parties to the agreed machinery of negotiation. The Employers' domestic agreements covering manual workers had been negotiated with six officially recognised trade unions, namely the A.E.U., the Electrical Trades Union, the Heating and Domestic Engineers' Union, the National Union of Vehicle Builders, the Transport and General Workers' Union and the United Patternmakers' Association: all of them were in membership of the Confederation of Shipbuilding and Engineering Unions....

15. The A.E.U. shop stewards informed the Employers that the recognition of the Association would prejudice the negotiating rights on behalf of toolmakers accorded by domestic agreement, custom and practice to the A.E.U., and on the 7 July 1963 that Union's District Secretary wrote to inform the Employers that, unless the A.E.U. members who had signified their intention of resigning to join the Association rescinded their proposed resignation by the 31 July, there would be a complete withdrawal of all A.E.U. members....

19. The Engineering Employers' Federation invoked the assistance of the Ministry of Labour on the 31 July 1963 and throughout August

the Employers, their local Association and the Engineering Employers' Federation continued to make every possible effort to resolve the dispute.

20. When those efforts failed the Employers decided, during the first week of September 1963, that they could no longer retain the 37 suspended toolmakers, and they were given one week's pay in lieu if notice, in accordance with the Works rules. By the 30 September, all but three of the 37 men had returned to the Employers' service without loss of seniority, having rescinded their resignation from the A.E.U....

23. Having no quarrel with their workpeople nor with the two Unions concerned the Employers, nevertheless, had had no choice but to act as they did to avoid a major strike, officially backed by the recognised Unions, which would have had repercussions throughout the country.

Award

24. Having given careful consideration to all the evidence and submissions put before them the Court find that the claim that the Employers are in breach of the requirements of the Fair Wages Resolution passed by the House of Commons on the 14 October 1946 has not been established.

NATIONAL UNION OF DYERS against WILLIAM DENBY & SONS LTD

Industrial Court   Case 3071

William Denby & Sons Ltd entered a contract with the War Department ('Contract No. 78/Clothing/7800/CT2B') which provided that the contractor would observe and fulfil the obligations specified in the Fair Wages Resolution. The National Union of Dyers alleged a breach of clause 1 (*a*) because the company sometimes employed workers over the weekend contrary to agreements which covered all process-workers: and also a breach of clause 4 because the company refused to negotiate with the union. Neither of the questions having been disposed of after complaint to him, the Minister referred them to the Industrial Court.

Main submissions on behalf of the Union

7. It was submitted that the terms and conditions of employment of all process workers in the Textile Dyeing and Finishing Industry were governed by Agreements reached between the Textile Finishing Trades Association and the Union. Those Agreements, consolidated with effect

from the 14 February 1955 and subsequently amended, had at all material times been contained in a booklet entitled 'Textile Finishing Trades Conciliation Board Labour Agreement'....

9. It was contended that the Company were completely misinterpreting those provisions of the Agreement relating to daily hours of work and overtime,...The provisions relating to maximum hours and overtime were mandatory and not permissive....

10. It was also the Union's contention that the Company had failed to observe the requirements of clause 4 of the Fair Wages Resolution, which stated that 'the contractor shall recognise the freedom of his workpeople to be members of Trade Unions'. Although that clause did not expressly state that employers should recognise trade unions, the Union believed that such recognition was implicit in its terms. In their view the freedom of a worker to belong to a union was pointless unless his union were enabled to carry out effectively the functions of representing their members and negotiating on their behalf. For some twenty-three years up to January 1964 the Company had in fact recognised the Union and had frequently consulted with them on a wide range of industrial problems. Since that date, however, the Company had refused to meet the Union to negotiate or even to discuss outstanding problems.

11. The Company's changed attitude, it was stated, arose from a long and bitter dispute with the Union. On the 30 October 1963 the Company sent dismissal notices to the whole of its productive labour force (then 250 in number), offering at the same time terms of re-engagement which in the Union's submission were designed to encourage non-unionism, and on the 4 November 1963 the Company advertised in the local Press for '50 non-union operatives'. Copies of the letter of dismissal and of the advertisement referred to were placed before the Court: both documents were relied on by the Union as evidence of non-observance by the Company of clause 4 of the Resolution.

12. The Company had subsequently attempted to justify their refusal since January 1964 to negotiate with the Union on the grounds that the Union were insisting that all non-union labour should be dismissed. In the Union's submission, however, correspondence between the Parties during the period from the 21 May to the 11 August 1964 (copies of which were placed before the Court) showed clearly that the Union were advocating a compromise settlement. Their object was not the dismissal of non-union labour but the reinstatement of as many as possible of their members. The Company, however, in dismissing the

Union's members and advertising within a very few days specifically for non-union labour were, it was claimed, attempting to replace what had been for twenty-three years a 'closed shop' by a 'non-union shop'....

Main submissions on behalf of the Company

15. It was stated that the Company accepted that the terms and conditions of employment applicable to workers in the Textile Finishing Industry were those set out in the Agreement and that, in accordance with clause 1(a) of the Resolution, they were required to pay rates of wages and to observe hours and conditions of labour not less favourable than those established by the Agreement....

19. The Company interpreted the provisions referred to above as meaning that the normal working week should not include more than 12 hours work on any day from Monday to Friday and, where a $5\frac{1}{2}$-day week was in operation, should not extend beyond 12 noon on a Saturday; but that overtime within the specified limits could be worked outside the normal working week....

21. With regard to the Union's contention that the Company were not observing clause 4 of the Fair Wages Resolution it was stated that the Company did recognise the freedom of their workpeople to be members of trade unions, and in fact 23 of their present employees were members of one or other of six different unions. Furthermore they still employed some 30 workers who had formerly been members of the Union but who had been expelled from membership since the Company had been declared 'black' by the Union. The Company did not discriminate against members of the Union when engaging labour, but in order that such applicants for employment should not unwittingly risk losing their Union membership they did warn such applicants that they would probably be expelled from the Union if they decided to work for the Company. In the early days of the dispute a Director of the Company had personally visited at their homes a large number of ex-employees who were Union members and had asked them to return to work.

22. It was stated that the dispute arose when on the 30 October 1963 the Company's employees walked out of the factory and staged an un-official strike. This was not the first time this had happened and the men were accordingly given notice of dismissal. Negotiations with the Union broke down and on the 2 November the strike was made official by the Union. The Company advertised for non-union labour on the 4 November (see paragraph 11 above) because they urgently required

operatives if they were not to close down and they realised that they could not recruit members of the Union with whom they were officially in dispute. The only labour which it was open to them to recruit was non-union labour. The advertisement in question was headed 'Open Shop' and this, it was contended, showed that the Company had not adopted an attitude of hostility to trade unions.

23. Negotiations between the Parties continued for several months after the beginning of the dispute and resulted in an offer by the Company to re-employ most of the dismissed Union members. The Company had been not only willing but extremely anxious to take back the majority of their Union employees, although not certain men whom they regarded as trouble-makers. It was only when, in March 1964, the Company was declared 'black' and there were no longer any Union members in their employment that they refused to enter into further discussions with the Union. In their submission it was the Union's insistence on a 'closed shop' which had led to a position of deadlock. The Company had publicly stated that they were prepared to renew negotiations is the Union agreed to recognise their right to maintain an 'open shop', and this was still their position.

Award

24. Having given careful consideration to the evidence and submissions of the Parties the Court find an Award as follows:

(1) It has been established that the Company have not observed the requirements of clause 1(a) of the Fair Wages Resolution in that, by employing occasionally certain of their employees on productive work on Saturday afternoon or Sunday, they have observed hours and conditions of labour less favourable than those established by the Agreement referred to in paragraph 7 above. In the course of the hearing it was stated on behalf of the Company that if the Court were to find against them on this issue they would not in future carry on productive work on Saturday afternoon or Sunday.

(2) It has not been established that the Company have failed to observe the requirements of Clause 4 of the Resolution.

SUGAR ACT, 1956

24. *Wages and conditions of employment of employees of Corporation.* (1) The wages to be paid by the Corporation to persons employed by them, and the conditions of employment of persons so employed, shall,

unless agreed upon by the Corporation and by organisations representative of the persons employed, be no less favourable to the persons employed than the wages which would be payable, and the conditions which would have to be observed, under a contract which complies with the requirements of any resolution of the House of Commons for the time being in force applicable to contracts of Government departments; and if any dispute arises as to what wages ought to be paid, or what conditions ought to be observed, in accordance with this section, it shall, if not otherwise disposed of, be referred by the Minister of Labour and National Service to the industrial court for settlement.

(2) Where any award has been made by the industrial court upon a dispute referred to that court under this section, then, as from the date of the award or from such other date, not being earlier than the date on which the dispute to which the award relates first arose, as the court may direct, it shall be an implied term of the contract between the Corporation and workers to whom the award applies that the rate of wages to be paid, or the conditions of employment to be observed, under the contract shall, until varied in accordance with the provisions of this section, be in accordance with the award.*

ROAD TRAFFIC ACT, 1960†

152. *Wages and conditions of employment of persons employed in connection with public service vehicles.* (1) The wages paid by the holder of a road service licence to persons employed by him in connection with the operation of a public service vehicle and the conditions of their employment shall not be less favourable to them than the wages which would be payable and the conditions which would have to be observed under a contract which complied with the requirement of any resolution

---

* For a complete list of similar statutes, see Evidence of Ministry of Labour to the Royal Commission on Trade Unions and Employers' Associations (H.M.S.O. 1965) p. 112. Consider, *e.g.*, s. 16 Television Act, 1964; and compare s. 23 *ibid*.

† Here, at the instigation of the trade union (but not an individual worker) the employer's licence may be suspended or revoked under s. 178, *ibid*. Compare the statutory scheme for goods vehicle drivers employed for a firm's own purposes. (For road haulage undertakings the Wages Councils Act, 1959, *post*, p. 366, applies.) A 'fair wages' scheme is imposed for such drivers under ss. 4 and 5, Road Haulage Wages Act, 1938, and provides for the usual procedures: complaint to the Minister; attempt at voluntary settlement; ultimate reference to the Industrial Court; and an Award of that court which becomes a term of the employment contracts of the workers concerned. But the process can be set in motion here by either the union or an individual worker: s. 4(1). For a decision on this scheme see Case 2675, *Robert Johnston Duncan* against *R. C. Cessford*. A conviction for the offence of failing to observe the Road Haulage Wages Act, under s. 7 thereof, can also be the cause of revocation of a carrier's licence: Road Traffic Act, 1960, s. 178(1)(c).

of the House of Commons for the time being in force applicable to contracts with Government departments.

(2) Any organisation representative of the persons engaged in the road transport industry may make representations to the traffic commissioners to the effect that the wages paid to, or the conditions of employment of, any persons employed by the holder of a road service licence are not in accordance with the requirements of the foregoing subsection, and if the matter in dispute is not otherwise disposed of it shall be referred by the Minister of Labour to the Industrial Court for settlement.

(3) Where a matter is referred to the Industrial Court under the last foregoing subsection the Court, in arriving at its decision, shall have regard to any determination which may be brought to its notice relating to the wages or conditions of service of persons employed in a capacity similar to that of the persons to whom the reference relates and contained in a decision of a joint industrial council, conciliation board or other similar body, or in an agreement between organisations representative of employers and workpeople.

(4) If it is decided by the Industrial Court that a person has been guilty of a breach of the provisions of this section, he shall be liable to be dealt with in all respects as if he had failed to comply with a condition attached to his road service licence.

SECTION F

THE 'EXTENSION' OF RECOGNISED TERMS AND CONDITIONS*

TERMS AND CONDITIONS OF EMPLOYMENT ACT, 1959

8. (1) Where a claim is duly reported to the Minister under this section:

(a) that terms or conditions of employment are established in any trade or industry, or section of a trade or industry, either generally or in any district, which have been settled by an agreement or award, and

(b) that the parties to the agreement, or to the proceedings in which

* Note: The jurisdiction of the Industrial Court under s. 8 of the 1959 Act is preserved and not transferred to the Industrial Tribunals, even if the claim relates to terms and conditions concerning redundancy payments: s. 12, Redundancy Payments Act, 1965.

the award was made, are or represent organisations of employers and organisations of workers or associations of such organisations, and represent (generally or in the dictrict in question, as the case may be) a substantial proportion of the employers and of the workers in the trade, industry or section, being workers of the description (hereinafter referred to as 'the relevant description') to which the agreement or award relates, and

(c) that as respects any worker of the relevant description an employer engaged in the trade, industry or section (or, where the operation of the agreement or award is limited to a district, an employer so engaged in that district), whether represented as aforesaid or not, is not observing the terms or conditions (hereinafter referred to as 'the recognised terms or conditions'),

the Minister may take any steps which seem to him expedient to settle, or to secure the use of appropriate machinery to settle, the claim and shall, if the claim is not otherwise settled, refer it to the Industrial Court constituted under Part I of the Industrial Courts Act, 1919: Provided that:

(i) no claim shall be reported under this section as respects workers whose remuneration or minimum remuneration is fixed (otherwise than by the employer, with or without the approval of any other person) in pursuance of any enactment other than this section or in the case of whom provision is made by or under any enactment other than this section for the settlement of questions as to remuneration or minimum remuneration;

(ii) no claim shall be reported under this section as respects terms or conditions fixed as aforesaid.

(2) For the purposes of this section a claim, to be duly reported, must be reported to the Minister in writing by an organisation or association being, or represented by, one of the parties mentioned in paragraph (b) of the foregoing subsection; and if in the opinion of the Minister the report of a claim does not contain sufficient particulars he may require further particulars to be given, and if he does so the report shall not be treated as having been duly made until the Minister is satisfied that the particulars required have been given.

(3) If on a reference under this section the Industrial Court is satisfied that the claim is well founded, then unless the Court is satisfied that the terms or conditions which the employer is observing are not less favourable than the recognised terms or conditions the Court shall make an award requiring the employer to observe the recognised terms or

conditions as respects all workers of the relevant description from time to time employed by him.

(4) An award under this section shall have effect as an implied term of contract of employment, and shall have effect from such date as the Industrial Court may determine, being a date not earlier than the date on which, in the opinion of the Court the employer was first informed of the claim giving rise to the award by the organisation or association which reported the claim to the Minister; and an award under this section shall cease to have effect on the coming into operation of an agreement or award varying or abrogating the recognised terms or conditions.

(5) For the purposes of this section the carrying on of the activities of public or local authorities shall be treated as the carrying on of a trade or industry.

LAMINATED AND COIL SPRING WORKERS'
UNION against WAIN

Industrial Court   Case 3006

The Laminated and Coil Spring Workers' Union (with some 245 members) claimed that with reference to a collective agreement made between themselves and a manufacturers' association two men—Sykes and Gilman—employed by a Mr Wain of Cluntergate, Horbury, had been underpaid in respect of statutory and annual holidays, after July 1962. Also in the case of Sykes, who had been away because of an industrial injury, they said Wain had not observed the new rates for time worked which he did apply to Gilman.

Main submissions on behalf of the Union...

8. Since 1945 the Union had made a practice of informing the Employer of the changes made from time to time to the Agreements relating to the Industry, and although the Employer did not acknowledge those notifications he had in fact observed the appropriate terms and conditions of employment until July 1962....

12. As the Employer took no action despite the Union's letters matter was referred to the Ministry of Labour's Industrial Relations Officer. The latter's efforts to arrange a meeting between the Parties were unsuccessful and the claim was consequently referred to the Court.

Submissions on behalf of the Employer

13. The Employer (who was not represented at the hearing) stated in a letter dated the 21 January 1964 addressed to the Court that he had received no sick note or doctor's certificate from Mr Sykes on any occasion since the latter had injured his foot in November 1962, despite the fact that at different times he was (1) being treated for other than an injured foot; (2) attending an Industrial Rehabilitation Centre; and (3) on his own admission capable of work on the 20 August 1963. During that period Mr Sykes had been in receipt of National Insurance Benefits.

14. The Employer suggested that the Union's contention that Mr Sykes had not been paid at the appropriate datal rate was not correct and stated that this man had never started before 8.30 a.m., or worked beyond 5 p.m., or had less than one hour for lunch, without being paid at the rate of time-and-a-half of his datal rate.

Award

15. Having given careful consideration to the evidence and submissions of the Parties, the Court find that the recognised terms and conditions of employment applicable to the workers concerned in the claim were at all material times those laid down in the Agreement relating to datal rates dated the 19 July 1962 and in the Agreement relating to paid annual and statutory holidays, re-drafted on the 10 April 1963, between the Laminated Railway Spring Manufacturers' Association and the Union. They further find that the Employer, who after notification by letters dated the 3 May 1963 and the 8 August 1963 as to the proper payments to be made for annual and statutory holidays failed to make proper payment thereof to Mr H. Sykes and Mr F. Gilman, is not observing the recognised terms and conditions of employment. The Court require the Employer to observe the recognised terms and conditions of employment (and any subsequently agreed amendments thereto) as respects all employees from time to time employed by him. This Award shall have effect from the 4 May 1963.

D.A.T.A. against TUBEWRIGHTS LTD

Industrial Court   Case 3086

The Draughtsmen's and Allied Technicians' Association claimed that Tubewrights Ltd were not observing an informal agreement made between the union and the Engineering Employers' Federation which provided for a reduction in the normal working week. The company, a subsidiary of Stewart and Lloyds, claimed it was observing terms not less favourable; and also said that it should abide by the policy of the Group to which it belonged.

Main submissions on behalf of the Association...

12. It was stated that although the Company were a subsidiary of the Stewart and Lloyds Group, who were members of the Iron and Steel Federation, they were in fact engaged in engineering. Whereas, in the Association's submission, companies within the iron and steel industry were engaged in producing steel and various steel products, the Company, according to a description of their activities taken from a diary, were producers of material handling equipment, traffic engineering materials and special structures for building towers and gantries. The Association were not in dispute with any other company within the Stewart and Lloyds Group on the question of the working week because the other companies within that Group had reduced their normal weekly hours from 39¾ to 37½. The Association, it was submitted, were not inconsistent in raising the present issue with the Company since the latter, although operating a 37½-hour week, had made no reduction at all.

13. The Company had observed the provisions of an agreement concluded on the 22 December 1964 between the Federation and the Confederation of Shipbuilding and Engineering Unions whereby the working week of manual workers had been reduced to 40 hours. They had also undertaken to conform to national engineering agreements relating to wages. In the Association's view their refusal to observe the 1965 Agreement was therefore illogical and had led to a deterioration in the relative position of the employees concerned in comparison with employees in comparable undertakings in the same area....

Main submissions on behalf of the Company

15. It was stated that the Company did not dispute that they were engaged in the Engineering Industry although they were a subsidiary of Stewart and Lloyds, who were members of the Iron and Steel Federation. As they were not members of the Engineering Employers' Federation the Company were not parties to the 1965 Agreement, but they were aware of its provisions.

16. As far as was practicable the Company followed the policy of the Stewart and Lloyds Group as regards terms and conditions of employment.

Their normal working week was at present one of 37½ hours, daily working hours being from 9.0 a.m. to 5.30 p.m. Monday to Friday with one hour for lunch. The Company had operated a 37½-hour week since their inception in 1954, but within the Stewart and Lloyds Group working hours had been standardised at that level only in November 1964.

17. It was the Company's contention that they should abide by their Group's policy as regards those terms and conditions of employment which were not governed by any local consideration. The Company considered that most of the conditions they observed, in conformity with that policy, were generous: one indication of this was the fact that they allowed unofficial tea-breaks in the drawing office. It was submitted that the Association's members could not reasonably expect to enjoy whichever were the more favourable of the terms and conditions provided by the Stewart and Lloyds Group and by the engineering agreements respectively.

18. The Company also submitted that they were observing in respect of the employees concerned terms and conditions of employment which were in general not less favourable than those laid down in the national agreements in the Engineering Industry, in that they provided four additional days of statutory holiday, making a total of ten days a year. . . .

Award

20. Having given careful consideration to the evidence and submissions of the Parties the Court find and Award as follows:

(1) The recognised terms and conditions of employment in relation to the normal working week which are applicable to the workers concerned in the claim (hereinafter referred to as the recognised terms and conditions) are those laid down in the 1965 Agreement. . . .

(2) The Company are not observing the recognised terms and conditions, or terms and conditions not less favourable.

(3) The Court accordingly require the Company to observe the recognised terms and conditions.

(4) This Award shall take effect from the beginning of the first full pay period following the date hereof.

AMALGAMATED SOCIETY OF WOODWORKERS
against RIPLEY U.D.C.

Industrial Court   Case 3056

The Amalgamated Society of Woodworkers argued that Ripley U.D.C. were not observing the terms of employment in respect of overtime laid down by the Joint Committee for Local Authorities' services. The Council claimed that they were observing terms which were as favourable because the weekly wages of the man—a housing repairs foreman—reflected overtime whether he worked it or not.

Award

15. Having given careful consideration to the evidence and submissions of the Parties the Court find and Award as follows:

(1) The recognised terms and conditions applicable to the worker concerned in the claim (hereinafter referred to as the recognised terms and conditions) are those laid down in the National Agreement.

(2) The Council are not observing the recognised terms and conditions in that they are not paying to the worker concerned overtime calculated on the basis provided for under those terms and conditions.

(3) It is not known what would be the appropriate rate of pay for the worker concerned under the recognised terms and conditions, since this is a matter for agreement between the Parties or, failing such agreement, for determination by the Conciliation Committee. It follows that it cannot at present be shown whether the terms and conditions which the Council are observing are more or less favourable than the recognised terms and conditions, and that the Council have not satisfied the Court that the terms and conditions which they are observing are not less favourable.

(4) The Court accordingly require the Council to observe the recognised terms and conditions.

(5) This Award shall take effect from the beginning of the first full pay period following the date hereof.

VARIETY ARTISTES' FEDERATION against B.B.C.

Industrial Court   Case 2994

The Variety Artistes' Federation concluded a collective agreement covering artistes employed by the four major Independent Television Companies and nine regional ones. It then claimed that the B.B.C., with whom it was in dispute over a new fee structure for artistes, was not observing the established terms or conditions of employment because it was offering a minimum fee far below that of the Independent Television Agreement.

Main submissions on behalf of the Federation

5. It was the Federation's contention that the B.B.C. should engage Variety Artistes in the medium of television under terms and conditions of employment similar to those applicable to the Independent Television Programme Companies, since both Employers were engaged in the Television Section of the Entertainment Industry...

9. The Federation recognised that the claim could not succeed unless it satisfied the provisions of the Act, as to which their submissions were in substance as follows:

(1) The contention advanced by the B.B.C. that the claim was defeated by proviso (ii) to s. 8(1) of the Act (see paragraph 10(1) below) was misconceived; and s. 17 of the Television Act 1954, on which the B.B.C. placed reliance in this connection, was really concerned with securing the compliance of programme contractors with the wage standards required by the Fair Wages Resolution and had no relevance to the present case.

(2) In applying to the facts of the present case the expression 'any trade or industry, or section of a trade or industry' in s. 8(1) of the Act, the relevant industry was the Entertainment Industry and the relevant section of it was the Television Section; and the B.B.C. were wrong in saying that the case was concerned with the variety section of the television industry. The entertainment industry comprised various sections—television, sound radio, theatre, cinema and the like. The B.B.C. were engaged in two principal sections, television and sound radio, and separate departments of the B.B.C. made separate contracts for engagements in each of these sections.

(3) As to the question whether the terms and conditions of employment relied on by the Federation were such as to satisfy the provisions of s. 8(1)(a) of the Act, the Federation submitted that they were. The Independent Television Agreement established terms and conditions of employment for Variety Artistes in television broadcast programmes generally and/or in any district. The Independent Television Agreement was agreed with 13 employers, while the B.B.C. were only one employer. It could not be said that the B.B.C. were in a special position all their own.

The Federation recognised that there were difficulties in applying the pay terms of the Independent Television Agreement, as they stood, to the B.B.C., and they also realized that there was a difference in the 'fiscal' side of two channels. They were more than willing to help in solving these problems, and suggested that the Court might make some assessment of what the pay terms might be.

(4) As to the question whether the Independent Television Agreement was such as to satisfy the provisions of s. 8(1)(b) of the Act, the only question in dispute was whether the parties with whom the Federation had entered into the Independent Television Agreement were or represented an organisation of employers. That Agreement had been negotiated on behalf of the Independent Television Programme Companies by the Independent Television Labour Relations Committee, although the Committee on the one hand and the Federation's representatives on the other had to report back to the Companies and the Federation respectively. The Committee, it was believed, functioned under a written constitution derived from the Independent Television Companies Association, and could properly be regarded as an organisation of employers. As to the point made that it was not the Committee but the Independent Television Companies themselves who were parties to and signed the Independent Television Agreement, the Federation submitted that the Companies had grouped themselves together for the purposes of securing agreement and should consequently be regarded as an organisation of employers.

Main submissions on behalf of the B.B.C.

10. The Corporation agreed with the Federation that the Parties were before the Court because they had been unable to agree upon a new fee structure for Variety Artistes. The Corporation did not propose to enlarge on the reasons for this failure. The only question for the Court was whether the present claim was well-founded in that it satisfied the provisions of s. 8 of the Act. The onus of establishing this was on the Federation: the Corporation submitted that that had not been done and could not be done and that the claim was clearly not well founded. The substance of their submissions was as follows:

(1) The Independent Television Agreement was made and the remuneration of the artistes covered by it was fixed in pursuance of s. 17 of the Television Act 1954. Further or alternatively the terms or conditions of employment fixed by the Agreement related to workers in the case of whom provision for the settlement of questions as to

remuneration was made by the aforesaid Section. Accordingly proviso (ii) to s. 8(1) of the Act applied.

(2) The Corporation's own view was that, for the purposes of the present reference, the relevant industry was the television industry and the relevant section of it the variety section. They had considered that this view was more favourable to the Federation's claim than the Federation's own view (as to which see paragraph 9(2) above) since the television industry (or section of an industry) covered artists (such as musicians, actors, opera singers and others) who were not Variety Artistes and could not be covered by the Independent Television Agreement. There was however probably nothing between the Parties on those forms of words.

(3) As to whether the terms and conditions of employment relied on by the Federation were such as to satisfy s. 8(1)(a) of the Act, the Corporation submitted that it would be quite unreasonable to say that terms and conditions established for artistes employed by the Independent Television Companies were established generally in the television industry (or section of an industry). The television industry really consisted of two industries (or sections) or two distinct parts of an industry (or section), as to which quite separate considerations applied. On the one hand there was the Corporation, which was incorporated by Charter for the purpose of providing a public service, including the obligation to provide fair and accurate Parliamentary reports and the like, and which was dependent for its finance on a proportion of licence fees and accountable for its expenditure to Parliament through the Postmaster General, with an obligation to charge no private fees and to take on no sponsored programmes. On the other hand there was the Independent Television Authority and Companies which could charge as much as they liked for advertisements and in their charges and their payments were subject only to commercial limitations. This distinction had plainly been recognized by Equity and by the Musicians' Union, who had negotiated for actors and musicians performing for the B.B.C. lower rates of remuneration than for those performing for the Independent Companies.

The distinction was moreover demonstrated by the Independent Television Agreement itself, which could only be applied in relation to the Independent Companies: the provisions for rates of pay for performance, for example, or for weekly rates, were framed with reference to groups of Independent Companies, and could not be applied with reference to the B.B.C.

(4) As to the question whether the Independent Television Agreement was such as to satisfy the provisions of s. 8(1)(b) of the Act, it was conceded that one party to that Agreement, namely the Federation, were an organisation of the required kind. The other party to the Agreement, however, simply consisted of the Independent Companies themselves who were principals and who alone could be regarded as the party to the Agreement. As the Federation had conceded, the Independent Television Labour Relations Committee had no plenary powers, and after negotiating tentative terms had to report back to the Companies who were their principals. It could not be said that the Companies were or represented an organisation of employers or an association of such organisations...

Award

12. After giving careful consideration to the evidence and submissions of the Parties the Court find, and so Award, that the terms and conditions relied on by the Federation, namely those contained in the Agreement made on the 1 March 1962 between the Federation and the Independent Television Companies therein named, are not such as to satisfy the provisions of s. 8(1)(a) of the Act, and further that the said Agreement is not such as to satisfy the provisions of s. 8(1)(b) of the Act, and that accordingly the claim is not well founded.

For the purposes of this Award: (a) The Court have assumed, without deciding the point, that a Variety Artiste engaged in television can properly be regarded as a worker, and the Corporation or an Independent Television Company as his employer, and the relationship between them as one of employment, within the meaning of the Act.

(b) The Court have not found it necessary to decide whether the relevant industry is the entertainment industry and the relevant section of it is the television section or whether the relevant industry is the television industry and the relevant section of it is the variety section: the Award applies in either case.

R. *v.* INDUSTRIAL DISPUTES TRIBUNAL *ex parte*
COURAGE & CO. LTD

[1956] 1 W.L.R. 1062; [1956] 3 All E.R. 411

In a case under the Industrial Disputes Order 1951, about whether a particular trade union asking for a wage rise for its members at one brewery represented a substantial proportion of workers in the section of trade or industry concerned, ORMEROD, J. said:

With regard to the third point which has been made on behalf of the applicants, that the trade union were not representing a substantial proportion of a section of the trade or industry concerned, I respectfully agree with the construction which the Lord Chief Justice has put on that part of the Order. It appears to me that the term 'section of trade or industry' refers to function rather than to geographical situation and, in those circumstances, those particular words in article 1 (*b*) do not apply to this case; but even if they did, the figures which are before the court are that some 50 or more members of this trade union are included in the 350, the total number of employees in this brewery, and apart from any other consideration that could be regarded as a substantial proportion of the workmen engaged in this particular section of the industry. But I do not agree that the contention of Mr Hobson is the correct one. I think the words that apply here are that the trade union 'represents a substantial proportion of employers or workers, as the case may be, in the trade or industry'.

AMALGAMATED SOCIETY OF WOODCUTTING MACHINISTS AND ANOTHER against TILGATE PALLETS LTD

Industrial Court   Case 3064

Two unions reported Tilgate Pallets Ltd for not observing the terms and conditions established for the Packing Case Industry in Scotland by agreements between the unions and a Scottish manufacturers' federation. The firm claimed it was not engaged in that 'industry' because it only made pallets.*

Main submission on behalf of the Unions...

8. It was stated that the Unions rejected the Company's argument that a pallet was neither a box nor a case and that pallet making was accordingly not part of the Packing Case Industry. It was the essence of the Unions' case that, even if in a literal view a pallet was not a case or box, nevertheless by custom and usage in that Industry a pallet was regarded as a container and a container was regarded as a case or

---

* Note, too, that a group of workers in an enterprise may be held to fall within an 'industry' or 'section of an industry' different from that in which the majority of workers fall: see Cases 2808 (*Avon India Rubber Co. Ltd* and *A.E.S.D.*: a group of draughtsmen in a rubber manufacturing company fell within the national engineering agreement); and 2924 (*Parnall Ltd* and *N.U.F.T.O.*: a small group of upholstery workers in a general engineering factory were brought within the national Furniture Manufacturing Agreement).

box. It was pointed out that although the mechanical handling of loads by means of the fork lift had been introduced only about 12 years ago, pallets had been made by the Packing Case Industry for many years before that time. The main function of the pallets was to replace the containers which had formerly been used to transport goods from one place to another...

10. It was understood that the Company had observed and were observing the rates of pay and conditions of employment laid down by the J.I.C. in respect of pallet makers in their Crawley works. This showed, it was submitted, that in Crawley they had accepted that pallet making was part of the Packing Case Industry. The Unions could see no reason, therefore, why the Company should not observe the Scottish Agreement in respect of their pallet makers in Scotland...

11. It was pointed out that the fact that the Company were paying less than the established rates for the Packing Case Industry in Scotland had been brought to the Unions' attention by the Scottish National Federation of Packing Case Manufacturers (hereinafter referred to as 'the Federation'). Of that Federation, it was stated, over 50 per cent. of the members (including 15 employers in Glasgow alone) were engaged in the manufacture of pallets...

Main submissions on behalf of the Company...

15. It was explained that when the mechanical handling industry started to develop some twelve years ago, wooden pallets became much in demand. This need was met by box and packing case makers, who diversified their existing production to supply that new market. It was for that reason that pallet making had become associated, quite wrongly in the Company's view, with box and case making. The emergence of such a large and thriving industry had called for specialised techniques and methods of manufacture of a much more comprehensive standard, which, it was submitted, had taken pallet making right out of the realm of box and packing case making.

16. The Company, which commenced business in Crawley, Sussex in 1959, had originally operated a homegrown timber sawmill under the name of Tilgate Sawmills Ltd. In October 1964 they changed their name to Tilgate Pallets Ltd, a designation they had already used as a trade name for more than three years. The Company had never had any association with box and case making. When, some four years ago, it was decided to cease timber milling and to specialise in pallet making, the machinery and techniques employed were designed to

facilitate only pallet making, and in consequence the Company were not, and never had been, equipped or set up to manufacture boxes or cases...

17. It was submitted that the Company were not eligible for membership of the Scottish National Federation of Packing Case Manufacturers...

18. The Federation had been unwilling to supply a copy of the Scottish Agreement and the Company had been unable to obtain one from the Ministry of Labour. The Unions, it was true, had sent them an extract relating to wages, but the Company had not seen the booklet entitled 'Working Rules and Conditions of Apprenticeship' before the present hearing, and they had been unable until now to find out what were the precise terms of the Scottish Agreement...

21. Because pallet making required less skill than case making the Company's economy was pitched at a different level. Their markets were far more restricted than those for the box and packing case makers: they were confined to selling their products to those companies who owned fork lift or hand lift trucks. This necessarily limited the market and gave the Company a narrower economy in which to operate. It was submitted that the whole basis of the pallet making industry was quite different from that of box and case making, and was based on the employment of unskilled workers at appropriate rates of pay...

Award

26. Having given careful consideration to the evidence and submissions of the Parties the Court find and Award as follows:

(1) The recognised terms and conditions of employment applicable to the workers concerned in the claim (hereinafter referred to as the recognised terms and conditions) are those laid down in the Scottish Agreement.

(2) The Company are failing to observe the recognised terms and conditions, or terms and conditions not less favourable, in respect of sawyers, woodmachinists and other workers actually engaged in the making of pallets.

(3) The Court accordingly require the Company to observe the recognised terms and conditions.

(4) This Award shall take effect from the beginning of the first full pay period following the date hereof.

NATIONAL SOCIETY OF METAL MECHANICS
against NEWTOWN POLISHING CO. LTD (No. 2).

Industrial Court   Case 3069

The National Society of Metal Mechanics, a small union, claimed that the Newtown Polishing Co. Ltd was not observing recognized terms and conditions in respect of polishers whom it claimed to be members. In an Award (3026) the Court appeared to accept the argument to the extent of enforcing on the employers the 'recognition' and 'procedure' clauses as 'terms and conditions of employment'. Such a finding would have opened the gates to use of the 1959 Act for unions to compel recognition by legal means. The present Award 're-interprets' (and in effect reverses) that aspect of Award 3026.

1. A question having arisen as to the interpretation of Award No. 3026 dated the 29 July 1964, the matter was brought before the Court under the provisions of Rule 7 of the Industrial Court (Procedure) Rules 1920 at the request of one of the Parties concerned, namely the National Society of Metal Mechanics.

2. Award No. 3026 is a decision of the Court relating to a claim reported to the Minister of Labour on the 9 April 1964 by the National Society of Metal Mechanics (hereinafter referred to as 'the Society') under s. 8 of the Terms and Conditions of Employment Act 1959, that the Newtown Polishing Co. Ltd (hereinafter referred to as 'the Company') were not observing as regards engineering workers in their employ the established terms and conditions of employment. The decision of the Court was as follows:

Award

'14. Having given careful consideration to the evidence and submissions of the Parties the Court find that the recognised terms and conditions of employment applicable to the workers concerned in the claim are those laid down in the Agreements referred to in paragraph 2 above. The Court further find that the Company are not observing the aforesaid recognised terms and conditions of employment in that they are not paying the workers concerned the appropriate overtime and nightshift rates and holiday pay entitlements. The Court are not satisfied that the terms and conditions of employment which the Company are observing are not less favourable than the recognised terms and conditions. They require the Company to observe, with effect from the 19 June 1964, the recognised terms and conditions in respect of all employees of the category specified.'

3. Paragraph 2 of Award No. 3026, which was referred to in the above-quoted paragraph 14, is in the following terms:

'2. The claim concerns some 30 polishers employed in the Polishing Shop of the Newtown Polishing Co. Ltd, Birmingham (hereinafter referred to as "the Company"), a firm engaged in the Engineering Industry. The National Society of Metal Mechanics (hereinafter referred to as "the Society") are claiming that the Company are not observing the terms and conditions of employment laid down for the workers concerned in the Agreements between the Engineering Employers' Federation and the Confederation of Shipbuilding and Engineering Unions, namely (a) the Procedure Agreement dated the 2 June 1922, amended on the 10 August 1955, (b) the Overtime and Nightshift Agreement dated the 30 July 1956 (as amended) and (c) the Agreement on Holidays dated the 18 January 1961. Copies of the relevant Agreements were placed before the Court.'

4. The question in respect of which the interpretation of the Court is asked is whether or not the provisions of the Agreement referred to at (a) in the above-quoted paragraph 2 (which Agreement is hereinafter referred to as 'the Procedure Agreement') form part of the recognised terms and conditions of employment which the Court required the Company to observe...

6. In the course of the hearing reference was made to a recent Award of the Court (No. 3059 dated the 1 March 1965), in paragraph 27 of which there were quoted certain passages from the judgment of the Court of Appeal in R. v. *Industrial Disputes Tribunal, Ex parte Portland U.D.C.*, 1955 3 *A.E.R.* 18. In that case the Court of Appeal took the view that a position in the relevant agreement which related to procedure for the settlement of differences was not one of the terms and conditions of employment.

Main submissions on behalf of the Society

7. It was stated that, after examining carefully the terms of Award No. 3026, the Society had formed the opinion that the Court had clearly found in paragraph 14 of the Award that the recognised terms and conditions of employment applicable to the workers concerned were those laid down in the Agreements referred to in paragraph 2 of the Award. Since the Procedure Agreement was one of the Agreements referred to in the said paragraph 2, the Society took the view that the

Award had established that the Procedure Agreement was one of the terms and conditions of employment which the Court had required the Company to observe.

8. In their submissions to the Court at the hearing which led to Award No. 3026 the Society had not claimed that the Company, who were not parties to the Procedure Agreement, should observe all its provisions. It had been, and still was, their contention that the Company should observe the general principles which were set out in Section I of the Procedure Agreement in the following terms:

I. *General Principles*

(a) The Employers have the right to manage their establishments and the Trade Unions have the right to exercise their functions.

(b) In the process of evolution, provision for changes in shop conditions is necessary, but it is not the intention to create any specially favoured class of workpeople.

(c) The Employers and the Trade Unions, without departing in any way from the principles embodied in Clause (a) above, emphasise the value of consultation, not only in the successful operation of the Procedure set out in Section II but in the initial avoidance of disputes. In the Society's view (a) and (c) of those general principles required that the Company should enter into discussions with the Society, but the Company had rejected all their requests for such discussions.

9. With reference to the decision of the Court of Appeal referred to in paragraph 6 above, it was submitted that the Contracts of Employment Act 1963, which came into operation on the 6 July 1964, might have a bearing on the question as to whether provisions relating to procedure were part of the terms and conditions of employment. (A copy of that Act was before the Court.) It was the Society's submission that under paragraph 6(2) of Schedule 2 to that Act an employee who failed to observe any procedural provisions for the avoidance of disputes and who took part in an unofficial stoppage of work would be disqualified from receiving the benefits provided for by the Schedule. In the Society's submission this supported their contention that such procedural provisions were part of an employee's terms and conditions of employment.

Decision

10. Having given careful consideration to the submissions, the Court decide as follows:

The first sentence of paragraph 14 of Award No. 3026 described what were (for purposes relevant to the claim) the recognised terms and conditions of employment applicable to the workers concerned in the claim. In line 4 of the said paragraph 'the Agreements referred to in paragraph 2 above' meant and were intended to mean the Agreements referred to in paragraph 2 in so far as they laid down terms and conditions of employment. The Agreements referred to at (*b*) and (*c*) in the said paragraph 2 contain terms and conditions of employment relating respectively to overtime and nightshift and to holiday pay entitlements and it is in respect of those matters, and no others, that the Court found that the Company were not observing the recognised terms and conditions of employment. The Court's view was and is that none of the provisions of the Procedure Agreement referred to at (*a*) in the said paragraph 2, which provisions consist of a short Section headed 'General Principles' and a longer Section headed 'Procedure for Dealing with Questions Arising', constitute terms or conditions of employment or, consequently, recognised terms or conditions within the meaning of s. 8 of the Terms and Conditions of Employment Act, 1959. The question whether or not the Company were or were not observing the said provisions did not therefore arise for the Court's decision.

NATIONAL UNION OF VEHICLE BUILDERS
against FAIRVIEW CARAVANS LTD

Industrial Court   Case 3059

The National Union of Vehicle Builders complained that Fairview Caravans Ltd were failing to observe recognised terms and conditions for the vehicle building industry, as established in the Agreement between United Kingdom Joint Wages Board of Employers for the industry on the one side, and the Union and the Amalgamated Society of Woodcutting Machinists on the other. The complaint related especially to the 'procedure' clauses in the Agreement.

27. Reference was made during the hearing to the decision of the Court of Appeal in *R. v. Industrial Disputes Tribunal, Ex parte Portland U.D.C.*, 1955 3 *A.E.R.* 18. In that case the main question at issue had

been whether a local authority ought, under the Industrial Disputes Order of 1951 (which was the predecessor of s. 8 of the Act of 1959 and contained provisions which for relevant purposes were closely similar to those of the Section), to observe in relation to one of their employees the 'recognised terms and conditions' relied on by the trade union concerned. The local authority had not been paying to that employee the remuneration provided for in the agreement containing the recognised terms and conditions. It was, however, part of the local authority's case in the appeal that the agreement in question contained (in paragraph 25 (2)) a provision the effect of which was that the question at issue should be dealt with under the procedure laid down for the settlement of differences; that this provision was part of the recognised terms and conditions relied on; that the local authority were willing to abide by this provision; and that it could not therefore be said that they were not observing the recognised terms and conditions. This argument was rejected by the Court of Appeal. Lord Justice Denning, as he then was, said (at p. 23): 'Furthermore paragraph 25 (2) is not, properly speaking, one of the "terms and conditions of employment" at all. It is only machinery for settling a difference. The existence of such machinery is no bar to a report to the Minister.' And Lord Justice Romer said (at p. 28): 'I do not regard paragraph 25 (2) as forming a part of the "recognised terms and conditions" within the purview of that phrase as used in article 2 of the Order of 1951. The scheme admittedly formulates a complete code of terms and conditions, but that is not to say that a term or condition of employment emerges from every paragraph of the scheme. No such term or condition emerges from paragraph 25 (2), which does no more than provide administrative machinery for the purpose of settling questions whether or not an employee is in fact an officer to whom the scheme applies. From this it follows that the purported adoption by the local authority of paragraph 25 (2) does not enable them to say that they are conforming to even one of the recognised terms and conditions of employment and they cannot therefore displace the application of article 2 of the Order on that ground.'

Award

28. Having given careful consideration to the evidence and submissions of the Parties the Court decide and Award as follows:

(1) The recognised terms and conditions of employment established in the Vehicle Building Industry are contained in the Agreement

between the United Kingdom Joint Wages Board of Employers for the Vehicle Building Industry and the National Union of Vehicle Builders and the Amalgamated Society of Woodcutting Machinists, dated the 14 June 1961 and subsequently amended.

(2) The Agreement also, however, contains provisions which are not terms or conditions of employment, or recognised terms or conditions, within the meaning of s. 8 of the Act. Into this category fall the provisions set out in the Appendix hereto, which are the only provisions which it is claimed that the Company are not observing. The terms of those provisions are, moreover, such that they are inapplicable where, as in this case, the workers concerned are not employed in an establishment by a member of one of the Employers' Organisations parties to the Agreement.

(3) The claim, therefore, that as respects the workers concerned the Company are not observing the established terms or conditions of employment is not well founded.

APPENDIX

PROVISIONS IN THE AGREEMENT RELIED ON BY THE UNION

Provisions for the avoidance of disputes. With a view to the avoidance of disputes, deputations of workmen shall be received by their employers by appointment, for the mutual discussion of any question in the settlement of which both parties are directly concerned. Where the point of difference is not so disposed of the matter shall be referred to a Works Conference, to be held within seven days, at which representatives of the Employers' Organisation and the Trade Union may be present with representatives of the employer and the workpeople concerned.

Where it may seem desirable to either party, the point at issue may be referred from the initial stage direct to Local Conference, as outlined below, omitting the Works Conference stage.

In the event of a settlement not being reached at the Works Conference the case shall be referred to a Local Conference to be arranged between the Branch Secretaries of the Employers' Organisation and of the Trade Union, where such regional organisation exists, within ten days.

In the absence of regional organisation either of employers or workpeople or in the failure of the Local Conference to effect a settlement the matters at issue may be referred to National Conference to be arranged by the Secretary of the Wages Board and the General Secretaries of the Trades Unions.

National Conferences, which shall be held within 21 days of the receipt of the application by either Secretary (National holiday periods being excluded from those 21 days) may also be arranged, at the request of either party, for the discussion of questions of a general character.

There shall be no stoppage of work or lockout, of a partial or of a general character, but work shall proceed under the conditions prevailing prior to the question being raised until either side, at the National Conference, declares disagreement.

SHOP STEWARDS—REGULATIONS REGARDING THE APPOINTMENT AND FUNCTIONS OF SHOP STEWARDS

1. *Appointment of Shop Stewards*

(*a*) Workers, members of the above named Trades Unions, employed in an establishment by a member of one of the Employers' Organisations parties to this Agreement, may elect representatives from the members of the Unions employed in the establishment to act on their behalf in accordance with the terms of this Agreement.

(*b*) The representatives shall be known as Shop Stewards.

(*c*) Each Trade Union, party to this agreement, may have Shop Stewards.

(*d*) Shop Stewards shall be elected to speak on behalf of members in the particular shop, department or group—by members in that particular shop, department or group—in which the Shop Steward is employed.

(*e*) The names of the Shop Stewards and particulars of the shop, department or group in which they are employed, and the Trade Union to which they belong, shall—on election—be notified officially by the Trade Union concerned to the Management.

2. *Functions and Procedure*

The functions of Shop Stewards shall be exercised in accordance with the following procedure:

(*a*) A worker or workers desiring to raise any question in which he/they is/are directly concerned shall, in the first instance, discuss the same with his/their foreman, accompanied by the appropriate Shop Steward if the worker(s) so desire(s);

(*b*) Failing settlement, the appropriate Shop Steward and one of the workers directly concerned shall take the matter up with the Works Manager (or other Official of the Company nominated by the Management) through their own Foreman;

(*c*) If no settlement is arrived at the question may, at the request of either party, be further considered at a joint meeting of the Management and representatives of the Shop Stewards. (NOTE: In establishments where Shop Stewards have been appointed this (3rd) stage of domestic procedure takes the place of the first stage of the procedure under the 'Provisions for the Avoidance of Disputes' set out above); and

(*d*) Failing settlement, the question may be taken through the remainder of the procedure laid down in the 'Provisions for the Avoidance of Disputes'.

3. *General*

(*a*) Shop Stewards shall be subject to the control of the Trades Unions, and shall act in accordance with the Rules and Regulations of the Trade Union and Agreements with the Employers so far as these affect the relation between employer and workpeople.

(*b*) Shop Stewards shall be afforded the necessary facilities for carrying out their functions as defined in this Agreement. In all other respects Shop Stewards shall conform to the same working conditions as their fellow workers.

They may not visit any other shop, department or group without the previous consent of the Management obtained through their own Foreman such, consent not to be unreasonably withheld. The Foreman of the shop, department or group so visited must be made aware of the purpose of the visit by the visiting Shop Steward before proceeding further.

(*c*) Negotiations under this Agreement may be instituted either by the Management or by the Workers concerned.

(*d*) Employers and Shop Stewards shall not enter into any Agreement which is inconsistent with Agreements between the United Kingdom Joint Wages Board and the above named Trades Unions.

(*e*) For the purpose of this Agreement the expression 'establishment' shall mean the whole establishment or sections thereof according to whether the Management is unified or sub-divided.

(*f*) Any dispute between the Management and the Workers as to the appropriate number of Shop Stewards to be elected in any establishment shall be dealt with in accordance with Clause 2, paragraphs (*a*), (*b*), (*c*) and (*d*) of this section.

It is a recommendation by all parties to this Agreement that the number of Shop Stewards in any one establishment be kept as small as possible consistent with proper representation of the Trade Union members concerned.

Section G

WAGES COUNCILS

WAGES COUNCILS ACT, 1959

1. *Establishment of wages councils.* (1) Subject to the provisions of this Part of this Act, the Minister may by order establish a wages council to perform, in relation to the workers described in the order and their employers, the functions specified in the subsequent provisions of this Act.

(2) An order establishing a wages council may be made by the Minister either

(a) if he is of opinion that no adequate machinery exists for the effective regulation of the remuneration of the workers described in the order and that, having regard to the remuneration existing among those workers, or any of them, it is expedient that such a council should be established; or

(b) if he thinks fit, to give effect to a recommendation of a commission of inquiry made on the reference to them, in accordance with the following section, of an application made in accordance therewith for the establishment of a wages council; or

(c) if he thinks fit, to give effect to the recommendation of a commission of inquiry made in a case where the Minister, being of opinion that no adequate machinery exists for the effective regulation of the remuneration of any workers or the existing machinery is likely to cease to exist or be adequate for that purpose and a reasonable standard of remuneration among those workers will not be maintained, refers to the commission the question whether a wages council should be established with respect to any of those workers and their employers...*

2. *Applications for wages council orders.* (1) An application for the establishment of a wages council with respect to any workers and their employers may be made to the Minister either

(a) by a joint industrial council, conciliation board or other similar body constituted by organisations representative respectively of those workers and their employers; or

(b) jointly by any organisation of workers and any organisation of employers which claim to be organisations that habitually take part in the settlement of remuneration and conditions of employment for those workers,

on the ground, in either case, that the existing machinery for the settlement of remuneration and conditions of employment for those workers is likely to cease to exist or be adequate for that purpose...

(5) In considering for the purposes of s. 1 of this Act whether any machinery is, or is likely to remain, adequate for regulating the remuneration and conditions of employment of any workers, the commission shall consider not only what matters are capable of being dealt with by that machinery, but also to what extent those matters are covered by the agreements or awards arrived at or given thereunder,

* *Note:* Where a Wages Council is established, the 'extension' procedures of s. 8. Terms and Conditions of Employment Act, 1959, *ante*, p. 345, are excluded.

and to what extent the practice is, or is likely to be, in accordance with those agreements or awards...

3. *Proceedings on references as to establishment of wages councils.* (1) Where the Minister makes to a commission of inquiry any such reference as is mentioned in paragraph (*b*) or (*c*) of subsection (2) of s. 1 of this Act, it shall be the duty of the commission to consider not only the subject matter of the reference but also any other question or matter which, in the opinion of the commission, is relevant thereto...

10. *General duty of wages councils to consider references by government departments.* (1) A wages council shall consider, as occasion requires, any matter referred to it by the Minister or any government department with reference to the industrial conditions prevailing as respects the workers and employers in relation to whom it operates, and shall make a report upon the matter to the Minister or, as the case may be, to that department.

(2) A wages council may, if it thinks it expedient so to do, make of its own motion a recommendation to the Minister or any government department with reference to the said conditions and, where such a recommendation is so made, the Minister or, as the case may be, that department, shall forthwith take it into consideration...

11. *Power to fix remuneration and holidays.* (1) Subject to and in accordance with the provisions of this section, any wages council shall have power to submit to the Minister proposals (hereafter in this Act referred to as 'wages regulation proposals')

(*a*) for fixing the remuneration to be paid, either generally or for any particular work, by their employers to all or any of the workers in relation to whom the council operates;

(*b*) for requiring all or such workers as aforesaid to be allowed holidays by their employers...

(4) Where the Minister receives any wages regulation proposals, he shall make an order (hereafter in this Act referred to as a 'wages regulation order') giving effect to the proposals as from such date as may be specified in the order:

Provided that the Minister may, if he thinks fit, refer the proposals back to the council and the council shall thereupon reconsider them having regard to any observations made by the Minister and may, if it thinks fit, re-submit the proposals to the Minister either without amendment or with such amendments as it thinks fit having regard to those observations; and where proposals are so re-submitted, the

like proceedings shall be had thereon as in the case of original proposals
...*

12. *Effect and enforcement of wages regulation orders.* (1) If a contract
between a worker to whom a wages regulation order applies and his
employer provides for the payment of less remuneration than the
statutory minimum remuneration, it shall have effect as if for that less
remuneration there were substituted the statutory minimum remuneration
and if any such contract provides for the payment of any holiday
remuneration at times or subject to conditions other than those specified
in the order, it shall have effect as if for those times or conditions
there were substituted the times or conditions specified in the order.

(2) If an employer fails to pay a worker to whom a wages regulation
order applies remuneration not less than the statutory minimum
remuneration, or fails to pay to any such worker holiday remuneration
at the times and subject to the conditions specified in the order or fails
to allow to any such worker the holidays fixed by the order, he shall
be liable on summary conviction to a fine not exceeding twenty pounds
for each offence, and where the employer or any other person charged
as a person to whose act or default the offence was due has been found
guilty of an offence under this section consisting of a failure to pay
remuneration not less than the statutory minimum remuneration, the
court may order the employer to pay such sum as is found by the court
to represent the difference between the amount which ought to have
been paid to the worker by way of remuneration, if the provisions of
this Part of this Act had been complied with, and the amount actually
so paid.

(3) Where proceedings are brought under the foregoing subsection
in respect of an offence consisting of a failure to pay remuneration not
less than the statutory minimum remuneration, then, if notice of
intention so to do has been served with the summons, warrant or
complaint:

(*a*) Evidence may, on the employer or any other person charged
as a person to whose act or default the offence was due having been
found guilty of the offence, be given of any like contravention on the
part of the employer in respect of any period during the two years
immediately preceding the date of the offence; and

(*b*) on proof of the failure, the court may order the employer to
pay such sum as is found by the court to represent the difference

---

* But under Prices and Incomes Act, 1966, Part IV, s. 31, the Minister was given
temporary relief from his duty under this subsection.

between the amount which ought to have been paid during that period to the worker by way of remuneration, if the provisions of this Part of this Act had been complied with, and the amount actually so paid.

(4) The powers given by this section for the recovery of sums due from an employer to a worker shall not be in derogation of any right to recover such sums by civil proceedings.*

* *Note:* Furthermore the Ministry of Labour Wages Inspector may institute proceedings on the worker's behalf: *ibid.* s. 19. On the work of the Inspectors see *The Worker and the Law* (1965) p. 133; (1966) p. 128. On Wages Councils generally see C. W. Guillebaud, *The Wages Councils System in Great Britain;* F. J. Bayliss, *Wages Councils;* and Evidence of the Ministry of Labour to Royal Commission on Trade Unions and Employers' Associations (H.M.S.O., 1965) Fifth Memorandum, pp. 114–22. See too now the proposals made by the National Board for Prices and Incomes to change the Wages Councils system in order to effectuate a 'national incomes policy', in Report No. 27, *Pay of Workers in the Retail Drapery, Outfitting and Footwear Trades,* 1967: Cmnd. 3224.

CHAPTER 4

INDUSTRIAL CONFLICT*

SECTION A

THE EARLY COMMON LAW; AND STATUTORY PROVISIONS

R. v. JOURNEYMEN TAILORS OF CAMBRIDGE
(1721) 8 Mod. 10; 88 E.R. 9

Several journeymen tailors of Cambridge were indicted for a conspiracy among themselves to raise their wages. They were convicted.

The Court said: The indictment, it is true, sets forth, that the defendants refused to work under the wages which they demanded; but although these might be more than is directed by the statute, yet it is not for the refusing to work, but for conspiring, that they are indicted, and a conspiracy of any kind is illegal, although the matter about which they conspired might have been lawful for them, or any of them, to do, if they had not conspired to do it.

(Counsel):....this indictment ought to conclude *contra formam statuti;* for by the late statute 7 Geo. 1, c. 13, journeymen-taylors are prohibited to enter into any contract or agreement for advancing their wages, &c. And the statute of 2 & 3 Edw. 6, c. 15, makes such persons criminal.

It was answered, that the omission in not concluding this indictment *contra formam statuti* is not material, because it is for *a conspiracy*, which is an offence at common law. It is true, the indictment sets forth, that the defendants refused to work under such rates, which were more than enjoined by the statute, for that is only two shillings a-day; but yet these words will not bring the offence, for which the defendants are indicted, to be within that statute, because it is not the denial to work except for more wages than is allowed by the statute, but it is for *a conspiracy* to raise their wages, for which these defendants are indicted. It is true, it does not appear by the record that the wages

* For an introductory discussion of the law concerning conflict, see Chapters 7 and 8, Wedderburn, *The Worker and The Law* (Pelican, 1965; McGibbon and Kee, 1966).

demanded were excessive; but that is not material, because it may be given in evidence.

The Court: This indictment need not conclude *contra formam statuti*, because it is for *a conspiracy*, which is an offence at common law.

R. *v.* DUFFIELD

(1851) 5 Cox C.C. 404

A Wolverhampton employer, Mr Perry, received a demand from a London union that he should raise the wages of his men, their present wages being 30 per cent below the average. He refused but instead made all the men enter contracts to serve him for six months at the present rate. The union put the three defendants outside his works. Workmen began to disappear so that the number of employees fell from 85 to 25 'not being of the most able kind', and Mr Perry had to import French and German workers who also disappeared. The basic charge was for a conspiracy to obstruct Perry in the conduct of his business.

ERLE, J., in summing up, said: I may say, gentlemen, that with respect to the law, relating to combinations of workmen, nothing can be more clearly established in point of law than that workmen are at liberty while they are perfectly free from engagement, and have the option of entering into employ or not, nothing can be more clear than that they have a right to agree among themselves to say we will not go into any employ unless we can get a certain rate of wages. But I think, gentlemen, it would be most dangerous if that proposition were carried at all wider than the terms in which I put it; that is to say: where workmen are perfectly free from engagement, having the option whether they will hire themselves or not, each man for himself may say, 'I will go into no employ unless I can get a certain rate of wages,' and all of them, if they choose, may say, 'We will agree with one another that in our trade, as able-bodied workmen, we will not take employ unless the employers agree to give a certain rate of wages'. But, gentlemen, I think it would be most dangerous indeed if that rule of law, so in favour of workmen protecting their own interests, were at all construed to extend to that which is charged upon this indictment, and which the counsel for the prosecution supposes is made out by the evidence, and in respect of which your verdict is to be given; that is to say: to suppose that workmen, who think that a certain rate of wages ought to be obtained, have a right to combine together to induce men, already in the employ of other masters, for the purpose of compelling those masters to raise their wages. The indictment charges in one class of the counts, and that to which I think your attention should be most prominently directed, that they conspired to obstruct Mr Perry in the carrying out of his business, by persuading and inducing workmen, that had been hired by him, to leave his service in order to force him to change the mode of carrying on his business. There are no threats or intimidations supposed to have been used towards the workmen, but there is a class of counts founded upon that, and I take it to be perfectly clear in points of law, and I lay it down to you for the purpose of your verdict, that if that class of counts is made out you will find the defendents guilty upon that class of counts, that they conspired to obstruct Mr Perry by persuading his workmen to leave him in order to induce him to make a change in the mode of conducting and carrying on his business. Some of the counts charge that they conspired to obstruct Mr Perry by this mode; other counts charge that they conspired to molest Mr Perry by this mode; and I take it for granted that if a manufacturer has got a manufactory, and his capital embarked in it for the purpose of producing articles in that manufactory, if persons conspire together to take away all his workmen, that would necessarily be an obstruction to him that would necessarily be a molesting of him in his manufactory; therefore, if you find that these counts are established (that is, the first set of counts), you will say they are guilty upon that set of counts. . . . Gentlemen, the second class of counts to which I would draw your attention is that with relation to the freedom of the workmen themselves. The workmen have a right to agree that none of those who make the agreements will go into employ unless they are to receive a certain rate of wages; but with respect to their fellow-workmen they have no right at all to agree to molest, or intimidate, or annoy other workmen in the same line of business, who refuse to enter into the agreement, and who choose to go and work for the employers at a lower rate of wages than that which the parties agree to rely on.

R. *v.* ROWLANDS

(1851) 5 Cox C.C. 436, 466

The facts in this case are the same as in *R. v. Duffield* except that a different branch of Perry's works was concerned. Rowlands was the local agent of the London Union.

ERLE, J., in summing up, said: I state that the law is clear that workmen have a right to combine for their own protection, and to obtain such wages as they choose to agree to demand. I say nothing at present as to the legality of other persons, not workmen, combining with them to assist in that purpose. As far as I know, there is no objection in point of law to it, and it is not necessary to go into that matter, but I consider the law to be clear only to that point—while the purpose of the combination is to obtain a benefit for the parties who combine—a benefit which by law they can claim. I make that remark, because a combination for the purpose of injuring another is at once a combination of an entirely personal nature, and the law, allowing them to combine for the purpose of obtaining a lawful benefit to themselves, gives no sanction to combinations which have for their immediate purpose the injury or the hurt of another.... Taking it clearly to be a combination to force the assent to a uniform book of prices, it might be put as a proposition, the assent to certain wages for the workmen. If it stood merely there, it might be doubtful, in point of law, how far such a combination was lawful; but if they combine to bring about that purpose by any unlawful means, unquestionably the indictment would be sustained. I think the three classes in respect of which the law is perfectly clear, are, 1st,—If the purpose of the combination was to be effected by intimidation. There is a statute that secures those right to the labourers, but prohibits any intimidation to the other labourers....

There is another class of counts very much to the same purpose. You will have to consider whether there is upon the evidence proof, to your satisfaction, that the defendants combined for the purpose of forcing this assent of Messrs Perry, and intended to bring about that assent by intimidation to Mr Perry. These counts allege that he was molested or obstructed. If they intended to create alarm in the minds of Messrs. Perry, and so to force their assent to any alteration in the mode of carrying on their business, they would clearly, in my opinion, have violated the law, and be guilty on those counts.... I think, with respect to any intimidation to Mr Perry, there does not seem to be anything like a direct threat of personal violence, or anything like a direct threat of actual violence to his property; but if a powerful body intimate that his lawful freedom of action will be interfered with unless he consents to certain terms, it will be for you to consider whether he might not be reasonably said to be intimidated if such matters occurred to him.

WALSBY v. ANLEY

(1861) 3 E. & E. 516; 121 E.R. 536

Defendant gave notice to his employer of a resolution passed by 30 workmen that unless two fellow workmen who had signed 'the declaration' were dismissed, the men would cease work immediately. 'The declaration' was an undertaking not to belong to any union. He was convicted under 6 Geo. IV, c. 129, (Combination Act, 1825) s. 3.*

CROMPTON, J.: I doubted very much, on first reading the case, whether the conviction was right; because the threats and intimidation used by the workmen did not point to the commission by them of an act in itself unlawful; the threat being that they would do that which, taken by itself, they had a perfect right to do; namely, leave the employment. Although, however, I think that any workman has a right to go to his master and say, 'It is my whim not to work in company with so and so', I think that several workmen have no right to combine to procure the discharge of persons obnoxious to them by threatening to leave the employment at once in a body, unless those persons are forthwith discharged. It is a matter of common learning, that what a man may do singly he may not combine with others to do to the prejudice of another. Stat. 6 Geo. 4, c. 129, by repealing all the previous statutes on the subject, appears to me to have re-established the common law effecting combinations of masters or workmen. I adhere to the opinion that, at common law, all such combinations are illegal, and that Grose, J. rightly states the law in the passage to which I referred in the course of the argument.[1] That being so, it was necessary, by ss. 4 and 5 of the

---

[1] In *Rex* v. *Mawbey*, 6 T.R. 619 at p. 636.

* This statute was not repealed until the Criminal Law Amendment Act 1871. Under s. 3 a wide variety of activity ambiguously described could become criminal if the court chose to make it so, including: 'Threats or Intimidation or... molesting or in any way obstructing another' in order to 'force' a workman to depart from his hiring; or hand back his work before completion; or prevent any person from accepting work or employment; or induce any person to belong to any 'Club or Association'; or pay any fine levied through a refusal to join or to comply with regulations about action concerning wages, hours, or manner of work; or 'endeavour to force any Manufacturer or Person carrying on any Trade or Business' to conduct his business in a particular way, or limit the number of his workers. It is to be remembered that until 1875, various Master and Servant Acts also created criminal offences out of an employee's breach of contract: *ante*, p. 87. Furthermore, it is instructive to compare the offence of 'intimidation' created by the Trade Disputes and Trade Union Act, 1927, repealed by the Act of the same name in 1946. Section 3(2) in 1927 added to the definition of 'intimidation' under s. 7 of the Conspiracy and Protection of Property Act 1875, *post*, p. 383, the causing of reasonable apprehension of injury, including 'injury to a person in respect of his business, occupation or employment or other source of income'. This was repealed in 1946. But a wider notion of *civil* 'intimidation' was resurrected by the House of Lords in *Rookes* v. *Barnard* in 1964, *post*, p. 503.

statute, to render legal the combinations of workmen and masters therein referred to respectively, and which would, at common law, have been illegal. The combination charged in the present case is one by workmen to threaten to leave the respondent's service if he did not dismiss certain other workmen. That is a combination not within the protection of s. 4, and falling within the prohibition in s. 3 against endeavouring by threats or intimidation to force an employer to limit the number or description of his workmen.

HILL, J.: I entirely agree with what the Lord Chief Justice has said as to the right of an individual workman, or any number of workmen, to tell their employer that they decline to continue to work with particular men to whom they object. If, however, they act in combination, not honestly or independently, but by way of a conspiracy in order to coerce their employer to dismiss the men obnoxious to them, that combination is illegal.

COCKBURN, C.J. delivered a concurring judgment; WIGHTMAN, J. was absent.

UNWIN v. CLARKE

(1866) 35 L.J.R. (M.C.) 193

C. contracted to serve U. (and U. alone) as a cutler for two years at a specified wage. Later, the 'large majority' of cutlery-manufacturers in Sheffield gave their cutlers a rise; but U. refused to do this. C. refused to work for him and was sent to prison for three weeks hard labour. When he came out, he believed his contract to be at an end and refused to work for U., claiming his tools. He was charged a second time under one of the Master and Servant Acts.*

BLACKBURN, J.: This act was, no doubt, passed for the protection and assistance of masters against their workmen. It has been said that it was a one-sided piece of legislation, but we have only to do with its meaning. If it be a one-sided piece of legislation, the best thing we can do is to enforce the observation of it, in order that its defects may be made notorious....Now, the first question with regard to these words is, has the respondent 'absented himself' within the meaning of the section?.... We have to say whether this second refusal was an 'absenting himself' within the meaning of the statute. It seems to me that it was. The contract, which was a contract to serve for two years,

* These Acts, revised in 1867, were finally repealed by s. 17, Conspiracy and Protection of Property Act, 1875. That put an end to the general criminal sanction against breach of the employment contract as such, and left only exceptions such as those in ss. 4 and 5 of the 1875 Act, *post* p. 383.

had not been performed; and the respondent refuses to work, and stays away when it is still in force. It has been contended on his behalf that the contract having been once broken was rescinded, and that his obligation to serve was at an end, so that he could not be imprisoned a second time. But in all the cases that I can remember, a breach of a contract, accompanied by a declaration of an intention not to complete it, was held to give an option to the person injured, if he pleased, to rescind, but to give no rights to the wrong-doer.... I have no hesitation in saying that the respondent has absented himself without lawful excuse within the meaning of the statute.

MELLOR and SHEE, J.J., delivered concurring judgments.

SKINNER v. KITCH

(1867) L.R. 2 Q.B. 393

The secretary to a branch lodge of a carpenter's union served K, a master builder, with a notice which said: 'I am requested by the committee...to give the men in your employ notice to come out on strike against (a fellow employee) unless he become a member of the society'. He was charged with and convicted of having endeavoured by threats to force K. to limit the description of his workmen contrary to 6 Geo. 4, c. 129, s. 3 (Combination Act, 1925).

BLACKBURN, J.: The principal object of the statute was to protect both masters and workmen from all dictation as to whom they will employ or serve; and a greater piece of tyranny cannot well be conceived than to force the respondent, by the threat of striking, to consent to punish Jordan, by discharging him, unless he will join the union, nor a more proper case for a conviction. I do not want any authority for my opinion; but the question, in effect, has been decided already by the cases of *Walsby* v. *Anley*,[1] and *Shelbourne* v. *Oliver*,[2] in both of which the endeavour was to prevent the employment of men who were obnoxious to the union simply for not conforming to their rules.

LUSH, J.: I cannot conceive that the legislature could have used more apt words to designate what they meant to prevent, than by saying it shall be unlawful by intimidation to force a master to limit the description of his workmen, when they meant to prevent the unlawful combining of a union of workmen for the purpose of coercing an employer to employ only the members of their club.

SHEE, J., delivered a concurring judgment.

[1] 30 L.J. (M.C.) 121; 3 E. & E. 516.   [2] 13 L.T. (N.S.) 630.

SPRINGHEAD SPINNING COMPANY *v.* RILEY

(1868) L.R. 6 Eq. 551

Workmen withdrew their labour after their wages were cut. Their union circulated placards 'blacking' the employers until the dispute was settled. The employers sought an injunction to restrain the union from doing this (a remedy available to them if this was a civil wrong, whether or not it was a crime). The injunction was granted.*

MALINS, V.C.: The jurisdiction of this Court is to protect property, and it will interfere by injunction to stay any proceedings, whether connected with crime or not, which go to the immediate, or tend to the ultimate, destruction of property, or to make it less valuable or comfortable for use or occupation.... It is distinctly charged by this bill, and it is consequently admitted by the demurrers, that the acts of the Defendants which are complained of do tend to the immediate destruction of the value of the Plaintiffs' property. The 30th and 31st paragraphs of the bill go distinctly to this point, and in the 17th paragraph it is stated that these placards and advertisements are, in fact, part of a scheme of the Defendants whereby they, by threats and intimidation, prevent persons from hiring themselves to or accepting work from the Plaintiffs. If the Defendants *Riley* and *Butterworth* had carried on a manufactory in the neighbourhood of the Plaintiffs' works, and had by any process poured noxious vapours into the Plaintiffs' mill to such an extent as to render it impossible for them to procure workmen to carry on their operations, that would have been a nuisance tending to the destruction of the Plaintiffs' property which this Court would have restrained by injunction...

In the present case, the acts complained of are illegal and criminal by the Act of Geo. 4, and it is admitted by the demurrers that they were designedly done as part of a scheme, by threats and intimidation, to prevent persons from accepting work from the Plaintiffs, and, as a consequence, to destroy the value of the Plaintiffs' property. It is, in my opinion, within the jurisdiction of this Court to prevent such or any other mode of destroying property, and the demurrers must, therefore, be overruled... In the meantime I would only make this

---

* Doubts were later expressed whether an injunction was a proper remedy in such circumstances: *Prudential Assurance Ltd* v.*Knott* (1875) 10 Ch. App. 142. But when 'labour injunctions' came to be used more freely twenty years later, such procedural objections met short shift: *Collard* v. *Marshall* [1892] 1 Ch. 571, *Lyons* v. *Wilkins* (*post*, p. 424). See A. W. J. Thompson in (1966) 19 Industrial and Labour Relations Review 213.

observation, that by the Act of Parliament it is recited that all such proceedings are injurious to trade and commerce, and dangerous to the security and personal freedom of individual workmen, as well as the security of the property and persons of the public at large; and if it should turn out that this Court has jurisdiction to prevent these misguided and misled workmen from committing these acts of intimidation, which go to the destruction of that property which is the source of their own support and comfort in life, I can only say that it will be one of the most beneficial jurisdictions that this Court ever exercised.

R. *v.* DRUITT

(1867) 10 Cox C.C. 592

Workmen employed by master tailors, went on strike for more wages. Their employers then took on non-union men; and a picket was established to deter the non-unionists from continuing in this work. No violence was used. Proof only of insulting expressions and gestures was led. Phrases such as 'Is he not a dung?' and 'That's him' were used. Counsel for the defence said 'It was all very well to say that their conduct had been the means of frightening individuals, but where was one that had been so terrified.... There was not even a suggestion of loss of custom'. They were indicted for a conspiracy.

BRAMWELL, B., said to the jury: The public had an interest in the way in which a man disposed of his industry and his capital; and if two or more persons conspired by threats, intimidation, or molestation to deter or influence him in the way in which he should employ his industry, his talents, or his capital, they would be guilty of a criminal offence. That was the common law of the land, and it had been in his opinion re-enacted by an act of Parliament, passed in the 6th year of the reign of George IV, which provided in effect that any person who should by threats, intimidation, molestation, or any other way obstruct, force, or endeavour to force, any journeyman to depart from his hiring, or prevent any journeyman from hiring, should be guilty of an offence. That act was passed forty-one years ago, and by a statute of 1859 it was enacted that no workman merely by reason of his endeavouring peaceably and in a reasonable manner, and without threat or intimidation, direct or indirect, to persuade others from working or ceasing to work should be guilty of an offence under the former act of Parliament.... He was of opinion that if picketing could be done in a way which excited no reasonable alarm, or did not coerce or annoy those who were the subjects of it, it would be no offence in law. It was perfectly lawful to endeavour to persuade persons who had not hitherto acted with them to do so, provided that persuasion did not take the shape of compulsion or coercion. What was the object of this picketing? Was it that the names and addresses of the non-striking workmen might be found out, with the view to their being addressed by reasonable argument and persuasion; or was it for the purpose of coercion and intimidation? Even if the jury should be of opinion that the picket did nothing more than his duty as a picket, and if that duty did not extend to abusive language and gestures such as had been described, still, if that was calculated to have a deterring effect on the minds of ordinary persons, by exposing them to have their motions watched, and to encounter black looks, that would not be permitted by the law of the land.

R. *v.* BUNN

(1872) 12 Cox C.C. 316

The employees of a Gas Company threatened to withdraw their labour without notice and in breach of contract, when a fellow employee was dismissed for trade union activity.

They were indicted for conspiracy to coerce; and convicted.

BRETT, J. said to the jury: I tell you that the mere fact of these men being members of a trade-union is not illegal and ought not be pressed against them in the least. The mere fact of their leaving their work— although they were bound by contract, and although they broke their contract—I say the mere fact of their leaving their work and breaking their contract—is not a sufficient ground for you to find them guilty upon this indictment. This would be of no consequence of itself, but only as evidence of something else. But if there was an agreement among the defendants by improper molestation to control the will of the employers, then I tell you that that would be an illegal conspiracy at common law, and that such an offence is not abrogated by the Criminal Law Amendment Act,* which you have heard referred to. This is a charge of conspiracy at common law, and if you think that there was an agreement and combination between the defendants, or some of them, and others, to interfere with the masters by molesting them, so as to control their will; and if you think that the molestation which was so agreed upon was such as would be likely, in the minds of men of ordinary nerve, to deter them from carrying on their business

* 1871. See note on the statutes *post*, p. 384.

according to their own will, then I say that is an illegal conspiracy, for which these defendants are liable. That, gentlemen, is as to the first set of counts. But this conspiracy is charged in another form, and in that other form the real charge is that they either agreed to do an unlawful act, or to do a lawful act by unlawful means; and it seems to me more naturally to fall under the latter class. I shall, therefore, ask you whether there was an agreement or combination between the defendants and others to hinder and prevent the company from carrying on and exercising their business, by means of the men simultaneously breaking the contracts of service which they had entered into with the company. And I tell you that the breach without just cause of such contracts as have been proved in this case is an illegal act by the servant who does it. It is an illegal act, and what is more, it is a criminal act— that is to say, it is an act which makes each of them liable to the criminal law—and therefore if they did agree to interfere with the exercise of their employers' business by simultaneously breaking such contracts— even if you were to suppose that to interfere with the exercise of their employers' business was a lawful thing for them to do—yet if they agreed and combined to do that lawful act by the unlawful means of simultaneously breaking all these contracts, they were then agreeing to do that which may be assumed to be a lawful act by unlawful means, and that would bring them within the definition of a conspiracy.... Then, do you think that was done by an improper threat or molestation? And in order to arrive at this, I tell you there would be an improper molestation if anything was done with an improper intent which you think was an unjustifiable annoyance and interference with the masters in the conduct of their business, and which in any business would be such annoyance and interference as would be likely to have a deterring effect upon masters of ordinary nerve. Therefore, do you think that the defendants agreed to force their masters to carry on their business in a manner against their will by improper molestation—that is to say, by annoyance or interference which in your minds was so unfair as to be unjustifiable, and which would in your judgments deter masters of ordinary nerve from carrying on their business as they desire, such molestation being of this kind: 'Inasmuch as we know you are a gas company lighting a great part of the metropolis, we suggest to you this—Suppose we all leave work at the same moment; if we do, you cannot carry on your business; you must then throw every district into darkness. You dare not do that against your customers and against the public, and therefore you must yield to what we demand'.

R. *v.* HIBBERT

(1875) 13 Cox C.C. 82*

A firm of cabinet makers informed their employees that instead of being paid by the hour for their work they would be paid for piecework at 'living prices'. The men went on strike; and a picket was set up for five weeks, patrolling outside the factory talking to everyone who came to the factory to apply for work. The defendants were charged with conspiracy to molest and obstruct workmen and masters with a view to inducing them respectively to quit their employment and to change their mode of business. (This case came after the repeal of the 1859 Act and after the enactment of the 1871 Act. There was no statutory enactment in force which expressly 'legalized' peaceful picketing: see *post*, p. 384, note.)

The men were convicted.

CLEASBY, B.: It has been contended on behalf of the defendants that the prosecution have not satisfactorily established the intention of the defendants to coerce. This is not a point upon which I can reserve a case, as I think it is your duty to determine where persuasion ends and coercion begins. Coercion might either be effected by physical force or by the operation of fear upon the mind. It is possible that there might be such a molestation by watching and besetting premises as might be expected to and would operate upon the mind so as to take away liberty of will, by giving rise to a fear of violence by threats, or to some apprehension of loss or ruin, or to feelings of annoyance. Picketing, that is the watching and speaking to the workmen, as they come and go from their employment, to induce them to leave their service, is not necessarily unlawful; nor is it unlawful to use terms of persuasion towards them to accomplish that object; but if the watching and besetting is carried on to such a length and to such an extent that it occasions a dread of loss, it would be unlawful.

CONSPIRACY, AND PROTECTION OF PROPERTY ACT, 1875

3. An agreement or combination by two or more persons to do or procure to be done any act in contemplation or furtherance of a trade dispute...shall not be indictable as a conspiracy if such act committed by one person would not be punishable as a crime.

* The Recorder's charge to the jury in this case can be found at [1899] 1 Ch. p. 262 n.

Nothing in this section shall exempt from punishment any persons guilty of a conspiracy for which a punishment is awarded by any Act of Parliament.

Nothing in this section shall affect the law relating to riot, unlawful assembly, breach of the peace, or sedition, or any offence against the State or the Sovereign.

A crime for the purposes of this section means an offence punishable on indictment, or an offence which is punishable on summary conviction, and for the commission of which the offender is liable under the statute making the offence punishable to be imprisoned either absolutely or at the discretion of the court as an alternative for some other punishment...

4. Where a person employed by a municipal authority or by any company or contractor upon whom is imposed by Act of Parliament the duty, or who have otherwise assumed the duty of supplying any city borough town or place, or any part thereof, with gas or water,* wilfully and maliciously breaks a contract of service with that authority or company or contractor, knowing or having reasonable cause to believe that the probable consequences of his so doing, either alone or in combination with others, will be to deprive the inhabitants of that city, borough, town, place, or part, wholly or to a great extent of their supply of gas or water, he shall on conviction thereof by a court of summary jurisdiction, or on indictment as herein-after mentioned, be liable either to pay a penalty not exceeding twenty pounds or to be imprisoned for a term not exceeding three months, with or without hard labour.

Every such municipal authority, company, or contractor as is mentioned in this section shall cause to be posted up, at the gasworks or waterworks, as the case may be, belonging to such authority or company or contractor, a printed copy of this section in some conspicuous place where the same may be conveniently read by the persons employed, and as often as such copy becomes defaced obliterated or destroyed, shall cause it to be renewed with all reasonable despatch...

5. Where any person wilfully and maliciously breaks a contract of service or of hiring, knowing or having reasonable cause to believe that the probable consequences of his so doing, either alone or in combination with others, will be to endanger human life, or cause serious bodily injury, or to expose valuable property whether real or personal to destruction or serious injury, he shall on conviction thereof by a

* And now electricity since the Elecricity Supply Act 1919, s. 31.

court of summary jurisdiction, or on indictment as herein-after mentioned, be liable either to pay a penalty not exceeding twenty pounds, or to be imprisoned for a term not exceeding three months, with or without hard labour...

7. Every person who, with a view to compel any other person to abstain from doing or to do any act which such other person has a legal right to do or abstain from doing, wrongfully and without legal authority,

(1) Uses violence to or intimidates such other person or his wife or children, or injures his property; or,

(2) Persistently follows such other person about from place to place; or

(3) Hides any tools, clothes, or other property owned or used by such other person, or deprives him of or hinders him in the use thereof; or

(4) Watches or besets the house or other place where such other person resides, or works, or carries on business, or happens to be, or the approach to such house or place; or,

(5) Follows such other person with two or more other persons in a disorderly manner in or through any street or road,

shall, on conviction thereof by a court of summary jurisdiction, or on indictment as herein-after mentioned, be liable either to pay a penalty not exceeding twenty pounds, or to be imprisoned for a term not exceeding three months, with or without hard labour...*

---

* *Note*: the section as enacted contained the following additional words: *Attending at or near the house or place where a person resides, or works, or carries on business, or happens to be, or the approach to such house or place, in order merely to obtain or communicate information, shall not be deemed a watching or besetting within the meaning of this section.*

These were replaced in 1906 by the modern protection for peaceful picketing, s. 2 Trades Disputes Act, 1906, *post*, p. 385.

In assessing the earlier cases the reader must have in mind the exact state of the statute law. Between 1875 and 1906, the above formula was in operation and it was this that was interpreted in *Lyons* v. *Wilkins* (*post*, p. 424). Between 1871 and 1875, certain provisions of the Criminal Law Amendment Act 1871, s. 1, held the field; but they were largely ineffective after the decision in *Bunn* (*ante*, p. 380). Between 1859 and 1871, the Molestation of Workmen Act, 1859, operated, providing: That no Workman or other Person, whether actually in Employment or not, shall, by reason merely of his entering into an Agreement with any Workman or Workmen, or other Persons or Persons, for the Purpose of fixing or endeavouring to fix the Rate of Wages or Remuneration at which they or any of them shall work, or by reason merely of his endeavouring peaceably, and in a reasonable Manner, and without Threat or Intimidation, direct or indirect, to persuade others to cease or abstain from Work, in order to obtain the Rate of Wages or the altered Hours of Labour so fixed or agreed upon or to be agreed upon, shall be deemed or taken to be guilty of 'Molestation' or 'Obstruction', within the Meaning of the said Act, and shall not therefore be subject or liable to any

TRADE DISPUTES ACT 1906

1. The following paragraph shall be added as a new paragraph after the first paragraph of s. 3 of the Conspiracy and Protection of Property Act, 1875:

'An act done in pursuance of an agreement or combination by two or more persons shall, if done in contemplation or furtherance of a trade dispute, not be actionable unless the act, if done without any such agreement or combination, would be actionable.'

2. (1) It shall be lawful for one or more persons, acting on their own behalf or on behalf of a trade union or of an individual employer or firm in contemplation or furtherance of a trade dispute, to attend at or near a house or place where a person resides or works or carries on business or happens to be, if they so attend merely for the purpose of peacefully obtaining or communicating information, or of peacefully persuading any person to work or abstain from working.

(2) Section seven of the Conspiracy and Protection of Property Act, 1875, is hereby repealed from 'attending at or near' to the end of the section.

3. An act done by a person in contemplation or furtherance of a trade dispute shall not be actionable on the ground only that it induces some other person to break a contract of employment or that it is an interference with the trade, business, or employment of some other person, or with the right of some other person to dispose of his capital or his labour as he wills.

4. (1) An action against a trade union, whether of workmen or masters, or against any members or officials thereof on behalf of themselves and all other members of the trade union in respect of any tortious act alleged to have been committed by or on behalf of the trade union, shall not be entertained by any court.

(2) Nothing in this section shall affect the liability of the trustees of a trade union to be sued in the events provided for by the Trades Union Act, 1871, s. 9, except in respect of any tortious act committed by or on behalf of the union in contemplation or in furtherance of a trade dispute.[*]

Prosecution or Indictment for Conspiracy: Provided always, that nothing herein contained shall authorise any Workman to break or depart from any Contract or authorize any Attempt to induce any Workman to break or depart from any Contract.

But its provisions were largely sidestepped by judicial interpretations of the crimes of 'molestation', 'intimidation' and the like under the Combination Act, 1825, s. 3: see, for example, *ante*, p. 375 and p. 377.

[*] For s. 9, Trade Union Act, 1871, see *post*, p. 540.

5. (1) This Act may be cited as the Trade Disputes Act, 1906, and the Trade Unions Acts, 1871 and 1876, and this Act may be cited together as the Trade Unions Acts, 1871 to 1906.

(2) In this Act the expression 'trade union' has the same meaning as in the Trade Union Acts, 1871 and 1876, and shall include any combination as therein defined, notwithstanding that such combination may be the branch of a trade union.

(3) In this Act and in the Conspiracy and Protection of Property Act, 1875, the expression 'trade dispute' means any dispute between employers and workmen, or between workmen and workmen, which is connected with the employment or non-employment, or the terms of the employment, or with the conditions of labour, of any person, and the expression 'workmen' means all persons employed in trade or industry, whether or not in the employment of the employer with whom a trade dispute arises....

TRADE DISPUTES ACT, 1965

[See *post*, p. 520]

PRICES AND INCOMES ACT, 1966

[For s. 16(4) and (5), see *ante*, p. 261. Both s. 16 and s. 17 apply to Part IV of the Act as well as to Part II: s. 28(4) (6). Furthermore, after Part IV was activated, they applied even though Part II had not itself been activated by Order: s. 25(9).]

17. The expression 'trade dispute' as defined by s. 5(3) of the Trade Disputes Act, 1906 shall include any dispute between employers and workmen, or between workmen and workmen, which is connected with the restrictions imposed by this Part of this Act, and 'dispute' shall include any difference of opinion as to the manner in which account is to be taken of the provisions of this Part of this Act.

THE EMERGENCY POWERS ACT, 1920

1. *Issue of proclamations of emergency.* (1) If at any time it appears to His Majesty that any action has been taken or is immediately threatened by any persons or body of persons of such a nature and on so extensive a scale as to be calculated, by interfering with the supply and distribution of food, water, fuel, or light, or with the means of locomotion, to deprive the community, or any substantial portion of the

community, of the essentials of life, His Majesty may, by proclamation (hereinafter referred to as a proclamation of emergency), declare that a state of emergency exists.

No such proclamation shall be in force for more than one month, without prejudice to the issue of another proclamation at or before the end of that period.

(2) Where a proclamation of emergency has been made the occasion thereof shall forthwith be communicated to Parliament, and, if Parliament is then separated by such adjournment or prorogation as will not expire within five days, a proclamation shall be issued for the meeting of Parliament within five days, and Parliament shall accordingly meet and sit upon the day appointed by that proclamation, and shall continue to sit and act in like manner as if it had stood adjourned or prorogued to the same day.

2. *Emergency regulations.* (1) Where a proclamation of emergency has been made, and so long as the proclamation is in force, it shall be lawful for His Majesty in Council, by Order, to make regulations for securing the essentials of life to the community, and those regulations may confer or impose on a Secretary of State or other Government department, or any other persons in His Majesty's service or acting on His Majesty's behalf, such powers and duties as His Majesty may deem necessary for the preservation of the peace, for securing and regulating the supply and distribution of food, fuel, light, and other necessities, for maintaining the means of transit or locomotion, and for any other purposes essential to the public safety and the life of the community, and may make such provisions incidental to the powers aforesaid as may appear to His Majesty to be required for making the exercise of those powers effective:

Provided that nothing in this Act shall be construed to authorise the making of any regulations imposing any form of compulsory military service or industrial conscription:

Provided also that no such regulation shall make it an offence for any person or persons to take part in a strike, or peacefully to persuade any other person or persons to take part in a strike.

(2) Any regulations so made shall be laid before Parliament as soon as may be after they are made, and shall not continue in force after the expiration of seven days from the time when they are so laid unless a resolution is passed by both Houses providing for the continuance thereof.

THE EMERGENCY POWERS ACT, 1964

1. *Amendment of s.* 1(1) *of Emergency Powers Act,* 1920. In s. 1(1) of the Emergency Powers Act 1920 (by virtue of which Her Majesty may by proclamation declare that a state of emergency exists if at any time it appears to Her that any action has been taken or is immediately threatened by any persons or body of persons of such a nature and on so extensive a scale as to be calculated, by interfering with the supply and distribution of food, water, fuel or light, or with the means of locomotion, to deprive the community, or any substantial portion of the community, of the essentials of life), for the words from 'any action' to 'so extensive a scale' there shall be substituted the words 'there have occurred, or are about to occur, events of such a nature'.

SECTION B

THE 'GOLDEN FORMULA' IN TRADE DISPUTES

(i) THE COURTS AND S. 5(3) (*ante*, p. 386)

LARKIN *v.* LONG

House of Lords   [1915] A.C. 814

All the stevedores in Dublin, except the plaintiff, joined together to form the 'Stevedores' Association' whose aim was to obtain higher rates from the shipowners. This was supported by the Irish Transport Union (I.T.U.) who with a view to improving the conditions of employment of its members, undertook that none of its men would work for stevedores who did not join the association. The plaintiff refused to join and in consequence the I.T.U. brought out its men on strike. In an action against officials of both organisations, the question arose whether this was a trade dispute.

LORD ATKINSON: It was plain upon the evidence that the only dispute which existed was a dispute between the members of the Stevedores' Association and the plaintiff. The Association sought to force the plaintiff to enter its ranks in order that he might thereby be compelled to adopt the scale of remuneration for any dock labourers he might employ which this Association had adopted. Larkin, Hopkins, and Redmond, at the request of the Association, came to their aid, and sought to bring pressure to bear upon the plaintiff to force him to enter it, by refusing to permit the dock labourers who were members of the Transport Union to work for him.

But these officers of the union of employees by so aiding the association of employers in its contest with the plaintiff, another employer, did not change the character of the original dispute. It was from the first a dispute between an individual stevedore and an association of stevedores.

The Trade Disputes Act of 1906 has no application to such disputes. It only deals with disputes between employers and workmen and workmen and workmen. This dispute was neither of these. This defence, therefore, wholly fails.

LORDS DUNEDIN, PARKER OF WADDINGTON, SUMNER and PARMOOR delivered concurring speeches; VISCOUNT HALDANE, L.C. agreed with the speech of LORD ATKINSON.

BRIMELOW *v.* CASSON

[1924] 1 Ch. 302

The plaintiff—Jack Arnold of the King Wu Tut Tut Revue—ran a travelling theatrical company. Five theatrical trade unions combined together to deal with 'any bogus person engaged in the industry'. The plaintiff paid his chorus girls so little that in many cases they were driven to prostitution; one for instance, aged eighteen, 'was living in immorality with another member of the company, a tiny, deformed creature, a dwarf...She had not enough money to live on'. The five unions instructed the defendants to induce theatre owners to break their contracts with the plaintiff.

RUSSELL, J.: That they would have the sympathy and support of decent men and women I can have no doubt. But have they in law justification for those acts? As has been pointed out, no general rule can be laid down as a general guide in such cases, but I confess that if justification does not exist here I can hardly conceive the case in which it would be present. These defendants, as it seems to me, owed a duty to their calling and to its members, and, I am tempted to add, to the public, to take all necessary peaceful steps to terminate the payment of this insufficient wage, which in the plaintiff's company had apparently been in fact productive of those results which their past experience had led them to anticipate. 'The good sense' of this tribunal leads me to decide that in the circumstances of the present case justification did exist....This decision renders it unnecessary to consider the defence raised by them under s. 3 of the Trade Disputes Act, 1906, but in case the opinion of a higher Court is sought, it may be convenient to indicate shortly my views thereon. The plaintiff urged various points against this defence. He said that the case of actors was not within the section at all, because by the definition section the words 'trade dispute' mean a dispute in which workmen are concerned, that is, 'persons employed in trade or industry', and that acting is neither a trade nor an industry. This appears to me a narrow view of the section. There is no definition of 'trade or industry' in the Act, but it seems to me that the business of presenting histrionic performances to the public for profit may fairly be described as a trade or industry in which many persons, including actors, are employed. It was further said that there was no trade dispute in fact. I do not agree. There was a dispute between the Actors' Association and the plaintiff upon the question that the plaintiff was employing actors at wages below the minimum wage.

NATIONAL ASSOCIATION OF LOCAL GOVERN-
MENT OFFICERS v. BOLTON CORPORATION

House of Lords   [1943] A.C. 166

A dispute arose between the plaintiff union and the defendant corporation as to whether it should be a condition of the employment of local government officers that the Corporation should, under a power given to it by an Act of 1939, make up the difference between the civil pay and military service pay of officers who left to undertake war service. The question arose whether this was a 'trade dispute' under a war-time arbitration Order (1305) which used the same definition of 'trade dispute' as the 1906 Act (with the addition of the words 'or difference') and the same definition of 'workman' as the Industrial Courts Act 1919, (ante, p. 30 and p. 247).

VISCOUNT SIMON, L.C.: First, as to the meaning of 'trade dispute' in this connexion. Having regard to its definition for present purposes, and to the wide definition of 'workman' which has to be read into it in order to ascertain its ambit, I think that the phrase can cover a dispute as to conditions of service of officers of a municipal corporation. Mr Turner strenuously argued that such an interpretation gives no effect to the limiting word 'trade'. The answer is that the definition of 'trade dispute' introduces no such limitation. It does not speak of disputes or differences connected with the employment or non-employment of persons 'in trade' or 'in trade or industry', but deliberately omits such limitation, though the limitation is to be found in the definition of 'workman' in the Trade Disputes Act, 1906. If there can be a 'trade' union to which the higher grades of officers of a municipal corporation can belong, it does not seem an impossible use of language to say that a dispute concerning their conditions of service may be a 'trade' dispute. It was further urged on this point that administrative, professional and technical officials of the respondents are not 'workmen'. In the ordinary sense, they are not, but here again the definition provides the answer. They are, in my opinion, persons who have entered into contracts with the respondents 'whether the contract be by way of manual labour, clerical work, or otherwise'.

LORD WRIGHT: These definitions are identical with, and, in my opinion, have the same meaning as, the definitions contained in the Industrial Courts Act, 1919. The appellants contended that they include the members of the appellant trade union. The respondents disputed this because, they said, the definitions do not include employees of a public or local authority like the respondents, and, in particular, such employees who are engaged in professional, technical or administrative services. In my opinion, the respondents' contention would unduly narrow and limit the wide connotation which should here be given to 'trade' and to 'workman'. Section 11 of the Act of 1919 shows that 'trade' is used as including 'industry' because it refers to a trade dispute in the industry of agriculture. The same inference appears from the short title. It is described as an Act to provide for the establishment of an industrial court in connexion with trade disputes. Trade and industry are thus treated as interchangeable terms. Indeed, 'trade' is not only in the etymological or dictionary sense, but in legal usage, a term of the widest scope. It is connected originally with the word 'tread' and indicates a way of life or an occupation. In ordinary usage it may mean the occupation of a small shopkeeper equally with that of a commercial magnate. It may also mean a skilled craft. It is true that it is often used in contrast with a profession. A professional worker would not ordinarily be called a tradesman, but the word 'trade' is used in the widest application in the appellation 'trade unions'. Professions have their trade unions. It is also used in the Trade Boards Act to include industrial undertakings. I see no reason to exclude from the operation of the Industrial Courts Act the activities of local authorities, even without taking into account the fact that these authorities now carry on in most cases important industrial undertakings. The order expressly states in its definition section that "'trade or industry" includes the performance of its functions by a public local authority'. It is true that these words are used in Part III, which deals with 'recognized terms and conditions of employment', and in Part IV, which deals with 'departures from trade practices' in 'any industry or undertaking', and not in Part I, which deals with 'national arbitration' and is the part material in this case, but I take them as illustrating what modern conditions involve—the idea that the functions of local authorities may come under the expression 'trade or industry'. I think the same may be said of the Industrial Courts Act and of reg. 58 AA, in both of which the word 'trade' is used in the very wide connotation which it bears in the modern legislation dealing with conditions of employment, particularly in relation to matters of collective bargaining and the like.

I think, therefore, that the appellants are right in their construction of the word 'trade' as used in the order. I also think that they are right in their construction of the word 'workman', which they contend, as used in the order and in the Industrial Courts Act, includes professional, technical and administrative workers, as well as manual or clerical workers. From another point of view it may be said that every person who seeks to dispose of his services is a trader in that respect.…

It would be strangely out of date to hold, as was argued, that a trade union cannot act on behalf of its members in a trade dispute, or that a difference between a trade union acting for its members and their employer cannot be a trade dispute.*

LORDS ATKIN, PORTER and THANKERTON delivered concurring speeches, the last however dubitante on the correct interpretation of 'trade dispute'.

BRITISH AND IRISH STEAMPACKET CO. LTD *v.*
BRANIGAN

High Court of Ireland   [1958] I.R. 128

A dispute arose between the Commissioners for Carlingford Lough and a union about the employment by the Commissioners of a man to whose qualifications the union objected. The defendant members of the unions' executive committee blacked the plaintiff's ship which was due

---

* This point of agency was really settled in *White* v. *Riley*, 1921, *post*, p. 470. On the question of 'workmen' see Goddard, L.C.J. construing the 1951 Order in *R.* v. *Industrial Disputes Tribunal, Ex parte East Anglian Trustee Savings Bank* [1954] 2 All E.R. 730, where he thought that the business of banking was a 'trade' and therefore a dispute between the bank and its clerks could be a 'trade dispute'.

to discharge its cargo at the Lough. The plaintiff's employees all abandoned service of the ship. The plaintiff company sued for inducing breach of contract and the action succeeded.

DIXON, J.: The scope of the phrase, 'trade or industry', used in the Act of 1906 has never been precisely defined, but, in several cases, there have been *dicta* to the effect that the Act should be given a somewhat strict construction. These *dicta* are referred to, with approval, by Mr Justice Kingsmill Moore in *Smith* v. *Beirne*;[1] and the other members of the majority of the Court in that case adopted a similar approach to the Act. Viewing the Act in the same way, I find it impossible to accept that it could be held to have contemplated, in the phrase used, activities of the kind carried on by the Carlingford Lough Commissioners which consist solely in making and keeping the navigation of the Lough easier and safer. Even in the ordinary use of language, I think it would occur to very few people that such an activity could be characterised a trade or an industry.

It makes no difference to this view of mine that, by s. 9 of the order relating to Carlingford Lough, contained in the Schedule of Orders in the Pier and Harbour Orders Confirmation Act, 1884 (47 and 48 Vict, c. ccxvi), the Commissioners were given power to let on hire their steam or other vessels, matters, and things, mentioned in s. 22 of the Order of 1864. This was merely an extension of the power given in that s. 22 to sell and dispose of various articles and materials which, by the section, they were empowered from time to time to purchase, lease, provide or hire. These were, clearly, merely ancillary and necessary powers to enable the Commissioners to carry out the purposes of the Order and were, in no sense, a main object or activity, either actual or contemplated, of the Commissioners.

In my view, therefore, the Commissioners cannot be regarded as engaged in trade or industry within the meaning of the Trade Disputes Act, 1906, and their employees, accordingly, are not employed in trade or industry and are not, therefore, 'workmen' within the meaning of that Act. One of the necessary parties to a trade dispute is lacking and no 'trade dispute' exists. In *Smith and Another* v. *Beirne and Others* I have already rejected the view that the Union, as such, could supply the place of the missing and essential party, and I adhere to that view.

[1] 89 I.L.T.R. 24 at p. 24.

ROUNDABOUT LTD *v.* BEIRNE

High Court of Ireland   [1959] I.R. 423

The owners of licensed premises whose employees all joined the defendants' union, dismissed the staff, closed the premises and leased them to the plaintiff company, the directors of which were the owners their accountant and their three barmen. The premises re-opened with no person being employed by the directors and the barmen-directors being paid an annual sum.* The defendants were picketing the premises both when they were closed and when they reopened. The plaintiff company successfully sought an injunction.

DIXON, J.: The new company here is not an employer. It is true that it is a potential employer in the sense that it may well in the future be compelled by circumstances to take on staff, but at present it is not, and never has been, an employer in the sense in which that term is used in the Trade Disputes Act, 1906. It is true that the directors of the company do work in the licensed premises, but a distinction must be observed between directors who do work for a company and workmen who are employed by the company. The former cannot be regarded as working in pursuance of any contract of employment, and, therefore, cannot be regarded as workmen of the company. The fact that the company may at some future time be an employer is not sufficient to entitle me to hold that it is at present an employer, so as to entitle the defendants to claim the protection of the Trades Disputes Act, 1906.

The onus of establishing the existence of a trade dispute lies on the persons alleging its existence; in my view no trade dispute has been shown to exist between the plaintiffs, Roundabout Ltd, and the defendants, and accordingly the plaintiffs are entitled to have the interim injunction continued in a more permanent form.

BEETHAM *v.* TRINIDAD CEMENT LTD

Privy Council   [1960] A.C. 132; [1960] I All E.R. 274.

The jurisdiction of a Board of Inquiry set up to inquire into a trade dispute in Trinidad, was challenged on the ground that there was no trade dispute (the definition of which was the same as in s. 5(3) of the 1906 Act with the addition of the words 'or difference' after 'dispute'). A cement company refused absolutely to give any recognition to a trade union which represented two hundred of their three hundred or so men.

* On 'directors' as 'employees' or 'workmen' see *ante*, p. 21.

They dismissed two union employees and ignored all requests of the union to discuss this.* Was there a trade dispute?

LORD DENNING: By definition, a trade dispute exists wherever a 'difference' exists; and a difference can exist long before the parties become locked in combat. It is not necessary that they should have come to blows. It is sufficient that they should be sparring for an opening. And it seems to their Lordships that the parties had reached that point here, even in regard to the claim for bargaining status. The union had applied for bargaining status. The company had ignored the request, just as it had ignored previous requests. The union had sought the mediation of the Commissioner of Labour; but when he came forward, the company rejected his approach out of hand, just as it had rejected his previous approach. 'We have no intention of becoming involved in any way with the union concerned.' When this statement is taken in its setting—with the background of repeated refusal by the company to recognize the union over the two dismissals—the position at 16 April 1956, can be put simply thus: 'Here is this union knocking at the door of the company asking to be let in to negotiate; and the company time and time again refusing to open it, nay more, keeping it locked and barred against the union.' That was clearly a difference between them which subsisted at that very time.

But then it was said that this was not a difference between the company and *the workmen*, as the ordinance requires, but only a difference between the company and *the union*; and attention was drawn to the statement by Bennett, J., that a dispute between such bodies is not a trade dispute: see *R. v. National Arbitration Tribunal, Ex parte Bolton Corpn.*[1] To this their Lordships think that Lord Wright gave a sufficient answer when that case reached the House of Lords. He said:[2] 'It would be strangely out of date to hold, as was argued, that a trade union cannot act on behalf of its members in a trade dispute, or that a difference between a trade union acting for its members and their employer cannot be a trade dispute.' Accepting this statement, however, it was said that, in this case, the trade union was not acting *for its members*, but for itself. The claim for bargaining status was never authorized or approved, so it was said, by any of the members of the branch at Claxton Bay. It was done by the head office acting on its own initiative.

---

[1] [1941] 2 All E.R. 800 at p. 815; [1941] 2 K.B. 405 at p. 421.
[2] [1942] 2 All E.R. 425 at p. 435; [1943] A.C. 166 at p. 189.

* It was made clear by the Privy Council in *Bird* v. *O'Neal* [1960] A.C. 907, that the dismissal of one employee, even if lawful, can be the subject matter of a trade dispute.

And reliance was placed on observations in some of the cases that, if a trade union acts 'on a frolic of its own', there is not a trade dispute: see *R. v. National Arbitration Tribunal, Ex parte Keable Press, Ltd,*[1] *R. v. Industrial Disputes Tribunal, Ex parte Courage & Co., Ltd.*[2] Their Lordships cannot accept this argument. The claim was made by the executive committee who were, by the rules, entrusted with the general management of the union; and it was clearly within the scope of their authority to put forward a claim for bargaining status. If the union were able to obtain bargaining status, it would be able to promote the interest of its members far better than if it were unrecognised. Moreover, the claim had been brought to the attention of the branch who may fairly be assumed to have approved of it. The union can, therefore, properly be considered as acting for its members; and in consequence, the difference was one 'between employers and workmen'.

SHERRIFF *v.* McMULLEN

Irish Supreme Court   [1952] I.R. 236

A dispute arose between the plaintiff, an owner of saw mills, and a union to which the defendants belonged. While the matter was being considered by the Labour Court the plaintiff's employees resigned from the union. Union members who became employed by the plaintiff also resigned. Although the ex-members wrote and said their resignations were voluntary the union blacked the plaintiff's goods. Later two employees rejoined the union. The plaintiff sought an injunction and damages and was successful.

MURNAGHAN, J.: Mr McMullen's letter, dated the 10 June 1949, addressed to the plaintiff is brief, but it contains a vibrant message. It reads: 'We are informed that you have promised your men an increase and constant employment if they leave the Union. If this is true you will pay them for doing nothing as we will not allow our members in any part of the country to handle your products.' I think this letter means, and means only, one thing. It was written with the object of vindicating the Union's alleged right of maintaining its own members free from persuasion by an employer to induce them to leave the Union. The Union in its dealing with the plaintiff did not insist that the plaintiff should employ only Union labour. The Union was satisfied if the plaintiff would raise no objection to his employees joining the Union and only sought for a notice to this effect to be displayed in the

---

[1] [1943] 2 All E.R. 633.   [2] [1956] 3 All E.R. 411.

plaintiff's factory. There may, I think, be occasions on which members of a trade union may have a trade dispute with an employer although no one of the latter's employees is a member of the union; but it is not every dispute with a trade union which is a trade dispute. Was the dispute dealt with in the letter of the 10 June one connected with the employment or non-employment or the terms of employment or with the conditions of labour of any person ? On the evidence at the trial, the plaintiff did not make it a condition of employment that the men should cease to be members of the Union. In order to come within the protection given by the Trade Disputes Act the defendants must prove that a trade dispute did in fact exist—it is not enough to allege the existence of a trade dispute which did not in fact exist.

GAVAN DUFFY, P., delivered a concurring judgment; MAGUIRE, C.J., agreed with the judgment of MURNAGHAN, J.*

GASKELL v. LANCASHIRE AND CHESHIRE MINERS' FEDERATION

Court of Appeal   (1912) 28 T.L.R. 518

The defendant union wanted there to be only one miners' trade union in Lancashire and Cheshire. The three plaintiffs belonged to another trade union. The defendants told the plaintiffs and their employers that unless the three plaintiffs changed to the defendant union (nearly all the men did belong to it) the rest of the men would be called out.

The plaintiffs alleged by their statement of claim that at various times during February and March 1911, the defendants, by Mr Twist or their agents, verbally informed and threatened the plaintiffs that, if they did not resign from the rival association, and voluntarily become members of the Federation, the defendants would compel them to join or would fetch out all the men from the Bamfurlong mines and compel the employers to close them in order to make the plaintiffs join the Federation; that on or about 24 February 1911, the defendants verbally informed the employers by their manager, Mr Stephenson, that if they continued to employ the plaintiffs the executive committee of the Federation had decided to call the men out.

It appeared that the employers had continued to employ the plaintiffs

* The modern Irish cases are not necessarily a good guide to the interpretations of problems concerning trade disputes. In *Educational Co. of Ireland Ltd* v. *Fitzpatrick* [1961] I.R. 345, the Supreme Court went so far as to declare the provisions of the Trade Disputes Act, 1906, void as being repugnant to the Constitution, in so far as the statute protected trade union action (by picketing and the like) aimed at inducing non-union workers to join the union.

and thereupon the Federation gave 14 days' notice to expire on 14 March 1911, terminating the contracts of service in the mines of all members of the Federation. These members comprised all the men employed in the mines except about 40, so that the result of this action by the Federation would have been to close down the mines. This notice was subsequently postponed for a time, but matters came to a head on 22 March 1911, and the defendants definitely informed the employers that, unless the plaintiffs were at once withdrawn from employment, the rest of the men would be called out. Thereupon the employers suspended the plaintiffs from further work, and subsequently discharged them.

COZENS HARDY, M.R. said that the action had been brought by the plaintiffs against the Miners' Federation of Lancashire and Cheshire and two individuals seeking relief in respect of acts said to have been done by the Federation and by the individuals, of whom only one was now left, Mr Twist, the action against Mr Ashton having been abandoned. Two points had been raised which presented no difficulty whatever, and there was a third point which was more deserving of consideration.

The plaintiffs were non-union men engaged at the Bamfurlong Collieries, which employed a considerable number of men, the majority of whom were union men. They were anxious to get all the men engaged at the collieries into the union. A ballot was taken and there was a large majority in favour of a strike unless the non-union men either came into the union or were got rid of. The Bamfurlong union was a branch of the Federation, and in accordance with the rules the men would not get strike pay unless they got the sanction of the Federation to the action which the branch proposed to take. The first point that had been taken was that there was no trade dispute. No trade dispute when the whole substance of the thing was whether non-union men should be employed at the colliery! His Lordship thought this came as plainly as possible within the definition of trade dispute contained in the Trade Disputes Act, 1906, and he felt not the slightest doubt that there was in this case a trade dispute and that the Act applied.

FARWELL and KENNEDY, L.JJ., delivered concurring judgments.

HODGES *v*. WEBB

[1920] 2 Ch. 70

The defendant trade unionists, members of the Electrical Trade Union, were in dispute with their employers as to whether the plaintiff, whom they regarded as a non-unionist though he belonged to the National

Association of Supervising Electricians, should continue to be employed alongside them.

PETERSON, J.: But it is said that in this case there was no trade dispute within the meaning of the Act, and that this was a quarrel between two Unions, and that the decision in *Valentine* v. *Hyde*[1] compels me to hold that the defendant is not protected by s. 3 of the Trade Disputes Act, 1906....In my view, there was a dispute between the employers, represented by the London section of the National Federated Electrical Association, of which Messrs Tyler & Freeman were members, and the Electrical Trades Union on the question whether non-unionist labour in general and members of the National Association of Supervising Electricians in particular, should be employed in connection with members of the Electrical Trades Union. The workmen by their Union objected to working with members of the National Association of Supervising Electricians, or to the employment of the members of that Association on jobs on which the members of the Union were engaged. The dispute was one which was connected with the employment of members of the Association whom the Union persisted in regarding as in all essentials non-unionists. Whether the Union was right in this view appears to me to be immaterial for the purposes of this case. It is sufficient that it objected to members of the Association being employed on jobs on which members of the Union were engaged. No doubt this attitude involves a contest between the National Association and the Electrical Trades Union, as it necessarily tends to draw men away from the Association. But this consequence does not convert a trade dispute into something which is not a trade dispute. If it did, non-unionists would only have to form themselves into an association in order to prevent the operation of s. 3 of the Act in cases in which the authorized officials of recognized trades unions have called out their members in consequence of the employment of non-unionists. As in my opinion there was a trade dispute between employers and workmen, it is not necessary for me to consider whether there was also a dispute within the meaning of the Trade Disputes Act, 1906, between workmen and workmen which was connected with the employment or non-employment of any person....

'Coercion' is a word of ambiguous import. In one sense, anyone is coerced who under pressure does that which he would prefer not to do; but a reluctant debtor who pays under stress of proceedings is not coerced within the legal meaning of the word....

[1] [1919] 2 Ch. 129.

There remains the question whether the defendant threatened the plaintiff in such a way as to entitle the plaintiff to relief in this action. There are two possible threats on which the plaintiff relies: (a) that before withdrawing the men the defendant told the plaintiff that as the plaintiff refused to join the Electrical Trades Union he would have to call the men off the job, and that they would not return so long as he remained; (b) that after the men had ceased work, the defendant, when the plaintiff refused to join the Union, stated to him that similar trouble would arise on any job on which he was employed. Threats and coercion are not protected by s. 3 of the Trade Disputes Act, 1906: *Conway* v. *Wade*.[1] But what is a threat, and what kind of threat is actionable? We have been instructed on high authority to have regard to the difference between a threat and a warning: *Conway* v. *Wade* and *Santen* v. *Busnach*.[2]...I am not able to see that any great advantage is to be derived from the distinction between a threat and a warning. The question depends on what was said or written, and not on the favourable or unfavourable nature of the epithet by which the words may be described. The question is whether the defendant has employed unlawful means.*

CONWAY v. WADE

House of Lords   [1909] A.C. 506

The defendant told the foreman at the plaintiff's place of work that unless the plaintiff was dismissed the men would come out on strike, which was not true. The defendant did this to punish the plaintiff for not paying an eight-year-old fine or perhaps to deprive him of the position he had been promoted to. The plaintiff lost his job.

LORD LOREBURN, L.C.: 'Trade dispute' is a familiar phrase in earlier Acts of Parliament, and is defined in this Act. I do not know that the definition is of much assistance. If this section is to apply there must be a dispute, however the subject-matter of it be defined. A mere personal quarrel or a grumbling or an agitation will not suffice. It must be something fairly definite and of real substance....

I come now to the meaning of the words 'an act done in contemplation or furtherance of a trade dispute'. These words are not new in an Act of Parliament; they appear in the Conspiracy and Protection of

---

[1] [1909] A.C. 506.
[2] 29 Times L.R. 214 (*post*, p. 501).

* The distinction between 'threats' and 'warnings' or 'information' is long-standing: see, e.g., *Wood* v. *Bowron* (1867) L.R. 2 Q B.21. It is, however, very difficult to apply in practice. See, now, *Rookes* v. *Barnard*, *post*, p. 503.

Property Act, 1875. I think they mean that either a dispute is imminent and the act is done in expectation of and with a view to it, or that the dispute is already existing and the act is done in support of one side to it. In either case the act must be genuinely done as described, and the dispute must be a real thing imminent or existing. I agree with the Master of the Rolls that the section cannot fairly be confined to an act done by a party to the dispute. I do not believe that was intended. A dispute may have arisen, for example, in a single colliery, of which the subject is so important to the whole industry that either employers or workmen may think a general lock-out or a general strike is necessary to gain their point. Few are parties to, but all are interested in, the dispute. If, however, some meddler sought to use the trade dispute as a cloak beneath which to interfere with impunity in other people's work or business, a jury would be entirely justified in saying that what he did was done in contemplation or in furtherance, not of the trade dispute, but of his own designs, sectarian, political, or purely mischievous, as the case might be. These words do, in my opinion, in some sense import motive, and in the case I have put a quite different motive would be present. If the jury so found, the meddler would not be protected by the third section of the Act of 1906. But I have no doubt that an act done with a single eye to the dispute, 'in contemplation or in furtherance' of it, would not be actionable on any of the grounds specified in the section.

LORD ATKINSON: It is impossible to suppose, I think, that the Legislature ever intended that where perfect peace prevailed in any factory or establishment, and an intruder, a mere mischief-maker, actuated by greed, or some feeling of revenge, interfered, and by threats and molestation stirred up strife and disputes which neither employer nor workmen theretofore thought of, he should be made irresponsible because of the very mischief he intended and hoped to stir up.

On this, the true construction, as I think, of the words 'done in furtherance and contemplation of a trade dispute', occurring in the third section of the Act of 1906, borrowed as they are from the Conspiracy and Protection of Property Act, 1875, it would appear to me that there is no inconsistency whatever between the finding of the jury on the first question left to them and their findings on questions 6 and 7.[1] The fact that the defendant, being what he was, interfered in order

---

[1] The jury found (1) that there was no trade dispute existing or contemplated by the men; (6) that what the defendant did was done in order to compel the plaintiff to pay arrears of fine, and (7) in order to punish the plaintiff for not paying the arrears.

to compel the plaintiff to pay the old arrears he owed, and also in order to punish him for not paying them, does not, in my view, at all establish that his interference was an act done 'in contemplation of a trade dispute' within the meaning of the statute.*

LORDS JAMES and SHAW delivered concurring speeches; LORDS MACNAGHTEN and GORELL agreed with the opinion of LORD LOREBURN, L.C.

BENT'S BREWERY CO. LTD v. HOGAN

[See *ante*, p. 104, for the facts]

[1945] 2 All E.R. 570

LYNSKEY, J.: The next question I have to decide is whether the document was sent out by the defendant, or on his behalf, in contemplation or furtherance of a trade dispute. Long and detailed particulars were given by the defendant as to trade disputes alleged to be existing or in contemplation. I do not propose to go through these particulars or the evidence relating to them, as, in my opinion, they do not disclose any dispute either in being or imminent. The document was sent out to managers of brewery companies. No demand has been made for either better conditions or increased wages by any manager to any of the plaintiff brewery companies. No such demands had been made by the defendant, or his union, on behalf of such managers. The defendant in his evidence before me said he sent out the document containing the questionnaire to find out whether there was a trade dispute, and to find out whether the conditions and wages were satisfactory. In my opinion, a dispute cannot exist unless there is a difference of opinion between two parties as to some matter. There is no evidence before me that any dispute existed. The highest that it can be put on the evidence in favour of the defendant is that the document was sent out to obtain information which, after consideration of the information obtained, might lead to a request which, if not granted, might result in a dispute. There was no dispute when the document was sent out which was a real thing, either imminent or existing. There was a possibility of a dispute at some future time, but no certainty that such a dispute would arise. In my view

---

* Note: the true cause of action at common law probably rested on the presence of a fraudulent and deceitful element in the threat. Wade had threatened to bring the men out when he would have had no power to do that. See Lord James' speech at p. 513. Certainly a threat to do acts which were wholly lawful could not have been a tort, and *Allen* v. *Flood* (*post*, p. 497) was expressly argued. This is undoubtedly why Lord Reid referred explicitly to Wade's 'deceitful threat' in *Rookes* v. *Barnard* [1964] A.C. at p. 1176.

there was no dispute at the time this questionnaire was sent and the result is that the protection given by s. 3 of the Act does not help the defendant.

HUNTLEY v. THORNTON

[1957] 1 W.L.R. 321;
[1957] 1 All E.R. 234

The plaintiff's union called a twenty-four hour strike, in which the plaintiff refused to join. He consequently became involved in a number of stormy meetings with the District Committee, from the last of which he walked out shouting 'You are only a shower'. The District Committee recommended his expulsion from the union, but the Executive Council (who alone could do this) refused to sanction it. The District Committee treated him as expelled although he was not, and prevented him from getting jobs. Its members were liable for conspiracy. But two officials who helped to implement the policy were exculpated because, not knowing about the irregularities, they did not 'participate' in the conspiracy to injure, since their predominant motive was to forward union interests.

[It is to be noted that the question whether the defendants were acting 'in furtherance of a trade dispute' is distinct from the different, though similar, question whether their objects were legitimate for the purpose of the common law concerning conspiracy to injure, discussed *post*, p. 443.]

HARMAN, J.: Two questions arise out of this: first, was this a trade dispute; and, secondly, were the actions of the district committee done in furtherance of it?... It was not argued that these acts were 'in contemplation' of a trade dispute, and the plea in the defence that the dispute was as to the 15 per cent increase in wages then being demanded by the union was not persisted in. Further, in my judgment the employers were in no way parties to any dispute. But was it a dispute within the meaning of the Act, and, if so, was it one between workmen and workmen? According to the defendants the contestants were the district committee on the one side and the plaintiff on the other, and the subject whether the plaintiff (a member of the union) should be allowed to earn his living as an engineer in a closed shop in the district. It was contended for the plaintiff that the members of the committee did not act in their capacity as workmen. I feel the force of this point, but on the whole feel bound to reject it. The committee consisted of elected representatives of the workmen in the district who were members of the union. There are a number of cases to show that if the plaintiff had not been a member of the union and his right to work had been contested on that ground, this would have been considered a trade dispute. A more persuasive argument for the plaintiff is that the committee embarked on a policy of embargo entirely unauthorized by the rules of the union, and that they cannot escape the consequences of a wrong which was of their own invention by labelling it a trade dispute. This is to say that there was no 'dispute' at all. It was argued nonetheless for the defendants that the words of the definition clause cover the case: it was a dispute, say they, 'as to the employment of the plaintiff' within the words of the clause.

The plaintiff's contention derives some support from the speeches in *Conway* v. *Wade*....It seems to me that this case does not cover the present, for the question here is not whether sinister motives disentitle the defendants to rely on the Act but whether a trade dispute existed at all....On the whole I have come to the conclusion that this was not a trade dispute. The defendants were not asserting a trade right, for they knew that they could not procure the plaintiff's expulsion from the union. The dispute, if it could be so called, had become an internecine struggle between members of the union and no interests of 'the trade' were involved. It was a personal matter.

Behind these considerations lies a more fundamental point, namely, whether the committee's actions were 'in *furtherance* of a trade dispute'. In my judgment this raises the same question as the issue of conspiracy. If, as I have held, the paramount object of the committee was to injure the plaintiff, then that was the object in furtherance of which they acted. They did not intend to further the dispute arising out of the plaintiff's refusal to strike—that was settled by higher authority; they intended to injure the plaintiff in his trade by their embargo, and it was to that end that their actions were directed. They were not furthering a trade dispute, but a grudge; the Act does not protect them.*

DALLIMORE v. WILLIAMS

Court of Appeal   (1) (1912) 29 T.L.R. 67;
Court of Appeal   (2) (1913) 30 T.L.R. 432

The defendant trade union officials were sued by the plaintiff, D., proprietor and conductor of the Ex-Guards Band, for inducing members of the band to refuse to perform at the agreed rates. He alleged the use of circulars, oral statements, threats of expulsion from the union, the making of false statements, pickets and crowds: he also alleged that it was a sham dispute to vent their malice against himself.

---

* Compare the *dicta* in *Camden Exhibition Ltd* v. *Lynott, ante,* p. 306.

(1) COZENS HARDY, M.R.: Then came the question of the effect of the finding of spite. Counsel for the appellants had not been heard in reply, but his Lordship thought that there was abundant evidence to support the finding of spite. Then came this proposition: If there was a trade dispute, was the case taken outside the protection of the Trade Disputes Act if there was a finding that, though the act complained of was done in furtherance of a trade dispute, the defendant was also influenced by malice? His Lordship could not think it necessary for any person in order to get the protection of the Trade Disputes Act to say that the act done was entirely in furtherance of a trade dispute and that his mind was altogether free from malice. His Lordship could not find that in the Act.

FARWELL and HAMILTON, L.JJ., delivered concurring judgments.

(2) LORD SUMNER: Then, were the acts of which the plaintiff complained done in contemplation or furtherance of a trade dispute? Whatever might have been the motives of the defendants—and he would assume that the jury had found that they were sinister and improper—it was apparent on the plaintiff's own case that the defendants did in fact get up a trade dispute. Except by confusing the motive of an act with the act itself, he was unable to see how it could be said that the acts complained of were not done in contemplation or furtherance of a trade dispute. The argument for the plaintiff involved reading the Act as though it spoke of an act 'honestly' or 'solely' done in contemplation or furtherance of a trade dispute.

KENNEDY, L.J., and BRAY, J., delivered concurring judgments.

STRATFORD & SON LTD v. LINDLEY

[1965] A.C. 269

[See *post*, p. 478. The House of Lords, reversing the Court of Appeal, rejected the view that union defendants had acted in furtherance of a trade dispute. Three strands may be found in this decision: (i) that there was no live 'dispute'; (ii) that it was not 'about' terms of employment and the like (whereas the Act requires 'connection with' them); and (iii) that the element of inter-union rivalry had ousted the other elements to such an extent as to cause the union's action to fall outside s. 5(3).

See Wedderburn (1965) 28 M.L.R. 205.]

NATIONAL SAILORS' AND FIREMEN'S UNION v. REED

[1926] 1 Ch. 536

A government subsidy was withdrawn from the coal industry. As a result the coal owners enforced a wage reduction on the miners. A bitter struggle resulted, in which the T.U.C. called upon all affiliated unions to cease work if required to do so. In the event, nearly two million workers were brought out.

The present case was an application by a union for an injunction to restrain certain branch secretaries from calling a strike in support of the T.U.C.

On the question of whether the 'general strike' was legal, ASTBURY, J., merely said this:* I will endeavour now to state what I apprehend is the law upon this matter. To take the more general ground first, it is evidence that has been filed that members of the plaintiff Union have been placed in a position of doubt and danger, and it is my duty, as I have been requested by the plaintiffs and defendants to do, to state shortly their rights and those of their Union. The so-called general strike called by the Trades Union Congress Council is illegal, and persons inciting or taking part in it are not protected by the Trade Disputes Act, 1906. No trade dispute has been alleged or shown to exist in any of the unions affected, except in the miners' case, and no trade dispute does or can exist between the Trades Union Congress on the one hand and the Government and the nation on the other. The orders of the Trades Union Congress above referred to are therefore unlawful, and the defendants are acting illegally in obeying them, and accordingly (for the reason I shall state under the other head) can be restrained by their own Union from doing so.

* The fault in this argument was analysed well by Goodhart in [1927] 36 Yale Law Jo. 464 (reprinted in his 'Essays in Jurisprudence and the Common Law' chap. XI). The admixture of a 'political' element does not vitiate a trade dispute any more than the presence of 'spite' or inter-union rivalry. If the latter elements become dominant, however, the courts may decide that the connexion with or furtherance of the trade dispute has been lost.

(ii) SOCIAL SECURITY LAW: 'NEUTRALITY' IN TRADE DISPUTES

NATIONAL INSURANCE ACT, 1965

22. *Disqualifications and special conditions.** (1) A person who has lost employment in an employed contributor's employment by reason of a stoppage of work which was due to a trade dispute at his place of employment shall be disqualified for receiving unemployment benefit so long as the stoppage of work continues, except in a case where, during the stoppage of work, he has become bona fide employed elsewhere in the occupation which he usually follows or has become regularly engaged in some other occupation:

Provided that this subsection shall not apply in the case of a person who proves (*a*) that he is not participating in or financing or directly interested in the trade dispute which caused the stoppage of work; and (*b*) that he does not belong to a grade or class of workers of which, immediately before the commencement of the stoppage, there were members employed at his place of employment any of whom are participating in or financing or directly interested in the dispute....

(6)...(*b*) the expression 'trade dispute' means any dispute between employers and employees or between employees and employees which is connected with the employment or non-employment or the terms of employment or the conditions of employment of any persons, whether employees in the employment of the employer with whom the dispute arises or not.

* Identical to its predecessor, s. 13 of the Act of 1946. In addition to the illustrations which follow, many decisions have probed the difficulties of the wording. See e.g.: On stoppage 'due to' a dispute, R(U) 32/57 (sympathetic strike to support dismissed workers); R(U) 1/65 (employer's decision not to re-employ). On 'participating' and 'financing': R(U) 19/55 (claimant who sees other workers on strike goes home without positively presenting himself for work; held to be participating); R(U) 32/53 (one member of the union among the strikers is enough to disqualify all other union members unemployed in consequence). On 'directly interested': R(U) 17/61 (stoppage caused by compulsory pension scheme; claimant interested even though he approved of it and would have paid voluntarily). On 'grade or class': R(U) 32/53 (*supra*); R(U) 17/51 (compositors thrown out of work, of whom only three belonged to union on strike; all in the same grade or class; all disqualified); R(U) 26/53 (electricians not in same grade or class as other workers who might do an unskilled part of their work); R(U) 22/55 (worker temporarily doing unusual work held to be in the grade or class of his normal work).

PUNTON v. MINISTRY OF PENSIONS & NATIONAL INSURANCE (No. 2)

Court of Appeal [1964] 1 W.L.R. 226

This was an appeal against the Commissioner who had decided that the claimant was directly interested in a trade dispute and thus disqualified from benefit. The claimant appealed to the Court of Appeal on an originating summons for a determination whether on the facts the Commissioners' decision was right in law and for a declaration that he was entitled to benefit. The Ministry claimed that the court had no jurisdiction to grant the relief claimed on the basis principally that the National Insurance Act, 1946, made the Commissioner the final arbitrator of law and fact.* The dispute arose from stoppages of work by skilled workers, platers and shipwrights involved in a demarcation dispute in a shipyard where the plaintiffs worked as 'platers' helpers'. They lost their employment for many weeks on account of the stoppages but were disqualified from unemployment benefit.

SELLERS, L.J.: The argument against jurisdiction by way of originating summons for a declaration was further advanced by the submission that the supervisory jurisdiction by use of a declaration can only be used to deal with a decision of an inferior tribunal which is void or a nullity, or made without jurisdiction, or possibly which flows from a contract. Such procedure, it was submitted, cannot be used to deal with the decision of a tribunal acting within its powers and given within those powers even though it might, on investigation, be regarded as erroneous in law because the court would be assuming an appellate jurisdiction not given by statute and which the court cannot give to itself.

It is true that the Court of Queen's Bench has an inherent jurisdiction to control inferior tribunals in a supervisory capacity and to do so by certiorari (which would be the relevant procedure in this case), which enables the court to quash the decision if the inferior court can be shown to have exceeded its jurisdiction or to have erred in law. Neither certiorari nor mandamus usurp the function of a tribunal but require it, having quashed its decision, to hear the case and determine it correctly....

Apart from certiorari there is no machinery for getting rid of the decision of the National Insurance Commissioner and, what is more important, no way of substituting an effective award on which the claims could be paid. It would be out of harmony with all authority to

* See now ss. 67–82 National Insurance Act, 1965.

have two contrary decisions between the same parties on the same issues obtained by different procedures, as it were, on parallel courses which never met or could meet and where the effective decision would remain with the inferior tribunal and not that of the High Court. I conceive that to be the case here and it seems to me to lead to a conclusion against the jurisdiction of the High Court in this particular matter. The tribunal is wholly independent and the Commissioner or a deputy commissioner has to be a barrister or advocate of not less than ten years' standing, and an appeal may be heard if thought desirable by more than one member of the tribunal, and we were told that the tribunal does sometimes sit in banc. It is a statutory judicial tribunal to deal with a special subject-matter where the decisions will frequently be on mixed law and fact and where finality and the minimum of delay are sought to be achieved. There is much to lead to the implication that the jurisdiction of the courts was intended to be excluded and very little to be set against such a conclusion. . . .

I am most reluctant to [express a view of the law] and will go no further than saying, without expressing a final opinion, that the words 'directly interested in the dispute' cannot be improved on or made clearer by using other words in their place. The ultimate decision is one of mixed law and fact and, as at present advised, I would not disagree with the Commissioner when he says: 'Indeed, without the assistance of any authority, I should have come to the conclusion that. . .it cannot possibly be held that any of the claimants or their association have proved that neither they nor any of the other platers' helpers were directly interested in the dispute in question.'

DANCKWERTS, L.J., agreed with the opinion of SELLERS, L.J.,; DAVIES, L.J., delivered a concurring judgment.

R(U) 14/64

A plater's helper lost employment by reason of a stoppage of work which was due to a demarcation dispute between platers and shipwrights at the shipyard where he was employed. The platers' helpers took no part in the dispute, but the amount of work which would in future be available for them depended on the outcome of it.*

The decision of the Commissioner was as follows:

10. On behalf of the claimants it was urged that the dispute was one between the shipwrights and the platers. It was no concern of the platers' helpers. They stood neither to gain nor to lose by it. Whatever the result

* This was the decision which was the subject of *Punton's* case: *ante*, p. 408.

of it was, there would be the same amount of semi-skilled or labouring work to be done by someone. They were members of a general trade union as opposed to a skilled workers' union and there was no difficulty from a union point of view in transferring to the other general union, to which the erectors belonged. Also it was possible for them to remain in their own union doing the same work as labourers helping the ship-wrights. Accordingly it was urged that they had no direct interest in the dispute.

11. I am afraid that I do not feel able to accept these arguments. The evidence shows that on average a platers' helper is paid more than a labourer, and an erector is paid more than either of them and on a different basis. I am not satisfied that transfers were by any means so simple from the employers' point of view.... Further I am fully satisfied that, if the platers' contentions in the dispute had prevailed to the full extent, all the disputed work would have been done by platers and their helpers; whereas if the shipwrights' contentions had prevailed to the full extent, that same work would have been done by shipwrights, with perhaps very minor assistance from others, and no help at all from platers' helpers. The result of the dispute either way would therefore have involved a transfer of work as between platers' helpers and ship-wrights and only to a lesser extent between platers' helpers and erectors....

13. In order to escape disqualification in the present case it is neces-sary for the claimant or his association to prove not merely that none of the platers' helpers were participating in or financing the trade dispute (which is proved) but also that none of them were directly interested in the trade dispute. The question is not whether they were directly interested in the stoppage; no doubt many persons employed in the yard, who became redundant owing to it, were very much interested in the stoppage; but that is not the same thing as being directly interested in the dispute. (This may explain why members of other grades, who also became redundant, were not disqualified.) There are several ways in which a grade can be directly interested in a dispute in which it is not participating, as is illustrated by many wage dispute cases. One example is where one grade is contending for an increase in wages not only on behalf of itself but for all other grades as well. In that event the other grades are directly interested. That is not this case. Another example however is where one grade is contending on behalf of itself, but the result will in the circumstances probably affect other grades (Decision R(U) 3/56, paragraph 8). Counsel contended that in that and some other

cases too strict a test had been applied, and that mere probability was not sufficient. I am not satisfied that this criticism of the decision is justified, but in any event this case goes much further, since I am satisfied that it is quite certain that the amount of work available for platers' helpers must depend on the outcome of this dispute. Counsel also contended that a person was not directly interested unless he knew that he was directly interested, and that Decision R(U) 22/57 was wrongly decided. I am not satisfied that that decision was wrong, but in any event the contention appears to me to break down on the facts. It would not be sufficient for the purposes of this argument if each of the claimants had proved that *he* did not know that he was directly interested. It would be necessary to prove that none of the platers' helpers knew the facts which constituted such an interest, which in the circumstances of this case in my view cannot possibly be said to be proved.

R(U) 6/61

The claimant was a welder who lost employment when riveters went on strike at the shipyard where he was employed. The strike arose from a dispute concerning the transfer of redundant riveters to work performed by other tradesmen, including welders. The principle of interchangeability had been agreed by the executive of the claimant's trade union, and the claimant contended that the dispute was solely between the employers and the riveters about rates of pay of the latter. There was evidence, including reports of meetings, that, notwithstanding the agreement, the rank and file of union members refused to accept the redundant riveters.

Held: that the claimant was disqualified. The dispute which caused the stoppage of work was about interchangeability in practice. Members of the claimant's grade or class clearly participated and were directly interested in that dispute. In the matter of direct interests, an interchangeability dispute is on a par with a demarcation dispute (Decision R(U) 1/60).

R(U) 26/59

Because their foreman withheld a sum of money which was due to a fellow-worker by way of income tax rebate nineteen employees left their place of employment in protest. As a consequence the employers closed the site for several weeks.

The decision of the Commissioner was as follows:

1. My decision is that the claimant is not disqualified for receiving unemployment benefit on the ground that he lost employment by reason of a stoppage of work due to a trade dispute at his place of

employment; the claimant is disqualified for receiving unemployment benefit for three days from and including the 7 October 1958 on the ground that he lost his employment through his misconduct. . . .

7. In Case No. 2031/36 (reported at page 38 of U.I. Code 8B 1936) which was a case decided under the Unemployment Insurance Act, 1935 (now repealed) the then Umpire dealt with a case in which some thirty-four fillers alleged, when they received their pay notes, that the amount stated thereon as due to them for work which they had previously performed was understated. The fillers refused to descend the pit until what they alleged were the correct amounts were credited to them. Eventually, they decided to resume work on the Monday and to leave the redress of their grievances in the hands of the official of their association. On those facts the insurance officer disallowed claims for unemployment benefit on the ground that the claimants lost employment by reason of a stoppage of work due to a trade dispute. That decision was upheld by the court of referees. On appeal therefrom the Umpire referred to certain unreported decisions of the Umpire and, in particular, to an unreported decision (Decision 14400/32) in which the Umpire said 'There was no trouble in these cases about the terms of payment under the contracts of employment or as to what should be the terms of future employment, but whether the claimants had been underpaid or overpaid for work actually done. As the claimants could not induce the employer to pay what the claimants regarded as a debt due to them they refused to continue work.' The Umpire said 'In my view this was not a dispute which was "connected with the employment or non-employment, or the terms of employment, or with the conditions of employment, of any persons" within the definition of a trade dispute.' I here observe that s. 13(6)(b) is in identical terms. The Umpire recounted that the court of referees had taken the same view, but had disallowed benefit on the ground that the claimants had been notified that employment was available for them and refused to accept such employment without good cause. He observed that it might equally have been held that the claimants had voluntarily left their employment without just cause. In referring to the case which he was then deciding the Umpire said 'the claimants in the present case belong to an association which was well able, as subsequent events showed, to look after their interests and the claimants were not justified in giving up their employment without first taking steps to have their grievances adjusted by means of their association.'

8. In the light of these decisions of the Umpire to which I have referred and with which I respectfully agree I find that the claimant did not lose employment by reason of a stoppage of work due to a trade dispute at his place of employment. There is no evidence that there was any 'dispute' about the employment of the foreman and the question of income tax rebate did not concern future terms and conditions of employment of any persons. It was a sum of money due to J. under P.A.Y.E. arrangements in respect of the period during which he was absent from work owing to sickness and for which he received benefit which is not taxable. There was no dispute between the claimant and the foreman, but only a feeling of great annoyance and dissatisfaction at the foreman's conduct in withholding from J. what was due to him.

9. I do not doubt that the action of the claimant was improper, that is to say, it was improper of him and his colleagues to walk off the site, instead of referring their grievance to their trade union, and for this behaviour they must incur disqualification for unemployment benefit on the ground that they lost their employment through their misconduct. They were grievously provoked, however, and, therefore, the period of disqualification may be limited to that shown in paragraph one hereof.

R(U) 17/52

Owing to shortage of material a workman was given notice. Other employees saw the manager and were given notice because they were regarded as trouble-makers. As they were key-men the work of the factory came to a standstill.

Held that the stoppage of work was due not to a trade dispute but to the determination of one or both parties to have no further relations with each other.

R(U) 11/63

A stoppage of work occurred at a small factory when the claimant and most other employees went on strike because the management refused to deal with their trade union. On various dates during the next three months the company re-engaged the only four employees who sought re-employment, and also took on new workers. The insurance officer then decided that the stoppage had come to an end, the labour force having built up (as was thought) to 14 compared with the normal 20. The claimant contended that certain statements made by the managing director much earlier in the stoppage meant that, in effect, the company had severed relations permanently with most of the employees. Relying on Decision R(U) 17/52 it was argued that the stoppage ceased to be due to a trade dispute as soon as those statements were made.

Held that the claimant's contention paid too little regard to the actual facts and events and could not be accepted. The trade dispute remained the effective cause of the stoppage throughout. It was never settled, and the stoppage was never ended by formal agreement. The insurance officer's determination of the end of the stoppage reflected a liberal view but the Commissioner does not disturb it.

The decision of the Commissioner was as follows:

11. The claimant's trade union rely heavily upon Decision R(U) 17/52, a decision of a tribunal of Commissioners. In that case, although there was a smouldering trade dispute on the question of terms of work, this was held not to be the cause of a stoppage of work. On the facts of that case (which were described in paragraph 12 of the decision as 'somewhat exceptional') it was held that the stoppage was due to the employer's determination to dismiss summarily and for good, at a time when work was short owing to a scarcity of materials, the claimant and others whom he regarded as trouble-makers. They were key men and this brought the factory to a stand-still. The claimant later obtained judgment and damages against the employer for wrongful dismissal. The gist of the decision is that, even though there be a trade dispute in the background, a stoppage which is *really* due to an employer's taking advantage of an opportune time to rid himself for ever of trouble-makers will not be held to be due to the trade dispute. It is pointed out in paragraphs 9 to 11 of that decision that, to be due to a trade dispute, a stoppage must be in the nature of a strike or lock-out, that is it must be a move in a contest between employer and employees the object of which is that employment shall be resumed on certain conditions. Even when the stoppage is originally caused by a trade dispute, if the position is reached that the employer or the whole body of employees are no longer willing to employ, or be employed by, the other party on any terms, the stoppage will not be due to the trade dispute but to the determination of one or both parties to have no further relations with the other....

14. That submission is, in my view, ill-founded. The letter of the 14 November was only a move in furtherance of the original dispute. Mr B. was offering re-engagement upon terms that the employee renounced trade union membership. He was certainly not there breaking off all possibility of future re-employment but was offering re-employment on specified terms.

15. As to the 22 November, it was submitted that, when Mr B. publicly announced in the newspaper the withdrawal of his offer to re-

employ strikers, this amounted to a refusal to re-employ them on any terms; it was a complete and final severance of relations with the bulk of his former employees. This, it was submitted, introduced a new cause for the ensuing stoppage, viz. the employer's determination to have no further relations with the ex-employees on any terms, irrespective of the original cause of dispute, and the stoppage could not be said thereafter to be due to the trade dispute.

16. Again I cannot accept that submission which appears to me to attach too great weight to the newspaper report and to Mr B.'s letter to the trade union of the 26 November and too little to the actual facts and events. Although Mr B. has never repudiated the newspaper report by words he certainly did so by his deeds. On Monday the 26 November 1962, only 4 days after the report was published, he did in fact re-engage two strikers. I think this fact must have become generally known among strikers. He said at the hearing that he had been ready to re-engage any strikers who renounced union membership, even after the publication of the newspaper report, and in fact he did re-engage all who applied, who were only four altogether. I myself feel no doubt that the only obstacle which prevented a full resumption of work even after the 2 November was, not the newspaper report, but the very same cause as gave rise to the trade dispute in the first place, that is the adherence by the bulk of ex-employees to their union membership on the one side and Mr B.'s refusal to employ members of that union on the other. I feel sure that if either side had yielded on the point in dispute, the bulk of the strikers would have been re-engaged immediately and work would have been generally restarted. Many of the strikers were trained employees, too valuable to be easily let go, and Mr B. would have been glad to have them back on his own terms, that is as non-unionists. In my view the trade dispute, which was the original cause of the stoppage, remained in fact the effective cause of the stoppage throughout and was not replaced by some new or different cause.

17. Whether a stoppage of work, which was due to a trade dispute, has come to an end, and on what date it came to an end, are in truth questions of pure fact, though the facts may sometimes be difficult and complicated. When considering or applying earlier decisions of the Umpire or the Commissioner on this topic there is, I think, some danger of treating what are essentially decisions of fact as though they enunciated principles of law. One may however safely say that in applying s. 13(1) it is always necessary to keep the trade dispute distinct in one's mind from the stoppage of work. A trade dispute may be settled, but the

resulting stoppage of work and disqualification may persist after the settlement, for instance if a factory is disorganised by the trade dispute or the employer cannot re-engage enough workers. Or the dispute may never be settled, but the resulting stoppage may come to an end through a general resumption of work by the old employees or others engaged to replace them, or by the merger and obliteration of the stoppage in a general closure owing to bad trade.

18. In the present case I think it is perfectly plain that the trade dispute which caused the stoppage has never been settled. Mr B. is as firmly resolved as ever he was that he will never employ members of the claimant's trade union. The claimant for her part and nearly all the members of her trade union who were formerly employed at the toy factory refuse to renounce their membership and have not applied for re-engagement. The conflict still exists. The trade union representative submitted that when Mr B. announced in the newspaper his intention never to re-engage a striker the dispute was at an end. I cannot take that view. It seems to me that if two parties are in dispute, a refusal by one ever to have anything more to do with the other is not a settlement but a perpetuation of the dispute. In the present case, I feel confident in holding that the trade dispute remained in being and that the stoppage of work resulting from it continued certainly after the 22 November 1962.

19. Since, in my view, the trade dispute has never been settled and the stoppage has never been ended by any formal agreement, it is necessary to decide whether the stoppage has come to an end, and if so, when. It was decided in Decision R(U) 25/57 (following an earlier Umpire's decision) that where there is no formal settlement of a dispute, but workers return to work by driblets or are replaced by others, 'the stoppage of work comes to an end when the employers have got all the workers they require, that is, when work is no longer being stopped or hindered by the refusal of workers to work on the employers' terms or the refusal of employers to employ the workers on the workers' terms.' It was suggested to Mr B. in cross-examination that, owing to seasonal slackness of trade after the 18 December and his absence at a toy fair early in January, the factory would in any event have been closed for a week or more in January, and that early in the New Year the need for labour would be much reduced. He denied this. He said that if there had been no stoppage the factory would have worked to full capacity after Christmas and that there would have been no redundancies. I accept that to be the fact. The factory evidently required a labour force

of about 20 for normal working. I think the insurance officer took a liberal view in holding that, when the labour force reached 14 as (on her information) it did on the 18 February, work was no longer being stopped or hindered by the trade dispute. I see no reason for differing from that conclusion. It appears to me that the stoppage of work continued until the 16 February 1963.

R(U) 20/57

Claimant was discharged from a shipyard the day before a stoppage of work began there. Under the 12 days' rule a presumption arose that he had lost employment by reason of the stoppage.

Held that the presumption was rebutted. The inference from the evidence was that the claimant's employment had terminated and was not merely indefinitely suspended. The 12 days' rule reaffirmed.

The decision of the Tribunal was as follows:

4. On the 5 March 1957 the Shipbuilding and Ship-repairing Employers' Federation finally rejected a claim for an increase of wages covering all workers in the shipbuilding and ship-repairing industry which had been made by the Confederation of Shipbuilding and Engineering Unions of which the claimant's association was a member. On the 7 March 1957 a meeting of the executives of the trade unions affiliated to the above-mentioned Confederation decided that a national withdrawal of labour should begin at noon on the 16 March 1957. The claimant's employers had begun to discharge workers from the 11 March 1957. The stoppage of work began on the 18 March and lasted up to and including the 3 April 1957. As the claimant was discharged on a day before the stoppage began his claim makes it necessary to consider the application of the principle laid down in decisions of the Umpire under the former Unemployment Insurance Acts which was referred to in those decisions as 'the 12 days' rule'. This principle was applied for so many years in the interpretation of the provisions in previous Unemployment Insurance Acts which are reproduced in s. 13(1) that in our opinion the legislature must be taken to have intended the principle to be applied in the interpretation of s. 13(1). This principle was that an employee whose employment is indefinitely suspended within 12 working days of a stoppage of work at premises at which the employee habitually seeks work must *prima facie* be presumed to have lost employment by reason of the stoppage.

5. An employee's employment is treated as indefinitely suspended within the meaning of this rule notwithstanding that his employment

14

WCA

has in form been terminated by his employer if he habitually seeks work at premises at which the stoppage of work is in force.

6. It was, however, pointed out in the Umpire's decisions that this presumption might be rebutted by definite evidence to the contrary. (See Umpire's Decision 18901/31 applying the principle explained in Umpire's Decision 7712/20.)...

R(U) 12/60

The claimant had participated in a national trade dispute in the printing industry, and had lost employment from 20 June 1959 to 5 August 1959, when that dispute ended. He and other employees were prepared to resume work on 6 August, but by that time the management had formally dismissed them and said that in future only non-union employees would be engaged. The employees did not accept that condition, and as a consequence the stoppage at their place of employment continued until work was resumed on 21 August. The question at issue was whether the stoppage of work which began on 20 June, and which was originally due to a trade dispute, continued to be due to a trade dispute from 6 August to 20 August.

Held that the claimant was disqualified for that period: he continued to lose employment as a consequence of a trade dispute even though that dispute was not the dispute which caused the original stoppage. The fact that formal notice of dismissal had been given was not in itself important. Whatever the merits of an employee's or employer's attitude towards trade union membership in relation to other provisions of the National Insurance Act, 1946, they have no relevance to the trade dispute disqualification: a conflict between employers and employees as to whether the employees shall or shall not be members of a trade union falls inescapably within the terms of the statutory definition of 'trade dispute'.

R(U) 4/58

Claimant was employed loading stones on to a ship. He lost employment during a stoppage of work due to a trade dispute in the shipyards. It was contended that his place of employment was the ship on which he was working and there was no stoppage there; and that although he subscribed to a union which was paying strike pay, he was not financing the dispute as the strike pay was not paid out of subscriptions but out of interest from the union's investments.

The decision of the Commissioner was as follows:

6. The claimant was represented at the oral hearing of this appeal by an officer of his trade union who submitted that the claimant's place of employment within the meaning of s. 13(6)(*a*) of the National Insurance Act, 1946, was the ship which he was engaged in loading and that there was no stoppage of work at that 'place'. In my opinion this submission

is clearly fallacious. The claimant is doubtless called upon to work at different parts of Surrey Docks from time to time and clearly his place of employment within s. 13(6)(a) must include any such parts and cannot be confined to the particular ship on which he happens to be working when the stoppage of work begins. (See Decisions R(U) 30/57 and R(U) 26/57 and compare Umpire's Decisions 1953/25 and 9731/33.)

7. The claimant's representative stressed the fact that the claimant and other riggers and lumpers had not withdrawn their labour and argued that there was thus no dispute between them and their employers. Section 13(6)(b) of the National Insurance Act, 1946, however defines trade dispute 'as any dispute between employers and employees or between employees and employees' not merely any dispute to which the claimant concerned is himself a party: it follows that unless the claimant can bring himself within the exception contained in the proviso to s. 13(1) the fact that he had not himself withdrawn his labour would not assist him. To qualify for the exception the claimant must prove that neither he nor any member of his grade or class was participating in or financing or directly interested in the dispute. The local tribunal held that the claimant satisfied all three requirements. At the hearing before me attention was concentrated on the question whether the claimant or any member of his grade or class was financing the dispute. In my opinion the claimant failed to prove that he was not doing so since he was admittedly a subscribing member of his union who were financing the dispute by paying strike pay from their funds. The claimant's representative urged (as I understood his argument) that the claimant and his grade or class ought not to be regarded as financing the dispute because the subscriptions were used for the expenses of administration and strike pay was paid out of the interest on the union's investments. This argument is in my view plainly untenable; the burden of proving that neither he nor any member of his grade or class was financing the dispute rests on the claimant and he could only discharge that burden by showing that no subscriptions by any members of his grade or class were expended on the investments from the interest on which the strike pay was made. No evidence was offered to establish such a contention.

REDUNDANCY PAYMENTS ACT, 1965

[Certain sections of this Act pursue the policy of attempting to 'neutralise' industrial conflict in so far as redundancy payments are concerned. Among them may be noted the following:

Section 7 deals with the calculation of periods of short time and lay off which may entitle a worker to a payment; having provided that the weeks may be partly of one and partly of the other, proceeds:]

(3) For the purposes mentioned in the last preceding sub-section no account shall be taken of any week for which an employee is laid off or kept on short-time where the lay-off or short-time is wholly or mainly attributable to a strike or a lock-out, whether the strike or lock-out is in the trade or industry in which the employee is employed or not and whether it is in Great Britain or elsewhere....

See too s. 10(1) Where at any such time as is mentioned in the next following sub-section, an employee who (a) has been given notice by his employer to terminate his contract of employment, or (b) has given notice to his employer under sub-section (1) of s. 6 of this Act, takes part in a strike, in such circumstances that the employer is entitled, by reason of his taking part in the strike, to treat the contract of employment as terminable without notice, and the employer for that reason terminates the contract as mentioned in sub-section (2) of s. 2 of this Act, that sub-section shall not apply to that termination of the contract.

(2) The times referred to in the preceding sub-section are (a) in a case falling within paragraph (a) of that sub-section, any time within the obligatory period of the employer's notice (as defined by s. 4(5) of this Act), and (b) in a case falling within paragraph (b) of the preceding sub-section, any time after the service of the notice mentioned in that paragraph.

(3) Where at any such time as is mentioned in the last preceding sub-section an employee's contract of employment, otherwise than by reason of his taking part in a strike, is terminated by his employer in the circumstances specified in sub-section (2) of s. 2 of this Act, and is so terminated as mentioned in the said sub-section (2), and on a reference to a tribunal it appears to the tribunal, in the circumstances of the case, to be just and equitable that the employee should receive the whole or part of any redundancy payment to which he would have been entitled apart from the last-mentioned sub-section, the tribunal may determine that the employer shall be liable to pay to the employee (a) the whole of the redundancy payment to which the employee would

have been so entitled, or (*b*) such part of that redundancy payment as the tribunal thinks fit.

(4) Where an employee terminates his contract of employment without notice, being entitled to do so by reason of a lock-out by his employer, s. 3(1)(*c*) of this Act shall not apply to that termination of the contract.

[With this section the reader should compare the complex s. 40: if, during the period of notice given to an employee, a strike occurs, the employer can serve a 'notice of extension' requiring the employee to come back and work out the time lost by striking in the notice period. The tribunal has a discretion to judge the reasonableness of an employee's refusal to do so in awarding the whole or part of a redundancy payment.

See too, s. 37 of the Act. Under the Contracts of Employment Act, 1963, Schedule 1, paragraph 7, strikes in breach of contract ruptured continuity of employment; but the 1965 Act altered that exception:]

37. (1) Sub-paragraph (2) of paragraph 7 of Schedule 1 to the Contracts of Employment Act, 1963 (which preserves continuity of employment where an employee takes part in a strike, except where in doing so he breaks his contract of employment) shall have effect, subject to the following provisions of this section, with the omission of the words from 'except' to the end of the sub-paragraph.

(2) For the purpose of computing a period of continuous employment in accordance with Schedule 1 to this Act, the amendment made by the preceding sub-section shall have effect in relation to any week beginning after the commencement of the Contracts of Employment Act, 1963, whether before or after the passing of this Act.

SECTION C

CONDUCT OF TRADE DISPUTES: PICKETING*

AGNEW *v.* MUNRO

Court of Session   [1891] 2 White 611

The defendant, a butcher, was charged with a contravention of s. 7 of the Conspiracy and Protection of Property Act, 1875. It was alleged that he had tried to compel various persons to abstain from working by

---

* For Conspiracy and Protection of Property Act 1875, s. 7, and Trade Disputes Act, 1906, s. 2, see *ante,* p. 384 and p. 385.

threatening them variously by saying that one would 'wear sore bones for it one of these nights'. Another if he did not abstain would be 'made to do so', and others would be thrown into the dock.

THE LORD JUSTICE CLERK: The complaint is well drawn, and sets forth the offence under the statute. It alleges that the accused did 'wrongfully and without legal authority'—using the words of the statute—'intimidate'—still using the words of the statute—certain people; and then it describes how the intimidation was committed—namely, by threats, which were plainly on the face of them threats of personal violence. Now, sub-section 1 of s. 7 says, 'uses violence to or intimidates such other person.' The use of violence would, of course, necessarily come under the statute whether successful in preventing the person from going to work or not. I do not suppose that anyone doubts that an offence would be committed under the statute in the case of a man who threw a stone at an engine-driver and cut his head. It would not cease to be an offence that the engine-driver tied up his head with a handkerchief and went on with his work. If, instead of throwing a stone, the offender went on to the engine, and told the engine-driver that he would get his head broken that night if he did not come off, that is as clearly intimidation as the other is violence; and in neither case would it matter in the least whether the man to whom the violence was used or who was intimidated was thereby induced to abstain from doing that which he had a legal right to do. I think the clause would be rendered practically nugatory if it were read in the sense in which the Sheriff-Substitute read it, viz.: that in every case the prosecutor was bound to aver that the violence or intimidation was successful in producing the results intended. The object and intention of that section of the statute, as I read it, and as I think everyone who considers it carefully must read it, was to prevent people from endeavouring by such means to induce others to give up doing that which they had a right to do. Of course the intimidating conduct must be of a serious character. The person intimidated must be intimidated by threats which may be supposed to affect a person of common sense, and raise a natural alarm of personal violence or of violence to his family. That such threats were used here is certain.

LORD MCLAREN, LORD TRAYNER and LORD WELLWOOD concurred.

GIBSON *v.* LAWSON; CURRAN *v.* TRELEAVEN

[1891] 2 Q.B. 545

A member of one trade union (A) informed a fellow-employee, who belonged to another trade union (B), that unless he changed his trade union from B to A there would be a strike. The appellant refused to change, and his employer dismissed him to avoid trouble. There were no threats of violence.

The respondent was charged in substance with unlawfully intimidating the appellant under s. 7 of the Act of 1875, but was acquitted.

The Court held that 'intimidation' in the Criminal Law Amendment Act, 1871, meant a threat of violence or the like; and that the Conspiracy and Protection of Property Act, 1875, had not extended the meaning more widely.

LORD COLERIDGE, C.J., delivering the judgment of the court (MATTHEW, CAVE, A. L. SMITH, and CHARLES, JJ.) said: The statute [of 1871] is not, indeed, conceived in any weak spirit of tenderness to workmen, but the second sub-section of the first section limits 'intimidation' in that sub-section to such intimidation as would justify a magistrate in binding over the intimidator to keep the peace towards the person intimidated—in other words, to such intimidation as implies a threat of personal violence. Of such intimidation there is in this case, no evidence whatever; but it is truly said that this statute is repealed and is of importance only so far as its objects and language may throw light upon the existing statute—the statute under which the summons was issued. It seems clear, however, that, looking at the course of legislation, and keeping in mind the changing temper of the times on this subject, the word 'intimidate' in the seventh section of the latter Act [1875] cannot reasonably be construed in a wider and severer sense than the same word in the second sub-section of the first section of the earlier Act [of 1871]. 'Intimidate' is not, as has been often said by judges of authority, a term of art—it is a word of common speech and everyday use; and it must receive, therefore, a reasonable and sensible interpretation according to the circumstances of the cases as they arise from time to time. We do not propose to attempt an exhaustive definition of the word, nor a complete enumeration of the cases to which it may be properly, nor of those to which it may be improperly, applied. It is enough for us to say that in this case it appears to us all that there was nothing which, under any reasonable construction of the word 'intimidate' could be brought within it....

This, however, does not entirely dispose of the question; for we were very properly reminded of the cases of *Reg.* v. *Druitt*[1] and *Reg.* v. *Bunn*,[2] in which Lord Bramwell and Lord Esher (then Bramwell, B., and Brett, J.), are both said to have held that the statutes on the subject have in no way interfered with or altered the common law, and that strikes and combinations expressly legalised by statute may yet be treated as indictable conspiracies at common law, and may be punished by imprisonment with hard labour. Neither of those cases is very satisfactorily reported; in neither was there any motive for questioning the dicta of the judges; in the one tried by Lord Esher (then Brett, J.), there was no opportunity, in consequence of the prisoner having been acquitted on all the counts to which the alleged ruling applied. We are well aware of the great authority of the judges by whom the above cases were decided, but we are unable to concur in these dicta, and, speaking with all deference, we think they are not law. It seems to us that to hold that the very same acts which are expressly legalised by statute remain nevertheless crimes punishable by the common law is contrary to good sense and elementary principle, and that the reports, therefore, cannot be correct. If the dicta are law, they render the statutes passed on these subjects practically inoperative; these statutes might as well not have been passed.... As we said in an earlier part of the judgment, we do not propose to enter upon an exhaustive enumeration of all the possible acts which do, and of those which do not, constitute intimidation within the section. But we say that, to tell an employer that if he employs workmen of a certain sort, the workmen of another sort in his employ will be told to leave him, and to tell the men, when the employer will not give way, to 'leave their work, use no violence, use no immoderate language, but quietly cease to work and go home' (we quote the language of the Recorder), is certainly not intimidation within any reasonable construction of the statute.

J. LYONS & SONS *v.* WILKINS

Court of Appeal   (1) [1896] 1 Ch. 811;
Court of Appeal   (2) [1899] 1 Ch. 255

The Society of Fancy Leather Workers tried to persuade J. Lyons and Sons to raise the wages of their employees and to alter their system of employment from part piece-work and part time-work to a system of all piece-work or all time-work. J. Lyons refused. The union ordered a strike and several men gave notice. A picket of two men was set up

---

[1] 10 Cox C.C. 592.   [2] 12 Cox C.C. 316.

which peacefully attempted to request and persuade men not to work for the firm until the dispute was settled. They also picketed an outworker of Messrs Lyons, named Schoenthal. It was admitted that no violence, intimidation or threats were used.

Lyons sought an injunction against the secretary and a member of the committee of the union under s. 7 of the 1875 Act, *ante* p. 384.

(1) LINDLEY, L.J.: I understand the meaning to be as follows: 'That every person who, with a view to compel any other person to abstain from doing or to do any act which such other person has a legal right to do, or abstain from doing, wrongfully and without legal authority watches or besets the house or other place where such other person,' and so on, 'shall on conviction' be liable to a penalty; but in construing this language and giving effect to it, Courts are not to treat as 'watching or besetting' any 'attending at or near a house in order merely to obtain or communicate information'. That is to be allowed; and picketing (if you call it so) for that limited purpose, and conducted in that way for that simple object, is not made a criminal offence, and must therefore be taken to be a lawful act. Accordingly, one cannot say as an abstract proposition that all picketing is unlawful, because if all that is done is attending at or near a house in order merely to obtain or communicate information, that is lawful. But it is easy to see how under colour of so attending a great deal may be done which is absolutely illegal. It would be wrong to post people about a place of business or a house under pretence of merely obtaining or communicating information, if the object and effect were to compel the person so picketed not to do that which he has a perfect right to do; and it is because this proviso is often abused and used for an illegal purpose that such disputes as these very often arise.... Now, they are not there merely to obtain or communicate information: that is not their function. They are there to put pressure upon Messrs Lyons by persuading people not to enter into their employment; and that is watching or besetting within clause 4, and is not attending in order merely to obtain or communicate information. Under these circumstances they have gone too far, and have gone beyond what the Act of Parliament authorizes, and I do not hesitate to say that it is a case in which from the necessity of the thing a quick remedy is actually and absolutely required.

KAY, L.J.: This is an appeal from an interlocutory injunction, and in all these cases of interlocutory injunctions where a man's trade is affected one sees the enormous importance that there may be in interfering at once before the action can be brought on for trial; because during the interval, which may be long or short according to the state of business in the courts, a man's trade might be absolutely destroyed or ruined by a course of proceedings which, when the action comes to be tried, may be determined to be utterly illegal; and yet nothing can compensate the man for the utter loss of his business by what has been done in that interval. Such a case as that may happen, and I am not at all sure that this is not one of that very kind. I can well understand that immense and almost irreparable damage may be done to Messrs Lyons & Co. if what is now taking place is allowed to continue until the action comes on to be tried.

A. L. SMITH, L.J., concurred.

(2) LINDLEY, M.R.: The great point made by the appellants' counsel turned on the word 'wrongfully' in s. 7 and on the effect of *Allen* v. *Flood*[1] on the meaning of that word....

The truth is that to watch or beset a man's house with a view to compel him to do or not to do what is lawful for him not to do or to do is wrongful and without lawful authority unless some reasonable justification for it is consistent with the evidence. Such conduct seriously interferes with the ordinary comfort of human existence and ordinary enjoyment of the house beset, and such conduct would support an action on the case for a nuisance at common law: see *Bamford* v. *Turnley*,[2] *Broder* v. *Saillard*,[3] per Jessel, M.R., *Walter* v. *Selfe*[4] and *Crump* v. *Lambert*.[5] Proof that the nuisance was 'peaceably to persuade other people' would afford no defence to such an action. Persons may be peaceably persuaded provided the method employed to persuade is not a nuisance to other people.

Another point made by the appellants' counsel was that what was done to Schoenthal gave the plaintiffs no cause of action. This point was raised and considered and decided by the Court on the former appeal, and I might say no more. But as I do not remember whether the particular argument urged by Mr W. H. Cozens-Hardy was used on that occasion, I will add that, in my opinion, his contention cannot be supported. It is based on the expression 'such other person'. It is said that to beset one person's house with a view to compel someone else is not within the section. Such a construction would render the Act nugatory in a great number of cases clearly within the mischief intended to be remedied. But a more direct answer to the argument is that 'such other' means 'any other'. This seems plain if attention is paid to the

[1] [1898] A.C. 1.   [2] 3 B. & S. 62.   [3] 2 Ch. D. 692, 701.
[4] 4 De G. & Sm. 315.   [5] L.R. 3 Eq. 409.

language of the first part of the section where these words first occur. Moreover, the word 'person' in the singular must be read so as to include 'persons' in the plural (see 52 & 53 Vict, c. 63, s. 1), and if this is borne in mind the argument is seen at once to be untenable.... As regards the facts, the evidence was amply sufficient to prove the plaintiffs' case. The whole object of what was done was to compel the plaintiffs to comply with the terms contained in a circular put forth by Mr Wilkins, and although there was no violence or overt threat of violence, it is quite plain that the relays of men set to watch and beset the plaintiffs' house (and the house of Schoenthal, who worked for him) were sent to do, and that they did, a great deal more than 'attend' where they were 'in order merely to obtain or communicate information'.

CHITTY, L.J.: Mr W. H. Cozens-Hardy, in his argument for the appellants, fastened on the words 'wrongfully and without legal authority', and contended that they showed that the watching or besetting mentioned in the fourth sub-section were acts lawful in themselves, unless it were shown in some way other than by proof of the facts of watching or besetting with the view mentioned at the beginning of the section that the acts done were done wrongfully or without legal authority. But this argument cannot be sustained. 'Wrongfully and without legal authority' applies equally to all the five sub-sections; and to take (by way of illustration) the first sub-section, the using of violence, or intimidation, or injury to property, there specified, are all of them unlawful acts in themselves. No just or sound construction of the section would permit words which in terms apply to all the sub-sections being confined to one sub-section only.

But further, the acts of watching or besetting here proved in reference to the fourth sub-section, and done with the view mentioned, were acts in themselves unlawful at common law, and are not made lawful by the Legislature. In my opinion they constitute a nuisance at common law. True it is that every annoyance is not a nuisance; the annoyance must be of a serious character, and of such a degree as to interfere with the ordinary comforts of life. To watch or beset a man's house for the length of time and in the manner and with the view proved would undoubtedly constitute a nuisance of an aggravated character. It must be borne in mind that the seventh section, although it probably arose out of trade disputes, is not confined to trade disputes or to disputes between masters and men. It applies equally to all Her Majesty's subjects of every class. It would embrace the case of besetting a man's house with a view to compel him not to receive guests or visitors.... On this appeal

Mr W. H. Cozens-Hardy raised what may have been a new point founded on the words 'such other person' which run throughout the seventh section. It was urged that besetting the house of one person with a view to compel another is not within the section. I think it is. Grammatically, 'such other' refers to 'any other person', the immediate antecedent. Besetting a workman to compel a master and besetting a master to compel a workman are both within the mischief aimed at. Schoenthal was an outworker for the plaintiffs.

VAUGHAN WILLIAMS, L.J., delivered a concurring judgment.

CHARNOCK v. COURT

[1899] 2 Ch. 35

During a strike in Halifax, employers brought in 13 Irishmen to replace the men on strike. The Irishmen were met at the landing-stage and railway station by trade union officials who told them about the strike and said that if they went elsewhere, the union would pay their expenses and find them work. Only four Irishmen reached the employers. An interlocutory injunction against the trade union officers was sought, and granted.

STIRLING, J.: First of all it is decided that watching or besetting is unlawful within the meaning of s. 7, subs. 4, unless it is in order merely to obtain or communicate information;* and, secondly, that watching or besetting a house or other place where the workmen are is unlawful, if done in order to compel a master to do or abstain from doing what he has a legal right to abstain from doing or to do.... It seems to me that that is watching a place where the workmen happened to be. There is nothing in the statute which defines the duration of the watching. It may be, it seems to me, for a short time, and as to that I refer to the words of the proviso itself, which speaks of attending at or near a house or place where the person resides, or works, or happens to be. The word 'attending' does not necessarily imply any lengthened attendance upon the spot; nor is there anything in the statute to limit its operation to a place habitually frequented by the workman, such as the house where he resides or the place where he works. On the contrary, the words 'place where he happens to be' seem to me to embrace any place where the workman is found, however casually.

* See note *ante* p. 384.

THOMPSON-SCHWAB v. COSTAKI

Court of Appeal [1956] 1 W.L.R. 335

The plaintiff successfully sought an injunction to restrain the defendants from using their premises next door for the purpose of prostitution. The evidence was that the defendants patrolled the street outside the plaintiff's home, thereby seriously depreciating the value of his house and interfering with his comfortable enjoyment of it.

In the course of his judgment ROMER, L.J. said: The second point on which the defendants rely is that nothing can constitute a private nuisance at law unless it affects the reasonable enjoyment of other premises in a physical way. This is only an interlocutory application, and at the trial no doubt that point will be taken again and may be argued at greater length, but my present impression is that it is unsound. It appears to be an unwarrantable gloss on the law on the subject as formulated in the textbooks and, what is perhaps more important, it appears to be inconsistent with the judgments of this court in *Lyons & Sons* v. *Wilkins*,[1] which was the picketing case. Consequently I am not prepared to accept either of the principal submissions on which the defendants are founding their case on this appeal.

WARD LOCK v. OPERATIVE PRINTERS' ASSISTANTS' SOC.

Court of Appeal (1906) 22 T.L.R. 327

The defendant union picketed the Botolph Printing Works with two aims: to induce the men employed there to join their union, and then for the new unionists to give in notice and abstain from working for the employers. The aim was to get the employers to employ only union men. The court held that there was no evidence of violence, obstruction or any other common law nuisance: nor of the pickets inducing the men to break their contracts.

VAUGHAN WILLIAMS, L.J.: Now, if the defendants by their conduct were guilty of an offence under s. 7, subs. 4, of the Conspiracy and Protection of Property Act, 1875, the plaintiffs would have a good cause of action by civil process. But, in my opinion, such conduct as I have described of the defendants does not constitute a criminal offence within subsection 4. When the Act of 1875 was passed the employers had a good cause of action for various forms of nuisance. The Legislature,

---

[1] [1899] 1 Ch. 255.

by the Act of 1875, gave in respect of some of these nuisances, as to which there was a civil remedy, a summary remedy by summons before a magistrate for acts done for which previously there was only a civil remedy. And it seems to me that the words in the first clause of the section, 'wrongfully and without legal authority', were introduced for the very purpose of limiting the remedy by criminal prosecution to cases so tortious as to give a civil remedy. The summons before the magistrate and the punishment on conviction were enacted by way of an additional remedy to the civil remedy before existing.

LORD JUSTICE MOULTON: I will now deal with the head of claim relating to picketing, which I use as a convenient term for what is included in the phrase 'watching or besetting or causing to be watched or beset the plaintiffs' premises or the approaches thereto', which appears in the first question left to the jury. In connexion with that part of the case which relates to picketing frequent reference has been made to s. 7 of the Conspiracy and Protection of Property Act, 1875, and I propose therefore to examine the meaning of that section and its bearing on the matters in issue in this action before dealing with the facts. Giving to that section the most careful consideration in my power, I come to the same conclusion as is expressed in the judgment of my Lord. I cannot see that this section affects or is intended to affect civil rights or civil remedies. It legalizes nothing, and it renders nothing wrongful that was not so before. Its object is solely to visit certain selected classes of acts which were previously wrongful, i.e., were at least civil torts, with penal consequences capable of being summarily inflicted. This interpretation appears to me to satisfy the whole language of the section, and I can find no indication in it of any intention to do more. The classes of acts are set out in the five several subsections, each of which must, of course, be read with the opening words of the section. The restriction that the acts referred to must in themselves be at least civil torts is plainly expressed by the presence of the word 'wrongfully', which applies equally to all the classes, and the penal consequences which are by the section attached to these wrongful acts, as well as the procedure by which they are to be inflicted, are clearly set forth. What, then, is the effect of the exception which is made by the last paragraph of the section? In my opinion, that part of the section does exactly what its language expresses and no more. It expressly excepts a sub-class of acts (which otherwise might be held to be within the class specified in subsection 4) from the operation of the section, i.e., it does not attach the additional penal consequences to acts which come within that sub-class. It leaves them exactly as they were before. If they were civil torts, they remain so. If they were previously criminal in their nature, their criminality and its punishment are unaffected by the section. In thus restricting the application of the section to acts in themselves wrongful I am following the high authority of Lord Justice Lindley in his well-known judgment in the case of *Lyons and Sons* v. *Wilkins* ([1899] 1 Ch. 255). But he arrives at it in a different way. He construes the word 'compel' in the opening words of the section in such a sense as to make the act of compelling wrongful in itself, and therefore considers the presence of the word 'wrongfully' as superfluous, or at least as only an indication of the phraseology to be used by the pleader. I see no reason why we should treat so lightly a word of such importance. In my opinion, the Legislature inserted the word 'wrongfully' expressly, because it did not intend to leave this all-important limitation of the ambit of the clause to the chance that a Court might construe the word 'compel' in such a restricted sense.

I am therefore of opinion that in support of the plaintiffs' claim with regard to picketing, it must be shown that the defendants or one of them were guilty of a wrongful act, i.e., that the picketing constituted an interference with the plaintiffs' action wrongful at common law, or, as I think it may accurately be phrased, were guilty of a common law nuisance....I wish to add that, in my opinion, there is throughout a complete absence of evidence of anything in the nature of picketing or besetting which could constitute a nuisance. It appears that the discharged workmen loitered about for a day or two after leaving work—a thing which is not unlikely to happen—and that they were at times joined by others, but there is no suggestion even by the plaintiffs' witnesses that any annoyance or molestation took place, and the evidence to the contrary is overwhelming. At the request of the plaintiffs the police placed special patrols outside the premises during the whole period of the dispute, and the police therefore would be in a position to give independent evidence as to what occurred. The plaintiffs did not call any of the police as witnesses....I am therefore of opinion that there was no evidence to go to the jury in respect of any cause of action against the defendants, or either of them, based on alleged picketing, and that the verdict and judgment in respect of this head of claim should be set aside and judgment thereon entered for the defendants.

STIRLING, L.J., held that there was no evidence of unlawful picketing.

FERGUSON LTD *v.* O'GORMAN

Supreme Court of Ireland   [1937] I.R. 620

During a dispute between the proprietors of a hair-dressing business and a trade union to which the defendants belonged over the employment of non-union labour and the dismissal of an employee, Busby, all the staff were dismissed and the premises closed down. A new company was formed to take over the business and it invited applications for re-employment. The defendant members of the former staff did not ask for re-employment but peacefully picketed the premises walking up and down outside, two abreast, carrying placards. The plaintiff company sought an injunction claiming a declaration that the picket was a trespass to the plaintiff's rights in the soil of the highway. The action failed. It was conceded in the Supreme Court that this was a trade dispute within s. 5(3) of the Trade Disputes Act 1906. Counsel for the Company argued that s. 2 of the Act did not justify a trespass.

SULLIVAN, C.J. referred to earlier judgments which made it clear that s. 2 does not legalise a trespass on private property and went on: But I do not think that either of these learned Judges had present to his mind a trespass on the soil of a highway by the user of it in a manner that is not the reasonable and usual mode of using a highway as such, and accordingly I do not think that their judgments can be relied on as indicating their opinion that such a trespass could not be justified under the section in question. If it could not, then I find it difficult to give any reasonable interpretation to the section. When the Legislature declared it lawful for persons to attend at or near a house or place where a person resides, or works, or carries on business, it cannot reasonably have contemplated that such a house or place would be situated in a waste or no man's land. The usual approach to a residence or place of business is by a public highway and unless the right to attend at or near a residence or place of business is a right to attend on a public highway I do not see how such right can be exercised at all, consistently with the decisions in *Larkin's Case*[1] and *McCusker's Case*[2] that private property may not be invaded. I am, therefore, driven to the conclusion that s. 2 of the Trade Disputes Act authorises the user of a highway by the person and for the purpose described in that section, and that it therefore justifies a user of the highway which would consitute a trespass at common law. Whether the user proved in any particular case is such a user as can be justified under the section will depend on

[1] [1908] 2 I.R. 214.   [2] [1918] 2 I.R. 432.

the particular circumstances, including the acts and conduct of the alleged trespassers.

In the present case it was admitted that the defendants who took part in the picketing of the appellants' premises were acting on their own behalf or on behalf of a trade union. Meredith J. was satisfied that they acted in furtherance of a trade dispute, the existence of which is now not denied, and that they attended outside the appellants' premises merely for the purpose of peacefully obtaining or communicating information, or of peacefully persuading persons to abstain from working, and that in fact they acted peacefully.

FOWLER v. KIBBLE

Court of Appeal   [1922] 1 Ch. 487

The plaintiffs were mineworkers, and members of an unregistered union, and the defendants were members of unions affiliated to the Miners' Federation. This Federation had an agreement with the mineowner that only union labour was to be employed, and for this purpose the plaintiffs were non-unionists. The defendants told the men who handed out safety lamps not to give any to the plaintiffs and they told those plaintiffs who had lamps to give them back which they did. In consequence the plaintiffs were not allowed down into the mines. They brought an action against the defendants for an injunction and damages, claiming that they were entitled to maintain an action against the defendants for breach of the obligations imposed by s. 7 of the Conspiracy and Protection of Property Act 1875.

WARRINGTON, L.J.: It is not now in controversy that there was at the time in question a trade dispute, and that the acts done by the defendants were in furtherance of that dispute. Consequently by reason of s. 3 of the Trade Disputes Act, 1906, if the acts done by the defendants were actionable on the ground only that they interfered with the employment of the plaintiffs or their right to dispose of their labour as they willed, then no action could be brought in respect of those acts. The learned judge has decided that the acts done by the defendants were actionable only on the grounds I have stated, and that so far as the Trade Disputes Act, 1906, was concerned, or by reason of the provisions of that Act, no action could be brought in respect of them, and it is not disputed now that the decision of the learned judge was right except in one respect. The plaintiffs maintain that the acts done were not only actionable on the grounds mentioned in the Trade

Disputes Act, 1906, but that they were also actionable, because they constituted breaches of a statutory prohibition imposed by s. 7 of the Conspiracy, and Protection of Property Act, 1875. That section provides: [His Lordship read the section.] In the first place does that section create a new actionable wrong? In my opinion it does not. The learned judge decided on the construction of the Conspiracy, and Protection of Property Act, 1875, that the element of violence was essential to the offences specified in the Act, and that inasmuch as violence was absent in the present case the Act had no application to the acts done by the defendants. I am not sure that the learned judge's view of the construction of the Act is, in the terms in which he expressed it, accurate, but I am also not sure that it is not merely a verbal difference between the view I take and that which the learned judge expressed.

In *Ward, Lock & Co.* v. *Operative Printers' Assistants' Society*[1] it was decided by the Court of Appeal that the Trade Disputes Act, 1906 did not render wrongful anything that was not previously wrongful; but that all it did was to add the sanction of a penalty to that which previously was nothing but a civil wrong. The point is put with extreme clearness by Fletcher Moulton L.J.[2] where he says: 'I cannot see that this section affects'—that is s. 7 to which I have referred—'or is intended to affect civil rights or civil remedies. It legalizes nothing, and it renders nothing wrongful that was not so before. Its object is solely to visit certain selected classes of acts which were previously wrongful, i.e. were at least civil torts, with penal consequences capable of being summarily inflicted'. If that is so, then on that ground—namely, that there is no statutory right of action—the plaintiffs would fail, but I think they also fail for the reason that what the defendants did was not within the statute at all. Now in the present case I cannot see that what the defendants did, which has been described by my Lord, deprived the plaintiffs of the use of their lamps. Section 7 of the Act of 1875 does not say 'causes to be deprived' of the use of the tools, and at the outside all that the defendants did was to persuade the lamp man whose duty it was to hand out the lamps that it would be better under the circumstances of the case not to hand the lamps to the plaintiffs, but in that I cannot see that there was any 'wrongful (which is essential) depriving' of the plaintiffs of the use of the lamps to the use of which they allege they were entitled. Then if I am right with regard to the construction and effect of the section (and I must be right, speaking

[1] 22 Times L.R. 327.　　　　[2] Ibid. 329.

in this Court, because I am only following the decision of the Court of Appeal in *Ward, Lock & Co.* v. *Operative Printers' Assistants' Society*), that there is no new right of action created by the statute itself, then the only right of action is that to which I referred at the beginning of my judgment—a right of action on the sole ground that the act of the defendants, among other things, interferes with the employment of the plaintiffs and with the right to dispose of their labour as they will, and an action founded on such a ground since the Trade Disputes Act, 1906, can no longer be maintained.

YOUNGER, L.J.: Now I will assume, but again without deciding, that the acts proved against the defendants in this case constituted in normal circumstances actionable wrongs at the instance of the plaintiffs. But I then ask myself the question why so much can be said of them, and I can think of no more appropriate answer than this: that they amounted to an interference with the employment of the plaintiffs, or with the right of the plaintiffs to dispose of their labour as they would. I can myself, as I have said, think of no more strictly appropriate answer than one stated in that form of words and no other more closely relevant reply to the question was suggested by counsel for the plaintiffs. If therefore the acts in question be in normal circumstances actionable at all they are so actionable because they amount to an interference with the employment of the plaintiffs, or with the right of the plaintiffs to dispose of their labour as they will and for no additional reason in itself sufficient to make them actionable. But it is admitted that these acts were here committed in furtherance of a trade dispute, and if they were so committed and were actionable only for the reason I have stated, it becomes clear, under s. 3 of the Trade Disputes Act, 1906, that they ceased to be actionable in the circumstance in which they were committed.

LORD STERNDALE, M.R., delivered a concurring judgment.

PIDDINGTON v. BATES

[1960] 3 All E.R. 660

During a trade dispute, pickets were placed outside the employers' premises. The employer rang up the police. A police officer on arrival decided that two pickets at each of the two entrances was sufficient. P. arrived and was told by the police constable that two pickets were enough. P. said 'I know my rights' and, going to join the pickets, pushed gently past the policeman and was 'gently arrested'. He was charged with obstructing a police officer in the execution of his duty contrary to s. 2, Prevention of Crimes Amendment Act, 1885. There was no evidence that P. knew the number of people in the building at the time or the normal full complement of staff.

LORD PARKER, C.J.: The question here is whether the constables were acting in the course of the execution of their duty when, so it is said, they were obstructed. The court has been referred to a great number of cases, both Irish and English, dealing with the position when a police constable can be said to contemplate a breach of the peace and to take action to preserve it, but I find it unecessary to refer to those cases. It seems to me that the law is reasonably plain. First, the mere statement by a constable that he did anticipate that there might be a breach of the peace is clearly not enough. There must exist proved facts from which a constable could reasonably have anticipated such a breach. Secondly, it is not enough that his contemplation is that there is a remote possibility but there must be a real possibility of a breach of the peace. Accordingly, in every case it becomes a question whether, on the particular facts, there were reasonable grounds on which a constable charged with this duty reasonably anticipated that a breach of the peace might occur...It is said that there must be something more than a mere possibility. For my part, I agree with that, but I do not read the finding of the magistrate in the case as saying that here it was just a mere remote possibility. I think that he was referring to it as what I may call a real possibility. The other point goes to an analysis of the evidence, from which it is said that no reasonable man could possibly anticipate a breach of the peace. It is pointed out there was no obstruction in the street; there was no actual intimidation; and that there were no threats or intimations of violence. It is said that there was really nothing save the fact that picketing was going on to suggest that a breach of the peace was a real possibility.

Every case must depend on its exact facts, and the matter which influences me in this case is the matter of numbers. It is, I think, perfectly clear from the wording of the case, although it is not expressly so found, that the police knew that in these small works there were only eight people working at the time. They found two vehicles arriving with eighteen people, milling about the street, and trying to form pickets at the doors and, for my part, on that ground alone, coupled with the telephone call which I should have thought intimated some sense of urgency and apprehension, the police were fully entitled to think as reasonable men that there was a real danger of something more than mere picketing to obtain or communicate information or to peaceably persuade. I think that, in those circumstances, the respondent had reasonable grounds for anticipating that a breach of the peace was a real possibility. The real criticism, I think, is this: 'Well, to say that only two pickets should be allowed is purely arbitrary. Why two? Why not three? Where do you draw the line?' For my part, I think that a police officer charged with the duty of preserving the Queen's peace must be left to take such steps as, on the evidence before him, he thinks are proper. I am far from saying that there should be any rule that only two pickets should be allowed at any particular door. There, one gets into an arbitrary area, but, so far as this case is concerned, I cannot see that there was anything wrong in the action of this respondent.

ASHWORTH, J. and ELWES, J. concurred.

R. *v.* WALL

Irish Assizes   (1907) 21 Cox C.C. 401

On an indictment under s. 7 of the Conspiracy and Protection of Property Act, 1875, for persistently following employer and watching his place of business and his private residence with a view to coerce him to take back a dismissed *employee* into his employment, the evidence being that the defendants with other persons had continually watched and walked up and down before the prosecutor's business premises, and had followed him through the streets to his private residence.

Held: that under the circumstances if the acts of 'watching' and 'persistently following' were done with the intention of coercing the employer to take back the dismissed *employee*, the defendants ought to be found guilty.

Held: also, that s. 2, subs. 1, of the Trade Disputes Act, 1906, did not apply as regards the 'watching' of the private residence.

PALLES, C.B., in the course of his charge to the jury said: Workmen have a right of combining, like employers, but must do so in a lawful manner. They have a right to resent dismissal, but not to resent it by doing certain overt acts prohibited by statute. They must not do so by persistently following an employer with a view to coercing him into doing a certain act—to take back a former employee into his employment. It is not denied that the defendants persistently followed Deevy. Did they do so with the object of compelling him to take back Wall into his service? If you believe they did you should find them guilty on the first count. If you convict on this you need not consider the other counts. But if you acquit on this, then consider the count for 'watching' the prosecutor's house in the suburbs. The defendants were not entitled to watch with a view to compel Deevy to take back Wall. Watching involves persistent watching. They rely on their right under the Trades Disputes Act, 1906, s. 2(1) to 'attend at the house for the purpose of peaceably persuading other employees to abstain from working'. The Trades Disputes Act, 1906, refers to a 'mere attending' which is more temporary than 'watching'. In any case it is not suggested that there were any workmen there to be persuaded, as this count relates to watching the house in the suburbs, not the business premises in the city. If you believe that the watching was done with the object of compelling Deevy to take back Wall you should convict on this count.

The jury returned a verdict of guilty on the count of 'persistently following'.

TOPPIN v. FERON

Irish Assizes   (1909) 43 I.L.T.R. 190

A theatre company, of which Sir Alfred Dobbin was a director, had dismissed two employees. Two of the defendants called upon him to reinstate the men; but he declined. On 17 November 1908, one defendant said to a group gathered near the theatre: 'We will make Sir Alfred Dobbin bleed through the pocket for this'. That same evening a picket was placed on the theatre, one of the defendants shoving away a boy who made to enter. Police cautioned defendants speaking to other customers entering the theatre, and warned them that they were an obstruction. On 24 November, a picket including the defendants walked up and down, causing an obstruction, and speeches were made calling on the public to boycott Dobbin and his theatre. By the 26th, over 200 persons were on the picket line; the defendants told police officers they would go on until the employees were reinstated, but also entered into a guarantee at Cork Police Court not to cause any obstruction or violence. On 30 November (the only date mentioned in the summons) the evidence was that there was no breach of the peace. Prosecuted under s. 7(4) of the 1875 Act, the defendants objected to evidence being admitted of acts prior to 30 November; and counsel said: We rely strongly on the Trade Disputes Act, 1906, s. 2(1). The defendants were simply engaged in 'picketing'.

[PALLES, L.C.B.: Preventing people going into the theatre is not, I think, within the saving clause of the Act.]

'Working', we say, means carrying on any business transaction. They were there for the purpose of persuading the people not to deal with Sir Alfred Dobbin.

PALLES, L.C.B., in delivering judgment, said that the case was quite clear. The Court were of opinion that the magistrates were quite wrong on two different matters. They were clearly wrong when they said in the case stated that the facts deposed to as having taken place on 24 November should not now be acted upon owing to the guarantee that had been entered into. In reference to transactions of that kind, where the Court was obliged to find the mind and intention of the parties, they were at liberty to refer to antecedent transactions to ascertain what was the intention of the parties, and, therefore, in that first ruling of the magistrates, in which he was extremely glad to see the resident magistrate did not concur, his Lordship was plainly of opinion they were wrong in point of law. As to the second ground of their decision, his Lordship was of opinion that even if they were to put out of consideration what took place prior to 30 November, yet, having regard to the number of persons who were assembled there, evidently for the purpose of coercing and intimidating Sir Alfred Dobbin into doing an act which he did not wish to do, and which it was his lawful right to refuse to do, the mere character of that meeting, its numbers, and the mind in which the people went there, were all evidence that they were not acting lawfully—that they were not acting merely for the purpose of peacefully obtaining or communicating information or of peacefully persuading any person to work or abstain from working. Taking all the circumstances of the case into consideration, as the magistrates ought to have done—viz. the evidence in the case before 30 November, and the evidence of the acts on 30 November —his Lordship was of opinion there was a very strong case against these parties showing that they were acting illegally.

TYNAN v. BALMER
[1966] 2 W.L.R. 1181; [1966] 2 All E.R. 133

The defendant was leading 40 pickets round and round in a continuous circle outside a factory. Police Constable O'Hare decided that this was an obstruction and intimidation and asked him to stop them. The defendant refused. He was arrested and convicted for wilfully obstructing a police constable in the execution of his duty. The judge found that they were on the public highway, that there was never any risk of violence, and that they were 'decent, well-mannered, orderly people'.

WIDGERY, J.: In my judgment, the proper way to approach this question, and it is a way which may well have commended itself to the recorder also, is to ask whether the conduct of the pickets would have been a nuisance at common law as an unreasonable user of the highway. It seems, in my judgment, that it clearly would have been so regarded. One leaves aside for the moment any facilities enjoyed by those acting in furtherance of a trade dispute, and if one imagines these pickets as carrying banners advertising some patent medicine or advocating some political reform, it seems to me that their conduct in sealing off a part of the highway by this moving circle would have been an unreasonable user of the highway.

In so far as it is a question of fact, the recorder takes the same view, and has, as I read his judgment, found that it was an unreasonable user of the highway. Indeed, Mr Pain, appearing for the appellant today, does not seek to argue the contrary.

In my judgment, therefore, if one ignores s. 2 of the Trade Disputes Act, 1906, for the moment and considers the position at common law, this action would have been an unreasonable use of the highway, admittedly a nuisance, and a police officer would be fully entitled to take action to move the pickets on.

If one can start from that foundation, it seems to me that the sole question in this case is whether the activity was authorised and made legal by s. 2 of the Act of 1906....As Mr Pain has suggested, it would seem that the genesis of that section is the decision of the Court of Appeal in *J. Lyons & Sons* v. *Wilkins*. It is not necessary to take time by looking at that report in detail, but it is of great interest to see that in that case it was accepted as possible at common law that watching and besetting a man's house would be a nuisance and a wrongful act, quite apart from any obstruction of the highway thereby caused. One should not, in my judgment, therefore regard s. 2 as being primarily a highway section, because there may be many other wrongs which could be committed by citizens which are now authorised by that section. But what in my view one must do is to look carefully at s. 2 and see exactly what it authorises. It authorises in its simplest terms a person to attend at or near one of the places described if he does so merely for the purpose of peacefully obtaining or communicating information or of peacefully persuading any person to work or abstain from working.

The recorder has found as a fact that the pickets in this case were not attending merely for the purposes described in the section. He has found as a fact that their object at any rate in part was to seal off the highway and to cause vehicles approaching the premises to stop. In my judgment that finding of fact is quite enough to require this court to say that as a matter of law the recorder's judgment in this case should be upheld.

Mr Pain, however, submits that a somewhat different test must be applied. He says that s. 2 has put beyond doubt that picketing is a lawful user of the highway, and that as a lawful user of the highway it is not the subject of interference by a constable, provided the picket has reasonable regard for the rights of others. In this case, as I understand him, he says that as the pickets did not in fact cause any actual obstruction to any person, the fact that they were circling in the road had not brought them to the point at which it was proper for the police to interfere. In particular, he says that the police might have properly interfered half an hour later when workpeople were coming out for their lunch and might be obstructed, but had no right to interfere at the time when police constable O'Hare took action in this case.

I cannot accept that this is a proper approach to the problem. Once one accepts that independently of s. 2 this action was unlawful and a nuisance, the only question left is whether s. 2 by its terms authorises it or not. On the recorder's finding s. 2 clearly did not authorise this conduct and it therefore seems to me that this appeal should be dismissed.

LORD PARKER, C.J.: I also agree, and I would only add this in deference to Mr Pain's argument, that, despite the finding here that one of the objects was to ensure that vehicles were brought to a stop, even so that was permitted, if I may use that term, by s. 2 of the Trade Disputes Act, 1906, because the rights conferred by that section involve, as he would say, the stopping of a vehicle for the purpose, for instance, of communicating information. Mr Pain conceded that no right was conferred of stopping a pedestrian, apparently on the basis that you could communicate your information by walking alongside him, but he suggested that when you get to a vehicle the section authorised and permitted the stopping of vehicles. I am quite unable to accept that argument, and on the findings of the recorder in this case I am quite clear that an offence was committed.

SACHS, J. agreed.

SMITH v. THOMASSON*

[1891] 62 L.T. 68

The appellant, who was on strike, was posted outside works at which he had been engaged as a picket, and when the workmen who had taken the place of the strikers came out of the works silently followed the respondent at a short distance down two streets. A crowd which had been waiting outside the works also followed the respondent with hostile words and gestures. The justices convicted the appellant under s. 7(2), Conspiracy and Protection of Property Act, 1875.

POLLOCK, B.: I have no doubt that what the defendant did in this case infringed the provision of the Act of Parliament.... The Legislature does not intend in the 2nd sub-section to deal with intimidation by a crowd of people. The act of one person is sufficient to constitute an offence. Further, it is very clear that the Legislature intended to prevent mere acts, though done without any expressed intention. It was for the magistrates to say whether the act complained of was in fact an act of intimidation. There was here plenty of evidence that the defendant in silently dogging the footsteps of the workman committed the act which the statute defines as 'persistently following'. There were the further facts before the magistrates that many other persons were pursuing a common course with the appellant. I think the magistrates were right, and that the appeal must be dismissed.

HAWKINS, J. It is impossible to define generally what is 'persistent following' within the meaning of the Act of Parliament. I will confine myself to the evidence which the justices had before them, and which was enough to justify their decision. It seems that some of Messrs Cooke's men were out on strike. The respondent had gone in to supply the place of one of the men. The appellant with other pickets was stationed opposite a gate, out of which the respondent had to come. When the men got out of the gate, there was a cry raised 'They are coming'. The men then went down the street followed by the defendant and a crowd. Now the defendant was not accidentally mixed up in this crowd, but had been with the pickets watching the door. This crowd followed the workmen with hostile action and gestures, and the respondent was frightened. Whichever way the workmen went the crowd and the appellant followed. Under these circumstances I have no doubt but that the justices were right in the conclusion at which they arrived.

* Note the terms too of s. 7(5) of the 1875 Act: *ante*, p. 384. The 'disorderly following' like the 'persistent following' in this case, and the other acts in the section, becomes an offence only if done with 'a view to compel': R. v. *McKenzie* [1892] 2 Q.B. 519.

Section D

STRIKES: COMMON LAW LIABILITIES AND THE STATUTES

(i) CONSPIRACY TO INJURE

QUINN v. LEATHEM

House of Lords   [1901] A.C. 495

The plaintiff, a flesher, employed non-union men. The defendants told the plaintiff and one of his best customers, a butcher, that unless he dismissed these men from their jobs, there would be a strike both at his and the customer's place of work. As a result he lost this customer. The plaintiff sued for conspiracy, alleging a 'combination to injure'.

LORD BRAMPTON: It has often been debated whether, assuming the existence of a conspiracy to do a wrongful and harmful act towards another and to carry it out by a number of overt acts, no one of which taken singly and alone would, if done by one individual acting alone and apart from any conspiracy, constitute a cause of action, such acts would become unlawful or actionable if done by the conspirators acting jointly or severally in pursuance of their conspiracy, and if by those acts substantial damage was caused to the person against whom the conspiracy was directed: my own opinion is that they would... I feel that such unlawful conduct as has been pursued towards Mr Leathem demanded serious attention. I think the law is with him, and that the damages awarded by the jury are under the circumstances very moderate. It is at all times a painful thing for any individual to be the object of the hatred, spite, and ill-will of any one who seeks to do him harm. But that is as nothing compared to the danger and alarm created by a conspiracy formed by a number of unscrupulous enemies acting under an illegal compact, together and separately, as often as opportunity occurs regardless of law, and actuated by malevolence, to injure him and all who stand by him. Such a conspiracy is a powerful and dangerous engine, which in this case has, I think, been employed by the defendants for the perpetration of organized and ruinous oppression.

LORD LINDLEY: My Lords, the case of *Allen* v. *Flood*[1] has so important a bearing on the present appeal that it is necessary to ascertain

---

[1] [1898] A.C. 1 [*post*, p. 497].

exactly what this House really decided in that celebrated case.... My Lords, this decision, as I understand it, establishes two propositions: one a far-reaching and extremely important proposition of law, and the other a comparatively unimportant proposition of mixed law and fact, useful as a guide, but of a very different character from the first.

The first and important proposition is that an act otherwise lawful, although harmful, does not become actionable by being done maliciously in the sense of proceeding from a bad motive, and with intent to annoy or harm another.

The second proposition is that what Allen did infringed no right of the plaintiffs, even although he acted maliciously and with a view to injure them. I have already stated what he did, and all that he did, in the opinion of the majority of the noble Lords. If their view of the facts was correct, their conclusion that Allen infringed no right of the plaintiffs is perfectly intelligible, and indeed unavoidable.

I will pass now to the facts of this case,... What the defendants did was to threaten to call out the union workmen of the plaintiff and of his customers if he would not discharge some non-union men in his employ. In other words, in order to compel the plaintiff to discharge some of his men, the defendants threatened to put the plaintiff and his customers, and persons lawfully working for them, to all the inconvenience they could without using violence. The defendants' conduct was the more reprehensible because the plaintiff offered to pay the fees necessary to enable his non-union men to become members of the defendants' union; but this would not satisfy the defendants. The facts of this case are entirely different from those which this House had to consider in *Allen* v. *Flood*. In the present case there was no dispute between the plaintiff and his men. None of them wanted to leave his employ. Nor was there any dispute between the plaintiff's customers and their own men, nor between the plaintiff and his customers, nor between the men they respectively employed. The defendants called no witnesses, and there was no evidence to justify or excuse the conduct of the defendants. That they acted as they did in furtherance of what they considered the interests of union men may probably be fairly assumed in their favour, although they did not come forward and say so themselves; but that is all that can be said for them. ... The defendants were doing a great deal more than exercising their own rights: they were dictating to the plaintiff and his customers and servants what they were to do. The defendants were violating their duty to the plaintiff and his customers and servants, which was to leave them in the undisturbed enjoyment of their liberty of action as already explained. What is the legal justification or excuse for such conduct? None is alleged, and none can be found. This violation of duty by the defendants resulted in damage to the plaintiff—not remote, but immediate and intended. The intention to injure the plaintiff negatives all excuses and disposes of any question of remoteness of damage. Your Lordships have to deal with a case, not of *damnum absque injuria*, but of *damnum cum injuria*...

It was contended at the bar that if what was done in this case had been done by one person only, his conduct would not have been actionable, and that the fact that what was done was effected by many acting in concert makes no difference. My Lords, one man without others behind him who would obey his orders could not have done what these defendants did. One man exercising the same control over others as these defendants had could have acted as they did, and, if he had done so, I conceive that he would have committed a wrong towards the plaintiff for which the plaintiff could have maintained an action. I am aware that in *Allen* v. *Flood* Lord Herschell expressed his opinion to be that it was immaterial whether Allen said he would call the men out or not. This may have been so in that particular case, as there was evidence that Allen had no power to call out the men, and the men had determined to strike before Allen had anything to do with the matter. But if Lord Herschell meant to say that as a matter of law there is no difference between giving information that men will strike and making them strike, or threatening to make them strike, by calling them out when they do not want to strike, I am unable to concur with him...

Black lists are real instruments of coercion, as every man whose name is on one soon discovers to his cost. A combination not to work is one thing, and is lawful. A combination to prevent others from working by annoying them if they do is a very different thing, and is *prima facie* unlawful. Again, not to work oneself is lawful so long as one keep off the poor-rates, but to order men not to work when they are willing to work is another thing. A threat to call men out given by a trade union official to an employer of men belonging to the union and willing to work with him is a form of coercion, intimidation, molestation, or annoyance to them and to him very difficult to resist, and, to say the least, requiring justification. None was offered in this case.

My Lords, it is said that conduct which is not actionable on the part of one person cannot be actionable if it is that of several acting in concert. This may be so where many do no more than one is supposed to do. But numbers may annoy and coerce where one may not. Annoyance and coercion by many may be so intolerable as to become actionable, and produce a result which one alone could not produce.... Intentional damage which arises from the mere exercise of the rights of many is not, I apprehend, actionable by our law as now settled. To hold the contrary would be unduly to restrict the liberty of one set of persons in order to uphold the liberty of another set. According to our law, competition, with all its drawbacks, not only between individuals, but between associations, and between them and individuals, is permissible, provided nobody's rights are infringed. The law is the same for all persons, whatever their callings: it applies to masters as well as to men; the proviso, however, is all-important, and it also applies to both, and limits the rights of those who combine to lock-out as well as the right of those who strike. But coercion by threats, open or disguised, not only of bodily harm but of serious annoyance and damage, is *prima facie*, at all events, a wrong inflicted on the persons coerced; and in considering whether coercion has been applied or not, numbers cannot be disregarded.

EARL OF HALSBURY, L.C. and LORDS MACNAGHTEN, SHAND and ROBERTSON delivered concurring speeches.

REYNOLDS *v.* SHIPPING FEDERATION

[1924] 1 Ch. 28

The defendant shipowners federation agreed with the National Union that they would employ on their ships only those persons belonging to that union. The shipowners, in pursuance of this agreement, instructed their ships' officers to employ only those persons holding the union card. It was a 'closed shop' agreement formed to establish 'a single supply of sailors and firemen controlled by employers and employed' and it was governed by reference to the National Maritime Board.

The plaintiff belong to the A. union which had refused to accept or join the N.M.B. He refused to join the National Union and consequently failed to obtain employment on a ship. He brought this action alleging conspiracy preventing him from obtaining employment on a ship under the defendant's control. He sought a declaration that the agreement for a closed shop was void as being against public policy and an injunction to prevent further interference with his obtaining employment and damages for harm suffered.

SARGANT, J.: Mr Grant for the plaintiff relied on *Temperton* v. *Russell*[1] and *Quinn* v. *Leathem*,[2] and, while admitting that neither of these cases completely covered the ground, argued that they established principles sufficient to entitle the plaintiff to succeed here. But in my judgment the present case differs in at least two vital respects from either of those cases. In the first place, the agreement or combination here was not against a particular individual, but merely operated to exclude such individuals as might not from time to time satisfy a qualification which was within the reach of any one who desired employment. The exclusion, that is, was against a class, and that a class to which any one at any time might cease to belong. And in the second place, the motive of the exclusion was not a malicious desire to inflict loss on any individual or class of individuals, but a desire to advance the business interests of employers and employed alike by securing or maintaining those advantages of collective bargaining and control which had been experienced since the institution of the National Maritime Board. In both these respects the present case markedly resembles the *Mogul Steamship Case*,[3] and in my opinion the principles laid down in the judgments there are entirely applicable here, and are fatal to the plaintiff's claim.

SORRELL *v.* SMITH

House of Lords   [1925] A.C. 700

The plaintiff, a retail newsagent, transferred his custom from one wholesale newsagent (R.) to another (W.). He did this at the request of his trade union who were trying to limit the number of retail news-agents in the area, and had not been consulted when several new newsagents had opened up and obtained their papers from R. The defendants were a committee of newspaper proprietors who tried to make the plaintiff return to R. by threatening to cut off the supply of papers to his new wholesale agent W. They did this purely to protect their trade and were not actuated by spite. The plaintiff unsuccessfully sought an injunction to restrain the defendants from interfering with his right to continue contractual relations with W.

LORD DUNEDIN: That brings me to what I consider the leading heresy which is to be found in some judgments and text writers—namely, to use the words of McCardie, J., in *Pratt* v. *British Medical Association*,[4] when, in speaking of *Quinn* v. *Leathem*, he says: 'The element of

---

[1] [1893] 1 Q.B. 715.   [2] [1901] A.C. 495.   [3] [1892] A.C. 25.
[4] [1919] 1 K.B. at p. 260.

conspiracy seems to have been a merely incidental feature of that case'. Practically the same was said in this case by Russell J. In rejecting such a view, I entirely concur with what was said by Atkin L.J. in *Ware and De Freville.*[1] 'It appears to me,' he says, 'to be beyond dispute that the effect of the two decisions in *Allen* v. *Flood* and *Quinn* v. *Leathem* is this: that on the one hand a lawful act done by one does not become unlawful if done with an intent to injure another, whereas an otherwise lawful act done by two or more in combination does become unlawful if done by the two or more in combination with intent to injure another.'...

To sum up. There are some observations in Lord Lindley's judgment which might seem to point to another ground of action, and Lord Halsbury proceeds on the grounds of threats, which in that case he regarded as illegal means or, in other words, tortious acts, as well as a conspiracy to injure. But as regards the others, Lord Macnaghten demolished in terms every finding as the basis of the verdict except the finding of the conspiracy, and in the judgments of all the others, all, save conspiracy, has passed out of sight. In fact, I endorse what was said by Atkin, L.J. in *Ware and De Freville.*[1] 'The case seems to me not to turn in any degree on the evidence as to threats. The foundation of the decision was the principle, expressly reserved in the decision in *Allen* v. *Flood*, that a combination to injure may be unlawful where the intention by one is not.'

My Lords, it may seem self confident to be positive when so many learned persons have expressed other views, but candidly I never held a clearer opinion than the one I now express, that the effect of *Allen* v. *Flood* and *Quinn* v. *Leathem* is to settle beyond dispute that in an action against an individual for injury he has caused to the plaintiff by his action, the whole question is whether the act complained of was legal, and motive or intent is immaterial; but that in an action against a set of persons in combination, a conspiracy to injure, followed by actual injury, will give a good cause for action, and motive or intent when the act itself is not illegal is of the essence of the conspiracy...

What I have to do is to fancy myself a juryman, faced with the question with which I began this opinion, and which, I think, still remains: Was there here a conspiracy to injure Sorrell? I hold there was not. I entirely agree with the way that the learned judges of the Court of Appeal have looked at the facts. Sorrell had volunteered to take action as a piece of policy on behalf of the federation. The action of

[1] [1921] 3 K.B. 90.

the circulation managers was a defensive action to protect their own trade against being dictated to by the federation; it was, in no sense, a conspiracy to injure Sorrell, and here I again repeat my apology for my hypercriticism. I agree so thoroughly with what the learned judges of the Court of Appeal said; only I look at the inquiry into the facts, not as a means of arriving at the conclusion whether there was justification of what, without justification, would be an illegal action, but as evidence of whether there was any proof of illegal action, i.e., a conspiracy to injure, and I find as a juryman, that there was none. As I am attempting to deal with the whole subject, I should say something as to the meaning of the expression 'threats', which, as I have noticed above, Lord Halsbury in some of his remarks in *Quinn* v. *Leathem* considered as in that case equivalent to a tortious act. The matter is discussed at some length by Scrutton and Atkin, L.JJ. in *Ware and De Freville*, and with their views I generally agree. Expressing the matter in my own words, I would say that a threat is a pre-intimation of proposed action of some sort. That action must be either *per se* a legal action or an illegal, i.e., a tortious action. If the threat used to effect some purpose is of the first kind, it gives no grounds for legal proceeding; if of the second, it falls within the description of illegal means, and the right to sue of the person injured is established.

VISCOUNT CAVE, L.C. and LORDS SUMNER and BUCKMASTER delivered concurring speeches; LORD ATKINSON agreed with the opinion of VISCOUNT CAVE, L.C.

McKERNAN v. FRASER

High Court of Australia (1931) 46 C.L.R. 343

After an exhaustive review of the authorities on civil conspiracy, EVATT, J. continued: It is obvious from such divergent opinions upon the same set of facts, that it is almost always possible to regard trade union action to prevent the employment in the industry of non-unionists or rival unionists, from two points of view, first as a combination for the purpose of damaging or injuring the non-unionists, secondly as a combination to protect or advance the interests of the union...

Before liability can attach to defendants for conspiracy to injure, there must be evidence to support a finding of fact as to the object or motive animating the parties to a combination which intentionally causes temporal harm to a plaintiff. Three possible types of case may arise:

I. Where the agreement to cause damage or loss is made solely with the object or motive of causing such damage. It is not easy to picture such a case, because it supposes the deliberate entry by persons into an agreement and its execution, for no reason at all beyond the mere infliction of injury. The whole thing would be stamped with wantonness, almost with absence of meaning or significance. But if such a case arose, the defendants would, no doubt, be held liable, and the combination would be regarded as possessing the necessary malicious character.

II. Where the agreement to cause damage or loss is made, *all* the parties seeking to carry out some object or satisfy some motive, beyond the mere infliction of damage. This case assumes the existence of a similar object or motive in all the parties to the agreement.

III. Where the agreement to cause damage or loss is made, each one of the parties seeking to carry out some object or satisfy some motive beyond the mere infliction of damage, but one or more acting solely from one object or motive, others acting solely from a different object or motive, and others still, acting from more than one object or motive.

I pause here to refer to the suggestion of Lord Sumner in *Sorrell* v. *Smith*[1] that the terms 'object' and 'purpose' in relation to the 'aggressive action of a combination', stand in need of strict definition. He added that 'the tests, by which the definition is to be applied, seem to me not to have been as yet sufficiently examined'.[2]

In the present examples, I am assuming that the defendants have combined to do certain acts which must necessarily cause temporal harm or injury to a plaintiff or a class of which the plaintiff is one. I have also assumed that the harm to the plaintiff is 'intended' by all parties to the agreement. The infliction of such harm may also be called their 'object' or 'purpose'. Each of these two words indicates the conscious pursuit of some end or goal, or the presentation to the actors of such end or goal as a desirable thing. It may be more accurate to call the immediate end or goal the 'purpose' of the combination and the ultimate end or goal sought, the 'object' of the person who enters the combination. If each party has the same ultimate 'object', that is also the 'object' of the combination. In this sense, the 'object' desired by each and all, is also the 'motive', both of each individual and of the combination. It may be that the 'intention' or immediate 'purpose' of the persons combined is to inflict harm, but their 'motive' or ultimate 'object' is the furtherance of their trade interests. It may be,

---

[1] (1925) A.C. 700.   [2] (1925) A.C. at pp. 741–742.

on the contrary, that the 'motive' or ultimate 'object' beyond the immediate 'purpose' or 'intention' of the combination, is to do harm because the plaintiff is hated for some personal reason and his harm or ruin is desired as an end to be achieved by means of inflicting harm upon him.

I am quite aware that with this terminology, many psychologists would not rest satisfied. But the difficulty is, as the references I have already given show, that the Courts have not separately defined a number of these expressions. In certain relations, the words employed tend to have the same meaning, but in other relations, they have meanings which are quite distinct.

'Though it is easy,' said Lord Dunedin, 'on the strict view of the meaning of the words to draw a distinction between motive and intention yet the meaning of the one who runs into the other, and in the set of cases I have quoted I think they are used as synonymous' (*Sorrell* v. *Smith*[1]).

So long, however, as the meaning of the words used is kept clear, the substance of Lord Sumner's suggestion will be followed. I therefore return to the illustrations already enumerated.

Further information is required before it is possible to pronounce of either case II or case III whether any or all of the parties are liable to a plaintiff who sustains injury through the carrying out of the agreement. If in case II the common object or motive be the satisfaction of a personal hatred or grudge by means of the ruin or impoverishment of the plaintiff, liability is clear. If it be the protection or advancement of trading, professional or economic interests common to the defendants, there is no liability. If it be the carrying out of some religious, social or political object, the law prefers to examine the motive or object in each case before pronouncing an opinion. The pursuit of economic ends is most favoured.

It will be noted that case II assumes that all the parties intend to inflict damage. The existence of such agreement or common design assumes that damage is inflicted deliberately and not accidentally. Not only was such deliberate infliction of injury characteristic of the *Mogul Case*[2]; the fact of agreement itself excludes the possibility that the injury inflicted is accidental and not designed. Before the defendants can be held liable, we must ascertain the object or motive of the combination beyond the immediate intention or purpose of inflicting injury. The question requires closer examination.

[1] (1925) A.C. at p. 724.   [2] (1892) A.C. 25.

Case III is typical, even of the cases where, if all parties had the one object or motive, there would either be clear liability or clear absence of it. Take the following illustration: A, B, C, D, E and F agree to inflict damage on X. A and B agree, because they desire to protect the standards of the professional body to which A, B, C, D, E and F all belong, and have no other object or motive. C and D wish to revenge themselves on X for some personal quarrel, concealing this motive from the other parties to the agreement and from each other. E and F act from mixed motives: they genuinely wish to maintain the professional ideals of their body, but they also have a strong dislike to X and it can truly be said that they are gratifying it when they enter into the agreement.

In such case, the only state of mind which is *common* to A, B, C, D, E and F is the immediate intention or purpose of inflicting damage upon X. But there are the other facts mentioned. Who is liable for conspiracy to injure? In my opinion A and B, not knowing of the malicious motives animating C and D or the strong dislike felt to X by E and F, are not liable. C, D, E and F are not the agents of A and B so as to alter the nature and character, the object or motive, of the common agreement.

The example presented by the position of E and F is typical of these group activities. But it is convenient first to examine the question of liability in C and D. Each has agreed with five others, and each is inspired by personal malice. But the fact of the existence of such malice is not made known by either to the other, and it is also unknown to the other parties to the agreement. It is not possible to say that C and D *alone* are liable for conspiracy to injure, except on the basis that there has been an agreement come to by them alone. But the only agreement entered into, has six parties not two. The position might be different, if it could be shown that C and D, for the purpose of satisfying their hatred of X, agreed between themselves to procure acts to be done by A, B, E, F, and themselves all in association, for the purpose of causing harm to X. Such agreement would be a separate conspiracy to injure, carried out by using the other persons as instruments for effectuating their own design. In such a case C and D would be liable. But, in the absence of such a separate agreement between them, the uncommunicated existence of an evil motive in each towards X, would not make themselves alone liable to X. This view is, however, subject to a further contention shortly to be mentioned, and, I hope, disposed of. Upon the same footing, E and F would not be liable, because no separate understanding between them is shown. In case III therefore, subject to the same contention, neither A, B, C, D, E, nor F is liable as for 'conspiracy to injure'...

Sir Godfrey Lushington said, in special reference to combined action against employers or non-unionists on the part of unionists, that to ask the question whether they acted to defend their own trade interests or to injure their economic adversary for the time being, is equivalent to asking of a soldier who shoots to kill in battle, whether he does so for the purpose of injuring his enemy or of defending his country. The analogy is sound, because combined strike action is usually undertaken for the purpose, both of causing harm to the employers and for the improvement or maintenance of the standard of the unionists.

Dixon, J. delivered a concurring judgment, with which Rich and McTiernan, JJ. agreed. Gavan Duffy, C.J., and Starke, J. delivered a joint dissenting judgment.

CROFTER HANDWOVEN HARRIS TWEED v. VEITCH

House of Lords   [1942] A.C. 435

Millowners on the Island of Lewis who made and sold tweed cloth were unable to agree to employ 100 per cent union labour because of competition from local producers who obtained cheap yarn from the mainland, wove it into cloth, and sold it at a lower price than the millowners. The millowners and the union, the Transport and General Workers Union, combined together; and the T.G.W.U. instructed dockers in the port to refuse to handle yarn coming in for the local producers. The latter sued union officials for a conspiracy to injure. There was no breach of employment contracts by the dockers.

Lord Wright: The concept of a civil conspiracy to injure has been in the main developed in the course of the last half century...The rule may seem anomalous, so far as it holds that conduct by two may be actionable if it causes damage, whereas the same conduct done by one, causing the same damage, would give no redress. In effect the plaintiff's right is that he should not be damnified by a conspiracy to injure him, and it is in the fact of the conspiracy that the unlawfulness resides. It is a different matter if the conspiracy is to do acts in themselves wrongful, such as to deceive or defraud, to commit violence, or to conduct a strike or lock-out by means of conduct prohibited by the

Conspiracy and Protection of Property Act, 1875, or which contravenes the Trade Disputes and Trade Unions Act, 1927. But a conspiracy to injure is a tort which requires careful definition, in order to hold the balance between the defendant's right to exercise his lawful rights and the plaintiff's right not to be injured by an injurious conspiracy. As I read the authorities, there is a clear and definite distinction which runs through them all between what Lord Dunedin in *Sorrell* v. *Smith* calls 'a conspiracy to injure' and 'a set of acts dictated by business interest'. I should qualify 'business' by adding 'or other legitimate interests', using the convenient adjective not very precisely....

In effect, it was said, the union were bribed by the millowners to victimize the appellants in their trade by the promise of help in the matter of the union membership, which was entirely foreign to the question of the importation of yarn. These considerations, it was said, constituted 'malice' in law, even if there was no malevolence, and prevented the respondents from justifying the injury which they wilfully did to the appellants' trade, because they could not assert any legitimate interest of their union which was relevant to the action taken. Actual malevolence or spite was, it was said, not essential. There was no genuine intention to promote union interests by the stoppage of importation. The interference with the appellants' trade by stopping import of yarn was wilful and ultroneous action on the part of the union supported by no relevant union interest. It was malicious or wrongful because it was intentionally and unjustifiably mischievous, even though not malevolent.

Before I refer to the authorities, there are some preliminary observations which I desire to make. I shall avoid the use of what Lord Bowen described as the 'slippery' word 'malice' except in quotations. When I want to express spite or ill will, I shall use the word malevolence. When I want to express merely intentional tortious conduct I shall use the word wrongful. As the claim is for a tort, it is necessary to ascertain what constitutes the tort alleged. It cannot be merely that the appellants' right to freedom in conducting their trade has been interfered with. That right is not an absolute or unconditional right. It is only a particular aspect of the citizen's right to personal freedom, and like other aspects of that right is qualified by various legal limitations, either by statute or by common law. Such limitations are inevitable in organized societies where the rights of individuals may clash. In commercial affairs each trader's rights are qualified by the right of others to compete. Where the rights of labour are concerned, the rights of the employer are conditioned by the rights of the men to give or withhold their services. The right of workmen to strike is an essential element in the principle of collective bargaining. . .

It is thus clear that employers of workmen or those who like the appellants depend in part on the services of workmen, have in the conduct of their affairs to reckon with this freedom of the men and to realize that the exercise of the men's rights may involve some limitation on their own freedom in the management of their business. Such interference with a person's business, so long as the limitations enforced by law are not contravened, involves no legal wrong against the person. In the present case the respondents are sued for imposing the 'embargo', which corresponds to calling out the men on strike. The dockers were free to obey or not to obey the call to refuse to handle the appellants' goods. In refusing to handle the goods they did not commit any breach of contract with anyone; they were merely exercising their own rights. But there might be circumstances which rendered the action wrongful. The men might be called out in breach of their contracts with their employer, and that would be clearly a wrongful act as against the employer, an interference with his contractual right, for which damages could be claimed not only as against the contract-breaker, but against the person who counselled or procured or advised the breach. . . .

But in *Allen* v. *Flood*,[1] this House was considering a case of an individual actor, where the element of combination was absent. In that case, it was held, the motive of the defendant is immaterial. Damage done intentionally and even malevolently to another, thus, it was held, gives no cause of action so long as no legal right of the other is infringed. . . . Thus for purposes of the present case we reach the position that apart from combination no wrong would have been committed. There was no coercion of the dockers. There were no threats to them. They were legally free to choose the alternative course which they preferred. In *Quinn* v. *Leathem*[2] a wide meaning was given to words like threats, intimidation or coercion, especially by Lord Lindley, but that was not the *ratio decidendi* adopted by the House. These words, as R. S. Wright pointed out in his book on Criminal Conspiracy, are not terms of art and are consistent either with legality or illegality. They are not correctly used in the circumstances of a case like this. In *Allen* v. *Flood, Ware and De Freville, Ltd* v. *Motor Trade Association*[3]

[1] [1898] A.C. 1. [2] [1901] A.C. 495, 510.
[3] [1921] 3 K.B. 40

and *Sorrell's* case[1], a more accurate definition was given. I should also refer to the admirable discussion by Peterson, J. in *Hodges* v. *Webb*.[2] There is nothing unlawful in giving a warning or intimation that if the party addressed pursues a certain line of conduct, others may act in a manner which he will not like and which will be prejudicial to his interests, so long as nothing unlawful is threatened or done.... The fact that the sole trader employed servants or agents in the conduct of his business would not *per se* in my opinion make these others co-conspirators with him. The special rule relating to the effect of a combination has been explained on the ground that it is easier to resist one than two. That may appear to be true if a crude illustration is taken, such as the case of two men attacking another, but even there it would not always be true if, for instance, the one man was very strong and the two very weak....

A conspiracy to injure involves *ex vi termini* an intention to injure, or more accurately, a common intention and agreement to injure. Both 'intention' and 'injure' need definition. The word 'injure' is here used in its correct meaning of 'wrongful harm', *damnum cum injuria*, not *damnum absque injuria*. That obviously raises the question, when is the harm wrongful? 'Intention' is generally determined by reference to overt acts and to the circumstances in which they are done. ...A perfectly lawful strike may aim at dislocating the employer's business for the moment, but its real object is to secure better wages or conditions for the workers. The true contrast is, I think, between the case where the object is the legitimate benefit of the combiners and the case where the object is deliberate damage without any such just cause. The courts have repudiated the idea that it is for them to determine whether the object of the combiners is reasonably calculated to achieve their benefit. The words 'motive', 'object', 'purpose', are in application to practical matters difficult strictly to define or distinguish. Sometimes mere animus, such as spite or ill will, malevolence or a wanton desire to harm without any view to personal benefit is meant. But motive is often used as meaning purpose, something objective and external, as contrasted with a mere mental state. 'Object' is, I think, the most appropriate word....I may add that a desire to injure does not necessarily involve malevolence. It may be motivated by wantonness or some object not justifiable. As to the authorities, the balance, in my opinion, is in favour of the view that malevolence as a mental state is not the test. I accordingly agree with the appellants'

[1] [1925] A.C. 700. [2] [1920] 2 Ch. 70.

contention that they are not concluded by the finding that the respondents were not malevolent.... The appellants must establish that they have been damnified by a conspiracy to injure, that is, that there was a wilful and concerted intention to injure without just cause, and consequent damage...

I have attempted to state principles so generally accepted as to pass into the realm of what has been called jurisprudence, at least in English law, which has for better or worse adopted the test of self-interest or selfishness as being capable of justifying the deliberate doing of lawful acts which inflict harm, so long as the means employed are not wrongful. The common law in England might have adopted a different criterion and one more consistent with the standpoint of a man who refuses to benefit himself at the cost of harming another. But we live in a competitive or acquisitive society, and the English common law may have felt that it was beyond its power to fix by any but the crudest distinctions and metes and bounds which divide the rightful from the wrongful use of the actor's own freedom, leaving the precise application in any particular case to the jury or judge of fact. If further principles of regulation or control are to be introduced, that is matter for the legislature....

In *Sorrell* v. *Smith* the judge's view was 'that the defendants were well meaning busybodies, who intimated third parties and so meddled with the plaintiff's business in a matter which was no business of theirs' because, as he held, they wanted a controlling decision in the dispute. The Court of Appeal and this House reversed the decision of the judge on the short ground that the real purpose of the newspaper proprietors was to promote the circulation of their papers, and that they did so by lawful means.

I think this line of reasoning applies here to answer the appellants' contention that the respondents or the union had no direct interest in the importation of yarn. On the facts found, rightly as I think, they were of opinion that the prosperity of the industry in Harris tweed was jeopardized by the importation. It is not for the court to decide whether this opinion was reasonable or not. It was a genuine opinion. It cannot be said that it was a mere sham intended to cloak a sinister desire to injure the importers. The respondents had no quarrel with the yarn importers. Their sole object, the courts below have held, was to promote their union's interests by promoting the interest of the industry on which the men's wages depended. On these findings, with which I agree, it could not be said that their combination was without sufficient justification. Nor would this conclusion be vitiated, even though their motives may have been mixed, so long as the real or predominant object, if they had more than one object, was not wrongful. Nor is the objection tenable that the respondent's real or predominant object was to secure the employers' help to get 100 per cent. membership of the union among the textile workers. Cases of mixed motives or, as I should prefer to say, of the presence of more than one object, are not uncommon. If so, it is for the jury or judge of fact to decide which is the predominant object, as it may be assumed the jury did in *Quinn's* case, when they decided on the basis that the object of the combiners was vindictive punishment, not their own practical advantage.... It was objected that there could be no combination between the employers and the union because their respective interests were necessarily opposed. I think that is a fallacious contention. It is true that employers and workmen are often at variance because the special interest of each side conflicts in a material respect as, for instance, in questions of wages, conditions of hours of work, exclusion of non-union labour. But apart from these differences in interest, both employers and workmen have a common interest in the prosperity of their industry, though the interest of one side may be in profits and of the other in wages. Hence a wider and truer view is that there is a community of interest. That view was acted upon in the present case in regard to the essential matter of yarn importation. As to the separate matter of the union membership, while that was something regarded as important by the respondents it was probably regarded by the employers as a matter of indifference to them. It was, in any case, a side issue in the combination even from the respondents' point of view. I may add that I do not accept, as a general proposition, that there must be a complete identity of interest between parties to a combination. There must, however, be sufficient identity of object, though the advantage to be derived from that same object may not be the same...

I need add merely a few words on the objection that the embargo was the act of the dockers for the benefit, not of themselves, but of the textile workers. It is enough to say that both sections were members of the union, and there was in my opinion a sufficient community of interest even if the matter is regarded from the standpoint of the men, as individuals, and not from the standpoint of the respondents, who were the only parties sued. Their interest, however, was to promote the advantage of the union as a whole.

VISCOUNTS SIMON, L.C., and MAUGHAM, and LORDS THANKERTON and PORTER delivered concurring speeches.

DEANE v. CRAIK

The Times, 16 March, 1962

The plaintiff brought an action against the defendant trade unionists for a malicious conspiracy to injure the plaintiff's professional standing by having all his work black-listed. The plaintiff was a film-producer. The defendants blacked his goods when he failed to pay money which he owed to three members of the union following filming on location in Portugal.

SALMON, J. said: The position was that on 13 October 1960, Mr Deane knew he owed about £550 and had owed it for nearly two months. He replied to a letter from Mr Craik, and the plaintiff's letter bore the hall mark of a letter written by a man bent upon delaying and defeating his creditors as long as possible. Finally, after further letters and meetings, instructions were sent out to all laboratories and all shop stewards to black all work of the plaintiffs.

As a result of that action, Kay Laboratories refused to handle the plaintiff's work and until that ban was lifted, as a result of an interlocutory injunction obtained in this action, the plaintiffs suffered some loss. That loss was small and did not exceed £50.

In this action the plaintiffs contended that all the defendants conspired against them and as a result of that conspiracy they suffered damage. Two points therefore arose for decision: (1) Were the defendants liable at common law for the tort of conspiracy? (2) Were the defendants protected by the Trade Disputes Act, 1906?

The first question depended largely on the motive, purpose or object upon which the defendants acted. It was now clear law that if two or more combined for the sole purpose of injuring another, and in pursuance of that combination caused him damage, the combiners had committed the tort of conspiracy notwithstanding that the act causing the damage was not unlawful. It was equally clear law that if persons combined with the sole purpose of furthering some legitimate object of their own they committed no tort, even if in carrying out that object they in fact caused damage to another, providing that act was lawful. Difficulties had arisen because men's motives were rarely solitary and obvious, but varied and complex. Most of the difficulties had been resolved by the decision in Crofter Hand Woven Harris Tweed v. Veitch ([1942] A.C. 435) that if the predominant purpose of those combining was to protect their lawful interest it was not a tortious conspiracy.

Counsel for the plaintiff had contended that the defendants' predominant purpose was to injure Mr Deane or to obtain payments for their three members. He contended on the authority of Giblan's Case ([1903] 2 K.B. 600) that if persons combined to compel the payment of a debt by industrial action the law presumes that the dominent purpose was to intrigue since such compulsion could never be lawful.

The predominant purpose of the defendants was to keep their industry clean by protecting technicians against defaulting producers. The defendants were very conscious of the history of their industry and the perils to which technicians were exposed before the trade union came into existence. They believed that if Mr Deane was allowed to act as he had done other producers would probably follow his example and other technicians would suffer.

No point arose under the Trade Disputes Act, 1906, as the defendants had incurred no liability at common law. If, however, the defendants were liable at common law then they were protected, by the provisions of that Act, because there was a trade dispute. The Act defined a trade dispute as 'any dispute between employers and workmen...which is connected with...the terms of the employment'. There was a dispute between the three members and Mr Deane as to the terms of their employment at the time that the defendants acted and the defendants were protected by the Trade Disputes Act, 1906.

HUNTLEY v. THORNTON

[1957] 1 W.L.R. 321

[For facts see *ante*, p. 403.]

HARMAN, J. referred to the *Crofter* case (*ante*, p. 453) and went on: Lord Simon sums up his conclusions in these words[1]: 'I am content to say that, unless the real and predominant purpose is to advance the defendants' lawful interests in a matter where the defendants honestly believe that those interests would directly suffer if the action taken against the plaintiffs was not taken, a combination wilfully to damage a man in his trade is unlawful'.

Lord Maugham, in the same case,...points out also[2] that the absence of spite or malice does not preclude a finding of conspiracy, and that it is not enough to justify wrongful acts to show that the predominant motive was not the injury of the plaintiff. He formulates the question thus[3]: 'Was the real or predominant purpose of the combination to forward or defend the trade or business interests of the trade union

---

[1] [1942] A.C. 435, 446.   [2] [1942] A.C. 435, 451.   [3] Ibid. 452.

and its members and of the mill owners? If the answer is in the negative it would be necessary very carefully to examine "the real purpose" or "the true motive" (which I think is the same thing) of the combination and to consider whether there was in the eyes of the law a just cause or excuse for taking or directing acts in combination which will destroy the present means of subsistence of the appellants. On this point, if it arises, there is little authority to guide us, but I will add that when the question of the real purpose is being considered it is impossible to leave out of consideration the principle that men are in general to be taken as intending the direct consequences of their acts'.

Was there then a conspiracy on the part of the Hartlepool District Committee to injure the plaintiff? In my judgment there was, because the acts of these defendants were 'without justification', to use Lord Cave's words. It might be arguable that in the early days the members of the district committee honestly took the view that nothing would uphold the prestige of the union in the district but the plaintiff's expulsion, though this is a view so wrong-headed that it would be hard to accept it. The only element in the charges against the plaintiff relevant here is his disobedience to the instruction to stop work on 2 December, and that is indeed the charge made in the letter summoning him before the district committee on 11 December. But the recommendation to expel relies not only on that but on the new charge of 'coercing' other members, a charge of which no notice was given and which was entirely unsupported by evidence. The third ground is the 'arrogant attitude' of the plaintiff. If this refers to the fact that the plaintiff insisted on questioning the validity of the summons to strike it is a denial of the right to hold an opinion. It would be no ground even if the plaintiff was mistaken; it becomes grotesque when, as I have shown, he was probably right. If it be a reference to the plaintiff's use of bad language, it is enough to point out that the rules themselves provide a penalty of a fine of 2s. 6d. for that offence (rule 22(3)).

The matter does not end there. When the executive council declined to sanction expulsion for disobedience of the strike summons the district committee persisted in asking for expulsion for the plaintiff's 'disrespectful attitude' to themselves. This looks very like punishment for personal reasons.

Be this as it may, all question of expulsion was closed by the general secretary's letter of 6 January 1954. The district committee then knew that nothing more than a reprimand and perhaps a fine would be countenanced by the executive council. Nevertheless by the resolution of 15 January, and still more clearly by that of 25 January, they sought to flout the executive council's decision and to produce by other means, at any rate within their own district, and as the letter to Mr Thornton shows also on Tees-side, all the effects of expulsion. It is an ironic comment that while pretending to visit the plaintiff with a penalty for disloyalty to the union they were themselves guilty of that very offence.

In my judgment it is true to say that by this time the district committee had entirely lost sight of what the interests of the union demanded, and thought only of their own ruffled dignity. Probably the publicity given to the affair in the press was largely responsible, but in saying this I cast no reflection on that organ which was reporting fairly enough on a matter of public interest. It had become a question of the district committee's prestige; they were determined to use any weapon ready to their hand to vindicate their authority, and grossly abused the quite frightening powers at their command. The threat 'to withdraw all labour' from any employer daring to engage one of their own members whom they had been elected to protect was, as events showed, effective enough, even though they had as they well knew, no right to take any such step. The district committee had no power to call a strike.

The matter does not end there. It was none of their business to interfere in another district, and the letter to Thornton was only justifiable if the plaintiff was or was about to be expelled. This is the inference that Thornton drew, and in my judgment was intended to draw....That damage was suffered by the plaintiff cannot be questioned, so all the elements of a civil conspiracy are present.

In view of this finding I need not consider whether the actions of any member of this group was in itself a tortious act against the plaintiff. Assuming that what was done might not be a legal wrong if done by an individual, it is clear that the combination may make the act wrongful...

When I turn to consider the case against the officials of the Tees-side district, the defendants Thornton and Langford, the picture is at once seen to be very different....No doubt Thornton and Langford lent themselves to their co-defendants' plan, but I have no evidence that their motive was to injure the plaintiff rather than to forward the interests of the union as they saw them. They had none of their co-defendants' personal reasons for attacking the plaintiff, who was in fact unknown to them. I cannot hold them to be participators in the conspiracy I have found to exist. It was suggested that they might themselves have formed a separate conspiracy. No doubt they acted in concert, but I cannot find that their predominant motive was to injure the plaintiff.

SCALA BALLROOM (WOLVERHAMPTON) LTD *v.* RATCLIFFE

Court of Appeal [1958] 3 All E.R. 220

The plaintiffs excluded coloured persons from their ballroom. The Musicians Union, of which the defendants were officials, boycotted the ballroom in protest against the colour bar. The plaintiffs applied for an injunction on the ground of a conspiracy to injure. The union had coloured members but could not prove any immediate material interest which they were pursuing. The court nevertheless held that the object of the combination was legitimate as a furtherance of union interests, particularly in the light of an affidavit sworn by one official of the union in which he insisted on the 'insidious effects' of a colour bar imposed on the audience because 'it is impossible for musicians to insulate themselves from their audience'.

HODSON, L.J.: I am not prepared, at any rate, for the purposes of this provisional opinion to say that the interests which can lawfully be protected are confined to the material interests in the sense of interests which can be exchanged for cash. Lawful interests in my judgment may and I think do extend further than that; but reading the affidavit... it seems to me that *prima facie* at any rate the defendants in this case, who represent the members of the Musicians Union, which includes amongst its members a great many coloured people, have a lawful interest to protect in looking after their members' interests and, taking the long view, in looking after their livelihood as well.

MORRIS, L.J.: ...But it seems to me that, if the defendants honestly believe that a certain policy is desirable and that it is the wish of their members that that policy should prevail and that there should be no colour bar discrimination, it can be said that the welfare of the members is being advanced, even though it cannot be positively translated into or shown to be reflected in detailed financial terms.*

SELLERS, L.J. delivered a concurring judgment.

* *Note*: In all the recent judgments, an honest belief in pursuit of normal union interests, as understood today, has been sufficient to escape liability for common law 'conspiracy to injure'. See e.g. *Rookes* v. *Barnard* (*post*, p. 503) and *Stratford* v. *Lindley* (*post*, p. 478) where, even though their Lordships were not prepared to hold that the defendants had acted in furtherance of a genuine trade dispute, but in pursuit

(ii) INDUCING BREACH OF CONTRACT

[*Note*. Section 3 Trade Disputes Act, 1906, provides a limited protection in respect of this tort: *ante*, p. 385.* See too the extension in Trade Disputes Act, 1965, *post*, p. 520. The protection of s. 3 extends to all types of remedy: *Camden Exhibition Ltd.* v. *Lynott*, *ante*, p. 306.]

LUMLEY *v.* GYE

2 E. & B. 216 [118 E.R. 749]

The plaintiff, manager of the Queen's Theatre, had a contract with an opera singer, Miss Wagner, whereby she agreed to sing at his theatre for thrcc months and not to sing anywhere else during that time. The plaintiff sued the defendant alleging that he induced Miss Wagner to break her contract by getting her to sing at Her Majesty's theatre instead.

CROMPTON, J.: Whatever may have been the origin or foundation of the law as to enticing of servants, and whether it be, as contended by the plaintiff, an instance and branch of a wider rule, or whether it be, as contended by the defendant, an anomaly and an exception from the general rule of law on such subjects, it must now be considered clear law that a person who wrongfully and maliciously, or, which is the same thing, with notice, interrupts the relation subsisting between master and servant by procuring the servant to depart from the master's service, or by harbouring and keeping him as servant after he has quitted it and during the time stipulated for as the period of service, whereby the master is injured, commits a wrongful act for which he is responsible at law.

ERLE and WIGHTMAN, JJ. delivered concurring judgments; COLERIDGE, J. dissented.

of inter-union rivalry, they nevertheless held that the union officials acted 'to forward what they believed to be the interests of the union and fundamental trade union principles' (Lord Reid) so that no conspiracy to injure *simpliciter* was made out. As to political objects, see further O. Kahn-Freund (1959) 22 M.L.R. 69.
* On the problematical relationship of 'Limb 1' and 'Limb 2' of s. 3, see Wedderburn in (1964) 27 M.L.R. 257, continuing (1962) 25 M.L.R. 513 and (1961) 24 M.L.R. 572; and Hoffman (1965) 81 L.Q.R. 116. The section must now be read in the light of the House of Lord's speeches in *Rookes* v. *Barnard*, *post*, p. 503.

SOUTH WALES MINERS' FEDERATION v.
GLAMORGAN COAL COMPANY LTD

House of Lords   [1905] A.C. 239

This appeal arose from an action by the respondents for damages for wrongfully and maliciously inducing colliery workmen to break their contracts of employment with the Glamorgan Coal Co. Ltd and others. The colliery workers, who were represented by the appellant Federation, were paid on a sliding scale agreement, rising and falling with the price of coal. In defence to the above charges, the Federation pleaded an honest desire to further the interests of the workmen; that there was lawful justification for their activities. They feared a further reduction in wages.

EARL OF HALSBURY, L.C.: Now it is sought to be justified, first, because it is said that the men were acting in their own interest, and that they were sincerely under the belief that the employers would themselves benefit by their collieries being interrupted in their work; but what sort of excuse is this for breaking a contract when the co-contractor refuses to allow the breach? It seems to me to be absurd to suppose that a benefit which he refuses to accept justified an intentional breach of contractual rights. It may, indeed, be urged in proof of the allegation that there was no ill-will against the employers. I assume this to be true, but I have no conception what can be meant by an excuse for breaking a contract because you really think it will not harm your co-contractor.

I absolutely refuse to discuss the cases which have been suggested widely apart from the question of what pecuniary advantage may be reaped from breaking a contract, where, upon moral or religious grounds, people may be justly advised to refuse to perform what they have agreed to do.

Some cases may be suggested when higher and deeper considerations may, in a moral point of view, justify the refusal to do what has been agreed to be done. Such cases may give rise to the consideration whether, in a moral or religious point of view, you are not bound to indemnify the person whom your refusal injures; but a Court of law has only to decide whether there is a legal justification.*

Again, I refuse to go into a discussion of the duty or the moral right to tender advice. The facts in this case show nothing in the nature of

---

* Consider *Brimelow* v. *Casson, ante*, p. 389. The whole of the common law relating to 'justification' in this tort was reviewed in Canada by Gale J. in *Posluns* v. *Toronto Stock Exchange* (1964) 46 D.L.R. (2d.) 210, pp. 270–271.

advice, even if the supposed duty could be created by people who made them their official advisers who were to advise them even to break the law. But, so I have said, these are peremptory orders given by the official superiors of the body, and it has been found by the learned judge who tried the case that the body sued was responsible for the interference with the workmen.

LORD JAMES: The intention of the defendants was directly to procure the breach of contracts. The fact that their motives were good in the interests of those they moved to action does not form any answer to those who have suffered from the unlawful act. During the arguments that have been addressed to your Lordships I do not think quite sufficient distinction was drawn between the intention and the motives of the defendants. Their intention clearly was that the workmen should break their contracts. The defendants' motives, no doubt, were that by so doing wages should be raised. But if in carrying out the intention the defendants purposely procured an unlawful act to be committed, the wrong that is thereby inflicted cannot be obliterated by the existence of a motive to secure a money benefit to the wrong-doers.

LORDS MACNAGHTEN and LINDLEY delivered concurring speeches.

DENABY AND CADEBY MAIN COLLIERIES LTD *v.* YORKSHIRE MINERS' ASSOCIATION

House of Lords   [1906] A.C. 384

This case arose out of the same strike as *Yorkshire Miners' Association* v. *Howden* [see *post*, p. 594]. Following a dispute about bag dirt and a 10 per cent reduction in wages, workmen at a colliery came out on an unauthorised and unofficial strike at the instigation of branch officials. Their union pointed out to them that they were in breach of contract and told them to go back to work.

The Home Secretary had issued some new regulations on timbering which various people thought *ultra vires*; and the men were offered re-employment on terms which embodied these regulations. Supported by their union the men declined to sign on again on these terms. Strike pay was then made to the men for six months until restrained in *Howden's* case. The strike then ended. The collieries then sued the union for damages, claiming *inter alia* that it was liable as principal for the act of its agents—the officials—in procuring the strike in breach of contract; and that it was liable for maliciously aiding by unlawful means a strike of the plaintiff's union. The action was unsuccessful.

Lord Loreburn, L.C. examined the union rules and said:

The net result of these provisions is that all strikes of a branch are prohibited unless the prescribed majority of branch members is obtained; that no strike pay is to be granted except the strike be sanctioned by the central council after peaceful efforts have been exhausted, but that a plebiscite of the entire association may adopt a strike after it has commenced.

On the other hand, if any branch is locked out in consequence of any action lawfully taken by the association to remedy grievances the men are entitled to maintenance equal to strike pay. Can it be said in the face of these rules that the association is liable in damages for the action of delegates or of branch officials or committees in procuring a strike (whether accompanied or not by breach of contract) without a ballot, without the sanction of the council, and without a registered vote of the entire association? In my opinion the association is not so liable. The delegates are agents of the branches to represent them in the council. When acting in the council they are agents of the entire association to do the business of the council. They are not agents of the association to represent it or act for it in their localities, either as to strikes or other matters.

Branch officials and committees are elected by members of the branch, who are engaged in a common service under one particular employer. If they quarrel with the employers about the conditions of their service they have a right to strike. The association does not confer that right, which is derived from the general law, but it restricts the right by rules requiring a prescribed majority as the indispensable preliminary. I do not see how either the officials or committees thereby become agents of the association to procure a strike even if it were lawful and regular, still less to procure it contrary to the rules and contrary to the law in breach of existing contracts.

It is true that on certain conditions the association is bound to furnish strike pay. Will that circumstance create the agency for which Mr. Bankes contends? I will suppose that the employers also are members of an association of coalowners, as we were told they are, and that the coalowners' association bind themselves to support each other with money in the event of any one member locking out his workmen after certain conditions had been observed. If such member locked out his men without giving the notice prescribed by contract it would seem very strange to suppose the other members were liable to damages for an act over which they had no control and which was contrary to the conditions. Yet the cases are precisely the same.

In my opinion the first head of claim entirely fails.

The second head of claim advanced by the plaintiffs is to be found in questions 6, 7 and 8, and relates, not to the initiation of the strike, but to its maintenance by the defendant association after it had been commenced. It amounts to this, that after the strike had commenced the defendant association, by its officials or by the members of the committees of the Denaby and Cadeby branches, assisted and maintained the strike by means of intimidation in order to prevent the men who were still working from continuing to work, by inducing others not to enter the plaintiffs' service and by granting strike pay against rules of the association. I find no evidence in support of any material part of this charge against the defendant association.

LORD DAVEY: My Lords, the appellants were perfectly within their right in electing to treat the absence of the men from work since 29 June as a recission of their contracts and requiring them to enter into new contracts of service before resuming work. But they cannot have it both ways. If these men were no longer in the employment of the colliery owners the original vice which infected the initiation of the strike on 29 June was purged, and the men were no longer in the position of 'playing' (to use their own expression) in breach of their contracts, but were henceforth men who declined to enter into contracts of service with the colliery owners on the conditions offered them, which they had a perfect right to do. Then came the important question of strike pay. Mr Pickard appears to have thought that the situation resembled a lock-out by the colliery owners, and strike pay could properly be paid in accordance with the rules. And on 24 July a resolution was passed at a special council meeting that strike pay be paid from the first day when the men presented themselves for work, and Mr Chambers would not allow them to resume work unless they signed a new contract. Strike pay was accordingly paid out of the funds of the association until February 1902, when it was stopped by injunction in Howden's action, and the strike collapsed.

My Lords, it has been held in this House, affirming the decision in the Courts below, that the payment of strike pay to the Denaby and Cadeby strikers was unauthorized by the rules of the association, and therefore illegal: *Yorkshire Miners' Association* v. *Howden*.[1] There is no evidence impugning the good faith, both of Mr Pickard and the

---

[1] [1905] A.C. 256 (H.L.).

council, but they made a grievous mistake. The payment was *ultra vires* as regards not only the council, but also as regards the association itself. In other words, it was not the act of the association, and was incapable of ratification by the members of the association. And I have some difficulty in seeing under these circumstances how the unauthorized employment of the association's money by its trustees can prejudice or create any liability against the association.

LORD JAMES: It was further contended on the part of the plaintiffs that the acts of the defendants' union in granting strike pay and some individual acts established liability on account of what was termed maintaining the strike existing at the Denaby and Cadeby Collieries. Importance must be attached to this argument in consequence of the judgment given by the learned Master of the Rolls upon the point thus raised. In relation to it consideration should be given to the term 'maintaining the strike'. If one assists in procuring the commission of an unlawful act, doubtless liability follows, and so if the defendants had done anything, by assistance or otherwise, to induce the branch workmen to break their contracts the union would have been liable. But no such inducing to break a contract was proved. When the assistance was given, that is, when strike pay was voted, the unlawful acts had been committed, all the contracts of employment were terminated, and employers and employed were in respect of contracts entirely unconnected. So that the effect of the grant of strike pay was not to cause or induce the commission of an unlawful act, but to place the workmen in the position of being able to maintain themselves without entering into a new contract of labour with the plaintiffs or with anyone else. This is no more than the subscribing to a strike fund. Within the last few years we have had instances of the public contributing largely towards the maintenance of men who had ceased to work under conditions which constituted what is called a strike. Were these subscribers liable to an action? It surely must be admitted that they were not, even if the workmen had broken their contracts.*

LORDS ROBERTSON and ATKINSON delivered concurring speeches; LORD MACNAGHTEN agreed with the opinion of LORD LOREBURN, L.C.

---

* Note that liability may not arise from 'harbouring' or assisting an employee who left his job in breach of contract but who refuses to return to it, because the original employer cannot prove any damage: *Jones Bros. (Hunstanton) Ltd.* v. *Stevens* [1955] 1 Q.B. 275 (C.A.).

WHITE v. RILEY

Court of Appeal   [1921] 1 Ch. 1

Members of the Curriers' union employed by D. informed D. that unless the plaintiff transferred to their union or left the shop they would come out on strike.* D. gave the plaintiff notice.

WARRINGTON, L.J.: The only so-called threat of which any evidence was given consisted of a letter signed by the defendant Riley, and written on behalf of the men who had been present at the shop meeting. [His Lordship read the letter and continued:] No other threat is alleged except that, at a subsequent meeting between the men and the employers, the men, through their spokesman, determined to adhere to the notice which they had already given.

Now the question arises, is the giving of a notice of that kind on behalf of the men a wrongful act, I mean at common law quite independently of the Trade Disputes Act, 1906? That an act of that kind done by an individual is not at common law a wrongful act is I think quite plain from the decision in *Allen* v. *Flood*.[1]...They did not conspire by any threat to obtain his dismissal from his employment: What they did seek to do was to secure that if he remained in the employment he should become a member of the Curriers' Union. What they did they did by means which, in my opinion, were perfectly lawful.

The second finding of fact by the learned judge is, that they were guilty of inducing and intentionally obtaining severally and in combination a direct breach by the employers of the plaintiff's agreement for service. That again, if possible, is even less to be supported on the evidence than the previous finding.

What happened was this. It was not proved what were the terms of the employment so far as concerns the right of the employers to terminate it; but it seems to have been assumed on both sides that the employers had the right to determine it either by giving a week's notice or in the alternative paying a week's wages, and when it was intimated to the men that the employers might have to pay the week's wages in lieu of notice and so avoiding a breach of contract, the men in effect said to the employers: 'We will pay the wages; if you pay them you may deduct them from our wages in the following week.' It is true that the employers for some reason best known to themselves and which

---

[1] [1898] A.C. 1.

* The notice of strike was probably long enough to be equivalent to the obligatory period for the men's notice to terminate employment: see the calculation in (1962) 25 M.L.R. p. 519, n. 53.

was not explained to us, did not subsequently carry that proposal into effect. They did not pay the week's wages to the plaintiff. But that was no fault of the men. The men intended that the contract which they believed to be the true contract should be carried out by the employers and that they should terminate the plaintiff's service in the way in which he was in their view, and apparently in the view of all the parties concerned, entitled to have it terminated—namely, by payment to him of a week's wages in lieu of notice. The answer therefore to that claim is that the defendants did not knowingly and intentionally endeavour to induce or succeed in inducing the employers to commit a breach of that contract. What they intended was to avoid a breach of contract.... That being so it is really unnecessary to consider the question of the construction and effect of the Trade Disputes Act, 1906.... In the present case there was, I think, quite plainly a dispute between workmen and workmen and it was a dispute as to whether or not the plaintiff should, in the position in which he then stood in relation to the unions, be employed by the particular employers. In my opinion that was a dispute connected with the employment or non-employment of the plaintiff. It was also a dispute connected with the employment or non-employment of the other workmen because they were unwilling to continue in the employment if the plaintiff was also in that employment. On this point, I wish to say for myself that I cannot appreciate the reasoning of Astbury, J. in *Valentine* v. *Hyde*.[1] He treats the matter as if the dispute was whether or not the workman in question should join the particular union. In my judgment that is only an incident in the dispute. The dispute is whether while he is not a member of the union to which the other men belong he should be employed by the employers. It is really a dispute as to the terms upon which he should continue in the employment. On this point I very much prefer the reasoning of Peterson, J. in *Hodges* v. *Webb*[2] to the reasoning of Astbury, J. in *Valentine* v. *Hyde* and in the present case.

LORD STERNDALE, M.R. and YOUNGER, L.J. delivered concurring judgments.

NOTE: TWO PROBLEMS CONNECTED WITH THIS TORT

A. Who is the proper plaintiff in actions based on this tort? In *Boulting* v. *Association of Cinematograph, Television and Allied Technicians* (*post*, p. 567) Upjohn, L.J. said:

[1] [1919] 2 Ch. 129.   [2] [1920] 2 Ch. 70.

If A procures B to break his contract with C, C can complain because A commits a well-established tort against C. But B has no right at law to restrain A from attempting to suborn him from his duty to C. He must resist A's efforts by strength of will. If B succumbs to A's blandishments and contracts with him in breach of his duty to C, B can have no right to complain of A's conduct if A performs his contract with B which the latter has so wrongly entered into.

Similarly, see Russell, L.J. in *Camden Exhibition Ltd* v. *Lynott* (*ante*, p. 309). On this basis, the employer in dispute with a union would not usually be a competent plaintiff in an action for inducing breach of commercial contracts. The plaintiff would have to be one of the commercial customers. The point does not seem to have been taken in *Square Grip Reinforcement Ltd* v. *Macdonald* (*post*, p. 495). Consider, too, *Stratford Ltd* v. *Lindley* in this connection (*post*, p. 478).

B. It has recently been suggested in some judgments that an injunction might be issued against a third party to prevent his joining and assisting in the breach of a contract, on equitable principles, without strict proof of all the ingredients of the tort now under discussion. See for example *Printers & Finishers Ltd* v. *Holloway* [1964] 3 All E.R. 731 and 738 n.; and the C.A. in *Sefton* v. *Tophams* [1965] Ch. 1140 (a point not discussed when the H.L. reversed the decision [1966] 1 All E.R. 1039).

Compare the possible liability after *Rookes* v. *Barnard* (*post*, p. 503) for conspiracy to break a contract: discussed in Excursus A, p. 525.

D. C. THOMSON & CO. LTD *v.* DEAKIN

Court of Appeal [1952] Ch. 646

D. C. Thomson ran a non-union shop, and dismissed a man who joined a union (N.A.T.S.O.P.A.). A boycott was organized and men employed at Bowaters Sales Ltd, who supplied D. C. Thomson with paper, told Bowaters that they might not be prepared to deliver paper to Thomson. Bowaters never ordered the men to deliver the paper; but instead told Thomson & Co. that they would not be able to deliver the paper which they had contracted to do. D. C. Thomson & Co. sought an interlocutory injunction against officials of various unions concerned to restrain them from procuring any breach by Bowaters of their contract with D. C. Thomson & Co. There was no allegation of a conspiracy to injure.

EVERSHED, M.R.: It was suggested in the course of argument by Sir

Frank Soskice and by Mr Lindner, that the tort must still be properly confined to such direct intervention, that is, to cases where the intervener or persuader uses by personal intervention persuasion on the mind of one of the parties to the contract so as to procure that party to break it.

I am unable to agree that any such limitation is logical, rational or part of our law. In such cases where the intervener (if I may call him such) does so directly act upon the mind of a party to the contract as to cause him to break it, the result is, for practical purposes as though in substance he, the intervener, is breaking the contract although he is not a party to it....

I find it for myself exceedingly difficult to suppose that, the exercise of the right of way by the persons persuaded being lawful, the intervener would be liable according to the principles of the law for having persuaded them to do that lawful thing. The persons using it might, or might not, themselves have been innocent of any desire to cause damage to A; they might be innocent of any knowledge of the existence of a contract between A and B. If they were so innocent, they themselves would, in my view, clearly not be under any liability. If they knew of the existence of a contract and intended to cause its breach, another question might arise (and this is a matter to which I shall have later to return) whether they would in any circumstances be themselves liable. Another instance may be quoted which was taken by my brother Jenkins earlier in the case. Let it be supposed that A had made a contract to supply certain goods to B and that the intervener, knowing of the contract and intending to deprive B of its benefit, had proceeded to go into the market and buy up all the goods that he could find of that character, so as to render it impossible for A in fact to perform the contract. Again, I think it is impossible to say, according to the principles of our law, that the intervener in such a case was acting tortiously....

I come then to such formulation of the result as seems to me to be correct; but I should first add this. The argument that this tort should be confined to such direct intervention or interference as is illustrated, for example, in *Lumley* v. *Gye*[1] introduces this strange difficulty. A limited liability company, a persona ficta, can only act through agents or servants. If the intervention has to be of so direct a kind, it would obviously create strange problems in the case of a limited liability company. No doubt, if I approach some person in the company who

[1] 2 El. & Bl. 216.

has authority on the company's behalf to make contracts, I may be said to be approaching the company direct. I think that the illustration of the company emphasizes the anomaly which would result if, in the case of a limited company, a tortious act were only committed if the person approached or induced had a particular office or responsibility (actual or perhaps ostensible) in the company.

Dealing first with individual contractors, it seems to me that the intervener, assuming in all cases that he knows of the contract and acts with the aim and object of procuring its breach to the damage of B, one of the contracting parties, will be liable not only (1) if he directly intervenes by persuading A to break it, but also (2) if he intervenes by the commission of some act wrongful in itself so as to prevent A from in fact performing his contract; and also (3) if he persuades a third party, for example, a servant of A, to do an act in itself wrongful or not legitimate (as committing a breach of a contract of service with A) so as to render, as was intended, impossible A's performance of his contract with B.

In the case of a company, the approach to or the persuasion of a managing director, or of some person having like authority, may be regarded as being in all respects equivalent to the direct approach of the individual contractor, as found in *Lumley* v. *Gye* and in the *Glamorgan* case; but, if the approach is made to other servants of the company, the case, in my view, becomes parallel to an approach made not to the contracting party himself, but to some servant of the contracting party, so that the intervener will only be liable if the act which he procures the servant to do is either a breach of contract towards the servant's master or is otherwise tortious in itself....If that be the law, I must now come to the facts and see what the conclusion must be. I have already indicated that there is, in my opinion, no sufficient case made out for a conspiracy. I must, therefore, deal with each of the defendants in turn.

[His Lordship considered the evidence against each defendant in turn and held that in each case the evidence did not establish such action as would constitute the tort of wrongfully procuring the breach of the contract in question. His Lordship continued:] As to the whole of the defendants, it follows accordingly that, in my judgment, there is not on this motion proved any procuring of any wrongful act by any member of any of the unions concerned.

I need only add that there was, on the evidence, no breach of contract by any workmen, since Bowaters, for reasons which I doubt not were prudent, took the line that they would not order any man either to load or to drive paper for the plaintiffs. They accepted the situation as they found it and made no attempt to contrive to get the paper to the plaintiffs by any other means. It is true, if my analysis is correct, that there was, in the case of the first three defendants, what might be called a direct approach to Bowaters, but, so far as I understand the evidence, I cannot see that that direct approach amounted to anything more than a statement of the facts, as the members of the union understood them to be. In particular, there was a reference to picketing which was obviously of great significance; and, whether that reference was correct or incorrect, there is no suggestion that it was not made in the *bona fide* belief of its truth.

I appreciate that in these matters there is a difficult question of distinguishing between what might be called persuasion and what might be called advice, meaning by the latter a mere statement of, or drawing of the attention of the party addressed to, the state of facts as they were. In the case of *Camden Nominees Ltd.* v. *Forcey*[1] before Simonds, J., it was held that the advice given was of such a nature (was of a character obviously intended to be acted upon) that it was for all practical purposes equivalent to persuasion; but, if the matter be advice merely (in the ordinary sense of that word), it seems to me that there can be no complaint about it; nor do I think that Mr Beyfus can derive any substantial assistance by saying that Bowaters proved themselves merely chicken-hearted and that the ease with which a person may be persuaded is not a relevant consideration in determining whether the persuader was wrongful in what he was doing. That may, as a general proposition, be true; but in this case the evidence on this motion, whatever may emerge when the matter is fully investigated, falls too far short of any proof of what is required to constitute a cause of action such as would entitle the plaintiffs to an injunction. Put another way, I cannot see that the evidence establishes that there was anything done by Bowaters *vis-à-vis* the plaintiffs which is fairly attributable to any such pressure, persuasion or procuration on the part of any of these defendants, as would in any event cause them to be liable in tort....

I have referred already to the absence of proof of direct procurement or attempted procurement of wrongful acts on the part of the workmen. There were, in fact, so far as I can see, no wrongful acts at all on the workmen's part. There is, moreover, no evidence that there was actual

[1] [1940] Ch. 352.

knowledge, on the part of any of the persons charged, of the contract or of any contract between Bowaters and the plaintiffs, assuming such contract to have been broken; or at least, if these persons thought that there might be or was some contract, any knowledge of the terms of that contract....If all else were satisfactorily proved, it might well be (having regard to common knowledge about the way business is conducted) that absence of such strict proof would not suffice to prevent the grant of relief; but, when the whole matter is generally regarded, it seems to me that the case is a very different case from anything that was contemplated by Lord Macnaghten in *Quinn* v. *Leathem*[1] and approved in subsequent cases in which *Quinn* v. *Leathem* has been applied.

Having reached that conclusion, it is unnecessary for me to express concluded opinions on the matters raised in regard to the Trade Disputes Act, 1906, particularly on the point of great difficulty which emerges in reference to s. 3 of that Act....Having read the section, it is pertinent to observe that it would not, as I follow it, having regard to Mr Beyfus' concession, be a wrongful or actionable act on the part of these defendants *vis-à-vis* Bowaters to cause workmen belonging to their respective unions to break their contracts of employment; but, if that be so, it does not follow, nor is it in my judgment the case, that, if the workmen did break their contracts, they, the workmen, did not do an unlawful act, in the sense of committing a breach of contract. I should, therefore, be prepared to hold that the defendants would not be entitled to resist the plaintiffs' claim merely by saying that their own procuration of the workmen's breach of contract was *vis-à-vis* Bowaters protected by s. 3.

JENKINS, L.J.: I see no distinction in principle for the present purpose between persuading a man to break his contract with another, preventing him by physical restraint from performing it, making his performance of it impossible by taking away or damaging his tools or machinery, and making his performance of it impossible by depriving him, in breach of their contracts, of the services of his employees. All these are wrongful acts, and if done with knowledge of and intention to bring about a breach of a contract to which the person directly wronged is a party, and, if in fact producing that result, I fail to see why they should not all alike fall within the sphere of actionable interference with contractual relations delimited by Lords Macnaghten and Lindley in *Quinn* v. *Leathem.*

But, while admitting this form of actionable interference in principle,

[1] [1901] A.C. 495.

I would hold it strictly confined to cases where it is clearly shown, first, that the person charged with actionable interference knew of the existence of the contract and intended to procure its breach; secondly, that the person so charged did definitely and unequivocally persuade, induce or procure the employees concerned to break their contracts of employment with the intent I have mentioned; thirdly, that the employees so persuaded, induced or procured did in fact break their contracts of employment; and, fourthly, that breach of the contract forming the alleged subject of interference ensued as a necessary consequence of the breaches by the employees concerned of their contracts of employment.

I should add that by the expression 'necessary consequence' used here and elsewhere in this judgment I mean that it must be shown that, by reason of the withdrawal of the services of the employees concerned, the contract breaker was unable, as a matter of practical possibility, to perform his contract; in other words, I think the continuance of the services of the particular employees concerned must be so vital to the performance of the contract alleged to have been interfered with as to make the effect of their withdrawal comparable, for practical purposes, to a direct invasion of the contractual rights of the party aggrieved under the contract alleged to have been interfered with, as, for example (in the case of a contract for personal services), the physical restraint of the person by whom such services are to be performed....

If by reference to the form of actionable interference with contractual rights now propounded, general exhortations issued in the course of a trade dispute, such as 'Stop supplies to X', 'Refuse to handle X's goods', 'Treat X as "black" ', and the like, were regarded as amounting to actionable interference, because persons reached by such exhortations might respond to them by breaking their contracts of employment and thereby causing breaches of contracts between their employers and other persons, and because the person issuing such exhortations must be taken constructively to have known that the employers concerned must have contracts of some kind or other with other persons, and that his exhortations (general as they were) might lead to breaches of those contracts through breaches of contracts of employment committed by persons moved by his exhortations, then, the proposition must be accepted, that it is an actionable wrong to advocate objects which can be achieved by lawful means, because they can also be achieved by unlawful means; and to that proposition I decline to subscribe.

Furthermore, as the judge in effect pointed out in his judgment, almost every strike, if to any extent successful, must cause breaches of contracts between the employer against whom it is directed and the persons with whom he is doing business, the very object of the strike being to bring his business to a standstill or himself to terms. Again, many a strike embarked on in support of a strike in progress in some other concern must have had for its immediate object the cutting off of supplies to, or prevention of distribution of the products of, or the application of similar pressure upon, that other concern....

Finally, not every breach of a contract of employment with a trading or manufacturing concern by an employee engaged in services required for the performance of a contract between his employer and some other person carries with it as a necessary consequence (in the sense above indicated) the breach of the last mentioned contract. For instance, A induces B, C's lorry driver, to refuse, in breach of his contract of employment, to carry goods which C is under contract to deliver to D, and does so with a view to causing the breach of C's contract with D. C could, if he chose, engage some other lorry driver, or arrange alternative means of transport, but does not do so. He fails to deliver the goods, telling D he is prevented from doing so by B's breach of contract. In such circumstances, there has been no direct invasion by A of C's rights under his contract with D, and, although A has committed an actionable wrong against C, designed to bring about the breach of C's contract with D, and a breach has in fact occurred, it cannot be said that the breach has in fact been caused by A's wrongful act, and therefore D cannot, in my view, establish as against A an actionable interference with his rights under his contract with C.

MORRIS, L.J. delivered a concurring judgment.

STRATFORD & SON LTD v. LINDLEY

Court of Appeal   [1965] A.C. 269

Lightermen who manned barges in the Port of London belonged either to the T.G.W.U. or to the Watermen's Union, mainly to the latter. B.K. Ltd, was an employer in the port, employing 45 members of the T.G.W.U. and 3 members of the Watermen's Union. Both unions together repeatedly approached B.K. Ltd, to seek recognition but without success. The T.G.W.U. then tried alone and got recognition. When the Watermen's Union discovered this they were 'very upset about it...there was every likelihood that the Watermen's Union would be squeezed out' (Lord Denning, M.R. in the Court of Appeal). In reply they struck at the plaintiff company which was a subsidiary of B.K. Ltd, both companies being controlled by one man, Jack Stratford.

The plaintiff company hired out barges generally, and repaired barges belonging to the Port of London Authority... The Watermen's Union told their members not to handle barges belonging to or being repaired by the plaintiff company. This brought the plaintiff's trade to a standstill. The plaintiff did not employ any men belonging to the union. The defendants did not tell B.K. Ltd about the embargo, although they gave notice of it to an employers Association of which the plaintiff was a member.

The plaintiff sought an interlocutory injunction. The Court of Appeal refused, but the House of Lords granted, the injunction.

Court of Appeal

LORD DENNING, M.R.: The first point is whether the acts done by Lindley and Watson were done 'in contemplation or furtherance of a trade dispute': for if they were, the defendants are entitled to the protection of ss. 1 and 3 of the Trade Disputes Act, 1906. It seems to me that *prima facie* the evidence points to a 'trade dispute'. Whenever a trade union claims recognition (or negotiation rights, as it is sometimes called) on behalf of its members, and an employer declines to recognise the claim, there is a trade dispute within the Act. It is not necessary that there should be a dispute between any individual workman and his employer. Suffice it that the union, on behalf of all its members, desires to be able to negotiate terms of employment, and the employer refuses to recognise it. There is thereupon a dispute between employers and workmen which is connected with the terms of employment, see *Beetham* v. *Trinidad Cement Ltd.*[1] The acts done by Lindley and Watson were clearly done 'in contemplation of' such a dispute. It must have been quite obvious to them that a dispute was imminent. Bowker & King had made an agreement with the transport union behind the backs of the watermen's union. That was an ominous portent. It looked much as if Bowker & King were granting recognition to the transport union and would refuse to grant it to the watermen's union. Mr Stratford had previously declined to enter into negotiations with *both* unions —he says so in his affidavit—so it was reasonable inference that he would not recognise the watermen's union as well. Clearly a dispute was likely:

[1] [1960] A.C. 132.

and the acts were done in contemplation of it.... The important thing to notice is that under s. 3 it is not actionable for a person, in contemplation or furtherance of a trade dispute, to *induce* some other person to break a contract of employment. Note the emphasis on the word 'induce'. It is the *inducement by one person of another* which is not actionable. It is still actionable for a person to *break his own* contract of employment. It seems to me that the same must apply to threats. It is not actionable for one person to *threaten to induce* some other person to break his contract. But it is still actionable for one person in concert with others, to *threaten to break* his own contract. *Rookes* v. *Barnard*[1] was of the latter class.... To show how special was that case, I want to take the everyday case where there is no special contract forbidding a strike. Suppose that a trade union officer gives a 'strike notice'. He says to an employer: 'We are going to call a strike on Monday week unless you increase the men's wages by £1 a week'—or 'unless you dismiss yonder man who is not a member of the union'—or 'unless you cease to deal with such and such a customer'. Such a notice is not to be construed as if it were a week's notice on behalf of the men to terminate their employment, for that is the last thing any of the men would desire. They do not want to lose their pension rights and so forth by giving up their jobs. The 'strike notice' is nothing more nor less than a notice that the men will not come to work. In short, that they will break their contracts: see what Lord Devlin said in *Rookes* v. *Barnard*. In these circumstances it seems to me that the trade union officer, by giving the 'strike notice', issues a threat to the employer. He *threatens to induce the men to break* their contracts of employment unless the employer complies with the demand....

In my judgment, in the instances I have put, the acts of the trade union officer are protected by s. 3 of the Trade Disputes Act, 1906. That section makes it clear that it is not an actionable wrong to *induce* some other person to break a contract of employment. If it is not actionable to *induce* such a breach, I cannot see that it is actionable to *threaten* to induce it. And that is all the trade union officer has done.

SALMON, L.J.: ...It is not, in my judgment, unlawful to procure the breach of a contract of employment by lawful means in contemplation or furtherance of a trade dispute: Trade Disputes Act, 1906, s. 3. Accordingly to threaten to do so is not to threaten an unlawful act.

[1] [1964] A.C. 1129; [1964] 2 W.L.R. 269; [1964] 1 All E.R. 367, H.L. (E.) *post*, p. 503.

House of Lords

LORD REID: It is convenient first to consider the question whether the respondents or their union were acting in furtherance or contemplation of a trade dispute as defined in s. 5(3) of the Trade Disputes Act, 1906. That definition is not always easy to apply, and we do not know yet all the facts which may prove to be relevant. But I do not think that any sufficient *prima facie* case has been made out by the respondents. There was no actual dispute between their union and Bowker and King or the appellants when the embargo was imposed. No doubt they acted in contemplation of a dispute, but what the nature of that dispute was to be I find it difficult to determine. Taking the matters referred to in the definition in s. 5, it was not connected with the employment or non-employment of any person, and I cannot find sufficient grounds for holding that it was connected with the terms of employment or with the conditions of labour of any person. As I have already said, the terms of employment and conditions of labour of all the employees of Bowker and King had been settled in agreement with the transport union. I do not rule out the possiblity that facts proved at the trial may show that the respondents' union acted in contemplation of a dispute which could be brought within the scope of the definition, but I was unable to gather from the able argument of the respondents' counsel how that was to be done.

I must therefore consider the position at common law. I do not think that there is any *prima facie* case of conspiracy because I find nothing in the evidence to indicate that the executive committee or the respondents acted from any motive other than to forward what they believed to be the interests of the union and fundamental trade union principles.

The next question is whether the principle of *Lumley* v. *Gye*[1] has any application. I think that it has. The respondents acted with the intention of preventing barges out on hire from being returned to the appellants and those barges were in fact immobilised so that they could not be returned. The respondents knew that barges were always returned promptly on the completion of the job for which they had been hired, and it must have been obvious to them that this was done under contracts between the appellants and the barge hirers. It was argued that there was no evidence that they were sufficiently aware of the terms of these contracts to know that their interference would

---

[1] [1853] 2 E. & B. 216.

involve breaches of these contracts. But I think that at this stage it is reasonable to infer that they did know that. So I need not consider whether or how far the principle of *Lumley* v. *Gye* covers deliberate and direct interference with the execution of a contract without that causing any breach.

In addition to interfering with existing contracts the respondents' action made it practically impossible for the appellants to do any new business with the barge hirers. It was not disputed that such interference with business is tortious if any unlawful means are employed. It was made clear to the barge hirers that if they ordered their men to handle barges affected by the embargo the men would refuse to obey. If such refusal would have been in breach of the men's contracts of service, then inducing them to break their contracts would be using unlawful means. . . . Accordingly I am of the opinion that the appellants have made a *prima facie* case that the respondents threatened to induce the men of their union to break their contacts and thereby threatened to use unlawful means to interfere with the appellants' business.

VISCOUNT RADCLIFFE: As to the first point, I do not think that the defendants were acting in furtherance or contemplation of a trade dispute. Of course, a union can be a party to such a dispute: It can even bring about one and be the promoter of such a dispute. It can act on behalf of the employer's workmen or other workmen in starting or pursuing such a dispute. But, because it can, it does not follow that it always does. Has it got a dispute before it here? The only controversy that appears is between one union and another. There was no dispute about the pay or terms or conditions of employment of Stratford's workmen or Bowker and King's workmen, and if there was present or contemplated a dispute with any other workmen we certainly have not been allowed to know who they were. It is plain enough from the affidavit sworn by the defendants that the embargo was imposed for the purpose of 'making an example' of Stratford, but of what he was to be an example I do not know. In the past he had not recognised either the defendants' union or the Transport and General Workers' Union. Then he came to an agreement with the latter union which he applied to all Bowker and King's crews. No one seems concerned to say that that was not a satisfactory agreement. The defendants' union did not even ask Stratford after that whether he was prepared, having recognised one union, to recognise the other; they just put an embargo on his barges without more ado. Evidently they considered that the prestige of their union required this course. Whether its prestige was to be enhanced by punishing Stratford or by warning him or by compelling him, through the damage to his business, to 'recognise' their union I do not know, because the facts do not show it....

To embargo Stratford barges that were in service, then, and to require them to be tied up as soon as they became empty, wherever they might then be, instead of allowing them to be taken back to their base, was to bring about breaches of Stratford's contracts with its customers and I think that the terms of the embargo itself show that this result was foreseen and intended. The subsequent refusal of union officials, when appealed to, to allow the embargo to be lifted for this limited purpose of securing safe return bears out the nature of their original intention. On the evidence as it is before us, the defendants must, in my opinion, be treated as possessing a sufficient knowledge of the existence and nature of these hiring contracts and as having intended to bring it about that they should be broken.

The case comes before us as one in which the defendants have inflicted injury on the plaintiffs in the conduct of their business and have resorted to unlawful means to bring this about. It cannot be denied that to induce breaches of contract is to employ unlawful means. If the defendants were within the protection of s. 3 of the Trade Disputes Act their interference with their members' contracts of employment would not in itself be wrongful or unlawful, but even so, the procuring of the breaches of the hiring contracts would be against them; and where, as here, there does not appear to be even a trade dispute in contemplation of which the defendants can be said to have acted, they have two sets of tortious or unlawful acts which the plaintiffs can pray in aid against them....

LORD PEARCE: The question now to be decided is whether the plaintiffs have made out a *prima facie* case. If they have done so, there are strong reasons which make this a clear case for maintaining the *status quo* until the trial. First, if there is no injunction, very great damage will be done. Secondly, the damage will be irreparable since the defendants admittedly cannot pay the damages if they lose the case. Thirdly, an injunction will not cause any damage to the defendants. If it turns out that the plaintiffs have no remedy, the only inconvenience that the defendants will have suffered is a delay of some months in implementing their scheme for putting pressure on Bowker & King by damaging the plaintiffs and thereby enhancing or maintaining their trade union prestige as against the rival trade union.

The plaintiffs put their case first on the *Lumley* v. *Gye* principle that the defendants have knowingly without lawful justification induced the plaintiffs' customers to break their contracts with the plaintiffs....

On the present state of the evidence I do not find any reality in the argument that this was not a breach of contract, that the hiring remained in force until such time as the barges could be returned, and that, voluntarily, the plaintiffs chose to waive their rights to have the barges returned. The defendants' union maintained their refusal to allow the barges to be returned, and the plaintiffs obviously could not, from a practical point of view, insist on their return; they had to acquiesce in the termination of the hiring without it. That was the situation that the defendants intended to produce. They cannot have envisaged that the contracts of hiring would remain in force while the barges were idle, thus enabling the plaintiffs, whom they wished to injure, to continue collecting the hiring charges to the detriment of the hirers, whom they did not wish to injure. Such a view would not, I think, be reconcilable with the terms of the defendants' letter in which they announced the embargo to the Association of Master Lightermen or with their persistence in spite of the letter of the plaintiffs' solicitors of 10 December 1963. On the evidence in its present stage, therefore, it appears that the hirers broke their contracts with the plaintiffs.

Did the defendants have sufficient knowledge of the terms of the hirers' contracts? It is no answer to a claim based on wrongfully inducing a breach of contract, to assert that the defendants did not know with exactitude all the terms of the contract. The relevant question is whether they had sufficient knowledge of the terms to know that they were inducing a breach of contract. At present there is considerable indication that they had the knowledge. Moreover, it seems unlikely that they would be ignorant of the simple commonplace obligation of the hirers under the course of dealing whereby they had a duty to return the barges to the plaintiffs. But this is a point which the evidence at the trial will no doubt illuminate further. Did the defendants induce the breach? Albeit with expressions of regret, the defendants made it clear to the Association of Master Lightermen, which in effect represented the hirers (by letter of 8 November 1963), that the hirers could not return the barges to the plaintiffs. The fact that an inducement to break a contract is couched as an irresistible embargo rather than in terms of seduction does not make it any the less an inducement. The defendants were in effect saying to the hirers: 'You shall not carry out your contract with the plaintiffs, and we have taken steps which will make it impossible, though we regret the inconvenience to you.' If thereby the hirers were induced to break the contract, the tort is established.

It was argued that the plaintiffs have not shown that the hirers' breach was a necessary consequence, since they might have tried to employ men belonging to other unions. I find that argument quite unreal, since I would think that in practice they were bound to run into great difficulties. Moreover, if the defendants intended to procure the breach, and successfully procured it as a reasonable consequence of their acts and their communications to the hirers through their association and in answer to subsequent inquiries on the telephone, it is not, in my opinion, a defence to say that the hirers could have somehow avoided the breaches. In *Lumley* v. *Gye*[1] it was not necessary for Miss Wagner to break her contract; but the defendant was liable because he successfully persuaded her. *Thomson (D.C.) and Co. Ltd* v. *Deakin*[2] was a somewhat different case from the present. In that case.[3] 'There never was any direct action between the defendants or agents on their behalf and Bowaters with the object of persuading or causing Bowaters to break their existing contracts with the plaintiffs' (*per* Upjohn, J.). In a case where the defendant does not communicate any direct pressure or persuasion to the contract-breaker, but merely procures indirectly a situation which causes the breach, I am inclined to agree with the dictum of Jenkins, L.J.[4] that it must be shown 'that breach of the contract forming the alleged subject of interference ensued as a necessary consequence of the breaches by the employees concerned of their contracts of employment.' But that is not this case. The facts of this case, therefore, on the evidence in its present stage constitute, in my opinion, an inducement by the defendants to the hirers to break the contracts of hiring.... Since the hiring contracts were not contracts of employment, s. 3 does not protect an inducement of their breach. The first limb of the section clearly cannot apply, and for the reasons succinctly put by Upjohn, J. in *Thomson (D.C.) & Co. Ltd* v. *Deakin*[5] the second limb does not apply.

Moreover, I do not think in the present state of the evidence that any trade dispute is made out even 'in contemplation'. The definition of 'workmen' is extremely wide and certainly covers this case. But the reference to the subject-matter of the dispute is, by contrast, more precise: viz. 'which is connected with the employment or non-employment, or the terms of the employment, or with the conditions of labour,

---

[1] 2 E. & B. 216.   [2] [1952] Ch. 646.   [3] [1952] Ch. 646, 662.
[4] Ibid. 697.   [5] [1952] Ch. 646, 664.

of any person...'. Those words show an intention to prescribe with some accuracy the matter to which the dispute must pertain if it is to come within the definition of 'trade dispute'.

When a union makes a genuine claim on the employers for bargaining status with a view to regulating or improving the conditions or pay of their workmen and the employers reject the claim, a trade dispute is in contemplation even though no active dispute has yet arisen (see for instance *Beetham* v. *Trinidad Cement Ltd*).[1] Here, however, it would seem that at the material time there was no such claim and refusal. A request had been made on Bowker and King by the two unions acting jointly in 1956, 1961 and 1962. It had been refused by the employer and the matter had apparently lapsed. Then in July 1963 the predominant union to which some 90 per cent of the men belonged made a separate approach and came to an agreement which protected all Bowker and King's crews. The employer was not even asked by the defendants whether he had changed his mind with regard to them as he had with regard to the T.G.W.U. There was here no practical need for any intervention by the defendants. The three men who belonged to their union were, on one view of the evidence, wholly satisfied with their conditions and they were, from a practical point of view, adequately protected by the assurance given to the T.G.W.U. It would appear on the evidence so far given that the defendants were contemplating merely the advancement of their union's prestige in rivalry with another union. With this object they put a serious and damaging embargo on a company that had no dealings with any of their members....

It was suggested in argument that *Rookes* v. *Barnard* went a long way further than it was, in my opinion, intended to go. It was, for instance, suggested by Mr Pain that it withdrew from the protection of s. 3 the threats of a trade union official to the employer to call a strike in breach of the contract of employment. It certainly does not do that, and I agree with the observations of Pearson, L.J. on that subject. The apparent object of s. 3 was to protect a trade union official in just such a situation against an action by the employer. The only person who could sue him for his conduct 'on the ground only that it induces some other person to break a contract of employment' would be a party to the contract—namely, the employer. And it was the position between him and the employer with which the first limb of s. 3 was dealing. He is, therefore, not liable to the employer for inducing a

[1] [1960] A.C. 132.

breach of contract which would otherwise be an actionable tort. It follows that he is not liable to the employer for threatening to induce a breach of contract. And it must follow, I think, that since he is protected as between himself and the employer from liability to the employer for threatening to induce a breach of the contract of employment he is similarly protected as between himself and the employer from an action by the employer for intimidation based on the unlawfulness of that threat. Different considerations apply, however, when a third party is deliberately injured by unlawful threats to the employer. *Rookes* v. *Barnard* held that s. 3 was no protection against such intimidation. The fact that the first limb of the section is dealing only with the position between union official or unofficial agitator and the employer is further emphasised by the fact that it refers only to the tort of inducing a breach of contract. The actual breach of contract by the workmen remains actionable.

LORD UPJOHN: Plainly it is just and convenient to order an interlocutory injunction to preserve the *status quo* until judgment in the action so as to prevent further interference by the respondents with the contracts now made by the appellant company with their customers or which they may make with their customers in the future before judgment in the action. I cannot accept the argument that an injunction ought in some way to be limited so as to affect only existing contracts; such a limitation would fail to give the appellant company the protection, to which they have satisfied me they are entitled, of preserving the *status quo* until judgment so as to enable them to carry on business in the usual way by entering into new contracts from time to time with their customers.

The form of injunction granted by Marshall, J. is not, in my view, entirely appropriate and I would propose an injunction in this form: 'An injunction restraining the respondents and each of them until judgment or further order from doing (whether by themselves or by their servants agents or workmen or any of them or otherwise howsoever) any act which causes or procures a breach or breaches by customers of the appellant company of contracts made now or hereafter between the appellant company and such customers for the hiring of barges of the appellant company.'

LORD DONOVAN: It is desirable, I venture to think, that the minimum necessary to refuse or to restore the injunction should alone be decided. I am glad that it is so: for some of the propositions advanced on behalf of the appellant I find very far reaching. For example, the argument that there is a tort consisting of some undefinable interference with business contracts, falling short of inducing a breach of contract, I find as novel and surprising as I think the members of this House who decided *Crofter Hand Woven Harris Tweed Co. Ltd* v. *Veitch* would have done. Moreover, I should take much convincing that the mere notification of an existing state of affairs (e.g. the embargo in the present case) was itself a 'threat' which could found a claim for intimidation....

I can, if I may say so, understand the annoyance of the watermen's union when they found that this had been done, so to speak, behind their backs. But it was this that was their real grievance: their three members in Bowker and King were now covered by an agreement arrived at in accordance with trade union principles, and there is no evidence that they were dissatisfied. What remained, of course, was the blow to the watermen's union's prestige. They felt it so keenly that without seeking any explanation they struck at the appellants with the embargo. But ruffled feelings of this kind, however rightly resented, are not a trade dispute within the statutory definition. The matter can, no doubt, be put in this way: 'We, the watermen's union, had three members in Bowker and King. We claimed the right to negotiate on their behalf and it was refused. It is not to the point that some other union negotiated on behalf of the remaining employees, and that Bowker and King voluntarily extended the benefits of the resulting agreement to our members. We were still denied the right to negotiate, even if on behalf of three only out of 48 employees, and even if those three were already content.' Such a claim, if put forward, might disqualify itself as a trade dispute by reason of its own extravagance. But however that may be, such a claim was never put forward here. Originally the claim for recognition as a negotiating body was put forward by the watermen's union as a joint claim, i.e. with the T.G.W.U.: and when the latter obtained recognition on its own, no separate similar claim was made by the watermen's union. Should it be said that if put forward it would inevitably have been rejected, so that a trade dispute was at any rate 'in contemplation', the answer is that upon the facts of this case the dispute was not *prima facie* at any rate concerned with the matters specified in the statutory definition of 'trade dispute', but was concerned with inter-union rivalry....

Prima facie the respondents procured breaches of contracts of employment on the part of their members. It is an engaging picture to visualise a dock worker turning up each day, and each day representing that he is making a conditional offer of his services, the condition being that he shall not be asked to handle particular barges. All that was in his mind was that the union had told him he was not to handle them, and he was going to obey. Of course a conditional offer may be inferred from conduct, but I doubt if that is the reality of the matter here. The employer did not accept some conditional offer. The evidence shows that he expected his normal reasonable orders to be obeyed, but meeting with objection so far as concerned Stratford's barges, accepted the objection. I find the facts, so far as at present ascertained, to be much more consistent with the waiver of a breach of contract than with the acceptance of a conditional offer.

As regards the customers' hiring contracts I agree with the views of my noble and learned friend, Lord Pearce, on this point, and need add nothing to them.

BOWLES & SONS LTD AND METROPOLITAN SAND CO. LTD *v.* LINDLEY AND OTHERS

[1965] 1 Lloyd's Rep. 207

The first and second plaintiffs were both wholly-owned subsidiaries of one company. The first plaintiff owned two motor vessels and was concerned with dredging material from the sea-bed. The second plaintiff then took this material from the first plaintiff and sold it to regular customers. Though there was apparently no express contract between the parties, the court implied one from their course of dealings. A recognition dispute arose between the first plaintiff and the defendant union (the Watermen's Union). As a result, crew members who belonged to the union refused to sail, in breach of the Merchant Shipping Act, and were discharged. The first plaintiff then had to acquire substitute crews, which took over a month. During this time the union picketed and 'blacked' the second plaintiff. Both plaintiffs were losing a lot of money. They sought interim injunctions against the union. The injunctions were refused, but the defendants gave undertakings not to take unlawful action in pursuit of the dispute.

FENTON ATKINSON, J.: The point is raised whether I have power, legally, to grant any form of injunction against a trade union. As the law stands at the moment, two of the greatest lawyers, many years past, namely Lord Justice Scrutton and Lord Justice Atkin, expressed the view in *Ware and de Freville Ltd* v. *Motor Trade Association and Others*, [1921] 3 K.B. 40, that such relief cannot be granted against a union.

More than 40 years later, in *Boulting and Another* v. *Association of Cinematograph, Television and Allied Technicians*, [1963] 2 Q.B. 607, Lord Upjohn and Lord Justice Diplock expressed a contrary view. All those expressions of view were, in fact, unnecessary to the particular decision, and that of course poses a problem for the Judge of first instance. But for myself, if a *prima facie* case can be established, I would prefer, for the reasons given by Lord Upjohn, to follow *Boulting, sup.*, rather than *Ware and de Freville Ltd* v. *Motor Trade Association....* As a matter of law, I think it is quite plain that if any member of the crew of either of those vessels refuses to sail when he was due to do so, he would commit an offence under s. 221 or s. 225 of the Merchant Shipping Act, 1894, and any person who persuaded him to refuse to proceed to sea in accordance with his duty would also be committing an offence—for which I think he could be fined a maximum of £10—under s. 236 of the Merchant Shipping Act, 1894....

Whether one likes the particular steps taken against Metropolitan is quite beside the point, but in my judgment there is no material which enables me to say that in the action directed against Metropolitan from 23 November onwards there is any *prima facie* case that the predominant motive was to injure Metropolitan, or was otherwise than a motive to advance the legitimate interests of the defendants. That being so, it seems to me that any claim based upon conspiracy to injure, as it was put in this Court, must go.

Then I have to come on to consider the second ground, so far as Metropolitan is concerned, and there it is submitted by Mr Lawson on their behalf that this is a case of a tort of unlawful interference with business relationships. As I understand the position, there are three different cases established by authority where one can find this tort of unlawful interference with business relationships. First of all on the basis that A and B have a contract, and C knows of that contract, if C without lawful justification induces or procures B to break his contract with A—for example, by threatening him with labour troubles if he does not break that contract with A—then that behaviour would be actionable at the suit of A. That would be the *Lumley* v. *Gye*, (1853) 2 E. & B. 216, principle, but I see no evidence in the affidavits before me here of the defendants', without lawful justification, inducing or procuring anyone to break a contract with Metropolitan.

A second recognized form of this tort appears to be if, instead of procuring B to break the contract, C (by some unlawful means) makes it impossible for the contract to be performed—for example, by some form of physical interference which prevents A from delivering, or something of that kind. That again would be actionable at the suit of A. That necessitates the use of unlawful means.

The third apparently recognized form of this tort is if C persuades some third party to do an unlawful act, which makes it impossible for A to fulfil his contract. I think finally it is really under that head that Mr Lawson sought to bring this case.

Then I must ask myself: Are there any other heads of this tort? It seems to me there are not, and I rely here on the judgment of Lord Justice Jenkins in the case I have already referred to, namely *D. C. Thomson & Co. Ltd* v. *Deakin and Others*, [1952] 1 Ch. 646. I do not want to prolong this judgment by reading the whole passage, but the part of Lord Justice Jenkins's judgment that I find most helpful on this starts with the paragraph just below the middle of p. 696, carries on over to p. 697 and then to p. 698.*

It seems to me, on reading the judgment in *Thomson* v. *Deakin* (*supra*), as a whole, the tort of unlawful interference with business relationships must really be limited to those three specific types of action to which I have just referred....

The real point of Mr Lawson's argument here was the interference with the contract between Bowles and Metropolitan, broken, it was said, by the defendants conspiring with the crews to break their contracts of employment. I think I have already disposed of that by what I said on the facts, and in the face of the defendants' affidavits, I do not think here there is a *prima facie* case that the defendants, or any of them, did conspire with the crews of the *Bowbelle* or the *Bowqueen* to break their contracts of employment. That being so, it seems to me that no legal basis is left for an interlocutory injunction at the suit of Metropolitan.

There remains the question of Bowles's application to continue the injunction granted by Mr Justice Stirling last week.†...It seems to me that I have to consider there whether it is shown that there is some real probability, in the absence of a continuance of that injunction, that the substituted crews of these vessels will be exhorted or persuaded to leave that employment illegally—that is to say, without giving notice, which they are entitled to give, in the case of one vessel 24 hours and

---

* See *ante*, p. 477 where this is quoted.

† In the Vacation Court, Stirling, J. had granted an injunction against the union officials and the *union itself* (see *post*, p. 527) 'restraining them from interfering with the subsisting or future crews of the vessels...in their employment by the plaintiffs'.

in the case of the other vessel 48 hours—because it is only if they were exhorted or persuaded to refuse to sail contrary to the legal provisions of the Merchant Shipping Act, that there could be ground to intervene by injunction (it being admitted here that there was in fact a trade dispute)....But I think I should be slow to apprehend that the defendants, or any of them, would commit an offence under s. 236 of the Merchant Shipping Act, and induce these men to act in any unlawful way, when they could quite simply give 24 hours' or 48 hours' notice to terminate their employment quite lawfully.

EMERALD CONSTRUCTION CO. v. LOWTHIAN

Court of Appeal   [1966] 1 W.L.R. 691

A 'labour only' contract is a contract whereby a sub-contractor agrees to supply 'labour only' to a main contractor thus relieving the latter of direct responsibility for employing the men. The defendants were officers of the Amalgamated Union of Building Trade Workers, a union which had for long objected to these contracts because the sub-contractors had sometimes turned out to be men 'here today and gone tomorrow' to the detriment of the union members. It maintained its objections even though the N.J.C. for its industry had accepted these contracts. The plaintiff was a 'labour-only sub-contractor' under a contract which provided for termination in the event of failure to maintain reasonable progress. The defendants who knew of the existence of this contract but not, initially, of its precise terms, told the main contractors, Messrs Higgs and Hill Ltd, that unless the workers were directly employed and the sub-contract terminated, then there would be a strike. Industrial action followed. This was a successful action for an interlocutory injunction restraining the defendants from causing or procuring, by intimidation or otherwise, a breach of the labour-only contract.

LORD DENNING, M.R.: Such being the facts, how stands the law? This 'labour only' sub-contract was disliked intensely by this trade union and its officers. But nevertheless it was a perfectly lawful contract. The parties to it had a right to have their contractual relations preserved inviolate without unlawful interference by others: see *Quinn* v. *Leathem*, by Lord Macnaghten. If the officers of the trade union, knowing of the contract, deliberately sought to procure a breach of it they would do wrong: see *Lumley* v. *Gye*. Even if they did not know of the actual terms of the contract, but had the means of knowledge—

which they deliberately disregarded—that would be enough. Like the man who turns a blind eye. So here, if the officers deliberately sought to get this contract terminated, heedless of its terms, regardless whether it was terminated by breach or not, they would do wrong. For it is unlawful for a third person to procure a breach of contract knowingly, or recklessly, indifferent whether it is a breach or not. Some would go further and hold that it is unlawful for a third person deliberately and directly to interfere with the execution of a contract, even though he does not cause any breach. The point was left open by Lord Reid in *J. T. Stratford & Son Ltd* v. *Lindley*.[1] It is unnecessary to pursue this today. Suffice it that if the intention of the defendants was to get this contract terminated at all events, breach or no breach, they were *prima facie* in the wrong.

The evidence at present before us points in this direction. The object of the defendant officers was plain. It was to get Higgs & Hill Ltd to terminate this 'labour only' sub-contract; and the evidence suggests that they did not care how it was terminated, so long as it was terminated. The two letters of ultimatum contain an unequivocal demand. They did not inquire what were the terms of the contract. They did not request that it be terminated by lawful notice. They made the straight demand that it be terminated within the time limit—or else there would be a strike. When Higgs & Hill Ltd refused the demand, the defendants called a strike and did their best to get the contract terminated by that means. Even when they or their advisers got to know of the terms of the contract, they still continued the strike. All goes to show that they were determined to bring this contractual relationship to an end if they could, regardless of whether it was done in breach or not. At any rate, that is the inference I would draw until the contrary is shown. It may be that, as a result of the strike, Emerald have failed to maintain reasonable progress and Higgs & Hill Ltd can now terminate the contract; but the defendants cannot rely on this if it was brought about by their own wrongful act.

The Trade Disputes Acts, 1906 and 1965, do not avail the defendants, for although this may have been a 'trade dispute', nevertheless this 'labour only' sub-contract is not, as it appears to me at present, a 'contract of employment' within s. 3 of the Trade Disputes Act, 1906, or s. 1 of the Trade Disputes Act, 1965. The words 'contract of employment' in this context seem to me *prima facie* to denote a contract between employer and workman; and not a contract between an

---

[1] See *ante*, p. 478.

employer and a sub-contractor, even though he be a sub-contractor for labour only.

DIPLOCK, L.J.: The plaintiffs' case is put in a number of ways. The first is simple and based on the well-established principle of law laid down in *Lumley* v. *Gye*, which, as is shown by the recent decision of the House of Lords in *J. T. Stratford & Son Ltd* v. *Lindley*, applies to trade union officials as it does to other men, unless the contract of which the breach is procured is a contract of employment. The plaintiffs claim that the acts of the defendants which they threaten to continue were and are intended to procure a breach by the main contractors of their 'labour only' sub-contract with the plaintiffs. Upon the claim framed in this way there is no real dispute as to the law applicable. There are three essential elements in the tort of unlawful procurement of a breach of contract: the act, the intent and the resulting damage. In a *quia timet* action such as this, it is sufficient to prove the act and the intent and the likelihood of damage resulting if the act is successful in procuring a breach of contract. The only issue on this part of the case is one of fact as to the defendants' intent. At all relevant times they knew of the existence of a 'labour only' sub-contract for brickwork between the main contractors and the plaintiffs, but until it was disclosed to them on the interlocutory application to the judge in chambers for an injunction, they did not know its precise terms. They say in somewhat equivocal language that they assumed that it could be lawfully terminated by the main contractors on short notice and that such lawful termination was all that they insisted on. But ignorance of the precise terms of the contract is not enough to show absence of intent to procure its breach. The element of intent needed to constitute the tort of unlawful procurement of a breach of contract is, in my view, sufficiently established if it be proved that the defendants intended the party procured to bring the contract to an end by breach of it if there were no way of bringing it to an end lawfully. A defendant who acts with such intent runs the risk that if the contract is broken as a result of the party acting in the manner in which he is procured to act by the defendant, the defendant will be liable in damages to the other party to the contract.

On the evidence as it now stands I think the inference is irresistible that such was the defendants' intention. The one thing on which they were determined was that the plaintiffs' work under their 'labour only' sub-contract with the main contractors should cease. Whether this involved a breach of contract by the main contractors was a matter of indifference to them. The judge declined to draw this inference. Even on the evidence before him, I myself should have been inclined to draw it; but now there is additional evidence. Ever since the proceedings before the judge, the defendants have known the terms of the plaintiffs' sub-contract, and despite this have continued to act as they did when they were ignorant of its precise terms. This throws considerable light on their earlier attitude....

The plaintiffs put their case on other grounds as well. These involved novel and far-reaching propositions of law, the validity of which I do not think it necessary or desirable to determine on this interlocutory application. Briefly, these contentions were that the defendants' action in threatening to procure the plaintiffs' workmen to strike was itself unlawful upon a number of alternative grounds. It was an attempt to procure a breach by the plaintiffs of their sub-contract with the main contractor and was actionable at the suit of the plaintiffs. It was a threat to procure breaches of contracts of employment by the plaintiffs' workmen with the unlawful object of procuring a breach by the plaintiffs of their own 'labour only' contract with the main contractors. It was a threat to procure breaches of contracts of employment by the plaintiffs' workmen in breach of a contract to which the defendants' trade union was itself a party. None of these, it is contended, are protected by the Trade Disputes Act, 1965. These are interesting and ingenious propositions. They may be right; but in my view they are much too doubtful to form the grounds of an interlocutory injunction. The proper time to decide these questions of law is at the trial.

RUSSELL, L.J. delivered a concurring judgment.

SQUARE GRIP REINFORCEMENT CO. LTD v. MACDONALD

Court of Session (Outer House)   (1966) S.L.T. 232

A company which applied the principle of direct negotiation with their employees received a communication which purported to come from 'an organizer on behalf of the T.G.W.U.' informing them that the union 'had established union organization' with their employees in a certain factory. A meeting thereafter took place between the company and the union representatives. The company adhered to their policy of direct negotiation and posted a notice in the factory telling the employees that an approach had been made by the union, indicating that the company maintained its attitude, and inviting employees who could not accept the company's policy to seek alternative employment. Employees who were members of the union resigned, other than two who stayed on. Approaches were then made by representatives of the union to other employers of labour who had dealings with the company, exhorting men belonging to the union not to handle goods destined for or coming from the company. The company maintained that these actions were designed deliberately to bring about, through withdrawal of labour, conditions in which those other employers who were in contractual relationships with the company would break, or be compelled to break, their contracts with the company. The company sought interdict against the union representatives.

Held that interim interdict should be continued.

LORD AVONSIDE: Obviously, then, the first question is whether on these embryo pleadings there is shown to be a trade dispute within the meaning of the Act and that is what the respondents claim.... To my mind it is somewhat remarkable that in the pleadings as they presently stand there is no suggestion whatsoever that prior to entry of this union upon the scene there was any difference of opinion in regard to working conditions, conditions of employment or the like between the petitioners and those men who were employed by them. It is equally, in my opinion, somewhat surprising, even at this stage of the pleadings that the only reference made by the respondents to a trade dispute occurs in one of their pleas-in-law. I find nowhere in the pleadings, any clear description or attempt to define what precisely is the dispute which they say is in issue. The question of whether or not there is a trade dispute within the meaning of the Act to my mind is a very difficult one and where there are disputes and obvious gaps in the pleadings the matter is the more difficult. I am not prepared at this stage to accept that a trade dispute has been so clearly made out on the pleadings as to lead to the conclusion that the Act applies.

Quite apart from that there is another point. If one assumed that there was a trade dispute nonetheless the action of the type which the petitioners say had taken place would, in my opinion, clearly not be covered by s. 3 of the Act which is the section to which they resorted. That section is, as is well known, in two parts. The first part deals with the subject of persons who break contracts of employment, but there is clearly a strong line of authority to the effect that the second part which is couched in general terms does not cover the procuring of the breach of other types of contracts. It is perhaps sufficient for me at this stage and in this regard to refer to the case of *J. T. Stratford & Sons Ltd* v. *Lindley* [1965] A.C. 269....

The matter, therefore, to my mind at this stage resolves itself into an inquiry as to whether counsel for the respondents is right in saying that there are no relevant or at least no specific averments pointing to the unlawful procuring of breaches of contract by the respondents. In his approach to this matter he relied materially and very properly on passages from the judgment of Lord Justice Jenkins in *Thomson's* case to which I have just referred. It would be quite impertinent of me to attempt to criticise in this short judgment observations of Lord Justice Jenkins but I feel compelled to say, with the greatest respect, that I think the passage relied upon lays down too strict a definition and indeed that it may now be somewhat doubtful looking to what was said by various members of the House in the case of *Stratford (supra)*, to which I have just referred....

Finally, the matter of balance of convenience arises. Counsel for the respondents, very properly, did not press on this matter. I should perhaps say that in a case of this kind I would not for one moment consider recalling an interim interdict if I thought there was any substance in the petitioners' case, or even if I had more doubts than I have. Damage to the petitioners might be disastrous and irreparable. Damage, if any, to the respondents would be minimal.

(iii) INTIMIDATION; UNLAWFUL CONSPIRACY; AND RESIDUAL LIABILITY*

ALLEN v. FLOOD

House of Lords [1898] A.C. 1

A boiler-makers' union objected to the practice of employing shipwrights to repair ironwork on ships. When the plaintiff shipwrights were employed to repair woodwork on a certain ship, members of the boiler-makers' union discovered that they had previously been repairing ironwork on another ship and objected to their continued employment. Their union representative, the defendant, had an interview with the manager, and as a result the plaintiffs were lawfully dismissed. The defendant had told the manager that unless the plaintiffs were discharged, the men would be called out. There was evidence of an intention to punish the plaintiffs for what they had done in the past.

* *Post* at p. 525 and p. 526 the reader will find two short discussions in Excursus A and B on problems which arise from the material in Section D of this chapter.

There would apparently have been no breach of contract by the men had they come out on strike. The action was brought for maliciously inducing the company to break their contract or, at least, not to enter into any new contract of employment for intimidation and 'coercion'; and for conspiracy to injure. At the trial the evidence of any conspiracy was completely rejected. Before the House of Lords the issue was narrowed to the question whether the defendant could be liable because of his 'malice', if all the acts which he had done were in themselves lawful. The majority of the House rejected the notion that he could be under any such liability.*

LORD WATSON: Although the rule may be otherwise with regard to crimes, the law of England does not, according to my apprehension, take into account motive as constituting an element of civil wrong. Any invasion of the civil rights of another person is in itself a legal wrong, carrying with it liability to repair its necessary or natural consequences, in so far as these are injurious to the person whose right is infringed, whether the motive which prompted it be good, bad, or indifferent. But the existence of a bad motive, in the case of an act which is not in itself illegal, will not convert that act into a civil wrong for which reparation is due. A wrongful act, done knowingly and with a view to its injurious consequences, may, in the sense of law, be malicious; but such malice derives its essential character from the circumstance that the act done constitutes a violation of the law....

The root of the principle is that, in any legal question, malice depends, not upon evil motive which influenced the mind of the actor, but upon the illegal character of the act which he contemplated and committed. In my opinion it is alike consistent with reason and common sense that when the act done is, apart from the feelings which prompted it, legal, the civil law ought to take no cognizance of its motive....

There are, in my opinion, two grounds only upon which a person who procures the act of another can be made legally responsible for its consequences. In the first place, he will incur liability if he knowingly and for his own ends induces that other person to commit an actionable wrong. In the second place, when the act induced is within the right of the immediate actor, and is therefore not wrongful in so far as he is

---

* But compare Lord Lindley in *Quinn* v. *Leathem, ante*, p. 443. And even Lord Devlin in *Rookes* v. *Barnard, post*, p. 516, showed signs of not accepting this doctrine. Nevertheless, after the *Crofter* case, *ante*, p. 453, it seems clear that the courts could not go back on *Allen* v. *Flood* in any way; and, indeed, the decision in *Rookes* v. *Barnard* itself, that a threat can be civilly actionable as the tort of 'intimidation' only if the act threatened is itself 'unlawful', is in accord with it.

concerned, it may yet be to the detriment of a third party; and in that case, according to the law laid down by the majority in *Lumley* v. *Gye*,[1] the inducer may be held liable if he can be shown to have procured his object by the use of illegal means directed against that third party.

LORD HERSCHELL: In *Temperton* v. *Russell*,[2] the further step was taken by the majority of the Court, A. L. Smith, L.J. reserving his opinion on the point, of asserting that it was immaterial that the act induced was not the breach of a contract, but only the not entering into a contract, provided that the motive of desiring to injure the plaintiff, or to benefit the defendant at the expense of the plaintiff, was present. It seems to have been regarded as only a small step from the one decision to the other, and it was said that there seemed to be no good reason why, if an action lay for maliciously inducing a breach of contract, it should not equally lie for maliciously inducing a person not to enter into a contract. So far from thinking it a small step from the one decision to the other, I think there is a chasm between them. The reason for a distinction between the two cases appears to me to be this: that in the one case the act procured was the violation of a legal right, for which the person doing the act which injured the plaintiff could be sued as well as the person who procured it; whilst in the other case no legal right was violated by the person who did the act from which the plaintiff suffered: he would not be liable to be sued in respect of the act done, whilst the person who induced him to do the act would be liable to an action.

I think this was an entirely new departure. A study of the case of *Lumley* v. *Gye* has satisfied me that in that case the majority of the Court regarded the circumstance that what the defendant procured was a breach of contract as the essence of the cause of action....

It is said that the statement that the defendant would call the men out, if made, was a threat. It is this aspect of the case which has obviously greatly influenced some of the learned judges. Hawkins, J. says that the defendant without excuse or justification 'wilfully, unlawfully, unjustly, and tyrannically invaded the plaintiffs' right by intimidating and coercing their employers to deprive them of their present and future employment', and that the plaintiffs are therefore entitled to maintain this action. But 'excuse or justification' is only needed where an act is *prima facie* wrongful....

The proposition is therefore reduced to this, that the appellant invaded the plaintiffs' right by intimidating and coercing their employers.

[1] 2 E. & B. 216.　　　　　[2] [1893] 1 Q.B. 715.

In another passage in his opinion the learned judge says that there is no authority for the proposition that to render threats, menaces, intimidation or coercion available as elements in a cause of action, they must be of such a character as to create fear of personal violence. I quite agree with this. The threat of violence to property is equally a threat in the eye of the law. And many other instances might be given. On the other hand it is undeniable that the terms 'threat', 'coercion', and even 'intimidation', are often applied in popular language to utterances which are quite lawful and which give rise to no liability either civil or criminal. They mean no more than this, that the so-called threat puts pressure, and perhaps extreme pressure, on the person to whom it is addressed to take a particular course. Of this again numberless instances might be given. Even then if it can be said without abuse of language that the employers were 'intimidated and coerced' by the appellant, even if this be in a certain sense true, it by no means follows that he committed a wrong or is under any legal liability for his act. Everything depends on the nature of the representation or statement by which the pressure was exercised. The law cannot regard the act differently because you choose to call it a threat or coercion instead of an intimation or warning....

It is not for your Lordships to express any opinion on the policy of trade unions, membership of which may undoubtedly influence the action of those who have joined them. They are now recognised by law; there are combinations of employers as well as of employed. The members of these unions, of whichever class they are composed, act in the interest of their class. If they resort to unlawful acts they may be indicted or sued. If they do not resort to unlawful acts they are entitled to further their interests in the manner which seems to them best, and most likely to be effectual.

If, then, the men had ceased to work for the company either of their own motion or because they were 'called out', and the company in order to secure their return had thought it expedient no longer to employ the plaintiffs, they could certainly have maintained no action. Yet the damage to them would have been just the same. The employers would have been subjected to precisely the same 'coercion' and 'intimidation', save that it was by act and not by prospect of the act; they would have yielded in precisely the same way to the pressure put upon them, and been actuated by the same motive, and the aim of those who exercised the pressure would have been precisely the same. The only difference would have been the additional result that the company also might have suffered loss. I am quite unable to conceive how the plaintiffs can have a cause for action, because, instead of the ironworkers leaving, either of their own motion or because they were called out, there was an intimation beforehand that either the one or the other of these courses would be pursued. The ironworkers were employed on the terms that they might leave at the close of any day, and that on the other hand the employers might, if they saw fit, then discharge them. The company had employed the men knowing that they were members of the union, and they had on one occasion, at least, dealt with the appellant as its delegate. They had no ground for complaint if the men left, as they were by contract entitled to do, whether the men left of their own motion or followed the instruction of their union leaders. It is said that the company were in the power of the men because of the business loss to which the withdrawal of the men would subject them. But to what was this due, if not to the act of the company themselves in employing these men under a contract which either party might any day determine? Under such circumstances, to compare the act of the company to that of the traveller who, on a pistol being presented to his head, hands his purse to the highwayman, appears to me grotesque.

LORDS MACNAGHTEN, SHAND, DAVEY and JAMES OF HEREFORD delivered concurring speeches; LORD HALSBURY, L.C. and LORDS ASHBOURNE and MORRIS dissented.

SANTEN v. BUSNACH

Court of Appeal (1913) 29 T.L.R. 214

The plaintiff, on entering the employment of Mr Phillips, was told by the defendant that she had to leave her union and join the same one as all the other employees or they would not work with her. She refused to join. The defendants then told their employer that the plaintiff refused to join and that their union instructed them that if she stayed they would not stay there. Mr Phillips did not want his employees to go out so he lawfully dismissed the plaintiff.

LORD JUSTICE VAUGHAN WILLIAMS, after stating the facts, said that it was common ground that no breach of contract was induced and that the cause of action was limited to 'ceasing to employ the plaintiff'. There was no suggestion of any conspiracy in the claim, and when he came to the evidence not only was there no evidence of any conspiracy but the case was conducted as one in which there was no charge of conspiracy. In these circumstances he held that there was no evidence of any conspiracy either alleged in the particulars or suggested by the evidence. Then it was said that there was evidence of threats or intimidation. He could find no such evidence. He could really only find words which conveyed what had been called in *Allen* v. *Flood* a warning to the employer of the resolution which had been arrived at by the trade unionists, who with the exception of one person—namely, the plaintiff —formed the whole staff of Godfrey Phillips and Co.

He thought that this resolution was one of the kind described by Lord Watson in *Allen* v. *Flood* when he said that if men had passed a resolution to the effect that if a certain man was not discharged they would resign it was *prima facie* only an intimation which was beneficial to their master and which it was their duty to give. Lord Herschell had expressed himself to the same effect at p. 130 of the same case. He (the Lord Justice) thought that that applied to the facts of the present case. It was not suggested that the defendants had done anything illegal in giving the notice determining the contract. He could not see the faintest evidence of any threat. It was simply a warning given by the defendants to their employer without any violence or anger of their resolution to leave his employ. Neither was there any evidence that the defendants had personally anything to do with the matter. They simply intimated to their employer that such a resolution had been passed and that resolution imported a perfectly lawful act. Admittedly the mere giving of the notice to discontinue work and to withdraw from the employ was in no sense illegal. He wished, however, to make this perfectly plain. He was not saying that a person might not give a notice which was perfectly legal and against the wording of which nothing could be said, in such a manner and under such circumstances as to constitute a threat. There was no evidence of anything of that sort here. He thought the natural *prima facie* meaning of the words used here was a simple warning.

KENNEDY, L.J. and JOYCE, J. delivered concurring judgments.*

---

* *Note on Threats.* (i) In the early part of this century it was still uncertain how far 'threats' or 'coercion' could by themselves be causes of action, even if no unlawful act were done or threatened. Although accepted by some judges, the view that the common law knew of such an action was increasingly rejected after *Hodges* v. *Webb*, 1920, (*ante*, p. 398), until Lord Dunedin in *Sorrell* v. *Smith*, 1925, could call it the 'leading heresy' (*ante*, p. 447). After the *Crofter* case, 1942, it was clear that to be tortious the threat had to be a threat of an unlawful act. But this left the problem: which acts are 'unlawful' for this purpose? (ii) Through the cases concerned with 'threats' runs the distinction between 'threat' and 'warning'. This is, perhaps, parallel to the distinction between 'inducement' and 'advice' in the tort of inducing breach of contract; but the distinction has never been clarified and does not seem to rest on any sound philosophical footing.

ROOKES v. BARNARD

House of Lords [1964] A.C. 1129

B.O.A.C. and the draughtsmen's union (A.E.S.D.) had an informal 100 per cent membership agreement. Rookes was employed by B.O.A.C.; and in 1955 he resigned from the union. Feeling among the men ran strongly against him. Two unpaid union officials—Barnard and Fistal—who were employed by B.O.A.C., and a union official— Silverthorne—who was employed full-time by the union, told B.O.A.C. that unless Rookes was removed within three days the men would withdraw their labour. Rookes was given notice and lawfully discharged. He sued the three men for conspiracy to do a wrongful act and intimidation. He succeeded before Sachs J.

If there had been a strike, each man would have been in breach of his contract of employment for two reasons: (1) he would not have given the required notice to terminate his contract of employment; (2) it was *conceded* by counsel for the defendants that a no-strike clause in a formal collective agreement made in 1949 between B.O.A.C. and A.E.S.D. was incorporated into each individual contract of employment.

(*a*) Extracts from the Court of Appeal [1963] 1 Q.B. 623

DONOVAN, L.J.: There can be few strikes which do not involve a breach of contract by the strikers. Until a proper notice is given to terminate their contract of service, and the notice has expired, they remain liable under its terms to perform their bargain. It would, however, be affectation not to recognise that in the majority of strikes, no such notice to terminate the contract is either given or expected. The strikers do not want to give up their job; they simply want to be paid more for it or to secure some other advantage in connection with it. The employer does not want to lose his labour force; he simply wants to resist the claim. Not till the strike has lasted some time, and no settlement is in sight, does one usually read that the employers have given notice that unless the men return to work their contracts will be terminated, and they will be dismissed. If a threat to break one's own contract of service be 'unlawful' the actual breach of it must surely be 'unlawful' too. Yet no one seems yet to have thought that a strike itself in breach of contract is unlawful, and at this time of day I do not think it is. Otherwise there would have been countless actions against strikers before now, on the ground that they had conspired to secure their ends by unlawful means; and that on this hypothesis the provisions of ss. 1 and 3 of the Trade Disputes Act, 1906, were of no avail. In *Hodges* v. *Webb*[1] there was in fact a lightning strike of employees designed to secure the dismissal of a non-unionist and the strike seems to have lasted a month. No one apparently thought of suing the strikers for conspiracy involving unlawful means. And Peterson, J., in a judgment which has commanded high approval was able to say: 'No one doubts that the men could have ceased work because they objected to working with the plaintiff, or were entitled to refuse to return to work with the plaintiff.'

If that be the true position, as I think it is, then the situation is reached, if the plaintiff be right, that a strike is not unlawful, but the threat to do so is. In other words, the policy which workmen should pursue in order to avoid liability is to strike first and negotiate afterwards. One has the further anomaly that while a breach of the contract of service would give the present plaintiff no right to sue, since he was not a party to the contract, the mere threat to do so has.

If the present judgment stands it is clear that the protection hitherto thought to be afforded by ss. 1 and 3 of the Trade Disputes Act, 1906, is largely illusory. In almost all trade disputes there is a prior threat of a strike: and if strikes of themselves involve a breach of contract—as I think many of them must—then the threat will constitute the employment of unlawful means, thus taking away the protection of the Act. If this be so, I find it astonishing that in England at any rate no one seems to have thought of the point before....

I reach the conclusion that no unlawful means were employed by Barnard and Fistal; because 'unlawful' in the context of this kind of case means in my view unlawful as being criminal or tortious; and the threat to break their own contract of service by the first and third defendants was neither.

With regard to Silverthorne, who could not threaten to break his own contract since he did not possess one, I think the notion that the threats by Barnard and Fistal to break *their* contracts become threats in which Silverthorne joined pursuant to the alleged conspiracy is somewhat unreal....

If I am wrong in thinking that Barnard and Fistal employed no unlawful means, then in my opinion the second limb of s. 3 provides them with a defence. They clearly interfered with the plaintiff's employment, but in furtherance of a trade dispute. Why, then, do the plain words of the section not apply? It is said because they refer only

[1] [1920] 2 Ch. 70.

to lawful acts. But the first limb of the section protects inducements to break a contract and thus protects something which is ordinarily unlawful as being tortious. If the second limb refers only to lawful acts, that is something that anyone could do anyway, why bother to enact it?...

If, therefore, the second limb of s. 3 was intended to have any effect at all, it cannot have been meant to refer to interference caused by acts the legality of which was beyond question: and I find it impossible to suppose that the legislature in 1906 did not realise that interference with the trade or business or employment of another would probably involve breaches of contract of some kind. That, after all, is what the first limb of the section is concerned with: and if one may procure the breach of another's contract with impunity in a trade dispute it is certainly odd if one cannot even threaten to break one's own. It is significant too that when Parliament specified in 1871 what means were *not* to be employed to cause an employer to dismiss a workman, a breach of contract was not among them. They were violence, threats, molestation, and such acts as would justify a binding over to keep the peace. Whatever may be said, therefore, about these means of interference with trade, business, or employment (being breaches of the criminal law which all have an interest in upholding), I would hold that a breach of one's own private contract, even if 'unlawful', does not of itself involve a forfeiture of the protection of the second limb of s. 3: and *a fortiori* a mere threat of such breach does not do so.

PEARSON, L.J.: Should this obscure, unfamiliar and peculiar cause of action, which has its roots in cases of physical violence and threats of violence, be extended to cover a case in which there is only a threat to break a contract? If the extension were made, it would overturn or outflank some elementary principles of contract law. If A breaks his contract with B, A is liable in damages to B, but he is not liable to C for damage caused to him by that breach of contract even if such damage is foreseeable or even intended by A. The contract between A and B is *res inter alios acta* so far as C is concerned....A by entering into the contract with B has assumed liabilities towards B but not towards anyone else, and business is conducted on the basis of contractual liability being limited in that way and not extending to include liability to third parties. Otherwise it would be too perilous to make a contract. ...C would not have any such cause of action in respect of the actual breach if it occurred. Then if A began by threatening the breach of contract and went on to commit it, surely the result would not be that C, though having no cause of action in respect of the damage caused by the actual breach of contract, nevertheless would have a cause of action in respect of any severable part of the damage which could be attributable to the previous threats.... It seems inherently absurd to say that a mere threat to do something is actionable, when the actual doing of it is not, so that the minor act has a greater effect than the major act.

(b) Extracts from the House of Lords   [1964] A.C. 1129

[*Note* that their Lordships reversed the Court of Appeal on the law, but sent the case back for retrial on the issue of damages since they considered the award made at the trial as one based upon bad principles about punitive damages. The retrial never took place because the parties agreed on a lower figure. No extracts are included here on the question of damages.]

LORD REID: It has often been stated that if people combine to do acts which they know will cause loss to the plaintiff, he can sue if either the object of their conspiracy is unlawful or they use unlawful means to achieve it. In my judgment, to cause such loss by threat to commit a tort against a third person if he does not comply with their demands is to use unlawful means to achieve their object....

The appellant in this case could not take a benefit from contracts to which he was not a party or from any breach of them. But his ground of action is quite different. The respondents here used a weapon in a way in which they knew would cause him loss, and the question is whether they were entitled to use that weapon—a threat that they would cause loss to B.O.A.C. if B.O.A.C. did not do as they wished. That threat was to cause loss to B.O.A.C. by doing something which they had no right to do, breaking their contracts with B.O.A.C. I can see no difference in principle between a threat to break a contract and a threat to commit a tort. If a third party could not sue for damage caused to him by the former I can see no reason why he should be entitled to sue for damage caused to him by the latter. A person is no more entitled to sue in respect of loss which he suffers by reason of a tort committed against someone else than he is entitled to sue in respect of loss which he suffers by reason of breach of a contract to which he is not a party. What he sues for in each case is loss caused to him by the use of an unlawful weapon against him—intimidation of another person by unlawful means. So long as the defendant only threatens to do what he has a legal right to do he is on safe ground. At least if there is no conspiracy he would not be liable to anyone for doing the act, whatever his motive might be, and it would be absurd to make him liable for threatening to do it but not for doing it. But I agree with Lord Herschell (*Allen* v. *Flood*[1]) that there is a chasm between doing what you have a legal right to do and doing what you have no legal right to do, and there seems to me to be the same chasm between threatening to do what you have a legal right to do and threatening to do what you have no legal right to do. It must follow from *Allen* v. *Flood* that to intimidate by threatening to do what you have a legal right to do is to intimidate by lawful means. But I see no good reason for extending that doctrine. Threatening a breach of contract may be a much more coercive weapon than threatening a tort, particularly when the threat is directed against a company or corporation, and, if there is no technical reason requiring a distinction between different kinds of threats, I can see no other ground for making any such distinction....

One of the difficulties facing Parliament was the uncertain state of the law with regard to liability for interfering with a person's trade or employment. It is exceedingly difficult to determine just what was decided in *Quinn* v. *Leathem*,[2] and I neither need nor intend to embark on that vexed subject. But there were at least two theories about what the law really was. One was that an individual was free to take any steps he chose so long as he used no means to achieve his end which were unlawful for some reason other than that they interfered with some other person's trade or employment; and that a combination had the same freedom, provided that their conduct was not dictated by a desire or intention to injure the plaintiff. The other theory was that any action intended or known to be likely to interfere with the trade or employment of another person was unlawful unless it could be justified in some way. I might note that so late as 1908 Sir Frederick Pollock wrote in his *Law of Torts* (1908), 8th ed., pp. 325–6: 'The present writer confesses to great difficulty in understanding why, in *Quinn* v. *Leathem*, before the House of Lords...it was necessary to say so much about conspiracy; for the cause of action was, in effect, ruining the plaintiff's business by coercing his customers not to deal with him, which is well within a line of old authorities....It is submitted that the discussion would be materially simplified if it were understood that all damage wilfully done to one's neighbour is actionable unless it can be justified or excused.' So it is reasonable to suppose that the intention was to draft the Act of 1906 so that it would be equally effective whichever theory ultimately prevailed.

---

[1] [1898] A.C. 1, 121.　　　　[2] [1901] A.C. 495.

The only difficulty about s. 1 is to discover what is meant by 'unless the act, if done without any such agreement or combination, would be actionable.' In the present case, and I have no doubt in many others, the precise act complained of could not have been done without previous agreement. The act complained of in this case was presenting to B.O.A.C. a resolution of all the members of the union to which the respondents were parties. There was an argument that the section requires us to suppose that each respondent merely told B.O.A.C. that he would himself cease work if they did not get rid of the appellant. But that would have been an entirely different act and probably quite ineffective as a threat. The section cannot reasonably be held to mean that no action can be brought unless the precise act complained of could have been done by an individual without previous agreement or combination. In my view, the section requires us to find the nearest equivalent act which could have been so done and see whether it would be actionable. In the present case I think we must suppose that one of the respondents had said to B.O.A.C.: 'I am acting alone but I think I can and I intend to induce the men to break their contracts and strike if you do not get rid of Mr Rookes.' If the opinion which I have already expressed is right, that would have been actionable if B.O.A.C. had succumbed to that threat and got rid of the appellant in the way they did. So s. 1 does not help the respondents.

LORD HODSON: In the past there has been much discussion in the conspiracy cases about the word 'threat', but there is now no necessity to be careful to distinguish between a threat and a warning on the basis that one is a threat to do an illegal act and the other a warning to do something lawful. As Lord Dunedin put it in *Sorrell* v. *Smith*:[1] '...a threat is a pre-intimation of proposed action of some sort. That action must be either *per se* a legal action or an illegal, i.e. a tortious action. If the threat used to effect some purpose is of the first kind, it gives no ground for legal proceeding; if on the second, it falls within the description of illegal means, and the right to sue of the person injured is established.' This language, while making clear that the word 'threat' of itself is neutral, does nothing to support the contention of the appellant that breach of contract was the kind of unlawful act which could be envisaged by the tort of intimidation. Illegal is treated as equivalent to tortious by the use of the link *id est*....

It would, I think, today be more anomalous to draw the line short of breach of contract than beyond it. In the old days the question of

[1] [1925] A.C. 700, 730.

breach of contract by workmen simply did not arise for the reason that they did not have contracts of employment, as a rule, to break. Now the situation is different, and in this case the employees not only agreed to a fixed period of notice on either side for termination of the employment but also not to strike, which I take it means not to take part in any concerted withdrawal of labour, with or without notice.

It would be strange if threats of violence were sufficient and the more powerful weapon of a threat to strike were not, always provided that the threat is unlawful. The injury and suffering caused by strike action is very often widespread as well as devastating, and a threat to strike would be expected to be certainly no less serious than a threat of violence. That a breach of contract is unlawful in the sense that it involves the violation of a legal right there can be no doubt.

LORD DEVLIN: My Lords, on 16 March 1956, the appellant's employment, which had lasted nine years with B.O.A.C., was lawfully determined by notice. The reason why it was terminated was because on 10 January 1956, the members of the A.E.S.D., a trade union to which the appellant belonged and from which he had resigned, served notice on B.O.A.C. 'that if the non-unionist Mr D. E. Rookes, is not removed from the design office by 4 p.m. Friday, 13 January 1956, a withdrawal of labour of all A.E.S.D. membership will take place'. On 13 January the appellant was suspended from his employment and the strike thereby averted; and thereafter notice terminating his employment altogether was given to him, as I have said. The three respondents were officials of the union and two of them were employed by B.O.A.C.

It is not disputed that the notice constituted a threat of breach of contract by the members of A.E.S.D. It is true that any individual employee could lawfully have terminated his contract by giving seven days' notice and if the matter is looked at in that way, the breach might not appear to be a very serious one. But that would be a technical way of looking at it. As Donovan, L.J., said in the Court of Appeal, the object of the notice was not to terminate the contract either before or after the expiry of seven days. The object was to break the contract by withholding labour but keeping the contract alive for as long as the employers would tolerate the breach without exercising their right of rescission. In the second place, there was an agreement in force between A.E.S.D. and B.O.A.C. in which the former undertook that no strike of its members would ever take place; and it is admitted that that term formed part of the contract of service of each member with B.O.A.C....

Since all that the respondents did was admittedly done in the furtherance of a trade dispute, it is idle to inquire what possible causes of action there are available to the appellant at common law without inquiring at the same time to what extent they are curtailed by statute. Conspiracy, which suggests itself at once as a possible cause of action, is covered by s. 1 of the Trade Disputes Act, 1906. There are, as is well known, two sorts of conspiracies, the *Quinn* v. *Leathem*[1] type which employs only lawful means but aims at an unlawful end, and the type which employs unlawful means. Section 1 of the Act contains the formula which negatives the first type as a cause of action where there is a trade dispute. In the latter type, which in my opinion is not affected by the section, the element of conspiracy is usually only of secondary importance since the unlawful means are actionable by themselves.

Section 3 provides a second barrier for the appellant to surmount. It grants immunity in respect of certain acts which include, it is said (I shall have later to examine carefully the language in which the immunity is granted), an inducement of 'some other person to break a contract of employment' and 'an interference with the trade, business or employment of some other person'....

My Lords, in my opinion there is a tort of intimidation of the nature described in chapter 18 of Salmond on the *Law of Torts*, 13th ed. (1961), p. 697. The tort can take one of two forms which are set out in Salmond as follows:

(1) *Intimidation of the plaintiff himself....*

(2) *Intimidation of other persons to the injury of the plaintiff....*

As your Lordships are all of opinion that there is a tort of intimidation and on this point approve the judgments in both courts below, I do not propose to offer any further authorities or reasons in support of my conclusion. I note that no issue on justification was raised at the time and there is no finding of fact upon it. So your Lordships have not to consider what part, if any, justification plays in the tort of intimidation.... The line must be drawn according to the law. It cannot be said that to use a threat of any sort is *per se* unlawful; and I do not see how except in relation to the nature of the act threatened, i.e. whether it is lawful or unlawful, one could satisfactorily distinguish between a lawful and an unlawful threat.

This conclusion, while not directly in point, assists me in my approach to the matter to be determined here. It is not, of course, disputed that if the act threatened is a crime, the threat is unlawful. But otherwise is it enough to say that the act threatened is actionable as a breach of contract

[1] [1901] A.C. 495.

or must it be actionable as a tort? My Lords, I see no good ground for the latter limitation. I find the reasoning on this point of Professor Hamson[1] (which Sellers, L.J.,[2] sets out in his judgment though he does not himself accept it) very persuasive. The essence of the offence is coercion. It cannot be said that every form of coercion is wrong. A dividing line must be drawn and the natural line runs between what is lawful and unlawful as against the party threatened. If the defendant threatens something that that party cannot legally resist, the plaintiff likewise cannot be allowed to resist the consequences; both must put up with the coercion and its results. But if the intermediate party is threatened with an illegal injury, the plaintiff who suffers by the aversion of the act threatened can fairly claim that he is illegally injured.

Accordingly, I reach the conclusion that the respondents' second point fails and on the facts of this case the tort of intimidation was committed. I do not share the difficulties which the Lords Justices felt about the idea of admitting breach of contract into the tort of intimidation.... I think that in one form or another they all stem from the error that any cause of action by the third party, that is the appellant, must in some way be supplemental to or dependent upon a cause of action by B.O.A.C. Thus, it is said to be anomalous that on the facts of this case the appellant should be able to sue the respondents when B.O.A.C. could not. The best way of answering that is to grant that B.O.A.C. would not be able to sue and to assert, as I shall seek to show, that there is nothing anomalous about it. But there was introduced into the argument a suggestion that B.O.A.C. could in fact have sued because although there was no actual breach of contract, one was threatened and therefore there was an anticipatory breach. Against that, it was said that B.O.A.C. could not have sued for an anticipatory breach unless they first elected to rescind, which they never did. I dare say that is right, but I do not think it matters at all whether B.O.A.C. could sue or not. The two causes of action—B.O.A.C.'s and the appellant's—are in law quite independent; and in fact they are virtually alternative because it is difficult to visualise (except in one case) a set of facts on which both could sue.

This last statement is best examined in relation to a threat of physical violence which would unquestionably constitute intimidation. If A threatens B with physical violence unless he harms C, B can either resist or comply. If he resists, B might obtain an injunction against A (as he

[1] Prof. C. J. Hamson, *Camb. Law J.* November 1961, pp. 189, 191.
[2] [1963] 1 Q.B. 623, 666.

could also in the case of a threatened breach of contract if the contract were of a kind that permitted that remedy); or if A carries out his threat, B can sue for assault and obtain damages. In neither case can C sue because he has suffered no harm. If B complies with the threat, B cannot sue for damages because *ex hypothesi* there has been no assault; and he is not likely to obtain an injunction against the execution of a threat which he has already taken other means to avoid. But C will be able to sue because through B's compliance he has been injured. There is no anomaly about this; and if one substitutes 'breach of contract' for 'physical violence', the position is the same. The only case in which B and C are both likely to sue is if they both sue for the tort of intimidation in a case in which B has harmed himself by also harming C.

Then it is said that to give C a cause of action offends against the rule that one man cannot sue on another's contract. I cannot understand this. In no circumstances does C sue on B's contract. The cause of action arises not because B's contract is broken but because it is not broken; it arises because of the action which B has taken to avert a breach.

Then it is asked how it can be that C can sue when there is a threat to break B's contract but cannot sue if it is broken without a threat. This means, it is argued, that if A threatens first, C has a cause of action; but if he strikes without threatening, C has no cause of action. I think that this also is fallacious. What is material to C's cause of action is the threat and B's submission to it....*

So if in the present case A.E.S.D. went on strike without threatening, they would not achieve their object unless they made it plain why they were doing so. If they did that and B.O.A.C. then got rid of the appellant, his cause of action would be just the same as if B.O.A.C. had been threatened first, because the cause of the injury to the appellant would have been A.E.S.D.'s threat, express or implied, to continue on strike until the appellant was got rid of.†

---

* Note that in *Stratford* v. *Lindley* [1965] A.C. 269, Lord Denning, M.R. in the Court of Appeal said of intimidation as a tort: 'It is essential to the cause of action that the person threatened should comply with the demand'. But he went on to say that if the threatener went on to do damage by executing his threat, 'the party threatened can sue for the unlawful act'. Lord Denning's example in that passage was a threat of violence, and the execution is then assault. But what if the threat is of a breach of contract? The logic of the arguments in *Rookes* v. *Barnard* appears to be that a party who has resisted but to whom damage is then done by intentional breach, can sue even though he is a third party to the contract. But this is contrary to the most fundamental rules of English contract law. See the conclusion accepted [1964] *Camb. Law J.* 225; and criticism of the House of Lords decision in (1964) 27 M.L.R. 257.

† Compare the reasoning of Fullagar, J. in *Williams* v. *Hursey* (1959) 103 C.L.R. 30, pp. 80–3.

Finally, it is said that if a threat of breach of contract constitutes intimidation, one party to a contract could be sued for intimidation if he threatened reprisals. Suppose, for example, A has agreed to deliver goods to B in monthly instalments but has not made payment for the first a condition precedent to delivery of the second. If he threatens to withhold the second until payment has been made for the first, is he intimidating B? I doubt it. But the case introduces questions not in issue here—whether a threat in such circumstances would be justifiable and whether it is intimidation to try to force a man into doing what the law, if invoked, would compel him to do.

I find therefore nothing to differentiate a threat of a breach of contract from a threat of physical violence or any other illegal threat. The nature of the threat is immaterial....All that matters to the plaintiff is that, metaphorically speaking, a club has been used. It does not matter to the plaintiff what the club is made of—whether it is a physical club or an economic club, a tortious club or an otherwise illegal club. If an intermediate party is improperly coerced, it does not matter to the plaintiff how he is coerced.

I think, therefore, that at common law there is a tort of intimidation and that on the facts of this case each of the respondents has committed it, both individually (since the jury has found that each took an overt and active part) and in combination with others. I must add that I have obtained no assistance from the numerous data cited to show what constitutes 'unlawful means' in the action of conspiracy. In some of the dicta the language suggests that the means must be criminal or tortious and in others that breach of contract would do; but in no case was the point in issue. Moreover, while a decision on that point might have been most illuminating, it is not the point I have been considering. I have not been considering what amounts to unlawful means in the tort of conspiracy. I am not saying that a conspiracy to commit a breach of contract amounts to the tort of conspiracy; that point remains to be decided. I am saying that in the tort of intimidation a threat to break a contract would be a threat of an illegal act. It follows from that that a combination to intimidate by means of a threat of a breach of contract would be an unlawful conspiracy; but it does not necessarily follow that a combination to commit a breach of contract simpliciter would be an unlawful conspiracy....

The argument on s. 1 is that in order to find on the facts of this case sufficient proof of the tort of intimidation, it is necessary, so it is said, to bring in agreement or combination by the back door; and that is forbidden by s. 1. The argument is applied in particular and in general. In particular, it is applied in the case of Silverthorne, the respondent who is not an employee. He had therefore no contract to break; he cannot be sued (this is admittedly plain from s. 3) for procuring a breach by others; therefore the only cause of action against him is conspiracy or joint intimidation, involving either agreement or combination. In general, the argument is applied in the following way. To sustain the tort of intimidation, it must be shown that there was an operative threat. Damage is an essential part of the cause of action and it must be shown that the damage was caused by the threat. The threat of any single man to stop work would not have influenced B.O.A.C. It was the power of the combination that did that; and that makes proof of the combination (which s. 1 will not allow) an essential part of the appellant's cause of action against all three respondents.

The first part of this argument, i.e. its application in particular to Silverthorne, in my opinion reads too much into s. 1. To establish a cause of action of any sort a plaintiff must show an injurious act. If the act that injures him is not by itself actionable, the plaintiff can succeed at common law only if he shows that it was 'done in pursuance of an agreement or combination' to injure him. He is then setting up a *Quinn* v. *Leathem* cause of action and if that is his position, s. 1 prevents him from suing. But if the injurious act is actionable without the allegation of conspiracy, that is, if it is by itself unlawful, s. 1 does not apply at all. It does not prevent the plaintiff from suing the doer of the act and the conspirators, if any, as well. Section 1 does not prevent actions of conspiracy altogether; it restricts them.

I turn now to the second part of the argument...the question becomes one of the true interpretation and effect of the language of s. 1. It turns on what exactly is meant by 'actionable' and what is the test of actionability to be imposed. The section may mean that in the particular case to which it is being applied, the action will fail unless the plaintiff can prove that a single person has in fact committed the tort of intimidation. Or it may mean that the nature of the act must be such as to make it actionable even if done without any agreement or combination. If the former view is right, then on the assumption of fact that, as is probable, B.O.A.C. would not have been coerced by any individual threat, this appeal must fail. If the latter is right, it is sufficient that intimidation is not of its nature a tort that cannot be committed by a single person and therefore it is of its nature actionable if done without agreement or combination. I have reached the conclusion that the second interpretation should be preferred. This is consistent with the view I have already expressed about this section, namely, that its object is to exclude *Quinn* v. *Leathem* conspiracies in trade disputes. It is distinguishing between wrongs that can be committed singly and those that cannot.

The defence based on s. 3 also turns on the interpretation and effect of the section, the material words being 'actionable on the ground only that'. There are two limbs in the section and I agree that 'only' covers both.... The problem of interpretation to which this section gives rise is, I think, broadly similar to the problem created by s. 1. Is it dealing with the requisites of a cause of action in a given case or is it dealing with the nature of the tort which it is designed to exclude?...

If, then, one treats the section as dealing with the requisites of a cause of action, one finds oneself in difficulties with the cardinal phrase 'actionable on the ground only that'. This speaks of a sole ground. The tort of inducing a breach of contract—and this is true of most torts—is not based on a single ground. An act of inducement is not by itself actionable. One may induce another to take a certain course without the least idea that the other had pledged himself not to take it: that is not actionable at common law and needs no absolution from the statute....

What alternative is there—still on the assumption that the section is dealing with the requisites of a cause of action? An alternative is to treat *the only ground* as meaning *an essential ground*. This reading means that if a plaintiff cannot establish a cause of action without setting up as part of it an act of inducement, the action is barred by the section. If this reading is applied to the second limb, it is fatal to the appellant here since an essential part of his cause of action is injury done to him by interference with his employment.

If the section has to be interpreted on the assumption that it is dealing with the requisites of a cause of action, this reading of it is, I think, preferable to a literal reading. But undoubtedly it is straining the language to read the section as if for the words 'on the ground only' there was substituted 'if it is an essential ground'. The two phrases are quite different in their import and would produce quite different results in their application to the first limb. Suppose that a defendant slandered a plaintiff so as to induce the plaintiff's employer by that means to dismiss him. It seems extremely unlikely that Parliament intended to authorise the use of foul means in the furtherance of a trade dispute....

In the light of these considerations and having found that the proper construction of s. 1 requires one to read it as dealing with the nature of the act and not with the requisites of a cause of action in a given case, it is natural to ask whether 'actionable' should not be given the same sort of meaning in both sections; and whether s. 3 also should not be interpreted as dealing with the nature of the tort.

On such a reading 'the ground' is not used to define an ingredient in a tortious cause of action but to define the whole tort by reference to the essential ground by which the tort is usually described....I think that this is the way in which the section in its first limb deals with the tort of inducing a breach of contract. Standing alone the tort is insufficient where there is a trade dispute; but if the defendant has also committed the tort of intimidation, he can be sued. It does not matter that what was achieved by the intimidation was a breach of contract.

The same reasoning must, I think, be applied to the second limb, if it is assumed (as I shall start by assuming) that there is a tort of malicious interference with trade, business or employment. The section must be designed to deal with both torts in the same way. If as a result of the respondents' action B.O.A.C., instead of giving the appellant lawful notice, had dismissed him summarily, it would follow that he could have sued the respondents for intimidation, though not for inducing a breach of contract, and it would be no answer to say that the damage was done by means of a breach of the contract of employment....

What is said to be fatal to this reasoning is that there is in law no such tort as the tort of malicious interference done by a single person. Parliament, it is argued, cannot have intended to take away by statute a right of action that does not exist at common law. So the second limb, notwithstanding that there is no hint in the section of any different approach to it, cannot be construed in the same way as the first, and some other meaning must be found for it. What is suggested is, that since interference is not by itself actionable at common law, you must find some other element that added to interference makes it actionable at common law, and then you must give effect to the section by construing it as taking away that right of action....In order to weigh the merits of this argument, I do not think that it is necessary for the House to decide whether or not malicious interference by a single person with trade, business or employment is or is not a tort known to the law. But I must at least say what I mean by such a tort. I mean, putting it shortly, *Quinn* v. *Leathem* without the conspiracy. If one man, albeit by lawful means, interferes with another's right to earn his living or dispose of his labour as he wills and does so maliciously, that is, with intent to injure without justification, he is, if there is such a tort, liable in just the same way as he would undoubtedly be liable if he were acting in combination with others. The combination aggravates but is not essential.

As I say, I do not think your Lordships need decide this point. You are considering the construction of a statute passed in 1906 and endeavouring to interpret it in the light of what Parliament must be taken to have intended.... If it was perfectly clear in 1906 that the decision in *Quinn* v. *Leathem* depended on the element of conspiracy, s. 1 of the Act got rid of it. But if conspiracy was not essential to the decision, something more was necessary: and that something more is supplied by the second limb of s. 3. Moreover, the method chosen is that which one would expect Parliament in such circumstances to use. Statutes are not in this respect expressed conditionally. The draftsman cannot be expected to say by way of preface: 'If it be held that interference is wrongful'. He would assume for the purpose of the enactment that it was. If it was not, the enactment would be otiose but harmless; if it was, the enactment would achieve the object desired. I am not at all sure that it can be said even now with certainty what *Quinn* v. *Leathem* decided; but I am quite sure that in 1906 the matter was still in doubt....

I have therefore reached the conclusion that the true effect of s. 3 is that in a trade dispute it deprives the plaintiff of any cause of action he may have on the facts for inducing a breach of contract and any cause of action he may have on the facts or in law for interference with his employment by lawful means; but that in neither case does it countenance the use of tortious means. So the appellant's cause of action in intimidation is not barred by the statute.

This leads to the conclusion that this appeal should succeed. But there is one argument, or at least one consideration, that remains to be noticed. It is that the strike weapon is now so generally sanctioned that it cannot really be regarded as an unlawful weapon of intimidation; and so there must be something wrong with a conclusion that treats it as such. This thought plainly influenced quite strongly the judgments in the Court of Appeal. To give effect to it means either that illegal means ought not to include a breach of contract; or that the statute ought to be construed as wide enough to give protection. The Court of Appeal tended, I think, to apply the argument to both points indiscriminately.

I see the force of this consideration. But your Lordships can, in my opinion, give effect to it only if you are prepared either to hobble the common law in all classes of disputes lest its range is too wide to suit industrial disputes or to give the statute a wider scope than it was ever intended to have....

It may, therefore, as a matter of policy be right that a breach of contract should not be treated as an illegal means within the limited field of industrial disputes. But can your Lordships get that out of the words of the Act? Section 3 gives immunity from action for procuring a breach of contract but not for the breach itself. In the Court of Appeal Donovan, L.J.,[1] said with great force: '...if one may procure the breach of another's contract with impunity in a trade dispute it is certainly odd if one cannot even threaten to break one's own.' The section could easily have read—'shall not be actionable on the ground only that it *is a breach of contract or* induces some other person' etc.; but it is not so written. It may be that, as Mr Gardiner suggests, Parliament thought it very unlikely that an employer would resort to action against workmen individually for breaches of contract and that he would get very little from it if he did: see on this point *National Coal Board* v. *Galley*.[2] Or it may be that Parliament did not anticipate that a threat of breach of contract would be regarded as an intimidatory weapon. Whatever the reason, the immunity is not in the statute; the section clearly exempts the procurer or inducer and equally clearly does not exempt the breaker. It is not suggested that the House can remove the oddity by reading words into the Act that are not there.

So your Lordships cannot construe the Act to give protection in the case of a threat of a breach of contract unless you also make it wide enough to protect the threatener of physical violence....The essence of the difficulty lies in the fact that in determining what constitutes the tort of intimidation your Lordships have drawn the dividing line not between physical and economic coercion but between lawful and unlawful coercion. For the universal purposes of the common law, I am sure that that is the right, natural and logical line. For the purpose of the limited field of industrial disputes which is controlled by statute and where much that is in principle unlawful is already tolerated, it may be that pragmatically and on grounds of policy the line should be drawn between physical and economic pressure. But that is for Parliament to decide.

LORD PEARCE: The question whether 'means that are illegal in themselves' include threats of breach of contract is not directly covered by authority except in the two Irish cases *Cooper* v. *Millea*[3] and *Riordan*

---

[1] [1963] 1 Q.B. 623, 685.
[2] [1958] 1 W.L.R. 16, 27; [1958] 1 All E.R. 91, C.A.
[3] [1938] I.R. 749.

v. *Butler*,[1] which held that a threatened breach of contract constituted illegal means....

Businesses are run on the basis of contracts. The threat by an important supplier to withhold the supplies under a long-term contract on which a manufacturer relies might be tantamount to a threat of ruin and compel him to accede to the supplier's demands. It would seem strange if the law should disregard intimidation by such potent contractual weapons, while taking cognisance on intimidation by less potent tortious weapons....

At first sight, there is compelling force in the respondents' argument that Parliament cannot have intended the second limb to be merely declaratory that interference with employment (which is not a tort) shall not be actionable. But at the date when the Act was passed the law was in some confusion. It was thought by some well-informed opinion that there was a tort of mere unjustifiable interference with trade. This appears from the report of the Royal Commission which preceded the Act. On this view of the law (which was subsequently shown to be wrong) it would be reasonable for Parliament to enact the second limb of s. 3 for the purpose of ensuring that no conduct should be unlawful on the ground only that it interfered with trade—meaning that it was protected if it was tortious for that reason and for no other reason....

A strong argument (to which Donovan, L.J., in his forceful judgment subscribed) is urged on the respondent's behalf to the effect that threats of lawful action (i.e. by giving notice) as opposed to threats of unlawful action (i.e. by stopping work in breach of contract) are inconvenient and unsuited to modern industrial disputes, since neither side wishes the contracts to be determined and the termination of contracts would give rise to confusion in respect of superannuation schemes and other matters. I see the force of this, as a matter of convenience, but I feel some doubt as to how far it is a useful argument as to what Parliament intended in 1906 under the existing conditions....

One cannot read the words of the section literally as defining the components of a cause of action since in that case the protection against an action 'on the ground only that it induces some other person to break a contract of employment' is meaningless. For no action could ever lie on that 'ground only'; it would need the addition of knowledge and damage. I see the attractions of paraphrasing the section as referring to the substantial essential requirements of an action. One might, for

[1] [1940] I.R. 347.

instance, so read a section that said no spoken words shall be actionable on the ground only that they refer to a man in the way of his trade. LORD EVERSHED delivered a concurring speech, *dubitante* as to the interpretation of s. 3, 'Limb' 2.*

THE TRADE DISPUTES ACT, 1965†

1. *Certain acts not actionable in tort or as delicts.* (1) An act done after the passing of this Act by a person in contemplation or furtherance of a trade dispute (within the meaning of the Trade Disputes Act, 1906) shall not be actionable in tort on the ground only that it consists in his threatening (*a*) that a contract of employment (whether one to which he is a party or not) will be broken, or (*b*) that he will induce another to break a contract of employment to which that other is a party; or be capable of giving rise to an action of reparation on the ground only that it so consists.

(2) An act done as aforesaid by a person before the passing of this Act shall not be actionable in tort as mentioned in the foregoing subsection unless proceedings in respect thereof have been instituted either before or within the period of six months beginning with the date of the passing of this Act or be capable of giving rise to an action of reparation as so mentioned unless proceedings in respect thereof have been so instituted.

GAGNON v. FOUNDATION MARITIME LTD

Supreme Court of Canada   [1961] S.C.R. 435

Where legislation controls the forms of collective bargaining, as in Canada, a combination which infringes those forms can be treated as an unlawful conspiracy.‡

* For discussion of the implications of *Rookes* v. *Barnard*, the reader is referred to the following articles: K. W. Wedderburn, *Intimidation and the Right to Strike* (1964) 27 M.L.R. 257 (continuing (1962) 25 M.L.R. 513 and (1961) 24 M.L.R. 572), and note in (1965) 28 M.L.R. 205, p. 209; O. Kahn-Freund, *Rookes* v. *Barnard* (1964) 14 *Federation News*, p. 30; I. Christie, note (1964) 42 *Can. Bar. Rev.* 464; C. J. Hamson, *Rookes* v. *Barnard* [1964] *Camb. Law J.* 159 (continuing [1961] *Camb. Law. J.* 189); L. H. Hoffman *Rookes* v. *Barnard* (1965) 81 L.Q.R. 116; J. A. Weir, Note on 'Economic Torts' [1964] *Camb. Law J.* 225; W. F. Frank *The Right to Strike Reconsidered* [1964] Jo. B.L.L. 199. See too *Morgan* v. *Fry*, *The Times*, March 18, 1967.
On the Trade Disputes Act, 1965, see Wedderburn (1966) 29 M.L.R. 53.
Many of the points made in these articles are still relevant to the problems of 'residual tort liabilities: see *infra*, Excursus B, p. 526.
† On the arguments concerning the limitations of the protection provided by this statute see Diplock, L.J., *Emerald Construction Ltd* v. *Lowthian* (*ante*, p. 492); Salmond *Torts* (14th ed. Heuston) p. 533; Wedderburn, *The Worker and the Law* (1965) p. 292, (1966) p. 281; and (1966) 29 M.L.R. p. 54.
‡ The legislature plainly attempted to control the growth of any such liabilities in Britain by enacting s. 16(5) Prices and Incomes Act 1966: see *ante*, p. 261.

RITCHIE, J. (delivering the judgment of himself and of KERWIN, C.J., and CARTWRIGHT, J.): In the case of *Therien* v. *International Brotherhood of Teamsters*,¹ Mr Justice Sheppard of the British Columbia Court of Appeal had occasion to consider whether breaches of the *Labour Relations Act* of that province by the defendant constituted 'illegal means' whereby the company there in question was induced to cease doing business with the plaintiff. In the course of his decision, Mr Justice Sheppard said at p. 680:

'In relying upon ss. 4 and 6 of the statute the plaintiff is not to be taken as asserting a statutory cause of action. The plaintiff is here founding upon a common law cause of action within *Hodges* v. *Webb* [1920] 2 Ch. 70 which requires as one of the elements that an illegal means be used or threatened. To ascertain whether the means was illegal enquiry may be made both at common law and at statute law.'

When the *Therien* case,² reached this Court, Mr Justice Locke, speaking on behalf of the majority of the Court, said at p. 280:

'I agree with Sheppard, J.A., that in relying upon these sections of the Act the respondent is asserting, not a statutory cause of action, but a common law cause of action, and that to ascertain whether the means employed were illegal inquiry may be made both at common law and of the statute law.'

In light of these observations, it becomes unnecessary to embark upon the difficult exercise of determining whether or not a breach of s. 22(1) of the *Labour Relations Act* gives rise to a statutory cause of action because when inquiry is 'made of the statute law' in the present case it discloses, as has been said, that the means here employed by the appellants were prohibited, and this of itself supplies the ingredient necessary to change a lawful agreement which would not give rise to a cause of action into a tortious conspiracy, the carrying out of which exposes the conspirators to an action for damages if any ensue therefrom.

LOCKE, J., delivered a concurring judgment; JUDSON, J., dissented, *inter alia* on the ground that the unlawful means must be found in nominate torts or crimes.*

¹ [1959], 16 D.L.R. (2d) 646, 27 W.W.R. 49.
² [1960] S.C.R. 265, 22 D.L.R. (2d) 1.

* On the Canadian experience of conspiracy or residual tort liabilities based on breach of statutes regulating collective bargaining, see I. M. Christie, 'The Liability of Strikers in the Law of Torts' (Ontario 1967), chapters III and V.

CUNARD STEAMSHIP CO. LTD *v.* STACEY

Court of Appeal [1955] 2 Lloyd's Rep. 247

The defendant seamen, employees of the plaintiff company, held meetings at which they exhorted their fellow-employees to go on strike. Various ships including the *Queen Mary* were unable to sail. The strike was unofficial. The plaintiffs successfully sought an injunction to restrain the defendants from persuading seamen to break their contracts or from conspiring so to persuade the seamen.

EVERSHED, M.R.: Before I pass to the Merchant Shipping Act, 1894, in order to examine that matter, I should state that from the evidence to which I have referred it seems to me clear that there is here a trade dispute—though it is not necessary to express a final view.

Now, the Merchant Shipping Act, 1894, is an Act, as was pointed out to us more than once, which contains a very large number of sections. It is an Act which comprehends almost all aspects of its title, merchant shipping. I have already referred to one of the sections which regulate the contracts of employment. There is also a fasciculus of sections beginning with s. 220, which bears the heading 'Provisions as to discipline', and it is these sections which put the seamen, at any rate in some respects, clearly in a different position from the workmen in other walks of life and from members of other Unions than the National Union of Seamen.... Section 226, to which Lord Justice Parker referred, provides that nothing in these sections relating to absence without leave 'shall take away or limit any remedy by action or by summary procedure before Justices which an owner or master would but for those provisions have for any breach of contract...'. Then finally comes s. 236(1): 'If a person by any means whatever persuades or attempts to persuade a seaman or apprentice to neglect or refuse to join or proceed to sea in or to desert from his ship, or otherwise to absent himself from his duty, he shall for each offence in respect of each seaman or apprentice be liable to a fine not exceeding ten pounds.'

Now, the point which plainly emerges from what I have read is this: Does the fact that the activities with which the defendants are charged— and I assume for the moment truly charged—take the case out of s. 3, on the ground that there is some basis, some cause of action, some wrong, other than the mere inducement of persons to break contracts, namely, offences committed under the Merchant Shipping Act, 1894? I have felt, I confess, and still feel, considerable doubt what the right answer to this question is....

I must, therefore, look at s. 3 of the Trade Disputes Act, 1906, in the light of the Merchant Shipping Act, 1894, and ask whether it is shown here that the acts complained of would only be actionable on the ground that they are inducements to others to break contracts and therefore covered by the former Act. If this point stood alone, I am not at all sure what my own conclusion would be; but it does not stand alone.

Since, however, I have referred to the Merchant Shipping Act, 1894, I must say that in the light of the passages I have read I do not think it right to say that, after the passing of the Act, the only remedy which an owner has against his seamen is that of prosecution under the Merchant Shipping Act....

The joint effect, therefore, of ss. 1 and 3 of the Trade Disputes Act, 1906, would clearly, as it seems to me, have *prima facie* afforded protection (assuming here a trade dispute) to the defendants against a charge of civil conspiracy. But then our attention was drawn by Mr Brown, in the course of his address, to s. 16 of the Act of 1875—which is not special to any particular part of the Act. It is a separate general provision following the definition section: 'Nothing in this Act shall apply to seamen or to apprentices to the sea service.'* There are other sections of the 1875 Act, particularly s. 7, which create statutory offences—for example, intimidation or annoyance by violence—and, in the case of *Regina* v. *Lynch and Jones* [1898] 1 Q.B. 61, to which we were referred, seamen (or persons who were said to be seamen) were charged with an offence under s. 7. They cited this s. 16 and said: 'It cannot apply to us, because we are seamen'. That is the only case in which any consideration appears to have been given to the extent of the word 'seamen'. As I have said, I do not pursue that point, because no argument has been addressed to us that the men with whom we are now dealing are other than seamen. But the curious and, if I may use the phrase, the rather topsy-turvy effect in this case is that s. 16 is now relied upon, not as exempting seamen from the offences of the 1875 Act, but as depriving them of the amendment to the law which s. 3 gave for the benefit of persons concerned in strikes. At first it seems a remarkable result; but I confess I have not yet seen the answer to it, though answer there well may be. On the face of it, Parliament has said 'Nothing in this Act shall apply to seamen'; so that you are led to the conclusion that the section which begins 'An agreement...by two or

---

* Note: Since s. 1 of the 1906 Act took effect as an addition to s. 3 of the 1875 Act, s. 16 of the 1875 Act prevents its application to seamen. But no such problem deprives seamen of the protection of the rest of the 1906 Act, including s. 3.

more persons' ought to be read as 'two or more persons, not being seamen' If that is so, seamen appear to remain subject to the liabilities for conspiracy, civil or criminal, which were said to subsist before the 1875 Act.

JENKINS, L.J., delivered a concurring judgment; PARKER, L.J., agreed with the opinions of JENKINS, L.J., and EVERSHED, M.R.

POST OFFICE ACT, 1953*

59. *Carelessness, negligence or misconduct of persons employed in carrying or delivering mail bags, postal packets, etc.* If any person employed to convey or deliver a mail bag, or a postal packet in course of transmission by post, or to perform any other duty in respect of a mail bag or such a postal packet:

(*a*) without authority whilst so employed, or whilst the mail bag or postal packet is in his custody or possession, leaves it, or suffers any person, not being the person in charge thereof, to ride in the place for the conveyance thereof, or to ride in or upon a vehicle so used and not licensed to carry passengers, or upon a horse used for the conveyance on horseback thereof;

(*b*) is guilty of any act of drunkenness whilst so employed;

(*c*) is guilty of carelessness, negligence or other misconduct whereby the safety of the mail bag or postal packet is endangered;

(*d*) without authority collects, receives, conveys or delivers a postal packet otherwise than in the ordinary course of post;

(*e*) gives any false information of an assault or attempt at robbery upon him; or

(*f*) loiters on the road or passage, or wilfully misspends his time so as to retard the progress or delay the arrival of a mail bag or postal packet in the course of transmission by post, or does not use due care and diligence safely to convey a mail bag or postal packet at the due rate of speed,

he shall be liable on summary conviction to a fine not exceeding twenty pounds.

* *Note:* A 'work-to-rule' is not normally a breach of an employee's contractual obligations, whereas a 'go-slow' usually is. *Quaere:* how far would the same distinction be the measure of liability under this statute?

EXCURSUS A

Strikes and Breach of Employment Contracts

After the speeches in *Rookes* v. *Barnard*, the question whether a strike is in breach of employment contracts is bound to assume increased importance. Even though the Trade Disputes Act, 1965 (p. 520), provides limited protection for 'intimidation', such breach of contract was dubbed by the House of Lords a fully 'unlawful' act. The following points are offered in the light of the materials in this section, and in chapters 1, 2 and 3:

(*a*) The absence from work is *prima facie* a breach of contract by the worker. Notice cannot normally be given merely to 'suspend' the contract unilaterally. If a 'no strike' or 'procedure' clause is incorporated into the contract of employment, an additional reason will arise for finding a breach. The breach will normally go to the root of the contract (see *ante*, p. 87, p. 143 and p. 468).

(*b*) Even the giving of notice equivalent to that required for termination cannot cure the breach involved in a limited stoppage— e.g. a 'one day' strike. The defendants did in fact advance to the House of Lords in *Stratford* v. *Lindley* [1965] A.C. at p. 315, the proposition that there is a common law right to strike by way of implied term in the contract of employment (see (1965) 28 M.L.R., p. 206, n. 6: and the full pleading in K. W. Wedderburn, *Evidence to Royal Commission on Trade Unions* (H.M.S.O. 1966, Day 31, paragraph 56)). Their Lordships plainly did not accept that view.

(*c*) Nevertheless, in many cases of an *unlimited* stoppage, notice to terminate employment contracts can be, and has been, given (see e.g. *Gaskell's* case *ante*, p. 397); and in many other cases the courts have assumed in favour of the workmen that such notice was, or would be given (see e.g. *White* v. *Riley*, *ante*, p. 470; *Santen* v. *Busnach*, *ante*, p. 501). Sometimes there is a special reason for the desirability of giving notice to terminate, e.g. avoidance of possible criminality (see e.g. ss. 4 and 5 Conspiracy and Protection of Property Act, 1875, *ante*, p. 383).

(*d*) A notice of an unlimited stoppage, however, may not be a notice to terminate employment contracts. (It has been argued that this is always its character by C. Grunfeld, *Modern Trade Union Law*, p. 330—but this does not seem to be the better view.) Many unions avoid giving notice to terminate; they give notice of a withdrawal of labour, which in legal terms must mean a notice of forthcoming breach of contracts. This is recognized in the *dicta* in *Rookes* v. *Barnard* of Donovan, L.J. (p. 503), Lord Devlin (p. 509), and Lord Pearce (p. 519); and in *Stratford* v. *Lindley* by Lord Denning, M.R. (p. 480). Readers are referred to these passages, which represent the authoritative judicial view. See too *Morgan* v. *Fry*, *The Times*, March 17, 1967.

(*e*) In cases where notice to terminate employment is given by union officials it should be borne in mind that they need the authority of their members to terminate the employment.

EXCURSUS B

Residual Tort Liabilities in the Modern Law

The reader will have noted in many of the passages in this chapter from modern judgments judicial *dicta* which suggest new possibilities in tort liability. The following points may be kept in mind by the reader considering new developments:

(*a*) New forms of conspiracy: The simplest is the 'conspiracy to break contracts'—either employment or commercial contracts—which, since *Rookes* v. *Barnard*, must be a combination to use unlawful means. (Lord Devlin's suggestion that this might not be so, see p. 513, has puzzled both critics and supporters of the rest of his Lordship's speech.) A conspiracy to use unlawful means of this kind would not be protected by the Trade Disputes Acts. (The reader is reminded of the remarks made on this area in *Bunn*'s case, *ante*, p. 380.) Furthermore, combinations to act in contravention of statutes are likely to assume greater importance with the growth of 'incomes policy' legislation, though we have already seen that s. 16(5), Prices and Incomes Act, 1966, has tried to stem this tide.

(On the use of conspiracy to do damage by means of breach of contract see: (1961) 24 M.L.R. p. 581, (1964) 27 M.L.R. p. 267.)

(*b*) Some commentators go so far as seeing intentional breach of contract as a tort—e.g. Weir [1964] Camb. Law J. 225; but this (though logical) seems an unlikely judicial tack.

(*c*) Lord Devlin has left open the question whether mere 'interference with business', done maliciously, could after all be a tort, *ante*, p. 516. The burden of authority is firmly against this view, for it is hard not to see it as in conflict with *Allen* v. *Flood* itself (p. 497).

(*d*) It has now been expressly left open both by Lord Reid (p. 482) and Lord Denning, M.R. (p. 493) whether there is a tort consisting in interference with contractual relations *without* actually causing a breach. The manner in which the later cases have extended the area of liability for inducing breach of commercial contract (see (1965) 28 M.L.R. 205; and the *Emerald Construction* case, *ante*, p. 492) suggest that the courts might develop such a liability. *Contra* Lord Donovan, *ante* p. 488.

(*e*) One of the liabilities in *Stratford* v. *Lindley* (*ante*, p. 478) was based upon the interference by unlawful means with *future* commercial contracts. The unlawful means there was the inducement of breach of employment contracts otherwise than in a trade dispute. The extension of the concept of 'unlawful means' in one of the various ways outlined above, might allow a court to impose such a liability even where the defendants had acted in furtherance of a trade dispute. (In this connexion, consider the *dicta* of Lord Pearce limiting s. 3 of the 1906 Act (*ante*, p. 486); but for a criticism of that view, based on Lord Devlin's speech in *Rookes* v. *Barnard*, see (1965) 28 M.L.R. p. 211, where the meaning of the word 'actionable' is put in issue.)

SECTION E

TORT IMMUNITY OF THE TRADE UNION

(s. 4 of the 1906 Act, see *ante*, p. 385)

VACHER & SONS LTD *v.* LONDON SOCIETY OF COMPOSITORS

House of Lords   [1913] A.C.107

The appellant printing company sued the defendant trade union and two of its officials for libels which it alleged were contained in a guide to London Printing Offices issued by the union and from which the appellant's name was missing and in a letter written to the United Committee of the Taxation of the Land. They claimed these meant that the appellant company was unfair in its dealing, that it treated its employees harshly, refused to employ union compositors and was not fit to be entrusted with orders. The question arose of whether under s. 4(1) of the Trade Disputes Act, 1906, this action was competent against the union. The House held it should be summarily dismissed.

Viscount Haldane, L.C.: Section 4, subs. 1, the section which has to be construed in the present appeal, does, however, relate exclusively to the case of a trade union. It enacts that an action against such a union, whether of workmen or masters, or against any members or officials of the union on behalf of themselves and all the other members, in respect of any tortious act alleged to have been committed by or on behalf of the union, shall not be entertained by any Court. I draw attention to the fact that this section differs from the three preceding sections not only in relating exclusively to the case of a trade union, but in that subs. 1 omits mention of any restriction which would confine the tortious act to one in contemplation or in furtherance of a trade dispute. Upon this point it has been contended by the learned counsel who addressed the House for the appellants that such a restriction ought to be implied. It is said that s. 5, which provides that the Act may be cited as the Trade Disputes Act, 1906, and the scheme of the first three sections, which deal only with trade disputes, show that the Act is to be interpreted as so confined, and that it cannot be supposed that the Legislature intended to free trade unions from liability to the extent which a literal reading of s. 4, subs. 1, would indicate.

My Lords, with this contention I am unable to agree. It is true that it is provided that the Act may be cited by the short title of the Trade Disputes Act, 1906. But the governing title is that which introduces the statute as an Act to provide for the regulation of trade unions and trade disputes. The first three sections regulate trade disputes. The fourth section appears to me to carry out the other intention indicated by the initial title by laying down new law as to trade unions. I find no context in the Act read as a whole which indicates an intention to cut down the literal meaning of the wide language of s. 4, subs. 1. For reasons which I have already assigned, I think that it would not only be beyond the functions of a Court of justice to presume that the Legislature could not when it passed the Act have intended to go as far as the plain words used say, but that if judges could speculate as to its intentions they would probably speculate wrongly.

I pass, therefore, to the next point which was made for the appellants. This turns on the effect of subs. 2 of s. 4, a subsection which, it is said, ought to be read as a proviso to subs. 1 restricting its operation. Section 4, subs. 2, is in these terms: 'Nothing in this section shall affect the liability of the trustees of a trade union to be sued in the events provided for by the Trade Union Act, 1871, section nine, except in respect of any tortious act committed by or on behalf of the union in contemplation or furthance of a trade dispute.'

The Act of 1871 enables trade unions to register, and provides by s. 9

that the trustees of a registered trade union may sue or be sued as such in cases concerning the property of the trade union. The Legislature appears to have desired to draw a distinction between the union and its trustees and to preserve the liability of the trustees under this section, even in the case of tortious acts committed by the union, damages arising out of which might, as pointed out by Lord Lindley in his judgment in the *Taff Vale Case*, have been made effective against property in the hands of the trustees. But a restriction is put on the liability of the trustees by excepting from it liability in respect of a tortious act committed by or on behalf of the union in contemplation or in furtherance of a trade dispute. Having regard to the distinction drawn in the wording of the statute between the liability of the trade union and the liability of its trustees, I see no justification for importing the provision restricting liability enacted in the latter subsection into the words of subs. 1, and I think that on the second point made the argument which was addressed to us to the effect that the words of exception in the second subsection must be read as qualifying the whole section cannot succeed.

LORD MACNAGHTEN, LORD ATKINSON, LORD SHAW and LORD MOULTON delivered concurring judgments.

WARE AND DE FREVILLE LTD *v.* MOTOR TRADE ASSOCIATION

Court of Appeal   [1921] 3 K.B. 40

The defendant trade union, an association of manufacturers of motor vehicles, placed the plaintiff company on a 'stop list' whereupon the plaintiffs brought an unsuccessful action for libel.

SCRUTTON, L.J., also considered s. 4 of the 1906 Act in the following passage (in which ATKIN, L.J., concurred): The cross-appeal by the plaintiffs is against the decision of Rowlatt, J., that the action will not lie against the Motor Trade Association because they are a trade union, in view of s. 4 of the Trade Disputes Act, 1906.... The cross-appeal was rested on the ground that this did not prevent an action for an injunction, and this in turn was supported by two Chancery decisions, *Attorney-General* v. *Hackney Local Board*[1] and *Flower* v. *Leyton Local Board*.[2] The latter case allowed proceedings for an injunction without complying with the formalities of s. 264 of the Public Health Act, 1875, which provided that a 'writ or process' should not be served without

---

[1] L.R. 20 Eq. 626.   [2] 5 Ch. D. 347.

one month's previous notice. The explanation of this may be that 'writ or process' was not the correct term to apply to a bill in equity. But I notice that when all these statutes imposing conditions on proceedings against public authorities were consolidated in the Public Authorities Protection Act, 1893, the language used was: 'Where any action...or other proceeding is commenced in the United Kingdom' certain conditions shall be fulfilled. In 1898 in *Harrop* v. *Ossett Corporation*[1] it was attempted to argue that the section only applied to the same actions as the Public Health Act, 1875, and did not prevent proceedings in the Chancery Division to obtain injunctions. But Romer, J., took the view that 'action' covered all actions in the Chancery Division, whether for an injunction alone, or accompanied with damages. In my view the word 'action' in the Trade Disputes Act, 1906, has the same meaning. The section however uses the terms 'an action...in respect of any tortious act alleged to have been committed.' I cannot think these words were intended to exclude an action 'in respect of' a tortious act threatened to be committed. The words 'in respect of' seem framed with intentional width to cover all remedies asked for in relation to a tortious act, whether committed or about to be committed. It was clearly intended that a trade union should as such be free from liability for damages for tort. A request for an injunction may be dealt with by the Courts leaving the party to his remedy in damages, which, however, could not be given against a trade union. I cannot think that Parliament intended to allow injunctions to be granted in respect of acts for which, when done, no damages could be claimed, and therefore, though I feel I am straining the language of the Act, I must read 'alleged to have been committed' as including allegations that trade unions are about to commit tortious acts.

BANKES, L.J., concurred in the decision but did not consider this point.

BOULTING v. ASSOCIATION OF CINEMATOGRAPH, TELEVISION AND ALLIED TECHNICIANS
Court of Appeal   [1963] 2 Q.B. 606

LORD DENNING, M.R. (who dissented on the main point in holding that the plaintiffs should succeed, *post* p. 567): What, then, is the remedy open to the Boulting brothers? Clearly the courts can grant a declaration that the rules are unlawful. I do not base this on the fact that the

---

[1] [1898] 1 Ch. 525.

Boulting brothers were members at the date of the writ. I base it on the power of the court in its discretion to make a declaration of right whenever the interest of the plaintiff is sufficient to justify it. The judge said that if the plaintiffs were right in their contentions, he would not hesitate to grant a declaration. Nor would I. I would grant a declaration. I would declare that the Boulting brothers are not eligible to be members of this union.

Now as to an injunction. It seems to me that if the union are threatening to do an unlawful act, namely, to compel the directors to join the union in breach of their duty to the company, they are threatening to commit a tort, for which the company, or I may add, the Boulting brothers themselves, could obtain an injunction, were it not for s. 4 of the Act of 1906. That section says that 'an action against a trade union... in respect of any tortious act alleged to *have been committed* by or on behalf of the trade union shall not be entertained by any court'. Strictly speaking, those words do not forbid an action for an injunction in respect of a tortious act which is about to be committed. But in *Ware and de Freville* v. *Motor Trade Association*, Scrutton, L.J., with the concurrence of Atkin, L.J., thought that the words should be so construed as to forbid injunctions also. I hesitate to differ from so great authority: and on this account I would not be prepared to grant an injunction. But a declaration I would grant, in the confident expectation that, once the law is declared, the union, or at any rate, their officers, would not seek to do anything contrary to it.

UPJOHN, L.J. (with whom DIPLOCK, L.J., agreed): The final point is this. On the footing that the union are threatening to commit a tort by procuring the plaintiffs to commit a breach of duty to Charter, and that the plaintiffs can complain of that at law, the question is whether the plaintiffs are precluded from bringing an action against A.C.T.T. in the courts to have that matter determined. A.C.T.T. say they cannot and rely on s. 4(1) of the Trade Disputes Act, 1906, which is in these terms: 'An action against a trade union, whether of workmen or masters, or against any members or officials thereof on behalf of themselves and all other members of the trade union in respect of any tortious act alleged to have been committed by or on behalf of the trade union, shall not be entertained by any court.'

I recognize that my remarks are *obiter*, but I am bound to confess that I have the greatest difficulty in understanding Scrutton, L.J., in *Ware & de Freville Ltd* v. *Motor Trade Association*, when he thought that that section covered apprehended injury. He agreed that his view involved a strained construction of the section, and, indeed, it plainly did, because it entirely gave the go-by to the words 'alleged to have been committed'.

I see much force in the argument of Mr Parker upon this point. If a tort has been committed, the injured party is without remedy against the union, though not against the individuals who commit the tort, whether they be servants or agents or not. The tort remains a wrong by the union, but a wrong for which there is no remedy against it. I think in those circumstances that a strict construction should be given to the section which, after all, is substantially interfering with the common law rights of the subject. I think the court is entitled to grant an injunction to prevent an apprehended injury, as it would in the ordinary case, and all the more so if the statute has provided that if in fact the tort is committed, he shall be left without remedy.

I think that unless prevented by clear words, and there are none present in s. 4, the court should be especially astute to prevent the commission of an unlawful act where the tortfeasor can by statute escape the usual consequences of his aggression once committed.*

LINAKER v. PILCHER, HEWLETT AND OTHERS
[1901] 17 T.L.R. 256

The defendants, trustees of the Amalgamated Society of Railway Servants, were sued as proprietors of the union newspaper, *Railway Review*, for a libel upon the plaintiff (the newspaper had imputed drunkenness to him). The trustees had not authorized publication of the libel.

The court held that they were liable as trustees and were entitled to be indemnified out of the funds of the society.

---

* *Note:* The views of the judges remain divided on the interpretation of s. 4(1). The older view of Scrutton, L.J. received support in *Camden Exhibition Ltd* v. *Lynott* (see *ante*, p. 306). But practice among High Court judges appears increasingly to favour the view of UPJOHN, L.J. in view of the words 'alleged to have been committed'. See, for example, *Bowles* v. *Lindley* (*ante*, p. 489); and *Olympic Airways S.A.* v. *International Transport Workers' Federation*, 1966 (unreported, except in *The Times*, 25 and 26 August) where injunctions were granted *ex parte* against three British trade unions and continued for a week until the hearing. One particular problem raised in *The Worker and the Law* (1965), p. 230; (1966), p. 222, still awaits an answer: Since from the time of Lord Cairn's Act, 1858, the courts have had a discretionary power to award damages in lieu of an injunction, does the new interpretation of s. 4(1) imply that such damages might be awarded against a trade union for *future* torts even though damages are prohibited in respect of torts already committed? This problem is not raised by the middle path trodden by Lord Denning, M.R. (*ante*, p. 531) to the effect that an injunction will not be granted but a declaration may be allowed.

MATTHEW, J. (construing s. 4(2) of the 1906 Act, and s. 9 of the Act of 1871, set out *post*, p. 540) said: It was admitted that the trustees were not personally liable in the sense that they authorized the libel in any way. There was no evidence that the trustees had anything to do with the conduct of the paper. It was said that if the Trade Union Act, 1871, was carefully examined there would appear to be clear indications that it was never intended to make the trade union responsible in respect of a cause of action against their trustees unless it came within the limits of the trust. Section 9 of the Act gave the trustees power to bring and defend actions 'touching or concerning the property right, or claim to property of the trade union'. It was said that this was for the protection of trade unions, and, if so, it would follow that for any breach of contract or tort for which the trustees were liable the union would enjoy complete immunity. It was said that it was noticeable that all that the trustees were empowered to do under this section was to bring or defend an action respecting the property, right, or claim to property of the trade union. It was said that this meant specific property—e.g. goods or land, and that as this was not an action in respect of specific property the liability would rest where it fell and could not be transferred to the trade union. This seemed an extremely narrow construction of the section. There seemed to be no reason why this disability should be imposed on the trustees in respect of any but specific property, and his Lordship was satisfied that there could be no such intention on the part of the Legislature. Reference had been made to certain *dicta* in the Court of Appeal in the case of the *Taff Vale Railway Company* v. *Amalgamated Society of Railway Servants*, [1901] 1 Q.B. 170 [*post* p. 541], where it was suggested by a learned Judge during the course of the argument that 'property' meant 'specific property', but attention had also been called to another part of the argument where the same learned Judge had expressed the opposite view. His Lordship, having deprecated the practice of referring to the remarks made by Judges during the course of an argument, as they merely expressed what was passing in their minds at the moment, went on to say that he thought that 'property' meant property generally, and that an action for a breach of contract entered into on behalf of the society would be an action touching their property, and likewise an action for damages for tort would be an action touching the property of the society. It followed that the construction put on the section by the defendants was not the correct one.

LONGDON-GRIFFITHS *v.* SMITH & OTHERS
[1951] 1 K.B. 295

The plaintiff had been general secretary of the National Deposit Friendly Society—a registered society. This was an action for damages for libel against the defendants who were trustees of the Society, the action being against them both as trustees and in their private capacities. They had prepared a report on the plaintiff which contained defamatory statements and which was read by one of them to the general committee of the Society. Were the defendants as trustees of the Society the proper defendants ?

SLADE, J., held that the action should be brought not against the trustees but against the society in its registered name. He thought that the remarks in *Linaker* v. *Pilcher* (*ante*, p. 532) had been impliedly overruled by the House of Lords decision in the *Taff Vale* case (*post*, p. 541). The provisions of the Friendly Societies Act, 1896, s. 94, were similar to those of the Trade Union Act, 1871, s. 9. His Lordship thought that s. 9 was 'inapplicable to a tort, or, at any rate, to a tort unconnected with property', in the narrow sense.

DRENNAN *v.* BEECHEY
[1935] N.I.R. 74

The trustees of a union were sued by the plaintiff, a carrier, for the alleged action of a shop steward. The action claimed that the steward was their servant or agent and that he had prevented the plaintiff from carrying out a contract for the supply of coal. The action was dismissed.

ANDREWS, L.J., said about s. 4(2): It is clear both from the language of this latter subsection and from the general policy of the Act that the subsection was not passed with the object of extending the then existing liability of the trustees of a trade union. On the contrary, whilst in general terms re-affirming the legal position of trustees under s. 9 of the Act of 1871, it restricts their liability in cases in which the tortious act is committed in contemplation or in furtherance of a trade dispute. In my opinion the subsection recognises clearly that the liability of trustees of a trade union arises under s. 9 of the Act of 1871; that this liability may sometimes result from a tortious act; and that some such tortious acts may be committed by or on behalf of the Union in contemplation or in furtherance of a trade dispute, whilst others may not be. If the Act be a tortious one of this character it is not excepted by subsection (2) from the general words of immunity contained in subsection (1). If it be not so committed no such protection exists.

As the first condition of the trustees' liability is that the case should fall within s. 9 of the Act of 1871 I turn to a consideration of the material provisions of that Act. Section 7 makes it lawful for a registered trade union to purchase or take land upon lease not exceeding one acre in extent in the names of the trustees. Section 8 vests the property of a trade union whether real or personal in its trustees for the use and benefit of such trade union and the members thereof. By s. 9 the trustees of a registered trade union are empowered to bring or defend any action or suit touching or concerning the property, right, or claim to property of the trade union. Accordingly, if the action touches or concerns the property of the trade union which is vested in them the trustees may sue or be sued. They are not only entitled to protect the property of the trade union so vested in them, but it is their duty to do so; and, accordingly, they are proper parties to any action which touches or concerns it. Such actions may be in contract or they may be in tort. The trustees must fulfil any contractual obligations in respect of it, such as the performance of a covenant in a lease. They must also refrain from the commission of any torts in respect of it. For example, they cannot so negligently use or maintain it as to injure others. Corresponding obligations also arise in connection with personal chattels of the Union which are likewise vested in the trustees. Trustees can sue or be sued in respect of the Union's property; but if the action does not touch or concern such property, and if they were not personally responsible for the commission of the alleged wrongful acts, they are not proper parties.

Does the present action 'touch or concern the property of the Union' within the meaning of the section? In my opinion it clearly does not. If 'property' means specific property, as in my opinion it does, notwithstanding the *dicta* to the contrary of Matthew, J., in *Linaker* v. *Pilcher & Others*,[1] clearly the present action does not fall within it. I refer to the learned judge's words as mere *dicta*, for the newspaper which had published the alleged libel in that case was vested in the trustees and constituted specific property. If, on the other hand, 'property' means property generally, the action cannot come within the section unless either the Union is liable and their general property is in peril to satisfy any damages that may be awarded, or the trustees are by some recognised principle of the common law or by statute liable

[1] 17 T.L.R. 256.

for the wrong alleged to have been committed. None of these alternatives exists in the present case. The Union is freed from liability by the express provisions of s. 4(1) of the Act of 1906; the trustees are not liable at common law, for Magill is admittedly not their agent but the agent of the Union; and, lastly, no statute has been or could be cited which so extends the general common law liability of principal and agent as to make the trustees legally responsible for the wrongful acts of a person who was neither their servant nor agent, and over whom they had no control.

BEST, L.J., concurred.

CHAPTER 5

TRADE UNIONS: ADMINISTRATION AND MEMBERSHIP

Section A

THE TRADE UNION—CAPACITY AND *ULTRA VIRES*—POLITICAL OBJECTS AND POLITICAL FUND

DEFINITION OF A TRADE UNION

(Drawn from Trade Union Acts, 1871 to 1940; but in particular from Trade Union Acts, 1913, s. 1(2) and s. 2(1); 1876, s. 16; and 1871, s. 23.)

The expression 'trade union' means any combination, whether temporary or permanent, the principal objects of which are under its constitution the 'statutory objects', i.e. the regulation of the relations between workmen and masters, or between workmen and workmen, or between masters and masters, or the imposing of restrictive conditions on the conduct of any trade or business, and also the provision of benefits to members, whether such combination would or would not, if the Trade Union Act, 1871, had not been passed, have been deemed to have been an unlawful combination by reason of some one or more of its purposes being in restraint of trade.

Provided that the Acts shall not affect: 1. Any agreement between partners as to their own business; 2. Any agreement between an employer and those employed by him as to such employment; 3. Any agreement in consideration of the sale of the goodwill of a business or of instruction in any profession, trade, or handicraft.

Provided that any combination which is for the time being registered as a trade union shall be deemed to be a trade union as defined by this Act so long as it continues to be so registered.

HORNBY *v.* CLOSE

(1867) L.R. 2 Q.B. 153

This was an action unsuccessfully brought by the President of the Bradford branch of the United Order of Boilermakers on behalf of the Society to recover £24 18s. 5½d. from a member of the union. The money belonged to the union. The union's rules were deposited with the Registrar of Friendly Societies. To come within this Act, it had to be 'A Friendly Society established...for any purpose which is not illegal'.

BLACKBURN, J.: Now, as the Lord Chief Justice has said, the purposes of a trades' union are clearly not analogous to those of a friendly society. A little deviation from the strict purpose of a friendly society might not take the society out of the scope of the act; but here a main object certainly—if not the main object, I think the main object—was that of a trades' union, and therefore the magistrates were fully justified in declining to act. Secondly, I go further, and think the rules illegal in the sense of void, according to the principle of *Hilton* v. *Ekersley*[1]—a case of combination by masters, but the same principle must apply to combinations of men—that they are not enforceable at law. The Court of Exchequer Chamber in that case carefully avoid going further, and saying whether or not the objects of the masters were illegal in the sense of being criminal; and, acting on the authority of that case in the Exchequer Chamber, and adopting the view of Crompton, J., in the court below, I wish to guard myself from being supposed to express any opinion on the present case. I do not say the objects of this society are criminal. I do not say they are not. But I am clearly of opinion that the rules referred to are illegal, in the sense that they cannot be enforced; and on this ground, also, I think the society not within s. 44, as not being 'for a purpose not illegal'. Whatever the inclination of my opinion, it is unnecessary to decide whether the illegality of any of the rules would taint the whole, because here the illegal objects formed not a small part, but a principal, if not the whole, object of the society.

COCKBURN, L.C.J., delivered a concurring judgment, and MELLOR, J., concurred.

[1] 6 E. & B. 47, 66.

THE TRADE UNION ACT, 1871

2. *Trade union not criminal.* The purposes of any trade union shall not, by reason merely that they are in restraint of trade, be deemed to be unlawful so as to render any member of such trade union liable to criminal prosecution for conspiracy or otherwise.

3. *Trade union not unlawful for civil purposes.* The purposes of any trade union shall not, by reason merely that they are in restraint of trade, be unlawful so as to render void or voidable any agreement or trust.

4. *Trade union contracts, when not enforceable.* Nothing in this Act shall enable any court to entertain any legal proceeding instituted with the object of directly enforcing or recovering damages for the breach of any of the following agreements, namely,

(1) Any agreement between members of a trade union as such, concerning the conditions on which any members for the time being of such trade union shall or shall not sell their goods, transact business, employ, or be employed:

(2) Any agreement for the payment by any person of any subscription or penalty to a trade union:

(3) Any agreement for the application of the funds of a trade union (*a*) To provide benefits to members; or (*b*) To furnish contributions to any employer or workman not a member of such trade union, in consideration of such employer or workman acting in conformity with the rules or resolutions of such trade union; or (*c*) To discharge any fine imposed upon any person by sentence of a court of justice; or

(4) Any agreement made between one trade union and another; or

(5) Any bond to secure the performance of any of the above-mentioned agreements.

But nothing in this section shall be deemed to constitute any of the above-mentioned agreements unlawful....

6. *Registry of trade unions.* Any seven or more members of a trade union may by subscribing their names to the rules of the union, and otherwise complying with the provisions of this Act with respect to registry, register such trade union under this Act, provided that if any one of the purposes of such trade union be unlawful such registration shall be void....

8. *Property of the trade unions vested in trustees.* All real and personal estate whatsoever belonging to any trade union registered under this

Act shall be vested in the trustees for the time being of the trade union appointed as provided by this Act, for the use and benefit of such trade union and the members thereof, and the real or personal estate of any branch of a trade union shall be vested in the trustees of such branch (or of the trustees of the trade union, if the rules of the trade union so provide) and be under the control of such trustees, their respective executors or administrators, according to their respective claims and interests, and upon the death or removal of any such trustees the same shall vest in the succeeding trustees for the same estate and interest as the former trustees had therein, and subject to the same trusts, without any conveyance or assignment whatsoever, save and except in the case of stocks and securities in the public funds of Great Britain and Ireland, which shall be transferred into the names of such new trustees; and in all actions, or suits, or indictments, or summary proceedings before any court of summary jurisdiction, touching or concerning any such property, the same shall be stated to be the property of the person or persons for the time being holding the said office of trustee, in their proper names, as trustees of such trade union, without any further description.

9. *Actions, etc., by or against trustees, etc.* The trustees of any trade union registered under this Act or any other officer of such trade union who may be authorised so to do by the rules thereof, are hereby empowered to bring or defend, or cause to be brought or defended, any action, suit, prosecution, or complaint in any court of law or equity, touching or concerning the property, right, or claim to property of the trade union; and shall and may, in all cases concerning the real or personal property of such trade union, sue and be sued, plead and be impleaded, in any court of law or equity, in their proper names, without other description than the title of their office; and no such action, suit, prosecution, or complaint shall be discontinued or shall abate by the death or removal from office of such persons or any of them, but the same shall and may be proceeded in by their successor or successors as if such death, resignation, or removal had not taken place; and such successors shall pay or receive the like costs as if the action, suit prosecution, or complaint had been commenced in their names for the benefit of or to be reimbursed from the funds of such trade union, and the summons to be issued to such trustee or other officer may be served by leaving the same at the registered office of the trade union.

TAFF VALE RAILWAY CO. *v.* AMALGAMATED SOCIETY OF RAILWAY SERVANTS

House of Lords [1901] A.C. 426

The appellant company sought an injunction in respect of tortious acts against the respondent union and its officers. It was argued for the union that, even though registered, it could not be sued in its own name either for damages or for an injunction. The Court of Appeal, reversing Farwell, J., held that it could not be so sued because the legislature had expressly refrained from incorporating or otherwise making a legal entity out of a union which chose to register under s. 6 of the 1871 Act. The House of Lords agreed with Farwell, J.

[The House of Lords' discussion still forms the starting point for modern examination of the legal status of a registered union, even though the force of the actual decision was largely negatived in respect of actions in tort by s. 4 Trade Disputes Act, 1906, *ante*, p. 385.]

FARWELL, J.: Now, the Legislature in giving a trade union the capacity to own property and the capacity to act by agents has, without incorporating it, given it two of the essential qualities of a corporation— essential, I mean, in respect of liability for tort, for a corporation can only act by its agents, and can only be made to pay by means of its property. The principle on which corporations have been held liable in respect of wrongs committed by its servants or agents in the course of their service and for the benefit of the employer—*qui sentit commodum sentire debet et onus*...is as applicable to the case of a trade union as to that of a corporation. If the contention of the defendant society were well founded, the Legislature has authorized the creation of numerous bodies of men capable of owning great wealth and of acting by agents with absolutely no responsibility for the wrongs that they may do to other persons by the use of that wealth and the employment of those agents. They would be at liberty (I do not at all suggest that the defendant society would so act) to disseminate libels broadcast, or to hire men to reproduce the rattening methods that disgraced Sheffield thirty or forty years ago, and their victims would have nothing to look to for damages but the pockets of the individuals, usually men of small means, who acted as their agents.... The proper rule of construction of statutes such as these is that in the absence of express contrary intention the Legislature intends that the creature of the statute shall have the same duties, and that its funds shall be subject to the same liabilities as the general law would impose on a private individual doing the same thing. It would require very clear and express words of enactment to induce me to hold that the Legislature had in fact legalised the existence of such irresponsible bodies with such wide capacity for evil. Not only is there nothing in the Acts to lead me to such a conclusion, but ss. 15 and 16 of the Act of 1871 imposing penalties on the trade union, and ss. 8 and 15 of the Act of 1876 point to a contrary intention; nor do I see any reason for saying that the society cannot be sued in tort in their registered name. Sections 8 and 9 of the Act of 1871 expressly provide for actions in respect of property being brought by and against the trustees, and this express intention impliedly excludes such trustees from being sued in tort. If, therefore, I am right in concluding that the society are liable in tort, the action must be against them in their registered name. The acts complained of are the acts of the association.

EARL OF HALSBURY, L.C.: My Lords, in this case I am content to adopt the judgment of Farwell, J., with which I entirely concur; and I cannot find any satisfactory answer to that judgment in the judgment of the Court of Appeal which overruled it. If the Legislature has created a thing which can own property, which can employ servants, and which can inflict injury, it must be taken, I think, to have impliedly given the power to make it suable in a Court of Law for injuries purposely done by its authority and procurement.

LORD MACNAGHTEN: The substantial question, therefore, as Farwell, J., put it, is this: Has the Legislature authorized the creation of numerous bodies of men capable of owning great wealth and of acting by agents with absolutely no responsibility for the wrongs they may do to other persons by the use of that wealth and the employment of those agents? In my opinion, Parliament has done nothing of the kind. I cannot find anything in the Acts of 1871 and 1876, or either of them, from beginning to end, to warrant or suggest such a notion. It is perhaps satisfactory to find that nothing of the sort was contemplated by the minority of the members of the Royal Commission on Trade Unions, whose views found acceptance with the Legislature. In paragraph 4 of their report they say: 'It should be specially provided that except so far as combinations are thereby exempted from criminal prosecution nothing should affect...the liability of every person to be sued at law or in equity in respect of any damage which may have been occasioned to any other person through the act or default of the person so sued.'

Now, if the liability of every person in this respect was to be preserved, it would seem to follow that it was intended by the strongest advocates of trade unionism that persons should be liable for concerted as well as for individual action; and for this purpose it seems to me that it cannot matter in the least whether the persons acting in concert be combined together in a trade union, or collected and united under any other form of association.

Then, if trade unions are not above the law, the only remaining question, as it seems to me, is one of form. How are these bodies to be sued? I have no doubt whatever that a trade union, whether registered or unregistered, may be sued in a representative action if the persons selected as defendants be persons who, from their position, may be taken fairly to represent the body. As regards this point, Mr Haldane relied on the case of *Temperton* v. *Russell*;[1] but *Temperton* v. *Russell*, as I said in *Duke of Bedford* v. *Ellis*,[2] was an absurd case. The persons there selected as representatives of the various unions intended to be sued were selected in defiance of all rule and principle. They were not the managers of the union—they had no control over it or over its funds. They represented nobody but themselves. Their names seem to have been taken at random for the purpose, I suppose, of spreading a general sense of insecurity among the unions who ought to have been sued, if sued at all, either in their registered name, if that be permissible, or by their proper officers—the members of their executive committees and their trustees....it seems to me that there would be no difficulty in suing a trade union in a proper case if it be sued in a representative action by persons who fairly and properly represent it.

The further question remains: May a registered trade union be sued in and by its registered name? For my part, I cannot see any difficulty in the way of such a suit. It is quite true that a registered trade union is not a corporation, but it has a registered name and a registered office.

LORD BRAMPTON: I think that a legal entity was created under the Trade Union Act, 1871, by the registration of the society in its present name in the manner prescribed, and that the legal entity so created, though not perhaps in the strict sense a corporation, is nevertheless a newly created corporate body created by statute, distinct from the unincorporated trade union, consisting of many thousands of separate individuals, which no longer exists under any other name. The very omission from the statute of any provision authorizing and directing that it shall sue and be sued in any other name than that given to it by

[1] [1893] 1 Q.B. 435.   [2] [1900] A.C. 1.

its registration appears to me to lead to no other reasonable conclusion than that in so creating it, it was intended by the Legislature that by that name and by no other it should be known, and that for all purposes that name should be used and applied to it in all legal proceedings unless there was any other provision which militated against such a construction, as, for instance, in the case of trustees, by s. 9 of the same Act, who hold real and personal property of the society.

LORD LINDLEY: My Lords, the problem how to adapt legal proceedings to unincorporated societies consisting of many members is by no means new. The rules as to parties to common law actions were too rigid for practical purposes when those rules had to be applied to such societies. But the rules as to parties to suits in equity were not the same as those which governed courts of common law, and were long since adapted to meet the difficulties presented by a multiplicity of persons interested in the subject-matter of litigation. Some of such persons were allowed to sue and be sued on behalf of themselves and all others having the same interest....

I have myself no doubt whatever that if the trade union could not be sued in this case in its registered name, some of its members (namely, its executive committee) could be sued on behalf of themselves and the other members of the society, and an injunction and judgment for damages could be obtained in a proper case in an action so framed. Further, it is in my opinion equally plain that if the trustees in whom the property of the society is legally vested were added as parties, an order could be made in the same action for the payment by them out of the funds of the society of all damages and costs for which the plaintiff might obtain judgment against the trade union.

I entirely repudiate the notion that the effect of the Trade Union Act, 1871, is to legalise trade unions and confer on them the right to acquire and hold property, and at the same time to protect the union from legal proceedings if their managers or agents acting for the whole body violate the rights of other people. For such violation the property of trade unions can unquestionably in my opinion be reached by legal proceedings properly framed. The Court of Appeal has not denied this; but the Court has held that the trade union cannot be sued in its registered name, and in strictness the only question for determination by your Lordships now is whether the Court of Appeal was right in holding that the name of the trade union ought to be struck out of the writ, and that the injunction granted against the trade union in that name ought to be discharged.

If I am right in what I have already said, this question is of comparatively small importance: it is not a question of substance but of mere form, and turns on the Trade Union Act, 1871 (34 & 35 Vict. c. 31), and the Act of 1876 (39 & 40 Vict. c. 32) amending it. The Act does not in express terms say what use is to be made of the name under which the trade union is registered and by which it is known. But a trade union which is registered under the Act must have a name: see ss. 14, 16, and Schedule 1; it may acquire property, but, not being incorporated recourse is had to the old well-known machinery of trustees for acquiring and holding such property, and for suing and being sued in respect of it (ss. 7, 8, 9). The property so held is, however, the property of the union: the union is the beneficial owner. Section 12 provides summary remedies for misapplications of the trade union's property, but there is nothing here to oust the jurisdiction of the superior Courts, and, there being nothing in the Act to prevent it, I cannot conceive why an action in the name of the trade union against its trustees to restrain a breach of trust or to make them account for a breach of trust already committed should be held unmaintainable or wrong in point of form. Further, ss. 15 and 16 of the Act of 1871, and s. 15 of the Act of 1876, impose duties on registered trade unions and penalties on them (and not only on their officials) for breach of those duties. The mode of enforcing these penalties is pointed out in s. 19 of the Act of 1871, but there is nothing there to show that the trade union on which the duty is cast and which has to pay the penalty could not be proceeded against in its registered name. Again, I apprehend that a mandamus could go against a trade union to compel it to perform the duties cast upon it by statute; and here again the obvious course would be to proceed against the union by its registered name unless there is something in the statute to prevent it. My Lords, a careful study of the Act leads me to the conclusion that the Court of Appeal held, and rightly held, that trade unions are not corporations; but the Court held further that, not being corporations power to sue and be sued in their registered name must be conferred upon them; and further that the language of the statutes was not sufficient for the purpose. Upon this last point I differ from them. The Act appears to me to indicate with sufficient clearness that the registered name is one which may be used to denote the unions as an unincorporated society in legal proceedings as well as for business and other purposes. The use of the name in legal proceedings imposes no duties and alters no rights: it is only a more convenient mode of proceeding than that which would have to be adopted if the name could not be used. I do not say that the use of the name is compulsory, but it is at least permissive.

Your Lordships have not now to consider how a judgment or order against a trade union in its registered name can be enforced. I see no difficulty about this; but, to avoid misconception, I will add that if a judgment or order in that form is for the payment of money it can, in my opinion, only be enforced against the property of the trade union and that to reach such property it may be found necessary to sue the trustees.

LORD SHAND concurred.

BONSOR v. MUSICIANS' UNION

House of Lords   [1956] A.C. 104

[See *post*, p. 643. The different views as to the modern juridical status of a registered trade union are to be found in the speeches of their Lordships in this case. In effect, Lord Morton and Lord Porter look upon the registered union as a quasi-corporate body, capable of being a party to a contract. Lord MacDermott, Lord Somervell and (probably) Lord Keith, take the traditional view that it is an unincorporated body with a special procedural capacity to sue or be sued in its registered name.]

NATIONAL UNION OF GENERAL AND MUNICIPAL WORKERS v. GILLIAN

Court of Appeal   [1946] K.B. 81

The plaintiff sued the General Secretary of another union claiming damages for libel.

SCOTT, L.J.: The defendants' contention below and before us is that a trade union registered under the Trade Union Acts has no right in law to bring any action for tort. I agree so completely with the reserved judgment of Birkett, J., that I should have been content to adopt it as my own but for the far-reaching importance of the legal questions at issue and the careful argument of Mr Paull. He invited us to say 'No' to each of these questions: (1) Can any trade union sue in respect of any tort? (2) if, generally, it can, can it sue for a libel? (3) if in some cases some trade union may be at liberty so to sue, can the plaintiff union sue for the libels set forth in the statement of claim? I will discuss these three questions in that order.

(1) All the Trade Union Acts, from 1871 to 1927, are, according to

their terms, to be read as one, but the only two that are directly relevant are those of 1871 and 1876, although s. 4 of the Trade Disputes Act, 1906, which prohibits actions for tort against trade unions, may have some indirect relevance. Mr Paull points out, justly, that a registered trade union as defined by s. 16 of the Amendment Act of 1876 is neither a natural person not a corporation, and he contends that, because it is neither of those, it can have no powers, and indeed no existence, except what may have been conferred in express terms by Parliament in the relevant statutes affecting registered trade unions. That argument is, however, fallacious. There is a *tertium quid*. A trade union has many activities; it has some existence, and it is something. The omission of Parliament to christen it with some new generic name is immaterial, for Parliament has absolute sovereignty and can make new legal creatures if it likes. It is able, for instance, to create a *persona juridica* not previously known to the law, if it so chooses, or to clothe an existing association of natural persons with what may be called co-operative personality so as to give it the status of a *persona juridica*. In my view that is just what it did in 1871. It expressly assumed the possession by every trade union, when duly registered, of so many of the main attributes of judicial personality that I find any other inference of the intention of Parliament impossible.

First of all, the primary object of the legislation was to validate and encourage the exercise by trade unions of a whole group of industrial functions with a view to the establishment and maintenance of good relations between employers and employed, an object of fundamental public importance to the United Kingdom, which was in 1871 the leading industrial nation of the world. The functions in question are those which fall under the general head of collective bargaining; and in construing trade-union legislation it should never be forgotten that trade unions might consist only of employers, only of employees, or of both combined, for all three types of association might be, and often were, directed to the unlawful restraints of trade, which the legislation was intended to validate.

Secondly, the legislation contains many specific examples of attributes of legal personality expressly conferred on the trade unions thereby legalized, for example: (1) the right to own property—only nominally vested in trustees: see s. 8 of the Act of 1871, 'All real and personal estate whatsoever belonging to any trade union registered,' etc.; (2) the right to register an identifying name, and to change it; (3) the right to amalgamate with another trade union; (4) the right to dissolve itself by appropriate machinery; (5) the right to bring or defend actions in the name of the trustees, the *cestui que* trust being *ex hypothesi* a person—to wit, the trade union itself (s. 9); (6) the right to hold its treasurer to account (s. 11); (7) the right to have complaints made on its behalf before a court of summary jurisdiction (s. 12). These illustrations from the Act of 1871 are, in my opinion, conclusive of the intention of Parliament to attribute legal personality to trade unions, and that quality or characteristic must of necessity connote the general power to act, or, in other words, to do at any rate many of those things which are inherent in the legal concept of personality.

That being the character of the legislation, I can see no *prima facie* ground for limiting by any implication the list of powers normally attendant on legal personality. On the contrary, it is for those who contend for a limiting interpretation to state the reasons for that view.... In truth the principle involved has been decided by the House of Lords in *Taff Vale Railway Co.* v. *Amalgamated Society of Railway Servants*,[1] for if the *persona juridica* is liable to be sued for infringing the rights of others, it must equally be able to sue to vindicate its own right.

MACKINNON, L.J., and UTHWATT, J., concurred.

RULES OF THE SUPREME COURT: ORDER 15, RULE 12

(of which, before 1965, the predecessor in similar terms was Order 16, Rule 9)

Representative Proceedings: 12. (1) Where numerous persons have the same interest in any proceedings, not being such proceedings as are mentioned in rule 13, the proceedings may be begun, and, unless the Court otherwise orders, continued, by or against any one or more of them as representing all or as representing all except one or more of them.

(2) At any stage of proceedings under this Rule the Court may, on the application of the plaintiff, and on such terms, if any, as it thinks fit, appoint any one or more of the defendants or other persons as representing whom the defendants are sued to represent all, or all except one or more, of those persons in the proceedings; and where, in exercise of the power conferred by this paragraph, the Court appoints a person not named as a defendant, it shall make an order under rule 6 adding that person as a defendant.

[1] [1901] A.C. 426.

(3) A judgment or order given in proceedings under this Rule shall be binding on all the persons as representing whom the plaintiffs sue or, as the case may be, the defendants are sued, but shall not be enforced against any person not a party to the proceedings except with the leave of the Court. . . .

BARKER v. ALLANSON

Court of Appeal [1937] 1 K.B. 463

In 1936 the plaintiff brought a representative action against four members of a union lodge representing the 841 members of the lodge, for the price of goods sold and delivered to 89 members of the lodge in 1921.

SCOTT, L.J.: Before deciding in any particular case whether a representative order under Order XVI, rule 9, should be made in regard to defendants, it is necessary to consider two questions: (1) What is the cause of action? and (2) What is the precise class of potential defendants who are to be represented by the defendants on the record for the purpose of imposing liability on them if judgment is given for the plaintiff? The vital thing to remember is that judgment against representative defendants means judgment against each individual person covered by the representation. It is because of this consequence of a representative judgment that the conditions upon which an order to represent may be made are those laid down by Lord Parker in the passage from his opinion in *London Association for Protection of Trade* v. *Greenlands, Ltd*,[1] which Greer, L.J., has quoted. The reason why the position of all represented defendants must be the same as that of those who represent them is simply because that is the hypothesis on which alone such an order is authorized by the rule. The rule is not a device for enabling a plaintiff to have an inquiry conducted by the Court for the purpose of drawing up a list of persons who may, or may not, be liable to him in respect of the cause of action alleged on the writ, and then deciding whether they are liable or not. Its purpose is strictly confined within the limits I have stated.

In the present case the form of relief claimed is a declaration, but the cause of action, on which the Court would base its declaration, is a claim for the price of goods sold and delivered to the various members of the Lodge who in the year 1921 received and consumed the goods. Construed on the principles I have stated the representative order made was accordingly one which enabled the plaintiff through the named representatives to sue all the individual members who had authorized

[1] [1916] 2 A.C. 15, 39.

the purchase of the goods supplied, and to get a judgment enforceable against them—so far as the word 'enforceable' is applicable to a declaratory judgment. Unless all the persons so to be represented by the named defendants stood in the same position *vis-à-vis* the plaintiffs as the named defendants, they would not be really 'represented' by them, and therefore could not come within the meaning of the rule. It follows necessarily...that the representative order as made was limited in its application to those individuals who were still members of the Lodge at the date when the writ was issued, and also had been members in 1921, and then as members could have authorized the ordering of the particular lots of the goods in question. For the purposes of our decision it is enough to say that, when the representation order was made, there were 841 members of the Chilton Colliery Lodge, but the majority of these had joined since 1921 and consequently had had nothing to do with the ordering of any of the plaintiff's goods at that time. In 1921 there were 1093 members, but only 89 of these received goods from the plaintiff—of these 89 some had died, some had ceased to be members, some had paid for their goods; and only 19 out of the 89 were still members at the date of writ issued. Even amongst these there may have been legal differences of position in regard to the Statute of Limitations, etc. The result, in my opinion, is that there was so little identity of position as between the representing and the represented defendants, that I do not think there was any ground for a representative order at all: *a fortiori* we could not interfere with the discretion of the learned judge.

I think it is perhaps desirable to add that we are not prejudging a wholly different type of case which may conceivably arise some day in the event of a trade union or friendly society or a club having a rule which (*a*) authorizes the distribution of goods by way of assistance in kind; and (*b*) treats the cash cost of supplying the goods as a charge upon the general fund of the changing body of members. If the Rules of the Durham Miners' Association had contained a rule authorizing the officers of the Lodge in their discretion, instead of granting money allowances to the members, to purchase equivalent amounts of goods and give assistance in kind to the members, with a further provision that the cost of paying for the goods should be a charge on the Lodge funds and defrayed by the members for the time being when money was wanted for such payments, irrespective of the question whether they had been members or not at the time when the goods were bought, different considerations would be present. That question, however, does not arise in this appeal because there is no such cause of action alleged in the statement of claim, nor for that matter is there any rule, at any rate in express terms, having any such effect: and I express no final opinion upon that hypothetical case.

GREER, L.J., and EVE, J., concurred.

YORKSHIRE MINERS' ASSOCIATION v. HOWDEN

House of Lords   [1905] A.C. 256

[See *post*, p. 594. The House of Lords clearly established that an application of trade union funds for purposes outside those permitted by the rules was *ultra vires* and void. A member, therefore, has a *prima facie* right to restrain such application by injunction. Application of the *ultra vires* doctrine goes to the capacity of the association concerned. It has no legal capacity to act outside the permitted purposes. No ratification by the members can, therefore, cure the defect: see the cases on *ultra vires* admission of members, *post*, p. 564.]

ASTLEY AND OTHERS v. ELECTRICAL
TRADES UNION

[1951] 95 Sol. Jo. 744

On 13 February 1951, an unofficial strike was started by members of the defendant union employed by the London Electricity Board. The plaintiffs, who had refused to take part in the strike, asked, *inter alia*, for a declaration that payments from the funds of the union to persons who participated in or promoted the strike were unlawful and *ultra vires*.

WYNN PARRY, J., said that the strike was not, and could not be, authorised under the rules of the union. During the course of the strike, efforts were made to induce the plaintiffs, who belonged to various branches of the union and were working on various sites, to join the strike, but without success. Notwithstanding that the strike was not, and could not be, authorised by the executive council under the rules, the executive council authorised what were called *ex gratia* payments to those engaged in the unofficial strike. Those payments amounted to approximately £50,000. The claim that the strike was illegal was based on the Conditions of Employment and National Arbitration Order, 1940 (as amended), which was then in force. The plaintiffs claimed that the so-called *ex gratia* payments were improperly made. The defendants disputed this. The question was purely one of construction of the rules of the union in the light of Schedule I to the Trade Union Act, 1871. The argument for the defendants was that rule 10, which contained a detailed set of provisions dealing with the circumstances in which an authorised strike could be called and the strike benefits which might be paid out, was not exhaustive as regards strikes but limited to strikes of a particular character. Rule 1 defined, among the objects of the union, assistance to members in sickness and distress, and it was said that a member who had ceased work—even through his own fault—was in distress and the executive council might vote, *ex gratia*, whatever sums they thought fit. He (his lordship) could not accept that argument; it rested almost wholly on the presence of the word 'distress' in rule 1. Rule 16 had to be regarded as an exhaustive code on the matter of strikes. The rules had to be considered as they stood, and if this decision of the court was contrary to the general opinion of the members their remedy in the future lay in altering the rules. The plaintiffs were entitled to a declaration that it was *ultra vires* the union for any payment to be made out of their funds in furtherance of a strike not authorised under rule 16 of the rules of the union.

AMALGAMATED SOCIETY OF RAILWAY SERVANTS *v.* OSBORNE

House of Lords   [1910] A.C. 87

The appellant trade union was registered under the 1871 Act; and one of its rules purported to give it power to levy contributions from members for the purpose of securing Parliamentary representation. The respondent, a member, sought a declaration that this rule was *ultra vires* and void.

LORD ATKINSON: Sir George Jessel in *Rigby* v. *Connol*[1] analysed the legislation passed to deal with trade unions and described its purpose and effect. Farwell, L.J., in his judgment in this case described with accuracy and fullness their present position, their rights and privileges. From these judgments it is clear, in my view, that they are, when registered, quasi-corporations, resembling much more closely railway companies incorporated by statute than voluntary associations of individuals merely bound together by contract or agreement, express or implied. And it is plain that, as soon as this character was given to them, and the rights and privileges they now enjoy were conferred upon them, it became a matter of necessity to define the purposes and objects to

---

[1] [1880] 14 Ch. D. at p. 489; *post*, p. 592.

which they were at liberty to devote the funds raised from their members by enforced contributions. A definition which permitted them to do the particular things named and in addition all things not in themselves illegal would be no definition at all and would serve no purpose at all. There must be some limit. The question for decision, therefore, is whether parliamentary representation falls within or without that limit, or, in other words, whether the Legislature, expressly or by fair implication, has conferred upon registered trade unions power and authority to subsidize, in the manner provided by the impeached rule a scheme of parliamentary representation.... Trade unions are in this respect in precisely the same position as all corporations, municipal or commercial, including in the latter all limited liability companies created under the Act of 1862. These bodies, like the trade unions, may by legislation be helped or hindered in carrying out the objects which they were formed to carry out. Their most vital interest may be seriously prejudiced by taxation which the Legislature may impose, or enabling statutes, general in character, may be introduced calculated to enlarge their powers, increase their privileges, or remove restraints upon their action, or again some of them may be under the necessity of promoting private Bills to meet their own special needs. If, despite all this, the intention never has been and cannot be imputed to the Legislature to confer upon such corporations as these power or authority to devote their funds to the procurement of parliamentary representation in the manner in this case contended for, how can such an intention be imputed to it in the case of quasi-corporations such as registered trade unions ? And if this intention cannot be imputed to the Legislature in the case of registered trade unions, as in my view it cannot be, there can be no such thing as an implied grant of the desired powers, because an addition to a grant is only introduced by implication in order to carry out the presumed intention of the grantor. During the argument I asked to be informed on what principle the case of registered trade unions was to be differentiated from that of other corporations such as I have named, and why the former were to be permitted, by an alteration of their rules, to convert themselves into political organizations, while a similar privilege was to be denied to the latter. No satisfactory reply was given to me, because none could, I believe, be given. I know of no such principle myself.

EARL OF HALSBURY and LORD MACNAGHTEN concurred. LORD JAMES and LORD SHAW also concurred on different grounds.

THE TRADE UNION ACT, 1913

1. *Amendment of law as to objects and powers of trade unions.* (1) The fact that a combination has under its constitution objects or powers other than statutory objects within the meaning of this Act shall not prevent the combination being a trade union for the purposes of the Trade Union Acts, 1871 to 1906, so long as the combination is a trade union as defined by this Act, and, subject to the provisions of this Act as to the furtherance of political objects, any such trade union shall have power to apply the funds of the union for any lawful objects or purposes for the time being authorized under its constitution.

(2) For the purposes of this Act, the expression 'statutory objects' means the objects mentioned in section sixteen of the Trade Union Act Amendment Act, 1876, namely, the regulation of the relations between workmen and masters, or between workmen and workmen, or between masters and masters, or the imposing of restrictive conditions on the conduct of any trade or business, and also the provision of benefits to members....

3. *Restriction on application of funds for certain political purposes.* (1) The funds of a trade union shall not be applied, either directly or in conjunction with any other trade union, association, or body, or otherwise indirectly, in the furtherance of the political objects to which this section applies (without prejudice to the furtherance of any other political objects), unless the furtherance of those objects has been approved as an object of the union by a resolution for the time being in force passed on a ballot of the members of the union taken in accordance with this Act for the purpose by a majority of the members voting; and where such a resolution is in force, unless rules, to be approved, whether the union is registered or not, by the Registrar of Friendly Societies, are in force providing:

(a) That any payments in the furtherance of those objects are to be made out of a separate fund (in this Act referred to as the political fund of the union) and for the exemption in accordance with this Act of any member of the union from any obligation to contribute to such a fund if he gives notice in accordance with this Act that he objects to contribute; and

(b) That a member who is exempt from the obligation to contribute to the political fund of the union shall not be excluded from any benefits of the union, or placed in any respect either directly or indirectly under any disability or at any disadvantage as compared with other members of the union (except in relation to the control or management of the political fund) by reason of his being so exempt, and that contribution to the political fund of the union shall not be made a condition for admission to the union.

(2) If any member of a trade union alleges that he is aggrieved by a breach of any rule made in pursuance of this section, he may complain to the Registrar of Friendly Societies, and the Registrar of Friendly Societies, after giving the complainant and any representative of the union an opportunity of being heard, may, if he considers that such a breach has been committed, make such order for remedying the breach as he thinks just under the circumstances; and any such order of the Registrar shall be binding and conclusive on all parties without appeal and shall not be removable into any court of law or restrainable by injunction, and on being recorded in the county court, may be enforced as if it had been an order of the county court. In the application of this provision to Scotland the sheriff court shall be substituted for the county court, and 'interdict' shall be substituted for 'injunction'.

(3) The political objects to which this section applies are the expenditure of money

(*a*) on the payment of any expenses incurred either directly or indirectly by a candidate or prospective candidate for election to Parliament or to any public office, before, during, or after the election in connexion with his candidature or election; or

(*b*) on the holding of any meeting or the distribution of any literature or documents in support of any such candidate or prospective candidate; or

(*c*) on the maintenance of any person who is a member of Parliament or who holds a public office; or

(*d*) in connexion with the registration of electors or the selection of a candidate for Parliament or any public office; or

(*e*) on the holding of political meetings of any kind, or on the distribution of political literature or political documents of any kind, unless the main purpose of the meetings or of the distribution of the literature or documents is the furtherance of statutory objects within the meaning of this Act.

The expression 'public office' in this section means the office of member of any county, county borough, district, or parish council, or board of guardians, or of any public body who have power to raise money, either directly or indirectly, by means of a rate.

(4) A resolution under this section approving political objects as an

object of the union shall take effect as if it were a rule of the union and may be rescinded in the same manner and subject to the same provisions as such a rule.

(5) The provisions of this Act as to the application of the funds of a union for political purposes shall apply to a union which is in whole or in part an association or combination of other unions as if the individual members of the component unions were the members of that union and not the unions; but nothing in this Act shall prevent any such component union from collecting from any of their members who are not exempt on behalf of the association or combination any contributions to the political fund of the association or combination.. . .

4. *Approval of rules.* (1) A ballot for the purposes of this Act shall be taken in accordance with the rules of the union to be approved for the purpose, whether the union is registered or not, by the Registrar of Friendly Societies, but the Registrar of Friendly Societies shall not approve any such rules unless he is satisfied that every member has an equal right, and, if reasonably possible, a fair opportunity of voting, and that the secrecy of the ballot is properly secured.

(2) If the Registrar of Friendly Societies is satisfied, and certifies, that rules for the purpose of a ballot under this Act or rules made for other purposes of this Act which require approval by the Registrar, have been approved by a majority of members of a trade union, whether registered or not, voting for the purpose, or by a majority of delegates of such a trade union voting at a meeting called for the purpose, those rules shall have effect as rules of the union, notwithstanding that the provisions of the rules of the union as to the alteration of rules or the making of new rules have not been complied with.

5. *Notice of objection to contribute towards political objects.* (1) A member of a trade union may at any time give notice, in the form set out in the Schedule to this Act or in a form to the like effect, that he objects to contribute to the political fund of the union, and, on the adoption of a resolution of the union approving the furtherance of political objects as an object of the union, notice shall be given to the members of the union acquainting them that each member has a right to be exempt from contributing to the political fund of the union and that a form of exemption notice can be obtained by or on behalf of a member either by application at or by post from the head office or any branch office of the union or the office of the Registrar of Friendly Societies.

Any such notice to members of the union shall be given in accordance with rules of the union approved for the purpose by the Registrar of Friendly Societies, having regard in each case to the existing practice and to the character of the union....

6. *Mode of giving effect to exemption from contributions to political fund.* Effect may be given to the exemption of members to contribute to the political fund of a union either by a separate levy of contributions to that fund from the members of the union who are not exempt, and in that case the rules shall provide that no moneys of the union other than the amount raised by such separate levy shall be carried to that fund, or by relieving any members who are exempt from the payment of the whole or any part of any periodical contributions required from the members of the union towards the expenses of the union, and in that case the rules shall provide that the relief shall be given as far as possible to all members who are exempt on the occasion of the same periodic payment and for enabling each member of the union to know as respects any such periodical contribution, what portion, if any, of the sum payable by him is a contribution to the political fund of the union.*

BIRCH *v.* NATIONAL UNION OF RAILWAYMEN

[1950] Ch. 602

The plaintiff, a member of the defendant union, did not contribute to its political fund. In 1946 he was elected chairman of the Woodford Halse branch of the union; but in 1948 the general secretary noted that under the rules a person who had contracted out of the fund was not eligible to serve as a branch officer.

The plaintiff appealed to the Registrar who had already approved the rules; the Registrar held that this decision of the general secretary was no 'breach of the rules'.

The plaintiff then sought a declaration that the rules themselves did not comply with s. 3(1) of the Trade Union Act, 1913. The rule in question stated: 'A member who is exempt from the obligation to contribute to the political fund of the union shall not be excluded from any benefits of the union, or placed in any respect, either directly or indirectly, under any disability or disadvantage as compared with other members of the union by reason of his being so exempt, except that such a member shall take no part in the control or management of the political

---

* *Note:* Where union subscriptions are deducted at source by way of 'check-off', the different ways of arranging the political levy may give rise to problems, e.g. under the Truck Acts, *ante,* p. 119. See generally on the political fund, Grunfeld, *Modern Trade Union Law,* chapters 15–17.

fund of the union and shall be ineligible to occupy any office or representative position involving any such control or management.' The plaintiff was granted the declaration.

DANCKWERTS, J.: In the present case the conditions as to approval of the furtherance of the objects by a resolution of the members of the union and the rules providing for a separate political fund and for exemption from contribution by notice and as regards admission to the union are satisfied. The difficulties arise in respect of paragraph (b) in the subsection, but the rules have received the approval of the Registrar of Friendly Societies. In *Forster's* case,[1] Eve, J., held that, where a question as to a breach of a rule had been referred to the registrar under s. 3, subs. 2 of the Act, it was not open to the parties to raise the same question in an action in the High Court of Justice. In the present case, therefore, I do think that I am bound to proceed on the footing that the effect of rule 21 (8) is to disqualify the plaintiff from holding the office of chairman of the branch, because that office involves the control or management of the political fund of the branch.

It is unnecessary, therefore, for me to consider in detail the rules which involve control or management of the political fund of the branch by the chairman. The point is that the same officers and committee manage both the general fund and the political fund. The issue in this action is not whether the plaintiff was unlawfully deprived of the office of branch chairman, but whether the political fund of the union is lawful. The registrar was solely concerned with the question whether there had been a breach of the rules, and he expressly disclaimed any intention to deal with the question whether the rule complied with the provisions of s. 3 of the Act. But the registrar did express the opinion that the rule, by making the plaintiff, as a non-contributing member, ineligible for the office of chairman, placed him under a disability as compared with other members of the union, and it appears obvious to me that this is so. The argument for the plaintiff is that the rule, so far from providing that the plaintiff, though exempted from contribution to the political fund, is not placed under any disability or ar any disadvantage as compared with other members, in fact, by its concluding two lines, places the plaintiff under such a disability or at such a disadvantage....

In subs. 1 of s. 3 there is merely a provision that the relevant rules are 'to be approved' by the registrar. It was contended on behalf of the defendants that such approval must be meant to have some effect,

[1] [1927] 1 Ch. 539, 546.

and that the intention is that trade-union officials might safely act on the rules and treat them as valid once they have been approved by the registrar. There is much force in this contention, and it is not unreasonable that trade-union officials should suppose that, when rules have passed the scrutiny of the registrar, they can be treated as effective. On the other hand, the cases to which I have referred show that certificates of approval under a number of statutes have been treated as effective only to prevent subsequent allegations of failure to comply with forms of procedure and not to prevent attack on the material validity of the rules. In the present case, the legislature has made it plain in other sections that certificates under this Act are to be conclusive, but has omitted any such provision in the present context. It seems to me that the approval mentioned in s. 3, subs. 1 cannot be treated as conclusive so as to preclude consideration by the court whether the conditions required by the subsection have been satisfied.

I have therefore to consider whether rule 21 (8) is in accordance with the requirements of paragraph (b) of the subsection. It is to be observed that, when first read, the rule appears to follow the requirements of that paragraph and confine discrimination and ineligibility to positions involving control or management of the political fund, which is the exception mentioned in the paragraph. It is not until it is discovered that an exempted member is disqualified from holding the office of chairman because that office involves control or management of the political fund as well as the general fund, that doubts begin to arise.

Sir Walter Monckton contended (as I understood his argument) that (1) as a matter of practical administration of the affairs of the branch it is necessary to combine the control and management of the general fund and the political fund in the hands of the same officials of the branch, and (2) accordingly, the exempted member must suffer the disability or disadvantage of exclusion from office by reason of the exception permitting disability or disadvantage where the control or management of the political fund is involved. There is, he said, no provision confining the exception to functions concerned with control or management of the political fund. This is an ingenious argument, but be it observed that the effect is to exclude an exempted member from any part in the affairs of his branch as an officer or a representative by reason of the fact that the same persons administer (as the rules are constituted) both the general and the political funds. This appears to me to be equivalent to the exception swallowing the provisions of paragraph (b) which were primarily designed to prevent disability from being imposed on the exempted member. In other words, as long as the constitution of the union fails to separate the control and management of the political fund from other functions of the union, there is no limit to the area of the exception and an exempted member might find himself excluded from practically all the activities of his branch. I cannot believe that this is the result of an exception introduced into a provision designed to protect the exempted member. It is entirely reasonable that a non-contributor should be excluded from control or management of the political fund; it is quite another matter that he should be excluded from any office in his union or branch.

I reach the conclusion, therefore, that rule 21 (8) in conjunction with the other rules of the union, offends against the provisions of paragraph (*b*) of subs. 1 of s. 3 of the Act....

Consequently the conditions laid down by that section are not satisfied, and application of the funds of the defendant union in further-ance of political objects is prohibited by the section. It is regrettable that a fund which has been administered in good faith for so many years should be found to be unlawful; but that is the result of the way in which the rules of this union have been drafted and its scheme of administration or government. It is the constitution of the union and its branches which cause rule 21 (8) to have an effect which was, I think, not anticipated, and which was not perceived when steps were taken to have the plaintiff disqualified from the office of chairman of the Woodford Halse branch of the union.

That being so, I think that the plaintiff is entitled to a declaration.

DECISION OF THE REGISTRAR: JOHNS AND THE NATIONAL UNION OF RAILWAYMEN, 23 NOVEMBER 1948

This is a complaint made to me by a member of a Trade Union to the effect that he has been aggrieved by a breach of the rules relating to the political fund of the union. The complainant Mr Harold Johns, is a member of the National Union of Railwaymen, a registered Trade Union having for the time being in force a valid resolution approving the furtherance of political objects as defined in s. 3 (3) of the Trade Union Act, 1913. In accordance with s. 3 (1) of that Act rules for the purposes of regulating matters relating to the political fund have also been approved. The rule of which a breach is alleged by the complainant is rule XXI(8) which reads as follows: 'A member who is exempt from the obligation to contribute to the political fund of the Union shall not be excluded from any benefits of the Union or placed in any respect, either directly or indirectly, under any disability or disadvantage as compared with other members of the Union by reason of his being so exempt except that such member shall take no part in the control or management of the political fund of the Union and shall be ineligible to occupy any office or representative position involving any such control or management.' The substance of the complaint is that Mr Johns who is exempt from contributing to the political fund has been placed under a disability.

The facts of the case are relatively simple. The National Union of Railwaymen is a union whose members are divided into certain local groups called branches, the constitution and management of which is provided for in rules X and XI of the union's rules. The complainant is a member of the Llanelly Branch. This branch, in accordance with rule X(5), made a number of by-laws for its governance in October 1946 and amongst those by-laws there was one numbered 17 which as far as it is relevant reads as follows: '...A member who does not contribute to the General and Political Funds of the Union is ineligible for election as a Branch Officer.' By reason of this by-law Mr Johns alleges that he, as one exempted from contributing to the political fund of the union, is debarred from holding any branch office and that he is thereby placed under a greater disability than is provided for in rule XXI(8). It is his argument in fact that the term 'a branch officer' is a far wider term than the term 'any office or representative position involving any...control or management' of the political fund as used in rule XXI(8) and that in consequence the branch and the general secretary of the union, who in accordance with rule X(5) has approved the by-law in question, have both broken rule XXI(8) by using the wider term and thus placing the complainant as a non-contributor to the political fund under a disability not permitted by the latter rule....

I think I ought to make one point clear at this stage. Rule XXI(8) is a rule amongst others which has been approved in accordance with s. 3(1) of the Trade Union Act, 1913. The consequence of this is that I am not entitled in an inquiry of this nature to question its validity by reference to the words of the section under which it was approved. By reason of its approval it is and must be as far as I am now concerned a valid rule and the disability provided for in that rule must be considered a perfectly legal and valid disability which a non-contributor may suffer. Very different considerations, however, apply to the by-law in question. It has not been, nor is intended to be approved under the Act of 1913. It was made under rule X(5) of the union's rules. Such by-laws are perfectly valid as far as the individual branch is concerned. They bind each branch member as do the rules each union member. But to bind each branch member they must be made strictly in accordance with that rule which gives to the branch the requisite power of making them, otherwise they are *ultra vires* and of no effect. Now rule X(5) reads as follows: 'Each branch may make by-laws for the government of its local affairs; such by-laws must first be approved of and signed by the Executive Committee or the General Secretary, and be strictly consistent with these general rules of the Union'. Now it is clear therefore that a branch has no power to make by-laws which are not strictly consistent with these general rules of the union and if it purports to make such a by-law it is *ultra vires* rule X(5) and of no effect. In other words a by-law cannot in any way bind members unless it is *intra vires*. Now if I were to find that by-law 17 is inconsistent with the general rules in so far as it extends the application of certain words used in rule XXI(8) beyond the limits clearly intended by that rule, I should be forced to the conclusion that that by-law is *ultra vires* rule X(5) and therefore without any power to bind the members of the branch that passed it, and I cannot see that an invalid by-law contrary to which any member or group of members can legally act, is one which can place the complainant under any disability. If on the other hand I find this by-law a valid and binding one I can only do so because it is strictly consistent with the general rules including rule XXI(8) of the union and in consequence there is no breach of which Mr Johns can complain. What Mr Johns is really complaining of it not a breach of rule XXI(8) but a breach of rule X(5) which is a rule not relating to the political fund and consequently one about which I cannot hear a complaint.

Mr Johns has further alleged that he has been told by the general secretary of the union that he is not eligible to be nominated for or elected to any branch office and that he has in this way been placed under a disability in breach of rule XXI(8). As to this allegation analogous considerations to those already made apply. Nowhere in the rules do I find that the general secretary has any power to bind members of a branch by issuing instructions as to who may hold office. The rules alone are the determining factor. The general secretary's statement may be an indication of future conduct, of the probability or certainty that a non-contributor's nomination to a branch office will not be accepted but until such non-acceptance has taken place the complainant has not been placed under a disability and no breach of the rule XXI (8) occurred. It may be that the general secretary has placed Mr Johns under a potential disability, a disability to be actualized by the branch carrying out the general secretary's instructions. But until the branch has finally committed itself by refusing Mr Johns's nomination to any branch office neither a statement by an officer of the union nor a by-law, which if it is inconsistent with the rules must be *ultra vires*, can place Mr Johns under such a disability as to constitute a breach of the rule in question.

In these circumstances I must dismiss Mr Johns's complaint.

DECISION OF THE REGISTRAR: IN THE MATTER OF W. F. HOBBS AND THE CLERICAL AND ADMINISTRATIVE WORKERS' UNION, 30 JULY 1956

Mr W. F. Hobbs, who is a member of the Clerical and Administrative Workers' Union and secretary of its Feltham Branch, has, on the instructions of his Branch, complained that he has been aggrieved by a breach of rule 82 of the Union's rules, which is one of its political fund rules. My jurisdiction to hear the complaint is conferred by s. 2(2) of the Trade Union Act, 1913.

Rule 82 provides as follows: 'A member who is exempt from the obligation to contribute to the Political Fund of the Union shall not be excluded from any benefits of the Union, or placed in any respect either directly or indirectly under any disability or disadvantage as compared with other members of the Union (except in relation to control or management of the Political Fund of the Union), by reason of his being so exempt.'

Mr Hobbs alleges that a breach of that rule was committed in the following circumstances. At the last Annual Conference of the Union, members who did not contribute to its political fund were permitted to vote on a resolution to nominate Mr Aneurin Bevan as Treasurer of the Labour Party, which resolution, Mr Hobbs contends, related to the control and management of the political fund of the Union.

I express no opinion on the latter contention but assume, for the purposes of argument, that it is well founded. A breach of rule 82 can have been committed only if rule 82 requires non-contributory members to be placed at a disability or disadvantage as compared with the other members of the Union in matters relating to the control and management of the political fund.

Rule 82 follows *verbatim* s. 3(1)(*b*) of the Trade Union Act, 1913, which lays down a general principle, i.e. that non-contributors must not be placed at a disadvantage *vis-à-vis* other members and, by the words in brackets—'(except in relation to the control and management of the political fund)'—specifies that in one matter that general principle is not to apply. The effect of the words in brackets is that the union may exclude non-contributing members from the control and management of the political fund. If, however, the union is to take advantage of its power of exclusion it must do so by passing a rule excluding the non-contributing members from such control and management. Rule 82 contains no provision prohibiting non-contributors from controlling or managing the political fund. I am therefore unable to find that the facts disclose a breach of that rule.*

Section B

MEMBERSHIP OF THE UNION

(i) ADMISSION

MARTIN *v.* SCOTTISH TRANSPORT AND GENERAL WORKERS' UNION

House of Lords   [1952] 1 All E.R. 691

The plaintiff wanted to join the defendant union in 1940. He was made to sign a letter saying the union would be entitled to expel him after the war. In 1948 the union purported to expel him and he claimed a declaration that he was still a member. Under its rules the only provision for expulsion was that the union could expel people who in the opinion of the executive failed to abide by the rules; and there was no provision for temporary membership. The purported admission to temporary membership was held to be *ultra vires* and void (and not, therefore, open to ratification by the union officials or membership).

LORD NORMAND: My Lords, in my opinion, the reasoning of the learned judges in the Inner House, particularly in the judgments of

* Note, too, that s. 3, Trade Union Act, 1913, does not protect members against union rules which discriminate against them on other grounds, e.g. because they are Communists, or 'disruptive' elements in the union: see *Cleger and London District of Amalgamated Union of Operative Bakers*, Registrar's Decision, 26 June 1935 (ban on nomination for office of 'disruptive' members).

Lord Cooper, Lord President, and Lord Carmont, is unassailable and conclusive of the action. The whole issue turns on the construction and effect of the letter of 19 August 1940, and on the construction and effect of the respondents' rules, and I turn first to a consideration of the construction of the letter. The first sentence is, in terms, an application for membership 'for the duration of the war' neither more nor less; the second sentence contains an express provision that the executive of the union should be entitled to require the appellant to forfeit his membership '...on or at any time after the signing of an armistice by His Majesty's government'.

Had the letter been a document drafted and adjusted by lawyers for the parties, there might have been difficult questions about the legal meaning of the 'duration of the war' and of 'the signing of an armistice by His Majesty's government', and the fact that hostilities ended, not by the signing of an armistice, but by the unconditional surrender of the King's enemies, would have given rise to special difficulty. But this was not a lawyer's document and the parties were agreed that it should not be made the subject of a legalistic interpretation. It was really common ground that 'for the duration of the...war' meant no more than 'till the end of hostilities' and that the 'signing of an armistice' has the same meaning. I think that that is the sensible and correct way to construe the letter. What the application had in view was that the appellant should have the right to remain a member till hostilities ceased and that after that he might remain a member till the union executive chose to terminate his membership. The respondents' counsel did, indeed, offer another construction, that the letter was an application for membership without qualification as to duration accompanied by a standing offer of resignation capable of being made effective by acceptance at any time after the cessation of hostilities. The language of the document is not capable of bearing such a construction, and that is all that need be said about it. What, then, is the effect of the letter? It is, on the appellant's own averments, the basis of his admission, or purported admission, to membership. The appellant was reluctant to sign, but in the end he gave way and signed the document put before him. He then and there paid his entrance fee and was handed his membership card, a copy of the union's rules, and his contribution card. We were invited to ignore the letter and to treat the other incidents as an implied application for membership and an implied acceptance which were independent of the letter. But it is impossible to wipe out the express application which was followed by an act of acceptance and to substitute for it an implication from the tender of the entrance fee which was itself a consequence of the signing of the application in agreed terms. The real question is whether the condition affecting the duration of the membership is separable from the remainder of the latter. Again, I have no doubt that the condition was integral and cannot be separated and severed so as to leave the letter standing as an unqualified application. Lord Carmont's observations on this aspect of the case are, in my opinion, most cogent. The learned judge says that the more the appellant emphasises his reluctance to accept the condition and his protests, the more he makes it impossible to adopt the suggestion that he put forward an overriding application for unqualified membership, the acceptance of which was qualified by a severable *ultra vires* condition. The first sentence in the letter, moreover, is incapable of being separated into an application unlimited in time with an added limitation. The two things are indissolubly connected grammatically. I, therefore, hold that the letter was the basis on which the appellant was admitted and that the condition as to duration was an integral suspensive condition in the sense that he would not have been admitted unless he had signed the letter containing the condition as an integral part of his application.

For a just appreciation of the respondents' rules it is important to consider the statutory provisions under which they were made. They are contained in the Trade Union Act, 1871, s. 14, and schedule I. Section 14 enacts: 'With respect to the rules of a trade union registered under this Act, the following provisions shall have effect: (1) The rules of every such trade union shall contain provisions in respect of the several matters mentioned in schedule I to this Act.'

Schedule I contains the following: '(2) The whole of the objects for which the trade union is to be established, the purposes for which the funds thereof shall be applicable, and the conditions under which any member may become entitled to any benefit assured thereby, and the fines and forfeitures to be imposed on any member of such trade union. (3) The manner of making, altering, amending, and rescinding rules.'

It follows that any rule governing the terms on which membership is granted must apply to all admissions until it is altered by the method prescribed by the rules themselves, and I, therefore, reject the argument put forward for the respondents that *esto* the rules in August 1940, provided only for the admission of members without any limit on the duration of their membership, some modification of the rule so as to provide for temporary membership could be brought about by an implied ratification of admissions purporting to have been made on a temporary basis. Now, rule 15 contains this: 'Every person upon being admitted a member of the union shall be deemed to agree to abide by the rules of the union in every respect, and be liable to forfeit membership at any time if in the opinion of the general executive council such person has failed to abide by the rules.'

There is no rule providing for the admission of members on a temporary basis or for forfeiture for any reason except that prescribed by rule 15. Rule 20 provides: 'No new rule shall be made, nor shall any rule herein contained or hereafter to be made (sic), or amended, or rescinded except in accordance with a resolution duly passed at the annual meeting of the general executive council.'

In spite of imperfections of drafting, the sense of this rule is clear. It is common ground that rule 15 was in force in August 1940, and that it was not hereafter altered by any resolution passed at the annual meeting of the general executive council. Therefore, the officials of the branch or of the union had no authority in August 1940, or later, to admit the appellant to membership subject to a limitation of time, and when they purported to do so they acted in excess of their powers and their act had and has no validity. I agree with the view expressed by Lord Carmont that there was an attempt to create a class of member outside the provisions of the rules and that it necessarily fails. The conclusion that the appellant never was a member may be inconvenient to both parties, because it may be difficult to work out the equitable adjustment of rights, but that is not a consideration which can affect the decision of the present appeal. I would dismiss the appeal with costs.

LORD REID, LORD TUCKER, LORD ASQUITH OF BISHOPSTONE and LORD COHEN concurred.

BOULTING *v.* ASSOCIATION OF CINEMATOGRAPH TELEVISION & ALLIED TECHNICIANS

Court of Appeal   [1963] 2 Q.B. 606

The plaintiffs were joint managing directors of 'Charter' a company which produced films. They were active on both the management and the technical sides of the company. Rule 7 (a) of the defendant union ran as follows: 'The association shall consist of all employees engaged on the technical side of film production...including film directors, employee producers, associate producers, scriptwriters, and all employees of the cine-camera,...departments.'

The plaintiffs were members of the union up till 1950; in that year they stopped paying their subscriptions. In 1959 the union claimed arrears of subscriptions from them, claiming they were members. The plaintiffs claimed a declaration that they were not eligible for membership while producing films and were incapable of entering a contract of membership. They sought an injunction to restrain the defendants from taking any action to compel them to join the union. The Court of Appeal, by a majority, rejected their contentions.

UPJOHN, L.J.: The whole difficulty in this case arises because, as in the case of very many other film producing companies, the Boulting brothers as managing directors perform from time to time the functions of all these offices, i.e. managing directors, executive producers, associate producers, film directors, editors and script writers. It cannot be disputed that they are most expert on the technical side as on the purely management and administration side. The judge reached the conclusion that since the Boulting brothers are employed by Charter as film directors and producers, they are, according to the plain meaning of the words of rule 7, eligible for membership of the union. Mr Parker, for the plaintiffs, challenges the correctness of this conclusion. In an able argument he points out that the Boulting brothers respectively are managing directors employed as such for one entire salary covering all their duties and are bound by their agreements to devote the whole of their time and attention to the affairs of the company and to promote the best interests of the company. He submits that it is as such managing directors that they perform all these functions. They are the executives whose managerial and technical skills combined make them the alter ego of Charter. They are, for example, concerned on behalf of Charter in negotiation with A.C.T.T. and the other employee unions concerned with the industry. If any industrial or trade dispute arises during filming and there is some stoppage, it will be the Boulting brothers in the studio who will be responsible on behalf of Charter for operating the conciliation machinery....

The true test is whether the plaintiffs are to be regarded as employees for the purposes of the rule and [counsel] relies by analogy upon *Trussed Steel Concrete Co. Ltd* v. *Green*.[1] I agree with that approach to the problem. He summarises his argument by posing the question: are managing directors, who are throughout performing their functions as such, within the rule merely because some of their functions may be technical functions, frequently, though not invariably, performed by persons duly and properly described as employees because they perform

[1] [1946] Ch. 115.

no higher functions? He submits that the Boulting brothers are not employees for the purposes of the rule.

Mr Gardiner for A.C.T.T. submits that when the Boulting brothers are in the studio acting, for example, as producers or as film directors, they are doing so as employees of the company and, as such, are eligible for membership of the union, and it matters not that they may also perform other non-technical, non-employee functions, such as managing directors or executive producers. Mr Gardiner further submits, somewhat naively, that A.C.T.T. is not concerned with their activities when performing these other functions, and the union does not seek to influence their managerial activities as such....

Those are the arguments, and the matter is not in my view susceptible of sustained exposition. I cannot myself escape from the conclusion that the position of the Boulting brothers, although anomalous perhaps, is strictly within the wording of rule 7, for they are in fact employees of Charter engaged on the technical side of film production. True it is as directors they are not employees, but it cannot, I think, be doubted that a managing director may for many purposes properly be regarded as an employee, and that, indeed, is not disputed by Mr Parker, and the Boulting brothers seem to me to fall fairly and squarely within the rule. It must be remembered that this rule is only dealing with eligibility, and in law it is not incumbent upon the plaintiffs to join the union any more than A.C.T.T. are bound to elect them. The sole question is whether they are eligible....

I turn, then, to the second question, which raises a question of general importance: is there any principle of law which makes this rule as to eligibility *ultra vires* or unlawful in so far as it purports to make those whose principal functions are managerial, eligible to join what is essentially an employees' trade union? Mr Parker prays in aid the well-known principle of equity stated by Lord Cranworth, L.C., in *Aberdeen Railway Co.* v. *Blaikie*:[1] 'And it is a rule of universal application, that no one, having such duties to discharge, shall be allowed to enter into engagements in which he has, or can have, a personal interest conflicting, or which possibly may conflict, with the interest of those whom he is bound to protect. So strictly is this principle adhered to, that no question is allowed to be raised as to the fairness or unfairness of a contract so entered into.' This was a Scottish case, but it is clear that in this respect the law of Scotland and of England is the same.

The principle is one of the most firmly established in our law of

[1] 1 Macq. 461, 471

equity and it has been repeatedly recognised and applied by the Lord Chancellors and by the House of Lords.... The rule in no wise depends upon fraud or absence of *bona fides*. The profiteer, however honest and well intentioned, cannot escape the risk of being called upon to account: *Regal (Hastings) Ltd* v. *Gulliver*,[1] *per* Lord Russell. This is important because of the argument addressed to us. The rule is not directed at corrupt or fraudulent bargains (though, of course, it brings them within its umbrella). The rule is one of principle which depends not at all on any corrupt *mens rea* in the mind of the person holding the conflicting capacity. It will be seldom, if ever, that it will be necessary to rely on the rule in the case of a fraudulent or corrupt bargain; simpler common law rules are normally available. This rule extends to all manner of relationships and the reports are full of examples of its application to many different circumstances. Like all rules of equity, it is flexible, in the sense that it develops to meet the changing situations and conditions of the time, and so Mr Parker rightly calls it in aid here.

The rule, however, is one essentially for the protection of the person to whom the duty is owed. Thus the company is entitled to the undivided loyalty of its directors; beneficiaries are entitled to the unpaid services of their trustees; the client is entitled to the services of his solicitor who may not charge more than he is legally entitled to, and must not put himself into a position where he may owe conflicting duties to different clients.... But the person entitled to the benefit of the rule may relax it, provided he is of full age and *sui juris* and fully understands not only what he is doing but also what his legal rights are, and that he is in part surrendering them. Thus the company may, in its articles of association, permit directors to be interested in contracts with the company. It may go further, and articles may validly permit directors to be present at board meetings and even to vote when proposed contracts in which they are interested are being discussed; provided, of course, that they make full disclosure of their interests....

To sum up the position, it is clear that the person entitled to the benefit of this positive rule is the person who is protected by it, but he, and he alone, can in proper circumstances relax it to such extent as he thinks proper. It cannot be used as a shield by the person owning the duty; that is clear; it is a sword and as such only can it be used by the person entitled to the benefit of it, and he may sheath the weapon....

Mr Parker says the result is to make rule 7 *ultra vires* or unlawful in so far as it purports to make the Boulting brothers as employers eligible for

[1] [1942] 1 All E.R. 378, 386.

election. The argument proceeds that this conflict renders contracts of membership of the Boulting brothers with A.C.T.T. corrupt, illegal and wholly void because the *Blaikie* principle is violated. As a member of the union the director is biased in his mind and his conflicting interests will lead him to act disloyally to the company to which his undivided loyalty is pledged. So the rule purporting to make them eligible is *ultra vires*. Alternatively, the rule has a tendency to compel them to commit an unlawful act, i.e. a breach of their duty to Charter, so the rule is unlawful. He submits that s. 6 of the Trades Union Act, 1871, and s. 1 of the Trade Union Act, 1913, make it clear that the rules of the trade union cannot validly contain an unlawful rule and must be expunged....

However, I think that in principle there are a number of answers to these submissions. First, applying the principles I have attempted to state, I do not see how the Boulting brothers can invoke the *Blaikie* rule at all. The rule is not for their protection but that of Charter. If they break the rule, they will be liable to Charter. They cannot claim the protection of the rule. Whether Charter could obtain an injunction against the Boulting brothers restraining them from joining A.C.T.T. is an interesting question which does not arise in these proceedings. But as between A.C.T.T. and the Boulting brothers, the position is that if their duty makes it unlawful to join, then they ought not to join; in law they cannot be compelled to join. Of course, pressure *de facto* to join will be brought upon them and no doubt they are seeking to introduce this principle of equity in their fight to rebut that pressure; I am not without sympathy for them, but that does not give them a cause of action. If A procures B to break his contract with C, C can complain because A commits a well-established tort against C. But B has no right at law to restrain A from attempting to suborn him from his duty to C. He must resist A's efforts by strength of will. If B succumbs to A's blandishments and contracts with him in breach of his duty to C, B can have no right to complain of A's conduct if A performs his contract with B, which the latter has so wrongly entered into. Secondly, for the reasons I have attempted to explain, I cannot see how an engagement entered into in breach of the principle renders the engagement corrupt and void. Of course, it may do so, but that depends on proof of a *mens rea* of some dishonest or corrupt intention. There is none here. A.C.T.T. cannot be accused of dishonesty or corruptness that because of their trade motives they want to get the Boulting brothers into their fold.

Thirdly, I have pointed out that Charter, as a person entitled to the benefit of the rule, has the right to relax it. Charter may think that, on the whole, it will serve its best interests if in fact the Boulting brothers do join A.C.T.T. and that, on the whole, this will make for happier industrial relationships between employer and employee. They are entitled, as I understand the law, not only to authorise but to encourage the Boulting brothers to join. If so, why should the Boulting brothers not be permitted to join if under the rules they are eligible. If Mr Parker's argument is right, there can be no such relaxation; the *Blaikie* rule is absolute and a rule as to eligibility in breach of it is incurably bad. The Boulting brothers cannot become members, however eligible and however much Charter and the Boultings themselves may desire it. This cannot be right.

Fourthly, if such a rule, which admits employer and employee to membership of a union, is bad, this great principle has lain hidden and dormant for over 90 years. Section 16 of the Trade Union Amendment Act, 1876, is in terms very general and appears to contemplate a combination consisting of masters and employees together, though truly it does not say so in precise terms. But there seems no reason why a combination of masters and workmen together should not be formed for the purpose of regulating their relations, and this has been done many times; it has been so interpreted for many years and many examples were given to us. I will quote only two. Every band leader, who normally employs the other members of the band, is compelled by the all-powerful Musicians' Union to be a member of it, unless he is content, in a most literal sense, to be a one-man band. Actor-managers belong to Equity. It seems to be clear that there is nothing illegal in a rule which makes both employer and employee eligible for election.

The Boulting brothers' case therefore fails. I would, however, add this. I have so far assumed that if they join A.C.T.T. a genuine conflict of duty and interest would arise.... I am not, however, very convinced by this evidence that there is a real conflict between the Boulting brothers' duties as directors and their interests as members of A.C.T.T. I think it is the greatest pity that this case was heard at first instance on an agreed statement of facts without agreeing upon this point, merely leaving the court to infer that there was a real genuine conflict of interest and duty. I should have liked to have heard the Boulting brothers' evidence on oath and to have heard them cross-examined on the real alleged conflict between their duty as managers and their interest as members of A.C.T.T. Is it more than a fanciful conflict? The battle lies between the Boulting brothers in their managerial capacity and A.C.T.T. as representing the employees. Does their membership of

A.C.T.T. give rise to a real additional conflict of duty and interest, of which a court would take notice? I am not unmindful of the fact that nearly all of the persons in the film industry in positions comparable to the Boulting brothers (many of them equally distinguished in the film industry) are members of A.C.T.T. and do not seem to find their dual roles unworkable, as Salmon, J., said.

DIPLOCK, L.J., delivered a concurring judgment; LORD DENNING, M.R., dissented.

FARAMUS v. FILM ARTISTES ASSOCIATION

House of Lords   [1964] A.C. 925

The appellant had been a member of the respondent society since 1950. On joining he signed an application form which asked 'Have you ever been convicted of an offence?' to which he replied 'No'. In fact he had been sentenced to three months hard labour in Jersey in 1938 when he was 17; and in 1940 during the German occupation he had been sentenced to six months hard labour. Rule 4(2) of the union stated: 'No person who has been convicted in a court of law of a criminal offence (other than a motoring offence not punishable by imprisonment) shall be eligible for or retain membership of the association'. In 1958 the union, which operated a closed shop, discovered his previous offences and claimed that he was not and never had been a member. The appellant unsuccessfully sought a declaration that he was a member and an injunction.

LORD EVERSHED: I repeat that, as I read the words of this sub-rule, and when I have regard to the fact that in the later rules to which I have referred there is no reference anywhere to the case of one who has been admitted to membership notwithstanding some prior conviction in a criminal court or after becoming a member commits a criminal offence, the result is that upon this matter of construction there is no answer to the respondents' submission as to its effect. Unless, therefore, the rule can on some other ground be avoided, the result is that in truth the unfortunate appellant, though the forms of election were properly gone through, was never in fact validly elected because he never had the essential qualification for membership.

Like the majority of the Court of Appeal, I am unable to see any ground upon which it could be seriously submitted that the rule could be disregarded by the court because of the vagueness of its terms or because its application in certain circumstances might not only be difficult of ascertainment but productive of embarrassment in the conduct of the association's business. Nor can it, as I think, be suggested that to a rule of this kind there can be applied any principle of natural justice. The case is in no sense analogous to the case of rules applicable to someone whose contract of membership is being terminated, where it may well be that for their validity the rules must make provision to enable such a person at any rate to have a proper opportunity to put his case. In the circumstances, therefore, the only ground upon which the appellant can, as I think, succeed is if he were able to establish that the terms of this rule operated as an unreasonable restraint of trade and that the rule was not saved by s. 3 of the Trade Union Act, 1871.

My Lords, the normal case in which the principles of unreasonable restraint of trade come under the review of the courts is that of a contract made between two persons whereby something in unreasonable restraint of the trade of one of them is imposed by the contract upon the happening of some event. True it is that the whole of the rules of the respondents' association here constitute a contract between the members. On this ground, therefore, it might no doubt be contended that the second part of the relevant sub-rule (that which provides that membership shall automatically cease upon the member being convicted of any criminal offences, however trivial, with one trifling exception) could be regarded as being unreasonably in restraint of the member's trade, particularly since, as your Lordships were told, the union has in fact achieved what is commonly called a 'closed shop' so that no film artiste within a radius of 50 miles of Charing Cross can obtain employment as such unless he is a member of the union. Upon this matter, however, I would for myself prefer to express no final view since it does not, in the event, matter to the result of this appeal. And I prefer also not to express a concluded opinion that the operation of the sub-rule as regards the appellant in the circumstances of his case should be said to amount to an unreasonable restraint of trade—that is, to an unreasonable restraint upon his right and power to earn his living as a film artiste. I do not forget that, as I have earlier observed, it is one of the objects of this association which has been at the present time achieved, that only members of the association can in fact obtain employment in the neighbourhood of London as film artistes. It is, however, no less clear from the facts stated to your Lordships that there is work available for only about one-fourth of the total number of persons who each year apply for membership as film artistes within the area defined. It follows, therefore, that the rules as to admission of membership must inevitably be in some degree arbitrary—for example, if they provided that the successful candidates were to be drawn by lot. I am unaware of any case in which the principles of unreasonable restraint of trade have been held to be applicable to the rules made by any institution or association laying down the qualifications of persons to become members of the institution or association. In this respect I apprehend that I share the view of Diplock, L.J., in the Court of Appeal. I will, however, assume nonetheless that the wide and vague terms of the sub-rule in question should and can properly be described as an unreasonable restraint of trade so as to be invalid at common law. The question then turns upon the application of s. 3 of the Trades Union Act, 1871, which is in the following terms: 'The purposes of any trade union shall not, by reason merely that they are in restraint of trade, be unlawful so as to render void...any agreement or trust.'

The learned Master of the Rolls was able to avoid the application of the section so as to save the rule by holding, first that the rule was merely part of the administrative machinery of the union and not therefore one of its purposes; and, second, that according to the terms of the section it was only the purposes which could be saved by operation of the section. My Lords, it is no doubt true that the rules are but part of th emachinery of the union's organisation as distinct from its objects or purposes. But the section, as I read its terms, goes further than validating only the purposes themselves. According to the language of the section, the effect is to give validity to any agreement which may be made as appurtenant to or in pursuance of the purposes of the union where the purposes themselves are in restraint of trade. The vital words of the section are the last words '...so as to render void...*any agreement*...'. Having regard particularly to the 'closed shop' objective of the respondents' union, I am prepared to assume and accept it that at common law the purposes of the union would be regarded as constituting a restraint of trade. The effect, however, as I understand it, of the section, is not merely to declare the purposes valid but to validate also 'any agreement', that is to say, any agreement which is relevant or directed to the purposes of the union. The point is indeed a short one and not, as I conceive, capable of useful expansion. I therefore accept unequivocally the view taken by the majority of the Court of Appeal, and say that if the contract constituted by the rules in this case be or contain (at any rate so far as this sub-rule is concerned) an unreasonable restraint of trade, nonetheless the rules (and sub-rule (2) of rule 4 in particular) are validated by the section. I add only that it is unreal and impossible, as I think, to sever this particular sub-rule from the rules as a whole and to treat it therefore as something quite distinct not only from the other rules but also from the purposes of the union to which, of course, it is essentially addressed. I add also, first, that I agree entirely with the view of the majority of the Court of Appeal, that there is here no true analogy between the rules of this union and the by-laws of some corporation which would entitle the court to treat the rule (as they could treat a by-law) as ineffective and invalid if outside the law-making power conferred upon the makers of the rules. I agree in this respect entirely with Diplock, L.J., in thinking that the law applicable in cases of by-laws is in truth an aspect of the principle of *ultra vires* and I found myself, as he did, upon the judgment of Lord Russell, C.J., in the case of *Kruse* v. *Johnson*.[1] Second, it seems to me quite impossible for the appellant successfully to contend that the respondent union has by any conduct of the union or of the executive committee become estopped from asserting the application to the appellant's case of the relevant rule 4(2): for, if the rule has the meaning which I attribute to it, then in truth the appellant was at all times disqualified from membership by the rules, and the respondent union could no more avoid the consequence of the rules than could the union in the case of *Martin* v. *Scottish Transport and General Workers' Union* be treated by the court as competent to elect members of a particular class, such class being altogether outside the scope of the union's rules.

LORD HODSON: I think that, as Diplock, L.J., said, the question of whether rule 4(2), which deals with qualification for membership of the respondent association, is invalid at common law as being in unreasonable restraint of trade, depends on what the purposes of the association are. Taken in isolation it might not be so since an organisation can be arbitrary in its selection of members without infringing the principle of unreasonable restraint of trade. It was conceded, however, that one of the purposes of the association is to operate a 'closed shop'. This is manifestly in restraint of trade and the whole contract of association, together with its rules, would, I should have thought, be invalid at common law.

This, as my noble and learned friend, Lord Evershed, has pointed out, is no more than an academic question since, as I understand it, all your Lordships are of the opinion, with which I agree, that s. 3 of the Trade Union Act, 1871, operates to save the agreement contained in the contract of association from invalidity notwithstanding that the purpose

[1] [1898] 2 Q.B. 91.

I have mentioned being in unreasonable restraint of trade would otherwise have rendered the contract as contained in the rules void.

LORD PEARCE: Since this union has a monopoly, exclusion from its membership prevents a man from earning his living in this particular profession. An absolute rule that so prevents any person who may have suffered a trivial conviction many years before is in restraint of trade and unreasonable. It is therefore void unless it is saved by s. 3 of the Trade Union Act, 1871, which provides that: 'The purposes of any trade union shall not, by reason merely that they are in restraint of trade, be unlawful so as to render void...any agreement or trust.'

It is argued that this rule is not a 'purpose of the union' and that therefore s. 3 does not touch it. But the rule clearly helps to achieve one at least of the objects of the association. It would be detrimental to the position and status of film artistes if they had among their numbers persons convicted of serious or frequent crimes of fraud. Also it might create trouble between member and managers or between member and member if such dishonest persons could roam the changing rooms as of right. Rule 4(2) in a more precise form is at least desirable for the objects of the association. Moreover, the evidence shows that one of the purposes of the union in support of its expressed objects is to cut down the number of persons engaged in this particular walk of life. For, if all who wished were admitted, there would not be an adequate living for any. This rule is partly directed to that purpose and it is no more unfair to keep out one man because he has been convicted albeit trivially and so to put another in his place, than to keep persons out simply because there is no room for them. Merely because a desirable rule is too far-reaching, it does not cease, in my opinion, to be one of the purposes of the union. The question here is, would the agreement (that is to say, the rules) or any part of it (or them) be void merely because the purpose of the union is in restraint of trade? If so, it is protected by s. 3. In my opinion rule 4(2) would be void merely for that reason and for no other, and it is therefore protected.

An argument was founded on the *Amalgamated Society of Railway Servants* v. *Osborne*[1] and in particular on the words of Lord Macnaghten: '...the powers to be used in furtherance of those objects (to repeat Lord Watson's words) must be "either 'expressly conferred or derived by reasonable implication from the provisions of the Act'."' He then quoted Lord Selborne's words in *Murray* v. *Scott*[2] that 'a power may be "not only consistent with but reasonably conducive to the

[1] [1910] A.C. 87, 96; 26 T.L.R. 177, H.L.   [2] (1884) 9 App. Cas. 519, 537, H.L.

19   W C A

proper objects" of a society, and yet not so necessary as to be implied when not expressly given.' In *Osborne's* case it was held by your Lordships' House that there was nothing in the Trade Union Acts from which it could be reasonably inferred that trade unions were meant to have the power of collecting and administering funds for political purposes. In 1913, however, Parliament in order to mitigate the effect of that decision passed the Trade Union Act, 1913, giving to trade unions liberty to pursue objects and powers under their constitution other than statutory objects. In the light of that Act I do not find it possible to say that the making of rule 4(2) was outside the power of the union in this case.

Nor can I find any general power in the court to nullify the rule on the ground merely that it is unreasonable. In *Kruse* v. *Johnson*[1] Lord Russell, C.J., explained the reason for the court's interference with unreasonable by-laws: 'If, for instance, they were found to be partial and unequal in their operation as between different classes; if they were manifestly unjust; if they disclosed bad faith; if they involved such oppressive or gratuitous interference with the rights of those subject to them as could find no justification in the minds of reasonable men, the court might well say, "Parliament never intended to give authority to make such rules; they are unreasonable and *ultra vires*".' As Upjohn, L.J., pointed out in the present case:[2] 'Such tests cannot be applied to a rule of eligibility for joining a trade union'. And so far as such tests reveal unreasonable restraint of trade, Parliament has sanctioned that defect. In *Lee* v. *The Showmen's Guild of Great Britain*[3] Denning, L.J., pointed out that certain limitations of public policy were imposed on the jurisdiction of a domestic tribunal founded on contract, express or implied, in that it must, for instance, in cases of expulsion observe the principles of natural justice; that it must give a man an opportunity of refuting a charge; and that the contract cannot stipulate for a power to condemn a man unheard. But cases of expulsion without a fair hearing come in a different category from cases of refusal of an applicant for membership. No case has been cited in which the court has intervened or been asked to intervene to relax unreasonable prohibitions against such entry. Since there is here a 'closed shop' which can only be entered through membership of this union the court would, in my opinion, intervene on the ground of unreasonable restraint of trade were it not for s. 3 of the Trade Union Act, 1871. But now it cannot.

---

[1] [1898] 2 Q.B. 91, 99.   [2] [1963] 2 Q.B. 527, 547.
[3] [1952] 2 Q.B. 329, 342.

The appellant's argument based on estoppel cannot stand. True, the union have treated the appellant as a member for many years. But it is somewhat doubtful in the light of *Martin* v. *Scottish Transport and General Workers' Union* whether any reliance can be placed on that fact. And in this particular case it was the appellant's own misrepresentation which brought about his years of membership and he cannot rely on them to create any sort of estoppel in his own favour.

LORD REID and LORD DEVLIN concurred.

NAGLE v. FEILDEN

Court of Appeal [1966] 1 All E.R. 689

This was an action brought by Mrs Nagle against the Stewards of the Jockey Club. The stewards controlled flat racing in Great Britain and in pursuance of their unwritten policy of refusing to licence a woman as a trainer they refused the appellant a trainer's licence. They had, however, granted licences to her head lad. Mrs Nagle sued for an injunction and a declaration that the practice was against public policy. She now appealed against the striking out of her statement of claim as showing no cause of action. [The Court of Appeal was concerned only with that preliminary issue, whether the plaintiff had an arguable case. The action was later settled when the Stewards allowed Mrs Nagle to have a licence.]

LORD DENNING, M.R.: In support of the appeal, counsel for Mrs Nagle seemed at first to accept that it was necessary for him to show that there was a contractual relationship between Mrs Nagle and the Stewards of the Jockey Club. He did this because there are statements in the books—and I have said it myself—that the power of the courts to intervene in these cases is founded on its jurisdiction to protect rights of contract. Accepting these statements, counsel submitted that there was here an arguable case in favour of a contract. First, he said that the stewards made an offer to all the world that they would consider applications from trainers for licences: and that Mrs Nagle accepted that offer by applying for a licence. I cannot accept that submission. The stewards made no contractual offer to all the world, but at most an invitation to treat. Secondly, he said that when the head lad was granted a licence by the stewards, the head lad was only an agent for Mrs Nagle, and so there was a contract between his principal, Mrs Nagle, and the stewards. I cannot accept this submission either. The stewards declined to contract with Mrs Nagle. They were only willing to contract with her

19-2

head lad, and she knew it. That excludes any possibility of a contract with her....

Now, I quite agree that if we were here considering a social club, it would be necessary for the plaintiff to show a contract. If a man applies to join a social club and is blackballed, he has no cause of action: because the members have made no contract with him. They can do as they like. They can admit or refuse him, as they please; but we are not considering a social club. We are considering an association which exercises a virtual monopoly in an important field of human activity. By refusing or withdrawing a licence, the stewards can put a man out of business. This is a great power. If it is abused, can the courts give redress ? That is the question....

It was urged before us that the members of a trading or professional association were like a social club. They had, it was said, an unrestricted power to admit, or refuse to admit, any person whom they choose: and that this was established by a case in 1825 concerning the Inns of Court. In *R.* v. *Lincoln's Inn Benchers*[1] Bayley, J., said: 'They make their own rules as to the admission of members; and even if they act capriciously upon the subject, this court can give no remedy in such a case; because in fact there has been no violation of a right.'

I venture to question this statement, notwithstanding the eminence of the judge from whom it fell. The common law of England has for centuries recognised that a man has a right to work at his trade or profession without being unjustly excluded from it. He is not to be shut out from it at the whim of those having the governance of it. If they make a rule which enables them to reject his application arbitrarily or capriciously, not reasonably, that rule is bad. It is against public policy. The courts will not give effect to it. Such was held in the seventeenth century in the celebrated *Ipswich Tailors' Case*[2] where a rule was made that no person should exercise the trade of a tailor in Ipswich unless he was admitted by them to be a sufficient workman. Lord Coke, C.J., held that the rule was bad, because it was 'against the liberty and freedom of the subject'. If, however, the rule is reasonable, the courts will not interfere. In the eighteenth century, the company of surgeons required as a qualification for an apprentice an understanding of the Latin tongue. The governors rejected an apprentice because on examination they found him to be totally ignorant of Latin. Lord Mansfield, C.J., declined to interfere with their decision (see *R.* v. *Surgeons' Co. (Master)*)[3].

---

[1] (1825), 4 B. & C. 855 at pp. 859, 860.
[2] (1614), 11 Co. Rep. 53a.   [3] (1759), 2 Burr. 892.

There are not many modern cases on the subject, but they support the principle which I have stated. In *Weinberger* v. *Inglis*[1] the rules of the Stock Exchange gave to the committee an absolute discretion to admit such persons as they 'shall think proper'. The House of Lords were not referred to the old cases but to the cases where directors are empowered in their discretion to refuse a transfer of shares, such as *Re Gresham Life Assurance Society, Ex parte Penney.*[2] The House were disposed to accept this analogy and to hold that, if the committee of the Stock Exchange were to act arbitrarily or capriciously, the courts could set aside their decision—see what Lord Buckmaster,[3] Lord Atkinson[4] and Lord Wrenbury[5] said. Then again in *Faramus* v. *Film Artistes' Association*, a trade union, which kept a 'closed shop', made a rule forbidding entry to any person who had been convicted of a criminal offence. Lord Pearce said:[6] 'Since the respondent union have a monopoly, exclusion from membership prevents a man from earning his living in this particular profession. An absolute rule that so prevents any person who may have suffered a trivial conviction many years before is in restraint of trade and unreasonable.'

We cannot, of course, decide the matter today. All I say is that there is sufficient foundation for the principle for the case to go to trial. We live in days when many trading or professional associations operate 'closed shops'. No person can work at his trade or profession except by their permission. They can deprive him of his livelihood. When a man is wrongly rejected or ousted by one of these associations, has he no remedy? I think that he may well have, even though he can show no contract. The courts have power to grant him a declaration that his rejection and ouster was invalid and an injunction requiring the association to rectify their error. He may not be able to get damages unless he can show a contract or a tort; but he may get a declaration and injunction. Thus in *Abbott* v. *Sullivan*[7] the corn porter (although he had no contract with the committee) obtained a declaration that he was entitled to be reinstated on the register: and this court would, I think, have granted an injunction but for the fact that he had already been reinstated before the judgment. In *Davis* v. *Carew-Pole*[8] the livery-stablekeeper (although he was not a member) obtained a declaration that

[1] [1919] A.C. 606.
[2] [1861–73] All E.R. Rep. 903; (1872), 8 Ch.App. 446.
[3] [1919] A.C. at p. 621.　　　　　　　[4] [1919] A.C. at p. 631.
[5] [1919] A.C. at p. 644.
[6] [1964] 1 All E.R. at p. 32; [1964] A.C. at p. 946.
[7] [1952] 1 All E.R. 226; [1952] 1 K.B. 189.　　[8] [1956] 2 All E.R. 524.

the decision of the stewards disqualifying him was void, and an injunction restraining them from treating him as a disqualified person. I know that in the later case of *Byrne* v. *Kinematograph Rentals Society, Ltd*,[1] Harman, J., thought that those two cases could be based on contract. But I think that could only be done by inventing a fictitious contract. All through the centuries courts have given themselves jurisdiction by means of fictions; but we are mature enough, I hope, to do away with them. The true ground of jurisdiction in all these cases is a man's right to work. I have said before, and I repeat it now, that a man's right to work at his trade or profession is just as important to him as, perhaps more important than, his rights of property. Just as the courts will intervene to protect his rights of property, so they will also intervene to protect his right to work.... When an association, who have the governance of a trade, take it on themselves to licence persons to take part in it, then it is at least arguable that they are not at liberty to withdraw a man's licence—and thus put him out of business—without hearing him. Nor can they refuse a man a licence—and thus prevent him from carrying on his business—in their uncontrolled discretion. If they reject him arbitrarily or capriciously, there is ground for thinking that the courts can intervene. I know that there are statements to the contrary in some of the cases. We were referred to one by myself in *Russell* v. *Duke of Norfolk*;[2] but that was seventeen years ago. The right to work has become far better recognised since that time. So has the jurisdiction of the courts to control licensing authorities. When those authorities exercise a predominant power over the exercise of a trade or profession, the courts may have jurisdiction to see that this power is not abused.

DANCKWERTS, L.J., and SALMON, L.J., delivered concurring judgments.*

---

[1] [1958] 2 All E.R. 579 at p. 596.
[2] [1949] 1 All E.R. at 109 p. 119.

* It is to be noted that these judgments were given on the preliminary issue. Taken to their logical conclusion, the remarks of Lord Denning, M.R., could be used to give the courts a new control over admission rules in the trade union rule-book. In the light of the *Faramus* case, *ante*, p. 573, it seems clear that the courts could not go so far. Indeed, one of the issues much canvassed before the Royal Commission on Trade Unions in 1966 was *whether* the courts, or the Registrar, should be given some such new power of control.

(ii) THE CONTRACT IN THE UNION RULE BOOK
(a) The Parties

[*Note:* On the question whether the contract is made between a registered union and its members, or between members *inter se*, or both, see *post*, p. 643: *Bonsor* v. *Musicians' Union* [1956] A.C. 104. Where the union is unregistered, the contract must be only among members *inter se*. As to unregistered unions, see *ante*, p. 548.]

(b) The Members' Right to Enforce the Contract: Irregularities

COTTER v. NATIONAL UNION OF SEAMEN

Court of Appeal [1929] 2 Ch. 58

The plaintiffs' union was asked by a deputation of miners to lend to the miners £10,000 free of interest so that they could form a Miners' Non-Political Movement, the plaintiffs' union being in the words of the deputation 'an organisation which had already put politics from their midst'. Despite strong opposition from various officials of the union including the plaintiffs', a resolution purporting to authorise the loan was passed at a special general meeting, and also a resolution suspending two of the plaintiffs from office. The plaintiffs unsuccessfully sought a declaration that the meeting was invalidly convened and that resolutions were therefore invalid.

RUSSELL, L.J.: Is that a resolution which it was within the powers of the trade union to pass? In my opinion, clearly it was, in view of the provision of sub-rule 1 of rule III, which includes amongst the objects of the union to provide funds to extend the adoption of trade union principles.

This being a resolution *intra vires* the trade union, the next question is this: is it open to individual members of the union to complain of that proposed *intra vires* application of the trade union funds?

In considering that question I am going to assume in favour of the plaintiffs that all and every the allegations of irregularities concerning both the meeting of the executive council on July 7 and 8, and concerning the special general meeting on August 1, are true allegations. I am not saying that they are, but I am going to assume they are, and upon that assumption let me repeat my question: Is it open to individual members of this trade union to complain of the proposed *intra vires* application of the union funds? In my opinion, no, the reason for the negative answer being the rule in *Foss* v. *Harbottle*;[1] and, as I understand that rule, it is this, that the only possible plaintiff in an action to stop an act *intra vires* the corporation is the corporation itself.

In reply to that it was suggested by Sir Henry Slesser that the rule in *Foss* v. *Harbottle* has no application to a registered trade union; because, as he alleged, the members of a registered trade union have a proprietary interest in the union's funds which they are individually entitled to protect; and for that he relies upon the words of s. 8 of the Act of 1871, which provides that—I read it shortly—'all the real and personal estate whatsoever belonging to any trade union registered under this Act shall be vested in the trustees for the time being of the trade union appointed as provided by this Act, for the use and benefit of such trade union and the members thereof.' That is the relevant portion of the section. But notwithstanding those words relating to the members, it is, in my opinion, clear, as was stated by Lord Lindley, in the *Taff Vale* case,[2] that the beneficial owner of the funds is the union and not the individual members of the union. Whatever the exact nature of the interest of the members may be, it is subject to the uncontrollable power of the union to apply the union funds for *intra vires* purposes, and so the opportunity for the application of the *Foss* v. *Harbottle* rule equally applies.

Then the second argument against the application of the *Foss* v. *Harbottle* rule was this, that in regard to this particular trade union it was inapplicable, because the general meetings were not meetings of the members of the union but were meetings only of delegates. That is a perfectly true allegation, because as I read rule XVII, the general meetings, whether they are annual general meetings or special general meetings, are composed of delegates appointed by the members, and are not composed of the body of members themselves. But, in my opinion, that makes no difference to the application of the rule. That appears to me to be only a question of the machinery by which, under the constitution of the particular union, the views and desires of the union are to be ascertained.

The rule in *Foss* v. *Harbottle* really works by means of something in the nature of a dilemma. The only possible plaintiff to stop an *intra vires* act is the corporation itself. If an individual is in a position to be able to use the name of the corporation then the majority are in agreement with him. If he is not in a position to use that name, then the

---

[1] 2 Hare, 461. [2] [1901] A.C. 426, 444.

majority are in disagreement with him, and he is not entitled to bring an action in his own name.

LORD HANWORTH, M.R., and LAWRENCE, L.J., delivered concurring judgments.

EDWARDS v. HALLIWELL

Court of Appeal   [1950] 2 All E.R. 1064

Two members of a trade union claimed a declaration that an alteration of the union rules adopted at a delegates' meeting was invalid because it altered the amount of regular contributions to be paid by employed members without the holding of a ballot of the members and the obtaining of a two-thirds majority—both of which the rules demanded. The action was brought by the plaintiffs on behalf of themselves and all other members of the branch.

JENKINS, L.J.: I will pass to the argument based on the reluctance of the court to interfere with the domestic affairs of a company or association on the ground of mere irregularity in form in the conduct of those affairs, and the argument based on the more general proposition commonly called the rule in *Foss* v. *Harbottle*. As to the contention that, even though the purported alteration of the tables of contributions was invalid, the court should not interfere because the omission to hold a ballot and obtain a two-thirds majority as required by rule 19 was a mere irregularity in point of form, in my judgment, that argument can be shortly dismissed by saying that this was not a matter of form. It was a matter of substance. The relevant part of rule 19, I conceive, was designed to protect members against increases in the rates of contributions unless those increases were agreed to by a particular majority of members on a vote obtained in a particular way—that is to say, a two-thirds majority on a ballot vote. It seems to me that the executive committee's disregard of that express provision in the rules was a wrong done to each individual member on a point of substance. I say 'on a point of substance', because it is *nihil ad rem* to point out that the increases in question were merely a matter of pence per week. In my judgment, this question should be viewed in precisely the same way as if the increase had been a matter of pounds, which might have made a substantial difference to the financial position of the members. In my judgment, the case cited on this part of the argument—*Amalgamated Society of Engineers* v. *Jones*[1]—has no bearing on the facts of the present case. In that case a meeting had been held and certain resolutions passed,

---
[1] (1913) 29 T.L.R. 484.

and it was suggested that the mode of convening the meeting was irregular. The learned judge was able to hold that there had been no wrong done as a matter of substance, but that there had been a mere irregularity in procedure and he took the view that, in those circumstances, the court should not interfere. For the reasons I have endeavoured to state, I regard the present case as an entirely different one.

The rule in *Foss* v. *Harbottle*, as I understand it, comes to no more than this. First, the proper plaintiff in an action in respect of a wrong alleged to be done to a company or association of persons is *prima facie* the company or the association of persons itself. Secondly, where the alleged wrong is a transaction which might be made binding on the company or association and on all its members by a simple majority of the members, no individual member of the company is allowed to maintain an action in respect of that matter for the simple reason that, if a mere majority of the members of the company or association is in favour of what has been done, then *cadit quæstio*. No wrong had been done to the company or association and there is nothing in respect of which anyone can sue. If, on the other hand, a simple majority of members of the company or association is against what has been done, then there is no valid reason why the company or association itself should not sue. In my judgment, it is implicit in the rule that the matter relied on as constituting the cause of action should be a cause of action properly belonging to the general body of the corporation or members of the company or association as opposed to a cause of action which some individual member can assert in his own right.

The cases falling within the general ambit of the rule are subject to certain exceptions. It has been noted in the course of argument that in cases where the act complained of is wholly *ultra vires* the company or association the rule has no application because there is no question of the transaction being confirmed by any majority. It has been further pointed out that where what has been done amounts to what is generally called in these cases a fraud on the minority and the wrongdoers are themselves in control of the company, the rule is relaxed in favour of the aggrieved minority who are allowed to bring what is known as a minority shareholders' action on behalf of themselves and all others. The reason for this is that, if they were denied that right, their grievance could never reach the court because the wrongdoers themselves, being in control, would not allow the company to sue. Those exceptions are not directly in point in this case, but they show, especially the last one, that the rule is not an inflexible rule and it will be relaxed where necessary in the interests of justice.

There is a further exception which seems to me to touch this case directly. That is the exception noted by Romer, J., in *Cotter* v. *National Union of Seamen*. He pointed out that the rule did not prevent an individual member from suing if the matter in respect of which he was suing was one which could validly be done or sanctioned, not by a simple majority of the members of the company or association, but only by some special majority, as, for instance, in the case of a limited company under the Companies Act, a special resolution duly passed as such. As Romer, J., pointed out, the reason for that exception is clear, because otherwise, if the rule were applied in its full rigour, a company which, by its directors, had broken its own regulations by doing something without a special resolution which could only be done validly by a special resolution could assert that it alone was the proper plaintiff in any consequent action and the effect would be to allow a company acting in breach of its articles to do *de facto* by ordinary resolution that which according to its own regulations could only be done by special resolution. That exception exactly fits the present case inasmuch as here the act complained of is something which could only have been validly done, not by a simple majority, but by a two-thirds majority obtained on a ballot vote. In my judgment, therefore, the reliance on the rule in *Foss* v. *Harbottle* in the present case may be regarded as misconceived on that ground alone.

I would go further. In my judgment, this is a case of a kind which is not even within the general ambit of the rule. It is not a case where what is complained of is a wrong done to the union, a matter in respect of which the cause of action would primarily and properly belong to the union. It is a case in which certain members of a trade union complain that the union, acting through the delegate meeting and the executive council in breach of the rules by which the union and every member of the union are bound, has invaded the individual rights of the complainant members, who are entitled to maintain themselves in full membership with all the rights and privileges appertaining to that status so long as they pay contributions in accordance with the tables of contributions as they stood before the purported alterations of 1943, unless and until the scale of contributions is validly altered by the prescribed majority obtained on a ballot vote. Those rights, these members claim, have been invaded. The gist of the case is that the personal and individual rights of membership of each of them have been invaded by a purported, but invalid, alteration of the tables of contributions. In those circumstances, it seems to me the rule in *Foss* v. *Harbottle* has no application at all, for the individual members who are suing sue, not in the right of the union, but in their own right to protect from invasion their own individual rights as members.

I would be content so to hold as a matter of self-evident principle, but the matter is not free from authority. It will, I think, be enough for the present purposes if I refer, briefly, to a passage in the judgment of Sir George Jessel, M.R., in *Pender* v. *Lushington*. There was a discussion in the course of the case whether the action was one which an individual shareholder could maintain and Sir George Jessel, M.R., said (6 Ch.D. 80): 'But there is another ground on which the action may be maintained. This is an action by Mr Pender for himself. He is a member of the company, and whether he votes with the majority or the minority he is entitled to have his vote recorded—an individual right in respect of which he has a right to sue. That has nothing to do with the question like that raised in *Foss* v. *Harbottle* and that line of cases. He has a right to say, "Whether I vote in the majority or minority, you shall record my vote, as that is a right of property belonging to my interest in this company, and if you refuse to record my vote I will institute legal proceedings against you to compel you." What is the answer to such an action? It seems to me it can be maintained as a matter of substance, and that there is no technical difficulty in maintaining it.'

In my judgment, precisely the same conclusions as are there expressed apply in the present case, and the rule in *Foss* v. *Harbottle* affords no answer to the action. It was sought to show that this was not a matter affecting the individual rights of any particular member of the union because all were subject to the same alteration of the tables and, therefore, it was a matter which affected the general body of members as a whole. I do not agree. For one thing, the contributions to be paid by any individual member would depend on the particular category of membership to which he belonged, but, for another thing and more important, it seems to me that, although all the members are liable to pay the subscriptions appropriate to their respective categories, the right of each member to maintain himself in membership by paying his subscription—that is to say, by paying whatever subscription appropriate to his case is validly fixed and for the time being in force under the rules—is an individual right of his own which he himself is entitled to protect by an action on his own behalf.

It was pointed out in the course of the argument (though the matter was not fully developed) that the vast majority of members of the union had, in fact, paid without demur subscriptions at the new and invalid rate. It was further pointed out that those who had become entitled to benefits had taken benefits at the enhanced rate. It was further pointed out that in practice rule 19(1) had never been resorted to for many years. Before Vaisey, J., these matters seem to have been put forward as amounting to such acquiescence as to make rule 19(1) a dead letter which could no longer be enforced. That argument was not pressed before us, but these considerations were put as showing that the case was without substance. It was said that the fact that the vast majority of members had paid the new rate of subscriptions without demur demonstrated that the will of the union as a whole was in favour of the new subscriptions and consequently the action was without substance. I cannot agree. I cannot regard the mere paying by individual members of the increased rates without demur as equivalent to a ballot vote at which a two-thirds majority was obtained in favour of the alteration. In my judgment, the scale of contributions as fixed in the rules before the disputed alteration must stand unless and until altered in accordance with rule 19. It not having been so altered, the rates so fixed remain the only rates properly exigible, and no member is bound to pay any other rate except as a matter of individual consent. It may well be that in most cases it would be found, when the particular member's account was gone into, that he had by his conduct in paying the new rate of subscription expressed his individual consent to the alteration and thereby become bound, but I see no ground in principle or in authority for holding that these individual assents arising from the conduct of individual members can have any binding effect at all on those members who say: 'We are prepared to pay the contributions validly exigible under the rules and no more.'

Sir Raymond Evershed, M.R., and Asquith, L.J., concurred.

McNAMEE v. COOPER

The Times, 8 September 1966

The plaintiff sought an injunction to stop his union delegation from voting at the T.U.C. conference in favour of the policy of the Government concerning 'incomes policy'. He alleged that the delegates and the union's general council were bound by the terms of a composite motion carried at the union congress which expressed opposition to such policies.

GOFF, J. said that the composite motion was overwhelmingly carried at the meeting of the union congress. At a meeting of the national executive committee of the union on 4 August 1966, it was resolved that support be given to the action of the General Council of the Trades Union Congress up to the present in acquiescing in the Government's proposals on the prices and incomes policy. The resolution was circulated to branches of the union by district secretaries. A special meeting of the General Council of the union was convened for 22 August 1966, in London for the purpose of discussing the action of the Government in relation to the Prices and Incomes Bill.

On a resolution on that day before the general council that the union should support the measures outlined in the Bill, the plaintiff moved an amendment to the effect that the policy of the union on the question had already been decided at the annual congress and should be adhered to. That amendment was defeated by 22 votes to two. The general council thereupon circulated by district secretaries to branches a statement of policy.

The plaintiff alleged that that policy was inconsistent with the composite motion because the motion rejected any standstill in the rates of pay of the lower paid industries and services and there was no mention of that in the resolution which said that that would be a question after the standstill.

The question really was one of the construction of the union rules. Rule 3(1) provided that the supreme authority of the union should be vested in the congress which should be held every year on dates to be determined by the national executive committee. Rule 4(2) provided that the business of the congress should be the consideration and determination of internal questions of policy affecting the general industrial, political and social welfare of the members; to receive reports from the general secretary; and the district secretaries and otherwise as in such subrule provided.

It was provided by rule 5(5) that the government of the union and the conduct of trade disputes should be vested in a general council. Rule 5(7) provided, among other things, that the general council might exercise all and any such powers and perform all such acts, duties and obligations as might be necessary to attain or were incidental to or conducive to the attainment of the objects and general interests of the union whether such powers, duties and obligations were specifically mentioned in the rules or not. Rule 5(15) provided that any matter not provided for in the rules should be decided by the general council.

On their construction the rules provided that what was admitted to the congress was internal matters and that congress must consider all matters on the agenda. The composite motion must have been determined as it was on the agenda, and was a matter rightly taken by the congress. Being a decision of the congress it was binding on the general council.

The question then was whether the Court ought to interfere. It was said for the plaintiff that he was being deprived of his proprietory right of casting a vote. Had the general council acted properly a congress would have been convened. As he was a member of the general council he was a member of the congress and was entitled to vote there. In such a case the matter would have been put to vote and he would have exercised his right.

The plaintiff had, in fact, voted and his vote had been counted. That argument could not be accepted. What was happening was that the general council was allegedly about to act contrary to the policy of the union laid down by the congress. It was said that that was an *ultra vires* act. As the general council was only acting, if what the plaintiff alleged was right, contrary to the composite motion and not outside the scope of the rules of the union it was in breach of the rules. Its acts could not be regarded as *ultra vires*.

As this was a breach of the rules the Court would not interfere unless property rights were affected. This was not a case where interlocutory relief ought to be granted.

NOTE ON INTERNAL IRREGULARITIES

Where the irregularity is one of a procedural character only, it is clear that the 'Rule in *Foss* v. *Harbottle*' operates, and the individual member cannot bring an action, even if the rules in the rule book are infringed. See for example *Chapple* v. *Electrical Trades Union*, *The Times*, 22 November 1961 (out of the fifty delegates, one from each division, at a rules revision conference, four had not been properly elected through minor irregularities; it was held that a member could not obtain an injunction based on these irregularities so as to render the whole proceedings invalid). But, as in company law, there is an uncertain area of exception concerning the 'individual rights' of each member. In *McNamee* v. *Cooper* (*ante*, p. 589) Goff, J. may have interpreted this area unduly narrowly. The individual rights in respect of which any member is entitled to bring an action include not merely specific rights of property or of voting. They appear also to include a right to *have the affairs of the association conducted in accordance with the rules* of the constitution in any matter which is not purely one of minor procedure. See for example the parallel rights of a shareholder to have the affairs of his company 'conducted in accordance with its articles of association': Jenkins, L.J., *Re Harmer* [1958] 3 All E.R. 689, 704; discussed in Wedderburn [1957] *Camb. Law J.* 194.

(c) The Problem of s. 4, Trade Union Act, 1871*

RIGBY *v.* CONNOL

(1880) 14 Ch.D. 482

The plaintiff alleged that he had been wrongfully expelled from a trade union and claimed a declaration that he was entitled to participate in the property and benefits of the union.

JESSEL, M.R.: The first question that I will consider is, what is the jurisdiction of a Court of Equity as regards interfering at the instance of a member of a society to prevent his being improperly expelled therefrom? I have no doubt whatever that the foundation of the jurisdiction is the right of property vested in the member of the society, and of which he is unjustly deprived by such unlawful expulsion. There is no such jurisdiction that I am aware of reposed, in this country at least, in any of the Queen's Courts to decide upon the rights of persons to associate together when the association possesses no property. Persons, and many persons, do associate together without any property in common at all. A dozen people may agree to meet and play whist at each other's houses for a certain period, and if eleven of them refuse to associate with the twelfth any longer, I am not aware that there is any jurisdiction in any Court of Justice in this country to interfere.... If that is the foundation of the jurisdiction, the Plaintiff, if he can succeed at all, must succeed on the ground that some right of property to which he is entitled has been taken away from him.

There was a great difficulty in suing and getting their property from

---

* *Note:* In *Edinburgh Master Plumbers' Assocn.* v. *Munro*, 1928, S.C. 565, the Court of Session held that an action to enforce an arbitrator's award, arising from an arbitration clause in a contract caught by s. 4, was not a legal proceeding brought to enforce the contract and, therefore, not barred by the section. But Streatfeild, J., has said that such an action on an award 'may well amount to a proceeding instituted with the object of directly enforcing an agreement' caught by the section: *Birtley District Co-operative Soc. Ltd* v. *Windy Nook and District Co-operative Soc. Ltd* [1960] 2 Q.B. 1 (overruled on other points *Bellshill and Mossend Co-op. Soc.* v. *Dalziel Co-op. Soc.* [1960] A. C. 832).

third persons, and one object of the Act was to enable these societies to sue in respect of their property, and also to enable them to hold property, such as a house or office, but it was not intended that the contracts entered into by the members of the society should be made legal contracts *inter se*, so that Courts of Justice should interfere to enforce them. If that had been intended the result would have been this, that an agreement between a number of workmen once entered into, compelling them to work in a particular manner, or to abstain from working in a particular manner, would have been enforceable according to law, and to a certain extent would have reduced some portion of the workmen to a condition of something like serfdom and slavery. Of course the Legislature, by interfering, had no idea of doing anything of that sort. Again, the Act recognises the principle that men may enter into any contract they think fit: there is an exception in the case of a contract for borrowing in this country, and I hope that exception will always remain in whatever form that contract may be expressed.

Then the Act goes on to provide...by s. 3, for the same reason, that the purposes shall not be unlawful so as to render void or voidable any agreement or trust. That applies to the rules of this union, and does not render them unlawful for being in restraint of trade, and then there comes this provision in s. 4: 'Nothing in this Act shall enable the Court to entertain any legal proceedings instituted with the object of directly enforcing or recovering damages for the breach of any of the following agreements.' Then it specifies what they are, and one of them is, 'any agreement for the application of the funds of a trades union to provide benefits for members.'

I am satisfied that the agreement contained in the rules is an agreement to provide benefits for members, and that, if I decide in favour of the Plaintiff, I directly enforce that agreement, because I declare him entitled to participate in the property of the union, and the only property they have is their subscriptions and fines, and I restrain the society from preventing that participation. It seems to me that is directly enforcing that agreement, in fact, it is in substance directing and enforcing the specific performance of it, nothing more or less.

WOLFE *v.* MATTHEWS

(1882) 21 Ch.D. 194

In an action brought by and on behalf of members of the London West End Farriers Trade Society for an injunction against the defendants, to prevent them from using union funds to carry out an amalgamation with another union rather than paying out benefits, it was argued that such an injunction would be a direct enforcement of an agreement for the application of the funds to provide benefits for members.

FRY, J.: Then I must look to see what is the nature of this application. The Plaintiffs say that having contributed to the common funds of this association they are entitled to the benefits which it was contracted they should have in return for such contributions; and they also claim these same benefits on behalf of other members of the *Association*; and on the ground that an inconsistent application of the funds is about to be made by the Defendants to some other persons, not according to the rules of the *Association*, they ask for an injunction to restrain such improper application.

Now it is plain that this is not an action to recover damages for the breach of an agreement, neither is it, in my judgment, an action to directly enforce an agreement, which proceedings are alone mentioned in the 4th section. An order that the Defendants should pay money to the Plaintiffs would be a direct enforcement of an agreement for the application of the funds, but all that is sought here is to prevent the payment of the moneys to somebody else. Either that is no enforcement of an agreement at all, or it is an indirect enforcement. To take a simple case, if there is a contract by A to pay £100 to B, that contract is directly enforced by a judgment of the Court directing A to pay to B. And the contract is only indirectly enforced or not at all by a judgment restraining A from paying the money to some one else. It is only by a stretch of language that such an order can be said to enforce A's contract; the utmost that can be said is, that it is then more likely that A will pay to B. For these reasons I am of opinion that the judgment of the Master of the Rolls in *Rigby* v. *Connol* does not apply to this case, and that the preliminary objection must be overruled, though it will remain to be seen whether the terms of the Act will eventually permit any relief to be given by the Court to the Plaintiffs.

YORKSHIRE MINERS' ASSOCIATION *v.* HOWDEN

House of Lords   [1905] A.C. 256

A dispute arose between colliers and their workmen as to whether the men should be paid extra for 'bag dirt', a substance which had to be removed before the coal could be got out. The men went on strike without official union sanction. This was later granted when it seemed to the union that the strike had become a lock-out. The union rules provided that its funds should be applied to carrying out the specific objects stated in the rules. The plaintiffs challenged the payment by the union of strike pay to the men in the collieries on the ground that there was no provision for the present situation where approval by the union was given after the cessation of work and the men were not thrown out of work as a result of the union's action. The plaintiff was granted an injunction.* [See too *ante* p. 466 and p. 551.]

LORD MACNAGHTEN: Was, then, the payment of strike-money in the present case authorized by the rules of the association? On this point your Lordships did not think it necessary to call upon the respondent. The question is fully discussed and completely disposed of by the opinions of the learned Lords Justices in the Court of Appeal, and I have nothing to add to what they said. Then if the action of the association, which was challenged by the plaintiff, was beyond the powers of the association, it seems clear, apart, of course, from any objection arising under the Act of 1871, that in an unincorporated society like this any single member suing alone would have a right to resist it and to call upon the Court to interpose by injunction. That was established in this House in the case of *Simpson* v. *Westminster Palace Hotel Co.*,[1] and is, I apprehend, beyond question.

So far it is all plain sailing. The difficulty, such as it is, is found in the Act of 1871. But the difficulty, if I may presume to say so, is, I think, not so much in the language of the Act as in the language of the learned judges who have expounded it. The commentaries are in fault rather than the text.

The Act of 1871 relieves trade unions from consequences which would otherwise result from the purposes of the union being in restraint of trade. That circumstance by itself is not to render void or voidable any agreement or trust. But, on the other hand, this concession to modern ideas is not to make all trade union contracts enforceable at law. Nothing in the Act is to 'enable any Court to entertain any legal proceeding instituted with the object of directly enforcing or recovering

---

[1] (1860) 8 H.L.C. 712.

* Compare *Sansom* v. *London and Provincial Union of Licensed Vehicle Workers* (1920) 36 T.L.R. 666. Members of the union who were on strike were entitled to dispute pay. In addition, there was a system whereby men on strike sold tickets to members still in work to raise an extra fund for striking members. The union used some of the 'ticket money' to pay ordinary dispute pay. The plaintiff members were granted a declaration and injunction to prevent the union so misapplying the 'ticket money'. But Bray, J., held that this money, though it was impressed with a special trust, was within the term 'union funds'; and that s. 4 therefore precluded him from granting the plaintiffs' request for a receiver and account of the money already paid out.

damages for the breach of' any of the several agreements which the enactment goes on to specify.

Now the first question that arises on this part of the enactment is, What is the meaning of the expression 'directly enforcing'? I cannot think that the Legislature intended to strike at proceedings for directly enforcing certain agreements, leaving untouched and unaffected all proceedings (other than actions for damages) designed to enforce those particular agreements indirectly. To forbid direct action in language that suggests that the object of the action so forbidden may be attained by a side-wind seems to me somewhat of a novelty in legislation. I venture to think that the word 'directly' is only put in to give point to the antithesis between proceedings to enforce agreements directly and proceedings to recover damages for breach of contract, which tend, though indirectly, to give force and strength to the agreement for breach of which an action may be brought. However, I need not dwell on this point, for it seems to me that for the present purpose the result must be the same whatever meaning or effect may be attached to the expression 'directly'.

The agreements which the Court is not at liberty to deal with are arranged under five headings or classes.... At first sight it is not very easy to see why the clause took this shape. I cannot help thinking that it comes from the apprehension which the leaders of the workmen then felt of the extreme danger to their combinations which might result from any attempt to separate the funds of the union, distinguishing between those collected or intended for benevolent purposes and those collected or intended for ordinary trade purposes.

Then I come to the question, What was the 'object' of the present litigation? Was it to enforce an agreement for the application of the funds of the union to provide benefits to members? I should say certainly not. The object of the litigation was to obtain an authoritative decision that the action of the union which was challenged by the plaintiff was not authorized by the rules of the union. The decision might take the form of a declaration or the form of an injunction, or both combined. But the decision, whatever form it might take, would be the end of the litigation. No administration or application of the funds of the union was sought or desired. The object of the litigation was simply to prevent misapplication of the funds of the union, not to administer those funds, or to apply them for the purpose of providing benefits to members.

I am aware that in expressing this view I am dissenting from the opinion of Sir George Jessel in the case of *Rigby* v. *Connol*.

LORD LINDLEY: But the Act of 1871 does more for trade unions than remove the consequences of being regarded as illegal societies; it allows them to a great extent to manage their own affairs free from the control of the ordinary Courts of the country (s. 4), and enables them to register themselves under a name (ss. 13, 14, and 1st schedule), and to obtain summary redress against their officials in cases of misconduct (s. 12). Further, it enables them to hold property by trustees (s. 8), and enables the trustees to sue and be sued in respect of such property (s. 9).

One thing, however, the Act of 1871 did not do. It did not incorporate trade unions even when registered under the Act with a name. A trade union holds property by trustees; but not being incorporated there is no one legal person or entity in whom the beneficial interest in the property of a trade union is vested. The beneficiaries are its members collectively and severally. This is plain from s. 8, which vests the property of every registered trade union in trustees for the use and benefit of such trade union and the members thereof. A trade union is, and its name is only a convenient designation for, an unincorporated society of individuals, and this observation must not be lost sight of on the present occasion. Prior to the decision of this House in the *Taff Vale Railway Co.* v. *Amalgamated Society of Railway Servants*,[1] it was doubtful whether a registered trade union could sue or be sued in its registered name. The House decided that it could be so sued in an action for an injunction against its agents. But care was taken in that case to point out that a trade union is not an incorporated society, although it may be sued in its registered name.

The Trade Union Act, 1871, contains a carefully framed scheme to enable trade unions to acquire and to hold through the medium of trustees funds for the benefit of their members who, as already observed, are expressly mentioned in s. 8. Unless something can be found in the Act to the contrary, the natural legal inference would be that the ordinary equitable machinery for preserving the trust property and for executing the trusts on which it is held would be available for the members....

But it is said that s. 4 of the Act of 1871 expressly excludes the jurisdiction of the Courts from interfering in this case. I confess I cannot adopt this conclusion. Before turning to the section let me remind your Lordships what the object of this action is, and what the judgment appealed from really does.

[1] [1901] A.C. 426, *ante*, p. 541.

The action is not to enforce a contract between the plaintiff and the defendants; its object is to vindicate a right to property. All trusts except those created by statute or by will may be said to be created by a contract between the parties to the instrument creating the trusts. But those trusts can be enforced in equity by any person entitled to the benefit of them. A suit by a *cestui que* trust against his trustee is not what is usually understood as a proceeding to enforce an agreement; if it were, the suit could only be maintained by some person who was a party to the agreement creating the trust.

But, further, the object of this action is not to distribute funds held in trust for the members of the trade union, nor to obtain payment of any money out of them, nor in any way to administer those funds. The plaintiff, who is a member of the trade union, and who is beneficially interested in its funds, complains that those who have control of them threaten and intend to apply them to purposes not authorized by the rules of the association; and the whole object of the action is to obtain an injunction to restrain that intended misapplication of the funds. The order appealed from does this, and when properly understood does no more....

The words are: 'Nothing in this Act shall enable any Court to entertain any legal proceeding instituted with the object of directly enforcing or recovering damages for the breach of any of the following agreements.' Pausing here for a moment, the words just quoted suggest the following observations: (1) The section extends not only to Courts of law, but also to Courts of equity. (2) The section does not prohibit any Court from exercising in any case jurisdiction which it could have exercised before the Act passed the section simply prevents any Court from extending its jurisdiction, and interfering in cases in which the Act would authorize interference if it were not for the direct prohibition contained in the section. (3) No legal proceeding which might be taken if the section did not prohibit it is prohibited, except a legal proceeding instituted with the object of directly enforcing or recovering damages for the breach of the specified agreements. The word 'directly' is important and limits the application of the section. Legal proceedings for other purposes than those specified are not prohibited, although they may indirectly affect agreements on which no action can be brought....My Lords, I am myself quite unable to see that these words include such an action as that which has been brought in this case. The object of this action is not directly to enforce any agreement for the application of the funds of the trade union in any of the ways specified under the third head. The object of the action is not to apply the funds, but to preserve them for future application; and to my mind this action is no more struck at by s. 4 than is an action brought by the trustees for the recovery of the funds of the trade union from some person wrongfully in possession of them.

EARL OF HALSBURY, L.C. and LORD ROBERTSON concurred; LORD DAVEY and LORD JAMES dissented.

GOZNEY v. BRISTOL TRADE AND PROVIDENT SOCIETY

Court of Appeal [1909] 1 K.B. 901

The plaintiff member was fined 2s. 6d., by way of deduction from sick pay to which his union rules entitled him, because of his alleged breach of the society's rules. The union was registered; various benefits were payable to members; but strike pay was payable only out of a special fund to which members were not compelled to contribute. He brought this action for a declaration that he had not broken the rules and for return of the 2s. 6d. The union argued that it was an association in restraint of trade and that the court was therefore precluded from entertaining the action by s. 4, Trade Union Act, 1871. The Court of Appeal rejected this argument on the ground that the union's rules were not unlawful at common law.*

BUCKLEY, L.J.: Looking at these rules, and having regard to the above considerations, my view of them may be shortly expressed by saying that, so far as trade benefits are concerned, the rules amount to no more than insurance of the members against the consequences of a strike. Provisions to encourage or procure a strike may be illegal. Provisions for the assistance of the victims of a strike may be perfectly legal. In these rules I can find no provisions addressed to the procurement or even the sanction of a strike. The rules do not, it is true, as did the rules in *Swaine* v. *Wilson*,[1] provide that one of the objects shall be to render assistance to members when out of employment, but rule 7 is really a rule in this direction. It contemplates that a member is in search of work, gives him assistance when out of employment, and provides by s. 4 that his allowance shall be stopped if he refuses work at the current rate except in an event, namely, that he is asked to fill the place of one fighting for better conditions. Here is a scintilla of

[1] 24 Q.B.D. 252.

* See O Kahn-Freund, 'The Illegality of a Trade Union' (1943) 7 M.L.R. 192.

assistance to maintaining a strike. This may fall into the observations which I have to make upon the principal rule in this connection, namely, rule 40. The effect of that rule, I think, is that if a strike takes place (s. 4) members are to have assistance, but that that assistance even is not available in the case of all strikes, but only (s. 2) in support of certain strikes, while by s. 6, which seems to me of first-class importance in this connection, it is provided that no officer or member shall take any active interest or aid in any way or otherwise assist any trade movement except in his private capacity. This is a direct veto upon procuring or inciting a strike. That the rules to a certain extent assist a strike by giving assistance to persons when there is a strike is true. But upon the authority of *Denaby and Cadeby Main Collieries, Ltd* v. *Yorkshire Miners' Association*[1] this is, within proper limits, not illegal. I find nothing here to exceed proper limits.

My conclusion, therefore, upon reading these rules, is that there is not here any such provision in restraint of trade as to render the society illegal. Under these circumstances, the questions which have been argued upon the several Acts of Parliament do not arise.

COZENS-HARDY, M.R. and FLETCHER MOULTON, L.J. concurred.

OSBORNE *v.* AMALGAMATED SOCIETY OF RAILWAY SERVANTS

Court of Appeal　　　　　　　　　　　　　　　　　　[1911] 1 Ch. 540

The plaintiff brought an action to obtain reinstatement as a member of the defendant Trade Union on the ground that his expulsion was *ultra vires* and void.

FLETCHER MOULTON, L.J.: To illustrate the combined effect of ss. 3 and 4 of the Act I will take an example which is quite outside the circumstances of the present case. Suppose that a trade union agrees to make a contribution to an employer in consideration of his acting in conformity with the rules or resolutions of the union. Such an agreement is valid under the provisions of s. 3 of the Act. To use the funds of the trade union for the purpose of making such a payment is neither *ultra vires* on the part of the officials of the trade union nor a breach of trust on the part of the trustees in whom those funds are vested. If the payments are made they are in the eye of the law payments made for valid consideration and can under no circumstances be recovered back. But such a contract comes within the provisions of clause 4. It

---
[1] [1906] A.C. 384.

follows that if the trade union, after making such an agreement (which, as I have said, is valid), chooses to refuse to make any of the stipulated payments, neither the aggrieved party nor any other person can compel it to do so. The law refuses its assistance in the matter, and thus in effect leaves it entirely at the option of the trade union whether it will or will not fulfil its engagement.

The only disabilities, therefore, under which a trade union or its members lie relate to the enforcement of contracts and not to their validity. In the present case we have to assume for the purposes of this argument that the plaintiff lawfully became and continued to be a member of the trade union, and that he has been wrongfully expelled therefrom. He comes to the Courts to have this wrong righted. If this had not been a trade union, but some society whose lawfulness did not depend on the Act of 1871, no one could have seriously contended that the Courts could not entertain his claim for reinstatement into his former position of membership.

Now trade unions and their members are, as I have said, in as good a position in all respects as other societies and their members, except as regards the enforcement of contracts, and there only if the contract which is sought to be enforced comes within one of the excepted classes. The contract of membership is the contract which the plaintiff seeks here to enforce. He says that he has been admitted to membership and has performed all conditions for his continuance therein. This is not denied for the purposes of to-day. But the defendants say that this demand for reinstatement is a legal proceeding instituted with the object of directly enforcing an agreement for the application of the funds of the trade union to provide benefits for members. If they are wrong in this, the appeal must be allowed and the action go to trial on the facts.

To test this, let us assume that the relief is granted, and that the plaintiff is declared a member of the trade union. Will the effect of that be to enforce an agreement for the application of the funds of the trade union to provide benefits for him? The only possible answer to this question is 'Certainly not'. By the statute that is the very thing which his membership does not entitle a man to do, and therefore declaring him a member simpliciter not only does not directly enforce an agreement for the application of funds for his benefit, but does not even help him in any future proceeding to enforce any such agreement. It seems to me to be a logical contradiction to say that to put a man in a position where he cannot enforce a particular agreement is enforcing it.

All that the Court is asked to do here is to declare that the plaintiff is entitled to the performance of the agreement to accept and to keep him as member, and inasmuch as this is not in itself an application of the funds of the trade union to provide benefits for a member and does not even enable the plaintiff by subsequent proceedings to enforce any agreement so to apply them, the subject-matter of this action appears to me to be entirely outside the excepted classes enumerated in s. 4.

BUCKLEY, L.J.: Notwithstanding that s. 3 has rendered contractual relations which include such terms lawful, the particular defined agreements are nevertheless to be unenforceable in any Court. Amongst those defined agreements is included 'any agreement for the application of the funds of a trade union to provide benefits to members'. The contention before us has been that this action is one in which the plaintiff asks the Court to entertain legal proceedings to enforce an agreement for such an application of the trade union funds and that the statute has precluded the Court from entertaining it.

The action is one brought by a plaintiff who was a member of the society and has been expelled therefrom. He asks for a declaration that the resolution for his expulsion is *ultra vires*, and an injunction to restrain the defendants from acting upon or enforcing it. He was a person who before his expulsion enjoyed certain contractual relations with the other members of the society, which even if the trade union was illegal at common law were by s. 3 of the Act lawful as matter of contract between him and his co-members. He enjoyed a vote as a member, a right to subscribe to certain funds, a right to benefits from those funds, an interest in common with his fellow members in the property of the society, a like right in all the advantages of membership, and, in case the society should be dissolved and the common purposes thus come to an end, a right to his distributive share of the assets. These rights were all, by virtue of s. 3, lawful, although some, but not all, were by virtue of s. 4 unenforceable. The right to have benefits from the funds was unenforceable; others seem to me to be clearly enforceable. There is nothing in s. 4 to forbid a Court to entertain legal proceedings to enforce the member's right to his vote or his right to his distributive share in winding up. It is quite plain that he had rights in respect of property. All the property of the society belonged to him and his co-members, and none the less because s. 4 renders unenforceable certain rights in respect of that property. His vote was property: *Pender* v. *Lushington*.[1] The jurisdiction of the Court is therefore not

---

[1] 6 Ch. D. 70.

excluded by any absence of rights of property. But it is said that an order to declare his expulsion *ultra vires* and a proper consequential injunction will be an enforcement of the agreement in the rules to apply the funds to provide him with benefits. I cannot follow the contention. The plaintiff was a member of a society with (amongst others) rights as regards those benefits which were unenforceable. How can an order to restore him to membership do more than make him what he was before, namely, a member with the same unenforceable rights? How does such an order enforce those rights? What benefit in the application of the funds is it that the order compels the society to give him? Obviously none. If he succeeds in the action he merely resumes the position in which he stood before. His rights by way of benefit are neither greater nor less than before his expulsion. The whole answer to the contention on this part of this case may be summarized in a sentence. An order to restore to membership with unenforceable rights is no order to enforce those rights.

COZENS-HARDY, M.R. concurred.

RUSSELL *v.* AMALGAMATED SOCIETY OF CARPENTERS AND JOINERS

House of Lords [1912] A.C. 421

This was an action brought by the widow and personal representative of the deceased, a carpenter, who had been a member of the respondent society for some 40 years before his death. The Society was a registered Trade Union and its trustees were also named as defendants. The action was a claim for money representing superannuation benefit to which, it was claimed, the deceased was entitled under the rules of the society at his death. In defence to the action it was pleaded that no contracts existed between the deceased and the union at the time of death. Alternatively if such contracts did exist they were in restraint of trade and unenforceable at law (s. 3 and s. 4, Trade Union Act, 1871).

LORD MACNAGHTEN: My Lords, the defendants are a registered trade union and certain officers of the union. The plaintiff is the widow of a deceased member of the society. As representative of her late husband, she claims a sum of money to which he appears to have been entitled at the time of his death under the terms and conditions of the society's agreement with him as contained in its certified rules. The defence, and the only defence we have to consider, at this stage of the proceedings is that the society was, and is, at common law an unlawful association by reason of its purposes being in restraint of trade, and that although those purposes are, according to the Trade Union Act, 1871, not unlawful so as to avoid the agreement and trust, in respect of which she is now suing, the Court is prohibited or prevented, by s. 4 of the Act, from entertaining her application.

If the defendants can make good the position on which their defence is founded they are undoubtedly entitled to the protection of the statute, and so the action must fail.

A trade union is merely an unincorporated society of individuals. The designation does not of itself import illegality. There have been many and probably there may be still some trade unions lawful in every point of view, and not depending for their legality or for their immunity on the Act of 1871. This proposition is recognized plainly in the definition of a trade union contained in the Act of 1876.

In the case of a trade union not dependent on the Trade Union Acts for its legality or immunity the law is open to the members of the society just as it is in the case of other voluntary societies for the purpose of enforcing contractual rights and trusts against the association.

The only question, therefore, seems to be this: Is this trade union, apart from the Act of 1871, a lawful association? The answer must depend on a consideration of its purposes as manifested in its rules.

It is not every restraint of trade that is unlawful. But I cannot doubt that restraint of trade which is unreasonable, oppressive, and destructive of individual liberty is unlawful. And I cannot help agreeing with the learned judges of the Court of Appeal that such is the character of some of the rules of this society, and further, that having regard to the constitution of the society, the powers vested in its executive officers, and the blending of its funds for all purposes, it is impossible to separate what is legal from what is not legal.

LORD ATKINSON: My Lords, the trade union in this case is sued in its registered name. It is true that in the *Taff Vale Case* it was held that a trade union might be sued in its trade name for wrongs committed by its agents; but when the judgments delivered in that case are examined, and especially the judgment of Farwell, J., which was unanimously approved of and adopted, it will be seen that that decision was based entirely upon the provisions of the Trade Union Act of 1871 as amended by the Act of 1876. The conclusion which, it appears to me, must necessarily be drawn from these judgments is this, that if the Act of 1871 had contained a provision to the effect that nothing in it should enable any Court to entertain any legal proceedings founded upon any tort committed by a trade union through its agents, the decision of this House in the *Taff Vale Case* would have been precisely the opposite of what it was, and that it would have been held that the trade union could not in that case have been sued *eo nomine*. But the provisions of s. 4, as regards the present action, are in effect similar to the hypothetical provisions above mentioned in their relation to such torts. All the reasoning based upon those provisions of the Act of 1871 upon which the judgments in the *Taff Vale Case* were founded is therefore inapplicable to this action.

This is an action based upon an agreement 'to provide benefits to members' and is instituted directly to enforce that agreement or to recover damages for the breach of it. The statute gives no support to such an action. Whether it can be instituted in its present form or not must depend upon the common law. It is not a representative action such as is frequently instituted in a Court of Equity. It is a common law action, and I am clearly of opinion that the defendant society cannot be sued in such an action in its registered name; nor can the trustees be sued in it in their character of trustees. Partners may no doubt be sued in the name of their firm, but that is under legislation in the form of the Rules and Orders of 1883.*

For these reasons I think the action must fail.

EARL LOREBURN, L.C. concurred in agreeing with LORD ATKINSON. LORD SHAW, LORD MERSEY and LORD ROBSON, also concurring agreed with LORD MACNAGHTEN.

* *Note on the Ambit of s. 4, Trade Union Act, 1871:* Many of the cases, as the reader will have noticed, assume that the only relevant section determining the ambit of s. 4 is s. 3 of the 1871 Act. That is to say, if a union is lawful at common law, its contracts are directly enforceable; but if the union needs s. 3 to validate its agreements, then s. 4 applies. This is obviously correct as far as it goes. But it is arguable that there is another factor of equal importance in s. 6 of the Act. Whenever a union sues or is sued by its registered name, this can be done *only* because the 1871 Act enabled it to have the status of litigant by setting up the voluntary register. Therefore, in any case where one of the parties is a *registered* union, s. 4 of the 1871 Act applies: see *The Worker and the Law* (1965) p. 310; (1966) p. 298. It has been questioned whether the word 'enables' in s. 4 is wide enough to carry this argument—by Grunfeld, *Modern Trade Union Law*, p. 71; but it is suggested that the Act in s. 6 'enables' a registered union to be a party to proceedings because of its interpretation in the *Taff Vale* case (*ante* p. 541; and see ss. 4 and 6, *ante* p. 539). Registration thus enables a union to sue or be sued in its registered name, when it otherwise could not do so, in exactly parallel fashion to the way in which the Act 'enables' it in s. 3 to carry its agreements outside the clutches of the doctrine of restraint of trade. What Lord Atkinson says inferentially supports this argument.

AMALGAMATED SOCIETY OF CARPENTERS *v.* BRAITHWAITE

House of Lords [1922] 2 A.C. 440

Lever Brothers Ltd set up a trust deed, to which no workers were party, under which certificates of £1 called 'partnership certificates' could be issued to meritorious workers who applied for them in writing and who promised they would 'loyally and faithfully further the interests of Lever Brothers Ltd, its associate companies and my co-partners'. The certificates, which could be cancelled for breach of this obligation, in return gave the worker certain rights of dividend which in practice were invested in shares of the company. The appellant union had power to expel members 'working on a co-partnership system when such system makes provision for the operatives holding only a minority of shares in the concern'. Acting under this rule, the union gave instruction that any member participating in the Lever Brothers Ltd scheme should be expelled. The plaintiff, a participant in the scheme who over eleven years had acquired 854 shares at 5s. each, sought an injunction against the union to restrain such expulsion. He was successful.

LORD BUCKMASTER: The first question that arises is whether such action can be maintained. It is alleged that it cannot, upon the ground that it is expressly prohibited by s. 4 of the Trades Union Act of 1871. ...It is said that this proceeding offends that section for two reasons: the first, that it is instituted with the object of directly enforcing an agreement between members of a trades union concerning the conditions on which they shall or shall not be employed; and secondly, because it directly enforces an agreement for the application of the funds of trades unions to provide benefits to members. I am of opinion that it does neither one thing nor the other. Looking at the words of the section alone, unaided and unembarrassed by previous decisions, I should have thought it plain that an action which in fact asks for nothing but a declaration as to the construction of a rule as to membership and as incident thereto, an injunction, was not an attempt to enforce directly any such agreement as that referred to in the statute. It is, of course, true that no such claim could lie unless there were some right of property possessed by the member by virtue of his membership. And one of the most obvious instances of such right is his right to share in the benefits provided for members. But in this action there is no direct attempt to interfere with the application of the funds at all. It is nothing but a declaration as to membership with an injunction in its support. It appears to me that it is a totally different proposition to say that a man claims to possess rights and that he seeks to enforce the obligations they create. The latter may be prevented by the statute; the former is not. Nor is he seeking to enforce an agreement with regard to the terms upon which workmen are to be employed. He says that the conditions imposed do not apply to the conditions of his labour, which is the exact opposite of any attempt to enforce such conditions.... In *Yorkshire Miners' Association* v. *Howden*[1], in a judgment which binds this House, it was decided that an application to prevent by injunction the application of the funds of a trade union for a purpose for which they were not authorized was an action which it was competent for any member of the union to maintain, and I find it impossible by any refinement of language or argument to accede to the present appellants' contention without disregarding the opinion of Lord Macnaghten [in that case]...

Again, in *Osborne* v. *Amalgamated Society of Railway Servants*,[2] a decision was reached which actually covers the present dispute, except so far as it relates to the conditions of labour; for there an expelled member was held entitled to maintain an action asking a declaration that the rule under which he was expelled was *ultra vires* and an ancillary injunction. It is, however, true that in the judgment of Buckley L.J. there are sentences[3] which suggest that an action in which the relief was based upon the construction of the rules would be one that it would not be possible for the Court to entertain, and he relies on the case of *Chamberlain's Wharf* v. *Smith*[4] as an illustration of this principle. The words I refer to are as follows: 'The point in *Chamberlain's Wharf* v. *Smith* was as follows: There was a rule in that case which fell within the words of s. 4, "agreement concerning the conditions on which any members...shall sell their goods". For a breach of the rule the plaintiffs were expelled in exercise of a power of expulsion in the rules. They asked for an injunction to restrain the defendants from acting on the resolution, alleging that they had not had a fair opportunity of being heard in their own defence. Their case, therefore, was that they had not broken the rule. To adjudicate in the action would have involved an investigation whether they had broken it or not. This the Court could not entertain'. I differ, with the greatest hesitation and reluctance, from any statement of the noble and learned Lord, but I

---

[1] [1905] A.C. 256, 265.
[3] [1911] 1 Ch. 569.
[2] [1911] 1 Ch. 540.
[4] [1900] 2 Ch. 605.

cannot accept this view of the statute and the authorities. *Chamberlain's Wharf* v. *Smith* was clearly based on the wider view of *Rigby* v. *Connol*[1]: see Lord Alverstone, M.R. at foot of p. 612; and Collins, L.J. at p. 615. And this view cannot, after the decision in [1905] A.C., be any longer accepted. To construe a rule is not directly to enforce any agreement between the members, and I am unable to see any reason why the words of the statute should be so extended as to exclude a trade union itself or any of its members from obtaining the advantage of having obscure words construed by a wholly independent and impartial tribunal....

Turning now to the words of the rule, I find it difficult to construe them as the appellants desire. It seems to me that the meaning of the words is that there must be a system which includes as part of its terms the allotment of shares and also makes no provision for the workmen holding more than a minority. I cannot, on any other reading, give an intelligible meaning to the words 'when such system makes provision for the operatives holding only a minority of shares in the concern', for these words seem to me to involve the proposition that the system itself provides for the allotment of some shares. And if this be right, the matter ends, because the present system makes no provision for the allotment of shares at all. I think also there is difficulty in showing that a workmen is working on a system of co-partnership at all when the terms of his employment as here create neither an obligation nor a right to obtain any partnership interest, although I appreciate the value of the argument that when once he has accepted the certificate he is then working on a system of which the certificate forms part. I do not, however, think it is necessary to decide this point. Finally, it was urged that this scheme was obviously within the object against which the rule was aimed, and I think this would be true.

LORD ATKINSON: The respondents never were in fact expelled from the society. Their expulsion was threatened, but not carried out. The effect, therefore, of this order is not to restore the respondents to a position which they occupied but were deprived of, but rather to quiet them in the enjoyment of the position they occupied before the threat was made, a position which they still continue to occupy with, in all cases, all their previously existing rights, privileges and disabilities. Any legal proceedings any of them could have instituted before the threat they can still institute. Any legal proceeding they were disabled from bringing before the threat they are still disabled from bringing;

[1] 14 Ch. D. 482.

and yet it is contended that a legal proceeding instituted by a person which secures for that person continuance in a position in which he is disabled from enforcing a particular contract is a proceeding directly enforcing that very contract. That appears to me to be, and I hope will always appear to me to be, a most illogical conclusion. In one sense the inflicting a pecuniary or other penalty upon a man for not doing something he is by contract or duty bound to do amounts to enforcing that contract or duty, because he will probably keep the contract or discharge the duty to avoid being mulcted in damage, but that is obviously not the sense in which the words 'directly enforcing' are used in s. 4 of the Act of 1871, since the indirect enforcement of an agreement by recovering damages for its breach is treated as a separate matter uncovered by the words 'directly enforcing'.

I do not think Lord Macnaghten, in the statement made in his judgment in *Yorkshire Miners' Association* v. *Howden*, ever meant to suggest that the word 'directly' was to have no force given to it, or that the words 'directly enforcing' include any kind of indirect enforcement of a contract other than a suit to recover damages for the breach of it.

LORD WRENBURY:...The matter may be stated tersely, I think, by saying that it is not enforcing an agreement against a party to grant an injunction to restrain him from tearing it up. When the injunction is granted and obeyed, the result is simply to leave the relations between the parties *in statu quo ante*, without enforcing them at all. It is plain that under the Act of 1871, a trade union is not outside the jurisdiction of the court altogether. It is within the jurisdiction as regards contractual obligations other than those specified in s. 4 of the Act of 1871, and is within the jurisdiction as regards the contractual obligations specified in s. 4 if the jurisdiction is invoked with an object which is not that of directly enforcing or recovering damages for the breach of the agreement...A declaration that an agreement is such that a man is a member, and an injunction in support of that declaration, are not enforcing an agreement to make him a member, or enforcing any rights which he has as a member.... If this action is confined to maintaining the contract unimpaired without enforcing it, there is nothing in the Act to stay the court from upholding it.

LORD CARSON and LORD SUMNER concurred.

BAKER *v.* INGALL

Court of Appeal   [1912] 3 K.B. 106

Rule 25 of a union provided that where a member was incapacitated for life he would be entitled to benefit of £100; but that a member receiving this benefit had to sign an agreement that if he returned to his trade he had to refund to the union all the accident benefit he had received, and that if he defaulted the council could sue to receive it. The plaintiff was severely injured and was granted this benefit; at the time of receiving it he signed an agreement in accordance with rule 25. Later he resumed work but did not repay the benefit. The union sued to recover it, but the court held the action to be unmaintainable in the light of s. 4 of the 1871 Act.

VAUGHAN WILLIAMS, L.J.: I cannot agree that the agreement of 29 August 1907, which the member has signed in pursuance of his promise contained in rule 25, sub-rule 6, is a separate and independent agreement; it is, I think, merely a part or a term of the original agreement contained in rule 25; and, if that is so, both the learned judges held that it was not enforceable in a Court of law: that is, indeed, common ground between us.

I now read the material portions of rule 25. Sub-rule 1 runs thus: 'Accident benefit. Any twelve-months' member owing not more than twelve weeks' contributions meeting with an accident, and thereby losing or disabling a limb, or suffering from bodily ailment, imperfect vision or blindness, not caused by old age, but the result of an accident to a previously healthy organ, and who, in consequence, is totally incapacitated from following his employment as a metal founder or general core maker for the remainder of his life, shall, if not disentitled according to rule, receive the sum of one hundred pounds'. Passing over sub-rule 2, I come to sub-rule 3, which says: 'Any member desiring to claim the accident benefit shall inform his branch secretary, who must bring the application before the next quarterly meeting, and if, after making the fullest inquiries, the branch is satisfied of the justice of the claim, they shall forward their report to the council for their consideration and decision'. The next that I need read is sub-rule 6, which says: 'All members receiving the accident benefit must sign an agreement that, in the event of their returning to the trade, they shall refund to the society the amount of accident benefit received. Failing to do so, the council shall be empowered to institute legal proceedings for recovery'.

In my opinion this rule 25, apart from any illegality in the society, and from the provisions of the Trade Union Act, to which I have already referred, would give to a member and to the society respectively rights which could be enforced by the one against the other. The agreement is entirely one agreement; every recital must be taken into consideration, and if an action is brought to enforce any part of it, it is an action brought to enforce an agreement for the application of the funds of the trade union and in particular an agreement for the application of trade union funds to provide benefits to members in pursuance of rule 25. That rule is headed 'Accident benefit'. I think it is impossible to divide the agreement into two parts and to treat the action as brought on the agreement to refund. I do not say that the agreement is unlawful, but I do say that it falls within s. 4, subs. 3, of the Trade Union Act, 1871.

BUCKLEY, L.J. delivered a concurring judgment; KENNEDY, L.J. dissented.

BRODIE *v.* BEVAN

(1921) 38 T.L.R. 172

The Executive Council of a union called a general ballot on the question of whether a levy on members should be raised, and the ballot was narrowly defeated. The council shortly afterwards called a second ballot to the same effect which was passed. The plaintiffs alleged this ballot was invalid because the voting papers were counted by the wrong people. They also claimed that a third ballot (taken on an alteration of the rules) was invalid, since the papers were numbered and the members' votes could be identified. The plaintiffs sought a declaration that the society could not refuse their weekly contributions when not tendered with the levy and that the second and third ballots were invalid. The action succeeded.

SARGANT, J.: There remained the question, which ought perhaps to have been decided first, whether the Court could entertain these actions at all. It had been argued on behalf of the defendants that the Court was precluded from entertaining these actions under s. 4 of the Trade Union Act, 1871...

Mr Rolt relied on subsection 2 of the section. The question under this was whether by declaring the ballots invalid he would be directly enforcing an agreement for payment of subscriptions. He was unable to see how that could be so. He was deciding not that the plaintiffs were bound to pay the levy, but that they were not bound to pay the levy under penalty of losing their membership of the society. It was urged by Mr Rolt that an agreement to pay necessarily included an agreement to receive. He (his Lordship) was unable to appreciate that, and he had drawn Mr Rolt's attention to the case of a bond. To that Mr Rolt had replied that a bond was a unilateral contract. If so, it was only a contract to pay. He did not think that there was anything in this provision to prevent his deciding that the defendants were not entitled to decline to receive the plaintiffs' contributions, so that by virtue of the non-payment arising from this refusal the plaintiffs would become liable to come out of benefit or cease to be members of the society. That, in his view, was the true object of both actions in this case.

As to the point taken by Mr Slesser under subsection 3 of s. 4, the argument as far as he understood it was that when funds were received they would be applied for benefits, and therefore that by interfering with the payment of funds to the society he would be interfering with the administration of the funds of the society. In his judgment that was not so. All that he was holding was that the society could not insist on members' paying the levy as a condition of their remaining members. He was in no way dealing with the subsequent application of the fund. He was of opinion that the defence founded on the Act of 1871 failed.

He would decide in favour of the plaintiffs that the result of the ballot of May 30 was not duly ascertained in accordance with the rules of the society, and that the plaintiffs were therefore not liable to pay to the society the levy affected to be authorized by that ballot as a condition of their remaining members of the society and receiving benefits from the society. He would further declare that the ballot of August 8 was not properly held in view of the marking of the ballot papers of the London members.

MILLER v. AMALGAMATED ENGINEERING UNION

[1938] I Ch. 669

The plaintiff, son and administrator of a deceased member of the defendant union, claimed a declaration that the union was bound to pay him arrears of superannuation benefit owing to the deceased at his death. The union successfully relied upon s. 4 of the Trade Union Act, 1871.

MORTON, J.: The first contention of counsel for the union is that at common law the union is an unlawful association because its objects are in unlawful restraint of trade, the result being, as he says, that the union could not have been sued at common law. He also says that, even if the union is a lawful association at common law, it could not have been sued at common law in its name, the only possible procedure being one against its officials: and he says that, this action having taken the form that it has, the union, even if it is a lawful association, cannot be sued except subject to the provisions of the Trade Union Acts, 1871 to 1927....As to the question whether the union is a trade union within s. 4 of the Act of 1871, counsel for the union says, first, that the union comes within the definition of a trade union in the Trade Union Acts; and, secondly, that, whether it does or does not come within that definition, it must be deemed to be a trade union for the purpose of the Act of 1871 by reason of certain provisions in s. 2 of the Trade Union Act, 1913.

In order to ascertain whether the union is a trade union within the meaning of the Act of 1871 and whether it is an association unlawful at common law, it is necessary to consider first of all the relevant statutory provisions; and, secondly, the union's rules....It is admitted that the union is for the time being registered as a trade union, and I think that the contention of counsel for the union that it is to be deemed to be a trade union for the purposes of s. 4 of the Trade Union Act, 1871, is well founded; but I propose to consider also, in the course of going through some of the rules, whether it is in fact within the definitions which I have read...

The rules of the union are somewhat voluminous, and I shall refer only to those which seem to me particularly relevant to the questions which I have to decide...[By rule 13] sub-rule 21 it is provided that: 'No member shall ask for or take work by any system of payment by results or contract in any firm or factory where such system of payment does not exist without the approval of, and in conformity with the conditions as laid down by the district committee'. It is apparent from the passages which I have read that the district committee and the shop committee have considerable control over the actions of the members of the union...

Rule 21 is, I think, of great importance. Rule 21, sub-rule 1, deals with the expulsion of a member in the following terms: 'Without prejudice to any other grounds of expulsion herein contained any member of the union who, in the opinion of his branch or the executive council, shall have injured or attempted to injure the union, or worked or acted contrary to the interests of the union or its members, or have attempted to break up or dissolve the union otherwise than as allowed by these rules, or otherwise brought the union into discredit or refused to comply with the order or decision of any committee, council, or conference having jurisdiction over such member under these rules or requested or taken work from any employer at any place where or when a trade dispute exists between such employer and the union or any branch thereof, or obtained or attempted to obtain any of the benefits of the union by means of misrepresentation, or have knowingly participated in or been a party to any fraud perpetrated upon the union, or any misappropriation or misapplication of its funds or the funds of any branch thereof, or whose conduct shall have been otherwise inconsistent with the duties of a member of this union, or who being an officer shall have refused to perform the duties imposed upon him by these rules or any of them, may be expelled by his branch, with the approval of the executive council, or he may be excluded by the executive council from the union, and shall thereupon, subject to his right of appeal as in these rules provided, cease to be a member thereof. Every expelled member shall cease to have any claim on the funds and benefits of the union, and shall forfeit all right to participate in the privileges thereof'. Then there is a provision as to giving notice of the intention to proceed against any member.

That, of course, is a very striking power which is vested in the officials of this particular union, and it seems to involve this: that any man, no matter how many contributions he may have paid to the funds, and no matter how much superannuation benefit he may thereby have become entitled to, must, if he disobeys the orders and decisions of any committee or council, be liable to forfeit every benefit which he would otherwise have had under the rules. That, of course, supplies a very strong weapon for compelling any man to take part, for example, in a strike, whether he desires to take such part or not, and it is a rule which is, in my opinion, of great importance in ascertaining whether at common law, and apart from the Trade Union Acts, the union is an unlawful association...

Reading the rules as a whole, I do not entertain the slightest doubt that the union is a trade union within the meaning of the Trade Union Acts; indeed, although the point was not, I think, conceded by Mr Baker, on behalf of the plaintiff, it was hardly seriously argued. Moreover, I do not see any flaw in Mr Hutchinson's argument that the union, being admittedly registered as a trade union under the Acts, must be deemed to be a trade union within the meaning of the Acts: nor did counsel for the plaintiff draw my attention to any flaw in that argument.

The next question which I have to determine is: Is this action a 'legal proceeding instituted with the object of directly enforcing an agreement for the application of the funds of a trade union to provide benefits for members' within the meaning of s. 4 of the Trade Union Act, 1871?...

It is, I think, plain that there is in the present action a direct attempt to interfere with the application of the funds, and it could not be said of this action, as was said by Lord Buckmaster in *Braithwaite's* case,[1] that the action seeks nothing but a declaration as to membership and an injunction in its support. On the contrary, the whole essence of this action is that the plaintiff is saying to the union: 'You owe me a sum under the rules, and you must pay it, and you owe me that sum by way of a benefit, and that benefit is to be paid out of the union's funds'. It is true that in this case there are certain alternative claims which, if they had stood alone and if the statement of claim had been framed in a very different way, might possibly have been outside the provisions of s. 4—as to that I express no opinion. But in my view the action, framed as it is, with the allegations of fact which the statement of claim contains and with the claims for money which the statement of claim contains, is a clear instance of an action seeking directly to enforce an agreement for the application of the funds of the trade union to provide benefits to members. I see no parallel between the present action and the action which Lord Buckmaster was considering...

The last question which I have to consider is this: Is the union an association unlawful at common law so that no action can be brought at common law to enforce payment of any sum which may be payable under its rules? It is clear that the union's rules impose very definite restrictions upon the way in which the members of it can carry on their trade, but as was said by Lord Macnaghten in *Russell* v. *The Amalgamated Society of Carpenters and Joiners and Others*[2] it is not every restraint of trade that is unlawful. The illegality at common law of the restraint of trade depends upon the nature and extent of the restraint. Counsel for the union has referred me to the case which I have just quoted, and has argued that if, as was held by Lord Macnaghten, Lord Shaw of Dunfermline, Lord Mersey and Lord Robson, in that case,

---

[1] [1922] 2 A.C. 440.　　　　[2] [1912] A.C. 421, 430.

the respondent society in that case was an unlawful association at common law, then *a fortiori* the union in the present case is an unlawful association at common law also. I do not propose to state in detail the facts of *Russell's* case or to compare the rules of the respondent society in that case with the union's rules in this case. It is sufficient to say that, having carefully considered both sets of rules, I am satisfied that the union in this case is no less an association unlawful at common law than was the respondent society in *Russell's* case.

(iii) DISCIPLINE AND EXPULSION—NATURAL JUSTICE— REMEDIES OF MEMBERS

WOLSTENHOLME *v.* AMALGAMATED MUSICIANS' UNION

[1920] 2 Ch. 388

The plaintiff, a Cardiff confectioner who was also employed as a flautist by Moss Empires Ltd, made charges of undercutting against members of the branch committee of the defendant union to which he belonged. He refused to retract these charges in writing and was expelled by the branch committee under rule 16(3) of the union. This empowered the committee to expel any member upon satisfactory proof being given that he had by his conduct 'brought the union into discredit'. The plaintiff unsuccessfully sought a declaration that this resolution was *ultra vires* and void.

EVE, J.: Upon this critical analysis of the rule and upon its position in the Book of Rules and the subject-matter with which it mainly deals, an argument was put forward on behalf of the plaintiff that the rule ought to be construed as one of procedure only—as one which vests in the Branch a power to expel on any of the grounds for which expulsion is the penalty but which does not in itself confer any power to expel upon grounds other than those mentioned in the specific rules to which I have just referred.

I do not think I should be doing right in so restricting the language of the rule. It is true that treated as an enabling rule, some of its language—as in not a few other cases in the Book of Rules—may be tautological, but, on the other hand, to restrict it to procedure involves the imposition of a very strained construction on the sentence dealing with conduct bringing the Union into discredit, and provokes the inquiry why the draftsman—if he intended the rule to extent to all cases of expulsion provided for in the rules—did not say so instead of specifying certain grounds and leaving the others to be deduced from the references to conduct bringing the Union into discredit—and not the less so because the specifically mentioned grounds would appear to be quite as much calculated to bring discredit on the Union as those which it is suggested are compendiously dealt with by the phrase 'conduct bringing the Union into discredit'.

I think I ought to read the rule as an enabling one as well as one dealing with procedure, and this brings me to the final question I have to consider, and that is whether there was evidence on which it could be found that the plaintiff had been satisfactorily proved by his conduct to have brought the Union into discredit. What is the meaning to be attached to this phrase? It cannot in an organization of this nature with its Head Office in Manchester and Branches in cities and towns all over the country, mean that the conduct must be such as to bring the whole Union into discredit. It is obvious there might be conduct discrediting one Branch and in no way affecting the Head Office or any other Branch. 'Bringing the Union into discredit' must, therefore, mean the Union, or any Branch of it. Any other construction would impose on the Branch seeking to exercise this power of expulsion the impossible task of obtaining satisfactory proof that the conduct had brought the whole Union into discredit. Moreover, the distributive construction is consonant with the fact that the exercise of this power is vested in each branch.

The next question is, Bring it into discredit with whom? The plaintiff says: 'The outside public, and in particular that part of it which has business or professional relations with members of the Union'. I agree, but why should it be restricted to this class? Is it not equally important that the credit of the Branch should be maintained with the Head Office and the other branches? I think it must be, and that conduct which has brought discredit on the Branch with the public, or any section of it, or with the other component parts of the whole organization comes within the rule.

On this footing is it possible to assert that the members of this particular Branch had not in the plaintiff's original letter— alleging, as I have held it does, misconduct of a discreditable character on the part of its members of the Committee—in the attitude assumed and persisted in by the Head Office towards the Branch in consequence of that letter, and in the plaintiff's persistent refusal to redeem his promise of 1 September, evidence on which it was competent for them to hold that the plaintiff had been satisfactorily proved by his conduct to have brought the Branch into discredit? I do not think it is—on the contrary, I think there were ample materials on which it was open to the Branch to come to the conclusion they did come to, and I cannot give the plaintiff the relief he asks in this action.

EVANS *v.* NATIONAL UNION OF PRINTING, BOOKBINDING AND PAPER WORKERS

Court of Appeal   [1938] 4 All E.R. 51

Rule 21 of the defendant union provided as follows:

'Should members leave their situations without proper notice to their employers (unless by mutual consent, or under circumstances which the branch committee may consider justifiable), or lose their employment through misconduct, it shall be within the power and discretion of the branch committee to suspend such offending members from out-of-work benefit for one or more weeks...'

'Any member refusing to accept work at the trade without a satisfactory reason being given shall be suspended from all benefits for such period as the committee may resolve upon, and shall not be allowed to sign the call-book during such period.'

The plaintiff, an employee of W. H. Smith & Son and a member of the union, absented himself from work with the result that a non-unionist was engaged to do his work. He was instructed by his union to accept the work ('six early mornings') but he still refused because he disliked it. He was summoned before the branch committee and expelled under rule 242(*f*) which rendered a member liable to expulsion...'if he has knowingly acted to the detriment of the interests of the union'. The decision was confirmed by the executive council. The plaintiff argued that the union could only suspend him from benefit: but the court, who viewed this as a disciplinary matter, held that the union had been entitled to act as it did.

GODDARD, L.J.: The branch committee held a meeting, and, as I must assume from their finding, they considered apparently—no one has challenged the honesty of their decision, and it would not really matter, because it went to the executive council—that Mr Evans' conduct amounted to knowingly acting to the detriment of the interests of the union—as, of course, it would be.

As I said in the course of the argument, the great benefit of a trade union is that you can have collective bargaining between employers and employed, and, if the union come to an arrangement or come to a decision regarding any man or body of men, and then that man or body of men refuses to be bound, it destroys the confidence that should exist between the employers and the union, and is to the detriment of collective bargaining. I have no doubt that that is the view which the committee took. When Evans refused to abide by their decision, and refused to accept the work which was offered him, the committee decided to recommend the national executive council to expel Evans. Then proper notice of the meeting of the national executive council was given to Mr Evans, who attended the national executive council. He laid a case before them, and the minutes show that the executive council considered this case very fully, and came to the conclusion that the recommendation of the branch committee should be adopted. I cannot see how they acted *ultra vires*. They decided, in other words, that, in defying the instruction given by the branch committee, and refusing to be bound by their direction, Mr Evans had knowingly acted to the detriment of the interests of the union. That was a decision to which they could come. There is nothing contrary to natural justice in it. They gave Mr Evans a hearing and came to that decision. I cannot interfere with their decision, and this action fails, and must be dismissed with costs.*

SPRING *v.* NATIONAL AMALGAMATED STEVEDORES AND DOCKERS SOCIETY

[1956] 1 W.L.R. 585; [1956] 2 All E.R. 221

After a dispute between the defendant union and another union affiliated to the T.U.C., the T.U.C. Disputes Committee made an award deciding that the defendant union should exclude from member-

* Compare now, *Silvester* v. *N.U.P.B.P.W.*, *The Times*, 28 October 1966. The plaintiff was a night driver for the *Daily Mail* where several types of overtime were worked, one of them of a routine character. In 1959, for domestic reasons, the plaintiff ceased to work even that type of overtime. His branch of the union fined him and ordered him to work overtime; and the union's Final Appeal Court upheld the branch decisions. Goff, J., decided that there was no term, express or implied, in the plaintiff's contract of employment which obliged him to work overtime. Even though the union might expect its members to work the routine 'guaranteed overtime', there could be no obligation owed by the plaintiff to his union to do so, as the rules stood. He granted a declaration that the decisions of the branch and Appeal Court were void. It is to be noted that the only rule of the union there expressly dealing with overtime was a rule prohibiting members from working more than eight' hours overtime, except under the terms of a trade agreement which would be negotiated by the national executive council. His lordship firmly rejected the argument that the branch could order the member to do overtime merely because his failure to do it was considered 'injurious' to the union, when he was not obliged to do it under his employment contract. No doubt, however, union rules could be drafted which would give a branch that power in another case.

ship all the members recruited at certain ports after a certain date. These members included the plaintiff. The union purported to exclude the plaintiff from membership. When sued, the union argued, *inter alia*, that it was an an implied term of the plaintiff's contract of membership that he could be expelled if this was required by the T.U.C. Disputes Committee under the Bridlington Agreement. The contention was rejected.*

STONE, V.C.: That brings me to the question of the implied terms raised in paragraphs 14 and 15 of the Defence, namely: that it was an implied term of the plaintiff's contract of membership of the defendant union that the union should have the right to do all things which may be necessary and proper to comply with its lawful and proper agreements; and further, an implied term that members would act in conformity with the lawful and proper agreements of the defendant union, meaning of course, thereby, the Bridlington Agreement...

To that line of defence several submissions have been made by counsel for the plaintiff. The first is that the plaintiff in his evidence, which I entirely accept, said that it was not until the recognition strike, that is to say, some five or six weeks after he had been accepted as a member of the defendant union, that he first heard of the Bridlington Agreement. Even in this court his ideas about its effect were quite inaccurate and imperfect. I have been referred to the well-known passage in the judgment of MacKinnon L.J. in *Shirlaw* v. *Southern Foundries (1926) Ltd*, where he said[1]...'If I may quote from an essay which I wrote some years ago, I then said: "*Prima facie* that which in any contract is left to be implied and need not be expressed is something so obvious that it goes without saying; so that, if, while the parties were making their bargain, an officious bystander were to suggest some express provision for it in their agreement, they would testily suppress him with a common 'Oh, of course!' " '

If that test were to be applied to the facts of the present case and the bystander had asked the plaintiff at the time he paid his five shillings

---

[1] [1939] 2 K.B. 206, 227.

* The grounds on which it was rejected are understandable. But should the union have been allowed ever to take the point at all ? The courts have elsewhere insisted that effect will be given only to *express* disciplinary terms in the contract of membership, and in particular that power to expel will not be implied. See for example *Luby* v. *Warwickshire Miners' Assocn*. [1912] 2 Ch. 371. An express rule permitting expulsion when required by the T.U.C. Bridlington Committee has now been adopted by many of the affiliated unions to meet the difficulty caused by *Spring's* case: see, e.g. *post*, p. 659; and R. Rideout, *The Content of Trade Union Disciplinary Rules* (1965) III Brit. Jo. Ind. Rels. 153.

and signed the acceptance form, 'Won't you put into it some reference to the Bridlington Agreement?,' I think (indeed, I have no doubt) the plaintiff would have answered 'What's that?' In my judgment, that is sufficient to dispose of this case, but as two further grounds have been argued with regard to the Bridlington Agreement being applied to the terms of this contract, I intend to express my views upon them out of deference to the arguments.

It is said that when the Bridlington Agreement is examined, every term of it contains something which a trade union as an entity must do or abstain from doing, and that there is nothing in it which a member of a trade union has to do or abstain from doing. That is so, and I do not know how a member who is intending to join a new union and does in fact join a new union can, by the importation of some implied term be made liable for some infraction by the trade union of principles which are laid down as a morally binding code of conduct in the relationship between trade unions. Further, there is no power of expulsion in the Bridlington Agreement. That code is concerned with the admission of new members and nothing at all is laid down in it about getting rid of them.

BLACKALL v. NATIONAL UNION OF FOUNDRY WORKERS

(1923) 39 T.L.R. 431

The plaintiff who had infringed an overtime ban was fined £2 by a meeting at which he was not present. In protest he refused to pay the fine or his contributions until he was heard in his own defence. The union then expelled him for failing to pay his contributions and advised the only other union which might take him not to do so. The plaintiff sought to restrain the union from expelling him.

COLERIDGE, J. said: The reinstatement by the Court of a member of a trade union alleged to have been rejected for non-compliance with a rule embodying an agreement within s. 4 of the Act of 1871 is not prohibited, because it does not directly enforce the agreement. The Court cannot do that, but it can reinstate the member and thereby make him what he was before—namely, a member with the same unenforceable rights. The Court is at liberty to construe the rules so as to see whether the jurisdiction is ousted. The trade union is bound to act according to its rules as interpreted by these Courts, which can enforce the rules if their enforcement is not prohibited by s. 4, subsection 2, of the Act as being a direct enforcement of the agreements or any of them enumerated in the section. If the Court is asked to enforce directly any such agreement, the Court must refuse to interfere, and cannot inquire into the justice or injustice, the rights or wrongs of the case.

The defendants purported to act under rule 27, s. 3, which runs: 'Any member owing over twenty weeks' contributions who has not been clear on the books over the same period, shall be suspended from all benefits and shall be excluded unless a satisfactory reason be given to the branch committee, who shall have discretionary powers as to the time such member shall be allowed to pay up all arrears...but in every case no exclusion shall be binding unless sanctioned by the council.'

This is a penal clause and must be construed strictly. The plaintiff had paid everything up to Saturday, 13 November 1920. Twenty weeks from then expired on 2 April 1921. By rule 26, s. 7, the contribution week is from Monday to Saturday. The liability to contribute was not a daily but a weekly contribution. Therefore, before the plaintiff could be over twenty weeks' contributions in arrears he must fail to contribute up to and including Saturday, 9 April. If on Saturday, 9 April, the plaintiff appeared and contributed all that was due on that day, he could not be excluded for being over twenty weeks in arrear. But the plaintiff was excluded on 7 April, and on 9 April, before the meeting on that day, he offered the full amount of his arrears to the shop steward, who, on instructions, refused to receive it. The exclusion, therefore, was not justified by the rules. The result is that there must be an injunction restraining the defendants from excluding the plaintiff.

ANNAMUNTHODO v. OILFIELD WORKERS' UNION

Privy Council　　　　　　　　　　　　　　　　　　　　[1961] A.C. 945

During two lunch hours the appellant attended meetings at which he alleged the President-General of the union had embezzled $25,000. He was charged under four headings with having broken union rules but the maximum penalty for each infringement was a fine. He attended the first hearing when evidence was taken but not the second hearing when sentence was passed, owing to a previous engagement. He was found guilty of the breaches charged; but was then expelled under a different rule, 11 (7), on the ground that he had been 'guilty of conduct prejudicial to the interests of the Union'. He appealed to the Annual Conference of Delegates who upheld the expulsion. The Judicial Committee held that rule 11(7) 'created a separate and distinct offence'.

LORD DENNING: Their Lordships have already observed that under none of those rules was there any power to expel Walter Annamunthodo. Yet when it came to sentencing him the General Council did expel him: and for this purpose they invoked another rule, namely, rule 11(7). He had not been charged with a breach of it, but nevertheless they claimed a right to expel him under it.... The first question is: Did rule 11(7) create a *separate and distinct offence* of 'conduct prejudicial to the interests of the "Union"'?—for in that case it ought to have been separately charged—or did rule 11(7) merely empower the General Council to impose *more severe penalties* for the various *other offences* specified in the rules provided that the conduct of which he was convicted under them was prejudicial to the interests of the union?—for in that case rule 11(7), so it was said, need not be separately charged, but only the other offences. Phillips, J. in the Supreme Court and Archer and Rennie, JJ. in the Federal Supreme Court thought that the rule 11(7) only empowered the General Council to impose *more severe penalties* and sought support for this view from some observations of Eve, J. in *Wolstenholme* v. *Amalgamated Musicians' Union*.[1] But Wylie, J. thought it created a *separate and distinct offence*, and their Lordships agree with him. As he said, 'it stands entirely on its own, authorising expulsion of a member who is proved to the satisfaction of the General Council "to have been guilty of conduct prejudicial to the interests of the Union".' In the opinion of their Lordships it should not have been invoked for the purpose of expelling Walter Annamunthodo unless he was given notice of the charge under it and had a fair opportunity of meeting it.

But even if rule 11(7) only empowered *more severe penalties*, nevertheless those severe penalties could only be imposed when the conduct was prejudicial to the interest of the union: and their Lordships think that, even on that view, the rule should not have been invoked without giving Walter Annamunthodo notice of it.

Mr Lazarus sought to treat the specific formulation of *charges* as immaterial. The substance of the matter lay, he said, in the *facts* alleged in the letter as to the meetings which Walter Annamunthodo had attended and the allegations he had made. Their Lordships cannot

[1] [1920] 2 Ch. 388, 400-1.

accede to this view. If a domestic tribunal formulates specific charges, which lead only to a fine, it cannot without notice resort to other charges, which lead to far more severe penalties.

The second question is this: Is Walter Annamunthodo debarred from complaining of rule 11(7) being invoked because he did not appear at the adjourned hearing? He had attended the first hearing on 9 June 1957, when the evidence was taken: but he did not attend at the adjourned hearing on 16 June 1957, giving as his reason that he had made a previous engagement to be the judge at a 'Mock Trial' sponsored by a Girl's Group. That seems a poor excuse. And it was said that, if he had appeared at the adjourned hearing, he could have been given notice in writing then and there of the intention to proceed under rule 11(7) and thus expelled without any violation of natural justice. This argument appealed to Wylie, J. who thought that, as he had been given an opportunity of appearing at the adjourned hearing and had not appeared, that was enough to satisfy natural justice. Their Lordships realise the force of this reasoning but they cannot agree with it. Walter Annamunthodo must be taken to have known that, at the adjourned hearing, the General Council might proceed to award the full penalty prescribed for the offences then charged against him—which was only a small fine—but he could not be expected to know that he might be dealt with for a separate and distinct offence which involved expulsion. When the General Council at the adjourned hearing desired to proceed under rule 11(7), and found that he was not present, they ought to have adjourned the hearing once again so as to give him notice of the fresh charge: and they would have had to do it in writing under rule 32(5). By failing to do so, they failed to observe the requirements of natural justice.*

The third question is whether Walter Annamunthodo has lost his right to complain by appealing to the Annual Conference of Delegates. As soon as he knew of his expulsion by the General Council, he gave notice of appeal under rule 11(7). He had the opportunity to

---

* Compare *Taylor* v. *National Union of Seamen*, [1967] 1 All E.R. 767: a union official appealed against dismissal and a decision by the union council rendering him, as member, ineligible for further office. The general secretary had addressed the council *after* conclusion of the arguments before it about matters on which the plaintiff had had no opportunity to speak, such as his communist affiliations. Ungoed-Thomas J. held that the decision was contrary to natural justice and the dismissal was wrongful. But Taylor had to be a member to be an official; although an employee, his employment was on the basis of the membership rules; his position had a "dual aspect". The full-time union official as such is often merely an employee, and open to dismissal according to the terms of his employment contract, without any right to be heard, etc.: *Lewis* v. *N.U.G.M.W. The Times*, 31 July 1948; *ante* p. 153-4.

put before the Annual Conference of Delegates all his objections to his expulsion. He does not complain of any failure of natural justice by that body. And they affirmed his expulsion. So can he now complain? This reasoning was accepted by Archer and Wylie, JJ. They held that, by appealing, he had lost his right to complain of rule 11(7) being invoked. Indeed, he himself invoked rule 11(7) so as to appeal under it. So how can he now repudiate it? Their Lordships recognise the force of this reasoning, but they cannot agree with it. Even if the order of expulsion were capable of being affirmed or disaffirmed their Lordships cannot regard an appeal as an act of affirmance. On the contrary, it is a disaffirmance—a complaint against the order of expulsion. If he had not appealed, it might have been said that he should have done so, that he should have exhausted all internal means of redress, before having recourse to the courts. Such a plea was upheld in the special circumstances that prevailed in *White* v. *Kuzych*.[1] It was therefore quite proper for him to appeal to the Annual Conference before coming to the courts, even though he was not bound to do so. But, having appealed and failed, he does not by so doing forfeit his right to redress in the courts. If the original order was invalid, for want of observance of the rules of natural justice, he can still complain of it, notwithstanding his appeal.

Mr Lazarus did suggest that a man could not complain of a failure of natural justice unless he could show that he had been prejudiced by it. Their Lordships cannot accept this suggestion. If a domestic tribunal fails to act in accordance with natural justice, the person affected by their decision can always seek redress in the courts. It is a prejudice to any man to be denied justice. He will not, of course, be entitled to damages if he suffered none. But he can always ask for the decision against him to be set aside.

MACLEAN *v.* THE WORKERS' UNION

[1929] 1 Ch. 602

The plaintiff was charged with having broken a union rule concerning approval by the executive committee of circulars before they were sent out. He was given notice of the complaint against him, and an opportunity to conduct his case before the executive committee, to call witnesses and to submit evidence. He was expelled from the union as a result of the hearing. The plaintiff attacked their decision on the ground that they were biased and were judges in their own cause.

[1] [1951] A.C. 585.

MAUGHAM, J.: The jurisdiction of the Courts in regard to domestic tribunals—a phrase which may conveniently be used to include the committees or the councils or the members of trade unions, of members' clubs, and of professional bodies established by statute or Royal Charter while acting in a quasi-judicial capacity—is clearly of a limited nature. Parenthetically I may observe that I am not confident that precisely the same principles will apply in all these cases; for it may be that a body entrusted with important duties by an Act of Parliament is not in the same position as, for example, the executive committee in the present case. Speaking generally, it is useful to bear in mind the very wide differences between the principles applicable to Courts of Justice and those applicable to domestic tribunals. In the former the accused is entitled to be tried by the judge according to the evidence legally adduced and has a right to be represented by a skilled legal advocate. All the procedure of a modern trial, including the examination and cross-examination of the witnesses and the summing-up, if any, is based on these two circumstances. A domestic tribunal is in general a tribunal composed of laymen. It has no power to administer an oath and, a circumstance which is perhaps of greater importance, no party has the power to compel the attendance of witnesses. It is not bound by the rules of evidence; it is indeed probably ignorant of them. It may act, and it sometimes must act, on mere hearsay, and in many cases the members present or some of them (like an English jury in ancient days) are themselves both the witnesses and the judges. Before such a tribunal counsel have no right of audience and there are no effective means for testing by cross-examination the truth of the statements that may be made. The members of the tribunal may have been discussing the matter for weeks with persons not present at the hearing, and there is no one even to warn them of the danger of acting on preconceived views.

It is apparent and it is well settled by authority that the decision of such a tribunal cannot be attacked on the ground that it is against the weight of evidence, since evidence in the proper sense there is none, and since the decisions of the tribunal are not open to any sort of appeal unless the rules provide for one. There is perhaps a question whether the decision can be attacked on the ground that there is no evidence (a word used presumably in a popular sense) upon which the tribunal could possibly come to such a conclusion....It is certain, therefore, that a domestic tribunal is bound to act strictly according to its rules and is under an obligation to act honestly and in good faith. It is not suggested in the present case that the rules as they stand have not been complied with, and on the evidence before me I am quite unable to hold that the committee acted otherwise than honestly and in good faith. Indeed I was not invited to do so. It is, however, contended that there are other implied rules or implied obligations, sometimes described as obligations of natural justice, which the plaintiff may invoke; for example, a rule that no person or persons should sit on the tribunal or be present at the hearing if he or they are in effect prosecutors or if he or they may fairly be suspected of a bias against the accused. It is, therefore, desirable to consider the principle on which these contentions must ultimately rest.

In such a case as the present, where the tribunal is the result of rules adopted by persons who have formed the association known as a trade union, it seems to me reasonably clear that the rights of the plaintiff against the defendants must depend simply on the contract, and that the material terms of the contract must be found in the rules. ...In the case I have before me (and I may add in such a case as a power of expulsion in a members' club) it seems to me reasonably clear that the matter can only depend on contract express or implied. If, for instance, there was a clearly expressed rule stating that a member might be expelled by a defined body without calling upon the member in question to explain his conduct, I see no reason for supposing that the Courts would interfere with such a rule on the ground of public policy. Moreover, it is well settled by decisions of the Court of Appeal that, if the parties to a contract agree that a person who may well be suspected of a bias or who may be deciding in his own cause shall be the judge in a dispute between the parties, the Courts will not interfere...

Eminent judges have at times used the phrase 'the principles of natural justice'. The phrase is, of course, used only in a popular sense and must not be taken to mean that there is any justice natural among men. Among most savages there is no such thing as justice in the modern sense.... The truth is that justice is a very elaborate conception, the growth of many centuries of civilization; and even now the conception differs widely in countries usually described as civilized.

A person who joins an association governed by rules under which he may be expelled, e.g. such rules as in the present case exist in rules 45 and 46, has in my judgment no legal right of redress if he be expelled according to the rules, however unfair and unjust the rules or the action of the expelling tribunal may be, provided that it acts in good faith. It is impossible to doubt that, if the rules postulate an inquiry the accused must be given a reasonable opportunity of being heard. The phrase, 'the principles of natural justice', can only mean in this connection the principles of fair play so deeply rooted in the minds of modern Englishmen that a provision for an inquiry necessarily imports that the accused should be given his chance of defence and explanation. On that point there is no difficulty. Nor do I doubt that in most cases it is a reasonable inference from the rules that if there is anything of the nature of a *lis* between two persons, neither of them should sit on the tribunal. But when it is sought to lay down elaborate rules, taken from decisions as to Courts of law, and to apply them in such a case as the present, I think it is prudent to remember that these more or less artificial principles have no application except so far as they can be derived from a fair construction of the rules, and that the implication can only be made if it is clear that the parties, who are laymen and not lawyers, must have intended it.

There are a large number of well known cases as to the disqualification of justices from adjudicating on matters in regard to which they are interested or where there is ground for a reasonable suspicion of bias.... In my opinion, however, these cases have no real application to the case of a domestic tribunal established by private contract and acting, as pointed out above, on a system and by methods so entirely different from those of a Court of justice. If we consider first the case of a pecuniary interest it is impossible in general to imply from the terms of the rules such a disqualification as regards the members of a domestic forum. For example, when members of a club expel another member under their rules, generally speaking, they all have a small pecuniary interest in the matter. Moreover the members of a domestic tribunal have other interests in the decision which may well render them something less than impartial. They have, for example, the interests of their association or body to protect, and may properly regard these interests as a matter of great importance. In many cases the tribunal is necessarily entrusted with the duty of appearing to act as prosecutors as well as that of judges; for there is no one else to prosecute. For example, in a case where a council is charged with the duty of considering the conduct of any member whose conduct is disgraceful and of expelling him if found guilty of such an offence, it constantly occurs that the matter is brought to the attention of the council by a report of legal proceedings in the press. The member is summoned to appear before the council. The council's duty is to cause him to appear and to explain his conduct. It may be said that in so acting the council are the prosecutors. In one sense they are; but if the regulations show that the council is bound to act as I have mentioned and to that extent to act as prosecutors, it seems to be clear that the council is not disqualified from taking the further steps which the rules require.

If I am right so far, the real and the only question that arises in this case is whether on the true construction of the rules any members of the executive committee were disqualified from acting in relation to the breach by the plaintiff of rule 45, that is, from imposing the penalty laid down in that rule if they thought fit. The plaintiff asked for leave to issue his election address in its original form, and treated with contempt the decision of the committee that it must be altered. It was then, I think, the duty of the committee to take the steps mentioned in the letter of 15 September 1927; and if in taking those steps they were prosecutors, the answer is that the rules in such a case contemplate that they should be...

I am satisfied that there is no ground for contending that either of them was in any real sense acting as a judge in his own cause on 28 September. It may perhaps be true to say that the plaintiff had a long standing dispute with them as regards the management of the defendant union; but what follows from that? It is impossible to infer from the rules that members of the executive committee who do not see eye to eye with him on a matter of trade union politics are not to act. Even if there were satisfactory evidence (which there is not) that Mr Lord or Mr Cardinal had had a personal quarrel with the plaintiff, I should doubt very much whether it would be right to infer from the rules that he was thereby disqualified from acting under rule 45 or 46. That I think would be a matter of good taste, not of a legal disqualification. A case may well arise in which the member has definitely quarrelled with every member of the committee. Such bias as may result in the minds of the members of the committee, even if it were (which I greatly doubt) within the principle of 'a challenge to the favour', cannot in my opinion constitute a disqualification from acting under rule 45.

WHITE AND OTHERS v. KUZYCH

Privy Council   [1951] A.C. 585

The respondent publicly opposed and campaigned against the appellant union's closed shop policy. He was expelled from the union. The rules provided for an appeal to the executive within 60 days of the decision; and on joining the union the respondent had agreed not to become a party to a lawsuit against the union until he had exhausted all the remedies of the constitution. Without appealing to the executive the respondent sought a declaration alleging, *inter alia*, that the decision was contrary to natural justice. The Judicial Committee of the Privy Council took the view that the member was bound to exhaust his internal remedies by way of appeal.

VISCOUNT SIMON delivered the opinion of the Privy Council: It would indeed be an error to demand from those who took part the strict impartiality of mind with which a judge should approach and decide an issue between two litigants—that 'icy impartiality of a Rhadamanthus' which Bowen, L.J., in *Jackson* v. *Barry Ry. Co.*[1] thought could not be expected of an engineer arbitrator—or to regard as disqualified from acting any member who had held and expressed the view that the 'closed shop' principle was essential to the policy and purpose of the union. What those who considered the charges against the respondent and decided whether he was guilty ought to bring to their task was a will to reach an honest conclusion after hearing what was urged on either side, and a resolve not to make up their minds beforehand on his personal guilt, however firmly they held their conviction as to union policy and however strongly they had shared in previous adverse criticism of the respondent's conduct...

But, while accepting and applying the view of Maugham, J., in *Maclean* v. *Workers' Union* that the conduct of a person charged might well be such that every other member of the union might have a strong animus against him, and agreeing that the court should not interfere merely because the committee and the general executive detested him, the judge went on to say, 'But the plaintiff's actions by no means justified the conduct that some of the committee and some of the main executive had been guilty of it. No resentment, however just, can excuse it'. And, after reviewing the evidence, he concluded that the expulsion was invalid and bad in law.

The two judges who were in the minority in the Court of Appeal, the Chief Justice and Bird, J.A., do not express any dissent from the adverse view on the merits taken by their colleagues, and their Lordships will deal with the matter on the basis that severe condemnation of the methods followed in the proceedings under review is fully justified. If these were the only relevant considerations, some difficult questions would arise. For example, is the conclusion of a judicial tribunal

---

[1] [1893] 1 Ch. 238, 248.

acting within its jurisdiction, which is arrived at in a way which amounts to a denial of natural justice, appealable, or, on the contrary is it simply void and thus not subject to appeal at all? And the further question would then have to be considered, namely, how far the law on the subject of bias or prejudice or failure to apply natural justice extends to such a tribunal as the trial committee and the general meeting which is considering the committee's report.

The answers to these questions would not, however, be decisive of the present case, if the view taken by the two judges who were in the minority of the Court of Appeal prevails. The respondent, after his condemnation by the general meeting, did not appeal to the Shipyard General Workers' Federation before invoking the court's jurisdiction although he was contractually bound not to institute any action against the union until he had exhausted all the remedies by the union's constitution and byelaws. The Chief Justice and Bird, J.A., took the view that on this ground the respondent's claim must fail. This issue has been elaborately and excellently argued before their Lordships by counsel on either side, and it remains to examine the contention.

The respondent sets up two answers to it. (*a*) He contends that the trial committee was not properly constituted. If this is proved to be so, any proceedings for hearing and deciding on the charges were a nullity; the general meeting had no valid report before them; the sentence of expulsion would be without authority under the byelaws; and there would be no basis for an appeal to the federation. (*b*) Even if the committee was properly constituted, he contends that the conclusion reached at the general meeting should not be regarded as a 'decision' on the ground that it was arrived at by methods which make it contrary to natural justice and that it is the result of bias and even intimidation.

The respondent relied on expressions in some English cases which would suggest that a conclusion reached by certain tribunals in such circumstances may depart so far from a judicial pronouncement as not to amount to a 'decision' at all. However this may be, a crucial question under this second head is whether the conclusion reached by the general committee was a 'decision' within the meaning of that word in the provision headed 'Appeals' above quoted...

Their Lordships, after receiving argument on issue (*a*) from both sides, intimated at the hearing that in their view the trial committee must be regarded as validly constituted. As to (*b*), the whole difficulty is to put the proper construction on the word 'decision' when the byelaw gives a right of appeal from the general meeting to the federation if a member found guilty or penalized by the former 'feels that the decision is unfair or the penalty too severe'. The view of the Chief Justice and Bird, J.A., is that the conclusion reached by the general meeting was a 'decision' within the meaning of that expression in the byelaws even though it was tainted by bias or prejudice, or arrived at in defiance of natural justice, and even though the voting of some members may have been affected by intimidation. According to this view, these circumstances, or the allegation of them, would be matter for the consideration of the appellate tribunal, and would not justify the contention that no appeal was possible because there was no 'decision' to appeal against.

After anxious reflection, their Lordships have reached the conclusion that this is the correct view. The meaning of 'decision' in byelaw 26 must be arrived at by examining the byelaws as a whole. The scheme of them manifestly is that members of the union design to settle disputes between a member and the union in the domestic forum to the exclusion of the law courts, at any rate until the remedies provided by the constitution and byelaws, including the opportunity for appeal to the federation, are fully exhausted. If the question had been asked of the respondent, or of any of his fellow-members, 'What was the decision of the general committee?' it cannot be doubted that the answer would have been, not that no decision had been given, but that the decision was to condemn and expel the respondent. And this would be so, not only because it is the natural reply for members of the union to give in the circumstances, but because it would be the right answer. 'Decision' in the byelaw means 'conclusion'. The refinement which lawyers may appreciate between a tribunal's 'decision' and a conclusion pronounced by a tribunal which, though within the tribunal's jurisdiction, may be treated, because of the improper way in which it was reached, as no decision at all and therefore incapable of being subject to appeal, cannot be attributed to the draftsman of these byelaws or to the trade-unionists who adopted them as their domestic code.

Their Lordships are therefore constrained to hold that the conclusion reached by the general committee was subject to appeal. And they must respectfully repudiate both the correctness and the relevance of the view that it would have been useless for the respondent to appeal because the federation would be sure to decide against him. They see no reason why the federation, if called on to deal with the appeal, should be assumed to be incapable of giving its honest attention to a complaint of unfairness or of undue severity, and of endeavouring to arrive at the right final decision. At any rate, this is the appeal which the respondent was bound by his contract to pursue before he could issue his writ. He has not done so, and on this ground their Lordships will humbly advise His Majesty that the appeal must be allowed.

LAWLOR v. UNION OF POST OFFICE WORKERS

[1965] Ch. 712; [1965] 2 W.L.R. 579

The Director of Personnel of the Post Office notified the general secretary of the union that it would be necessary in the London area to implement an agreement made with the union whereby part-time labour could be taken on if it was needed to maintain essential services. The plaintiffs, who constituted a majority on the committee of a sectional council in London, sought to implement a ban on overtime if part-time labour was brought in even though this was in opposition to the policy of the executive council. The committee members maintained this position when required by the general secretary to retract. After a debate, the executive council decided that the plaintiffs should be expelled from the union for unconstitutional action in violation of the National Rules.

The plaintiffs successfully sought a declaration that their expulsion was contrary to natural justice since they had not been told that disciplinary action was proposed, nor what the charges were, nor were they given a chance to defend themselves.

UNGOED-THOMAS, J., after reviewing the facts, said: So the decision here, in so far as it depends on the application of the rules of natural justice, depends on whether or not this is a case in which natural justice applies at all. If it does apply, it has not been observed. Is this, then, a case in which the rules of natural justice apply? And it is on this question that unfortunately the law on natural justice is most debatable.

There are authorities which suggest that the application of natural justice may be affected by such considerations as whether the decision was of a professional or trade body, or of such a social body as a club; whether the decision affects livelihood or reputation; whether the consequences are financial or social; whether the decision involves imputation or misconduct; and whether it involves an inquiry. On the one hand it has been regarded as a requirement of public policy overriding contract, and on the other hand as no more than a term, albeit implied, in a contract. Doubtless these considerations and differing views about them can be expanded. But the most restricted view of the application of natural justice is that which may be based on the observations of Lord Goddard, C.J. in the Jockey Club case, *Russell* v. *Duke of Norfolk*,[1] approved by Tucker, L.J. in the Court of Appeal.[2] This view, advanced by the union in this case, is to the effect that the rules of natural justice can only be applied in a contract: (1) if they are not inconsistent with what is expressed in the contract; and (2) if they are necessary to carry it out and therefore must have been intended by the parties, and not merely if the rules of natural justice make the carrying out of the contract more convenient and might have been included if the parties had thought about it. It was not controverted in the Jockey Club case, and it was accepted by the union before me, that if the contract contemplated an inquiry, that inquiry would, at any rate in the absence of express limitation by contract, import the rules of natural justice. Thus, on his most restricted view of the application of the rules of natural justice, the question becomes: (1) Are the express terms of the union rules about expulsion, which constitute the relevant contract in this case between the members, inconsistent with the rules of natural justice, and if not: (2) Is it necessary to the carrying out of the union rules about expulsion that the executive council should hold an inquiry, or that the persons proposed to be expelled by the executive council should be told of the charges against them and have an opportunity of being heard on those charges by that council?

In this case the expulsion is under rule 3 (*e*) of the National Rules, and that rule is in these terms. It is headed 'Expulsion', and continues: 'Any member shall be expelled from the union who in the opinion of the executive council is not a fit and proper person for membership, but he shall have a right of appeal to the next annual conference and the decision of the annual conference shall be conclusively binding on the parties. Such right of appeal shall subsist for only 28 clear days after the date of notification to the member of the decision of the executive council and such appeals shall be made in writing addressed to the general secretary of the union and shall be sent to him by prepaid registered post'.

Great emphasis was understandably placed by the union on the words 'who in the opinion of the executive council', and it was argued for them that those words indicated a subjective test on the part of the executive council, by which I understand is meant a test not requiring issue of fact or statement of reason. But in the course of argument it

---

[1] 64 T.L.R. 263; [1948] 1 All E.R. 488.
[2] 65 T.L.R. 225; [1949] 1 All E.R. 109, C.A.

was accepted, and in my view could not be disputed, that 'opinion' could refer to an opinion of such a judicial nature after due investigation and hearing as might result in or constitute the finding of a jury or decision of a judge. So 'opinion', unlike the words 'absolute discretion' in the context in the Jockey Club case, is, in my view, not inconsistent with an inquiry or the appreciation of the rules of natural justice.

Rule 3 (e) gives a right of appeal to the annual conference and it says that 'the decision' of the annual conference is to be 'conclusively binding'. The conference is a large body consisting of delegates from branches or groups of branches all over the country, and it would appear that members appealing against expulsion might well be completely unknown to many of them. Clearly they could not be expected to act without having the issues properly and fairly presented to them, that is, without due inquiry in accordance with the rules of natural justice. It is accepted, and indeed urged by the union, that before this 'decision' can properly be made at the annual conference, the rules of natural justice must be applied. But the subject of appeal is also referred to in the rule as the 'decision' of the executive council, and that decision, which might be upset on appeal, is, or follows from, the opinion that, and I quote again, 'a person is not a fit and proper person for membership'. So the conference on appeal might, like the executive council, have to form an opinion of the appellant's fitness for membership. But that opinion would have to be objectively and judicially formed as indicated by the nature of that body and its members' lack of knowledge of the possible appellants, as implicit in the union's recognition that the rules of natural justice would apply to the appeal.... Further, the rule provides that the right of appeal shall subsist only for 28 clear days after the intimation of the executive council's decision and that, and I quote, 'such appeals', shall be made in writing. To enable members to be in a position to decide whether to appeal at all, they should at least know the charges against them, and, in my view, the case made in substantiating those charges to the satisfaction of the executive council; and if that information is to appear only at the annual conference, it might involve the members and the annual conference itself in quite unnecessary trouble and expense and keep unknown charges hanging over the members for up to 12 months.... If there were no inquiry before the executive council, then a member could be excluded by the executive council from membership and office without hearing and without redress for up to 12 months, since there is no provision for any stay of the executive council decision pending appeal. Then, perhaps, on the first opportunity of knowing the charge and being heard, the appellant might be restored to membership. That very decision of the executive council might be one which the annual conference considered should never have been made at all, and one which might never have been made, if the appellants had been informed of the charges and heard on them.

All these considerations strongly indicate that the rules of natural justice apply to the making of an expulsion decision by the executive council under rule 3 (*e*). They are considerations which are particularly appropriate to such a non-technical business document as trade union rules, but I will also make a more technical and meticulous approach. An appeal, generally at any rate, implies the contention that the decision appealed against was wrong, and a successful appeal similarly implies the conclusion that the decision was wrong. But a subjective opinion and a decision laid down as the expression or consequence of a subjective opinion cannot by its very nature be wrong, as in the words of rule 3 (*e*), if the 'opinion' is subjective in the passage 'Any member shall be expelled from the union who in the opinion of the executive council is not a fit and proper person for membership,...' If 'opinion' is subjective, it is the opinion, and that is the end of the matter. But an appeal implies that the decision appealed against is of an appealable nature and not the expression of a subjective opinion but of an opinion that can be the subject of examination on appeal and, therefore, arrived at judicially and objectively. So this approach also, to my mind, indicates an inquiry and the rules of natural justice.

So, in view of all these considerations, it is incredible to my mind that these union rules should not necessarily contemplate that for the executive council to consider the expulsion of a member, the member should have a statement of charges or complaints and an opportunity of being heard by the council on them. The rules of natural justice are, in my view, necessarily implied into the making of an expulsion decision by the executive council under rule 3 (*e*), and those rules have not been observed in this case.

It was then submitted by the union that the plaintiffs were not entitled to relief from the courts until the domestic remedy by appeal within the union to the annual conference was exhausted. Reference was made to a statement in Norman Citrine's book on *Trade Union Law*, (1960) 2nd ed., p. 233, 'It is clear that where there is appeal machinery under the rules, the court will not interfere before that machinery has been used'. But that statement is not supported by authority, and in its present terms it is clearly too widely stated. Counsel referred me to *White* v. *Kuzych*,[1] where the Privy Council decided that a member of a trade union was bound to exhaust a right of appeal within the union before resorting to the courts. But in that case the member was contractually bound by express provision in the union by-laws to exhaust the domestic remedies before resorting to the courts, and that essential element is lacking here. In *Annamunthodo* v. *Oilfields Workers' Union*,[2] it was held that a trade union member who exercises a right of appeal within his union was not thereby precluded from having recourse to the courts. Lord Denning, in delivering the judgment of the Privy Council, referred to the 'special circumstances that prevailed in *White* v. *Kuzych*',[3] evidently referring to the express provision which I have mentioned limiting recourse to the courts. And he added that it was quite proper for the appellants to appeal to the annual conference before resorting to the courts 'even though he was not bound to do so'. The Privy Council thus seems to have been of the opinion that, in the absence of express provision to the contrary, a right of appeal to a domestic tribunal does not preclude resort to the courts before exercising that right. In *Bonsor* v. *Musicians' Union*,[4] the court intervened in favour of a trade union member where his expulsion was *ultra vires* the union rules despite his omission to exercise a domestic right of appeal within the union (see Lord Evershed, M.R.[5]).

Trade union rules clearly cannot oust the jurisdiction of the courts. Contracts, including a contract constituted by trade union rules, may provide that recourse to domestic tribunals shall be exhausted before there is recourse to the courts, and the courts may recognise and give effect to that contract; but that does not oust its jurisdiction. So in this case, the court has jurisdiction, and here there is no contractual provision requiring domestic remedies to be exhausted before resort to the courts. Should that jurisdiction be exercised now, or should it be withheld, in the circumstances, pending appeal to annual conference?

This case involves the construction of the rules of the trade union, and it is for the courts, and not a domestic body, to decide questions of construction, as matters of law. It involves questions of natural justice, which again are matters for the courts to decide. And pending the hearing of any appeal to the annual conference, which I am told

---

[1] [1951] A.C. 585.
[2] [1961] A.C. 945.
[3] [1951] A.C. 585.
[4] [1954] Ch. 479.
[5] [1954] Ch. 479, 485, [affd. [1956] A.C. 104].

will not be held until May 1965, the appellant would be excluded from membership and office in the union as, unlike the trade union constitution in *White* v. *Kuzych*,[1] the constitution of the union does not, as I have said, provide for any stay at all of expulsion pending the appeal. So the domestic appeal could not, in any event, provide all the relief which the court might provide; and if the court were to refuse relief until all domestic remedy had been exhausted, the remedy might be quite inadequate and substantial injustice might be suffered. Further, it is debatable whether improper failure to observe the rules of natural justice makes a decision void or voidable (see *White* v. *Kuzych*[2]). If it is void, it has been said to be not subject to appeal at all. But only the courts can decide whether it is void or voidable and whether, in this case, the executive council decision is a complete nullity and, therefore, not subject to appeal at all to the annual conference. So, in my judgment, this is not a case in which the court's jurisdiction is ousted or in which the court should decline to intervene on the ground that an appeal should first be made to and be heard by the annual conference of the union.

Then it is said that even though the rules of natural justice be applicable here and have been disregarded, and even though it is a case in which the court should not decline to intervene unless an appeal to the union annual conference has been heard, yet no sufficient case has been made for the interlocutory relief now claimed.

It is rightly pointed out that loss of membership of the union does not mean loss of job, so that the disadvantage to the plaintiffs is not of a financial character. But the disadvantage is more than merely social. The expulsion does affect the expelled member in his work. It affects his standing with and relation to other members. The trade union is concerned with members in their capacity as workers in their jobs, and expulsion excludes from the advantages which such membership confers. Trade unions, to their honour, also develop strong ties of loyalty amongst their members, and loss of membership, particularly amongst members of standing like some of the plaintiffs, strikes deep, and not the less so because it may not strike at the pocket. Failes, who is not himself a plaintiff, expresses that attachment when he says in his affidavit: 'My union card was my most treasured possession'. The plaintiffs have been elected to office by an electorate of 28,000 members to represent their interests, and such a position not only carries status and honour, but also responsibility to the members who have elected

[1] [1951] A.C. 585.　　　　　　　　[2] Ibid. 598.

them. Although so elected, and although an appeal to annual conference were unsuccessful, they would not, without the court's intervention, be able to stand for election next time, as I am told that that election occurs before the appeal to annual conference could be heard. And of course, if they were not to stand next time, their position in the union might be prejudiced, perhaps permanently. These considerations favour the granting of interlocutory relief.

But the general secretary has gone so far as to express the view that, if the relief now sought is granted, and I quote his words, 'it will be quite impossible to conduct reasonable meaningful negotiations' (that is, with the postal authorities) 'and there will be a very real risk of postal chaos and hardship to the general public'. I fully appreciate the difficulty of his responsible task, and the importance of the postal services. But for the plaintiffs it was submitted that failure to grant relief would exacerbate the dispute within the union to the public detriment. And I have the evidence of members of the executive council itself that a less drastic course than expulsion was sought; and that there was at any rate substantial support for a less drastic course had that not been ruled out of order as impossible under the rules. There have been put in evidence letters from the London District Postmaster to some of the plaintiffs, speaking well of their reasonable and helpful attitude in negotiation. To one of them he wrote: 'You are well known to us as an awkward talkative old "so and so," but in the last analysis you were always genuine, reasonable and helpful. We will miss you very much'. I am in no position to decide on these differences of view, and it is most undesirable that I should attempt to do so. My duty here is to the best of my ability to administer justice according to law. I am not concerned with the political or economic consequences of doing so. To do that would be to dabble in politics, and that is not my function here. I am only concerned with matters of public policy so far as they are expressed in legal principles of general application; and there is no legal principle that relief against ignoring natural justice must be denied if it is feared that it might prejudice industrial negotiations. Such fears are for others to deal with; and it may well be that there would be no great difficulty in dealing with them in this case. Nor am I trying the plaintiffs for being, in the parliamentary language of a civil servant, 'awkward so and so's'. I have merely to decide whether, *prima facie*, natural justice has wrongly been denied to the plaintiffs, and if so whether, within the well-established principles of the law, relief should be granted.

LEE v. SHOWMEN'S GUILD OF GREAT BRITAIN

Court of Appeal   [1952] 2 Q.B. 329

The plaintiff was expelled from the defendant union after he had failed to pay a fine. The fine was imposed because the area committee of the union decided that he had unfairly competed with another member, which was prohibited in the rules. The judge held that the plaintiff's conduct did not amount to 'unfair competition'. The defendants argued that provided the committee acting *bona fide* could reasonably take the view that the plaintiff's conduct was 'unfair competition' then the court should not interfere even if it disagreed. The judgment of the Court of Appeal is strictly based on a finding that the facts were not 'reasonably capable' of being 'unfair competition'. The defendants' appeal was dismissed.

DENNING, L.J. (after noting that the older cases rested the court's jurisdiction upon protection of the member's proprietary rights) said: The power of this court to intervene is founded on its jurisdiction to protect rights of contract. If a member is expelled by a committee in breach of contract, this court will grant a declaration that their action is *ultra vires*. It will also grant an injunction to prevent his expulsion if that is necessary to protect a proprietary right of his; or to protect him in his right to earn his livelihood: see *Amalgamated Society of Carpenters, etc.* v. *Braithwaite*[1]; but it will not grant an injunction to give a member the right to enter a social club, unless there are proprietary rights attached to it, because it is too personal to be specifically enforced: see *Baird* v. *Wells*.[2] That is, I think, the only relevance of rights of property in this connexion. It goes to the form of remedy, not to the right.

Although the jurisdiction of a domestic tribunal is founded on contract, express of implied, nevertheless the parties are not free to make any contract they like. There are important limitations imposed by public policy. The tribunal must, for instance, observe the principles of natural justice. They must give the man notice of the charge and a reasonable opportunity of meeting it. Any stipulation to the contrary would be invalid. They cannot stipulate for a power to condemn a man unheard...They can, of course, agree to leave questions of law, as well as questions of fact, to the decision of the domestic tribunal. They can, indeed, make the tribunal the final arbiter on questions of fact, but they cannot make it the final arbiter on questions of law.

[1] [1922] 2 A.C. 440.   [2] [1890] 44 Ch. D. 661, 675-6.

They cannot prevent its decisions being examined by the courts. If parties should seek, by agreement, to take the law out of the hands of the courts and put it into the hands of a private tribunal, without any recourse at all to the courts in case of error of law, then the agreement is to that extent contrary to public policy and void: see *Czarnikow & Co. Ltd* v. *Roth, Schmidt & Co.*[1] *In re Raven*[2] and *In re Wynn.*[3]

The question in this case is: to what extent will the courts examine the decisions of domestic tribunals on points of law? This is a new question which is not to be solved by turning to the club cases. In the case of social clubs, the rules usually empower the committee to expel a member who, in their opinion, has been guilty of conduct detrimental to the club; and this is a matter of opinion and nothing else. The courts have no wish to sit on appeal from their decisions on such a matter any more than from the decisions of a family conference. They have nothing to do with social rights or social duties. On any expulsion they will see that there is fair play. They will see that the man has notice of the charge and a reasonable opportunity of being heard. They will see that the committee observe the procedure laid down by the rules; but they will not otherwise interfere: see *Labouchere* v. *Earl of Wharncliffe*[4] and *Dawkins* v. *Antrobus.*[5]

It is very different with domestic tribunals which sit in judgment on the members of a trade or profession. They wield powers as great as, if not greater than, any exercised by the courts of law. They can deprive a man of his livelihood. They can ban him from the trade in which he has spent his life and which is the only trade he knows. They are usually empowered to do this for any breach of their rules, which, be it noted, are rules which they impose and which he has no real opportunity of accepting or rejecting. In theory their powers are based on contract. The man is supposed to have contracted to give them these great powers; but in practice he has no choice in the matter. If he is to engage in the trade, he has to submit to the rules promulgated by the committee. Is such a tribunal to be treated by these courts on the same footing as a social club? I say no. A man's right to work is just as important to him as, if not more important than, his rights of property. These courts intervene every day to protect rights of property. They must also intervene to protect the right to work.

But the question still remains: to what extent will the courts inter-

---

[1] [1922] 2 K.B. 478, 488.
[3] [1952] 1 Ch. 271.
[5] 17 Ch.D. 615, 630.

[2] [1915] 1 Ch. 673.
[4] (1879) 13 Ch.D. 346.

vene? They will, I think, always be prepared to examine the decision to see that the tribunal has observed the law. This includes the correct interpretation of the rules. Let me give an illustration. If a domestic tribunal is given power by the rules to expel a member for misconduct, such as here for 'unfair competition', does that mean that the tribunal is the sole judge of what constitutes unfair competition? Suppose it puts an entirely wrong construction on the words 'unfair competition' and finds a member guilty of it when no reasonable person could so find, has not the man a remedy? I think that he has, for the simple reason that he has only agreed to the committee exercising jurisdiction according to the true interpretation of the rules, and not according to a wrong interpretation. Take this very case. If the man is found guilty of unfair competition, the committee can impose a fine on him of a sum up to £250. Then if he has not the money to pay, or, at any rate, does not pay, within one month, the man automatically ceases to be a member of the guild: see rule 14. To be deprived of membership in this way is a very severe penalty on a man. It means that he will be excluded from all the fairgrounds of the country which are controlled by the guild or its members: see rules 11 (g) (ii) and 15 (a). This is a serious encroachment on his right to earn a livelihood, and it is, I think not to be permitted unless justified by the contract into which he has entered. The courts have never allowed a master to dismiss a servant except in accordance with the terms of the contract between them. So also they cannot permit a domestic tribunal to deprive a member of his livelihood or to injure him in it, unless the contract, on its true construction, gives the tribunal power to do so.

I repeat 'on its true construction', because I desire to emphasize that the true construction of the contract is to be decided by the courts and by no one else. Sir Frank Soskice argued that it was for the committee of the guild to construe the rules, and that, so long as they put an honest construction on them, their construction was binding on the members, even though it was a wrong construction. I cannot agree with that contention. The rules are the contract between the members. The committee cannot extend their jurisdiction by giving a wrong interpretation to the contract, no matter how honest they may be. They have only such jurisdiction as the contract on its true interpretation confers on them, not what they think it confers. The scope of their jurisdiction is a matter for the courts, and not for the parties, let alone for one of them.... In most of the cases which come before such a domestic tribunal the task of the committee can be divided into two parts: first, they must construe the rules; secondly, they must apply the rules to the facts. The first is a question of law which they must answer correctly if they are to keep within their jurisdiction; the second is a question of fact which is essentially a matter for them. The whole point of giving jurisdiction to a committee is so that they can determine the facts and decide what is to be done about them. The two parts of the task are, however, often inextricably mixed together. The construction of the rules is so bound up with the application of the rules to the facts that no one can tell one from the other. When that happens, the question whether the committee has acted within its jurisdiction depends, in my opinion, on whether the facts adduced before them were reasonably capable of being held to be a breach of the rules. If they were, then the proper inference is that the committee correctly construed the rules and have acted within their jurisdiction. If, however, the facts were not reasonably capable of being held to be a breach, and yet the committee held them to be a breach, then the only inference is that the committee have misconstrued the rules and exceeded their jurisdiction. The proposition is sometimes stated in the form that the court can interfere if there was no evidence to support the finding of the committee; but that only means that the facts were not reasonably capable of supporting the finding.

SOMERVELL, L.J. and ROMER, L.J. delivered concurring judgments.

BONSOR v. MUSICIANS' UNION

House of Lords   [1956] A.C. 104

The plaintiff was wrongly expelled from the defendant union when the branch secretary struck his name off the register without having authority to do so. The plaintiff was a musician and without membership of the union it was virtually impossible to get employment as a musician. He claimed damages from the union, and succeeded in obtaining them in addition to the remedy of an injunction. [The Court of Appeal had held in *Kelly* v. *NAT.S.O.P.A.* (1915) 84 L.J.K.B. 2236, that a member wrongly expelled might be granted a declaration or injunction, but would not be granted damages, for the reasons which Jenkins, L.J. best summarises in the passage cited below. The House of Lords reversed this long-standing rule, but in speeches which differed in their reasoning.*]

* See for discussions of the complexities of these speeches: D. Lloyd (1956) 19 M.L.R. 121; K. W. Wedderburn (1957) 20 M.L.R. 105; T. C. Thomas (1956) *Camb. Law J.* 67. See, too, for an illuminating account of the social and legal problems of such situations, W. E. J. McCarthy *The Closed Shop in Britain* (1964).

JENKINS, L.J.: But I may, perhaps, permit myself two observations on the merits of the decision in *Kelly's* case.[1] The first is that, given the premise that an action by a member of a registered trade union against the union in its registered name, for relief in respect of his wrongful exclusion or expulsion from the union in circumstances such as those of the present case, is an action against the members of the union (or the members of the union other than the plaintiff himself) based on breach of the contract of membership between themselves and the plaintiff, and not an action against the union as a distinct legal entity based on breach by that entity of a contract of membership between that entity and the plaintiff, the objections to allowing any claim to damages in an action so constituted are, to my mind, unanswerable.

The second is that, given the same premise, the alleged inconsistency in granting a declaration and an injunction while refusing damages, is by no means clear to me. In claiming a declaration and an injunction in a case such as this, the plaintiff member is in effect saying to his fellow members: 'Our common agent the secretary, duly appointed under the rules, has without our authority and in breach of the rules purported to exclude me from membership. I contend that such purported exclusion is a nullity, and that if you treat and act upon it as valid you will be committing a breach of the contract of membership subsisting between us. Accordingly, I am applying to the court for a declaration that my purported exclusion is invalid and an injunction restraining you from acting upon it, in order to protect my rights as a member'. To succeed in that claim the plaintiff need not bring home to any individual member any actual breach of his contract of membership.

But in claiming damages against his fellow members in the like case the plaintiff is in effect saying to his fellow members: 'Our common agent the secretary, duly appointed under the rules, has, without our authority and in breach of the rules, purported to exclude me from membership. I must admit that you did not authorize this wrongful act any more than I did, and that the offending secretary is my agent just as much as yours; and it is, of course, the foundation of my case that my purported exclusion by the secretary is a mere nullity. Nevertheless, I claim damages from each and every one of you on the ground that this wrongful and unauthorized act of the secretary in itself

[1] 113 L.T. 1055.

constituted a breach by you as his principals of the contract of membership subsisting between us'. It seems to me that the difficulties with which the claim in damages, so stated, is fraught do not attend the claim for relief by way of declaration and injunction.

The result might well be different if it could be held that in such cases the wrongfully expelled member's contract of membership was a contract between the wrongfully expelled member and the union as a legal entity distinct from its members, and the action an action against that entity based on breach of that contract. But the decision to the contrary in *Kelly's* case precludes us from so holding. Even if it was open to us so to hold, we could not do so without going the length of attributing full corporate status to a registered trade union, which, speaking for myself, I would hesitate to do.

In the House of Lords [1956] A.C. 104

LORD MORTON: My Lords, in my view the *Taff Vale* case[1] goes far to decide the question now before your Lordships' House. It may be that Lords Macnaghten and Lindley thought that an action against the union was an action against all the individual members—indeed, that view was expressed again by Lord Macnaghten in *Russell's* case[2] and by Lord Lindley in *Yorkshire Miners' Association* v. *Howden*[3]—but I am satisfied that it has never been more than a minority view, inconsistent with the relevant authorities from the *Taff Vale* case[4] onwards, with the solitary exception of *Kelly's* case[5]...

Finally, in the case of *National Union of General and Municipal Workers* v. *Gillian*,[6] the Court of Appeal, affirming Birkett, J., held that a trade union can sue for a libel on itself, and Uthwatt, J. said: 'That decision' (i.e., the decision in the *Taff Vale* case) 'involves, to my mind, that a registered trade union is recognized by the law as a body distinct from the individuals who from time to time compose it'. With that observation I agree, and all the cases to which I have referred, with the solitary exception of *Kelly's* case, lead me to the following conclusions:

(1) The respondent union, though it is not an incorporated body, is capable of entering into contracts and of being sued as a legal entity, distinct from its individual members.

(2) When Mr Bonsor applied to join the respondent union, and his

---

[1] [1901] A.C. 426.　　　　　　　　[2] [1912] A.C. 421, 429.
[3] [1905] A.C. 256, 280.　　　　　　[4] [1901] A.C. 426.
[5] 84 L.J.K.B. 2236.　　　　　　　　[6] [1946] K.B. 81.

application was accepted, a contract came into existence between Mr Bonsor and the respondent, whereby Mr Bonsor agreed to abide by the rules of the respondent union, and the union implied agreed that Mr Bonsor would not be excluded by the union or its officers otherwise than in accordance with the rules.

(3) The respondent union broke this contract, by wrongfully expelling Mr Bonsor, and Mr Bonsor sued the union as a legal entity. He did not sue either all the members of the union at the date of the writ than himself, many of whom must have joined since the breach of contract, or all the members of the union including himself.

(4) There is no reason in law why Mr Bonsor should not be granted against the respondent all the remedies appropriate to a breach of contract.

(5) The Court of Appeal in *Kelly's* case should have awarded damages to the plaintiff.

LORD PORTER: Apart from the question with whom did the member make his contract the Court of Appeal in *Kelly* v. *National Society of Operative Printers' Assistants* held that he was unable to sue because the agent of the society who had done him wrong was agent for himself as well as the other members, since the persons sued were an unincorporated body of which he was one. Looked at from this angle he was suing his own agent and therefore suing himself, a thing he could not do. If, however, there has been, as I think there has, a thing created by statute, call it what you will, an entity, a body, a near-corporation, which by statute has in certain respects an existence apart from its members, then I do not see why that body should not be sued by one of its members for a breach of contract.

The exact limits of the power of a trade union to bind itself need not be determined. It may well be that it does not possess the full powers of an incorporated society. Its position is perhaps best expressed by Farwell, J. in the *Taff Vale* case, and I am content to adopt his wording as expressing my own view of a trade union's status. It is true that in that case the plaintiff was an outside body and not one if its own members, but Farwell, J.'s words seem to me to be wide enough to embrace its liabilities not only to third parties but also to its members, inasmuch as they imply an existence of the body apart from the members of which it is composed.

LORD MACDERMOTT*: My Lords, I shall refer to the reasoning of *Kelly's* case later, but for the purposes of this narrative it will suffice

---

* With whom Lord Somervell largely agreed.

to say that it was based upon the view that a registered trade union is only an association of individuals, and that a member who sues it is suing the individuals who are his fellow-members. That view was challenged before the Court of Appeal on behalf of Mr Bonsor in a submission to the effect that a registered trade union was a juridical person in itself, a complete entity, a body with a legal personality separate from that of its members and as competent to contract with them as they were to contract with each other....

My Lords, if a registered trade union is a juridical person—and to avoid confusion I should say that I propose to use that expression as connoting the characteristics and attributes of the complete legal entity for which Mr Lester contended—it must be in consequence of the Trade Union Act, 1871, which provided for the voluntary registration of trade unions and conferred certain privileges upon unions taking advantage of that provision. There can be no question that a trade union which is not registered under that Act is not a juridical person. It is a voluntary association of persons, a combination for the purposes mentioned in the definition of 'trade union' in s. 23 of the Act of 1871, as modified by s. 16 of the Trade Union Act (1871), Amendment Act, 1876, and s. 2 of the Trade Union Act, 1913. The first step, therefore, in ascertaining the effect of registration on the nature of a trade union must be to consider such of the provisions of the Act of 1871 as appear to have a bearing on the point.

Sections 2 and 3 throw no direct light on the question, but they were enacted to deal with a situation which has to be kept in mind in construing the Act....Now, it is clear that s. 4, like ss. 2 and 3, is not confined in its application to unions which are registered under the subsequent provisions of the Act. It applies to trade unions within the definition to which I have already referred, and therefore to unions which are not registered and not juridical persons as well as to unions which are registered; and this, it may be added, holds good for all the classes of agreement which s. 4 specifies, for there is nothing in the text to restrict any of these classes to a particular type of union. On this account s. 4 can hardly be expected to furnish a positive answer to the question under discussion; nevertheless I think its description of class (1), though by no means conclusive, affords some indication of the intention of the legislature. That class of agreement is described in a manner which indicates that it was the policy of Parliament to keep the contracts of union members respecting the main purposes of their combination outside the jurisdiction of the courts. The description accords with what has long been the generally accepted view of the bond by which the members of a trade union are held in association, namely, the contract between members which is formed on admission by an acceptance of the union rules. But it does not refer to agreements between a union and its members. This omission seems natural if the only bond in contemplation was that just mentioned. But I do not think it is what one would expect if the intention was to make a juridical person of any union choosing to register, as in that case the registered union would, while the unregistered union would not, be free to circumvent this part of s. 4 by the simple expedient of doing what the union here is said to have done and framing its rules so that the members were bound contractually to it; and that would be contrary to the policy of s. 4, if I am right in the view already expressed that that section was meant to apply to trade unions generally and irrespective of registration...

I would agree with Denning, L.J. that a trade union may be regarded as an entity in fact. In common parlance the term is habitually used to connote something that is in some way different from the individuals who form the combination; and I think it is right to say that the Act of 1871 (including s. 4) speaks after this fashion and recognizes that a trade union and its membership may not always mean the same thing. But the same can be said of many groups which lay no claim to a legal personality, and since s. 4 applies to both registered and unregistered unions, the Act's recognition of the factual entity can, in my opinion, offer no sound ground for making the registered union a legal entity as well.

Section 6 provides for registration, but neither in it nor in the fasciculus of sections, beginning with s. 13, which deals with the machinery of registration and various obligations flowing therefrom, nor elsewhere, is any provision for incorporation to be found; this omission is all the more striking in view of s. 5 which enacts that certain statutes, including the Companies Acts, 1862 and 1867, 'shall not apply to any trade union, and the registration of any trade union under any of the said Acts shall be void'. Then s. 7 says that it shall be lawful for a registered trade union to purchase or take on lease in the names of its trustees any land not exceeding one acre and to sell, exchange, mortgage or let the same. And s. 8 enacts that all the real and personal estate belonging to a registered trade union shall be vested in its trustees for the time being 'for the use and benefit of such trade union and the members thereof'. At first glance the enabling form of s. 7 suggests that the legislature regarded a registered trade union as an entity apart from its members which, like certain incorporated bodies, required special authority to hold land. But against this must be set the provision made in both ss. 7 and 8 for the holding of union property by the union trustees, which was relied upon by the union as a clear indication that Parliament did not intend to make the registered trade union a juridical person, and as such capable of holding its own assets in its own name. Section 9 was said to point in the same direction.... If, as the appellant claims, this Act made the registered union a juridical person, in the sense in which I am using the expression, there seems no very convincing reason why it should not have been left to sue and be sued respecting its property without conferring these special powers upon its officers and trustees.... Section 13 deals with applications for registration, and s. 14 provides, *inter alia*, for the union having a name which can be registered. Section 15 requires a registered trade union to have a registered office, and s. 16 requires it to make annual returns. Each of these last two sections further provides that a trade union which fails to comply with its requirements shall be liable to a penalty. This was said to point to a registered trade union having a distinct personality as, at common law, an offender must be either a natural or an artificial person and must be named or otherwise identifies as a person in the charge.

Reference may also be made in this connexion to ss. 6 and 8 of the Act of 1876. Section 6 requires a registered trade union to be registered in that part of the kingdom where its registered office is, and provides that if it carries on business in another part of the kingdom it is not to enjoy there 'any of the privileges' of the Acts of 1871 and 1876 until the rules have been recorded by the registrar of that other part. Thus, if the act of registration creates a juristic person, it could happen, to take an example, that a union active through Great Britain, with one membership and one set of rules, might find itself at the same time an association of individuals in Scotland and an artificial person, a distinct entity, in England—or vice versa, according to the location of the registered office. The power of Parliament to do more than that cannot be questioned, but one would expect to find the intention to produce such an anomalous situation expressed in clear terms. Section 8 evokes a similar reflection. It makes provision whereby, *inter alia*, a registered trade union may have its certificate of registration withdrawn or cancelled at its request, and enacts that when this is done the union shall 'absolutely cease to enjoy as such the privileges of a registered trade union, but without prejudice to any liability actually incurred by such trade union, which may be enforced against the same as if such withdrawal or cancelling had not taken place'. I find it difficult to believe that the legislature ever intended that a trade union should be able to accomplish a fundamental change in its legal character by this simple procedure; yet such would be the result if the appellant's contention were well founded. It would be idle to say that these sections, considered in the context in which they must be placed, make an end of the matter; but their operation is relevant, and their language suggests a further way of stating the issue. Did Parliament intend registration to create a new sort of trade union with a legal personality of its own, or merely to confer the privileges for which the Acts provide the unions as they were?...

My Lords, having endeavoured to give [effect] to what has been said on the subject, both in the cases and at the Bar, I have come to the conclusion that the correct view is the view favoured by Lord Macnaghten and Lord Lindley[1] and by the Master of the Rolls and Jenkins, L.J. in the Court of Appeal. I base this opinion primarily on the statutes. The more closely they are examined the clearer it seems to be that the legislature, though minded to bestow upon registered unions some of the gifts and attributes of legal personality, had no intention of doing more and was, indeed, averse to the idea of going the whole length and making those unions new creatures, distinct in law from their membership, and fundamentally different from the 'combination' of persons which the definition requires all trade unions to be. I need not go over the various provisions of the Acts again. If they point in more than one direction, on balance they seem to me to lead away from the appellant's contention; and taken together it would, I think, be right to say of them that they make of registration and its results something of far less consequence than might fairly be expected had that process been meant to bring into being a new juridical person. The comparative ease with which the garb of registration may be donned and doffed hardly accords with the view that each exchange means the taking up or the laying down of a legal personality; there is, however, nothing so casual or anomalous about the position if all that happens is that the union concerned gains or loses, as the case may be, certain advantages or 'privileges' with their attendant responsibilities. But perhaps the most weighty consideration of all lies in the fact that Parliament has

---

[1] In the *Taff Vale* case, *ante*, p. 541, which speeches his Lordship had analysed closely. 'Effect' is misprinted as 'that' in the Appeal Cases report.

made no effort to incorporate the registered trade union. In the latter half of last century incorporation was the recognized and usual way of conferring upon an association of persons the status of a distinct legal entity, and it is clear that the draftsman of the Act of 1871 had the Companies Act of 1862 before him. Yet there is not a word about the members becoming, on registration, a body corporate, and the only reference to a seal is in relation to the work of the registry. Parliament is not, of course, restricted in its choice of possible methods for producing a given result. But when, as here, it studiously avoids a familiar and appropriate method without purporting to adopt another in its stead, its intention to reach that result may well be open to doubt. For these reasons I am of opinion that a registered trade union is not a juridical person.

Having come to this conclusion it is, I think, desirable to add some observations respecting the procedural consequences of the *Taff Vale* decision.[1] How a voluntary association of persons, such as a trade union, can be sued is hardly less important than its responsibility under the law. The numbers and the changing character of its membership may be such as to make it impracticable to sue the right persons individually and difficult to obtain an order appointing representative defendants. These difficulties are, perhaps, at their height in the case of trade unions of workmen where the membership often runs into many thousands and is subject to a constant fluctuation. Anyone—be he a member or an outsider—who seeks a remedy in the courts against an unregistered union of this nature may well be confronted at the outset with a formidable problem in determining how to constitute his suit. The *Taff Vale* decision removed this obstacle to the process of adjudication in the case of the registered union by holding that Parliament had allowed it to be sued in its registered name. Where this is done the party suing, if he is to succeed, has still, of course, to show that the union concerned is, as an organized combination, responsible for the act of which he complains; but he does not need to marshal the membership on any basis of individual liability as, for example, by excluding those who are infants or who have joined since his cause of action arose or who, as a minority, have voted in his favour; nor (if a member) has he, in my opinion, even to make it clear on the face of the record that he excludes himself. The peculiarity of this procedure, like that under the rules of court in England and Northern Ireland whereby a partnership may be sued in its firm name, lies in the fact that it sanctions

[1] [1901] A.C. 426.

proceedings at law in a name which is not that of a juridical person, either natural or artificial. But that, as Farwell J. pointed out and as this House held in the *Taff Vale* case, is the result of what Parliament has enacted and, anomalous though it may be, there can be little doubt that as a procedure it is a convenient and valuable aid to the administration of justice. It has, however, one consequence which ought not to be overlooked. If a union is sued to judgment in its registered name execution in respect of any sum it may be ordered to pay cannot, in my opinion, be levied on the assets of members and must be confined to the property of the union. That, as I read the judgment of Farwell, J., was his view, and it was also the view of Lord Lindley, who said at the end of his speech[1]: 'I will add that if a judgment or order in that form' —that is, against a trade union in its registered name—'is for the payment of money it can, in my opinion, only be enforced against the property of the trade union...' Lord Lindley did not state his reasons for this conclusion. Subsequently, in delivering the judgment of the Judicial Committee in *Wise* v. *Perpetual Trustee Co. Ltd*,[2] he said, speaking of unincorporated member clubs: 'They are societies the members of which are perpetually changing. They are not partnerships; they are not associations for gain; and which distinguishes them from other societies is that no member as such becomes liable to pay to the funds of the society or to anyone else any money beyond the subscriptions required by the rules of the club to be paid as he so long remains a member'. It may be, taking the view he did of the legal nature of a registered union, that Lord Lindley considered its members to be, in this respect, in a position similar to the members of a club. But I feel no certainty about that or as to whether the passage I have quoted was meant to apply to unliquidated claims. I have not, therefore, based my opinion on any analogy of this sort. I prefer to found it on what appears to me a simpler and less debatable ground. If the statutory right to sue a registered union in its registered name is exercised and a money judgment is obtained, there is no procedure available whereby execution may be levied on foot of such a judgment against the individual members. I find it hard to regard this omission as accidental but, however that may be, the fact is that Parliament has not provided any machinery for extending what I may call a registered name judgment so as to make it enforceable against members as such. The situation where the members are sued by name or by duly appointed representatives raises different and, as it seems to me, more difficult

---

[1] Ibid. 445.　　　　　　　　[2] [1903] A.C. 139, 149.

considerations, but as that situation does not arise here I express no opinion upon it.

My Lords, counsel for the union conceded—very rightly as I think—that s. 4 of the Act of 1871 did not apply to these proceedings.... My Lords, the salient facts in *Kelly's* case are so similar to those of the present appeal that I need not refer to them at length. In each case the party seeking redress had been actually expelled from his union; in each the expulsion was wrongful and in breach of the rules forming the contract between the members; and in each the union stood behind the expulsion and sought to justify it as warranted by the rules until it had to admit defeat on that issue before the Court of Appeal.... The second matter arises on that part of the judgment of Bankes, L.J. in which he says: 'Further than this, the very ground on which the plaintiff succeeds in obtaining an injunction is fatal to his claim for damages. He succeeds in that claim because he has established that the London committee and the executive committee in expelling him from the society acted without authority and in defiance of the rules. Having established that fact, it is not possible to contend that they were at the same time the authorized agents of his fellow members to do the acts which he complains of as constituting breaches of his contract'. I have no doubt that this point, which is not taken by the other members of the court, is outside the ratio of its decision; but I have considerable difficulty in seeing how it can be applied to the facts of *Kelly's* case if I have gathered them aright. Had the union there disavowed the action of the committee the reasoning of this passage would be plainer, but instead of doing that the union appears from the reports to have approved the views of the committee and to have adopted what it had done. Here the relevant facts preclude the point, if anything more clearly. There is little more the Musicians' Union could have done to identify itself with the expulsion of Mr Bonsor. It has made the act of the branch secretary its act and cannot now say that because the expulsion was unauthorized by the rules it has no responsibility for it.

With these points out of the way the ratio of *Kelly's* case is, I think, clear...Bankes, L.J. stated it more fully than the other members in saying: 'The plaintiff's case is that this contract has been broken, not by all the other members personally, but by the London committee acting as the agents of those other members. It is here, I think, that the plaintiff fails. It is true that both these bodies were appointed by the general body of members, and as such they are the agents of the members, but they are just as much the agents of the plaintiff as the agents of his fellow members whom he seeks to make liable under their collective name'.

My Lords, as I follow it, this reasoning is not based on any concept peculiar to the law of trade unions. It appears to be founded on a general proposition to the effect that a member of a voluntary association who is injured by some wrongful act done by an agent of the association on behalf of its members, including himself, cannot recover against his fellow members whose responsibility, in the circumstances, will be no greater than his own. For the purposes of this appeal I am prepared to accept that proposition without inquiry as to what, if any, are the limits to be put upon it. But one of its essential ingredients is that the act complained of should be done by the agent on behalf of the injured member. Was the Court of Appeal right in holding that the committee which expelled Mr Kelly was, in so doing, acting as his agent? In the present case Denning, L.J. answered that question thus[1]: 'I cannot', he said, 'understand this line of reasoning. I cannot understand, how it can be said that the committee, when they were excluding Kelly, were acting as 'agents on his behalf. They were acting against him, not for him'. My Lords, I think this criticism is well founded and I agree with it. Expulsion from membership of a trade union stands, as a breach of contract, in a special category. It may be that a union committee or official, while investigating a complaint against a member, can be said to be acting on his behalf. I do not need to decide that or to say where the line is to be drawn. We are now concerned with a later stage, with the act of expulsion, when what is being done is to thrust a party to the contract out of the combination on the ground that he is no longer entitled to any of the rights or privileges of membership. To say that that is done on behalf of the person expelled seems to me an unwarranted extension of the agency and quite out of keeping with reality.

For this reason I think *Kelly's* case was wrongly decided, and as I see nothing else to stand in the way of an award of damages, I would therefore allow the appeal and remit the case for the purpose of assessing the amount to be recovered.*

---

[1] [1954] Ch. 479, 513.

* The damages would be assessed in accordance with the ordinary principles of the law of contract. The plaintiff would be under a duty to mitigate his loss. Tax would normally be deductable from sums representing loss of earnings: see *Parsons* v. *B.N.M. Laboratories Ltd, ante*, p. 191. If the plaintiff proved a cause of action in tort, it is possible that higher damages could be awarded as 'aggravated' damages, though not,

LORD KEITH: My Lords, I think that the decisions of this House show that, in a sense, a registered trade union is a legal entity distinguishable at any moment of time from the members of which it is at that time composed. It remains a voluntary association of individuals but it is capable of suing and being sued in its registered name; it holds property, through trustees, against which a creditor holding a decree against it could levy execution; it acts by agents; and it has other rights and is subject to other liabilities set out in the Trade Union Acts. It differs from an unincorporated association in that it is unnecessary to consider who were the members at any particular time. For instance, it is immaterial who were the members at the time that any cause of action arose, or what members have joined the union since the cause of action arose. The registered trade union may be said to assume a collective responsibility for all members past, present and future, in respect of any cause of action for which it may be made liable, irrespective of the date of the cause of action. On the other hand, the judgment creditor can look only to the funds of such a trade union to satisfy his debt, and to the extent to which these may be augmented from time to time by contributions of members, whether new or old, they will still be available for the unsatisfied judgment creditor.

These are important attributes, or characteristics, of a registered trade union which, in my opinion, differentiate it from other voluntary associations and may entitle it to be called a legal entity, while at the same time remaining an unincorporated association of individuals. As an association its membership is constantly changing but as a registered trade union it has a permanent identity and represents its members at any moment of time. It would not, I think, be wrong to call it a legal entity...

In the result, then, my view is that Mr Bonsor's contract of membership was a contract between himself and the other members of the union. On the view I have endeavoured to express it may be regarded also as a contract with the trade union, for the trade union, in its registered capacity, is representative of all the members. So long as this is kept in view it is convenient to talk of a member's contract of membership as a contract with his trade union. Has, then, the plaintiff a right to sue the trade union for breach of contract?

The Court of Appeal has held itself bound by the decision *Kelly* v.

after *Rookes* v. *Barnard* [1964] A.C. 1129, 'exemplary' damages. Such a tort action might arise from a conspiracy to injure, as in *Huntley* v. *Thornton ante*, p. 460; or, perhaps, an unlawful conspiracy to expel the plaintiff in breach of contract: see, *The Worker and The Law* (1965) p. 323, (1966) p. 311.

National Society of Operative Printers' Assistants and the question is whether *Kelly's* case was rightly decided. That case was decided in the Court of Appeal by a strong court. On its facts it is indistinguishable from the present case. Kelly sought against a registered trade union a declaration, an injunction and damages in respect of illegal expulsion from the union. He was held entitled to a declaration and injunction, but his claim for damages was refused. I find it unnecessary to analyse the judgments in detail. The ratio of all the judgments appears to me to be that in complaining of the action of the officers of the union in expelling him the plaintiff was complaining of the conduct of agents of all the members of the union, including himself, and that in suing the trade union he was suing himself among others. In my opinion this reasoning suffers from an underlying fallacy. A simple example will illustrate the point. Take the case of a member who has been illegally expelled by a majority of members at a general meeting which is sufficient to bind the union. No question of agency arises here. The member may be entitled to sue the individuals of the majority for damages in some form of action. I do not find it necessary, however, to decide this point. He could not, it is clear, sue the individuals of the minority. But I see no reason why, if the union is bound by the voice of the majority, the member should not be able to sue the union as here for a declaration and injunction, and the question would then arise, clear of any question of agency, whether he could sue it for damages and recover against the union funds. If the expulsion takes place on the initiative of the union officials it appears to me that it reduces the position to an absurdity to say that the officials were acting as the expelled member's agents in the matter of the expulsion. They are no more his agents in the matter complained of than would be a majority who expelled him in a general meeting. There may be cases where a trade union disclaims the action of an official or officials and in which, accordingly, the conduct complained of cannot be said to be the act of that trade union. But in such a case the member would be speedily restored to his status as a union member and would, presumably, in the matter of any claim of damages, have to proceed against the individual or individuals concerned.

(iv) MATERIALS FROM UNION RULE BOOKS*

TRANSPORT AND GENERAL WORKERS' UNION

RULE II. BRANCHES...

...19. Any member violating any working rules, registration, or by-laws, disseminating false statements or any rumour which tends to depreciate the organisation, its officers, or any section appertaining to the Union, or circulating any business of the Union to unauthorised persons without authority, or who is guilty of other forms of misconduct shall be fined a sum not exceeding £5, or otherwise dealt with by the branch or authorised committee of the Union as may be deemed fit.

20. (a) Complaints against the conduct of members may be dealt with by the branch, branch committee (where so determined by the branch), divisional committee, regional committee or the General Executive Council. A member whose conduct is the subject of inquiry shall be given notice of the complaint in writing with an intimation of his right to be present at the hearing.

(b) If a branch, branch committee or divisional committee, as the case may be, imposes a fine for misconduct, or for any of the offences specified in clause 19, the member shall have a right of appeal to the regional committee, whose decision shall be final. Notwithstanding the foregoing provision a regional committee shall have power to impose fines for misconduct provided that in the event of a fine being imposed by a regional committee, a member shall have a right of appeal to the General Executive Council, whose decision shall be final.

(c) Notice of appeal under the preceding clause (b) must be in writing and sent to the regional secretary or the general secretary, as the case may be, within fourteen days from the date of receipt of notification of the fine, and the appeal shall be heard at the first meeting of the regional committee or the General Executive Council, as the case may be, held following the receipt of such notice.

(d) Where a question of expulsion arises for misconduct, or for any of the offences specified in clause 19, the investigation shall be conducted by the regional committee who shall make recommendations to the General Executive Council. A member whose conduct is the

---

* This small selection is not meant to be representative. Indeed, the rule books of unions vary so much that such a selection would be difficult to make. The object of this section is to add a few illustrative materials to those found in the judicial decisions on which discussion of legal problems may be based.

subject of complaint, shall be given notice of the investigation in writing and afforded an opportunity of appearing before the regional committee. The General Executive Council may act upon the recommendation of the regional committee or make further investigation or take such steps as, in the opinion of the General Executive Council, seem just.

21. Without prejudice to any other ground of expulsion contained in these rules, any member, or members, of the Union who, in the opinion of the General Executive Council shall have injured or attempted to injure the Union, or worked or acted contrary to the interest of the Union or its members, or whose conduct shall have been otherwise inconsistent with the duties of a member of this Union may be fined a sum not exceeding £5 and if holding office removed therefrom, or may be expelled by the General Executive Council from the Union and shall thereupon, subject to the right of appeal as in these rules provided, cease to be a member thereof...

RULE 20. MEMBERSHIP

1. All members of the amalgamating unions shall be members of the Union.

2. Persons of either sex may be admitted members of the Union, and upon being admitted shall be deemed to agree to abide by the rules of the Union in every respect. If, in the opinion of the General Executive Council, a person fails to abide by the rules at any time, that person shall be liable to forfeit membership...

4. The General Executive Council shall have power, on application from the appropriate committee, to establish by-laws for any particular section, port or district, governing the admission of new members, and/or determining the entrance fee to be charged. Such by-laws shall become binding on the branches within the section, port or district, as the case may be, and so remain until revoked by the General Executive Council.

5. Subject to the provisions of clause 4, every person applying for membership shall, on admission, pay his entrance fee and the first week's contribution at the appropriate rate provided in the schedules annexed to these rules.

6. Every member shall contribute as in such schedules provided...

12. (a) Any member wishing to transfer to another branch shall only do so if clear on the books. He shall apply to the secretary of the

branch he wishes to join, who shall forward a form to the secretary of the branch he then belongs to, who shall fill it in and return. Any branch secretary transferring a member of his branch without transfer form shall be fined 1*s*.

(*b*) Any member of another union desiring to transfer shall pay all arrears to the union he is about to leave before being accepted as a member; but owing to the exceptional circumstances prevailing in certain unions the General Executive Council shall have power to decide transfer arrangements to meet the conditions.

13. Any member going to sea shall remain in benefit for a period not exceeding six months provided that he clears his contribution card to date of sailing and shall before embarking notify in writing to the branch secretary or other permanent officer the name of his ship and probable period of absence, and the next branch meeting shall approve, and the General Executive Council shall endorse such approval. Such member shall report to the branch secretary or other permanent officer and bring himself into compliance by paying all arrears within seven days after return. No application for benefit shall be entertained unless arrears up to the date thereof shall have been paid.

14. Any national or regional trade group committee may submit for the approval of the General Executive Council such by-laws as may be necessary to govern the conduct of members in their trade group in connection with working conditions and the observance of working rules.

15. Notwithstanding anything in these rules the General Executive Council may, by giving six week's notice in writing, terminate the membership of any member if necessary in order to comply with a decision of the Disputes Committee of the Trades Union Congress.

16. Any member obtaining membership of the Union by false statement material to his admission into the Union or any evasion in that regard may be expelled from the Union by decision of the General Executive Council...

RULE 26. AMENDMENT OF RULES

1. No new rule shall be made, nor shall any rule herein contained or hereafter to be made be amended or rescinded, except in accordance with a resolution duly passed at a Rules Conference of the Union.

2. No new rule or amendment or rescission of a rule shall be valid until registered.

RULE 27. VOLUNTARY DISSOLUTION

The Union may be dissolved at any time by the consent of five-sixths of the members voting at meetings duly summoned for that purpose....

SCHEDULE I. ELIGIBILITY AND REQUIREMENTS OF DELEGATES, OFFICERS, ETC.

1. Every candidate for any office in the Union, i.e., officers, whether paid or not, or delegates to a Delegate Conference, the Rules Conference, or for membership of the General Executive Council, or of a national trade group, or a regional trade group, or a regional committee or other constitutional committee, shall have been a financial member of this Union for at least two years immediately preceding the date of application or nomination, subject to the provisions of rule 16, clause 1, rule 6, clause 10, and rule 17, clause 1, in the case of the general secretary, docks officer and the financial secretary, respectively. A candidate must be employed in or in connection with the trade he desires to represent provided always that for the purpose of suitable and efficient discharge of the duties of a paid officer the General Executive Council may, at its discretion, invite applications from other or all sections of the membership.

2. No member of the Communist or Fascist Parties shall be eligible to hold any office within the Union, either as a lay member or as a permanent full-time officer, this rule to take effect as and from the beginning of the 1950/51 electoral period...

BRITISH IRON, STEEL, AND KINDRED TRADES ASSOCIATION

RULE 43

...5. If any dispute shall arise between any member or any person who has ceased to be a member or any person claiming through such member or person or under these rules and the Association or the Executive Council, it shall, failing settlement by amicable negotiation, be referred to a court of arbitration as provided in this rule, and the decision of such court shall be final, conclusive, and binding upon all parties concerned, without any further right of appeal, and shall not be removable into any court of law or restrainable by injunction. The arbitration court shall have power to direct by whom the expenses of the arbitration shall be paid, and any such direction shall in like manner be binding upon all parties concerned.

Provided that nothing herein contained shall deprive any member or any person of any rights which are open to him to seek the decision of a court of competent jurisdiction upon any question arising out of the interpretation of these Rules or on a matter of law.

6. Twelve persons, being trade unionists and members of any organisation affiliated to the Trades Union Congress or to the Scottish Trades Union Congress, or to the Labour Party, and not being beneficially interested directly or indirectly in the funds of the Association, shall be elected at the first Executive Council meeting held in any year, and shall constitute a panel of arbitrators...

RULE 44

1. The Executive Council shall have power to impose the fines stated in these rules, and in addition to fine in any sum not more than forty shillings (and if an official of the Association to suspend or dismiss from office) or to expel any member upon satisfactory proof being given that such member has by his conduct brought the Association into discredit or has violated trade rules or rates of wages recognised by the Association, or has been fraudently receiving or misapplying the funds of the Association or the moneys of any members entrusted to him for payment to the Association, or has slandered or libelled another member in his capacity as a member or an official of the Association, or at any meeting of members of the Association has been guilty of using language of a vulgar and filthy nature, or of being drunk and disorderly, or has been guilty of using information obtained at any meeting or from any publication of the Association to the detriment of the Association or of any member thereof, or has advocated or taken legal proceedings not being arbitration proceedings under the provisions of Rule 43 against the Association, or has damaged or destroyed or improperly withheld any of the books or other property of the Association, or has in any other way sought to injure the Association.

NATIONAL UNION OF PRINTING, BOOKBINDING, AND PAPER WORKERS

RULE 26. CONTRIBUTIONS, FINES, ARREARS AND EXCLUSIONS...

...7. No member who is in regular employment shall do any work whatever for another employer without the consent of the Branch Secretary. Where permission has been given, all such cases to be reported to the Branch Committee at the following meeting.

Any member breaking this rule shall be liable to a fine not exceeding £20, as the Branch Committee may determine.

8. No member shall work more than eight hours' overtime in one week, unless provided for in trade agreements.

In special circumstances a Branch Secretary may grant an extension on application by an employer provided that there are no unemployed members available capable of doing the work.

Any member exceeding the overtime limit without sanction shall be dealt with by the Branch Committee, who shall have power to impose a fine not exceeding £20....

RULE 27. MISCONDUCT OF MEMBERS

Any member shall be liable to exclusion from the Union, a fine not exceeding £20, or a warning, as the Branch Committee may determine:

(*a*) If having insulted any officer or member, or otherwise abused them, either at meetings of the Union or elsewhere, by charging them with any act of injustice or improper conduct as to the discharge of their duty which they cannot prove.

(*b*) If having obtained admission into the Union by misrepresentation.

(*c*) If he has become indebted to the Union for unpaid contributions, according to rule.

(*d*) If having made a fraudulent claim for any financial benefits whatever.

(*e*) If having fraudulently received or misapplied the funds of the National Union, Branch or Chapel.

(*f*) For accepting a situation, or any work for less than the Union scale, or under conditions which are in contravention of the instructions of the Executuve Council or Branch Committee.

(*g*) If having acted to the detriment of the interests of the Union.

(*h*) If having attempted to break up or encourage the breaking up of any Branch of the Union.

(*i*) If he has been fined three times for offences under these Rules the penalty of expulsion may be immediately applied...

RULE 51. FINAL APPEAL COURT

1. The Final Appeal Court shall consist of 24 members, who shall be elected biennially from and by the delegates attending the Delegate Council. A member of the Exchange Council shall not be eligible to be a member of the Final Appeal Court. Members of the Final Appeal Court must not be over the age of 65 men and 60 women. Each division shall elect four members, except Division 1, who shall elect eight members: there to be not more than two representatives from any Branch, except in Division 1, where the maximum shall be three. In addition, Divisions 2, 3, 4 and 5 shall elect a fifth and sixth member, and Division 1 a ninth, tenth, eleventh and twelfth member, who shall be available for co-option to fill any vacancy occurring in the respective divisional representation. The members of the Final Appeal Court shall elect as Chairman one of their number, who shall have no vote. Not less than 12 members shall form a quorum. The General Secretary (or in his absence, the General President) shall have the right to attend by virtue of office at any appeal, and the General Secretary shall have power to call any necessary witnesses...

6. No member of the Final Appeal Court will be permitted to adjudicate on any case in which he is personally interested or in any case where he holds an administrative position in the Branch to which the appellant belongs. Where by virtue of the foregoing section of this rule a question is raised the decision of the Final Appeal Court shall be final...

8. (i) The Final Appeal Court shall determine all appeals in strict accord with the Rules.

(ii) The appellant shall be permitted to present his case to the Court either orally or in writing (at his discretion) and to call any witnesses whose evidence is relevant.

(iii) The appellant may be represented before the Final Appeal Court, but only by a member of the Union.

(iv) In the event of equal voting, the appellant shall be deemed to have succeeded in his appeal.

(v) The Final Appeal Court shall determine its procedure for hearing appeals except in so far as is provided by these Rules.

(vi) Where the final Appeal Court find in favour of an appellant it shall order the payment of the appellant's reasonable expenses in attending before it. The expenses of not more than two witnesses shall be met, whether or not the appellant's case is upheld.

UNION OF SHOP, DISTRIBUTIVE AND ALLIED WORKERS

RULE 36. ARREARS

1. Any member in arrears with ordinary contributions to the extent of six weeks or less, or in arrears with any levies due, on any date when a claim for benefit arises and is made, shall not be entitled to receive benefit until the whole amount of arrears has been actually paid by him or on his behalf.

2. Any member who is seven weeks or more, but not exceeding thirteen weeks, in arrears with ordinary contributions on any date when a claim for benefit arises and is made, shall not be entitled to receive benefit until all arrears are actually paid by him or on his behalf and a penalty waiting period of six weeks has elapsed from the date of arrears payment, and benefit shall not be paid retrospectively over the said waiting period, but only forward from the end of such period if the reason for the claim (sickness, disability, unemployment, etc.) still continues, and provided that the member is not again in arrears.

3. Any member whose contributions are over thirteen weeks in arrears shall be liable to be struck off the books if the Executive Council so decide, but if allowed to remain on the books shall be disentitled to any benefits for a period of thirteen weeks from the date on which such arrears are paid, and thereafter shall be entitled to benefit only if clear on the books....

RULE 38. CONNECTION WITH OTHER BODIES

1. No portion of the Union's funds (local or national) shall be expended directly or indirectly under this Rule or otherwise in further-ance of any of the political objects defined in the Trade Union Act, 1913, and set out in s. 1 (*a*) of Rule 39, (Part I of Rule Book), unless

and until the provisions of the Trade Union Act, 1913, have been complied with and Rules under that Act are duly in force.

NOTE: 'ILFORD-TYPE' AGREEMENTS, THE EMPLOYMENT CONTRACT, AND UNION RULES

A certain number of agreements now exist between employers and unions of the kind made in 1965 between Ilford Ltd and the National Union of General and Municipal Workers. The company, on its side, in this sort of collective bargain, accepts the principle of 100 per cent trade union membership for employees. In return, the union agrees to co-operate with management in various stated ways, including, in the Ilford Agreement itself, acceptance of 'job evaluation' as the basis of the wage structure, and a guarantee that locally bargained bonuses or other benefits would not be used on a 'comparability' basis as a lever for attempts to gain similar benefits in other plants of the company. More important, it is agreed that each and every employee shall sign an 'Undertaking'. In this he promises, as an employee of the company *and* as a union member, to abide by the union rules and by the Agreements made between the union and the company. In the event of breach of such undertakings, the company becomes free from its '100 per cent unionism' obligation. Limits are also placed upon the union's power to expel a member without first consulting the company.

The reader will notice that in situations of this kind, the legal institutions of the contract of employment, the contract of union membership, and the collective agreement, have been welded together in a novel fashion. The present writer has described the situation as one of a 'closed discipline' kind for the individual worker; since, if the company Works Rules and the union rules on expulsion are interwoven sufficiently closely, the worker can find that a breach of *either* his employment obligations *or* his union obligations can lead to the loss of both employment and union membership: Evidence to Royal Commission on Trade Unions: Day 31 (H.M.S.O. 1966) paragraph 100. It remains to be seen how many unions will bring their rule books and their members' contracts of union membership within the ambit of such relationship by negotiating such agreements.

[See too now *Silvester's* Case, *ante* p. 619, note.]

SECTION C

RELATIONS BETWEEN UNIONS*

THE TRADE UNION (AMALGAMATIONS, ETC.) ACT, 1964

(1) *Conditions necessary for amalgamations and transfers of engagements of trade unions.* (1) Subject to this section

(*a*) two or more trade unions may amalgamate and become one trade union, with or without a division or dissolution of the funds of any one or more of those unions, but shall not do so unless, in the case of each of the amalgamating unions, a resolution which approves an instrument of amalgamation approved by the Registrar has been passed on a vote taken in a manner which satisfies the conditions specified in subsection (2) of this section;

(*b*) a trade union may transfer its engagements to any other trade union which undertakes to fulfil those engagements, but shall not do so unless, in the case of the transferor union, a resolution which approves an instrument of transfer approved by the Registrar has been passed on a vote taken in a manner which satisfies the said conditions.

(2) The conditions referred to in the foregoing subsection are the following, that is

(*a*) every member of the union must be entitled to vote on the resolution;

(*b*) every member of the union must be allowed to vote without interference or constraint and must, so far as is reasonably possible, be given a fair opportunity of voting;

(*c*) the method of voting must involve the marking of a voting paper by the person voting;

(*d*) all reasonable steps must have been taken by the union to secure that, not less than seven days before voting on the resolution begins, every member of the union is supplied with a notice in writing approved for the purpose by the Registrar.

(3) The notice referred to in subsection (2) (*d*) of this section

(*a*) shall either set out in full the instrument of amalgamation or

---

* As to the enforceability in law of agreements between trade unions see *ante*, p. 278 and p. 539. As in the case of the Bridlington Agreement, their intention would frequently be not to create contractually binding obligations: *ante*, p. 277.

transfer to which the resolution relates, or give an account of it sufficient to enable those receiving the notice to form a reasonable judgment of the main effects of the proposed amalgamation or transfer; and

(b) if it does not set out the instrument in full, shall state where copies of the instrument may be inspected by those receiving the notice;

and both the instrument and the notice shall comply with the requirements of any regulations for the time being in force under this Act.

(4) Before a resolution to approve an instrument of amalgamation or transfer is voted on by the members of a trade union

(a) that instrument, and

(b) the notice proposed to be supplied to members of the union in accordance with subsection (2) (d) of this section,

shall be submitted to the Registrar, and the Registrar shall approve them respectively on being satisfied that they comply with the requirements of subsection (3) of this section.

(5) An instrument of amalgamation or transfer shall not take effect before it has been registered by the Registrar under this Act, and shall not be so registered before the expiration of a period of six weeks beginning with the date on which an application for its registration is sent to the Registrar...

2. *Manner of voting on, and majority required for, resolution.* (1) Section 1 of this Act shall apply in relation to every amalgamation or transfer of engagements notwithstanding anything in the rules of any of the trade unions concerned or in the following provisions of this section.

(2) For the purposes of the passing of a resolution to approve an instrument of amalgamation or transfer, the committee of management or other governing body of a trade union shall, unless the rules of that union expressly provide that this subsection shall not apply in relation to that union, have power, notwithstanding anything in the rules of the union, to arrange for a vote of the members of that union to be taken in any manner which that body think fit.

(3) Where, in the case of a trade union, a vote is taken (whether under arrangements made under subsection (2) of this section or under provisions in the rules of the union) on a resolution to approve an instrument of amalgamation or transfer, a simple majority of the votes recorded shall be sufficient to pass the resolution, notwithstanding anything in the rules of the union and, in particular, notwithstanding

anything in those rules which, but for this subsection, would require the resolution

(*a*) to be passed by a majority greater than a simple majority, or

(*b*) to be voted on by not less than a specified proportion of the members of the union:

Provided that the foregoing provisions of this subsection shall not apply in the case of a union whose rules expressly provide that this subsection shall not apply in relation to that union...

4. *Complaints to Registrar as regards passing of resolution.* (1) A member of a trade union which passes or purports to pass a resolution approving an instrument of amalgamation or transfer may complain to the Registrar on one or more of the following grounds, that is

(*a*) that the manner in which the vote on the resolution was taken did not satisfy the conditions specified in s. 1 (2) of this Act; or

(*b*) where that vote was taken under arrangements made under s. 2 (2) of this Act, that the manner in which it was taken was not in accordance with the arrangements; or

(*c*) where that vote was taken under provisions in the rules of the union, that the manner in which it was taken was not in accordance with those rules; or

(*d*) that the votes recorded did not have the effect of passing the resolution.

(2) A complaint under this section may be made at any time before but shall not be made after, the expiration of a period of six weeks beginning with the date on which an application for registration of the instrument of amalgamation or transfer is sent to the Registrar; and where a complaint is made under this section, the Registrar shall not register the instrument under this Act before the complaint is finally determined.

(3) Where a complaint is made under this section the Registrar may either dismiss it or, if after giving the complainant and the trade union an opportunity of being heard he finds the complaint to be justified, may either

(*a*) so declare, but make no order under this subsection thereon, or

(*b*) make an order specifying the steps which must be taken before he will entertain any application to register the instrument of amalgamation or transfer, as the case may be.

(4) It shall be the duty of the Registrar to furnish a statement, either written or oral, of the reasons for any decision which he gives on a complaint under this section.

(5) The Registrar may from time to time by order vary any order made under subsection (3) of this section, and after making an order under that subsection in relation to an instrument of amalgamation or transfer shall not entertain any application to register that instrument unless he is satisfied that the steps specified in the order (or, where the order has been varied, in the order as varied) have been taken.

(6) Schedule 1 to this Act shall apply in relation to complaints under this section.

(7) Subject to subsection (8) of this section, the validity of a resolution approving an instrument of amalgamation or transfer shall not be questioned in any legal proceedings whatsoever (except proceedings before the Registrar under this section or any proceedings arising out of such proceedings) on any ground on which a complaint could be, or could have been, made to the Registrar under this section.*

(8) In the course of proceedings on a complaint under this section the Registrar may, if he thinks fit, at the request of the complainant or the trade union, state a case for the opinion of the High Court on any question of law arising in the proceedings.

The decision of the High Court on a case stated under this subsection shall be final.

5. *Disposal of property on amalgamation or transfer.* (1) Subject to this section, where an instrument of amalgamation or transfer takes effect, the property held

(*a*) for the benefit of any of the amalgamating unions or for the benefit of a branch of any of those unions, by the trustees of the union or branch, or

(*b*) for the benefit of the transferor trade union or for the benefit of a branch of the transferor trade union, by the trustees of the union or branch,

shall without any conveyance, assignment or assignation vest, on the instrument taking effect, or on the appointment of the appropriate trustees, whichever is the later, in the appropriate trustees....

6. *Change of name of trade union.* (1) Subject to this section, a trade union may change its name by any method of doing so expressly provided for by its rules or, if its rules do not expressly provide for a method of doing so, by adopting in accordance with its rules an alteration of the provision in them which gives the union its name.

---

* The member retains his right to challenge the amalgamation in the courts if he has other grounds: *Booth* v. *Amalgamated Marine Workers' Union* [1926] Ch. 904.

(2) In the case of a registered trade union, a change of name shall not take effect until it is registered by the Registrar under this Act; and the Registrar shall not register a change of name if it appears to him that registration of the union under the proposed new name would be contrary to s. 13(3) of the Trade Union Act 1871 (which prohibits registration under a name identical with, or too nearly resembling, that of another registered trade union).

(3) Where a trade union changes its name, the change of name shall not affect any right or obligation of the union or of any of its members, and any pending legal proceedings may be continued by or against the trustees of the union or any other officer of the union who can sue or be sued on its behalf, notwithstanding its change of name.

TRADES UNION CONGRESS: CONSTITUTION

RULE 2. OBJECTS

(*a*) The objects of the Congress shall be:

To do anything to promote the interests of all or any of its affiliated organisations or anything beneficial to the interests of past and present individual members of such organisations.

Generally to improve the economic or social conditions of workers in all parts of the world and to render them assistance whether or not such workers are employed or have ceased to be employed.

To affiliate to or subscribe to or to assist any other organisation having objects similar to those of the Congress.

To assist in the complete organisation of all workers eligible for membership of its affiliated organisations and subject as hereinafter set forth in these Rules to settle disputes between the members of such organisations and their employers or between such organisations and their members or between the organisations themselves.

In pursuance of such objects the Congress may do or authorise to be done all such acts and things as it considers necessary for the furtherance of those objects and in particular shall endeavour to establish the following measures and such others as any Annual Congress may approve:

Public Ownership and control of natural resources and of services:

Nationalisation of land, mines, and minerals.

Nationalisation of railways.

The extension of State and municipal enterprise for the provision of social necessities and services.

Proper provision for the adequate participation of the workers in the control and management of public services and industries.

Wages and hours of labour:

A legal maximum working week of 40 hours.

A legal minimum wage for each industry or occupation.

Unemployment:

Suitable provision in relation to unemployment, with adequate maintenance of the unemployed.

Establishment of training centres for unemployed juveniles.

Extension of training facilities for adults during periods of industrial depression.

Housing:

Provision for proper and adequate housing accommodation.

Education:

To raise the school leaving age to 16 and to ensure that full educational facilities are provided by the State from the elementary schools to the universities.

Occupational accidents and diseases—

Adequate maintenance and compensation in respect of all forms of industrial accidents and diseases.

The promotion of legal standards of health, hygiene and welfare in all places of employment.

Pensions

Adequate State pensions for all at the age of 60.

Adequate State pensions for widowed mothers and dependent children and mothers whose family breadwinner is incapacitated.

(b) In the interpretation of the above objects the General Council shall have complete discretion subject only to the power of the Annual Congress to revise its decisions...

RULE II. INDUSTRIAL DISPUTES

(a) It shall be an obligation upon the affiliated organisations to keep the General Council informed with regard to matters arising as between them and employers, and/or between one organisation and another, in particular where such matters may involve directly or indirectly large bodies of workers. The General Council shall, if they deem necessary, disseminate the information as soon as possible to all organisations which are affiliated to the Congress, and which may be either directly or indirectly affected.

(*b*) The general policy of the General Council shall be that unless requested to do so by the affiliated organisation or organisations concerned, the Council shall not intervene so long as there is a prospect of whatever difference may exist on the matters in question being amicably settled by means of the machinery of negotiation existing in the trades affected.

(*c*) If however there is a likelihood of negotiations breaking down and creating a situation in which other bodies of workpeople affiliated to Congress might be involved in a stoppage of work or their wages, hours and conditions of employment imperilled the General Council may take the initiative by calling representatives of the organisation into consultation, and use their influence to effect a just settlement of the difference. In this connection the Council having ascertained all the facts relating to the difference, may tender their considered opinion and advice thereon to the organisation or organisations concerned. Should the organisation or organisations refuse the assistance or advice of the Council, the General Council shall duly report to Congress.

(*d*) Where the Council intervenes, as herein provided, and the organisation or organisations concerned accept the assistance and advice of the Council, and where despite the efforts of the Council, the policy of the employers enforces a stoppage of work by strike or lock-out, the Council shall forthwith take steps to organise on behalf of the organisation or organisations concerned all such moral and material support as the circumstances of the dispute may appear to justify.

RULE 12. DISPUTES BETWEEN AFFILIATED ORGANISATIONS*

(*a*) Where disputes arise, or threaten to arise, between affiliated organisations, the General Council shall use their influence to promote a settlement.

---

* *Note:* The problems of boundary questions arising between affiliated unions are still governed by the principles of the 'Bridlington Agreement'. The principles were first laid down in 1924, and revised at the Bridlington Congress of 1939. They provide that an application form of a union should contain an inquiry whether the candidate has been or is a member of another union and his financial relationship to that union. An inquiry should be addressed to a former union before a candidate is accepted into membership. No candidate should be accepted who is in dispute with his former union or under disciplinary action or penalty or who is in arrears. Nor should members be accepted from unions engaged in a trade dispute; and unions should inform other unions whose members are likely to be affected by industrial action they are about to

(b) Upon application from an affiliated organisation, the General Council shall also have the power to investigate cases of dispute or disagreement between affiliated organisations, whether relating to general industrial questions or demarcation of work.

(c) If the parties to a dispute fail to submit the case to the Disputes Committee of the General Council as provided by this Rule, it shall not be permissible for such disputes to be raised at any Annual Congress.

(d) The General Council shall have power to summon the contending affiliated organisations to appear before the Disputes Committee of the General Council, and to require such organisations to submit all evidence and information that the Disputes Committee may deem essential to enable it to adjudicate upon the case.

(e) If the result of such an inquiry be that the complaining organisation fails to prove the charge, it shall bear the whole cost of the investigation, including the expenses incurred by the defending organisation.

(f) Should any affiliated organisation not carry into effect any decision of the General Council in connection with cases under this Rule the General Council may at once issue a report to all affiliated organisations. If the decision of the General Council is still not carried out, the General Council may, at their discretion, adopt either of the following methods of procedure:

The General Council may report the matter to the next Annual Congress to deal with as may be decided upon; or

Deal with the organisation under Clauses (b), (c) and (d) of Rule 13, (set out *ante*, chapter 2, p. 277, *Spring's* case).

RULE 13. CONDUCT OF AFFILIATED ORGANISATIONS

(a) If at any time there appears to the General Council to be justification for an investigation into the conduct of any affiliated organisation on the ground that the activities of such organisation are detrimental to the interests of the Trade Union Movement or contrary to the declared principles and policy of the Congress the General Council shall summon such organisation to appear before them or their appropriate Committee by duly appointed representatives of such

take. Over all is the obligation not to begin organising workers of any grade at an establishment or undertaking where another union already has in membership the majority of such workers and negotiates on their behalf, at any rate unless prior arrangements with that union have been made. The Disputes Committee of the T.U.C. bases its deliberations on these principles.

organisation in order that such activities may be investigated. In the event of the organisation failing to attend, the investigation shall proceed in its absence....

REPORT OF THE 97TH ANNUAL TRADES UNION CONGRESS, 1965

RELATIONS BETWEEN UNIONS: DISPUTES COMMITTEE[*]

(9) *Amalgamated Engineering Union and Association of Supervisory Staffs, Executives and Technicians*

A Disputes Committee composed of Mr S. W. G. Ford (chairman), Mr L. Forden and Mr S. Hill met on 8 February 1965, to consider a dispute between the Amalgamated Engineering Union and the Association of Supervisory Staffs, Executives & Technicians about the trade union membership of staff engineers employed at John Dickinson Ltd, Apsley...For the Amalgamated Engineering Union it was said that the dispute concerned staff engineers—mostly machine adjusters—who were employed at Apsley Mills. Hourly-rated adjusters had been employed at the Mills for many years and their wages had been negotiated by the A.E.U. However, in recent years the firm had given staff status to some engineers including adjusters. This had been described by the firm as 'a reward for their personal attributes'. Many A.E.U. members had allowed their membership to lapse on receiving staff status: this had not been pursued at the time and it was recognised as a weak point in the A.E.U.'s case.

The A.E.U. said that although the firm had continued to grant staff status to their engineers many of those workers became disillusioned with their conditions. Approaches were made by them to the A.E.U. At that time discussions took place between the two unions and the A.E.U. were under the impression that A.S.S.E.T. intended to confine their recruitment to monthly-paid staff and foremen. Manual workers employed at the factory who were A.E.U. members obtained an agreement for a wage increase and the A.E.U. subsequently negotiated an agreement for staff engineers which gave them a £30 annual increase. The firm recognized the A.E.U. as the appropriate union for staff engineers and adjusters who use the tools of the trade. The firm had also said that adjusters with staff status were not supervisors: they were

[*] On the use of the Disputes Committee up to 1957, see S. Lerner, *Breakaway Unions and the Small Trade Union* (1961) chapter 2.

doing exactly the same work as adjusters on hourly-rates. It was therefore clear that in their recruitment of 70 workers who were not supervisors A.S.S.E.T. were in breach of Bridlington Principle No. 5. The present case could be compared with the 1941 agreement in the engineering industry between the A.E.U. and the Engineering Employers' Federation which defined a supervisor as a person having authority over other workers and not normally using the tools of the trade. Using this definition it was clear that the staff adjusters at Dickinson's were not supervisors.

The Association of Supervisory Staffs, Executives & Technicians denied that a breach of Bridlington Principles had occurred. Their recruitment at Apsley Mills began in September 1962 following an approach to them by a staff employee. Subsequently a number of staff workers met an official of A.S.S.E.T. and informed him that no real attempt had been made to organise staff workers at the factory and no union negotiated on their behalf. The workers had also said that staff engineers and adjusters were monthly paid and all of them had supervisory responsibilities. Officials of A.S.S.E.T. and A.E.U. met at a Confederation Shipbuilding & Engineering Union's meeting and the A.E.U. official was informed about A.S.S.E.T.'s intention to commence recruitment at Dickinson's. At this stage the A.E.U. raised no objections. However, on 31 December 1962, the A.E.U. district official informed A.S.S.E.T. that staff engineers and adjusters who worked with the tools of the trade should be advised that the A.E.U. was the appropriate union. By this time A.S.S.E.T. had accepted 70 workers, including foremen, staff engineers and adjusters. An inquiry form had been sent to the A.E.U. for one of these and clearance was given for him. Some others of the 70 had previously been in the A.E.U. but had given up their membership when they achieved staff status.

A.S.S.E.T. said that on a number of occasions during 1963 discussions had taken place between officials of the two unions but no settlement had been reached. In November the A.E.U. negotiated an agreement with Dickinson's for a salary increase for staff engineers, including adjusters. However, at this time the A.E.U. had in membership only seven of the total of 77 in this grade and A.S.S.E.T. had 47. In December 1963 A.S.S.E.T. approached the management for recognition but this was refused: the management said that the A.E.U. were the appropriate union for these workers. A.S.S.E.T. drew the attention of the A.E.U. to the membership position and suggested that it would be in the best interests of trade unionism if the staff workers who held A.E.U. membership transferred to A.S.S.E.T. In February 1964 officials of both unions spoke to a well-attended meeting of members of both unions in the grade. This meeting rejected the proposal that staff engineers should be in the A.E.U.

Further discussions and correspondence took place between the two unions at district and national level but the only result was an A.E.U. suggestion that staff adjusters should transfer from A.S.S.E.T. into the A.E.U. because they held the negotiating rights. This was unacceptable to A.S.S.E.T. who now had 88 members at John Dickinson Ltd, of whom 28 were foremen and 46 were staff engineers and adjusters. A.S.S.E.T. welcomed the reference of the case to a Disputes Committee. They denied they had commenced organising activities in a grade where the A.E.U. had a majority of the workers employed. Moreover when A.S.S.E.T. commenced recruitment no other union negotiated on behalf of the workers concerned. A.S.S.E.T. asked the Disputes Committee to award that the complaint had not been established and suggested the A.E.U. should transfer their small minority of members to A.S.S.E.T. which was the union freely chosen by a majority of the workers concerned...

Award

The Disputes Committee considered that the historical background they were given about the use of 'staff status' in the firm was relevant to the dispute. Of the various types of staff employees recruited by A.S.S.E.T. at Dickinson's the dispute was confined to those monthly-paid adjusters or engineers, who it was claimed by the A.E.U., performed the same work as hourly-paid adjusters and could therefore be regarded as within the same 'grade' in the terms of Bridlington Principle No. 5.

On the evidence presented to them the Disputes Committee find that the A.E.U. have not substantiated their charge that the recruitment by A.S.S.E.T. was in breach of Bridlington Principles but this finding will not itself solve the whole problem of organisation and representation of monthly-paid adjusters who are at present members of A.S.S.E.T. or of A.E.U. or of no union, nor of negotiations on behalf of the other staff grades who are members of A.S.S.E.T.

The Disputes Committee therefore advise the two unions to consider whether it is possible locally to differentiate between those monthly-paid adjusters or engineers who exercise supervision and those who do not—with a view to those (if any) who exercise no supervision being excluded from A.S.S.E.T. and invited to join the A.E.U. The two unions will need to obtain additional information about the responsibilities of monthly-paid adjusters to enable them to seek agreement on this point. However, if after considering this information, the unions are unable to reach agreement it will be open to them to ask the Disputes Committee to adjudicate upon it.

(10) Further Meeting

To carry out the latter part of the award the two unions met at Apsley Mill on 9 April but did not reach agreement. The hearing by the Disputes Committee was therefore resumed at Congress House on 20 May. Mr S. Hill was unable to be present and Mr A. E. Griffiths took his place on the committee. After hearing both sides the committee awarded as follows.

Award

The Disputes Committee have noted that representatives of the two unions who met at Apsley were unable to reach agreement on whether or to what degree staff adjusters exercise supervision. They have studied the opposing views on this put forward by the two unions and are unable to make a decision on this point. In coming to their conclusion the committee were aware both that A.S.S.E.T. have not obtained recognition from the employer and that A.S.S.E.T. acknowledge the problem this causes them. The Disputes Committee consider they should call the attention of the national executives of the two unions to the likelihood of similar disputes arising in other establishments and suggest that a national agreement should be sought about the respective spheres which each union would regard as appropriate to the other.

(11) Amalgamated Society of Woodcutting Machinists and National Union of Furniture Trade Operatives

A Disputes Committee composed of Mr S. W. G. Ford (chairman), Mr A. E. Griffiths and Mr L. Sharp met under Standing Order 12(b) on 3 May 1965 to consider a dispute between the Amalgamated Society of Woodcutting Machinists and the National Union of Furniture Trade Operatives about the trade union membership of three workers employed at the Stag Cabinet Co., Hucknall.

For the Amalgamated Society of Woodcutting Machinists it was said that N.U.F.T.O. had accepted three of their members without observing the requirements of Bridlington Principle No. 2. On

22 March 1964 N.U.F.T.O. sent inquiry forms concerning the three members to the Nottingham branch secretary of the A.S.Wc.M., who replied on 27 March that he was not prepared to transfer the members. The branch secretary had not used the official form to reply but the position of the A.S.Wc.M. had been made clear. At no time had the three members complained about the service given them by the A.S.Wc.M. nor had any applications for resignation been submitted: one of the members had said that he wanted to transfer because it was inconvenient to send his contributions some miles to the A.S.Wc.M. branch. All three were long-standing members of the A.S.Wc.M.: one joined in 1947 and the other two in 1955.

The A.S.Wc.M. said that the Stag Cabinet Co. had two factories: one in Nottingham and the other in Hucknall but both were closely linked. The three members concerned in the present dispute had been transferred to Hucknall from the Nottingham factory where the union had 80 members—almost all the woodcutting machinists employed. Moreover most woodcutting machinists in the Midlands area were members of the A.S.Wc.M. It was admitted that the three members were not under discipline or in arrears at the time they were accepted into N.U.F.T.O. but the A.S.Wc.M. were still able to represent them: one of the three had been a shop steward for the union while employed at the Hucknall factory. Correspondence had been exchanged at local and national level but N.U.F.T.O. had refused to return the members. The Disputes Committee were therefore asked to award that N.U.F.T.O. had acted in breach of Bridlington Principle No. 2 and should exclude the three members.

For the National Union of Furniture Trade Operatives it was said that inquiry forms on behalf of the members concerned were sent to the A.S.Wc.M. branch. It was admitted that the A.S.Wc.M. branch had written to the N.U.F.T.O. branch refusing permission for the transfers but the forms had not been returned. No attempts had been made to persuade these members to join N.U.F.T.O. nor had any pressure been put on them. After the complaint by the A.S.Wc.M. a careful examination was carried out but the N.U.F.T.O. head office could see no grounds for substantiating the claim that there was a breach of the Bridlington Principles. If any breach had occurred the contributions would have been returned immediately to the members.

N.U.F.T.O. said that the two factories of the Stag Cabinet Co. were separate establishments with separate managements: they were eight miles apart. The Hucknall factory had been open for ten years and

N.U.F.T.O. had 268 members out of a total work force of 276. The A.S.Wc.M. now had 3 members at Hucknall who were employed in the machine shop but N.U.F.T.O. had 19 members in this shop.

In answer to questions from the Disputes Committee, representatives of both unions said they had no agreement about spheres of influence on recruitment. They also said that both unions were represented on the national negotiating machinery covering the workers in the present dispute.

Award

The claim by the Woodcutting Machinists is that the acceptance by N.U.F.T.O. of the three members was contrary to Bridlington Principle No. 2. The Disputes Committee find that the claim has not been established and award accordingly.*

* See now on the modern history of inter-union arrangements, including use of the T.U.C. machinery: John Hughes, *Trade Union Structure and Government (Part 1)*, Research Paper No. 5 for Royal Commission on Trade Unions and Employers Associations (H.M.S.O., 1967).

CHAPTER 6

INJURY AT WORK

INTRODUCTORY NOTE

The number of workers injured or contracting an industrial disease in the course of their work increases annually, and legal measures so far taken do not appear to have been effective for accident prevention: see *The Worker and the Law* (1965) pp. 163–75; (1966) pp. 157–168. In his Annual Report for 1965, the Chief Inspector of Factories revealed that reported factory accidents rose from some 268,000 in 1964 to 293,717 in 1965 (Cmnd. 3080). Little progress is revealed in the field of voluntary measures for accident prevention; and a body of opinion is now turning to the suggestion that workers' safety delegates and committees should be made compulsory in all places of work. The coal mining industry has had experience of such workers' inspectors.

The student in a Labour Law course, however, is more often concerned with the legal effects of industrial injury than its prevention, though he should be made aware of the primary importance of prevention. As such, the lawyer finds this part an extension of the study which he has already made in the law of tort of the duties of the 'master' in respect of safety at work. Since, however, there is such a vast range of statutory material which affects health and safety at work, a selection has to be made. In the materials which follow, three areas have been selected for illustration.

First, Section A deals mainly with the approach of the common law. This is material with which the lawyer will be already familiar. Section B adds statutory and case law materials concerned with a few of the duties applying to occupiers of factories and offices. This restriction is, of course, arbitrary; but of all the statutory material, the Factories Act, 1961, is the most important and a thorough inspection of its more important sections may be as far as a Labour Law course can hope to go. Lastly, Section C includes materials relating to the recovery of industrial injury benefit under the national insurance scheme.

SECTION A

THE COMMON LAW*

WILSON'S & CLYDE COAL CO. v. ENGLISH

House of Lords   [1938] A.C. 57

The respondent was employed in the appellants' coal mine. At the end of a day shift, as he proceeded along one of the main underground haulage roads, the respondent was crushed when the haulage plant was put into motion. The respondent, in a common law action, claimed that it was a necessary part of a safe system of working that during the period of time when the men were being raised to the surface the haulage plant should be stopped.

Section 2(4) of the Coal Mines Act, 1911 required that only a qualified person could operate the technical management of this type of mine. The appellants claimed that they had effectively discharged their duty of providing a reasonably safe system of work by appointing a qualified manager and thus properly delegating their duty. Their contention was rejected by the House of Lords.

LORD WRIGHT: When I use the word absolutely, I do not mean that employers warrant the adequacy of plant, or the competence of fellow-employees, or the propriety of the system of work. The obligation is fulfilled by the exercise of due care and skill. But it is not fulfilled by entrusting its fulfilment to employees, even though selected with due care and skill. The obligation is threefold—'the provision of a competent staff of men, adequate material, and a proper system and effective supervision'; I repeat the statement of the duty by Lord M'Laren quoted with approval by Lord Shaw in *Black* v. *Fife Coal Co.*[1], and again approved in the *Lochgelly* case.[2]....

The well-established, but illogical, doctrine of common employment is certainly one not to be extended, and indeed has never in its long career been pushed so far as the Court of Appeal sought to push it. Even in *Farwell* v. *Boston Railroad Co.*,[3] the *fons et origo* (I almost add

---

[1] [1912] A.C. 149, 173.   [2] [1934] A.C. 1, 28.   [3] 4 Metcalf, 49.

* Persons other than the employer may of course be liable to the injured worker, but no materials are included in this book dealing exclusively with that problem. The reader is reminded of the Occupiers Liability Act, 1957, and the general duty of care in the law of tort. See, for example, *Clay* v. *Crump Ltd* [1964] 1 Q.B. 533 (employers, building contractors, liable to injured worker; but demolition contractors on site and architect in charge of work also liable for negligence); and *McArdle* v. *Andmac Roofing Co.* [1967] 1 All E.R. 583 (C.A.: liability of contractors and two sub-contractors).

'*mali*'), Shaw, C.J. reserved the question of an employer's obligations in respect of adequacy of plant and competence of fellow-workmen....

I think the whole course of authority consistently recognizes a duty which rests on the employer and which is personal to the employer, to take reasonable care for the safety of his workmen, whether the employer be an individual, a firm, or a company, and whether or not the employer takes any share in the conduct of the operations. The obligation is threefold, as I have explained. Thus the obligation to provide and maintain proper plant and appliances is a continuing obligation. It is not, however, broken by a mere misuse or failure to use proper plant and appliances due to the negligence of a fellow-servant or a merely temporary failure to keep in order or adjust plant and appliances or a casual departure from the system of working, if these matters can be regarded as the casual negligence of the managers, foreman, or other employees. It may be difficult in some cases to distinguish on the facts between the employers' failure to provide and maintain and the fellow-servants' negligence in the respects indicated.

LORDS ATKIN, THANKERTON, MACMILLAN and MAUGHAM delivered concurring speeches.

PARIS v. STEPNEY B.C.

House of Lords   [1951] A.C. 367

The plaintiff, a garage hand employed by the defendant council, had only one eye. This was injured during the course of his employment when he was hammering at a rust bolt on a car. He was not wearing goggles; but claimed that the employers were liable to him in negligence for failing to provide and require the use of goggles by him. It was not the ordinary practice for employers in the trade to supply goggles for such work.*

LORD MACDERMOTT: The proposition underlying the second conclusion is succinctly stated by Asquith, L.J., in a passage which, I believe, represented the unanimous opinion of the court. It reads as

* Proof that an employer was following a general practice of the industry is evidence that he was not negligent. Lord Dunedin once said that the employer following such a practice could, in cases of omission, be liable if it involved 'a thing which was so obviously wanted that it would be folly' to neglect it: *Morton* v. *Wm. Dixon* (1909) S.C. 807. But, after Lord Normand's speech in the *Paris* case, *supra*, proof of following a general practice does no more than raise a presumption which can be rebutted by proof that it was not the act of a reasonable man in the circumstances: see *Morris* v. *West Hartlepool Steam Navigation Ltd* [1956] A.C. 552 (H.L.): negligence when hatchways were left open as was the general custom at sea; *Cavanagh* v. *Ulster Weaving Ltd* [1960] A.C. 145 (H.L.): normal building industry methods of carrying cement on roof held to be negligent. See generally for this and other aspects of the employer's duty, Munkman, *Employer's Liability*, 5th ed., chapters 2 and 3.

follows[1]: 'The plaintiff's disability could only be relevant to the stringency of the duty owed to him if it increased the risk to which he was exposed. A one-eyed man is no more likely to get a splinter or a chip in his eye than is a two-eyed man.... A greater risk of injury is not the same thing as a risk of greater injury; the first alone is relevant to liability.'... I think it is enough to say that the employer's duty to take reasonable care for the safety of his workmen is directed—and, I venture to add, obviously directed—to their welfare and for that reason, if for no other, must be related to both the risk and the degree of the injury. If that is so and if, as was very properly conceded, the duty is that owed to the individual and not to a class, it seems to me to follow that the known circumstance that a particular workman is likely to suffer a graver injury than his fellows from the happening of a given event is one which must be taken into consideration in assessing the nature of the employer's obligation to that workman.

For these reasons I am of opinion that the Court of Appeal was wrong and that Lynskey, J., was right regarding the relevance of the respondents' knowledge of the appellant's eye defect.

LORDS NORMAND and OAKSEY delivered concurring speeches. LORDS SIMONDS and MORTON agreed with the principle stated but disagreed that the respondents were on the facts in breach of duty.

THE LAW REFORM (PERSONAL INJURIES) ACT, 1948

1. *Common employment.* (1) It shall not be a defence to an employer who is sued in respect of personal injuries caused by the negligence of a person employed by him, that that person was at the time the injuries were caused in common employment with the person injured....

(3) Any provision contained in a contract of service or apprenticeship, or in an agreement collateral thereto, (including a contract or agreement entered into before the commencement of this Act) shall be void in so far as it would have the effect of excluding or limiting any liability of the employer in respect of personal injuries caused to the person employed or apprenticed by the negligence of persons in common employment with him.*

---

[1] [1950] 1 K.B. 320, 324.

* Thus the employer cannot contract out of his vicarious liability for torts committed by one servant on another where they are in common employment. 'Collateral' agreements will include agreements made in respect of pension schemes: *Smith* v. *B.E.A.* [1951] 2 K.B. 893. Even if the injured plaintiff is an employee, the employer's vicarious

2. *Measure of damages.* (1) In an action for damages for personal injuries (including any such action arising out of a contract), there shall in assessing those damages be taken into account, against any loss of earnings or profits which has accrued or probably will acrue to the injured person from the injuries, one half of the value of any rights which have accrued or probably will accrue to him therefrom in respect of industrial injury benefit, industrial disablement benefit or sickness benefit for the five years beginning with the time when the cause of action accrued....

(4) In an action for damages for personal injuries (including any such action arising out of a contract), there shall be disregarded, in determining the reasonableness of any expenses, the possibility of avoiding those expenses or part of them by taking advantage of facilities available under the National Health Service Act, 1946, or the National Health Service (Scotland) Act, 1947, or of any corresponding facilities in Northern Ireland.

LATIMER v. A.E.C. LTD

House of Lords [1953] A.C. 643

During a particularly heavy rainstorm a factory floor was flooded and an oily liquid, which normally ran along a channel in the floor, mixed with the rain water. When the flood subsided the floor was slippery. All available sawdust was put down but some areas were not covered. The plaintiff, handling a heavy barrel, slipped and was injured. He claimed damages at common law and under the Factories Act, 1937, s. 25.*

LORD PORTER: Upon the issue of common law negligence as now presented the direction which should be given is not in doubt. It is that the duty of the tribunal is to determine what action in the circumstances which have been proved would a reasonably prudent man have taken. The probability of a workman slipping is one matter which must be borne in mind but it must be remembered that no one else did so. Nor does the possibility seem to have occurred to anyone at the time....

In my view, in these circumstances, the appellant has not established that a reasonably careful employer would have shut down the works or that the respondents ought to have taken the drastic step of closing the factory.

liability for torts of servants committed within the scope of their employment is still to be distinguished from his liability for failure to fulfil his personal duty to provide a safe system of work, etc.: *Staveley Iron and Chemical Ltd* v. *Jones* [1956] A.C. 627 (H.L.). The latter duty may be seen to rest upon contract (*Matthews* v.*Kuwait Bechtel Corporation* [1959] 2 Q.B. 57), and, in theory at least, it is still open to the employer to exempt himself from, or limit his liability here by contract with the employee.

* The modern equivalent is s. 28 of the Factories Act, 1961 (see p. 703).

The question whether there has been a breach of statutory duty turns upon the true construction of s. 25 of the Factories Act, 1937. That section provides that: 'All floors, steps, stairs, passages and gangways shall be of sound construction and properly maintained,' and s. 152(1) defines 'maintained' as meaning 'maintained in an efficient state, in efficient working order, and in good repair'....

It has still, however, to be determined what it is which has to be in an efficient state. Does it include the elimination of some matter which is temporarily superimposed upon the floor or is the requirement confined to the floor itself? To be efficient, the appellant contended, the floor must be fit for any of the purposes for which it is intended, e.g. for support and for passing over in safety. The difficulty of such a view is that it puts an excessive obligation upon the employer. Indeed, it was conceded that it could not be carried to the length of saying that a temporary obstruction, such as a piece of orange peel or the like, would make it inefficient. Once this concession is made it becomes a question of the degree of temporary inefficiency which constitutes a breach of the employer's obligation.

Primarily, in my opinion, the section is aimed at some general condition of the gangway, e.g. a dangerously polished surface or the like or possibly some permanent fitment which makes it unsafe. But I cannot think the provision was meant to or does apply to a transient and exceptional condition. If it had been directed to such a state of affairs it would have been easy to say so.

LORD TUCKER: In the present case the respondents were faced with an unprecedented situation following a phenomenal rain storm. They set 40 men to work on cleaning up the factory when the flood subsided and used all the available supply of sawdust, which was approximately three tons. The judge has found that they took every step which could reasonably have been taken to deal with the conditions which prevailed before the night shift came on duty, and he has negatived every specific allegation of negligence as pleaded, but he has held the respondents liable because they did not close down the factory, or the part of the factory where the accident occurred, before the commencement of the night shift.

My Lords, I do not question that such a drastic step may be required on the part of a reasonably prudent employer if the peril to his employees is sufficiently grave, and to this extent it must always be a question of degree, but in my view there was no evidence in the present case which could justify a finding of negligence for failure on the part of the respondents to take this step. This question was never canvassed in evidence, nor was sufficient evidence given as to the condition of the factory as a whole to enable a satisfactory conclusion to be reached... The problem is perfectly simple. The only question was: Has it been proved that the floor was so slippery that, remedial steps not being possible, a reasonably prudent employer would have closed down the factory rather than allow his employees to run the risks involved in continuing work? The learned judge does not seem to me to have posed this question to himself, nor was there sufficient evidence before him to have justified an affirmative answer.

LORDS OAKSEY, REID and ASQUITH OF BISHOPSTONE delivered concurring speeches.

DAVIE *v.* NEW MERTON BOARD MILLS LTD

House of Lords   [1959] A.C. 604

The plaintiff during the course and scope of his employment was using a metal drift belonging to his employers. The drift broke and a piece of metal flew into the plaintiff's eye. The drift had been supplied to the defendants—who employed the plaintiff—by reputable suppliers. Its defect was due to the negligence of the manufacturers but would not have been discoverable by ordinary inspection. The plaintiff claimed damages for negligence at common law.

VISCOUNT SIMONDS: The accident, it was said, was caused by the negligence of the respondents, their servants or agents, and their negligence consisted in this, that they failed to provide a suitable drift which could be hammered safely without the risk of pieces flying off. I have deliberately used the language of the statement of claim which has been repeatedly used in these proceedings. It may be relevant to observe that it is not strictly accurate. The accident occurred not through a failure to supply a suitable drift—a failure that could result in nothing—but through the supply of an unsuitable drift. Therein lay their alleged negligence, and I pause to analyse that allegation. It may mean one of two things. First, it may mean that it was the duty of the respondents to supply suitable drifts: they supplied an unsuitable one: they did not do their duty: therefore they were negligent. This is a bare statement of absolute obligation. But, secondly, it may mean that the supply of an unsuitable drift was due to a want of reasonable care on their part. It must, then, be shown wherein lay the want of reasonable care, and at once the question arises, for whose negligence, acts,

I suppose, of omission and commission, the employer is liable in the long chain which ends with the supply by him of a tool to his workman but may begin with the delving of the raw material of manufacture in a distant continent. In the case before us the chain is long enough. The respondents were not guilty of any negligence nor was any servant or agent of theirs nor was the reputable firm who supplied the drifts, but at the end of the claim were the manufacturers. The respondents stood in no contractual relation to them: so little connection was there between them that it was long in dispute whether the fatal drift had been manufactured by them and delivered by them to the suppliers. But it is for their negligence in manufacture that the appellant would make the respondents liable. Remembering, my Lords, that the essence of the tort of negligence lies in the failure to take reasonable care, I am constrained to wonder how this thing can be. But it is made clear by the powerful dissenting judgment of Jenkins, L.J. that, if such a result cannot commend itself to reason, it yet may find support in authority. I say that it cannot commend itself to reason; for, if indeed it is the law, every man employing another and supplying him with tools for his job acts at his peril: if someone at some time has been careless, then, for any flaw in the tools, it is he who is responsible, be he himself ever so careful. I observe that such a view of the law is usually accompanied by a disclaimer of any idea that an employer warrants the fitness of the tool he supplies and do not find the reconciliation easy....it is well to remember that we are dealing with a case of tort. The same act or omission by an employer may support an action in tort or for breach of an implied term of the contract of employment but it can only lead to confusion if, when the action is in tort, the court embarks on the controversial subject of implied contractual terms....

But, my Lords, as I have said, the difficulty arises, not on the primary statement of liability, but upon the question for whom is the employer responsible. Clearly he is responsible for his own acts, and clearly, too, for those of his servants. To them at least the maxims *respondeat superior* and *qui facit per alium facit per se* will apply. It is the next step that is difficult. The employer is said to be liable for the acts of his 'agents' and, with greater hesitation, for the acts of 'independent contractors'. My Lords, fortunately we are not troubled here with the word 'agent'. No one could say that a manufacturer who makes a tool and supplies it to a merchant who in turn sells it to an employer is in any sense an agent of the latter for providing his workman with a tool. Is he then an independent contractor? It is perhaps a striking commentary on the artificiality of this concept that it should for a moment be thought possible to regard as an independent contractor with an employer a manufacturer with whom he never contracted, of whom he may never have heard and from whom he may be divided in time and space by decades and continents. It may lead your Lordships to the conclusion that the liability of the employer in such a case can only be sustained if his obligation is absolute. But that *ex hypothesi* it is not....

As I have tried to show, the contention, as stated in its first form, that the employer is liable for the acts of himself, his servants and agents and, subject to whatever limitations might be thought fit, independent contractors, could not lead to success in this action: for the manufacturer could not by any legitimate use of language be considered the servant or agent of, or an independent contractor with, the employer who buys his manufactures in the market. It was then sought to reach the same result by a different road. The employer, it was said, was under a duty to take reasonable care to supply his workmen with proper plant and machinery. It was assumed that this included tools such as drifts, and I, too, will, without deciding it, assume it. It was then said that the employer could not escape responsibility by employing a third party, however expert, to do his duty for him. So far, so good. That is what Lord Maugham said, and I agree. But then comes the next step—but I would rather call it a jump, and a jump that would unhorse any rider. Therefore, it was said, the employer is responsible for the defect in goods that he buys in the market, if it can be shown that that defect was due to the want of skill or care on the part of anyone who was concerned in its manufacture. But, my Lords, by what use or misuse of language can the manufacturer be said to be a person to whom the employer delegated a duty which it was for him to perform? How can it be said that it was as the delegate or agent of the employer that the manufacturer failed to exhibit due skill and care? It is, to my mind, clear that he cannot.*...

It was said that an employer might, instead of purchasing tools of a standard design, either from the manufacturer direct or in the market, order them to be made to his own design. If he did so and if they were defective and an accident resulted, it was clear (so the argument ran)

---

* *Quaere:* whether after this decision the duty on the employer at common law in respect of his *premises* is higher than that of an occupier under the Occupiers' Liability Act, 1957? Compare *Naismith* v. *London Film Productions Ltd* [1939] 1 All E.R. 794 (C.A.); *Sumner* v. *Wm Henderson Ltd* [1964] 1 Q.B. 450 (set aside on other grounds in the C.A. [1963] 1 W.L.R. 823); Winfield, *Torts* (7th ed. Jolowicz) p. 342, n. 54; and now *Pisicani* v. *Post Office The Times*, 11 May 1967 (C.A.).

that he would be responsible. I agree that he would, if the fault lay in the design and was due to lack of reasonable care or skill on his part. There is no reason why he should not. A more difficult question would arise if the defect was not due to any fault in design (for which the employer was responsible) but to carelessness in workmanship. . . .

One more thing I must say. It was at one time suggested—I do not use a more emphatic word, for learned counsel was rightly discreet in his approach—that the House should take into consideration the fact that possibly or even probably the employer would, but the workman would not, be covered by insurance, and for that reason should be the more ready to fasten upon the employer's liability for an accident due neither to his nor to the workman's carelessness. I will only say that this is not a consideration to which your Lordships should give any weight at all in your determination of the rights and obligations of the parties. The legislature has thought fit in some circumstances to impose an absolute obligation upon employers. The Factories Acts and the elaborate regulations made under them testify to the care with which the common law has been altered, adjusted and refined in order to give protection and compensation to the workman. It is not the function of a court of law to fasten upon the fortuitous circumstance of insurance to impose a greater burden on the employer than would otherwise lie upon him.

LORDS MORTON, TUCKER, REID and KEITH delivered concurring speeches.

TAYLOR v. ROVER CO. LTD

[1966] 2 All E.R. 181

The plaintiff, in the course of his work for R. Co., was injured in the eye which he later lost, by a splinter of steel from a chisel which he was hammering. The chisel was made by S. Co. according to a specification provided by R. Co. from steel purchased from and specially hardened by C. Co. The leading hand in the works had previously suffered an injury from using one of the chisels. The plaintiff, succeeded against R. Co., his employers, because they had failed to withdraw the chisels from circulation after they knew (through their leading hand) of the danger. The defect in the chisel was caused by the neglect in its treatment by C. Co. The plaintiff also sued S. Co.

BAKER, J. held that there was no reasonable probability of intermediate examination by R. Co. before use of the chisel, in the period before the leading hand was injured. S. Co. were not liable to the plaintiff because after the defect had been actually discovered by the leading hand 'it was the keeping of the chisel in circulation with the knowledge that it was dangerous that caused the accident'. The chain of causation was broken. In any case, S. Co. was entitled to rely upon their independent contractors C. Co. as far as the hardening went, and could not be liable for their negligence.

GENERAL CLEANING CONTRACTORS *v.* CHRISTMAS

House of Lords   [1953] A.C. 180

The appellants sent the respondent to clean the windows of one of their customers. While doing this, the employee had his fingers caught when the sash came down and as a result lost his balance and fell. Safety belts were provided by the employers, but could not be used because no hooks were fixed to the premises to which the belt could be attached. The employee sued his employers for their failure to take reasonable care to provide a reasonably safe system of work.

LORD REID: The main case made for the respondent in his pleadings and at the trial was that this method of cleaning windows is in itself so unsafe that a master who requires his servants to adopt it is in breach of his duty to provide a safe system of working. . . .

A plaintiff who seeks to have condemned as unsafe a system of work which has been generally used for a long time in an important trade undertakes a heavy onus: if he is right it means that all, or practically all, the numerous employers in the trade have been habitually neglecting their duty to their men. The evidence in this case appears to me to be quite inadequate to establish either that the window sill method is so inherently dangerous that it cannot be made reasonably safe by taking proper precautions, or that the ladder method or the safety belt method are as a general rule reasonably practicable alternatives.

That brings me to what I have found to be the most difficult part of the case. The evidence does prove that the window sill method is often dangerous if no precautions are taken, and in this case no precautions were taken; and if the respondent is to succeed it must, I think, be on the ground that it was the duty of the appellants to devise for the window sill method a proper system of precautions and instruct their servants to follow that system, and that, if they had done so and their orders had been obeyed, this accident would, or at least would probably, have been prevented. No such case is made in the pleadings and no attempt was made to prove it at the trial. . . .

It does appear from the evidence that very simple tests after the accident showed that this sash was loose and ran down very easily. I think that this ought to have been discovered before the accident, and I think that I am entitled to assume that if it had been discovered some simple and effective precaution could have been taken. But I must confess that even in this case I make this assumption with some reluctance in the absence of evidence and I would not be prepared to do so in a less clear case.

The question then is whether it is the duty of the appellants to instruct their servants what precautions they ought to take and to take reasonable steps to see that those instructions are carried out. On that matter the appellants say that their men are skilled men who are well aware of the dangers involved and as well able as the appellants to devise and take any necessary precautions. That may be so but, in my opinion, it is not a sufficient answer. Where the problem varies from job to job it may be reasonable to leave a great deal to the man in charge, but the danger in this case is one which is constantly found, and it calls for a system to meet it. Where a practice of ignoring an obvious danger has grown up I do not think that it is reasonable to expect an individual workman to take the initiative in devising and using precautions. It is the duty of the employer to consider the situation, to devise a suitable system, to instruct his men what they must do and to supply any implements that may be required such as, in this case, wedges or objects to be put on the window sill to prevent the window from closing. No doubt he cannot be certain that his men will do as they are told when they are working alone. But if he does all that is reasonable to ensure that his safety system is operated he will have done what he is bound to do. In this case the appellants do not appear to have done anything as they thought they were entitled to leave the taking of precautions to the discretion of each of their men. In this I think that they were in fault, and I think that this accident need not have happened if the appellants had done as I hold they ought to have done.*

EARL JOWITT and LORDS OAKSEY and TUCKER delivered concurring speeches.

---

* The employer must do what is reasonable to instruct or supervise the worker in the safe system, appliance, etc. The duty is not higher than that: *Qualcast (Wolverhampton) Ltd* v. *Haynes* [1959] A.C. 743 (H.L.). An inexperienced man may have to be given more instruction than that of a skilled worker: *Byers* v. *Head Wrightson Ltd* [1961] 2 All E.R. 538; see too *McWilliams* v. *Sir Wm Arrol* [1962] 1 W.L.R. 295 (H.L.) *post*, p. 737. The courts have shown a restrictive approach in regard to the duty to skilled men since Viscount Simonds remarked that the employer's relation to him is not 'equivalent to that of a nurse and an imbecile child', *Smith* v. *Austin Lifts* [1959]

HUDSON v. RIDGE MANUFACTURING CO.

[1957] 2 Q.B. 348

This was an action by the plaintiff against his employers for failure to ensure a safe system of work. For some four years preceding this action a fellow employee of the plaintiff had gained a reputation for persistently engaging in skylarking activities—such as tripping up his fellows. The man had frequently been warned about these activities which were well known to the employers. This same employee, indulging in horseplay had tripped and injured the plaintiff. [On the distinction between the employer's personal and his vicarious liability in such a situation, see *ante*, p. 683, note.]

STREATFEILD, J.: As Mr Leigh put it in his opening, he does not contend that the employers are vicariously liable for any negligent act of a fellow servant, but that they are primarily liable because they were guilty of a breach of their common law duty to take care for the safety of their employees.

This is an unusual case, because the particular form of lack of care by the employers alleged is that they failed to maintain discipline and to take proper steps to put an end to this skylarking which might lead to injury at some time in the future. As it seems to me, the matter is covered not by authority so much as principle. It is the duty of employers, for the safety of their employees, to have reasonably safe plant and machinery. It is their duty to have premises which are similarly reasonably safe. It is their duty to have a reasonably safe system of work. It is their duty to employ reasonably competent fellow workmen. All of those duties exist at common law for the safety of the workmen, and if, for instance, it is found that a piece of plant or part of the premises is not reasonably safe, it is the duty of the employers to cure it, to make it safe and to remove that source of danger. In the same way, if the system of working is found, in practice, to be beset with dangers, it is the duty of the employers to evolve a reasonably safe system of working so as to obviate those dangers, and upon principle it seems to me that if, in fact, a fellow workman is not merely incompetent but, by his habitual conduct, is likely to prove a source of danger to his fellow employees, a duty lies fairly and squarely on the employers to remove that source of danger.

1 W.L.R. 100 p. 105. Note that the employer's failure to give adequate instruction or warning to an employee may involve him in liability to a third party who attempts reasonably to rescue the workman: *Baker* v. *Hopkins & Son Ltd* [1959] 3 All E.R. 225 (C.A.).

I agree with Mr Hodgson, for the defendants, that it is a matter of degree. Nobody would say that if Chadwick had merely tripped somebody up for the first time and had been at once reprimanded by the foreman and then did not do it again, that was such conduct, on an isolated occasion by a man, as would put upon the employers the duty of taking the extreme course of dismissing that workman in case he should do it again....

I think I am fortified in that view by the case, to which Mr Leigh drew my attention, of *Smith* v. *Crossley Brothers Ltd*,[1] in which Pearce, J., in the first instance, had found the employers liable because injury had been caused to the plaintiff, a boy of 16 years of age, through the conduct of two apprentices in the misuse of a compressed air pipe, which they put up this unfortunate plaintiff's rectum. It was found that the employers were liable, but Singleton, L.J., in allowing the appeal and finding the employers not liable, said: 'The defendants had no reason whatever to anticipate that the two apprentices in question would use it in that way.' They had never done it before....

Here is a case where there existed, as it were in the system of work, a source of danger, through the conduct of one of the defendants' employees, of which they knew, repeated conduct which went on over a long period of time, and which they did nothing whatever to remove, except to reprimand and go on reprimanding to no effect. In my judgment, therefore, the injury was sustained as a result of the defendants' failure to take proper steps to put an end to that conduct, to see that it would not happen again and, if it did happen again, to remove the source of it....

WINTER v. CARDIFF R.D.C.

House of Lords [1950] 1 All E.R. 819

The appellant was riding on one of the respondents' lorries when a heavy voltage regulator which it was carrying fell off carrying him with it and injuring him. It had been negligently secured by one of the respondents' charge hands. He sued for damages. The action failed.

LORD OAKSEY: My Lords, I agree that this appeal should be dismissed. In my opinion, the common law duty of an employer of labour is to act reasonably in all the circumstances. One of those circumstances is that he is an employer of labour, and it is, therefore, reasonable that he

---

[1] (1951) 95 Sol. Jo. 655. Cf. *O'Reilly* v. *National Rail and Tramway Appliance Ltd* [1966] 1 All E.R. 499; *post* p. 751, note.

should employ competent servants, should supply them with adequate plant, and should give adequate directions as to the system of work or mode of operation, but this does not mean that the employer must decide on every detail of the system of work or mode of operation.... Where the operation is simple and the decision how it shall be done has to be taken frequently, it is natural and reasonable that it should be left to the foreman or workmen on the spot. In the present case the question to be decided was whether to lash the regulator on the lorry or not to lash it, and both courts have held, as I think, rightly, that that was a matter for the decision of the charge hand on the spot. Transport of goods would, I apprehend, be impossible to carry on efficiently if the method of securing every load had to be decided by the employer. It might almost as well be suggested that the tying up of every parcel in a shop is a matter for the employer's decision. A good leader of men (and an employer is a leader of men) leaves to his men as much discretion as he can, otherwise unforeseen circumstances will upset the best laid plan. The question is in each case: Is it a matter for the employer's decision or for the man's ?, and I have no doubt that the courts below were right in holding that in the present case it was for the charge hand to decide whether this load should be lashed on the lorry or not.

LORD MACDERMOTT (having stated the facts): My Lords, unfortunately for the appellant, he received his injuries before s. 1 (1) of the Law Reform (Personal Injuries) Act, 1948, which abolished the doctrine of common employment, came into force. He cannot, therefore, succeed against the respondents merely by establishing negligence on the part of Hayman, for the latter was undoubtedly his fellow-servant. This was conceded, but the appellant contended that his injuries were also due to the negligence of the respondents, his employers, in failing to provide (a) proper plant and equipment for the job, and (b) a proper and safe system of working. If default of this nature was a cause of the accident, it is clear that the doctrine of common employment would not afford a defence, for the duties underlying these two types of negligence are and remain the personal obligations of the employer: see *Wilsons and Clyde Coal Co.* v. *English*. These duties, it may be well to add, are not absolute in nature. They lie within, and exemplify, the broader duty of taking reasonable care for the safety of his workmen which rests on every employer, and they may be more accurately described as (a) the duty to use reasonable skill and care to provide proper plant and equipment, and (b) the duty to use reasonable skill and care to provide a proper and safe system of working where the task is such as to call for the laying down of a system or mode of working in the interests of safety.

LORDS PORTER and REID delivered concurring speeches; VISCOUNT JOWITT, L.C., agreed with the opinion of LORD PORTER.

BAXTER *v.* CENTRAL ELECTRICITY GENERATING BOARD

[1965] 1 W.L.R. 200

The second defendants were installing a fuel mill in a power station of the first defendants. The plaintiff was employed by the first defendants. The plaintiff and an employee of the second defendants were trying to detect a fault in a heater which was being used to dry out the mill. They removed the wire mesh guard and adjusted the engine, while the engine was stopped. The plaintiff restarted the engine and then tried to make a further adjustment. He lost two fingers in a revolving fan. The plaintiff claimed damages against the second defendants—the company installing the mill—alleging breach of duty at common law and breach of statutory duty under the Building (Safety, Health and Welfare) Regulations 1948, regulation 85.

ASHWORTH, J. stated the facts and continued: It is perhaps convenient to deal first with the claim at common law which, in my judgment, must fail. One asks oneself: 'What duty did the second defendants owe to someone in the plaintiff's position, who was not employed by them?' It would be impossible, in my view, to hold that the second defendants owed generally to persons engaged on work within this building the special employer's duty which is owed to their own employees. I call it 'special duty,' although at the end of the day it can be expressed in simple language: a duty to take reasonable care in regard to place, equipment and system of work and to take reasonable care not to expose their servants to danger.

The plaintiff, as I have said, was not their servant but it is said that the plaintiff was, if not their servant, in the same position as if he had been a servant because on this particular Saturday evening the second defendants had left no fitter on the site. They ought to have contemplated that fitter's work might become necessary and that, in the ordinary course of things, their charge-hand electrician might, so to speak, enlist the temporary service of someone else who would become, *ad hoc,* the servant of the second defendants.

I cannot accept that argument at all. It seems to me that the second defendants had no reason whatever to contemplate that any work would become necessary in regard to this particular heater. They had had heaters of this type in operation, I think, for some little time before the date of the accident and no trouble had been caused by them. I feel, notwithstanding counsel for the plaintiff's argument, that it would be stretching the duty of employers far beyond anything that has so far been held, to reach the conclusion that, when the plaintiff was engaged in helping Miller, he had, so to speak, acquired the protection of the second defendants' duty to their own employees.

Even if I were wrong about that, it seems to me that there is cogent force in what counsel for the second defendants submitted as his second answer to this claim, namely, that even if a duty was owed in the nature of the employer's duty, there was no breach. This particular heater was not an article that the second defendants themselves had manufactured; it is an article that is on the market as the product of well-known and reputable manufacturers and the second defendants had bought it, and maybe others, for the purpose for which it was designed, namely, drying out equipment that had been in store. As counsel for the second defendants said, is it to be supposed that the second defendants in such a situation were required to take down or take to pieces this heater in order to satisfy themselves that, in the cylinder where the fan was placed, there was a guard?

I have a feeling that this case has some resemblance to the decision of the House of Lords in *Davie* v. *New Merton Board Mills Ltd*[1] where I regret I was the judge at first instance, but on this point I do not think I was corrected. I can see no breach of duty on the part of the second defendants, assuming they owed an employer's duty to the plaintiff. They had got equipment from a reputable source; it appeared to be perfectly well guarded by means of the mesh guard at the end and, in my view, there was nothing to lead them to suppose that there was any danger lurking within. Accordingly, at common law I decided, without hesitation, that this claim must fail....

His second contention is that the heater was not machinery. For my part, I find this a desperately difficult question. One finds in regulation 85 a reference to machinery and one finds in regulation 86 a reference to prime movers and machines....It rather looks as if you may have machines which are also machinery and I have, frankly, had some doubt as to the real answer when applying regulations 85 and 86 to the facts of this case. Regulation 85 was designed to protect people in respect of

[1] [1959] A.C. 604; [1959] 1 All E.R. 346, H.L.

machinery. I think one gets some assistance from its terms: 'Every fly wheel and every moving part of any prime mover, every part of trans-mission machinery and every dangerous part of other machinery (whether or not driven by mechanical power) shall be securely fenced....'

It may be that if the weather had been warmer, or if there had not been delay, it would have been quite unnecessary to make any use of these heaters at all. They were, in no sense, an integral part of the machinery, in the true sense of that word, which the second defendants were instal-ling. In my judgment, what the second defendants did was to introduce a machine for the purpose of drying out machinery. I do not regard the fact that this particular heater was portable as conclusive, but some guidance in the direction in which I am heading is to be derived from *Cherry* v. *International Alloys Ltd.*[1]

I would, therefore, hold on the second of these submissions that regulation 85 did not apply to this particular heater because it was not machinery. The third of his contentions was that there was no duty in any event, even if regulation 85 did apply, because the heater was not being used...It is fortified by reference to *Richard Thomas and Baldwins Ltd* v. *Cummings*[2] and *Knight* v. *Leamington Spa Courier Ltd.*[3]...it seems to be plain from those two decisions that, at the time when the plaintiff met with this accident, this particular heater was not in use but was under examination or repair. It may seem rather hard—and I confess I have some sympathy with the plaintiff and his advisers about this—that a machine which has been in use and is not going well is then examined and, for the purpose of examination, has to be kept running, can then be described by the defendants as not in use but merely under examination, but I think that that is the result of the authorities.

There is no provision, so far as I am aware, in the regulations cor-responding to the proviso of s. 16 of the Factories Act, and one asks oneself the simple question : 'Was this machine in use when the plaintiff was injured ?' I feel driven to hold that it was not.

Fourthly, it is said that, even if there was a duty and even if regulation 85 was applicable, there was no breach because this machine or mach-inery was securely fenced. Reliance is placed naturally upon the wire mesh guard at the back of the machine and, forensically, counsel for the second defendants asks: 'What more could be done to make it securely

---

[1] [1961] 1 Q.B. 136; [1960] 3 All E.R. 264, C.A. [*post* p. 717].
[2] [1955] A.C. 321; [1955] 1 All E.R. 285, H.L. [*post* p. 753].
[3] [1961] 2 Q.B. 253; [1961] 2 All E.R. 666, C.A.

fenced ?' One contemplates secure fencing as a protection for work-people when they are operating machinery and, in this instance, no one could suggest for one moment that this heater was any danger to anyone so long as it was being used as the makers intended and so long as it was in the condition in which it was up to the day of the accident. Until the plaintiff took the mesh guard off, I hold that the fan was securely fenced, no one could get to it, and I would also reinforce that by the consideration that, if it becomes necessary to take the heater to pieces for the purpose of examination or repair, one could normally contemplate that the presence of the fan and its position in relation to the engine would be such that further fencing would not be required. That is not the basis of my decision. I hold that it was securely fenced.

QUINN *v.* BURCH BROS (BUILDERS) LTD

Court of Appeal   [1966] 2 All E.R. 283

The plaintiff carried out building work for the defendants as their sub-contractor. It was an implied term of the contract that the defendants should supply equipment reasonably needed for the job, and in breach of that term they failed to supply the plaintiff with a step-ladder. To get on with the job, the plaintiff used a trestle instead, in a manner which he knew to be dangerous. The trestle slipped and he was injured. The defendants admitted that, in the absence of a ladder, it was foreseeable that the plaintiff would use the trestle in this dangerous manner. The plaintiff sued for damages for breach of contract. The Court of Appeal rejected his claim on the ground that the breach was not the cause of the damage.

SALMON, L.J.: The true nature of causation has long been debated by philosophers and lawyers. I do not think that it is necessary, or desirable, to attempt to add to the anthology of phrases that have been used with a view to describing the true nature of causation. Foreseeability of possible injury is, no doubt, the true criterion where negligence is in issue: *Thorogood* v. *Van den Berghs & Jurgens Ltd*[1] Similarly, when the question arises whether damages are too remote—damages, be it observed, which are admitted to have been caused by a breach of contract—the test is whether the damages which were actually sustained were reasonably foreseeable at the time the contract was entered into as likely to result from its breach: *Victoria Laundry (Windsor) Ltd* v. *Newman Industries Ltd.*[2] Although the foreseeability test is a handmaiden of the

---

[1] [1951] 1 All E.R. 682; [1951] 2 K.B. 537.
[2] [1949] 1 All E.R. 997 at p. 1002; [1949] 2 K.B. 528 at p. 539.

as law, it is by no means a maid-of-all-work. To my mind, it cannot serve the true criterion when the question is: how was the damage caused?...

All, I think, that the answers which the counsel for the plaintiff elicited in this case from the defendants' foreman really amount to is that the defendants realised that, if there was a breach of contract on their part to supply the step-ladder, that breach would afford the plaintiff the opportunity of acting negligently, and that he might take it and thereby suffer injury; but it seems to me quite impossible to say that in reality the plaintiff's injury was caused by the breach of contract. The breach of contract merely gave the plaintiff the opportunity to injure himself and was the occasion of the injury. There is always a temptation to fall into the fallacy of *post hoc ergo propter hoc*; and that is no less a fallacy, even if what happens afterwards could have been foreseen before it occurred. In my judgment, the learned judge in this case came to the only possible conclusion, and I am quite satisfied that the breach of contract cannot, in the circumstances of this case, be said to have caused the plaintiff's injury.*

SELLERS, L.J. and DANCKWERTS, L.J. delivered concurring judgments.

DOUGHTY v. TURNER MANUFACTURING CO. LTD
Court of Appeal [1964] 1 Q.B. 518

In the heat treatment room of the defendants' factory cauldrons of hot metal liquid were used for heating metal parts. An asbestos cement cover, purchased from reputable dealers, was used to cover each cauldron. A fellow employee of the plaintiff accidentally knocked one of the covers into its cauldron. It was not known that this could lead to dire consequences and nobody moved from the general vicinity of the cauldron. The molten liquid erupted—causing personal injuries to the plaintiff standing nearby. This was a common law action in negligence.

LORD PEARCE: In the present case the potential eruptive qualities of the covers when immersed in great heat were not suspected and they were not a known source of danger, but Mr James argues that the cause of injury was the escape of the hot liquid from the bath, and that injury through the escape of liquid from the bath by splashing was foreseeable.

---

* *Note:* Paull, J., in the court below, had held also that the defendant's breach of contract was not within the ambit of the word 'fault' in the Law Reform (Contributory Negligence) Act 1945, so that that statute could not have applied had the defendants been held liable. (See *post* pp. 737–751.)

Quaere: How far would the decision have been different if the plaintiff had been the employee of the defendants? Is this yet another area of law where the spread of 'self-employment' and 'sub-contracting' (see *ante*, p. 11) affects the legal duties? See now *McArdle* v. *Andmac Roofing Ltd.* [1967] 1 All E.R. 583 ('labour only' contractor employer made liable).

The evidence showed that splashes caused by sudden immersion, whether of the metal objects for which it was intended or any other extraneous object, were a foreseeable danger which should be carefully avoided. The falling cover might have ejected the liquid by a splash and in the result it did eject the liquid, though in a more dramatic fashion. Therefore, he argues, the actual accident was merely a variant of foreseeable accidents by splashing. It is clear, however, both by inference and by one explicit observation, that the judge regarded splashes as being in quite a different category. Moreover, according to the evidence, it seems that the cover never did create a splash: it appears to have slid into the liquid at an angle of some 45 degrees and dived obliquely downwards. Further, it seems somewhat doubtful whether the cover falling only from a height of four or six inches, which was the difference in level between the liquid and the sides, could have splashed any liquid outside the bath. And when (if ever) the plaintiff was in the area in which he could be hit by a mere splash (apparently the liquid being heavy, if splashed, would not travel further than a foot from the bath) the cover had already slid into the liquid without splashing. Indeed, it seems from the plaintiff's evidence that when he first came on to the scene the cover was already half in and half out of the liquid. On broader grounds, however, it would be quite unrealistic to describe this accident as a variant of the perils from splashing. The cause of the accident, to quote Lord Reid's words,[1] was 'the intrusion of a new and unexpected factor'. There was an eruption due to chemical changes underneath the surface of the liquid as opposed to a splash caused by displacement from bodies falling on to its surface. In my judgment, the reasoning in *Hughes* v. *Lord Advocate*[2] cannot be extended far enough to cover this case.

HARMAN and DIPLOCK, L.JJ. delivered concurring judgments.[*]

SMITH v. LEECH BRAIN & CO. LTD
[1962] 2 Q.B. 405

Part of the work of a galvaniser employed by the defendants involved lowering articles by means of an overhead crane into a tank containing molten metal. On 15 August 1950, whilst lowering an article into the

---

[1] [1963] A.C. 837, 845.　　　　　　[2] Ibid. 837.

[*] See, too, now on remoteness of damage *The Wagon Mound (No. 2)* [1966] 3 W.L.R. 498 (P.C.) where the test of foreseeability is reaffirmed. However, in personal injuries cases at least, it is not quite accurate to assert that 'the direct consequence doctrine...has therefore been overruled' (1966) 82 L.Q.R. p. 447. The tortfeasor still takes his victim as he finds him as is shown by *Smith* v. *Leech Brain & Co. Ltd (infra*, next case). and *Bradford* v. *Robinson Rentals Ltd.* [1967] 1 All E.R. 267.

tank, he turned round to see what he was doing, so that his head was outside the shield afforded by the corrugated iron, and a piece of molten metal struck him on the lower lip, causing a burn. The burn was the promoting agent of cancer, which developed at the site of the burn, and from which he died some three years later. The cancer developed in tissues which already had a pre-malignant condition. But for the burn, cancer might never have developed, although there was a strong likelihood that it would have done so at some stage in his life.

Held: (1) that the risk of a workman receiving a burn from the molten metal while operating the overhead crane, unless adequately protected, was one which any reasonable employer should have foreseen and the defendants, in that they had failed to provide adequate protection, were guilty of negligence at common law.

(2) That a tortfeasor must take his victim as he found him, and the test of the defendant's liability in respect of the death was not whether they could reasonably have foreseen that a burn would cause cancer and death, but whether they could reasonably foresee the type of injury suffered, namely, the burn; and that, therefore, since the cancer was merely an extension of the burn, which they should reasonably have anticipated, the defendants were liable in damages.

LORD PARKER, C.J.: This is a widow's claim under the Law Reform Act, 1934, and the Fatal Accidents Acts, 1846–1908, for damages arising out of an accident to her husband in the course of his employment by the first defendants. As a result of that accident he suffered a small burn on the lip, and subsequently died of cancer.... This accident occurred as long ago as 15 August 1950, which certainly does not make the case any easier for the widow, for the defendants or for myself....

On the issue of contributory negligence I have had some doubt because, as I have said, this is not the case of a man who was required to do a job for eight hours of the shift, but by a man who, maybe, was only doing it for five minutes in a night, and who knew full well all the dangers of putting his head outside the shield afforded by the temporary shelter. Nevertheless, it seems to me that this was something which was so foreseeable by the employers, for it is the most natural thing in the world for a man to turn round, as I feel this man did, that it would be wrong in this case for me to hold that he was in any substantial degree to blame for the accident. Accordingly, I find that contributory negligence is not made out....

The third question is damages. Here I am confronted with the recent decision of the Privy Council in *Overseas Tankship (U.K.) Limited* v.

Morts Dock and Engineering Co. Ltd (The Wagon Mound).[1] But for that case, it seems to me perfectly clear that, assuming negligence proved, and assuming that the burn caused in whole or in part the cancer and the death, the plaintiff would be entitled to recover.... For my part, I am quite satisfied that the Judicial Committee in the *Wagon Mound* case did not have what I may call, loosely, the thin skull cases in mind. It has always been the law of this country that a tortfeasor takes his victim as he finds him.... In those circumstances, it seems to me that this is plainly a case which comes within the old principle. The test is not whether these employers could reasonably have foreseen that a burn would cause cancer and that he would die. The question is whether these employers could reasonably foresee the type of injury he suffered, namely, the burn. What, in the particular case, is the amount of damage which he suffers as a result of that burn, depends upon the characteristics and constitution of the victim.

Accordingly, I find that the damages which the widow claims are damages for which the defendants are liable.

Section B

STATUTORY DUTIES IN FACTORIES AND OFFICES*

FACTORIES ACT, 1961

13. *Transmission machinery.* (1) Every part of the transmission machinery shall be securely fenced unless it is in such a position or of such construction as to be as safe to every person employed or working on the premises as it would be if securely fenced....

14. *Other machinery.* (1) Every dangerous part of any machinery, other than prime movers and transmission machinery, shall be securely fenced unless it is in such a position or of such construction as to be as safe to every person employed or working on the premises as it would be if securely fenced.

(2) In so far as the safety of a dangerous part of any machinery cannot by reason of the nature of the operation be secured by means of a

---

[1] (No. 1) [1961] A.C. 388; [1961] 1 All E.R. 404, P.C.

* The reader is referred also to other important safety statutes, especially the Mines and Quarries Act, 1954. Considerations of space caused the following selection of materials to be limited to factories and offices.

fixed guard, the requirements of subsection (1) of this section shall be deemed to have been complied with if a device is provided which automatically prevents the operator from coming into contact with that part...

16. *Construction and maintenance of fencing.* All fencing or other safeguards provided in pursuance of the foregoing provisions of this Part of this Act shall be of substantial construction, and constantly maintained and kept in position while the parts required to be fenced or safeguarded are in motion or use, except when any such parts are necessarily exposed for examination and for any lubrication or adjustment shown by the examination to be immediately necessary, and all such conditions as may be specified in regulations made by the Minister are complied with....

28. *Floors, passages and stairs.* (1) All floors, steps, stairs, passages and gangways shall be of sound construction and properly maintained and shall, so far as is reasonably practicable, be kept free from any obstruction and from any substance likely to cause persons to slip....

29. *Safe means of access and safe place of employment.* (1) There shall, so far as is reasonably practicable, be provided and maintained safe means of access to every place at which any person has at any time to work, and every such place shall, so far as is reasonably practicable, be made and kept safe for any person working there.

(2) Where any person has to work at a place from which he will be liable to fall a distance more than six feet six inches, then, unless the place is one which affords secure foothold and, where necessary, secure hand-hold, means shall be provided, so far as is reasonably practicable, by fencing or otherwise, for ensuring his safety....

76. (1) Where the Minister is satisfied that any manufacture, machinery, plant, equipment, appliance, process or description of manual labour is of such a nature as to cause risk of bodily injury to the persons employed or any class of those persons, he may, subject to the provisions of this Act, make such special regulations as appear to him to be reasonably practicable and to meet the necessity of the case....

143. (1) No person employed in a factory or in any other place to which any provisions of this Act apply shall wilfully interfere with or misuse any means, appliance, convenience or other thing provided in pursuance of this Act for securing the health, safety or welfare of the persons employed in the factory or place, and where any means or appliance for securing health or safety is provided for the use of any such person under this Act he shall use the means or appliance.

(2) No person employed in a factory or in any other place to which any provisions of this Act apply shall wilfully and without reasonable cause do anything likely to endanger himself or others.

155. *Offences.* (1) In the event of any contravention in or in connection with or in relation to a factory of the provisions of this Act, or of any regulation or order made thereunder, the occupier, or (if the contravention is one in respect of which the owner is by or under this Act made responsible) the owner, of the factory shall, subject to the following provisions of this Part of this Act, be guilty of an offence.

(2) In the event of a contravention by an employed person of the provisions of Part X of this Act with respect to duties of persons employed or of a contravention by any person of any regulation or order made under this Act which expressly imposes any duty upon him, that person shall be guilty of an offence and the occupier or owner, as the case may be, shall not be guilty of an offence, by reason only of the contravention of the said provisions of Part X of this Act, or the contravention of the provision imposing the said duty, as the case may be, unless it is proved that he failed to take all reasonable steps to prevent the contravention; but this subsection shall not be taken as affecting any liability of the occupier or owner in respect of the same matters by virtue of some provision other than the provisions or provision aforesaid.

175. *Interpretation of expression 'factory'.* (1) Subject to the provisions of this section, the expression 'factory' means any premises in which, or within the close or curtilage or precincts of which, persons are employed in manual labour in any process for or incidental to any of the following purposes, namely:

(*a*) the making of any article or of part of any article; or

(*b*) the altering, repairing, ornamenting, finishing, cleaning, or washing or the breaking up or demolition of any article; or

(*c*) the adapting for sale of any article;

(*d*) the slaughtering of cattle, sheep, swine, goats, horses, asses or mules; or

(*e*) the confinement of such animals as aforesaid while awaiting slaughter at other premises, in a case where the place of confinement is available in connection with those other premises, is not maintained primarily for agricultural purposes within the meaning of the Agriculture Act, 1947, or, as the case may be, the Agriculture (Scotland) Act, 1948, and does not form part of premises used for the holding of a market in respect of such animals;

being premises in which, or within the close or curtilage or precincts of which, the work is carried on by way of trade or for purposes of gain and to or over which the employer of the persons employed therein has the right of access or control.

(2) The expression 'factory' also includes the following premises in which persons are employed in manual labour (whether or not they are factories by virtue of subsection (1) of this section), that is to say, ...

[The subsection goes on to make special provision for: dry docks and shipyards; premises for sorting, washing, packing articles preliminary to factory work; certain laundries; premises for work on cloth or on transport vehicles; printing works; premises for work on theatrical properties (but not theatres themselves); net-mending works; certain repairing works; film studios; works for the making of building materials; and premises for storage of gas.]

(4) A part of a factory may, with the approval in writing of the chief inspector, be taken to be a separate factory and two or more factories may, with the like approval, be taken to be a single factory....

(6) Where a place situate within the close, curtilage, or precincts forming a factory is solely used for some purpose other than the processes carried on in the factory, that place shall not be deemed to form part of the factory for the purposes of this Act, but shall, if otherwise it would be a factory, be deemed to be a separate factory.

(7) Premises shall not be excluded from the definition of a factory by reason only that they are open air premises....

(9) Any premises belonging to or in the occupation of the Crown or any municipal or other public authority shall not be deemed not to be a factory, and building operations or works of engineering construction undertaken by or on behalf of the Crown or any such authority shall not be excluded from the operation of this Act, by reason only that the work carried on thereat is not carried on by way of trade or for purposes of gain.

OFFICES, SHOPS AND RAILWAYS
PREMISES ACT, 1963

1. (1) The premises to which this Act applies are office premises, shop premises and railway premises being (in each case) premises in the case of which persons are employed to work therein.

(2) In this Act: (a) 'office premises' means a building or part of a building, being a building or part the sole or principal use of which is as an office or for office purposes; (b) 'office purposes' includes the purposes

of administration, clerical work, handling money and telephone and telegraph operating; and (c) 'clerical work' includes writing, book-keeping, sorting papers, filing, typing, duplicating, machine calculation, drawing and the editorial preparation of matter for publication; and for the purposes of this Act premises occupied together with office premises for the purposes of the activities there carried on shall be treated as forming part of the office premises....

17. (1) Every dangerous part of any machinery used as, or forming part of the equipment of premises to which this Act applies shall be securely fenced unless it is such a position or of such construction as to be safe to every person working in the premises as it would be if securely fenced....

NEWTON v. JOHN STANNING & SON

[1962] 1 W.L.R. 30

The defendants occupied a factory where textiles were bleached and finished. In the curtilage of the factory there was a pump-house which contained transmission machinery used for pumping water under pressure into the mill of the factory. This was an essential part of the works. The machinery was admittedly unfenced and the information preferred against the defendants charged them with a failure to fence under s. 13 (1) of the Factories Act, 1937. In defence to the charge it was pleaded that the pump-house was not a factory within the meaning of s. 151 (1) of the 1937 Act thus placing it outside the requirements of that Act.

LORD PARKER, C.J.: There is no question here of the pump-house being a separate factory on its own, and the sole question is whether it was used solely for a purpose other than the processes carried on in the factory. It was suggested that the pumping of water was no more than a process of transportation or distribution and formed no part of the processes carried on in the factory.... I find it quite impossible to say that this pump-house must be treated as separate from the factory. It seems to me that therein was carried on a process which was undoubtedly for or incidental to the work of bleaching and finishing of textiles. Indeed, the justices found that it was an essential part of the works and accordingly, in my judgment, the offence was proved.

I should only add this, that the justices clearly felt that they were bound to hold otherwise by reason of the decision in Longhust v. Guild-ford, Godalming and District Water Board.[1] That case was tried by me;

[1] [1960] 2 Q.B. 265; [1960] 2 W.L.R. 383; [1960] 1 All E.R. 54.

it went to the Court of Appeal[1] and the House of Lords,[2] and so far as this particular point is concerned the decision has been the same in all courts. In that case there were within the one precincts a filter-house in which water was collected, filtered and chlorinated, and, separate to that, a pump-house in which the chlorinated water was taken out under pressure and pumped as part of the water supply to the individual houses. It was held that the pump-house had nothing to do with the process of chlorinating and filtering but was something separate and amounted to transportation and distribution of water that had already completed, as it were, its treatment in the factory. I cannot see that that decision has anything to do with this case where, as an integral part of the works, water is being pumped for the purposes of the bleaching and finishing. Accordingly, this case, in my judgment should go back to the justices with a direction to convict.

SLADE and WIDGERY, JJ. agreed with LORD PARKER, C.J.

PULLIN v. PRISON COMMISSIONERS

[1957] 1 W.L.R. 1186

The plaintiff after serving a three year prison sentence discovered that he had tuberculosis. While in prison he had worked in the workshops making mats. He claimed damages alleging that his condition had been caused *inter alia* by breaches of the Factories Act, 1937. The question arose whether the premises were a factory within the statute.

LORD GODDARD, C.J.: I think that for the Factory Act to apply there must be found to exist (except in certain express cases, as, for instance, apprentices, which are dealt with separately) the relationship of master and servant and employment for wages. There is no employment for wages in the case of prisoners. Prisons are put under the control of the Secretary of State, who exercises his control through the Prison Commissioners, and through visiting magistrates who visit the prisons to see that the provisions of the Prison Act, 1952, are being carried out.

A number of sections of the Factories Act, 1937, to which my attention was called show quite clearly that they cannot possibly apply to prisons. The work which is carried on in prisons is work which is penal in the sense that the prisoners are obliged to work as a consequence of their sentence. I do not find any section in the Act which faintly indicates in my opinion that a prison workshop can be a factory. I think that the

---

[1] [1961] 1 Q.B. 408; [1960] 3 W.L.R. 1059; [1960] 3 All E.R. 664, C.A.
[2] [1961] 3 W.L.R. 915; [1961] 3 All E.R. 545, H.L.

reasons given by Wrottesley, J. in *Weston* v. *London County Council*,[1] and the considerations which he applied to show that a technical institute, in which work was being carried on which, if it had been carried on by persons employed under a contractual relationship, would have made it a factory, was not a factory apply in the present case. If they did not make that institute a factory in that case, still less do they make a prison a factory in this case.

PAUL POPPER LTD *v.* GRIMSEY

[1963] 1 Q.B. 44

The defendants were a photographic agency who brought up negatives and sold prints of photographs together with the right to reproduce, mainly to the Press. Their premises consisted of offices, a library and two rooms where the prints were made. Two of the fifteen employees worked in these two rooms and their work involved manual labour. Were their premises 'a factory'? In a prosecution under the Factories Act it was held the entire premises were a factory.

LORD PARKER, C.J. (delivering the judgment of the court): The finished print is an 'article' which has been made by manual labour on the premises and so made for purposes of gain. It seems to us to be quite immaterial that the prints are returned to the defendants after use and not retained by the customer and, if one regards the glazing room and dark room as the 'premises' to which s. 151 is to be applied, we think it clear that those premises are a factory.

The defendants, however, further contend that the premises to which the definition must be applied are not the glazing room and dark room in isolation but the complete entity, which they occupy including the offices and library. They say that this entity is not a factory, because the employment of persons in manual labour is merely incidental to the general business carried on, and they found themselves on certain dicta of Lord Alverstone, C.J. in *Hoare* v. *Robert Green Ltd.*[2]...

We have come to the conclusion that the premises to be considered in this case are all the rooms occupied by the defendants, and not merely the glazing room and dark room. The definition of 'workshop' in the Factory and Workshop Act, 1901, directed attention to individual rooms in a building, but the definition of 'factory' in both Acts seems to us, *prima facie*, to refer to the whole of the premises within the curtilage of which the manufacturing activity is carried on, and, although we have

---

[1] [1941] 1 K.B. 608.   [2] [1907] 2 K.B. 315, D.C.

not been referred to any authority which in terms so decides, this seems to be implicit in many of the earlier cases....

In our opinion the language of the section supports this view, because it seems clear that if premises consist of a building occupied with land, forming its close, curtilage or precinct the existence of a manufacturing activity in the close, curtilage or precinct will make the whole of the premises a factory, unless some particular part of the premises is excluded by the terms of s. 151(6).* The very fact that it was thought necessary to enact subsection (6) supports the contention that subsection (1) would not by itself restrict the factory premises to those parts which were used for strict manufacturing purposes....

In our judgment, therefore, the magistrate applied a wrong principle if, by holding that the glazing room and dark room constituted a factory, he was thereby treating the rest of the premises as outside the ambit of the Act. On a literal interpretation of s. 151(1) the premises as a whole were a factory because persons were employed therein in manual labour in making an article for the purposes of gain....The purpose of the defendants' business was to provide photographic prints on loan to interested persons, and the physical production of those prints was the essence of that business. The manual labour employed in the glazing and dark rooms was not concerned with some incidental matter, but was the final stage in the substantial and only purpose for which the premises as a whole were used.

J. & F. STONE LIGHTING & RADIO LTD v. HAYGARTH

House of Lords   [1966] 3 All E.R. 539

The defendants were occupiers of a shop and workroom. In the shop a radio, television and electrical business was carried on; and in the workroom an engineer (Sayer) was employed to diagnose and repair the faults in goods hired and sold in the shop, and also to conduct a general repair service. The defendants were charged with offences against the Factories Act, 1961. Their defence was that the premises were not a factory within s. 175(1) of the Act.

LORD MORRIS: My lords, I cannot think that, if someone spends all his time, or at least the greater part of it, doing work with his hands, he is not to be regarded as employed in manual labour merely because he needs knowledge to do his work. I can find nothing in the wording of

* The predecessor of s. 175(6) Factories Act, 1961.

the Act of 1961 which suggests that, if manual labour needs knowledge for its performance, it is to cease to be regarded as manual labour.

It is clear that the mere fact that someone labours with his hands in a place does not make that place a factory. For that to be so (*a*) the person must be employed; (*b*) he must be employed in manual labour; (*c*) he must be so employed in a process for or incidental to a purpose of a kind designated in s. 175; (*d*) the place must be premises in which (or within the close or curtilage or precincts of which) the work is carried on by way of trade or for purposes of gain, and (*e*) the premises must be premises to or over which the employer of the person (or persons) employed has the right of access or control. Here we are only concerned with the words 'employed in manual labour'. The word 'employed' is clear. The words 'employed in' denote employed to do. The word 'manual' denotes something done with the hands. (As long ago as in 1884 Bowen, L.J., said in *Morgan* v. *London General Omnibus Co.*[1] that manual labour could only mean 'labour performed by hand'.) In one sense every person is employed in manual labour who is employed to do work with his hands; but nearly everyone who is employed must do some work with his hands. How then is a decision to be made as to whether an employed person is or is not employed in manual labour?

In so far as decided cases are being looked at for guidance it is to be remembered that they are often decisions on particular facts and furthermore that varying statutory phrases have been under consideration....

Problems have often arisen in cases where the work which a person has been employed to do is partly work to be done with the hands and partly work not to be done with the hands. It is here that the decided cases are of assistance. There is, I think, a clear and unbroken line of authority to the effect that in such a situation regard must be had to what is the main substantial work which a person is employed to do. Following this line of authority it seems to me that on the facts as found by the magistrates in this case and as recorded by them in the Case Stated the conclusion inevitably followed that Mr Sayer was employed in manual labour with the result (by reason of the other findings) that the place where he worked was a factory....

There are few employments which do not in some way involve some use of the hands in the performance of duties involved. Those who in various capacities are employed to evolve policies, to reach decisions, to direct affairs, or to guide and supervise others may all at certain moments need the use of their hands. Yet in so many cases the use of the

---

[1] (1884), 13 Q.B.D. 832 at p. 834.

hands would be of so incidental and subsidiary a nature that on a commonsense approach a decision could readily be reached that there was no employment 'in manual labour'.

My lords, in the present case on the facts as found it seems to me that it was not possible to say that Mr Sayer was not employed in manual labour. On the facts as found his use of his hands could not be said to be subsidiary or incidental. It was the whole purpose of his employment that by the use of his hands he should repair or adjust or replace. That was his essential work and for all practical purposes his only work. His labour was to be done by hand. This being so the facts of the present case do not give rise to the sort of problem which arose in many of the decided cases. Nor can a survey of particular decisions on particular facts be of value or call for an expression of approval or disapproval unless they reveal guidance as to what is denoted by the words 'employed in manual labour'.

In *Bound* v. *Lawrence*[1] (a case relating to s. 10 of the Employers and Workmen Act, 1875) the substantial nature of the employment was non-manual though some manual labour was incidental. Lord Esher, M.R., said that the court must not look at what a person does incidentally in the course of his employment, but must see what is his real and substantial work. In that case a grocer's assistant had the duty of serving customers in a shop. That did not involve manual labour; but he had also certain other duties which did involve manual labour. Those duties were held to be incidental to his real and substantial employment as a salesman.

Among the general purposes of the Factory Acts are those of ensuring health, safety and satisfactory conditions of work. In legislating in relation to those employed in manual labour it would seem reasonable to suppose that the legislature was contemplating those whose work involved to a substantial extent the use of their hands. If manual labour denotes working with the hands, I can find nothing in the Act of 1961 which requires that the work must be heavy work which demands great strength. Some manual labour may require much strength: other manual labour may require but little. Similarly there may be manual labour which requires much knowledge: other manual labour may require but little. Some knowledge may be generally possessed by most people: some knowledge may be specially possessed by a few. Furthermore that which yesterday was the special knowledge of the few may tomorrow be the commonplace knowledge of all. The Act of 1961 neither prescribes

[1] [1892] 1 Q.B. 226.

nor defines any varieties of manual labour. If therefore someone is employed to work with his hands, so that in a realistic way it can be said that such work with his hands forms his main or predominant activity (as opposed to work with his hands which is merely incidental to or accessory to work which is not so done), then he would be employed in manual labour. He would still be so employed even if his work required knowledge or skill or ability. The Act of 1961 is not limited to unskilled manual labour. There is no exemption for skilled manual labour. Were it so the Act of 1961 might cease to operate in some of the very places for which its provisions would seem to be appropriate....

The contention which the justices considered was expressed as being that the work on which Mr Sayer was employed was not manual work, since the high degree of ability required in fault finding and testing and the substantial proportion of time spent in this aspect of his work made that the substantial part of his work, to which the work of manual repair, replacement and adjustment was incidental. I have referred to and summarised what were the actual findings of fact which were arrived at by the justices and which included the finding that the greater part of Mr Sayer's time was spent in work of repair, replacement and adjustment. On these findings of fact their conclusion was that because of the knowledge that Mr Sayer needed to do his work the use of his hands was only a subsidiary part of his work. My lords, I agree with the Divisional Court that the justices misdirected themselves in thinking that, because Mr Sayer had to have knowledge to do his work, the use of his hands became a subsidiary part of his work. This would in my view be dangerous doctrine. If it were approved and upheld it would greatly restrict and limit the meaning of the words manual labour.

LORD PEARSON: There is no provision to the effect that, in order to constitute 'manual labour', the work must be physically arduous, or that it must be repetitive or of a routine character, or that it must be unskilled or involving only manual dexterity, or that it must be capable of being done without the exercise of intelligence, technical knowledge or artistic taste. The evident intention of the Act of 1961 is to protect persons engaged in the specified operations, provided their work is 'manual labour'. It is reasonable to expect that at any rate most persons engaged in specified operations of ordinary kinds will have the protection of the Act of 1961. It is helpful therefore to envisage a number of ordinary kinds of repair work, in order to see what faculties may have to be exercised, and what qualifications may have to be possessed, by persons doing repair work. Doubtless a great many examples could be given. Those which occur to me are repairs of boots and shoes, clothing, jewellery, carpets (including Persian carpets), furniture (including antique furniture), articles of china or earthenware, motor vehicles, firearms, musical instruments, clocks and watches, dolls in a 'dolls' hospital', mechanical toys, optical instruments and electrical domestic appliances. There are also in factories the millwrights, maintenance engineers and toolsetters who may have to repair and adjust intricate and complicated machinery. The uninitiated 'man in the street' would not be able to repair any of these things, not only from want of manual dexterity but also from want of technical knowledge. If the need for possessing and exercising technical knowledge in the course of their work disqualified persons from being regarded as 'employed in manual labour' within the meaning of s. 175, very few repairers would by virtue of their own employment be entitled to the protection of the Act of 1961. That does not seem right. Persons who are engaged in repairing articles by the use of their hands ought to be protected by the Act of 1961, however much technical knowledge they need to have and use in doing so. The extent of the technical knowledge brought to bear in the course of the work with the hands does not affect the need for protection of the workers in respect of health, welfare and safety....

There is however a principle which seems to be common to all the relevant cases under all the Acts, and it can be stated shortly in these terms. A person is not employed in 'manual labour' for the purposes of any of the Acts, if his occupation is primarily or substantially an activity of a different kind and the manual work that he does is merely ancillary or accessory to that activity. There are many decided cases illustrating the application of this principle. *Morgan* v. *London General Omnibus Co.*[1] (bus conductor not 'engaged in manual labour'); *Cook* v. *North Metropolitan Tramways Co.*[2] (tram driver not 'engaged in manual labour'); *Bound* v. *Lawrence*[3] (grocer's assistant not 'engaged in manual labour'); *Fullers, Ltd* v. *Squire*[4] (as above, 'manual labour'); *Hoare* v. *Robert Green, Ltd*[5] (girls engaged in making wreaths, crosses and bouquets behind a florist's shop were exercising 'manual labour'); *Re Dairymen's Foremen, Re Tailors' Cutters*[6] (held to be 'employed otherwise than in manual labour' within the National Insurance Act, 1911, as they were in substance employed as managers); *Re National*

---

[1] (1884), 13 Q.B.D. 832.
[3] [1892] 1 Q.B. 226.
[4] [1900–3] All E.R. Rep. 138; [1901] 2 K.B. 209.
[5] [1904–7] All E.R. Rep. 858; [1907] 2 K.B. 315.

[2] (1887), 18 Q.B.D. 683.

[6] (1912), 107 L.T. 342.

Insurance Act, 1911, *Re Lithographic Artists, Re Engravers*[1] (held to be exercising the highest degree of artistic intelligence and artistic skill, and to be employed 'otherwise than in manual labour'); *Jaques* v. *Owners of Steam Tug Alexandra*[2] (tug master employed 'otherwise than by way of manual labour' within s. 13 of the Workmen's Compensation Act, 1906, on the facts there set out); *Appeal of Gardner, Re Maschek, Re Tyrrell*[3] (modellers held not to be employed 'otherwise than by way of manual labour' for the purposes of the Unemployment Insurance Act, 1935); *Joyce* v. *Boots Cash Chemists (Southern), Ltd*[4] (dispenser at chemist's shop held not 'employed in manual labour').

There may be difficulty in applying the principle in particular cases (e.g. in the case of the dispenser at the chemist's shop, who seems to me a borderline case), but in general the principle is clear. Examples of activities which are primarily non-manual, though involving some manual work, are (i) the work of a painter, sculptor or lithographic artist; (ii) managerial or supervisory work; (iii) selling in a shop; (iv) clerical work; (v) driving a vehicle or acting as conductor of a public service vehicle. In the sphere of repairing there seems to be no decided case, but it can be suggested with, at any rate, plausibility, that an artist restoring or even cleaning a picture, an expert in oriental ceramics repairing a Ming vase, or an archaeologist piecing together fragments of an Egyptian papyrus or Linea B script, would not be held to be employed in manual labour. There ought also to be examples of primarily intellectual activities involving some incidental element of manual labour. Mathematicians, scientists, inventors, actors and musicians—even authors—may have to do some incidental manual work.

In my opinion, however, the present case wholly fails to come within the principle. There is no primary or substantial main activity to which Mr Sayer's work of repairing television and radio sets and electrical appliances by the use of his hands could be ancillary or accessory. He is a highly skilled craftsman using his technical knowledge in his manual work of repairing articles.

LORD UPJOHN delivered a concurring speech; LORD REID and LORD PEARCE dissented.

[1] (1913), 108 T.L. 894.   [2] [1921] 2 A.C. 339 at pp. 340, 341.
[3] [1938] 1 All E.R. 20.   [4] [1950] 2 All E.R. 719.

POWLEY v. BRISTOL SIDDELEY ENGINES LTD
[1966] 1 W.L.R. 729

The plaintiff was employed by the defendants at their premises, a greater part of which was a factory within s. 175(1) of the Factories Act, 1961, engaged in the production of aircraft engines. Within the perimeter of the premises there was a separate administration block which contained technical staff. In the course of his employment the plaintiff walked through the courtyard to the administration block and on returning the same way slipped on some ice and suffered personal injury. This was an action alleging breach of s. 28(1) of the Factories Act, 1961. The issue to be determined was whether the administration block and the place of the accident was prevented from being a part of the factory by s. 175(6) of the 1961 Act—if so, the defendants could not be made liable under s. 28(1).

MEGAW, J.: I come, therefore, to the question whether the administration block (which, as I have said, is agreed to include the scene of the accident) is or is not a place to which the Factories Act, 1961, applies. One thing at least can be stated with confidence: either the Factories Act applies, or else it does not apply, to the place where this accident happened. The question has to be answered. Whichever answer is given, that answer can be assailed as being absurd. It can be said that it is absurd that a courtyard surrounded by flower beds and hedges in front of a building containing administrative offices is a 'factory'. On the other hand, it can be said that it is absurd that the plaintiff's rights against his employers vary according to the apparently irrelevant consideration whether his fall happened to take place on these steps or on identical steps, perhaps only a few yards away, but technically outside the purlieus of the administration block. I do not think that considerations of the rationality of the result help much in arriving at the answer....

That subsection, or rather, its predecessor, s. 151(6) of the Act of 1937, has been the subject of a number of decided cases. I note that in *Thurogood* v. *Van den Berghs and Jurgens Ltd*,[1] the subsection's predecessor was referred to by counsel as 'an ineptly drawn subsection which plainly contained an ambiguity'. Yet the re-enactment in 1961 was in identical terms.

One difficulty which I find is the apposition of the words 'purpose' and 'processes': 'Where a place...is solely used for some purpose

[1] [1951] 2 K.B. 537.

other than the processes carried on in the factory'. Some words must, I think, be implied. Does it, perhaps, mean 'for some purpose other than the purpose of carrying on the processes carried on in the factory'? If that is right, one is entitled to inquire what processes, if any, are carried on in 'the place' and to compare those processes with the factory processes. That this is the right approach, or at least a permissible approach, is, in my view, implicit in the judgment of the Court of Appeal in *Thurogood's* case....In *Thurogood's* case the question was whether an engineering shop, being a separate building within the curtilage of a margarine-making factory, was excluded from being a part of that factory by reason of subsection (6). The engineering shop was used for the testing and repair of machinery used in the main factory. The Court of Appeal held that it was not excluded....The fact that the persons principally employed in 'the place'—the administration block— are not engaged in manual labour is not, as I see it, of any relevance in respect of the first part of subsection (6), with which I am here concerned. No doubt it would be highly relevant to the question involved in the latter part of the subsection, if it were to arise: that is, whether, if the place is excluded from 'the factory', it is itself a separate factory. Further, 'process' does not necessarily connote a 'manufacturing process'....

Accordingly, as I understand *Thurogood's* case, the question to be decided is whether any process, or activity, carried on in the administration block was the same as, or was incidental to, the process, or activity, carried on in the part of the premises where aircraft engines were physically manufactured. Are such activities as the designing, drawing and technical development of aircraft engines, carried out in the offices of the administration block, processes 'other than processes for, or incidental to, the purpose of the making of aircraft engines'? In my judgment, they are not 'other than'. They are, in any ordinary use of the words, 'incidental to' the making of aircraft engines. I hold that the administration block, including the actual place where the accident happened, is not excluded by virtue of s. 175 (6) from being a part of the factory which, by virtue of s. 175 (1), the rest of the premises unquestionably is. I assess the plaintiff's own share of the responsibility for his accident at 50 per cent.

LIPTROT v. BRITISH RAILWAYS BOARD

Court of Appeal   [1966] 2 Q.B. 253; [1966] 2 W.L.R. 841

The plaintiff was injured by a mobile crane while it was working in a scrap-metal yard. The question was whether this crane was 'machinery' within the Factories Act s. 14(1).

WILLMER, L.J.: Counsel for the defendants, in the course of his argument this morning, advanced the proposition that this mobile crane was really nothing more than a vehicle used for the transport of material from place to place, in much the same way as a lorry might be used to transport material from place to place. He will, I am sure, forgive me if I say that I think that argument was rather far-fetched. Coming back, however, to the question whether *Cherry's* case[1] does afford any guide to the solution of the problem in the present case, it seems to me that the two cases are quite different. In *Cherry's* case the truck with which the court was concerned was basically a vehicle, and nothing but a vehicle. In the present case the piece of equipment, to use a neutral phrase, with which we are concerned is basically a crane. The fact that it happens to be fitted with wheels which make it mobile is merely an irrelevant detail. Had this crane been mounted on a fixed pedestal, I do not see how it could be doubted but that it would have constituted factory machinery, so as to be capable of falling within s. 14 of the Act of 1961. It appears to me that it can make no difference to the nature of a piece of machinery that it happens to be mounted on a mobile chassis.

No case has been cited to us in which the exact question before us has been the subject of specific decision; but three cases have been called to our attention in which equipment of a similar character has been held to constitute 'machinery' within s. 14 of the Factories Act apparently without argument to the contrary. I refer first to the well-known and oft-quoted case of *Walker* v. *Bletchley Flettons, Ltd*,[2] a case concerning a mechanical excavator; *Fowler* v. *Yorkshire Electric Power Co., Ltd*,[3] a case concerning a crane which travelled on overhead rails, and *Biddle* v. *Truvox Engineering Co., Ltd*,[4] a case concerning an electric stacking truck. It seems to me that the mobile crane with which we are concerned in the present case is an object bearing certain quite striking similarities with the objects in those cases to which we have been referred. I can see no real answer to the contention advanced on behalf

---

[1] [1960] 3 All E.R. 264; [1961] 1 Q.B. 136. (*Cherry* v. *International Alloys Ltd.*)
[2] [1937] 1 All E.R. 170.   [3] [1939] 1 All E.R. 407.
[4] [1951] 2 All E.R. 835; [1952] 1 K.B. 101.

of the plaintiff that this crane constitutes part of the factory machinery, so as to be capable of being caught by s. 14 of the Act of 1961.

DANCKWERTS, L.J.: I find myself in disagreement. I think that the judge reached the right result, and I would dismiss the appeal. In this case I find myself caught between sympathy for the plaintiff and the injuries which he received, and exasperation at the artificial results produced by the provisions of the Factories Act, 1961. In the present case, however, no ordinary person would call this yard a factory.

In *Cherry's* case a very different kind of vehicle was involved. It was a Lister truck which apparently moved about in the factory, and it had not any lifting machinery. I cannot appreciate, however, why the absence of lifting machinery in that case and the presence of lifting machinery in the present case make the two cases in principle distinguishable.

It seems to me that one should apply common sense in these cases and apply a reasonable construction to the words which are found in the Factories Act in such a way that they do not produce an absurd and entirely unexpected result. The accident in the present case seems to me to be of a type which is not that which one would ordinarily associate with factory machinery at all. It was caused by the revolution of part of the main body of the crane so as to produce a space in which the plaintiff happened to be standing which was not wide enough for his body to be between the body of the crane and the wheel, thus causing him to suffer the severe injury which he did. I cannot believe that this machine, the travelling crane, is properly within the meaning of 'factory machinery' contained in the Factories Act, and, in particular, in s. 14, the section which we have been considering.

SALMON, L.J.: The premises at which this accident occurred were an open space, which I suppose no layman would regard as a factory. In my view, one's approach to the present problem tends to be bedevilled by that circumstance, for it is difficult to think of anything in that open space as being factory machinery. Nevertheless, that open space was a factory within the meaning of the Factories Acts, since it comes within the definition of a 'factory' in s. 175(2)(b).

The sole question that arises on this appeal is whether a mobile, mechanically-operated crane used in a factory of this kind is a machine to which the Act applies. It is conceded that, if the crane in this factory had been on a fixed platform, it would fall within the Act. I ask myself the question: Why should it make any difference, in considering whether a crane is part of the factory machinery, that it happens to be on wheels and movable? I confess that I find great difficulty in supplying any sensible answer to that question. In the cases to which Willmer, L.J., has referred it seems to have been assumed that mechanical excavators, travelling cranes and electric stacking trucks, if used in a factory, are machines or machinery within the Act.

In *Parvin* v. *Morton Machine Co. Ltd*[1] it was decided that machinery manufactured in a factory was not machinery within the Act. According to Lord Normand,[2] the Act applied only to '...machines or machinery for use in the factory in the processes of manufacture, or as ancillary to these processes'. The factory there being considered was a factory in which processes of manufacture took place. Here, it is a factory where processes of sorting take place. There can be no doubt that this mobile crane was used in this factory in the processes of sorting.

In my judgment, a crane used for sorting purposes in a factory such as the one under consideration in the present case is part of the factory equipment and falls within the provisions of the Factories Act whether it be mobile or static. That, as I desire to emphasise, is the only point that has been raised on this appeal. I emphasise that point because I do not wish it to be thought that I am deciding that the parts of the crane with which this unfortunate plaintiff came into contact are parts of machinery within the meaning of s. 14. I expressly desire to reserve that point. I have not even formed a provisional view about it. I am certainly not convinced that the parts in question are parts of machinery which are covered by s. 14. No point has been taken as to whether the wheel or the other part of the crane which came into contact with the plaintiff is a 'part of any machinery' to which s. 14 of the Factories Act applies.

[An appeal is pending to the House of Lords currently in this case.]

IRWIN v. WHITE, TOMKINS & COURAGE LTD

House of Lords [1964] 1 W.L.R. 387

The respondents were installing new machinery at their mill. Before the installation of all the machinery was complete and before it was put to commercial use the defendant was killed by part of it—a sack hoist—which in itself was complete and ready for use.

The House held that the Act* applied since the hoist was an independent machine and was 'in motion' at the time of the accident.

---

[1] [1952] A.C. 515. [2] Ibid. 520.

* The statutory provisions were the Northern Ireland equivalent of ss. 14 and 16, Factories Act, 1961.

LORD REID: Section 15(1) provides that: 'Every dangerous part of any machinery, other than prime movers and transmission machinery, shall be securely fenced...'. The exception and the proviso do not apply to this case. I agree with the respondents to this extent: there cannot be a dangerous part of any machinery until there is machinery, and machinery means machinery which has been installed as part of the equipment of the factory. There is no statutory obligation to fence while a machine is being erected; at that stage the employee can only rely on his employers' common law obligations. The respondents did contend that the hoist and conveyor belt were only parts of a single machine which was not yet complete, but I agree with Lord MacDermott, C.J., that the hoist was an independent machine—'it was a machine in its own right, as it were, and it had been erected and completed before the accident'...

Section 17 requires rather more detailed examination. It provides that fencing required by the Act shall be kept in position while the dangerous parts 'are in motion or in use'. There is an exception to this when the parts are exposed for examination, lubrication or adjustment: but then additional precautions prescribed by regulations must be taken. The respondents contend that the phrase 'in motion or in use' shows that the section cannot be intended to apply until the machine has been taken into use. But the phrase cannot mean in motion *and* in use, for then the exception would be unnecessary. It is not obvious why the words 'or in use' were added: it may be because parts which are not in motion may nevertheless be dangerous while the machine is in use....

Finally the respondents relied on the case of *Parvin* v. *Morton Machine Co. Ltd.*[1] There it was held that the fencing provisions of the Act do not apply to machinery which is being manufactured in a factory and which is not part of its equipment. The respondents rely particularly on the speech of Lord Normand but at the beginning of his speech he set out the question very clearly:[2] 'It is whether the provisions of ss. 14(1), 16 and 20 of the Factories Act, 1937, apply to machines or machinery manufactured in the factory or only to machines or machinery for use in the factory in the processes of manufacture or as ancillaries to these processes.' The machinery in this case was undoubtedly 'for use' in the factory. It is true that later in his speech Lord Normand used various forms of expression—'machinery used for

---

[1] [1952] A.C. 515; [1952] 1 T.L.R. 682; [1952] 1 All E.R. 670, H.L.
[2] [1952] A.C. 515, 520.

production',[1] 'machinery used in the process of production'[2] and 'machinery which is part of the factory and used in the 'manufacturing processes'. But he meant the same thing throughout. 'Used' could mean (i) used at the time of the accident, or (ii) which has been used in the process of production but is not being so used at the time of the accident, or (iii) which is intended to be so used in future, or all three. Lord Normand cannot have meant to exclude both (ii) and (iii), for that would be going back to the repealed Act of 1878. As between (ii) and (iii), I can see no virtue in the machine having been used in the past if it is not in use at the time of the accident, and nothing said by Lord Normand suggests any such distinction.

LORD HODSON, LORD GUEST, LORD DEVLIN and LORD PEARCE delivered concurring speeches.

SUMMERS (JOHN) & SONS v. FROST

House of Lords   [1955] A.C. 740

The respondent worked as a fitter in the appellants' steelworks and in the course of his work used a power-driven grindstone—this was an action for damages for personal injuries sustained whilst using the grindstone. The wheel revolved at 1,450 r.p.m. The back and top of the grinding wheel was fenced. Only a small area remained unfenced. It was in this area that the injury occurred. The action involved consideration of s. 14(1) of the Factories Act, 1937—were the employers in breach of the statute for failure to fence?

The House of Lords (VISCOUNT SIMONDS, LORD OAKSEY, LORD MORTON, LORD REID and LORD KEITH) decided that they were. In the course of his speech, LORD MORTON said: [Counsel] pointed out, however, that, according to the uncontradicted evidence of an expert at the trial, 'It' (i.e. the grinding wheel) 'is guarded as far as is practicable in order to allow the machine to be used at all', and he contended that the obligation imposed by s. 14(1) was only an obligation to fence to such an extent as will preserve the identity of the machine by permitting its use. 'If', said he, 'you cannot use the wheel, it ceases to be a grinding wheel in any real sense and becomes merely a museum piece.'

My Lords, I have felt, and still feel, great sympathy with this argument, but I feel unable to accede to it. The wording of the section places no limitation upon the words 'securely fenced'. An absolute

---

[1] Ibid. 521.   [2] Ibid. 522.

obligation is imposed and I am impressed by the fact that in a number of sections of the Act the duties imposed are qualified by the insertion of the words 'so far as is reasonably practicable' or other words to the same effect....On the other hand, in the section now under consideration and in many other sections no such qualification is inserted.

UDDIN v. ASSOCIATED PORTLAND CEMENT

Court of Appeal   [1965] 2 Q.B. 582

During working hours the plaintiff who worked in a cement-packing factory went into a part of the factory where he was not authorised to go. He was following a pigeon and, the judge said: 'Whatever were his designs towards the pigeon which he was stalking, they were not actuated by benevolence'. He attempted to grab the pigeon and got 'inexorably involved' in the machinery. He claimed damages alleging a breach of s. 14(1) of the Factories Act and this was upheld.

The court did not interfere with the judge's apportionment of blame, 20 per cent to the defendants and 80 per cent to the plaintiff.

LORD PEARCE: Mr Forrest argued that s. 14 was not intended to give any cause of action to a plaintiff in such circumstances. One can, he contends, derive an analogy from the law of vicarious liability. The master could not be liable for the act of a servant done (as that of the plaintiff was) on a frolic of his own, and not within the scope of his employment. That same concept should, he says, be imported into the words of s. 14....

The conditional clause relating to machinery which is safe by position makes it clear that the whole section is designed to procure safety for 'every person employed or working on the premises'. And the words 'on the premises' govern, I think, the word 'employed'. Either the fact that the person is employed on the premises, *or* the fact that he is working on the premises, qualifies him for protection. The draftsman could have written 'and', but he chose to write 'or'. Therefore, the defendants cannot rely on the fact that the plaintiff was not working, if he was at the relevant time employed on the premises.*

The words 'every person employed...on the premises' have no express limitation. The word 'every' shows a wide intention. It would have been easy to insert the limitation if that had been the intention of the legislature. Is it possible to import into the word 'employed' any implied exclusion of acts done on a frolic or not within the scope of

* Note: a self-employed person may not be a 'workman' within regulations made under s. 76, *ante* p. 703: *Herbert* v. *Harold Shaw Ltd.* [1959] 2 All E.R. 189.

employment? I think not. That concept was devised by the common law to achieve a measure of fairness and common sense on a difficult point in the doctrine of vicarious liability. That doctrine itself is not the product of logical or legal principle. Though its roots go back to ancient days, its present form was fashioned in the eighteenth and nineteenth centuries as a matter of social expediency and general justice. It is not a safe source of analogy, particularly for the interpretation of a statute. It certainly cannot be said that the word 'employed' in a statute automatically connotes an exclusion of periods when acts are done which are not within the scope of employment. Nor is there anything in the words of the section to suggest such a connotation....

Does a broader view of the Act as a whole support the gloss? In my view, it tells strongly against it. The Act relates to 'the safety, health and welfare of employed persons'. It deals extensively with the inevitable dangers in factories that may be caused to safety, health and welfare by machinery and other things. The Factories Acts would be quite unnecessary if all factory owners were at all times very careful and reasonable, and if they were so fortunate as only to employ persons who are never stupid, careless, unreasonable or disobedient, and who never have moments of clumsiness, forgetfulness or aberration. But a cross-section of humanity does not present that picture. Hence the necessity for legislation with the benevolent intention of enforcing precautions which will prevent avoidable dangers in the interests of those who might be injured by them. Factories and mechanisation which are to the material advantage of both employer and employed introduce dangers and lay obligations upon both, as s. 155 acknowledges.

It is true that the occupier may exculpate himself from failure to fence by showing that only a piece of unforeseeable folly could create danger in some particular piece of machinery, and that therefore it could not be called dangerous and he was not required to fence it. But once it has been shown to be dangerous and to have needed fencing, it seems to me that he should, under the general intention of the Act, be potentially liable to all employees who suffer from that failure. There is nothing to justify the view that the Act intended its protection for only the slightly stupid or slightly negligent, and intended to withdraw all protection from the utterly stupid and utterly negligent. Of course, when contributory negligence comes to be considered, the utterly stupid or utterly negligent man may find that a large proportion (or even the whole) of the fault is laid on his shoulders so as to diminish or extinguish his damages. But it seems out of accord with the general policy of the Act that he should be, at a certain stage of folly, outlawed from its protection and denied a cause of action.

WILLMER and RUSSELL, L.JJ., delivered concurring judgments.

HINDLE v. BIRTWISTLE

[1897] 1 Q.B. 192

It was the responsibility of the factory occupier under s. 6(2) of the Factory & Workshop Act, 1891 (predecessor of s. 14(1) of the 1961 Factories Act) to ensure that 'all dangerous parts of the machinery' in a factory must be securely fenced or otherwise rendered safe. The occupier of a cotton factory was summoned under the above section for failing to fence the shuttles of his looms. The evidence showed that in the weaving process shuttles occasionally flew out from the shuttle-race in a dangerous fashion. Sometimes this was caused by the negligence of the weaver in charge, or the presence of a foreign substance in the machine, or simply defective yarn.

WILLS, J.: It seems to me that machinery or parts of machinery is and are dangerous if in the ordinary course of human affairs danger may be reasonably anticipated from the use of them without protection. No doubt it would be impossible to say that because an accident had happened once therefore the machinery was dangerous. On the other hand, it is equally out of the question to say that machinery cannot be dangerous unless it is so in the course of careful working. In considering whether machinery is dangerous, the contingency of carelessness on the part of the workman in charge of it, and the frequency with which that contingency is likely to arise, are matters that must be taken into consideration. It is entirely a question of degree. As the recorder has not dealt with the matter from that point of view, the case must go back to him for reconsideration.

WRIGHT, J.: I am of the same opinion. The justices of the borough of Blackburn, who are presumably persons acquainted with these matters, came to the conclusion that these shuttles were dangerous. The recorder has reversed their decision on a view of the law which is in my judgment erroneous. It seems to me that the chances that the workmen will be negligent, that foreign material will get in, or that the yarn may be of bad quality, must all be taken into consideration. The mere fact that the shuttle will sometimes fly out, and that when it flies out it is dangerous, is not enough. It is a question of degree and of fact in all cases whether the tendency to fly out is a tendency to fly out often enough to satisfy a reasonable interpretation of the word 'dangerous'.

WALKER v. BLETCHLEY FLETTONS LTD

[1937] 1 All E.R. 170

The plaintiff worker, who was being taught to use an excavator, slipped when going to the tool box. His leg was caught in an unfenced wheel of the machine. Negligence was not alleged; but the plaintiff claimed that he had been injured by a part of the machinery made 'dangerous' by lack of fencing contrary to the Factory and Workshop Act, 1901, s. 10. His action succeeded.

Du Parcq, J.: It was rather suggested by [counsel] (and in my view it cannot be right) that in considering whether the defendants had been guilty of a breach of their statutory duty to fence all dangerous parts of machinery, the question was precisely the same as it would be if I were considering, apart from the statute, whether the defendants had been negligent in not fencing that machinery. Undoubtedly the questions are very nearly the same, and the matters to be considered may be sometimes very much the same, but there is clearly, in my view, a distinction to be drawn. I think if I were to venture to expand a little what was said by Wills, J. [in *Hindle* v. *Birtwistle, ante*, p. 724] I would say, and I think I am saying nothing inconsistent with what the learned judge said, that a part of machinery is dangerous if it is a possible cause of injury to anybody acting in a way in which a human being may be reasonably expected to act in circumstances which may be reasonably expected to occur.

MIDLAND AND LOW MOOR IRON AND STEEL CO. LTD v. CROSS

House of Lords   [1965] A.C. 343

The court had to decide under an information preferred against the appellants by an inspector of factories whether a certain piece of machinery was 'dangerous' within s. 14(1) of the Factories Act, 1961. The machine, which straightened out iron bars, consisted of two banks of four rollers one above the other, the four underneath being power driven. The rollers in the top row were not vertically above those in the bottom row: they were so placed that when a bar was inserted the bottom rollers would move it along causing the top rollers also to revolve as the bar was squeezed and straightened out.

The court held that it was dangerous.

Lord Reid: The purpose of the machine is to straighten bars. For this purpose the bar is fed in between two sets of grooved wheels at a speed of about 20 inches per second. The accident on the day in question occurred because the man who was feeding in the bar had his attention momentarily distracted and his hand was carried along by the moving bar and nipped between it and the first of the wheels.

It is not disputed that, if the Act requires us to consider the position when the machine is doing its usual work, the moving wheel was dangerous because the possibility of an accident like that which happened was reasonably foreseeable. But the justices dismissed the information on the ground 'that the only danger was created by a nip as a bar was going through the machine so that there could be a trapping between the bar and one of the leading in rollers, and that there was no duty to fence against a danger created by the juxtaposition of a moving piece of material and a part of the machine not in itself dangerous.' By 'not in itself dangerous' the justices mean that if the machine were running light doing no work there would be no danger: then the lower wheels would be revolving, being power driven, the upper wheels, being free, would be stationary, and there would be a sufficient gap between the upper and lower wheels to make it impossible for a man's hand or clothing to be nipped between them.

The purpose of this legislation is to promote the safety of workmen when they are at work and I would find it very surprising if the Act requires us to disregard dangers which arise out of the ordinary working of the machine, and only to have regard to dangers which can arise when the machine is running light before normal working begins.

LORD EVERSHED: It was the contention of Mr Everett, for the appellants, that there was not in the machine here in question any 'dangerous part' inasmuch as danger did not occur by the mere fact of putting the machine in operation but only resulted when a bar or rod was being passed through it; and in support of his argument Mr Everett referred to a number of other provisions of the Act, such as subsection (6) of s. 14, empowering the Minister to make regulations as regards the fencing of materials or articles which are dangerous while in motion in the machine, and similarly to s. 76, empowering the Minister to make regulations when satisfied that a 'process' of manual labour was liable to cause risk of bodily injury to the person employed; and he further contended that s. 19 of the Act, relating to self-acting machines, would be unnecessary, if the view of the Divisional Court was correct.

With all respect to Mr Everett's ingenious argument, I have been unable to accept it and, as already indicated, I agree with the view taken by the Lord Chief Justice in the Divisional Court. As it seems to me, the question whether it can properly be said that some part of a piece of machinery is dangerous must depend upon considering whether such danger exists and arises from the normal operation of the machine, that is, from the purposes of the mechanical work which the machine is specifically designed to achieve; and if a part of such a machine becomes undoubtedly dangerous from such normal and projected operation then it follows that such part of the machine is a dangerous part within the meaning of s. 14(1)....

In my judgment, for the purpose of determining whether s. 14(1) of the Factories Act, 1961, is applicable to a piece of machinery, the machine must be regarded not as a kind of exhibit, as an illustration of the art and skill of the designer to be judged by showing how in fact the machine is set in motion and, when set in motion, what parts of it revolve or otherwise move; but must, for the purpose of the section, be judged by observing what in fact mechanically occurs when the machine is performing the task for which it has been especially designed and in fact (as in the present case) executing that very task. It may be (as Mr Jukes said) that so judged a stationary part of a machine may be dangerous, for example, because an exposed part of it becomes excessively hot. But danger arising from stationary parts of a machine does not here arise and I express no view upon that problem. What does, to my mind, emerge and emerge inevitably from the facts of the present case is that when the Bigwood roller is set in motion to do the specific job for which it was designed and installed the two closely adjacent sets of rollers with the bar or rod passing through them were liable to trap and seriously to injure the operative's hand or arm if his attention became for any reason temporarily distracted....

But there remain difficult questions to which allusion was made in the course of the arguments in the present case—particularly questions as to the applicability of the Act to danger arising from work pieces (not themselves part of the machine) and other moving material when the machine itself or the relevant part of it is stationary. I must not be taken from my citations to have indicated any view upon these questions. They do not in the present case arise and I express no view upon them.

Although the question of foreseeability was not, as I understand, seriously argued before your Lordships, if there was here a 'dangerous part' of the machine within s. 14(1) of the Act then, like the Lord Chief Justice, I can have no doubt that the danger was foreseeable....

I conclude my judgment by respectfully reciting and adopting the passage from the judgment of the Lord Justice-Clerk, Lord Cooper, in the Scottish case of *Mitchell* v. *North British Rubber Co. Ltd*[1] which my noble and learned friend Lord Reid cited in his speech in the case of *John Summers & Sons Ltd* v. *Frost*[2] where your Lordships found that there was a duty to fence a grinding wheel in the machine there under consideration. The language of Lord Cooper was as follows: 'The test is objective and impersonal. Is the part such in its character, and so circumstanced in its position, exposure, method of operation and the like, that in the ordinary course of human affairs danger may reasonably be anticipated from its use unfenced, not only to the prudent, alert and skilled operative intent upon his task, but also to the careless or inattentive worker whose inadvertent or indolent conduct may expose him to risk of injury or death from the unguarded part?'

LORDS HODSON, DONOVAN and MORRIS delivered concurring speeches.

PEARCE v. STANLEY-BRIDGES LTD

Court of Appeal [1965] 1 W.L.R. 931

The plaintiff was injured when a pneumatic hoist which he was adjusting rose unexpectedly trapping his elbow between the top of the hoist and a conveyor belt. The judge at first instance found that the hoist rose because the plaintiff negligently left the switch at the 'on' position, that the 'nip' between the belt and the hoist was no danger to an operator carrying out his work normally, that it only became dangerous because of the plaintiff's folly and that a good employer could not reasonably have expected this accident to occur. The plaintiff's claim failed.

WILLMER, L.J.: The difficult question with which Mr Hooson has tried to grapple is to identify what is the dangerous part of machinery here which he contends ought to have been fenced. The only danger which has been suggested is the danger caused by the proximity of the platform when it is raised to the end of the conveyor apparatus. It has not been suggested (and I do not think that it could be suggested) that, of itself, the moving platform was a cause of any foreseeable danger.

In the result, Mr Hooson has been driven to contend that what ought to have been fenced was the gap between the moving platform and the end of the stationary structure supporting the conveyor apparatus. It seems to me, however, that to hold that there was a

---

[1] [1945] S.C. (J.) 69 at p. 73.   [2] [1955] A.C. 740 at p. 766.

duty to fence that gap would go far beyond any of the authorities in which s. 14 has been previously considered. No case has been cited to us in which it has ever been held that there is a duty to fence merely by reason of the proximity of a moving part of a machine to some extraneous object...

Apart from all that, however, I for myself would be disposed to agree with the view expressed by the judge below that the argument based on s. 14 in the present case fails on the test laid down by du Parcq, J. in *Walker* v. *Bletchley Flettons Ltd*,[1] as amended by Lord Reid in the more recent case of *Summers* (*John*) & *Sons Ltd* v. *Frost*.[2] I do not think that the alleged danger in the present case was 'a reasonably foreseeable cause of injury to anybody acting in a way a human being may be reasonably expected to act in circumstances which may reasonably be expected to occur.' As McNair, J. pointed out, it was not reasonably to be anticipated that an experienced maintenance fitter such as the plaintiff would try to adjust this air pressure valve with the switch left in the 'on' position. Moreover, even if one can get over that stile, I do not see that there was any really foreseeable possibility of an injury such as this being caused.

HARMAN, L.J. delivered a concurring judgment; WINN, L.J. agreed with WILLMER, L.J.

CLOSE v. STEEL CO. OF WALES

House of Lords   [1962] A.C. 367

The appellant was injured when the bit of an electric drill which he was using shattered and a piece flew into his eye. He sued *inter alia* under s. 14(1) of the Factories Act, 1937. The House of Lords unanimously held that the drill was not 'dangerous' within the meaning of the section. A majority of their Lordships also felt bound to hold that the section imposed no duty to fence in order to prevent the ejection of parts of a machine.

LORD DENNING: Applying the test enunciated in *Hindle* v. *Birtwistle* (*ante*, p. 724) I have come to the clear conclusion that the bit of this drill is not a dangerous part of machinery. This drilling machine is a well-known machine which is used by men at their own homes in doing things for themselves as well as in factories. It is true that the bit occasionally shatters, it may be as often as once a week in a factory like this. But there is no evidence of any previous accidents having

---

[1] [1937] 1 All E.R. 170.
[2] [1955] A.C. 740, 765–6; [1955] 2 W.L.R. 825; [1955] 1 All E.R. 870, H.L.

happened on that account. The reason is because fragments are so small and light that they usually go only a few inches or at most a foot or two. They have not sufficient force to penetrate clothing, and, although the judge thought there was a distinct possibility that a man's hands might be scratched or cut there was no evidence of even this having happened. No one had ever known of an accident to an eye before, and the chances of such a grave injury were, as the judge said, 'extremely remote'. No one ever used goggles for the work and there was no evidence to suggest that goggles should be worn. In these circumstances it seems clear that in the ordinary course of human affairs, danger could not reasonably be anticipated from the use of the drill unfenced. It cannot therefore be classed as dangerous.

LORD GODDARD: My Lords, the evidence in this case satisfies me that the risk of injury, serious and regrettable as it proved to be, was not reasonably foreseeable and I entirely agree with the Court of Appeal that on this ground alone the appellant's claim must fail, whether it is based on negligence at common law or on a breach of statutory duty.

The Court of Appeal, however, have asked your Lordships' guidance as to the extent to which, if at all, the decision of this House in *Nicholls* v. *F. Austin (Leyton) Ltd*,[1] ought now to be regarded as qualified. Concisely stated, that case decided that the Factories Act requires a dangerous part of a machine to be securely fenced, but for the purpose of preventing an operator from coming into contact with it and not for the purpose of keeping parts of the machine or of the material on which it is being worked from flying out. Reluctantly, I have come to the conclusion that *Nicholls* v. *F. Austin (Leyton) Ltd*,[2] reinforced as I think it was by *Carroll* v. *Andrew Barclay & Sons Ltd*,[3] cannot be regarded as qualified. The opinions of my noble and learned friends Lord Morton of Henryton and Lord Guest, which I have had the advantage of seeing, convince me that these decisions settled the law on this subject with regard to a cause of action under the Factories Act which can only be qualified by legislation, or perhaps, as at least some of their Lordships thought, by a regulation made by the Secretary of State.

LORD MORRIS OF BORTH-Y-GEST: My Lords, the speeches in *Nicholls* v. *F. Austin (Leyton) Ltd*[4] show clearly that in considering subsection (1) of s. 14 it must be decided whether there is a 'dangerous part' of a machine: if there is, then there is an obligation to guard so as to

[1] [1946] A.C. 493.   [2] Ibid.
[3] [1948] A.C. 477.   [4] [1946] A.C. 493.

prevent the body of the operator coming into contact with such dangerous part.

In the later case of *Carroll* v. *Andrew Barclay & Sons Ltd*[1] consideration was given to the requirement imposed by s. 13 that 'every part of the transmission machinery shall be securely "fenced"'. The injured worker operated a lathe which was $6\frac{1}{2}$ feet behind a motor which drove a main shaft. That shaft was operated from the motor by means of a belt. The belt did not ascend vertically to the shaft (which was at a height of 25 feet above the ground) but sloped at an angle away from the position of the worker. In his position at his lathe he would be in a direct line with the revolving belt. He was protected from the motor by a fence which was five feet high. The belt broke and lashed out over the fence and struck the worker. The breaking of a belt was itself a very infrequent occurrence but such an occurrence as a belt coming out from its guard and causing injury to someone who was outside the guard or fence enclosing the motor or belt had never been known to have happened. The motor and the belt and the shaft were all part of the 'transmission machinery' and it was held that there was no breach of s. 13. This was in accord with the reasoning in the earlier case in regard to the words 'securely fenced'. It was made plain that the obligation securely to fence is not one that can cover the contingency of the accidental breaking of machinery with a consequence that some piece or pieces of broken machinery may fly out and injure.

Lord Porter pointed out that all machinery is potentially dangerous because it may break, but that the Act is not concerned with danger in that sense but that it is 'danger in working' against which it is framed to give security...

My Lords, if it is a strange and unfortunate result that the words of the statute do not compel fencing where there is the ejection of fragments of some inserted material or substance upon which a machine is working this is not a matter which it is within the power of the courts to remedy.

LORD GUEST: The appellant argued that the obligation under s. 14 was not only to keep the operator from contact with the machine but also to prevent pieces of the machine which had been shattered in operation flying out and hitting the operator's eye, if the propensity of the machine to eject such pieces was known to the respondents. In my view such a construction of s. 14 is not open having regard to

[1] [1948] A.C. 477.

decisions of this House. A number of decisions of the Court of Appeal, commencing with *Hindle* v. *Birtwistle*,[1] were relied upon by the appellant in justification of his construction of s. 14. But in my opinion it is not necessary to go further back than 1946 to find the answer to the problem. In that year *Nicholls* v. *F. Austin (Leyton) Ltd*[1] was decided by this House. This case, which was under s. 14 of the Act of 1937, concerned material which flew out from the machine in the course of operation and injured the workman. But in deciding that s. 14 did not extend to guarding against dangerous materials ejected from the machine, the House had to consider in general the scope of this section. All their Lordships, with the exception of Lord Wright, indicated their view that the obligation was to guard against the employee coming in contact with the dangerous part. Lord Thankerton said that the obligation was to provide a guard against contact with any dangerous part of a machine. Lord Macmillan said: 'The obligation under s. 14 to fence the dangerous part of a machine, as I read it, is an obligation so to screen or shield the dangerous part so as to prevent the body of the operator from coming into contact with it....' Lord Simonds said: 'The fence is intended to keep the worker out, not to keep the machine or its product in'.

LORD DENNING dissented on the issue whether s. 14 imposed a duty in regard to the ejection of material; LORD MORRIS was in doubt upon this question; LORD MORTON OF HENRYTON delivered a speech concurring with LORD GUEST and LORD GODDARD, that there was no such duty.

SPARROW *v.* FAIREY AVIATION CO. LTD

House of Lords   [1964] A.C. 1019

The plaintiff was machining sealings for petrol filler caps on a fast moving lathe. The blade of the tool he was holding caught against the moving part of the lathe and his hand was injured by being thrown against a non-moving part of the machine. He brought an action under s. 14(1) of the Factories Act, 1937.

LORD REID: One might perhaps have expected that it would have been pleaded that the whole of the chuck, including the jaws, was a dangerous part of the machine in view of the speed at which it revolved. But it is only alleged that the jaws were dangerous and there may be some good reason for that. So we must decide the case on the footing that

---

[1] [1897] 1 Q.B. 192.   [2] [1946] A.C. 493.

no part of the appellant's body ever came into contact with the dangerous part of the machine. The accident was caused by the tool which he was holding coming in contact with the dangerous part and being thrown aside, so that his hand slipped forward and was injured by contact with a part which was not dangerous and which, therefore, there was no obligation to fence.

If I had simply to go to the words of the statute unaided by authority I would find it difficult to see any answer to the appellant's case. The jaws were dangerous. They were not fenced. And they were not as safe to the appellant as they would have been if securely fenced. The appellant was not negligent and in the course of his ordinary work his hand was injured as a result of the tool which he was using coming in contact with the jaws.

But this section has been the subject of three decisions of this House, and the respondents' contention is that those decisions establish that the only duty under the section is to fence against contact of any part of the worker's body with the dangerous part. They say that, owing to the position of the disc held by the jaws the man's hand could not come in contact with the jaws without some reckless act on his part, and so there was no duty to fence. Or, alternatively, they maintain that even if there was a duty to fence, they are not liable for the damage caused by this accident because they can only be liable for damage resulting from contact of some part of the worker's body with the dangerous part. I must therefore examine these authorities.

In *Nicholls* v. *F. Austin (Leyton) Ltd*[1] the worker was injured by a piece of the material on which the machine was working flying out and striking her, and it was held that there was no liability under the statute. Lord Simonds said: 'the fence is intended to keep the worker out, not to keep the machine or its product in'. In reaching that result much importance was attached to the proviso to subsection (1) and to subsections (2) and (3) of s. 14. I am bound to say that that surprises me. No one appears to have considered the earlier history of this section. The first general provision with regard to fencing was introduced in 1891 as amendment to particular provisions in the Act of 1878. Then, in the consolidating Act of 1901, s. 10(1) (c) is identical, apart from verbal changes, with the first part of s. 14(1) of the Act of 1937. But the Act of 1901 appears to contain nothing corresponding to the proviso to s. 14(1) or ss. 14(2) or 14(3) of the Act of 1937. So if the presence of those provisions turned the scale in *Nicholls'* case

[1] [1946] A.C. 493; 62 T.L.R. 320; [1946] 2 All E.R. 92, H.L.

—and an examination of the speeches in this House suggests to me that it may well have done so—that would mean that by inserting them Parliament narrowed the meaning of 'securely fenced' and thereby deprived workers of part of the protection they had enjoyed before these provisions were inserted. I find it impossible to believe that Parliament could have intended to do that.

The fact that a strong argument has not been taken into consideration may not diminish the authority of a decision of this House, but in my view it must at least entitle one to refuse to extend the decision so as to cover cases substantially different in their facts. And there were reservations about *Nicholls'* case[1] in *Carroll* v. *Andrew Barclay & Sons Ltd.*[2] But the recent decision in *Close* v. *Steel Company of Wales Ltd.*[3] appears to me to establish beyond question that s. 14 only requires a dangerous part of a machine to be fenced for the purpose of preventing a worker from coming in contact with it. That clearly appears from the speeches of all three noble Lords who formed the majority and there are frequent references to the body of the operator coming in contact with the dangerous part.

In all these cases the contrast was between injury to the worker by contact with the dangerous part of the machine and injury from something flying out from the machine. The present case does not fit either of these categories: the appellant's injury resulted from a tool which he was holding coming in contact with the dangerous part. But, in my view, *Closes'* case must be treated as a positive decision that the only duty under the statute is to fence against contact of the workers with dangerous parts of a machine and, therefore, the only question left is what can properly be regarded as contact of the worker with the dangerous part.

The appellant argues that this cannot be limited to contact between some part of his body with a dangerous part. Part of a man's clothing may be caught in an unfenced but dangerous part of a machine and this may cause him to fall in such a way that he sustains serious injury. I would agree that it would be absurd to say that such a man has no remedy under the Act merely because no part of his body actually touched the dangerous part of the machine. And then the appellant goes on to ask—if contact with a man's clothing is sufficient why is contact with a tool which he was holding insufficient? It was at that point that there was a difference of opinion in the Court of Appeal and

[1] [1946] A.C. 493.   [2] [1948] A.C. 477; [1948] 2 All E.R. 386, H.L.
[3] [1962] A.C. 367; [1961] 2 All E.R. 953, H.L.

I do not find this question at all easy to answer. I do not think that it can be answered satisfactorily in a logical way. It is too late to question the rule which this House laid down in *Close's* case, and we must do our best to apply it in a practical way. Fencing against a man's body and fencing against his clothing coming into contact with machinery would hardly differ. But fencing against anything which he is holding coming into contact with the machinery might be a very different matter. I appreciate the view of Sellers, L.J. that the section is for the protection of workers, and that *qua* worker a tool which a man is using is as much part of him as his clothing. But a line must be drawn somewhere and I could not distinguish between a small tool as used in this case and anything else which a man might be holding in the course of his work. I do not think that it would accord with the decision in *Close's* case to say that there is a duty to fence against anything that a man might have to use in the course of his work. Accordingly, with regret and some hesitation, I must move that this appeal be dismissed.

LORD MORRIS OF BORTH-Y-GEST: Even if the view be held that there was a failure to comply with the section in that there was no secure fencing which would have prevented physical contact between the operator and the dangerous part, it is not shown that there was any causal connection between any such breach of statutory obligation and the damage that in fact occurred unless it can be said that contact with a tool that is held by an operator is the same as physical contact with an operator. It may well be that clothing or protective covering which an operator wears could be regarded as being a part of him but, in my judgment, it is in general otherwise in the case of a tool that he is holding. I wish to reserve the question whether, in particular circumstances, some equipment or apparatus could be so attached to an operator that, in his capacity as an operator, such equipment or apparatus could rationally be regarded as being a part of him.

LORDS HODSON and GUEST delivered concurring speeches; LORD MACDERMOT dissented.

WIGLEY *v.* BRITISH VINEGARS LTD

House of Lords   [1964] A.C. 307

The appellant's husband, an independent contractor, was cleaning a window of the respondent's factory when he fell from the ladder and was killed. The window was a swinging window. No hooks to which a safety belt could be attached had been provided. The widow brought an action under the Factories Act, 1937 s. 26(2).* The respondents claimed there had been no breach and that anyway s. 26 did not apply to an independent contractor.

VISCOUNT KILMUIR: The real reason is: What is meant by the words 'any person' which appear in both subsections? They cannot be of entirely general application: I agree that a policeman who enters a factory in pursuit of a felon, or a fireman who enters to put out a fire, is not within the section, although he is a 'person' and he is 'working'. I think one must exclude, for example, the film actor who enters the factory where a scene in which he is playing is to be shot, though he again is a 'person' and the factory is a place in which he is to work. In my view, the true distinction is between those who are to work for the purposes of the factory and those who are not. Clearly, maintenance of the factory is work for the purpose of the factory, while the arrest of a felon or the putting out of a fire is not, though it may benefit the factory indirectly. Window cleaning is part of the maintenance of the factory and in my view the deceased was within the protection afforded by s. 26...

The fact is that anybody can fall off a ladder, even though the ladder itself is sound and is placed at a proper angle and is not liable to slip. The occupier of a factory must, as a matter of common sense, realise that this is a possibility which may occur to anyone working in the factory, but does that mean that, on each occasion that he sends a workman up a ladder to do a job, he must provide him with some extra means of safety if he is liable to fall more than 10 feet? I cannot think so—nor did I apprehend it to be contended by counsel for the appellant that this would constitute, in Mr Swanwick's phrase, a foreseeable and appreciable risk...

If your Lordships agree with me on this point, it is sufficient to dispose of the appeal. But, since it has been extensively argued before us, I propose to deal with the third question on which this case turns, namely, whether (on the assumption that the defendants were in breach of their statutory duty) such breach caused the accident. Since the hearing in the Court of Appeal, your Lordships have decided the case of *McWilliams* v. *Sir William Arrol & Co. Ltd*,[1] and it is now beyond dispute that both in England and Scotland it is for the plaintiff to

---

[1] [1962] 1 W.L.R. 295; [1962] 1 All E.R. 623, H.L. (Sc.).

* This section was equivalent to s. 29(2) of the Factories Act 1961. The distance specified was ten feet instead of six feet six inches, and it began 'Where any person *is* to work...' instead of 'Where any person *has* to work...'

prove on a balance of probabilities both that the safety measures would have been effective and that the injured person would have made use of them had they been available.

In the present case it was not disputed that a securely hooked belt would have saved the deceased. On the second part of the question Atkinson, J. and the Court of Appeal differed: the learned judge drew from the son's evidence the inference that, on a balance of probabilities, his father would have worn a safety belt had there been a hook to fasten it to. The Court of Appeal, on the other hand, held that this was not a legitimate inference from the evidence and that the probability was that the deceased would not have made use of a safety belt when working from a ladder even if hooks or bars had been provided on to which it could have been attached. I have already summarised the evidence on this question and in my view the judgment of Atkinson, J. cannot be supported on this point. His words '...from time to time the father did wear such belts' do not describe any situation which is relevant to the present case. The evidence fell far short of establishing a balance of probabilities in favour of the plaintiff's contention. On the contrary the balance was clearly the other way although, as this House decided in *McWilliams'* case, it is not necessary for the defendants to discharge any burden of proof on this issue.

LORDS HODSON, JENKINS and PEARCE agreed with the opinion of VISCOUNT KILMUIR.

McWILLIAMS *v.* SIR WILLIAM ARROL & CO. LTD

House of Lords   [1962] I W.L.R. 295

An experienced steel erector fell 70 feet during the course of his work and was killed. This was an action by his widow for damages against the employers, and against the occupiers of the site on the grounds that both had failed to supply the deceased with a safety belt and were liable in common law negligence. Against the occupier of the site it was also alleged that they had been in breach of s. 26(2) of the Factories Act, 1937. The evidence showed that both defendants had failed to discharge their duties but it was found as a fact that even if a safety belt had been provided the deceased would not have used it. The House found that there had been no failure to instruct or 'exhort' either steel erectors in general or the plaintiff in particular in the use of belts.

LORD DEVLIN: The courts below have held that the employers were in breach of their duty in failing to provide a safety belt, but that that was not the cause of the deceased's death since he would not have worn it if it had been provided. They have held also that there was no duty on the employers to instruct the deceased to wear it. On this second matter I cannot usefully add anything to the opinions already expressed by your Lordships with which I agree....The correct way of stating the appellant's case is, I think, as follows: The immediate cause of the deceased's death was that at the time of the fall he was not wearing a safety belt: but for the fault of his employers, he would have been wearing a safety belt: therefore the fault of his employers was an effective cause of his death. So stated, it is plain that the reason why the deceased was not wearing a safety belt must be a proper subject for inquiry.

Mr Stott relied upon the decision of the Court of Appeal in *Roberts* v. *Dorman Long & Co. Ltd.*[1] This also was a case in which the death of a steel erector was caused by his not wearing a safety belt, and his employers were in breach of duty in not making one available. The duty relied upon was created by regulation 97 of the Building (Safety, Health and Welfare) Regulations, 1948, which provided that 'there shall be available safety belts...which will so far as practicable enable such persons who elect to use them to carry out the work without risk of serious injury'. The court held that it was no answer for the employers in such circumstances to say that if they had made safety belts available, the deceased would not have used them; the fact that they were not available gave him no opportunity of exercising his election...

The second point raises the question of the burden of proof. The proposition, as I have stated it above, appears to put on the appellant the burden of showing why the deceased was not wearing a safety belt; she must prove her case, and it is part of her case that he was not wearing a belt because of the fault of his employers. But since *ex hypothesi* a prudent employer would provide a belt, it must follow that a prudent employee would wear it when provided. Any inquiry of this sort starts from the presumption that the pursuer or the defender, as the case may be, has done what is reasonable and prudent; and it is for the opposite party to displace that presumption by pleading and proving negligence or contributory negligence, as the case may be. So if there were no evidence at all to show why the deceased was not wearing a safety belt, it would be proper to conclude that the reason was because the employers had failed to provide one...

[1] [1953] 1 W.L.R. 942.

But here the question is not what the deceased did but what he would have done. That is a matter that is incapable of direct proof; it must be a matter of inference. His statement about what he would have done, if he were alive to make it, is only one of the factors which the court would have to take into consideration in its task of arriving at the correct inference. A man's actions in the past may well be a safer guide than his own forecast of his actions in the future.

In my judgment, the courts below were right to receive and consider the evidence that the deceased had never used a safety belt in the past when it was available. That is material from which it is permissible to draw the inference that he probably would not have used one if it had been provided on the day of his death. I think also, though with more hesitation, that the courts below were right in considering for what it was worth the evidence of the general practice of steel erectors, though without some evidence of the deceased's own attitude towards safety belts I do not think it would have been worth much.

Undoubtedly a court should be very careful about finding what one may call hypothetical contributory negligence. A defendant, whose negligence has prevented the matter in issue from being put directly to the proof, must expect that a court will be very careful to make sure that it is acting upon legitimate inference and not upon speculation. But in the present case the evidence, even if it were confined in the deceased's own past acts, is in my opinion conclusive.

VISCOUNT KILMUIR, L.C., VISCOUNT SIMONDS and LORD REID delivered concurring speeches; LORD MORRIS agreed with the speech of VISCOUNT KILMUIR, L.C.

GINTY v. BELMONT BUILDING SUPPLIES LTD

[1959] 1 All E.R. 414

The plaintiff, an experienced employee of the first defendant, was working on a roof of the second defendants' factory stripping off old asbestos sheeting. The second defendant (Pirelli Co.) agreed to supply duckboards and showed the plaintiff where to find them: when the plaintiff did not use them, servants of the second defendants placed the duckboards against a wall where the plaintiff could see them but they did not tell him they had done this. The plaintiff fell through the roof and was injured. He sued for damages for breach of Buildings (Safety Health and Welfare) Regulations 1948, and breach of s. 26 Factories Act, 1937 (predecessor of s. 29 of the 1961 Act).

PEARSON, J.: When reg. 4 and reg. 31(3) are read together, what is the effect? On whom are the several obligations imposed? Counsel for the Belmont company submitted that the only duty of the employer was to provide ladders, duck ladders or crawling boards; but that it was the duty, and solely the duty, of the employee—the sheeter or the workman—to use them. Certainly that is a possible contention, but in my view it is not right. In my view, the obligation to provide is the obligation of the employer, but the obligation to use is the obligation both of the employer and of the employee....I hold, therefore, that there was a breach of duty both by the employer (the Belmont company) and by the employee, the plaintiff, inasmuch as the crawling boards and duckboards were not used...

I have already held that the boards were provided for the use of the plaintiff and that he failed to use them; therefore, there was a contravention by him of s. 119(1).* There is also s. 119(2), which reads: 'No person employed in a factory or in any other place to which any provisions of this Act apply shall wilfully and without reasonable cause do anything likely to endanger himself or others'. It is part of the hardship of this case that the plaintiff, for reasons which one can fully understand, because he wanted to proceed with the work and to get it done quickly, took a risk. He did that wilfully, knowing that he was acting in breach of instructions and regulations, and I must hold that without reasonable cause he stepped on the roof without using boards— in other words, he did something which was likely to endanger his safety. So I must hold that there was a breach of s. 119(2) also.

What is the upshot of all that? This accident was caused manifestly by the plaintiff working on an asbestos roof, which was a fragile roof, without using boards. The special feature of this case is that the wrongful act of his constitutes a breach by him of his instructions and of the regulations as they apply to him; but it also constitutes, technically at any rate, a breach by his employer under his obligation under reg. 31(3)(a) to use the boards. The actual wrongful act was the plaintiff's wrongful act, but in one aspect it constitutes a breach by himself and in another aspect it constitutes a breach by his employer. So what is the position?

There has been a number of cases, to which I shall refer in a moment, in which it has been considered whether or not the employer delegated to the employee the performance of the statutory duty. In my view, the law which is applicable here is clear and comprehensible if one does

---

* Now s. 143, Factories Act, 1961; see *post*, p. 758.

not confuse it by seeking to investigate this very difficult and complicated question whether or not there was a delegation. In my view, the important and fundamental question in a case like this is not whether there was a delegation, but simply the usual question: Whose fault was it? I shall refer to some of the decided cases to demonstrate what I have said. If the answer to that question is that in substance and reality the accident was solely due to the fault of the plaintiff, so that he was the sole author of his own wrong, he is disentitled to recover. But that has to be applied to the particular case and it is not necessarily conclusive for the employer to show that it was a wrongful act of the employee plaintiff which caused the accident. It might also appear from the evidence that something was done or omitted by the employer which caused or contributed to the accident; there may have been a lack of proper supervision or lack of proper instructions; the employer may have employed for this purpose some insufficiently experienced men or he may in the past have acquiesced in some wrong behaviour on the part of the men. Therefore, if one finds that the immediate and direct cause of the accident was some wrongful act of the man, that is not decisive. One has to inquire whether the fault of the employer under the statutory regulations consists of, and is co-extensive with, the wrongful act of the employee. If there is some fault on the part of the employer which goes beyond or is independent of the wrongful act of the employee, and was a cause of the accident, the employer has some liability...

That being the position, we have here the case in which the fault of the employer—and it is a fault under the definition of 'fault' contained in the definition section, s. 4, of the Law Reform (Contributory Negligence) Act, 1945—was a breach of statutory obligation by the employer because, through the employee, the employer did not use the boards; but that fault of the employer consisted of, and was co-extensive with, that of the plaintiff, and in substance this unfortunate accident was due to the fault of the plaintiff in breach of, and in defiance of, his instructions and of regulations which were well known to him. He decided to do the work on this roof without the use of boards. It would not be right, however, to take too severe a view; he was not in any direct sense going to gain anything for himself; he was taking the risk for himself with a view to getting the work done. Yet it is quite impossible to impose a liability on his employer, because the plaintiff himself decided to take the risk and not to use the boards, and in those circumstances the plaintiff must fail.

ALLEN *v.* AEROPLANE & MOTOR ALUMINIUM CASTINGS

Court of Appeal   [1965] 3 All E.R. 377

A dangerous nip in a machine in the defendants' factory was not fenced; they were as a consequence in breach of s. 14(1) of the Factories Act, 1961. The plaintiff was injured in this nip which would not have occurred if it had been securely fenced. Although the nip was plainly the source of the injury there was considerable uncertainty as to the precise manner in which the accident occurred.

SELLERS, L.J.: [The judge] started off with the view that there was an undoubted breach by the defendants of s. 14(1) of the Factories Act, 1961. He had before him the evidence of the plaintiff who was at the time a recruit to industry, a boy of 15 who had recently left school, who had somehow or other got his fingers caught in a dangerous nip, which was the feature which brought about the breach of the Act of 1961. Nevertheless, the judge came to the conclusion, in the circumstances of the case, that he must enter judgment for the defendants. The basis of that was that the plaintiff had given to the judge a version of the accident which he could not accept and which was clearly, the judge thought, what the plaintiff was not doing. Therefore, the judge inferred that he was doing something which was 'a frolic of his own'. In those circumstances judgment was entered for the defendants...

[The plaintiff] gave an explanation of how his fingers got caught which was rejected, and the matter is left without anyone being able to find on the evidence—the judge or this court, or even counsel who had to make submissions—how this accident precisely came about. That is unusual. It is often said that a plaintiff who cannot give an acceptable version of the accident which befell him or her really cannot ask the court to start to find where liability lies. But this is an exceptional case: it is one where the facts show clearly that there was a breach of duty, and they show equally clearly that it was because of that breach, because of the dangerous nip, that this accident occurred. In those circumstances, I think that the law does not leave it open to the judge to come to the conclusion which he did.*

DIPLOCK and RUSSELL, L.JJ. delivered concurring judgments.

---

* Note however that this is an exceptional case. The plaintiff carries the burden of proving both breach of duty and causation. Contrast Willmer, L.J.: 'Employers are not insurers; they are under a duty at Common Law and under statute to take certain measures to protect their workmen, but a workman who seeks to recover damages must prove his case. The workman in the present case has not proved how the

ROSS v. ASSOCIATED PORTLAND CEMENT MANUFACTURERS LTD

House of Lords   [1964] 1 W.L.R. 768; [1964] 2 All E.R. 452

The plaintiff was told to repair a wire safety net, twenty two feet off the ground, and in bad condition. He was in charge of the job, which was an unusual job for a steel-erector; he was given no instructions as to how to do it and no proper equipment; he was not encouraged or told to ask the chief engineer for equipment or instructions, though he could have done so. While standing on a ladder leant against the netting, the plaintiff was catapulted to the ground when the netting partially collapsed. It was held that there was a clear breach of what is now s. 29(1) of the Factories Act, 1961.

LORD REID: I need not describe the circumstances in greater detail because the uncontradicted evidence of the only expert called was that it was obviously unsafe to use a ladder in this way. And it follows from that that there was a clear breach of what is now s. 29 of the Factories Act, 1961....Ross's working place was the place where he was working near the top of the ladder and there is nothing to show that it was not reasonably practicable for the respondents to provide the equipment which the expert says ought to have been used—a movable platform.

The respondents' case is that they were not at all to blame because they were entitled to leave it to Ross to decide what to do and to come to their chief engineer if he wanted further help or equipment. They say that the cause, and the sole cause of the breach and resulting accident was Ross's mistaken decision, or negligence, in using the ladder when he ought to have seen that it was unsafe. This defence was accepted by the learned trial judge and by the Court of Appeal, but it seems to me quite unrealistic, and in accepting it I think that the learned judges misdirected themselves in law in founding on what is called 'coterminous' fault.

The occupier of a factory cannot delegate his duty to carry out the statutory requirements. He can exempt himself from criminal liability under s. 161 if he proves that he has used all due diligence and that the actual offender committed the offence without his consent, connivance or wilful default. And he can avoid civil liability to the actual offender

accident occurred. The Court has to speculate and this is not sufficient': *Linton* v. *Colonnade Chrome Works Ltd, The Times*, 24 July 1964 (reversing the trial judge who had awarded damages even though he rejected the worker's account of the accident).

if he can show that the conduct of this offender was the sole cause of the breach and resulting injury to him. There are several cases to this effect.... Another typical case of avoiding civil liability was *Ginty* v. *Belmont Building Supplies Ltd*[1] ... [where Pearson J. said]: 'In my view, the important and fundamental question in a case like this is not whether there was a delegation, but simply the usual question: Whose fault was it?'

If the question is put in that way one must remember that fault is not necessarily equivalent in this context to blameworthiness. The question really is whose conduct caused the accident, because it is now well established that a breach of statutory duty does not give rise to civil liability unless there is proved a causal connection between the breach and the plaintiff's injury. With regard to what is to be regarded as a causal connection I may be permitted to repeat by reference my observations in *Stapley* v. *Gypsum Mines Ltd*.[2]

That approach appears to me to avoid the difficulty which has sometimes been felt in explaining why an employer, put in breach of a statute by the disobedience of his servant, can escape liability to that servant for injuries caused by the breach. If the employer exercised all due diligence, and the breach and resultant injuries were solely caused by the servant's conduct, the employer is liable vicariously for injuries sustained by a third party just as he would be for injuries caused solely by his servant's common law negligence: but he can say to the disobedient servant that his conduct in no way caused or contributed to that servant's injuries.

If the present case is approached in that way I have no doubt that the respondents cannot wholly escape liability. The owner of a factory who has given proper instructions and has provided proper equipment cannot make provision against disobedience either of his own servant or of the servant of a contractor who is working in the factory. But it is his responsibility to see that proper instructions are given and proper equipment is available. Where the work is to be done by a person fully skilled in that type of work he may say 'go and plan out the work and come back and discuss the matter if you have any difficulty, or cannot find the equipment you need'. But here Ross was only a chargehand, the respondents had no reason to suppose that he had ever done a job of this kind before, and there is nothing to show that the chief engineer gave him any encouragement to come back and discuss the

---

[1] [1959] 1 All E.R. 414.　　　[2] [1953] A.C. 663, 681; [1953] 2 All E.R. 478, H.L.
[See now *Donaghey* v. *O'Brien & Co.* [1966] 2 All E.R. 822, C.A.]

matter. No account has been taken of the reluctance which a man in Ross's position would naturally feel in going to a chief engineer un-invited to ask for extra equipment, the provision of which would entail at least some delay and expense. And no weight had been given to the very significant evidence of Boughen that the ladder 'was the only thing we could use at that moment'. If Ross had such skill that all decisions could properly be left to him, and if using a ladder was obviously dangerous, it seems a strange thing to say that his decision to use the ladder was a deliberate and unfettered decision and was the sole cause of his death. It cannot be suggested that Ross acted recklessly: his discussion of the problem with Boughen shows that he did not. He cannot be absolved from all blame, because he ought not to have been content to use makeshift equipment. But it appears to me that the failure of the respondents to take any steps to see that proper equipment was available contributed a great deal to the accident.

VISCOUNT SIMONDS and LORDS GUEST, UPJOHN and DONOVAN delivered concurring speeches.

IMPERIAL CHEMICAL INDUSTRIES LTD *v.* SHATWELL

House of Lords [1965] A.C. 656

The respondent, George, and his brother, James, were both shotfirers. Statutory regulations laid upon them a duty to take shelter before testing the circuit which connected up the explosives. In breach of these regulations the two men tested the circuit in the open and were seriously injured when it exploded. The respondent sued the employers, the appellants, claiming that they were vicariously liable to him for James' negligence and for James' breach of the statutory regulations, claiming that these had caused his injuries. The defence was (1) a denial of the causal connection claiming that the sole cause was the respondent's fault and (2) *volenti non fit injuria*.

LORD REID: More recently it appears to have been thought in some quarters that, at least as between master and servant, *volenti non fit injuria* is a dead or dying defence. That I think is because in most cases where the defence would now be available it has become usual to base the decision on contributory negligence. Where the plaintiff's own disobedient act is the sole cause of his injury it does not matter in the result whether one says 100 per cent contributory negligence or *volenti non fit injuria*. But it does matter in a case like the present.

If we adopt the inaccurate habit of using the word 'negligence' to denote a deliberate act done with full knowledge of the risk it is not surprising that we sometimes get into difficulties. I think that most people would say, without stopping to think of the reason, that there is a world of difference between two fellow-servants collaborating carelessly so that the acts of both contribute to cause injury to one of them, and two fellow-servants combining to disobey an order deliberately though they know the risk involved. It seems reasonable that the injured man should recover some compensation in the former case but not in the latter. If the law treats both as merely cases of negligence it cannot draw a distinction. But in my view the law does and should draw a distinction. In the first case only the partial defence of contributory negligence is available. In the second *volenti non fit injuria* is a complete defence if the employer is not himself at fault and is only liable vicariously for the acts of the fellow-servant. If the plaintiff invited or freely aided and abetted his fellow-servant's disobedience, then he was *volens* in the fullest sense. He cannot complain of the resulting injury either against the fellow-servant or against the master on the ground of his vicarious responsibility for his fellow-servant's conduct. I need not here consider the common case where the servant's disobedience puts the master in breach of a statutory obligation and it would be wrong to decide in advance whether that would make any difference...

I entirely agree that an employer who is himself at fault in persistently refusing to comply with a statutory rule could not possibly be allowed to escape liability because the injured workman had agreed to waive the breach. If it is still permissible for a workman to make an express agreement with his employer to work under an unsafe system, perhaps in consideration of a higher wage—a matter on which I need express no opinion—then there would be a difference between breach of a statutory obligation by the employer and breach of his common law obligation to exercise due care: it would be possible to contract out of the latter but not out of the former type of obligation. But all that is very far removed from the present case.

LORD PEARCE: Although in this action George alone is the plaintiff, each should be entitled, on the plaintiff's argument, to get damages from the employers on the ground that the other's negligence and breach of statutory duty renders the employers vicariously liable. And whatever precautions the employers had used to prevent the two men testing in the open, they would, if the men had managed to evade those precautions and blown themselves up, still be liable vicariously to the men for their negligence in doing so. That result offends against common sense.

A comparable absurdity would exist if a workman who deliberately breaks a regulation or duty which he is properly delegated to perform could, when injured solely through his own breach, claim damages on the ground that the employers are liable because they are vicariously in breach of duty or regulation in so far as the workman himself broke it. The law, has, however, dealt with and declined to accept this absurdity (*Smith* v. *Baveystock & Co. Ltd.*[1] and other cases).

The present case is really an extension of the same problem. Although the law has refused damages to a man who himself breaks a regulation so that he injures himself, can the man circumvent that difficulty by persuading a colleague to join him in doing the wrongful act? Can the two workmen then each say: 'My colleague was negligent along with me; our one joint explosion blew us both up; therefore *his* negligence caused *my* injury and *my* negligence caused *his* injury and our employer must pay damages to each of us accordingly'. It would be illogical and also I think against public policy if a workman, intending to commit a breach of regulation or duty, can thus ensure his getting some damages for any resultant accident by luring a fellow-worker to join him in the breach.

Is there some satisfactory answer which would break the chain of the plaintiff's argument, without having unjust repercussions on more meritorious claims?

Apportionment of loss through contributory negligence, which can so often provide a fair result, is of no avail in solving this problem. For if one of the men is held, owing to his greater fault, entitled only to 20 per cent of his loss, then as a general rule the other must be entitled to 80 per cent of his loss; and the total result would still offend against common sense...

At first sight it may seem odd that when two men mutually assent to do a dangerous act, it should be held that each has partially caused the injuries of the other. One workman owes a duty to another to take care not to injure him, but I doubt, as between equals, whether that duty is greater than or different from the duty of care not to injure someone other than a fellow-servant standing within the area of risk from his negligence. Different considerations, of course, apply when instructions are given by someone such as a foreman who is entitled to

[1] [1945] 1 All E.R. 531, C.A.

give instructions. When two men agree together to take a risk, a jury might well take the simple view that each caused his own injuries. The difficulty of the question is shown by the conflict of opinion in *Stapley's* case[1] between the Court of Appeal and the majority of your Lordships' House. In that case it could fairly be argued that the accident could not have happened had Dale gone on working on the roof as he should have done. In the present case, however, we have no knowledge what would have happened if James had refused. The question of causation is one of fact. But in view of the trial judge's decision and the reasoning which led to the decision in *Stapley's* case, I doubt if it is open to your Lordships to take a different view of the facts.

The doctrine of vicarious liability has not grown from any very clear, logical or legal principle but from social convenience and rough justice. The master having (presumably for his own benefit) employed the servant, and being (presumably) better able to make good any damage which may occasionally result from the arrangements, is answerable to the world at large for all the torts committed by his servant within the scope of it. The doctrine maintains that liability even in respect of acts which the employers had expressly prohibited (see *Canadian Pacific Railway* v. *Lockhart*[2]) and even when the employers are guilty of no fault themselves (*Staveley Iron & Chemical Co. Ltd* v. *Jones*,[3] and see *per* Fullagar J. in *Darling Island Stevedoring & Lighterage Co. Ltd* v. *Long*[4]). It follows that they are liable for the torts of one servant against another. In the present case, although George and James were acting wrongfully and in breach of the employers' prohibition, they were clearly acting within the scope of their employment...

In *Stapley's* case[5] the defence of *volenti non fit injuria* was not raised in any of the courts below nor in the respondents' case to your Lordships' House; nor was it discussed in the opinions. It has, however, been argued in the present case. One naturally approaches that defence with suspicion. For in the sphere of master and servant its role has been inglorious up to 1891, and, since that date, insignificant. In *Smith* v. *Baker and Sons*[6] it was laid down that the defence is not constituted by knowledge of the danger and acquiescence in it, but by an agreement to

---

[1] [1953] A.C. 663.
[2] [1942] A.C. 591; [1942] 2 All E.R. 464 P.C.
[3] [1956] A.C. 627; [1956] 1 All E.R. 403, H.L.
[4] (1957) 97 C.L.R. 36, 57 (Australia).
[5] [1953] A.C. 663, 665.   [6] [1891] A.C. 325.

run the risk and to waive any rights to recompense for any injury in which that risk may result.

The reason for the rarity of the defence thereafter was that it usually overlapped contributory negligence (and common employment) and produced the same result. In cases where there was real assumption of risk by the servant, he was on his part acting with negligence; and that negligence was a more practical and satisfactory issue than the implication of assumption of risk. So long as they were both total defences there was the same bias against them both. Since contributory negligence has ceased to be a total defence and it has become possible to produce a fair result by apportionment, the reluctance to find the total defence of *volenti non fit injuria* became more marked.

Moreover, the plea is in fact very rarely applicable to master and servant cases. It does not apply to consent obtained by any pressures whether social, economic, or simply habit. The master has an important duty of care for his servant; in general he has more skill in organisation, a wider foresight and more opportunity for innovation. So the assent of the servant to the master's failure very seldom in fact amounts to a real case of *volenti non fit injuria*. Nevertheless, the plea is a valid plea in the right setting. Is the present case one of the rare occasions in the sphere of master and servant when the plea may serve a fair and useful purpose? One must consider the plea in relation both to the cause of action in breach of statutory duty and also to that in common law negligence since the learned judge found that each had been proved.

Where Parliament has laid down that certain precautions shall be taken by the master to protect his workmen, a master is not and should not be entitled to neglect those precautions and then rely on an express or implied agreement between himself and the workman that the latter, if injured as a result of the neglect, will bear the loss alone. In *Wheeler* v. *New Merton Board Mills Ltd*[1] the Court of Appeal laid down that the defence of *volenti non fit injuria* was no answer to a claim by a workman against his employer for injury caused through a breach by the employer of a duty imposed on him by statute. They so held (with some reluctance, which I do not share) principally because the case of *Baddeley* v. *Earl Granville*[2] had stood for some 50 years. But in those cases the defendants were themselves in breach of statutory duty (as were the defendants in *Stapley's* case[3]). In the present case the defendants themselves were in breach of no statutory duty. The questions

[1] [1933] 2 K.B. 669.   [2] 19 Q.B.D. 423.   [3] [1953] A.C. 663.

of public policy and fairness which reinforced those decisions do not help the plaintiff in the present case but rather tell the other way. In my opinion, the rule which the courts have rightly created disallowing the defence where the employer is in breach of statutory duty should not apply to a case such as the present. The defence should be available where the employer was not himself in breach of statutory duty and was not vicariously in breach of any statutory duty through the neglect of some person who was of superior rank to the plaintiff and whose commands the plaintiff was bound to obey (or who had some special and different duty of care, e.g. *National Coal Board* v. *England*,[1] where a miner was injured by the shot firer firing the charge), and where the plaintiff himself assented to and took part in the breaking of the statutory duty in question. If one does not allow some such exception one is plainly shutting out a defence which, when applied in the right circumstances, is fair and sensible.

So far as concerns common law negligence, the defence of *volenti non fit injuria* is clearly applicable if there was a genuine full agreement, free from any kind of pressure, to assume the risk of loss. In *Williams* v. *Port of Liverpool Stevedoring Co. Ltd*[2] Lynskey, J. rejected the defence where one stevedore was injured by the deliberate negligence of the whole gang (to which the plaintiff gave 'tacit consent') in adopting a dangerous system of unloading. There was an overall duty on the master to provide a safe system of work, and it is difficult for one man to stand out against his gang. In such circumstances one may not have that deliberate free assumption of risk which is essential to the plea and which makes it as a rule unsuitable in master and servant cases owing to the possible existence of indefinable social and economic pressures. If the plaintiff had been shown to be a moving spirit in the decision to unload in the wrong manner it would have been different. But these matters are questions of fact and degree.

In the present case it seems clear that as between George and James there was a voluntary assumption of risk. George was clearly acting without any constraint or persuasion; he was in fact inaugurating the enterprise. On the facts it was an implied term (to the benefit of which the employers are vicariously entitled) that George would not sue James for any injury that he might suffer, if an accident occurred. Had an officious bystander raised the possibility, can one doubt that George would have ridiculed it?...

---

[1] [1954] A.C. 403; [1954] 1 All E.R. 546, H.L.
[2] [1956] 1 W.L.R. 551; [1956] 2 All E.R. 69.

The same result, so far as the breach of statutory duty is concerned, could be reached by accepting the reasoning of the High Court of Australia in *Darling Island Stevedoring & Lighterage Co. Ltd*,[1] where it was held that breach of a regulation laid on 'the person in charge' as defined by the regulations, did not create a vicarious liability on the employer of such person. It is not necessary to decide the point since the defence of *volenti non fit injuria* in the present case absolves the defendants. It was discussed but not decided in *Harrison v. National Coal Board*[2] and in *National Coal Board v. England*,[3] see *per* Lord Reid. I prefer to reserve the matter for future consideration.

Lords Hodson and Donovan delivered concurring speeches; Viscount Radcliffe dissented on the issue of causation but agreed with the opinion of Lord Pearce on the defence of *volenti non fit injuria.*[*]

LEACH v. STANDARD TELEPHONES & CABLES LTD

[1966] 2 All E.R. 523

The plaintiff, a Universal miller employed by the defendants, was given a job to do according to a lay-out. The lay-out specified the use of the Universal milling machine. The plaintiff started to do part of the job on a saw which would have taken 10 minutes for the job instead of 3¾ hours. He was not very familiar with the saw (only taking his thumb off when the metal he was sawing 'vibrated'). He lost the top joint of his left thumb. He was not authorised to use the saw. After the accident the foreman, Mr Brim said to him 'You was a bloody fool, Charlie' and the plaintiff replied 'Yes, I know I had no right to be on there'. The machine did have a fence, but it was not adjusted as closely as it might have been while the plaintiff was using it. If it had been properly adjusted it still would not have afforded complete protection.

---

[1] 97 C.L.R. 36.

[2] [1951] A.C. 639; [1951] 1 T.L.R. 1079; [1951] 1 All E.R. 1102, H.L.

[3] [1954] A.C. 403, 425.

[*] On the parallel reintroduction of *volenti non fit injuria* into areas of common law liability, from which it had been thought to be excluded in practice by cases such as *Smith v. Baker* [1891] A.C. 325 (H.L.), *Bowater v. Rowley Regis Corpn.* [1944] K.B. 476 (C.A.), and (although it was not there pleaded) *Stapley v. Gypsum Mines Ltd* [1953] A.C. 663 (H.L.), see now: *O'Reilly v. National Rail and Tramway Appliances Ltd* [1966] 1 All E.R. 499 (worker who hit live shell with sledgehammer at jocular instigation of T., a fellow workman; employers not liable since T. acted outside scope of employment; but, *per* Nield J., *volenti* would also be an available defence, p. 504); and *Bolt v. Wm Moss and Sons* (1966) 110 S.Jo. 385 (one of two workers who consistently disregard foreman's orders not to move scaffold when persons are on it injured when it is moved; held to have consented to risk of his own injury by Cantley, J.).

at this time, but nevertheless some qualification has been read into those words by the decisions of the courts. In *Richard Thomas & Baldwins Ltd.* v. *Cummings*[1] a machine was being moved by hand. The House of Lords held it was not in motion. In *Knight* v. *Leamington Spa Courier Ltd*[2] there was a printing machine with an 'inching button'. When the button was pressed the machine moved at a very slow speed, only five revolutions a minute. This court held that there the machine was not in motion. In *Irwin* v. *White, Tompkins & Courage Ltd*[3] a sack-hoist was being used at speed. The House of Lords held that it was in motion. Those cases seem to show that when a dangerous part is being moved slowly by hand, or by an 'inching button', it is not in motion: when it is being moved at speed, it is in motion... There is, I think, a broad distinction between a thing which is 'being moved' slowly and a thing which is 'in motion' at a fast pace. Accepting for present purposes that a thing which is being moved slowly is not in motion, I am of opinion that a cylinder going at the very high pace here was in motion.

The question whether a dangerous part is 'in motion' or not is a question of fact and degree. The primary facts here are not in dispute. We are in as good a position as the judge on this point. I am of opinion that this machine was in motion at the material time. It should have been fenced. It was not. I would hold that there is a breach of the Factories Act, 1961, and the defendants are liable accordingly.

DANCKWERTS, L.J. I agree. It is admitted that this piece of machinery is dangerous as regards the situation in question. We are told that there is no history of accidents. I can only conclude that that is due either to the skill of the operators or the intervention of providence. It seems that the courts have given rather limited meaning to the words of the section, which are 'in motion or in use' for this purpose. I should have thought, referring to some of the distinctions that have been made, that there was no difference in the meaning of the English words 'motion' and 'movement'. Be that as it may, I am not prepared to give the English language a further twist in the present case, and I think one must come to the conclusion that on the facts of this case the machinery was in motion, and therefore required to be fenced and protected by the fencing under the provisions of the Factories Act, 1961.

DIPLOCK, L.J. agreed with the judgments of LORD DENNING, M.R. and DANCKWERTS, L.J.

[1] [1955] A.C. 321.
[2] [1961] 2 Q.B. 253.   [3] [1964] 1 W.L.R. 387; [1964] 1 All E.R. 545.

MITCHELL *v.* WESTIN LTD

Court of Appeal   [1965] I W.L.R. 297

The plaintiff was tightening some screws on a lathe. He had removed the guard and in order to get them into a position where he could get at them he inched the machinery in question by pressing the starting button and then immediately pressing the stop button. While so doing he got one finger caught in some cogs. He could have used another method of getting at the screws without starting up the machine. He alleged negligence at common law and/or breach of statutory duty under ss. 14(1) and 16 of the Factories Act, 1961. The defendants denied negligence and the breach and alleged that the accident was wholly caused by the plaintiff's own negligence.

PEARSON, L.J.: I think that...one can deduce from *Richard Thomas & Baldwins Ltd* v. *Cummings*[1] these propositions. First, in ascertaining whether machinery in fact moving is 'in motion' for the purposes of the section, regard should be had to the character of the movement more than to its purpose. If machinery is revolving rapidly in a place where a workman may come in contact with it, the guard should be kept in place on the machinery whatever may be the purpose for which the movement is being made, whether it be production, examination, demonstration, adjustment, repairing, testing, or whatever the purpose may be. Secondly, the obvious and typical case of machinery in motion is, of course, machinery running in the usual way in its ordinary course of operation. Thirdly, there must, however, be other cases of machinery which is 'in motion', because the object of the statute is to protect the workman, and machinery may be running dangerously even though not in the ordinary course of operation or perhaps even though not running in the usual way. Fourthly, in deciding whether in a particular case the movement is or is not of such a character that the machinery is 'in motion', the factors to be taken into account include the speed of the movement, its duration, the method of starting the machinery, and probably to some extent or in some cases, also the purpose for which the movement has been instituted. Fifthly, when the factors are rightly taken into account, it must be a question of fact and of degree whether or not the machinery is 'in motion' within the meaning of the section.

SALMON, L.J.: When are parts of a machine which are actually moving not in motion? One might perhaps be forgiven, particularly at

[1] [1955] A.C. 321.

this season of the year, for supposing that this is a riddle or conundrum taken from a child's cracker. It is, however, nothing of the kind. It is the very question that arises in this case.

At first sight it does not perhaps seem to be a difficult question. I suppose that anyone other than a trained lawyer would answer it with some confidence by saying 'Never'. But he would be quite wrong, for the House of Lords has decided otherwise: *Richard Thomas & Baldwins Ltd* v. *Cummings*.[1] In that case it was decided that the words 'in motion' in s. 16 of the Factories Act of 1937 did not bear their ordinary and natural meaning but must be given some special and restricted meaning.

The reason for that decision is quite plain. Very often in industry, machinery has to be unfenced and set in motion (within the natural meaning of those words) for the purpose of repair or adjustment. If the words in the section were to be given their natural meaning, it would follow that factory owners would often be unable to repair or adjust their machinery without committing a criminal offence. Such a result would be patently ridiculous and unjust. It was, therefore, in order to avoid this absurdity and injustice that the House of Lords decided that the legislature must have intended the words 'in motion' to have some special meaning.

SELLERS, L.J. delivered a concurring judgment.

HORNE *v*. LEC REFRIGERATION LTD

[1965] 2 All E.R. 898

The deceased was using an electric drill inside a press when the cable of the drill caught the switch and turned on the machine, killing him. The deceased was familiar with the established safety routine which was to turn all the switches off and to remove the key from the safety key-switch: he also had to remove a fence. Apart from switching one switch off the deceased did not follow the safety-routine. His wife sued for breach of a statutory duty namely that when the press was 'in motion and in use' within s. 16 of the Factories Act it was not 'securely fenced' within s. 14.

CANTLEY, J. found that this was dangerous machinery within s. 14 but that it was not 'in use' within s. 16, saying: I was also referred to the judgment of Upjohn, L.J. in *Knight* v. *Leamington Spa Courier, Ltd*,[2]

---

[1] [1955] A.C. 321.
[2] [1961] 2 All E.R. 666 at p. 670; [1961] 2 Q.B. 253 at p. 264.

where he said: 'As a matter of common sense and ordinary use of the English language the machinery was not then in use. It was not being used for its ordinary commercial purpose; that is, printing. It was a slack period when the machine was not being used at all. The plaintiff, as the machine operator, was taking advantage of the slack period, as he did and as it was his duty to do two or three times a week, to clean the machine while it was not in use'. I agree with counsel's contention that this machine, at the material time, was not in use...

Thirdly, counsel for the defendants contended that the machine was not 'in motion' at the relevant time. 'Motion' is not in this branch of the law a synonym for 'movement', and he says that movement due to an accidental operation of the controls unforeseeable by an employer is not 'motion' any more than was the 'uncovenanted stroke' of the machine in *Eaves* v. *Morris Motors, Ltd*[1]...In the present case: (i) the machine was operated by a switch provided to produce the motion which occurred; (ii) the machine was moving in the same manner and place as in its normal working; and (iii) the machine was working at the same speed and to the same extent as in its normal working. In my view, this machine was in motion within the meaning of s. 16 of the Factories Act, 1961.

I, therefore, find that there was a breach of statutory duty, but I do not think that that by any means concludes the question of liability against the defendants. In my view, the sole cause of the breach was the deceased's conscious disregard of the prescribed safety procedure which he knew and understood. There was no breach of statutory duty when he unbolted the guard covering the press so that he might adjust the mould. The machine was not then in motion or in use. The breach of statutory duty occurred only when he caused the machine to be set in motion as a result of his own disregard of instructions, a matter which I feel bound to characterise in law on the evidence in this case as negligence. What fault of the defendants is to be superimposed on his negligence? I can find none...

In the circumstances of this case, although it is one in which one naturally feels the greatest sympathy, I have come to the conclusion, as a matter of law, that the sole fault which caused this accident was the conduct of the deceased, and that the claim must fail.

[1] [1961] 3 All E.R. 233; [1961] 2 Q.B. 385.

WRIGHT v. FORD MOTOR CO. LTD

[1966] 2 All E.R. 518

An unknown employee forced open a gate set in one side of a four foot high fence round a part of a large machine which contained a 'nip' that was dangerous within the Factories Act 1961, s. 14. The gate and the machine were both operated by the same key in such a way that normally the machine could not be set working unless the gate was locked, and could not be started while the gate was open. In the present case an employee found the gate open and wrongly assumed the machine could not be started while he was inside the fencing. An information was laid against the employers but was dismissed both by the justices and in the present appeal.

LORD PARKER, C.J.: The justices came to the conclusion that although s. 14(1) of the Factories Act, 1961, constitutes, as is well-known, an absolute offence, yet the respondents did have a defence by reason of the combined effect of s. 143(1), which puts an obligation on employees, and s. 155(2) dealing with offences under the Act of 1961.... There is no doubt, pausing there, as the justices find, that X, the unknown man, clearly contravened s. 143(1). One then turns to s. 155 creating offences.*

The point at issue that arises in this case is what is the offence referred to when it is said that the occupier shall not be guilty of an offence by reason only of the employee's contravention. I confess that, when I read this at first, I thought that the appeal here was really quite hopeless; commonsense seemed to demand that this was giving the respondents a defence, and was in effect saying: if the absence of the guard, in this case caused by the unlocking of the gate and, therefore, the offence of the occupier, occurred solely by reason of Mr X's contravention of s. 143(1), then the respondents were not guilty of an offence against s. 14(1) unless it was shown by the prosecution that they had failed to take all reasonable steps to prevent the employee's contravention. In other words, the offence there of which the employer is not to be guilty is, to take the present case, the absolute liability under s. 14(1). The argument which counsel for the appellant has raised in this appeal—a novel argument I confess to me, but others have greater experience—is that that is a wrong construction, and that the offence referred to, of which the employer is not guilty, is, to take this case, not the offence for which he was prosecuted, a breach of s. 14(1), but is, it is said, an

---

* For these sections see *ante*, p. 703.

offence which he, apart from these words, commits whenever a servant of his wilfully interferes with an appliance, contrary to s. 143(1). In other words, the conception here is one which is not only novel in practice, but novel in terms of an employer being criminally vicariously liable for an employee in regard to an offence for which the employee, on the face of s. 143(1), is alone made liable; in other words, it is surprising if the construction which the magistrates put on this is not right.

Counsel for the appellant's argument is really based entirely on the meaning of s. 155(1)....Counsel says, what is quite true, that this is *prima facie* referring to any contravention under the Act, and he would say any contravention by whomsoever committed, and that, under these wide words, the employer is liable for the offence committed by the employee. To take the present case, he says that, when one applies subsection (1), *prima facie* the respondents here are guilty of two offences one offence against s. 14(1) and, secondly, an offence against s. 143(1), although, as I have said, the obligation or the duties imposed under s. 143(1) are entirely those of the servant. For my part, I agree that those are very wide words, but I feel constrained in the circumstances of the case to interpret them in a way which will only make the employer liable for all contraventions under the Act other than those in respect of which the sole obligation to perform is imposed on the employee. To give it the other meaning seems to me to outrage one's sense of the criminal law in regard to vicarious liability of a master for crimes of his servant. If that construction is right, then counsel for the appellants I think, would agree that, when one gets to s. 155(2), there is no ground for reading an offence of which the employer is not to be guilty as an offence other than the offence charged under s. 14(1). For my part, I also see a further difficulty in counsel for the appellant's way, because, even accepting his argument under s. 155(1), I see no reason for reading the words 'an offence' in subsection (2) of s. 155 as meaning that offence, but rather that the words mean any offence; therefore, even if it is necessary to exempt the employer from a s. 143(1) offence on the basis that he has been made liable under s. 155(1), yet when one reaches s. 155(2), the words 'an offence' in subsection (2) are perfectly general and are capable of meaning not merely the s. 143(1) offence but also the s. 14(1) offence. That being the view which I take of this, and the prosecution having failed to show that the respondents failed to take reasonable steps to prevent contravention by Mr X, I would uphold these magistrates' opinion and dismiss the appeal.

Section C

INDUSTRIAL INJURY AND NATIONAL INSURANCE

NATIONAL INSURANCE (INDUSTRIAL INJURIES) ACT, 1965

1. *Persons to be insured.* (1) Subject to the provisions of this Act, all persons employed in insurable employment shall be insured in manner provided by this Act against personal injury caused after 4 July 1948 by accident arising out of and in the course of such employment....

5. (1) Subject to the provisions of this Act,* where an insured person suffers personal injury caused after 4 July 1948 by accident arising out of and in the course of his employment being insurable employment then:

(*a*) industrial injury benefit...shall be payable to the insured person if during such period as is hereinafter provided he is as the result of the injury incapable of work;

(*b*) industrial disablement benefit...if he suffers as the result of the injury from such loss of physical or mental faculty as is hereinafter provided;

(*c*) industrial death benefit...if the insured person dies as the result of the injury....

6. For the purposes of this Act, an accident arising in the course of an insured person's employment shall be deemed, in the absence of evidence to the contrary, also to have arisen out of that employment....

7. An accident shall be deemed to arise out of and in the course of an insured person's employment, notwithstanding that he is at the time of the accident acting in contravention of any statutory or other regulations applicable to his employment, or of any orders given by or on behalf of his employer, or that he is acting without instructions from his employer, if

(*a*) the accident would have been deemed so to have arisen had the

---

* See for the new graduated 'earnings-related' supplementary benefit, National Insurance Act, 1966: see J. Reid (1966) 29 M.L.R. 537. It is curious that the introduction of this scheme, and the retention in it of an industrial injury benefit at a rate higher than the ordinary sickness benefit, has not (apparently) been attacked by those who have argued for the abolition of the special injury benefit: see Wedderburn, *The Worker and The Law* (1965) p. 207, (1966) p. 199.

act not been done in contravention as aforesaid or without instructions from his employer, as the case may be; and

(b) the act is done for the purposes of and in connection with the employer's trade or business.

8. (1) An accident happening while an insured person is, with the express or implied permission of his employer, travelling as a passenger by any vehicle to or from his place of work shall, notwithstanding that he is under no obligation to his employer to travel by that vehicle, be deemed to arise out of and in the course of his employment, if

(a) the accident would have been deemed so to have arisen had he been under such an obligation; and

(b) at the time of the accident, the vehicle (i) is being operated by or on behalf of his employer or some other person by whom it is provided in pursuance of arrangements made with his employer; and (ii) is not being operated in the ordinary course of a public transport service.

(2) In this section references to a vehicle include references to a ship, vessel or aircraft....

10. An accident happening after 19 December 1961 shall be treated for the purposes of this Act, where it would not apart from this section be so treated, as arising out of a person's employment if

(a) the accident arises in the course of the employment; and

(b) the accident either is caused by another person's misconduct, skylarking or negligence, or by steps taken in consequence of any such misconduct, skylarking or negligence, or by the behaviour or presence of an animal (including a bird, fish or insect) or is caused by or consists in the insured person being struck by any object or by lightning; and

(c) the insured person did not directly or indirectly induce or contribute to the happening of the accident by his conduct outside the employment or by any act not incidental to the employment....

14. (1) The weekly rate of a disablement pension shall... be increased by an amount not exceeding the appropriate amount specified in paragraph 5 of Schedule 3 of this Act if as the result of the relevant loss of faculty the beneficiary

(a) is incapable and likely to remain permanently incapable of following his regular occupation; and

(b) is incapable of following employment of an equivalent standard which is suitable in his case....

R. *v.* INDUSTRIAL INJURIES COMMISSIONER, *EX PARTE* A.E.U.

Court of Appeal   [1966] 1 All E.R. 97

Culverwell was a factory employee entitled to a ten minute morning teabreak. Smoking was not allowed in the workshops so a small booth was set aside for this purpose. On the morning in question Culverwell found the booth full and he squatted in the passageway outside the booth waiting to go in and smoke. He had overstayed the teabreak by about five minutes when he was struck by a fork lift truck which ran into him. This was an application for an order of Certiorari to quash the decision of the Industrial Injuries Commissioner under the National Insurance (Industrial Injuries) Act, 1946, holding that the accident did not arise in the course of employment (see *post*, p. 765).

LORD DENNING, M.R.: Whilst he was there, squatting on the floor, a fork-lift truck was driven past, going from one part of the factory to another. The driver, coming along without looking, ran into Mr Culverwell and he was severely injured. He had a broken leg, a broken pelvis and a dislocated hip. We are told that he has made a claim at common law against his employers which has been settled by a payment to him. He claims that he is also entitled to industrial injuries benefit....

I think that it is right to say, as counsel for the insurance officer said, that (the words of the Act) are so very like the words of the old Workmen's Compensation Acts that it is legitimate to look for guidance to the decisions of the courts in the old days. But I would make it subject to the qualification that we do not fall into the errors which the courts did then. One of the principal mistakes was to interfere too much with the decisions of the arbitrators to whom the legislature had entrusted the administration of compensation....Nevertheless, I should like to say today that it would be unfortunate if, by means of applications for certiorari, the court should become engulfed in a stream of cases under this present Act. The other mistake which the courts made in the early days was to interpret the Workmen's Compensation Acts too narrowly. Even the House of Lords did not appreciate the social significance of this legislation. They debarred men from compensation when Parliament thought that they ought to have it....

As I listened to the argument today which counsel for the insurance officer has put forward, I felt that he was going back to the old narrow interpretations of this provision. He took us back to the early cases of

Parker v. *Black Rock (Owners)*[1] in 1915 and *St. Helens Colliery Co. Ltd* v. *Hewitson*[2] in 1924. Those decisions give me a shock even now, that the House should have decided them as they did. Counsel relied on them. He said that the rule of law still was, as stated by Lord Parker of Waddington in the *Black Rock* case,[3] 'In order to make it an accident arising out of the employment the absence from the vessel must be in pursuance of a duty owed to the employer.' This idea that a duty is necessary is all wrong. It does not stand with the decision of the House of Lords itself in *Armstrong, Whitworth & Co.* v. *Redford*,[4] where there was no duty on the young woman to go to and from the canteen, yet she was held to be in the course of her employment. Nor does it stand with the decision of the Court of Appeal in *Knight* v. *Howard Wall Ltd*[5] where a boy, who was having his midday meal in a canteen, was injured by a dart....I think it plain that a man can be acting in the course of his employment, even though he is doing something which it was not his duty to do. Thus, when Mr Culverwell went down for the break, when he was there waiting to go into the smoking booth, it was in the course of his employment, although he did not go in pursuance of any duty owed to his employer.

This point (whether a duty is necessary) seems to have played a part in the case of Mr Culverwell when it was before the local appeal tribunal....I am glad to see that on this ground the commissioner upheld the view of the dissenting member. The commissioner said: 'I assume in favour of the claimant that there would have been no interruption in the course of his employment if during the break period he had been smoking in the booth or had been waiting outside it, at the place where he was, intending to go into the booth to smoke.' The commissioner was there applying the very sensible rule that even though a person is not obliged to be in a certain place, but goes there for something incidental to his employment, such as for a meal to a canteen, he is acting in the course of his employment. So Mr Culverwell did not lose on that ground.

Now comes the crux of the commissioner's decision. He decided against Mr Culverwell because of the length of time which he had overstayed his break. What is the position when a man overstays his tea-break or his meal-break? I do not think that the mere fact of overstaying his time takes him out of the course of his employment:

---

[1] [1915] A.C. 725.
[3] [1915] A.C. at p. 729.
[5] [1938] 4 All E.R. 667.

[2] [1923] All E.R. Rep. 249; [1924] A.C. 59.
[4] [1920] All E.R. Rep. 316; [1920] A.C. 757.

certainly not when it is done without thinking. Even if it is done negligently or disobediently, it does not automatically take him outside the course of his employment. It is only taken out of the course of his employment when the circumstances show that he is doing something of a kind different from anything he was employed to do.

The course of employment *can* be interrupted in some circumstances: but not necessarily so. Take the first class where a man 'goes away from work for purposes of his own'. An illustration is where a man goes from one end of a factory to the other to compare notes on football pools. He is not acting in the course of his employment. It would be be different if he went to get a tool or to go to the lavatory. Now take the next class, where a man 'at his place of work does something which has nothing to do with his employment'. An illustration was given by Lord Atkin in *Noble's case*.[1] If the guard of a train takes it on himself to drive the train and is injured whilst driving, he is outside the course of his employment. Another illustration is the case which counsel for the insurance officer mentioned which was heard by the Divisional Court a little while ago where a man was employed to hook goods on to a crane and, instead, took it on himself to drive a fork-lift truck. There he was outside the course of his employment.

Take the third class where 'being away from his place of work, he does not return to it when he should'. An illustration can be taken from *Knight v. Howard Wall Ltd*.[2] Suppose the boy in the canteen, instead of going back to his work at the end of the meal, had stayed on for half an hour playing darts with the rest of the men in the canteen. By overstaying his visit to the canteen he would be taking himself completely out of the course of his employment, because he would be doing something of a kind different from anything he was employed to do.

All of those classes which the commissioner mentioned are, I think, justified when you remember that his words were: 'It *can*...be interrupted,' not *will* be interrupted.

Eventually this case comes down to this: Was what Mr Culverwell did (in overstaying his break in the morning) reasonably incidental to his employment? Was he merely overstaying the break negligently or even disobediently? Or was he doing something entirely different, using this extended break for purposes of his own for an indefinite time, quite unconnected with his employment? It must be remembered that five

---

[1] [1940] 2 All E.R. at p. 390; [1940] A.C. at p. 596.
[2] [1938] 4 All E.R. 667.

minutes had gone past after the end of the break and he was still waiting to smoke a cigarette. It might have been a long time, for all that appears before he returned.

This is one of those questions which, as it seems to me, the legislature has decided should not be brought up to the courts of law for decision, but should be entrusted to the specialised statutory authorities for determination. It may occasionally be of use, if there is a real error of law, for a case to be brought before this court, but not in such a case as this. No error of law is shown here.

I would agree that in the ordinary way if a man whilst at his place of work, during his hours of work, is injured by a risk incidental to his employment, then the right conclusion usually is that it is an injury which arises out of and in the course of the employment, even though he may not be doing his actual work but chatting to a friend or smoking or doing something of that kind. But he may take himself out of it if he does something of a kind entirely different from anything he was employed to do. That is what the commissioner found here. This man was overstaying his tea-break for so long that he was taking himself out of his employment. I would dismiss the appeal.

DAVIES, L.J.: Here, however, as I understand the decision of the learned commissioner, Mr Culverwell was outside his contract. Counsel for the applicants said in the course of his argument that this was nothing like a sit-down strike. I am not so sure. It was not a strike in the sense of a combination of workmen trying to bring pressure on their employers; but it was a strike in the sense that this man, knowing his tea-break finished at 10.40 a.m., decided that he was not going back to his work at 10.40 a.m. but was going to continue to sit down and have his smoke in time for which, no doubt, he would expect to be paid. I do not think that that is something very different from an individual strike, if such a thing is possible; and it shows that he was not in the course of his employment.

SALMON, L.J. delivered a concurring judgment.

Decision No. R(I) 4/66

A fitter's mate was injured while waiting outside a smoking booth in the factory where he was employed. The factory was subject to a special fire risk and the employees were not permitted to smoke anywhere except in the smoking booths. The accident happened at 10.45 a.m. although the permitted break was from 10.30 to 10.40 a.m. The claimant was clearly not on the point of returning to work at the time of the accident as he was still rolling his cigarette with a view to smoking it as soon as a seat should be free in the booth.

The decision of the Commissioner was as follows:*

1. My decision is that the claimant's accident on the 15 July 1963 did not arise in the course of his employment and that he is not entitled to industrial injury benefit....

8. The first matter which the claimant must establish if he is to succeed in this claim is that at the time of the accident he was in the course of his employment; in other words that the course of the employment had not been interrupted. It can of course be interrupted even during working hours and in the factory, if a claimant either goes away from work for purposes of his own, or at his place of work does something which has nothing to do with his employment, or if being away from his place of work he does not return to it when he should. The burden of proof is on the claimant to establish his case on balance of probabilities....

10. Having fully considered everything that has been said on behalf of the claimant I have come to a conclusion on the last of these matters, and it is therefore unnecessary for me to deal with any other points. I assume in favour of the claimant that there would have been no interruption in the course of his employment if during the break period he had been smoking in the booth or had been waiting outside it, at the place where he was, intending to go into the booth to smoke. But here the accident happened at 10.45 a.m. It was said by the claimant's solicitor that the claimant had overstepped the time by a very small amount. But on the other hand it was pointed out that an extra five minutes made the break half as long again. Moreover at the time of the accident the claimant was not even on the point of starting back to his place of work. He was still rolling his cigarette with a view to smoking it as soon as a seat (or perhaps 3 seats) should be free in the booth. Further, I found very unconvincing the various reasons which he

---

* Compare R(I) 3/62: A woman civil servant of 64 whose work involved standing and began at 8.30 a.m., preferred to arrive at the office at 7.0 a.m. in order to avoid the rush hour. She would then open the windows and read for an hour and a half. She was injured while opening a window at 7.10 a.m. *Held*: her accident arose out of and in the course of her employment. Her employers knew of her early arrival; and it was effected not for her own convenience but to conserve her strength for the better performance of her duties, and therefore incidental to the employment. Contrast a claim that failed: R(I) 1/59 (male nurse injured cycling to work an hour early, as he habitually did in order to have a game of billiards). See too R(I) 22/56: miner of 62 who, after his bath, went to the canteen to await later bus and avoid rush; the course of employment was held still to continue when he slipped on the way to the bus stop; and other cases discussed by J. Reid (1966) 29 M.L.R. 389.

alleged for not knowing the time: that the buzzer was often inaudible and that all the clocks in the works were different. I am not satisfied that he did not know that the break period had ended. The fact that the booth was full proves nothing, since process workers were allowed in it at any time irrespective of breaks. The conclusion to which I am driven, especially in view of the claimant's somewhat casual habits in this matter, is that there was here something definitely more than a mere trifling or inadvertent delay which could be disregarded. I do not think that extending a break so as to make it at least half as long again can fairly be regarded as a reasonable incident of the employment. I think that this case falls on the same side of the line as that which was the subject of Decision R(1) 44/57. In my judgment the claimant's action in remaining where he was at the time of the accident created an interruption in the course of the employment.

R(I) 8/61

Claimant, who was employed as a general labourer in the mechanics' shop of a dyeworks, was injured when, during working hours, attempting to remove a brush which had stuck in a chimney of his foreman's private house. The foreman had asked or told the claimant to do this job. The claimant's employers, while they knew of, and had not objected to, the men working under this foreman doing small odd jobs for him during working hours, had never expressly authorised this practice.

The decision of the Commissioner was as follows:

1. My decision is that the accident which befell the claimant on the 22 February 1960 did not arise out of and in the course of his employment: and accordingly he is not entitled to injury benefit in respect of the injury caused thereby....

6. I accept that the employers must have known, to some extent at least, of the practice whereby men from their works (including the claimant) were used by the foreman during working hours for work on his private property, and that (so far as they knew of it) they acquiesced in it. The last sentence of their letter quoted in paragraph 5 above (with its reference to 'trifling jobs') suggests however that they may not have realized the full extent of the practice. In any event, there is no suggestion that the employers expressly authorised either the practice in general or the claimant's visit to the foreman's house on the 22 February 1960 in particular....

7. If the claimant had determined, of his own initiative and without instructions from anybody, to go to the foreman's house and help to clear his chimney, it could not seriously be maintained, I think, that

in so doing he was acting within the scope of his employment. The question comes to be, therefore, whether (and if so to what extent) the situation is altered by the fact that the task was undertaken on the instructions of the foreman. The Commissioner has had to consider this situation in a number of cases, and the guiding principle is very clearly stated in Decision R(1) 36/55, at paragraph 8, as follows—'I appreciate...that it is difficult for an employee to refuse a request of this kind from his immediate superior; quite apart from the fear of possibly injury to his prospects...an employee would naturally desire to be co-operative in such a matter as this. But anxiety about his career or a desire for popularity or pure good nature may prompt a man to do work which is clearly outside the scope of his contract of service; when this happens the work will not be done in the course of man's employment unless it can be shown that it was done in response to an order or request made by or with the authority (actual or ostensible) of the employers and that it was the express or implied intention of both parties that the work should be done under the contract of service and not merely as an act of good nature or friendship....' Applying this principle to the facts of the present case: I do not think it can seriously be maintained that the task of clearing a chimney in the foreman's private house was within the scope of the claimant's contract of service. Nor is it shown that it was the express or implied intention of both parties that the work should be done under the contract of service. Simply put, it was an act outwith the scope of the claimant's employment, done to oblige the foreman, and done with the tacit acquiescence of the employers....

8. I suspect that it is not uncommon for persons in employment to be asked or instructed by persons in authority over them to perform tasks which are outwith the true scope of their employment. I think that persons who are minded to give such instructions (as well as those to whom the instructions are given) should remember that it is only accidents arising out of and in the course of a person's employment which are insured against under the National Insurance (Industrial Injuries) Acts. A person instructed to do work which is outwith the scope of his employment, who meets with an accident while engaged in that work, may well find that he is not entitled to benefit under these Acts.

R(I) 2/63

The claimant was injured by an explosion which occurred when, while in the course of his employment in a factory where (unknown to him) gas was escaping from an unlit blow-pipe, he attempted to relight his cigarette. The claimant's employers permitted smoking.

The decision of the Tribunal was as follows:

1. Our decision is that on the 27 November 1961 the claimant suffered personal injury caused by accident arising out of and in the course of his employment, and that he is entitled to injury benefit from the 27 November to the 9 December 1961, both days included....

6. In order to succeed in this appeal it is necessary for the claimant to establish on balance of probabilities that he suffered personal injury caused by accident arising out of and in the course of his employment (National Insurance (Industrial Injuries) Act, 1946, s. 7(1)). It is clear and not disputed that he suffered personal injury caused by accident arising in the course of his employment. The only question for decision is whether the accident arose out of it....

9. The association's second proposition was put forward at considerable length. We hope that we do no injustice to it if we summarise it briefly as follows. It was said that acts which formerly were not regarded as incidental to employment may now be so regarded. Smoking, if not forbidden, was such an act. It would follow that smoking did not interrupt the course of employment, and an accident resulting from smoking arose out of the employment, since 'employment' must mean the same in relation to both phrases....

10. This second proposition would have widespread consequences. It would mean that a man who burnt himself lighting his cigarette would without more have automatically suffered an industrial accident. Since smoking would be work, the place where he was smoking would be one of his places of work, and an accident arising from smoking would be an industrial accident, even though it was in no other way connected with the work. No decision directly supporting the proposition, either before or since 1948, was cited.

11. We have felt considerable doubt whether we ought to express any opinion on this second point. Since we feel able to allow the claim on the third ground, anything that we say is no more than *obiter dictum*. The question whether any act is not incidental to the employment will, we think, become increasingly important under s. 2(c) of

the Family Allowances and National Insurance Act, 1961,* where the
phrase appears for the first time in a statute dealing with this subject.
The association's solicitor however urged us to give a ruling on it, and
we therefore express our opinion. We think that to ask whether smoking
is incidental to employment is not to ask the right question....Nor are
we prepared to hold that smoking in this case was incidental *in that
sense* to this particular employment. Accordingly, in our opinion, the
claimant is not entitled to succeed simply because he was smoking or
attempting to smoke at work and an accident resulted from it, irrespective of any other circumstances connecting the accident with the
employment. We think it right to utter a warning about the use of the
word 'incidental' in cases of this type. We think that it is being used
in more senses than one. Sometimes it is used as meaning an act which
is incidental to the employment in the strict sense (as in *Davidson* v.
M'Robb)† so that anything arising out of the incidental act arises out
of the employment. It is however also sometimes used in the looser
sense of a neutral act, neither expressly permitted nor forbidden by the
employer, such as sucking sweets, smoking or knitting (e.g. in the case
of a telephone operator). We are by no means convinced that an accident
resulting solely from such an activity at work would arise out of the
employment, even though it arose in the course of it.

12. The association's third proposition raises in our opinion an
important question as to the test to be applied in a case such as this to
determine whether the accident arose out of the employment.

13. In a number of decisions, many of which are collected in the
published Index to Commissioner's Decisions under Group 31B, and
in particular in Decision R(I) 68/52, which was followed and applied
in Decisions R(I) 9/60 and R(I) 30/60, the test applied has been simply
whether the claimant's act was performed for his own personal purposes
rather than for the purposes of his employment.

14. The association contend that this is the wrong test. They submit
that the question is rather one of the causation of the accident, and that
the true test is whether the employment to a material extent contributed
towards causing the accident, using the word 'material' in the sense
in which it was used in *Bonnington Castings Ltd* v. *Wardlaw* [1956]
A.C. 613, at 620–1, where Lord Reid made clear that it included anything which did not come within the exception expressed by the words
de minimis non curat lex.

15. The insurance officer's legal representative does not attempt to

* Now s. 10 of the 1965 Act.   † [1918] A.C. 304.

support the view that the test is simply whether the claimant's action was performed for his own personal purposes. He agrees that the question is one of causation. He submits that the test is whether the employment was *an* efficient cause of the accident and not a mere condition, using 'efficient' in the sense in which it is used, interchangeably with 'effective', by Barry, J. in *Howgate* v. *Bagnall and another* [1951] 1 K.B. 265 at 271 to 273, and in connection with the question whether incapacity resulted from the relevant injury by a tribunal of Commissioners in paragraph 9(1) of Decision R(I) 3/56....

19. In this case we are concerned with the particular problem of smoking at work. This however is only part of the much larger problem of acts performed for personal purposes. This again is only part of the whole problem of accidents arising out of the employment. Having rejected the tests propounded by the association and the insurance officer, we think that it would be wrong for us to attempt the probably impossible task of formulating a test of general application. We must therefore emphasise that anything said in this decision applies only to cases of this type, viz. where a man at his place of work does something for his own personal purposes. It does not follow that the same considerations apply to other cases, e.g. where a man goes off to some other part of the factory to smoke....

23. Whereas the question whether an accident arises in the course of the claimant's employment is, generally speaking but not always, a question of time and place, the question whether the accident arises out of his employment is one of causation....

26. We think that in cases such as the present one the statutory authorities, when determining whether an accident arose out of the claimant's employment, may properly ask themselves whether a risk of the employment was a cause of the accident; and that, if it was, the accident may generally speaking be held to arise out of the employment, unless the claimant had added or created a different risk (for example by some act done for his own personal purposes and not those of his employment) and this different risk was the real cause of the accident.

27. We think that these questions should be considered in a broad commonsense manner (cf. *Cadzow's* case), as is now the rule in many other branches of the law (cf. *Yorkshire Dale Steamship Company Ltd* v. *Minister of War Transport* [1942] A.C. 691 at 706)...

29. Approaching the present case in this way, our conclusions are as follows. Looking at the matter in a commonsense fashion, there were in our judgment two causes of this accident: the act of the claimant in

operating his lighter and the presence of an explosive mixture of gas and air. The latter was dangerous, and the danger was clearly a risk of the claimant's employment. *Prima facie* therefore the accident arose out of the employment. The remaining question is whether the claimant's act, which was done for his own personal purposes, added a *different* risk, which was the real cause of the accident. In our judgment his act did not do so. The operation of the lighter and the relighting of the cigarette would have represented a minimal (if any) interference with the claimant's work. Smoking was permitted. The accident happened at the claimant's place, or one of his places, of work. There were numerous other flames which might have set the gas alight. One of the dangers of the presence of the gas was of fire or explosion. The claimant's act therefore converted the danger of an explosion into an actual explosion. It did not make it a different danger or create a fresh one. In our judgment there was here an amply sufficient causal connection between the employment and its risks on the one hand and the accident on the other. The accident arose out of the employment and the claim therefore succeeds. We have little doubt that the local appeal tribunal would have come to the same conclusion if they had not felt that they were bound by previous Commissioner's decisions to hold otherwise.

R(I) 3/63

The claimant's employers had made arrangements with a firm of caterers to do all the catering at their factory. Under these arrangements a trolley came round the factory each morning from which employees could purchase light refreshments to be consumed at their place of work during a short mid-morning break. The claimant was injured consequent upon eating, at her place of work during this break, a slice of toast, containing a piece or pieces of glass, purchased from the trolley. It was not in question that the claimant was in the course of her employment when the accident occurred, the issue being whether the accident arose out of her employment.

Held, allowing the appeal, that since the toast was supplied to the claimant at her place of work under a system arranged by her employers for supplying refreshment to employees, there was amply sufficient causal connection between the employment and the accident to warrant a finding that the accident arose out of the employment. (See R(I) 2/63). R(I) 90/53 was wrongly decided and is not to be followed*.

---

* Compare R(I) 4/64: cricket ball maker who was allowed to smoke at his work. A thread flicked hot ash into his eye. *Held*: as he was permitted to smoke, the risk was an employment risk and the accident arose out of the employment.

See too the cases on injury in the course of medical attention or the like: successful claims in: R(I) 24/63: checker at Royal Ordnance depot allowed by employers to visit

The decision of the Tribunal was as follows:

1. Our decision is that on the 13 April 1962 the claimant suffered personal injury caused by accident arising out of and in the course of her employment and that she is entitled to injury benefit from the 13 April to the 16 May 1962, both days included....

6. In order to determine whether this accident arose out of the employment it is necessary to consider whether there is any sufficient causal connection between the accident and the employment. (See the cases referred to in our Decision C.I. 48/62 given today.) In most of the cases decided about taking meals or eating food at work (which are collected in Group 31J in the published Index to Commissioner's Decisions) the question has been whether it involved an interruption of the course of the employment. In a number of cases, however, where there has been some connection between the accident and the employment, for example in relation to the state of the premises, where some part of them fell on the claimant, the accident has been held to arise out of the employment. (See Decision C.I. 34/50 (reported) and earlier decisions cited therein.) No case was cited to us however, except Decision R(I) 90/53, where the accident had resulted either from the food itself or from some foreign body in it.

7. In this case the toast was supplied to the claimant at her place of work on behalf of the employers (as to which see Decisions C.I. 34/50 above and R(I) 11/53) under a system arranged by the employers for supplying refreshments to the employees in the factory. On these facts we are satisfied that there was amply sufficient causal connection between the employment and the accident to warrant a finding that the accident arose out of the claimant's employment. One of the risks of eating the food supplied was that it might be defective in some way or might contain a foreign body. By eating it the claimant did not add a different risk (*Harris* v. *Associated Portland Cement Manufacturers* [1939] A.C. 71, 31 B.W.C.C. 434 (at pages 77 and 439 respectively) per Lord Atkin).

mobile X-ray unit temporarily stationed in the depot, injured in a waiting room in the medical centre. R(I) 16/62: injury during the course of free chiropody service provided on employers' premises. But an injury suffered during the use of a 'mere amenity' provided by the employer will not arise out of the employment, e.g. in playing volley ball: C.I. 17/50. Also contrast, R(I) 43/57: claimant complained of headache while in pit-head baths; a friend offered smelling salts and the contents splashed into his eye. His claim for benefit failed since the injury had nothing to do with the employers and did not arise out of the employment.

R(I) 7/66

The insured person was employed for the last 18 years of his life in the blasting department of a chemical factory, where he was more or less continuously exposed to E.G.D.N./N.G. He died suddenly at 10 a.m. on a Monday, which was a holiday, having done no work since the previous Friday. A full necropsy showed that there was nothing in the condition of his heart, or elsewhere, to explain his death.

Investigations by toxicologists, cardiologists and experts in industrial medicine have indicated that prolonged exposure to E.G.D.N., and N.G. can cause sudden death. Records of such deaths show that they usually occur not when a person is at work, but after a period of 2 days' absence from work, frequently on a Monday morning.

Held that the deceased's death was caused by his employment but that it had not been shown that there was personal injury 'by accident'.

The decision of the Commissioner was as follows:

1. My decision is that it is not shown that the claimant's late husband suffered personal injury by accident arising out of and in the course of his employment within the meaning of the National Insurance (Industrial Injuries) Acts and that accordingly the claimant is not entitled to industrial death benefit....

11. To establish a claim to industrial death benefit the claimant must show on balance of probabilities that the deceased suffered personal injury by accident arising out of and in the course of his employment and that he died as a result of the injury. (See s. 7 of the National Insurance (Industrial Injuries) Act, 1946 now replaced by s. 5 of the National Insurance (Industrial Injuries) Act, 1965). The Act itself does not mention the word 'process'. But the distinction between personal injury by accident and personal injury by process has been long established by decisions of the House of Lords and the Court of Appeal under the Workmen's Compensation Acts; these decisions have been applied to the same words repeated by the Legislature in the 1946 Act. It should always be remembered that where a claim fails by reason of the doctrine of process it does so, not because there was personal injury by process, but because there is not shown to have been personal injury 'by accident' within the meaning of the Act....

13. In the course of his argument the claimant's representative submitted that either the accident was the death and it should be treated as arising out of and in the course of the employment or the deceased suffered personal injury on Friday the 20 November 1964. He submitted that the deceased had not complained of anything wrong

with him during the last week of his life, and that the examination on that day established that the deceased was then completely healthy.... The insurance officer submitted that, the deceased having been exposed to these chemicals continuously for 18 years, this was not a case of personal injury by accident but one of process.

14. Having fully considered all the evidence and arguments, I do not feel able to accept the association's arguments. Although the manner in which these chemicals affect the body is known, I am satisfied as a matter of fact that the deceased's continuous exposure to them over a period of 18 years must have caused changes in his body which made him liable to die in the circumstances in which he did. I find therefore that his death was caused by his employment. In my judgment however the only possible conclusion from the evidence is that, to use Lord Porter's phrase, a time had come when the indefinite number of so-called accidents and the length of time over which they occurred took away the element of accident and substituted that of process. I can see no possible justification for holding that there was any accident on the 20 November 1964 any more than there was one on any of the other working days during the previous 18 years. In my judgment the claimant has not succeeded in showing, as she must, that there was personal injury 'by accident' (cf. paragraph 9 of Decision C.I. 83/50). I must therefore affirm the unanimous decision of the local appeal tribunal.

15. I do so with the utmost regret. If it be accepted that the first purpose of this legislation is to provide benefit when insured persons are injured or killed by their work, the result of the doctrine of process in this and a number of other cases is that that purpose is not fulfilled. The claimant must think the result of this case neither intelligible nor just. In view however of the decisions referred to above, including decisions of the House of Lords, it is not open to me to disregard the doctrine. The remedy, if one is needed, is in the hands of others.*

---

* The distinction between 'accident' and 'process' is of great complexity. Compare cases where the injury arose from an 'accident' even though the employee's work aggravated an existing bad condition of his body: e.g. R(I) 19/63: A bakehouse assistant with a pre-existing degenerative disc condition crouched and stretched to put some dishes under a table. She felt a click; had to leave work several times that day; and was incapable of work the following day because of a prolapsed disc.

Held: this was an accident within the Act, arising out of and in the course of the employment. The pain felt when her back clicked indicated that the movement of putting the dishes away was the 'last straw' which caused the complete prolapse of a partially prolapsed disc.

See too R(I) 19/56: leather stitcher transferred from machines to hand-stitching became incapable of work after three days by reason of osteoarthritis.

Held: this was a process not an accident. But after R(I) 43/61 it is possible to detect a narrowing of the concept of 'process'. Compare, for example, R(I) 4/62: develop-

R(I) 10/66

The claimant, a married woman, was regularly employed, owing to domestic circumstances, in part-time work, as a biscuit packer. As the result of the relevant loss of faculty she was incapable and likely to remain permanently incapable of following that regular occupation but she was capable of employment as a checker. She worked at this on a part-time basis because of her domestic circumstances although it was available to her full time. Whilst part-time work as a checker yielded less than as a part-time biscuit packer, full-time work as a checker was suitable and within her capacity and yielded more than work as a part-time biscuit packer.

The decision of the Commissioner was as follows:

1. My decision is that from and including the 3 June 1964, the claimant is not entitled to an increase of disablement gratuity under s. 14, as amended, of the National Insurance (Industrial Injuries) Act, 1946, now s. 14 of the National Insurance (Industrial Injuries) Act 1965....

3. I heard the two appeals on 9 August 1965 and adjourned for further argument which I heard on the 4 November 1965. I have since deferred my decision to await the result of the decision of the Court of Appeal in *Reg.* v. *Deputy Industrial Injuries Commissioner, Ex parte Humphreys*. The Divisional Court proceedings are reported in [1965] 3 W.L.R. 456 and the Court of Appeal proceedings not yet reported but I have had the advantage of reading an official transcript of the judgments, since reported in [1966] 2 W.L.R. 63; [1965] 3 All E.R. 885.

The short point in that case, as it may have affected this appeal, is that the Divisional Court by a majority decided that under s. 14, in considering the suitability of employment of an equivalent standard suitable in the case of a claimant, domestic circumstances do not come into consideration. On this aspect of that case the decision of the Court of Appeal agreed with the majority of the Divisional Court. That means that the domestic reasons for the claimant electing to work only part-time are not relevant in considering why she did not or could not work full-time. Whether or not she could work longer hours or full-time is relevant to consideration of whether or not she has a result of the degree of disablement due to the disease suffered a loss of earnings.

ment of ganglion in the employee's hand caused by exposure to heat and radiation over several days. The Commissioner refused to lay down any 'rigid rule', but held that this was an accident if the injury had developed over some days rather than on one ascertainable day.

In this connection I refer to the judgments in the Court of Appeal in which Lord Denning, M.R. said: 'What is meant by the words employment of "an equivalent standard"? They mean a standard of remuneration equivalent to his regular occupation.... What is meant by "suitable in his case"? It means, I think, employment suitable for him, in his disabled condition, having regard to his physical and mental capacity'

Salmon, L.J. said: 'The word "suitable" in s. 14(1)(b) and 14(4) relates to employment which is suitable to the workman's personal qualifications, including his physical and mental capacity and has nothing to do with suitability of employment from any other point of view'....*

6. In following the Court of Appeal decision and assisted as I have been by the earlier decisions, in my judgment, having regard to the wording of s. 14(1) and (4), the probable standard of remuneration in the insurable employment suitable in a claimant's case which he is likely to be capable of following as compared with that in his regular occupation has to do with capacity to earn and does not include such matters as the hours or conditions of work, or the rate of remuneration by the hour or by any other standard of time, piece rates or the like. Indeed such comparisons would often lead to anomalous results and in some instances it might prove impossible to achieve a comparison in occupations differing widely in their incidence of employment and methods of remuneration. The object of the section is to compensate for loss of earnings and the comparison of remuneration which has to be made is the amount earned before the relevant loss of faculty, plus appropriate increases, when applicable and the claimant's probable standard of remuneration afterwards in a suitable employment. This, for convenience, is often averaged into weekly, monthly or annual earnings as the circumstances may require. Many circumstances of differences can be envisaged in different occupations and the fact that different hours, length of shifts or scales of pay operate in different employments do not in themselves call for comparison; it is the probable amount which is *capable* of being earned which has to be compared with what the claimant might have earned in the regular occupation.

7. In the case of the claimant she worked part-time in the afternoons as a biscuit packer and has since worked part-time in the mornings as a

---

* Compare the interpretation of Redundancy Payments Act, 1965, s. 2, *ante*, p. 217 and of National Insurance Act, 1965, s. 22, *ante*, p. 199.

checker. If she worked longer hours as a checker she could earn as much as she did in her regular occupation. That she does not do so is because of domestic reasons which are not relevant factors to be taken into account. She does not therefore qualify for the increase under s. 14 and I can find no grounds for disagreeing with the unanimous decision of the local appeal tribunal.

[*Note on the finality of Commissioners' Decisions*: The House of Lords in *Minister of Social Security* v. *Amalgamated Engineering Union* [1967] 1 All E.R.210, held (Lord Wilberforce dissenting) that the decision of a Commissioner that a claimant had suffered personal injury caused by an accident arising out of his employment was final and conclusive not only for the claim to industrial injury benefit, but also for any subsequent claim to disablement benefit (by virtue of ss. 36(3) and 49(4) of the 1946 Act—now ss. 50(1) and 48(4) of the 1965 Act). In this case a worker had been injured when he lifted a heavy flagstone in the course of his work. The Commissioner made a favourable decision on a claim for injury benefit. But, in a subsequent claim for disablement benefit, a medical appeal tribunal and another Commissioner took a different view, in particular doubting whether injury had been caused by a relevant accident as required by the Act. These later decisions were quashed in an action for *certiorari*. The sections cited above make the Commissioner's initial decision on these matters final. But it must be noted that their Lordships point out that this was an unusual case. Normally, accident and injury are separate, as the Act envisages in speaking of 'injury caused by accident'. Here they were the same. 'There would be no accident but for the injury': *per* Lord Hodson. Here, therefore, in deciding whether there had been a 'loss of faculty' or 'disablement', the medical appeal tribunal could not take a different view of the accident or the injury.]

SUBJECT INDEX